Medieval Concepts of the Past

RITUAL, MEMORY, HISTORIOGRAPHY

Medieval Concepts of the Past demonstrates how the history of the Middle Ages is being reshaped by leading medieval historians in Germany and the United States in light of cultural and social-scientific investigations into ritual, language, and memory. These two national traditions of medieval scholarship, which have been largely separated over the course of the twentieth century, are drawing closer together through a common interest in issues of social science and linguistic theory as applied to the representation of the past. This book marks a significant step in the reconvergence of these two historiographical traditions.

Gerd Althoff is a professor of history at the University of Münster.

Johannes Fried is a professor of history at the University of Frankfurt.

Patrick J. Geary is a professor of history at the University of California at Los Angeles.

PUBLICATIONS OF THE GERMAN HISTORICAL INSTITUTE

The German Historical Institute is a center for advanced study and research whose purpose is to provide a permanent basis for scholarly cooperation among historians from the Federal Republic of Germany and the United States. The Institute conducts, promotes, and supports research into both American and German political, social, economic, and cultural history, into transatlantic migration, especially in the nineteenth and twentieth centuries, and into the history of international relations, with special emphasis on the roles played by the United States and Germany.

Recent books in the series

Norbert Finzsch and Dietmar Schirmer, editors, *Identity and Intolerance: Nationalism, Racism, and Xenophobia in Germany and the United States*

Susan Strasser, Charles McGovern, and Matthias Judt, editors, *Getting and Spending: European and American Consumer Societies in the Twentieth Century*

Carole Fink, Philipp Gassert, and Detlef Junker, editors, *1968: The World Transformed*

Manfred F. Boemeke, Roger Chickering, and Stig Förster, editors, *Anticipating Total War: The German and American Experiences, 1871–1914*

Roger Chickering and Stig Förster, editors, *Great War, Total War: Combat and Mobilization on the Western Front, 1914–1918*

Jürgen Heideking and James A. Henretta, editors, *Republicanism and Liberalism in America and the German States, 1750–1850*

Hubert Zimmermann, *Money and Security: Troops, Monetary Policy and West Germany's Relations with the United States and Britain, 1950–1971*

Medieval Concepts of the Past

RITUAL, MEMORY, HISTORIOGRAPHY

Edited by

GERD ALTHOFF
University of Münster

JOHANNES FRIED
University of Frankfurt

PATRICK J. GEARY
University of California at Los Angeles

GERMAN HISTORICAL INSTITUTE
Washington, D.C.
and
 CAMBRIDGE
UNIVERSITY PRESS

CAMBRIDGE UNIVERSITY PRESS
Cambridge, New York, Melbourne, Madrid, Cape Town, Singapore, São Paulo

Cambridge University Press
The Edinburgh Building, Cambridge CB2 8RU, UK

GERMAN HISTORICAL INSTITUTE
1607 New Hampshire Ave., NW, Washington, DC 20009

Published in the United States of America by Cambridge University Press, New York

www.cambridge.org
Information on this title: www.cambridge.org/9780521780667

First published 2002
Reprinted 2003
This digitally printed version 2008

A catalogue record for this publication is available from the British Library

Library of Congress Cataloguing in Publication data
Medieval concepts of the past : ritual, memory, historiography / edited by
Gerd Althoff, Johannes Fried, Patrick J. Geary.
p. cm. – (Publications of the German Historical Institute)
ISBN 0–521–78066–7
1. Historiography – History. 2. Middle Ages – Historiography. 3. Memory.
4. Rites and ceremonies. 5. Ritual. 6. Civilization, Medieval. I. Althoff, Gerd.
II. Fried, Johannes. III. Geary, Patrick J., 1948– IV. Title. V. Series.
D13.M3656 2000
907′.2 – dc21 00–023705

ISBN 978-0-521-78066-7 hardback
ISBN 978-0-521-06028-8 paperback

Contents

vii

Illustrations

Contributors

Gerd Althoff is a professor of history at the University of Münster.

John W. Bernhardt is a professor of history at San Jose State University.

Philippe Buc is a professor of history at Stanford University.

John B. Freed is a professor of history at Illinois State University.

Johannes Fried is a professor of history at the University of Frankfurt.

Patrick J. Geary is a professor of history at the University of California at Los Angeles.

Hans-Werner Goetz is a professor of history at the University of Hamburg.

Bernhard Jussen is a research fellow at the Max Planck Institute for History, Göttingen.

Felice Lifshitz is a professor of history at Florida International University.

David Nirenberg is a professor of history at Johns Hopkins University.

Amy G. Remensnyder is an associate professor of history at Brown University.

Bernd Schneidmüller is a professor of history at the University of Bamberg.

Beate Schuster is a research fellow of the Alexander von Humboldt Foundation at the University of Basel.

Hanna Vollrath is a professor of history at the University of Bochum.

Stefan Weinfurter is a professor of history at the University of Heidelberg.

Introduction

GERD ALTHOFF, JOHANNES FRIED, AND PATRICK J. GEARY

Although scholarship in general and historical scholarship in particular claim to be universal and international in their scope and methodology, national traditions, methods, and foci have developed in many fields, including medieval history. These national patterns have done little to encourage mutual cooperation and understanding: On the contrary, they often have been a real hindrance. Such obstacles, already observable in the nineteenth century, were made even more insurmountable by European political developments in the twentieth century. Two world wars, with their attendant alliances and oppositions, have made their contributions to deepening divisions and to complicating understanding and collaboration. These divisions have been particularly operative in American and German scholarship on medieval Europe.

A century ago, medieval historical studies in America were dominated by themes and methodologies developed in Germany. This influence was part of the more general influence exercised by German universities on American scholarship. Regardless of field, American historians looked to Germany for training, for inspiration, and for models of historical interpretation. For a variety of reasons, the investigation of which would take us far beyond the topic of this book, these close contacts dissolved in the course of the twentieth century.[1] World War I and its wave of anti-German sentiment in North America was certainly a major factor. So, too, was the general reaction in medieval German historiography against the integration of the social sciences into historical discourse, particularly in the 1920s and 1930s.

---

1 Patrick J. Geary, *Medieval Germany in America*, German Historical Institute, Washington, D.C., Annual Lecture series, no. 8 (Washington, D.C., 1995), 9–31; Edward Peters, "More Trouble with Henry: The Historiography of Medieval Germany in the Anglo-Literate World, 1888–1995," *Central European History* 28 (1995): 47–72.

Until the post-World War II era, German medieval history was to a great extent concerned with legitimating German contemporary politics with arguments drawn from history, as when scholars attempted, for example, to present the role of the medieval German kingdom as the "leading and exemplary power" in Europe. Such efforts led this sort of medieval national history into international isolation and marginality. In the aftermath of German defeat in 1919 the writing of German national history, with a few notable exceptions, became increasingly internal and conservative in its methods and its goals. German historians focused on the narrative political history of the German empire with special emphasis on the constitutional and ideological conflicts between empire and papacy that, in the dominant historiographical tradition, led to the failure of medieval Germany to develop the characteristics of a nation-state by the end of the Middle Ages.[2]

American medieval scholarship was no less affected by the hostility engendered by the world wars of the twentieth century, and it too had a primary focus: the origins of the modern state. Accepting the image of the "failure" of Germany to develop into a centralized state, American scholars interested in the development of the nation-state on the continent turned to the study of Normandy and France rather than to Germany. This was particularly true in the tradition of Charles Homer Haskins and his students such as Joseph Strayer and Charles Taylor.[3] These scholars were less concerned with the political events and ideological debates of French history than in the gradual development of state institutions tying together monarch and society. Moreover, at the same time that German scholarship "purified" itself from the influence of Max Weber and other theorists of social dynamics, American medievalists were increasingly influenced by the new social sciences, especially sociology and economics. This influence came primarily from the French-speaking world, through the work of the Belgian historian Henri Pirenne and, later, Marc Bloch.

---

2 Otto Gerhard Oexle, "Was There Anything to Learn? American Historians and German Medieval Scholarship: A Comment," in Geary, *Medieval Germany in America*, 32–44. As Oexle points out in this comment, there also were innovations in German medieval scholarship following World War I, particularly in the work of Otto Hintze. For examples of Hintze's work, see "Wesen und Verbreitung des Feudalismus" (1929); "Typologie der ständischen Verfassungen des Abendlandes" (1930); "Weltgeschichtliche Bedingungen der Repräsentativverfassung" (1931), in Otto Hintze, *Staat und Verfassung: Gesammelte Abhandlungen zur allgemeinen Verfassungsgeschichte*, 3d ed. (Göttingen, 1970).

3 Gabrielle M. Spiegel, "In the Mirror's Eye: The Writing of Medieval History in North America," in Gabrielle M. Spiegel, *The Past as Text: The Theory and Practice of Medieval Historiography* (Baltimore, 1997), 57–80.

The wave of Jewish and anti-Nazi German émigré intellectuals who profoundly changed American scholarship in modern history, art history, and the social sciences had little effect on the study of medieval German history in America. Those few medievalists who did come to this country, such as Gerhard Ladner, Stephan Kuttner, and Ernst Kantorowicz, were less interested in German history per se than in European cultural history or specialized areas such as canon law, pre-reformation history, or the history of the university, and their students for the most part continued this tradition. Before as after World War II mainstream American medievalists had little interest in or knowledge of German medieval historiography. At a few American institutions, most notably the University of California at Los Angeles, Robert Benson, a student of Kantorowicz and Theodore Mommsen, continued to send a trickle of students to Munich to work at the Monumenta Germaniae Historica, some of whom integrated into German *Reichsgeschichte* (history of the medieval German empire).[4] However, the state of American knowledge of medieval German history well into the 1970s is eloquently demonstrated by the fact that Geoffrey Barraclough's *Medieval Germany, 911–1250: Essays by German Historians*, first published in 1938, and his *The Origins of Modern Germany*, which appeared in 1946, were virtually the sole introductions for English readers to Germany in the Middle Ages.[5] For their part, German historians found nothing of interest in the directions of American medieval scholarship outside of canon law studies pursued primarily by their émigré contemporaries and a few hardy but lonely disciples. The reception of the work of James Westfall Thompson, the one American medievalist in the first half of the twentieth century to write medieval German history, was at best condescendingly patronizing.[6] One would be hard-pressed to find any American scholar cited by German scholars either for substantive, methodological, or theoretical contributions in the voluminous notes that darken the pages of German medieval scholarship.

Largely because of the presence in the United States of the great Austrian medievalist Gerhard Ladner and the widespread popularity of Heinrich Fichtenau's *Carolingian Empire*, albeit in a truncated form, the traditions of Austrian historiography developed in the Austrian Institute

---

4 See Richard A. Jackson, "Robert L. Benson," *Majestas* 5 (1997): 5–22.

5 *Medieval Germany, 911–1250: Essays by German Historians*, trans. Geoffrey Barraclough, 2 vols. (Oxford, 1938).

6 James Westfall Thompson, *Feudal Germany*, 2 vols. (New York, 1928; reprint, 1962). Concerning the reception of Thompson's work in Germany, see Bernhard Schmeidler's review in *Historische Zeitschrift* 140, no. 3 (1929): 591–5.

for Historical Research in Vienna continued to be known and appreciated in North America.[7] However, from the 1970s onward, the leading figure in this tradition, Herwig Wolfram, concentrated on the world of late antiquity and the ethnogenesis of the post-Roman world.[8] As a result, in the United States, the Austrian contribution was largely confined to the Early Middle Ages, and neither the earlier work of scholars such as Otto Brunner nor the high medieval work of Fichtenau and his students and colleagues penetrated American academic circles.[9] As for *Reichsgeschichte*, as practiced in Austria and Germany, outside of the narrow circle of Benson and his students, America evidenced virtually no interest.

But even whereas *Reichsgeschichte* remained the dominant focus of German historiography, new and important directions were being explored in pre- and postwar Germany, directions that would fundamentally transform German scholarship.[10] Percy Ernst Schramm and others began the analysis of royal and imperial ritual and systems of symbolic representation that, although little informed by the semiotics or ethnography informing the contemporary work of Marc Bloch on the royal touch in France, nevertheless opened new directions in the understanding of royal self-representation and ideology.[11] Gerd Tellenbach and his students and colleagues began to explore the world of aristocratic kindreds that made up the primary partners and opponents of the monarchy.[12] This new history of the nobility continued to emphasize the hierarchical relationships between king and nobility but led to an increasing interest in the structure, self-perception, and self-representation of these aristocratic kindreds. Tellenbach's students, notably Karl Schmid, began to exploit necrological and liturgical sources in order to identify the self-perceptions of group solidarities within the medieval aristocracy,

---

7 Heinrich Fichtenau, *The Carolingian Empire*, trans. Peter Munz (Oxford, 1957); Heinrich Fichtenau, *Ketzer und Professoren: Häresie und Vernunftglaube im Hochmittelalter* (Munich, 1992), translated as *Heretics and Scholars* (University Park, Pa., 1998); Patrick J. Geary, *Living with the Dead in the Middle Ages* (Ithaca, N.Y., 1994).

8 Herwig Wolfram, "The Shaping of the Early Medieval Kingdom," *Viator: Medieval and Renaissance Studies* 1 (1970): 1–20; Herwig Wolfram, *History of the Goths* (Berkeley, Calif., 1988); and Herwig Wolfram, *The Roman Empire and Its Germanic Peoples* (Berkeley, Calif., 1997).

9 Otto Brunner, *Land and Lordship: Structures of Governance in Medieval Austria*, trans. Howard Kaminsky and James Van Horn Melton, 4th rev. ed. (Philadelphia, 1992).

10 As Oexle points out, there were German scholars who had begun to undertake comparative histories of mentalities and comparative social and structural histories, especially Percy Ernst Schramm, Gerd Tellenbach, and Carl Erdmann. Oexle, "Was There Anything to Learn?" 43.

11 Percy Ernst Schramm, *Kaiser, Rom und Renovatio: Studien zur Geschichte des römischen Erneuerungsgedankens vom Ende des karolingischen Reiches bis zum Investiturstreit*, 3d ed. (1929; Darmstadt, 1962).

12 Gerd Tellenbach, *Libertas: Kirche und Weltordnung im Zeitalter des Investiturstreites* (Stuttgart, 1936); Gerd Tellenbach, *Königtum und Stämme in der Werdezeit des deutschen Reiches* (Weimar, 1939).

opening a new and complex tradition of the exploitation of liturgical sources for social history.[13] Both of these traditions still focused on the monarchy, but both went far beyond traditional legal constitutional perspectives.

Elsewhere, source critical studies of medieval historiography, traditionally connected to the elaboration of narrative political history, under the influence of Johannes Spörl and others, began to examine the mental horizons of the historians rather than simply mining such chronicles for their "historical" evidence.[14] More fundamentally, scholars such as Otto Brunner and Karl Bosl began to challenge the basic premises of narrative political history: Brunner through a conservative rejection of both social science methodology and the suppositions of liberal statist scholarship; Bosl by embracing sociology as a source for models in which to understand medieval social structures.[15] Finally, in the 1960s German medievalists began to reestablish ties with French colleagues and to develop ongoing relations with French institutions. The new French history became widely available to German readers through volumes such as the Fischer Taschenbuch edition of *Das Hohe Mittelalter* by Jacques Le Goff.[16] In addition, the German Historical Institute in Paris provided a forum in which French and German historians could meet to explore common ground. Particularly significant for medievalists was the work of its long-time director, Karl Ferdinand Werner, who wrote extensively on the origins of the high medieval French aristocracy in the Carolingian period, introducing French scholars to the potential importance of German prosopographical and onomastic studies for the understanding of their own regions.[17]

Medieval scholarship in postwar America began moving in some of the same directions, although under largely different impulses. The influence

---

13 Karl Schmid, *Gebetsgedenken und adliges Selbstverständnis im Mittelalter: Ausgewählte Beiträge: Festgabe zu seinem sechzigsten Geburtstag* (Sigmaringen, 1983). See also John B. Freed, "Reflections on the Medieval German Nobility," *American Historical Review* 91 (1986): 553–75.

14 Johannes Spörl, *Grundformen hochmittelalterlicher Geschichtsanschauung: Studien zum Weltbild der Geschichtsschreiber des 12. Jahrhunderts* (Darmstadt, 1968).

15 Brunner, *Land and Lordship*; Gadi Algazi, *Herrengewalt und Gewalt der Herren im späten Mittelalter: Herrschaft, Gegenseitigkeit und Sprachgebrauch* (Frankfurt am Main, 1996). For a review of the English edition of Brunner, see the book review by John B. Freed in *Speculum* 69 (1994): 112–15.

16 Jacques Le Goff, *Das Hochmittelalter* (Hamburg, 1965).

17 Karl Ferdinand Werner, "Untersuchungen zur Frühzeit des französischen Fürstentums (9.–10. Jahrhundert)," *Die Welt als Geschichte* 18 (1958): 256–88; 19 (1959): 146–93; and 20 (1960): 87–119; Karl Ferdinand Werner, "Bedeutende Adelsfamilien im Reich Karls des Grossen," in Helmut Beumann, ed., *Karl der Grosse: Persönlichkeit und Geschichte*, 5 vols. (Düsseldorf, 1965) 1:83–142, translated and reprinted in Timothy Reuter, ed., *The Medieval Nobility: Studies on the Ruling Classes of France and Germany from the Sixth to the Twelfth Century* (New York, 1979), 137–202.

of Kantorowicz was profound on those interested in ritual, but more influential were the French historical traditions associated with Marc Bloch, Lucien Febvre, and the *Annales* school. In the 1960s and 1970s, American medievalists, like American historians of other periods, became increasingly interested in social and economic history, focusing less on the history of kings and high aristocracy and more on the organization and structures of life affecting ordinary people. Historians applied the quantitative techniques of economics and the class analyses of sociologists to explore the history of the inarticulate. As in Germany, prosopography became an important tool, but the purpose to which this tool was put was the study of horizontal social structures rather than the vertical relations uniting ruler and the political elite. Within the area of cultural history, scholars turned from the articulated belief systems and ideological constructs of the elite to popular culture, seeking in popular hagiography, in heresy, and in vernacular literature the systems of implicit beliefs and practices that constituted a broader cultural system.

Of course, given the nature of medieval sources, much of this interest in social history focused on the structure and cultural world of the landholding elite, the nobility and lower knights. Such studies in America were profoundly influenced by the work of the postwar generation of French social historians, particularly Georges Duby, whose examination of the Mâconnais in the eleventh and twelfth centuries rapidly became a classic of the region. Few Americans, other than George Beech and Ted Evergates, actually undertook comprehensive regional studies on the model of Duby, but American medievalists became increasingly interested in questions about the organization of the nobility, their origins, kinship structures, landholding, and their access to power.[18] However, except for John Freed, none of these Americans connected their regional historical interests with German *Landesgeschichte*, which itself remained curiously isolated from French *histoire régionale*.[19]

Likewise, in part because medievalists in the United States tend to work across disciplines and thus historians have close relationships with scholars in the literatures, American medievalists were particularly interested in the

18 George Beech, *A Rural Society in Medieval France: The Gatine of Poitou in the Eleventh and Twelfth Centuries* (Baltimore, 1964); Theodore Evergates, *Feudal Society in Medieval France: Documents from the County of Champagne* (Philadelphia, 1993); Stephen White, *Custom, Kinship, and Gifts to Saints: The laudatio parentum in Western France, 1050–1150* (Chapel Hill, N.C., 1988); and Barbara Rosenwein, *To Be the Neighbor of Saint Peter: The Social Meaning of Cluny's Property, 909–1049* (Ithaca, N.Y., 1989).

19 John B. Freed, *Noble Bondsmen: Ministerial Marriage in the Archdiocese of Salzburg, 1100–1343* (Ithaca, N.Y., 1995).

development of chivalric cultural forms, that is, the mental and cultural horizons of the knightly elite. These questions, also enriched by similar questions of *mentalité* being explored by French scholars such as Jacques Le Goff, led historians to look beyond social and political structures toward the mental world of medieval aristocracies, both to understand cultural production and to recognize, in the patterns of life and thought, the implicit cultural rules governing social interaction. Increasingly, American historians looked to cultural anthropology for models of exploration and examination of the deeper processes that informed this distant and complex society. This led them to explore the areas of ritual and symbol, in part in the tradition of Kantorowicz, but also from the perspective of cultural anthropologists such as Victor Turner and Clifford Geertz.

Thus, by the 1970s, American and German scholars were increasingly working toward similar kinds of issues: a de-emphasis on narrative in favor of structure; history of the nobility; ritual, symbolism, self-representation. However, the two traditions had developed largely in ignorance of each other and with quite different goals. One of the few points of mediation was the French historical tradition, particularly the work of Georges Duby, who early on recognized the importance of Karl Schmid's analysis of aristocratic kinship structures as a key to understanding the transformation of the noble families in the Mâconnais.[20] His seminars at the Collège de France, frequented by Germans and Americans doing research in Paris, became the forum in which scholars to the east and west of France found their common interests. Still, few Americans working in social history or the history of popular culture read German with any fluency, and personal contacts, outside of the areas of intellectual history and traditional institutional history, were rare.

This situation began to change through the intervention of British scholars. In England, thanks to the presence of Karl Leyser at Oxford University and Walter Ullmann at Cambridge University, both scholarship focusing on the empire and the papacy and close contact with the new and emerging traditions of German scholarship had continued. In 1970 Leyser published two articles in *Past and Present* in which he discussed the work of Karl Schmid.[21] Although Leyser was dubious about

---

20 Georges Duby, "Lineage, Nobility and Knighthood: The Mâconnais in the Twelfth Century – a Revision," in Georges Duby, *The Chivalrous Society*, trans. Cynthia Postan (Berkeley, Calif., 1977), 59–80.
21 Karl Leyser, "The German Aristocracy from the Ninth to the Early Twelfth Century: A Historical and Cultural Sketch," *Past and Present* 41 (Dec. 1968): 25–53; Karl Leyser, "Debate: Maternal Kin in Early Medieval Germany. A Reply," *Past and Present* 49 (Nov. 1970): 126–34.

the full validity of Schmid's use of memorial texts for identifying kinship structures, his articles alerted English and American scholars to the undeniable importance of reconnecting with German-language scholarship. Not long after, in 1978, a much broader introduction to contemporary tendencies in German scholarship on the family appeared in the collection edited and translated by Leyser's student, the bicultural Timothy Reuter. Although Reuter's edited collection, *The Medieval Nobility: Studies on the Ruling Classes of France and Germany from the Sixth to the Twelfth Century*, contained some translations of French and Belgian scholars already well known to Americans, the access to the German essays had an immediate and far-reaching effect.[22] Although a few important articles had appeared in translations by scholars such as Frederic Cheyette, this was the first major, sustained introduction to those aspects of contemporary German history of most immediate interest and accessibility to American medievalists since Barraclough's 1938 collection.[23]

Second-hand knowledge of German scholarship led some Americans to seek out German contacts. Some of these connections were made in Paris through the German Historical Institute there. Others were facilitated by the Monumenta Germaniae Historica, the Max Planck Institute for History in Göttingen, and other research institutions in Germany, and supported by the generous policies of research grants made by the German government through the German Academic Exchange Service (DAAD) and the Humboldt Foundation. These contacts expanded into wider mutual interest. As a result, German historians began to appear in increasing numbers at the International Medieval Congress at Western Michigan University in Kalamazoo, Michigan. A critical stage was reached in 1993, when the University of Notre Dame sponsored a conference on medieval Germany at which a group of German and American scholars met to present papers and, more importantly, to begin to explore areas where direct collaboration was potentially fruitful.

At both the International Medieval Congress at Kalamazoo and the Notre Dame conference a group of German medievalists presented a survey of contemporary directions in German medieval historiography. American colleagues were invited to formulate responses in which they explained how these themes and research areas related to work on

---

22 Reuter, ed., *Medieval Nobility*.
23 Frederic Cheyette, *Lordship and Community in Medieval Europe: Selected Readings* (New York, 1968).

medieval Germany being done in the United States. The reaction to this arrangement, particularly on the part of younger American medievalists, was extremely positive. Hence was born the idea to continue contact of this sort and to bring together scholars from both countries at regular intervals.

The present book represents the next step in this collaboration. In September 1996, the German Historical Institute in Washington, D.C., sponsored a colloquium entitled "Image, Ritual, Memory, Historiography: Concepts of the Past," at the Internationales Wissenschaftsforum at the University of Heidelberg. The colloquium brought together nine American scholars and an equal number of Germans for a series of presentations and intense discussions of contemporary directions in medieval scholarship. The theme selected by the organizers – Gerd Althoff (University of Münster), Johannes Fried (University of Frankfurt), and Patrick J. Geary (University of California at Los Angeles) – recognized that in the last decade, both in Germany and in North America, medievalists have come to focus their attention on the representation and recollection of ritual action in narrative and archival texts, in popular literature, as well as in art and music. The German tradition has focused largely on historiography, on liturgical and extra-liturgical forms of the remembrance of the dead, and on royal and imperial ritual. Americans have applied approaches developed in process-oriented social and cultural anthropology to a wider social spectrum. However, both historical traditions are informed by French cultural and social history of the past quarter century and share important common epistemological concerns about the relationship between perception and representation, both by contemporaries and by modern historians. The colloquium offered representatives of both traditions the opportunity to learn from each other both in formal presentations and in animated discussions and debates. The intensive discussions of this conference demonstrated clearly that there were not two national concepts of medieval history. The papers rather elicited agreements and arguments entirely independent of the national origins of the participants. Collaboration continued in revising the papers for publication, with German participants sending their essays to American counterparts for assistance in preparing final drafts of their English texts. The present collection, which contains virtually all of the Heidelberg papers, demonstrates how well the two historical traditions have converged.

The lectures engaged the themes of the conference from multiple perspectives. Stephan Weinfurter (Chapter 1) and John W. Bernhardt (Chapter 2) represent the classic tradition of German ritual studies that seeks to derive imperial ideology from representations of imperial ceremony. In his essay Weinfurter examines a series of rituals, images, and prayer associations created by Henry II. He sees these as a privileged way of situating kingship within the working system of the realm, explaining ritual and ceremonial interactions during which the reciprocal relationship between magnates became visible. His focus is the question of how the seemingly firmly constructed ritual and ceremonial structure present in the interactions of the ruler on the one hand, and conceptions of royal rule on the other, behave with respect to one another. More generally, Weinfurter is interested in the question of interchange between established orders and mentally conceived orders. His approach is to read a program – a personal royal program – articulated in a complex iconographic tradition and in the specific language of royal chancery. Like Weinfurter, John Bernhardt too is interested in interaction of royal self-representation and historical memory in the representations of Henry II present in chronicles and in the iconography of the portrait of Henry II as Judge over Pandulf IV. His interest is in how different authors create their Henry in response to their own concerns as well as in the way that royal self-representation, ritual, and historical memory intersect in the development of imperial propaganda. For Bernhardt, reading the image of the submission of Pandulf IV to Henry, for example, is a process of deciphering a series of static, unambiguous iconographic elements. Pandulf, condemned to death for his disloyalty, knew the "rules of the game" and agreed to do ritual submission to Henry and endure a period of imprisonment as better than the alternatives.

Gerd Althoff (Chapter 3) is also interested in the "rules of the game" but in a different sense. He acknowledges that medieval public communication was ritual and demonstrative, demanding participation and audience. However, he focuses on the variability of rituals, arguing that ritual elements could be recombined in a wide variety of ways. Far from rigid and univocal procedures, ritualized action allowed room for innovation and modification either to fit the circumstances and persons involved, to evoke the past history of the issues and events giving rise to the ritual, or even spontaneously improvised by combining familiar gestures and actions on the spur of the moment. He examines a series of cases in which ambiguity, spontaneity, and disputed outcomes and meanings can be seen. He explores the paradox that "in order to fulfill its function the meaning of a ritual in public communication had to be unambiguous and easily understandable," and yet at the same time the changing patterns of combinations of ritual elements could communicate new meanings. Ritual thus becomes a communicative language made up of a limited stock of gestures and modes of behavior that could communicate a variety of new meanings. For Althoff, rituals are not univalent but rather are disputed fields of significance in which indeterminate results can develop. The "rules of the game" may apply in football, but they don't indicate who will win.

How to interpret the descriptions of ritual action in legal processes is the focus, in very different ways, of Hanna Vollrath (Chapter 4) and Patrick J. Geary (Chapter 5). Vollrath wants to find a way of understanding conflicts and their ways of being treated that avoids anachronistic legal frameworks derived from modern state categories or that falls into Otto Brunner's *völkisch* or structural history that refuses modern sociological analysis. She chooses to examine what have traditionally been seen as trials and judgments pronounced by kings against Margrave Ekbert II of Meissen, John Lackland, king of England and duke of Normandy, and Henry the Lion, for *contumacia*, refusal to appear in royal court to answer accusations against them. Vollrath sees the first two being summoned not to a judicial court but rather to participate in an open-ended negotiation and arbitration process. At such assemblies, she argues, although there were general ritual procedures that would be followed, the outcomes and the judgment of what the outcomes would mean was very fluid and ambiguous.

The ritual system could be a complex field of discourse in which a variety of outcomes might be anticipated. Ultimately, those on trial would be condemned not for failing to appear before the king who will judge them, but rather for refusing to participate in the normal, protracted process of negotiation and compromise that characterized the way the courts, whether royal or seigniorial, normally dealt with important matters. In the case of Henry the Lion, on the other hand, Frederick Barbarossa was indeed summoning him to what was to be a trial at which Frederick was prepared to adjudicate, not simply to arbitrate. His summons of the duke did not follow the rules of the game as usually played, and the duke must have seen it as an "outright provocation that left no room for the traditional rituals of noble society." Still, Vollrath does not imagine that Henry's condemnation was the advent of "modern" justice – it was rather a particular conjuncture of long-developing trends that came together at a moment: For once a ruler could enforce an unambiguous judgment against an isolated magnate. It showed the possibility of condemnation for *contumacia* in the twelfth century but neither its inevitability nor its future.

Patrick J. Geary's essay focuses on a much more local kind of court, local *placita* from tenth- and eleventh-century Provence and Septimania, to examine the interplay of oral and written testimony. Drawing on the theoretical work of German philologists and historians interested in vocality and in practical literacy, he emphasizes the performative aspect of court proceedings. Even in a region of deeply rooted Roman tradition, the past, whether preserved in texts or in people's memories, must be vocalized and performed in order to become a part of a dispute. This performance fictionalizes the past, making oral statements and texts read aloud by actors in a contemporary drama performed before people profoundly aware of the inadequacies of both to determine the future.

All of these essays take as their point of departure the written account of a ritual or a public performance, which the authors then seek to interpret. Philippe Buc (Chapter 6) takes the indeterminacy inherent in ritual procedures to the next level by questioning whether one can actually have access to medieval political culture as expressed by ritual at all since, just as John Bernhardt pointed out, our access is mediated by authors. Buc analyzes the alleged altercation between Emperor Louis II and Pope Nicholas that may have occurred in 864 before the steps of St. Peter's. Authors from differing political allegiances describe a clash between papal and imperial supporters that took place within the context of a ritual procession (whether penitential or a traditional *occursus* varies in the accounts). Each presents a heavily ideological position by the manner that it constructs the ritual circumstances in which the altercation is said to have occurred. In effect, just as rituals themselves could be manipulated, accounts of rituals were even more easily manipulated after the fact by propagandists. The result, Buc argues, is that the entirely subjective nature of our sources makes it possible to know that rituals were important ways of negotiating and disputing, but they prevent us from knowing how these rituals actually took place. What is more, "the more a political culture attributes an importance to rituals, the less one can trust its textual production to depict a ritual event as it actually happened." His larger point is that the medievalist must not attempt to analyze ritual action according to the norms of the ethnographer observer. The medievalist is imprisoned in texts, and must not forget that attempts to read rituals as texts amounts to reading texts as rituals.

This fundamental problem of hermeneutics, whether expressed in terms of traditional historiography or in more dynamic relationships

between present readers and past authors, provided a focus for a number
of the essays in this volume. Hans-Werner Goetz (Chapter 7) focuses on
the historiographical consciousness of time in the eleventh and twelfth
centuries, suggesting a tendency to place historical facts in right chronological order and establish precise dates, while at the same time neglecting vast distances in times and epochs. He contrasts the concern with the
proper ordering of events, of combining different threads of historiographical tradition (Roman, Christian, Frankish) into a unified chronology, and on the other hand, the lack of a sense of an epochal peculiarity.
The past was perceived as a temporal development corresponding to the
saeculum: While historical events might be ordered in time, the subject
matter of these events, the details of social custom, institutions, dress, and
the like might be detached from their chronological order. The reason
was the importance of inherent links with the present. The perception
of the past did not have an end in itself, but a chronological-genetic and
an exemplary concept of the past complemented each other. Cross-
chronological comparisons were typological comparisons, representation
of the past that was relevant for the present.

Bernd Schneidmüller (Chapter 8) too assumes that no one would
contest Goetz's conclusion that our present relates in a real sense to our
past. But just how this is done is not so easily defined. He examines
four forms of creation and maintenance of historical consciousness: history
of the imaginary – an institution, a dynasty, a people, and a city. His goal
is to assess the underlying interdependence between historical writings
and their contemporary sociopolitical context. The important question in
the creation of a direct line of royal succession is whether the genealogical adjustments and corrections to establish Carolingian and Capetian
continuity represent the ideals of the kings or just of clerical writers. He
argues from the royal registers that king-lists in the royal chancery registers show royal clerics working in the immediate circles of the Capetian rulers adjusting their genealogy, allowing their ninth-century
predecessors to disappear so that the continuity between the last Carolingians and Hugh Capet is established. The example of the Welfs shows
contradictory and differing strategies for constructing a family identity
that may at times be sacrificed to a regional identity. The case of the
"eternal freedom of the Frisian people" again shows a less easily identi-
fiable group assigning trans-temporal attributes and rights to the knightly
class, transposing social and political realities or corresponding postulates
onto the past. In his last example, urban memory, the patriciate emerges
with a God-given right to rule. For each of these, one must ask about

the concrete circumstances in which the historical materials were first collected. What was the purpose of these texts – in other words, their "place in the world"?

Expanding on the main theses of her *Remembering Kings Past*, Amy G. Remensnyder (Chapter 9) examines in still further detail the "place in the world" of monastic foundation legends. She discusses the construction of monastic foundation memories, focusing on how monastic traditions appropriated central figures (apostles, kings) and drew their own centrality from them. In this essay she discusses geographical centering, how monasteries made themselves the geographical center of a landscape sanctified by saintly royal foundation. The saintly royal founders are not royal saints appropriated to the task but they are sanctified because they are founders. The sanctification of Charlemagne in particular is a local phenomenon, not the result of the German cult or that of Charles V.

Finding the "place in the world" of textual traditions in light of the precarious and changing circumstances of the social environment is the goal of Bernhard Jussen (Chapter 10) and John B. Freed (Chapter 11). Jussen explores in the tradition of the "faithless matron of Ephesus" as transmitted in the Middle Ages the dilemma facing the medieval widow, obligated to remember her dead husband by remaining a widow and pressured to remarry and thus to "forget" her husband. The story originates in a radically different cultural sphere, that of the Roman world, in which such concerns were unknown and the widow was the personification of unbridled female libido. The medieval story is not about sex at all. Rather at stake was an aporia in the concept of the community of the living and the dead and the woman's role as wanderer between the two. Jussen's essay is thus an example of how to deeply contextualize a cultural artifact, even if its genealogy might imply "timelessness." The essential message is that such a myth is not "timeless" but deeply enmeshed in a specific nexus of social relations and cultural values.

John B. Freed also provides deep contextualization of constructed family pasts in literary and artistic representations, and in so doing represents an important and, in the context of this volume otherwise neglected German tradition, that of *Landesgeschichte* or regional history. He examines the portrait of Siboto IV of Falkenstein in his memorial book intended to transmit to his sons all that they needed to know about their past: fiefs, advocacies, genealogy, claims to castles, and the like. Freed examines how the past threatened Siboto's sons: disputed claims with relatives, disputed property usurped from monasteries, threats from powerful ducal neighbors. In this context the family portrait included in the memorial book, which enjoins the viewer or hearer to remember him, is presumably directed to the monks of Herrenchiemsee, his father-in-law, the five retainers he selected as his son's advisors, and other assumed audience of the codex. In his discussions of the Rodenegg Iwain frescoes and Ulrich of Liechtenstein's *Frauendienst*, Freed uncovers the tensions between free nobility and high ministerial backgrounds. In the former, he explains Arnold III of Rodank's ambivalence concerning the disparity between his unfree status and that of his noble wife; again, precarious status presented in chivalresque dress. Ulrich also presents an imagined youth when he could travel disguised as Arthur or Venus and contend as equal with the free nobility. All three are more programmatic than descriptive, representing how the author or commissioner wanted to be remembered.

The complexity of representation and identity is further explored by Beate Schuster (Chapter 12), who analyzes a particular historical text, the *De profectione Ludovici II in Orientem*, in order to show how a text, long a favorite of positivist historians because of its apparently naive and first-hand account by a young noble, is actually a carefully constructed theological text in which the persona of Odo of Deuil is created in an intertextual dialogue with other accounts of the crusade. Operating at multiple levels, the text draws the reader into doubt about the characterizations of the individuals and people who appear in the narrative. The key to understanding the text, she argues, is to displace one's identification with the narrator, to see him, and those he describes, as imperfect and his commentary on people and events as internally contradictory. Schuster concludes that the text was probably not by the historical Odo of Deuil but rather by the brilliant and complex Walter Map, who is using the persona of Odo to critique his own world in the aftermath of the Third Crusade.

Schuster's observations concerning the possibility that contemporary readers of the *De profectione* may have understood it in a way radically different from that of moderns raise a fundamental issue in the interpretation of historical sources addressed by David Nirenberg (Chapter 13) and Felice Lifshitz (Chapter 14). Not only must the complex contextualization of medieval authors and audiences be appreciated in interpreting medieval texts, but so too must those of modern interpreters. Nirenberg examines the accounts of the Rhineland massacres, not as the

Jewish means of creating a collective memory to preserve identity but as the result of an anxiety about memory that he situates in the past and, in a disjunctive way, in the twentieth century. His essay is a critique of a modern version of the blurring of epochs Goetz described as distinctively medieval. Since the 1930s, the memory of the persecution in Germany has made the medieval virtually continuous with the modern. The earliest chroniclers, facing the unheard of and unimaginable, groped for a Biblical tradition in which to place it. The accounts attempt to present the massacres as redemptive (atonement for collective guilt) and repetitive, repeating biblical typologies. But they are also a challenge to God as well as to people, to remember, and evoke the possibility that God's memory has been broken. In modern historiography these relatively minor massacres have elicited much more literature than the more extensive massacres of 1391. By the 1930s they had become the means by which one understood the present. Nirenberg questions the continuities established and the silences of more devastating slaughters.

Lifshitz likewise questions the relationship between twentieth-century scholars and their material in her analysis of the appearance of martyr cults in the later fourth century. She argues that in the first decades following Constantine's conversion, martyrs were not a conspicuous part of Christian worship. As in the case of Jews in the Middle Ages, since persecution was sporadic, one might have remembered the period as calm punctuated by sporadic persecution rather than as an age of persecution punctuated by moments of calm. However, martyrdom accounts were useful in detaching loyalty from a persecuting empire to the ecclesia. But the core of Lifshitz's argument is that Roman women provided the initiative for the initial development of most martyr cults, but bishops soon appropriated these cults to their own ends. More troubling is her assertion that the redefinition of legitimate cults as defined by Ambrose and other bishops in their efforts to appropriate these cults has been accepted uncritically by modern historians who fail utterly to recognize the gender implications of this appropriation. Interpretation of the past continues to be a means to assert one's "place in the world" within a context of competition and dispute.

Perhaps as important as the convergence of research themes among this group of scholars is the serious way in which many of the authors engage the problems and issues raised by each other and by other scholars from their colleagues' national traditions. This is less surprising in the case of Bernhardt's extensive use of Weinfurter's work, but present also in the papers of Althoff and Buc, both of whom address the work of

Geoffrey Koziol and which amount to the most direct debate within the volume.[24] Vollrath and Geary deal explicitly with issues developed in the American and German scholarly traditions respectively, although not otherwise represented in the volume. The historiographical chapters, too, indicate a developing knowledge of the scholarly traditions of each other's countries, although one might wish for a more direct engagement with their approaches to representing the past. The work of Karl Morrison informs Schuster's work on the *De profectione* and Schneidmüller takes into consideration the contributions of John Baldwin, Elizabeth Brown, and Gabrielle Spiegel. Jussen builds on and corrects the American contributions to the history of memory, and Felice Lifshitz appraises critically the scholarship of German scholars such as Arnold Angenendt, Rudolf Schieffer, and Bernard Kötting. We are gradually seeing a "reunification" of the two traditions divided for a century. Our hope is that this book will contribute to the continuation of this process.

The editors wish to thank all who have contributed to this project. These include the speakers and participants in the Heidelberg conference, the Wissenschaftszentrum Heidelberg for its hospitality and exemplary treatment of the participants, the German Historical Institute in Washington for its generous support of the conference and the publication, the anonymous readers who contributed to the improvement of the book through their criticisms, and, finally, Daniel S. Mattern, senior editor at the German Historical Institute, for his efforts in the preparation of the final manuscript.

---

24 Geoffrey Koziol, *Begging Pardon and Favor: Ritual and Political Order in Early Medieval France* (Ithaca, N.Y., 1992).

1

Authority and Legitimation of Royal Policy and Action

The Case of Henry II

STEFAN WEINFURTER

Almost a thousand years ago, in November 1007, King Henry II found himself in a strange situation. The archbishops and bishops of the realm had gathered at a synod in Frankfurt, and the king is said to have told them that he wanted to establish a new bishopric in Bamberg.[1] In this way, the king said, he wished to offer nearly all his possessions and the estates that he would acquire in the future to the eternal father.[2] Even so, the king had to reckon with difficulties. The bishop of Würzburg – also named Henry – who would have to give up portions of his diocese for this plan, had sent his chaplain Berengar to Frankfurt in order to lodge the strongest protest against the planned episcopal foundation. No diocese could be altered against the will of the affected bishop in his absence, argued Berengar. Now the synod was to decide the matter, and it became clear that the king's chances of success were not good. Yet on every occasion when a legal decision went against the king, Henry II, according to the chronicler Thietmar of Merseburg, threw himself onto the ground in a gesture of humility (*humiliatur*).[3] And in fact the bishops were unable

---

1 Thietmar, bishop of Merseburg, *Chronicon*, 2d ed., ed. Robert Holtzmann, in *Monumenta Germaniae Historica, Scriptores rerum Germanicarum*, n.s. 9 (Berlin, 1955), vol. 6, cc. 30–2, pp. 310–12; see Erich Frhr. von Guttenberg, *Die Regesten der Bischöfe und des Domkapitels von Bamberg* (Würzburg, 1932–63), nos. 33, 34; Harald Zimmermann, "Gründung und Bedeutung des Bistums Bamberg für den Osten," *Südostdeutsches Archiv* 10 (1967): 35–49.

2 Wilhelm Störmer, "Heinrichs II. Schenkungen an Bamberg: Zur Topographie und Typologie des Königs- und bayerischen Herzogsguts um die Jahrtausendwende in Franken und Bayern," in Lutz Fenske, ed., *Deutsche Königspfalzen: Beiträge zu ihrer historischen und archäologischen Erforschung*, vol. 4: *Pfalzen – Reichsgut – Königshöfe* (Göttingen, 1996), 377–408.

3 Thietmar, *Chronicon* 6.32, 312: "Inter haec quocies rex anxiam iudicum sententiam nutare prospexit, toties prostratus humiliatur."

to ignore this gesture of entreaty and humility; at its close, the synod
agreed to the foundation of Bamberg.

The story admittedly is not unknown, and it is commonly used as evidence for how sly and calculating this king was in his dealings with bishops.[4]
Medieval kingship was a game of tricks, or so it may almost appear to us.[5]

A king humbles himself not to do penance but to gain authority.[6] Not
before God or saints did he humble himself, but before men, that is, before
bishops. As far as I am aware, this is the first time in the history of the
Middle Ages that such a mode of action is recorded on the part of a ruler.[7]
The events at Frankfurt show us – for the first time – a kingship that
appears to draw its strength from a staged act of self-humiliation.[8] How are
we to situate such a kingship within the working system of the realm?

The observation that precisely during Henry II's reign the sources speak
of the terrors of a time without a king may not be unimportant in answer-
ing this question. "Woe to the people," exclaimed Thietmar of Merseburg
in a disastrous tone, taking Deuteronomy 17:14–15 as his text, when a ruler
does not have a son who can lead the kingdom without interruption.[9] The
comments of Wipo,[10] or Abbot Bern of Reichenau,[11] show that in 1024 as
well, the time without a king was regarded with particular dread, as a
danger to the unity and peace of the realm. The function of the king, so it
seems, is forcefully emphasized in the sources from these years: He wants to
preserve the peace and integrate the realm.[12]

---

4 More recently, see David A. Warner, "Thietmar of Merseburg on Rituals of Kingship," *Viator:
Medieval and Renaissance Studies* 26 (1995): 67–8.

5 See Johannes Fried, *Der Weg in die Geschichte: Die Ursprünge Deutschlands: Bis 1024*, Propyläen
Geschichte Deutschlands 1 (Berlin, 1994), 615–16.

6 See Lothar Bornscheuer, *Miseriae regum: Untersuchungen zum Krisen- und Todesgedanken in den
herrschaftstheologischen Vorstellungen der ottonisch-salischen Zeit*, Arbeiten zur Frühmittelalterforschung
4 (Berlin, 1968), 68–70.

7 Gerd Althoff, "Der König weint: Rituelle Tränen in öffentlicher Kommunikation," in Jan-Dirk
Müller, ed., *"Aufführung" und "Schrift" in Mittelalter und Neuzeit* (Stuttgart, 1997), 247–9, does not
name any earlier examples. Henry II's humble behavior cannot be seen as the penance of a ruler,
examples of which are of course known earlier. See Rudolf Schieffer, "Von Mailand nach Canossa:
Ein Beitrag zur Geschichte der christlichen Herrscherbusse von Theodosius d. Gr. bis zu
Heinrich IV.," *Deutsches Archiv* 28 (1972): 333–70. Likewise, a royal *deditio* does not have anything
to do with Henry's actions; on *deditio*, see Gerd Althoff, "Das Privileg der deditio: Formen
gütlicher Konfliktbeendigung in der mittelalterlichen Adelsgesellschaft," in Gerd Althoff, *Spielregeln
der Politik im Mittelalter: Kommunikation in Frieden und Fehde* (Darmstadt, 1997), 99–125.

8 The concept of multiple means of rituals might be important here; see Geoffrey Koziol, *Begging
Pardon and Favor: Ritual and Political Order in Early Medieval France* (Ithaca, N.Y., 1992), 307–11.

9 Thietmar, *Chronicon* 1.19, p. 24.

10 Wipo, *Gesta Chuonradi imperatoris*, 3d ed., ed. Harry Bresslau, *Monumenta Germaniae Historica,
Scriptores rerum Germanicarum* (Hannover, 1915), c. 1, p. 9.

11 Franz-Josef Schmale, ed. *Die Briefe des Abtes Bern von Reichenau* (Stuttgart, 1961), no. 10, pp. 36–7.

12 See Hagen Keller, "Die Investitur: Ein Beitrag zum Problem der 'Staatssymbolik' im Hochmittelalter," *Frühmittelalterliche Studien* 27 (1993): 76–7.

The research of the last years has made clear that at the turn of the millennium the realm had not yet developed any internal political unity, but rather it was in principle still a construct of various peoples.[13] Yet, it must be countered that the yearning for an integrative force clearly grew.[14] In this connection I would like to turn to Brun of Querfurt, whose statements in his *Life of Five Brothers* I interpret differently than has recently been done.[15] Brun reproaches Otto III for neglecting his duty to administer justice and law on behalf of the weak and the realm, and for generally failing to give sufficient attention to royal business.[16] He was a ruler who did not carry out his responsibilities – this criticism directed itself at the heart of the king's obligation to uphold the royal functions. Such criticism could hardly have been worded more sharply – the argument that Brun sought to explain Otto III's early death with these accusations does not change this.[17]

In sum, the sources from this time suggest that in the late Ottonian period the idea that the king ought to perform an integrating function grew stronger. Overcoming the gentile structure of the realm and building up its inner unity, it seems, surged ever more to the fore.

This process consequently entailed an increase of royal authority within the realm, for the power to bring things together came from this authority.[18] *Nostra (regalis) auctoritas*, such is the formula used for the ruler's power to effect his wishes as we find it countless times in the

13 Most recently, Knut Görich, *Otto III., Romanus Saxonicus et Italicus: Kaiserliche Rompolitik und sächsische Historiographie*, Historische Forschungen 18 (Sigmaringen, 1993).

14 See Hagen Keller, "Reichsstruktur und Herrschaftsauffassung in ottonisch-frühsalischer Zeit," *Frühmittelalterliche Studien* 16 (1982): 119.

15 In *Otto III*. Knut Görich correctly shifts the Roman and ecclesiastical orientation of Otto III to the center of things, but he goes probably too far if he wants totally to ignore the criticism of Otto regarding neglect of the realm.

16 Brun of Querfurt, *Vita quinque fratrum eremitarum*, ed. Jadwiga Karwasinka, Monumenta Poloniae Historica, n.s. 4, 3 (Warsaw, 1973), 43–4. The words "Peccatum regis hoc fuit" (p. 43) do not refer, as Görich, *Otto III*. (pp. 28, 50) claims, only to the preceding undertakings concerning the renewal of Rome and to the lack of respect paid the Apostle Peter, but just as well to the neglect of "Germany." In fact, the demonstrative pronoun *hoc* focuses, above all, on the following: "Terram sue natiuitatis, delectabilem Germaniam, iam nec uidere uoluit; tantus sibi amor habitare Italiam fuit." The criticism (p. 47) is even more pronounced, where it states: "that he, in human weakness, pursued an alien undertaking, not his own; meanwhile, he spent less time on law and justice, which he had to administer for the poor and the realm and – in so far as it is relevant – neglected royal business" ("quod humana fragilitate alienum non suum officium agebat, dimittens legem et iusticiam quam pauperibus et regno ministrare positus erat, et prope quantum ad rem pertinet, raro regalia fecit").

17 Görich, *Otto III*., 50; Jean-Marie Sansterre, "Otton III et les saints ascètes de son temps," *Rivista di storia della chiesa in Italia* 43 (1989): 377–412, believes that Brun of Querfurt saw Otto III's sin as the irreconcilable intermingling of empire and monastic spirituality.

18 Görich, *Otto III*., 25.

sources.[19] With royal *auctoritas* (authority) donations were made, protection and immunity granted, or *libertas* (liberty) guaranteed. The juridical act effected by the king was itself described as *auctoritas*, as was the royal diploma. The question is, however: On what was royal *auctoritas* based, what legitimized it in this period?

In the tense arena of rulership and conflict, royal authority in the Ottonian and Salian periods was able to support itself on solid, societally sanctioned norms.[20] Recent scholarship has brought to light the "rules of the game" used in this functional system and has brought out the meaning of ritual and performance in presenting and securing royal authority.[21] Through these ritual and ceremonial interactions, where the reciprocal relationship between magnates became visible, we can perceive the external framework of the sociopolitical order.

This system of ceremonial order had to be based on immutability.[22] This means, however, that by itself the system was unable to create increased royal authority, even when it had the ritual means to do so. Changes that upset the hierarchical structure of magnates had to be kept at bay – in any case at least until a new hierarchy of positions had established itself and had been anchored through ritual. Impulses that increased the authority of the grounds for royal action at the same time had to work themselves into the received system of rules from the outside. The case of Henry II allows us to see this clearly.

I have already argued elsewhere that it was the coronation ordo of Mainz – having up to this point described more the ideal of kingship than its reality – that first provided Henry with the conceptional basis for his kingship.[23] In 1002 Henry II was the first of the East Frankish-German

---

19 *Monumenta Germaniae Historica, Diplomata regum et imperatorum Germaniae 3: Heinrici II. et Arduini Diplomata*, ed. Harry Bresslau, Hermann Bloch, and Robert Holtzmann (Hannover, 1900–3; reprint, Munich, 1980), no. 47 (hereafter *MGH DH II* 47): "Et ut haec nostra regalis auctoritas nunc et in futuro firmior permaneat." The corroboration formula of the other charters, which refers to the *auctoritas* of the ruler, reads likewise or similarly.

20 Keller, "Die Investitur," 75–7.

21 See Gerd Althoff, "Königsherrschaft und Konfliktbewältigung im 10. und 11. Jahrhundert," *Frühmittelalterliche Studien* 23 (1989): 265–90; Gerd Althoff, "Demonstration und Inszenierung: Spielregeln der Kommunikation in mittelalterlicher Öffentlichkeit," *Frühmittelalterliche Studien* 27 (1993): 27–50; and Gerd Althoff, "Ungeschriebene Gesetze: Wie funktioniert Herrschaft ohne schriftlich fixierte Normen?" in Gerd Althoff, *Spielregeln der Politik im Mittelalter: Kommunikation in Frieden und Fehde* (Darmstadt, 1997), 282–304.

22 See Jan Assmann, *Das kulturelle Gedächtnis: Schrift, Erinnerung und politische Identität in frühen Hochkulturen* (Munich, 1992), 56–9, 142–4; Janet L. Nelson, *Politics and Ritual in Early Medieval Europe* (London, 1986).

23 Stefan Weinfurter, "Der Anspruch Heinrichs II. auf die Königsherrschaft 1002," in Joachim Dahlhaus and Armin Kohnle, eds., *Papstgeschichte und Landesgeschichte: Festschrift für Hermann Jakobs zum 65. Geburtstag* (Cologne, 1995), 121–34.

kings to fully develop his claim to royal office using the norms of this liturgical order.

That the coronation ordo draws an image of an Old Testament Levitical-Mosaic kingship is of great significance.[24] For this style of kingship, the first requirement was *paterna successio*, succession in the paternal line. The second step is even more important: Through the anointing performed by the bishops, that is, the consecration of the new king, the *paterna successio* became a *hereditarium ius*.[25] This means a hereditary right to the kingship originating with God. The *paterna successio* thus was differentiated from the *hereditarium ius*. We must take care not to confuse this distinction in the kingship's theory of heritability.

This idea of divine inheritance referred directly to Old Testament texts on the Levites, for whom, because of their anointment, as Deuteronomy 18:2 states, "The Lord is their heir."[26] Thus, the earthly claim to succession based on paternal descent only could lead to kingship when it was linked to the patrimony of the heavenly king, the *ius hereditarium*. It is probably at this point that we hit on the heart of Henry's understanding of kingship and his theory of authority: Henry II played on these connections in his well-known diploma, no. 34, dated January 15, 1003, which outlines the legitimation of his kingship. Henry II probably formulated the carefully crafted text in this document himself; nothing here was left to a notary's choice of phrase.[27] Using the coronation ordo as his point of departure, Henry made it clear that the *hereditaria successio* had been bestowed on him by divine Providence, and thus – as we can probably best translate – the succession in the kingship as heir to the heavenly king. Accordingly, he asserted that he had a right to the *regnum sine aliqua divisione*, that is, the whole and entire realm subject to his undiminished royal power, without any exception that could direct itself against the divine order.

The legitimation of Henry's kingship and his justification of authority by means of the Mosaic-Levitical conception of the royal office appear in

24 Cyrille Vogel and Reinhard Elze, eds., *Le Pontifical romano-germanique du dixième siècle. Le texte I* (Vatican City, 1963), 250–1, e.g., §11: "Moysi et Iosuae populo praelatis multiplicem victoriam tribuisti, humilemque David puerum tuum regni fastigio sublimasti, et Salomonem sapientiae pacisque ineffabili munere ditasti."

25 Vogel and Elze, *Le Pontifical*, 258: "Sta et retine amodo locum, quem hucusque paterna successione tenuisti, hereditario iure tibi delegatum per auctoritatem Dei omnipotentis et presentem traditionem nostram, omnium scilicet episcoporum ceterorumque Dei servorum."

26 "Dominus enim ipse est hereditas eorum." In this respect their *paterna successio* is absorbed into a larger entity; see *Deuteronomium* 18:8.

27 Hartmut Hoffmann, "Eigendiktat in den Urkunden Ottos III. und Heinrichs II.," *Deutsches Archiv* 44 (1988): 414–16.

a unique way in yet another source. This is the ruler portrait of Henry II found in the Regensburg sacramentary, a key source for Henry's conception of rulership (see Figure 1.1).

The Regensburg sacramentary[28] was made in the monastery of Saint Emmeram in Regensburg in 1002 or 1003 at the very beginning of Henry's reign.[29] Already during the time when he was still duke of Bavaria, Henry stood in a special relationship to Saint Emmeram, an important center for his ecclesiastical advisers.[30] His closest adviser and confidant, Tagino, had been raised in Saint Emmeram and had been a friend of Bishop Wolfgang of Regensburg, one of Henry's teachers.[31] The coronation picture, in my opinion, reflects the conception of rulership found in the closest circle around Henry II.

Furthermore, this appears to be – for the first time in the Middle Ages – a real coronation picture, that is, a representation that takes as its subject the constitutive act itself. All previous depictions, those of Otto II, Otto III, and those from the Carolingian period, are in my judgment simply ruler portraits, not real coronation pictures.[32] This is a very significant distinction, for it demonstrates that Henry II depended on the legitimization of his royal elevation, that is, on the act that defined his authority in an entirely new way.

In the coronation picture Henry II receives the crown from Christ standing – not yet enthroned! His head, shoulders, and chest rise into the

---

28 Ulrich Kuder, "Die Handschriften," in *Regensburger Buchmalerei: Von frühkarolingischer Zeit bis zum Ausgang des Mittelalters*, Bayerische Staatsbibliothek – Ausstellungskataloge 39 (Munich, 1987), 32–3; Jutta Held, "Das Krönungsbild im Sakramentar Kaiser Heinrichs II.: Zur Rekonstruktion seiner Bedeutungssysteme," *Aachener Kunstblätter* 59 (1991–3): 85–97; Susanne Künzel, *Denkmale der Herrschaftstheologie Kaiser Heinrichs II.*, Schriften aus dem Institut für Kunstgeschichte der Universität München 43 (Munich, 1989); Ulrich Kuder, "Bischof Ulrich von Augsburg in der mittelalterlichen Buchmalerei," in Manfred Weitlauff, ed., *Bischof Ulrich von Augsburg, 890–973: Seine Zeit – sein Leben – seine Verehrung: Festschrift aus Anlass des tausendjährigen Jubiläums seiner Kanonisation im Jahr 993* (Weissenhorn, 1993), 415–17; Stefan Weinfurter, "Sakralkönigtum und Herrschaftsbegründung um die Jahrtausendwende: Die Kaiser Otto III. und Heinrich II. in ihren Bildern," in Helmut Altrichter, ed., *Bilder erzählen Geschichte* (Freiburg im Breisgau, 1995), 84–91.

29 Joachim Ott, "Vom Zeichencharakter der Herrscherkrone: Krönungszeremoniell und Krönungsbild im Mittelalter: Der Mainzer Ordo und das Sakramentar Heinrichs II.," in Jörg Jochen Berns and Thomas Rahn, eds., *Zeremoniell als höfische Ästhetik in Spätmittelalter und Früher Neuzeit* (Tübingen, 1995), 561–70.

30 Karl Josef Benz, "Regensburg in den geistigen Strömungen des 10. und 11. Jahrhunderts," in Dieter Albrecht, ed., *Zwei Jahrtausende Regensburg: Vortragsreihe der Universität Regensburg zum Stadtjubiläum 1979* (Regensburg, 1979), 79–80; *St. Emmeram in Regensburg, Geschichte – Kunst – Denkmalpflege*, Thurn und Taxis-Studien 18 (Kallmünz, 1992).

31 Dietrich Claude, *Geschichte des Erzbistums Magdeburg bis in das 12. Jahrhundert*, vol. 1: *Die Geschichte der Erzbischöfe bis auf Ruotger (1124)* (Cologne, 1972), 221–4. Thietmar, *Chronicon* 5.42, p. 268, reported that Bishop Wolfgang had thought of Tagino as a son.

32 Regarding this important distinction, see Joachim Ott, *Krone und Krönung: Ihre Ikonographie und Auslegung von der Spätantike bis um 1200* (Mainz, 1997).

Figure 1.1 Coronation picture of Henry II in the Regensburg Cathedral sacramentary. Staatsbibliothek München (clm 4456), fol. 11r. Reproduced by permission.

mandorla, into the sphere of the divine. From above two angels hand him two insignia of rulership: the sword and the holy lance. The holy lance, moreover – this has often been pointed out – has a unique feature: Its handle is studded with buds. This can only mean that this is the rod of

Aaron, the rod of the chosen and of life, the rod that sprouted buds and blossoms, and which Moses, by the command of the Lord, was to keep near the ark of the covenant.[33] Henry II thus takes the rod of the chosen, as Moses had once done. We should note that the Moses idea also found an echo in the narrative sources, such as in the *Vita* of Adalbero of Metz,[34] the *Vita* of Burchard of Worms,[35] and the *Miraculae Sancti Emmerammi*.[36] Thus, Henry II entered the ranks of the leaders that God had set over the chosen people as they are listed in the Mainz coronation ordo: Moses, Joshua, David, and Solomon. The people entrusted to Henry accordingly assumed the role of the chosen people.

At Henry's right and left side stand the saintly bishops Emmeram of Regensburg and Ulrich of Augsburg. Just as it is described in the coronation ordo, they take the ruler by the left and right hands and lead him to the anointing and coronation.[37] In this way they transfer to him the *hereditarium ius*, the divine inheritance of the kingdom. For the first time in the Middle Ages – to emphasize this once more – we have before us a miniature of a ruler that makes a direct reference to the function played by the bishops in the coronation ordo, and that thereby shows that the king has entered into the qualitative likeness to the Levites.[38] Because

33 *Numeri* 17:1–13.

34 *Vita Adalberonis II.: Mettensis episcopi auctore Constantino abbate*, ed. Georg Heinrich Pertz, in *Monumenta Germaniae Historica, Scriptores* 4 (hereafter *MGH SS*) (Hannover, 1841), c. 16, p. 663: "Ecce, inquit, ecce, vos estis loca quidem sanctorum sacerdotum tenentes, et in meliori cathedra, quam sedisset Moyses, sedentes, utpote vices domini possidentes."

35 Heinrich Boos, ed., *Vita Burchardi*, Quellen zur Geschichte der Stadt Worms 3 (Berlin, 1893), cc. 18–19, pp. 117–21.

36 *Ex Arnoldi libris de sancto Emmerammo*, ed. Georg Waitz, in *MGH SS* 4 (Hannover, 1841), vol. 2, c. 40, p. 568: "Quinque autem altaria, in quibus totidem pyxides collocatae cum reliquiis, quas prenominatus heros de Lotharingia transtulit, quinque librorum Moysi principalem observantiam in memoria monent teneri, et in quinque sensibus corporis hortantur quinariam prudentiam semper haberi."

37 Vogel and Elze, *Le Pontifical*, §2, pp. 246–7.

38 A comparable representation exists in the Bamberg Pontifical of 1012–1014, which Henry II commissioned the monastery of Seeon to make for Bamberg (*Staatsbibliothek Bamberg, Msc. Lit. 53*, fol. 2ʳ). See Gude Suckale-Redlefsen, "Die Buchmalerei in Seeon zur Zeit Kaiser Heinrichs II.," in Hans von Malottki, ed., *Kloster Seeon: Beiträge zu Geschichte, Kunst und Kultur der ehemaligen Beneditkinerabtei* (Weissenhorn, 1993), 179–80, illus. no. 78. The ruler accompanied by two bishops in this manuscript clearly could also refer to Henry II. Decisive, however, is the illustration of the text in the Coronation Ordo. Also, one finds a corresponding representation from the same time in the Warmund Codex. See Adriano Peroni, "Il ruolo della committenza vescovile alle soglie del Mille: Il caso di Warmondo di Ivrea," in *Committenti e produzione artistico-letteraria nell'alto medioevo occidentale*, Settimane di Studio del Centro Italiano di Studi sull'Alto Medioevo 39, 2 vols. (Spoleto, 1992), 1:243–71. The pontifical of Schaffhausen (*Stadtbibliothek, Ministerialbibliothek Min. 94*), which likewise contains a picture of this kind, comes, however, from a later period (the end of the eleventh century) (see *Das Reich der Salier 1024–1125: Katalog zur Ausstellung des Landes Rheinland-Pfalz* [Sigmaringen, 1992], 421 and 424; Percy Ernst Schramm, *Die deutschen Kaiser und Könige in Bildern ihrer Zeit: 751–1190*, new ed. Florentine Mütherich (Munich, 1983), 237, illus. no. 165); Rolf Lauer, "Schaffhauser Pontifikale," in Michael Brandt and Arne

Henry appears as a new Moses chosen to bring the laws of God to the people of the Lord and to save God's people, the two bishops thus can be likened to Aaron and Hur, which has often been noted by scholars. These two supported Moses until the Israelites defeated the Amalekites, the enemies of God.[39]

When we keep these connections in mind, we can understand why Saint Emmeram and Saint Ulrich, the two victory-bringing saints of the East Frankish realm, are depicted. They both had secured the existence of the East Frankish realm, Emmeram – as the *Miraculae sancti Emmerammi* report[40] – as patronus (patron saint) in Arnulf of Carinthia's battles against the Moravians and Ulrich, who, as his *Vita* tells us, aided victory in 955 against the Hungarians.[41] These saints thus assume the place of Aaron and Hur and so project the biblical situation onto the East Frankish kingdom.

Actually, two other saints could have taken these places: Saint Maurice, the protector of the Saxon kingdom to whom Henry appealed for victory in the Polish campaigns, and Saint Lawrence, on whose feast day the battle of the Lechfeld had been won.[42] At that time Otto I had vowed to establish the bishopric Merseburg for Saint Lawrence in the event of a victory over the Hungarians on August 10, 955. This bishopric, founded in 968, thus was nothing less than a votive offering for the victory over the enemies of God and for the continued existence of the realm.[43] In this

---

Eggebrecht, eds., *Bernward von Hildesheim und das Zeitalter der Ottonen* 2 (Hildesheim, 1993), 176–8, no. IV-28.

39 *Exodus* 17:11–12. For a different interpretation, see Kuder, "Bischof Ulrich," 416–17 and note 13.

40 *Ex Arnoldi libris* 1.5, p. 551: (Arnulf of Carinthia) "Is namque sperans, deum sibi sic fore propitium, elegit beatum Emmerammum vitae suae ac regno patronum, adeoque illi adhesit, ut in vicinitate monasterii regio cultui aptum construeret grande palatium. Cum ergo huius patrocinium duris in negociis et in preliis multis satis haberet expertum, manifestius hoc sibi adesse sensit, quando Marahensi bello interfuit."

41 Gerhard von Augsburg, *Vita Sancti Uodalrici: Die älteste Lebensbeschreibung des heiligen Ulrich*, ed. Walter Berschin and Angelika Häse, Editiones Heidelbergenses 24 (Heidelberg, 1993), vol. 1, c. 12, pp. 192–202. It should also be noted that the victory over the Hungarians remained firmly embedded in the collective consciousness because of the yearly religious festival celebrated on the day of the victory (Aug. 10). This was the day on which God granted his Christian people victory over their worst enemy. See Hagen Keller, "Widukinds Bericht über die Aachener Wahl und Krönung Ottos I.," *Frühmittelalterliche Studien* 29 (1995): 400–1; Helmut Beumann, "Das Kaisertum Ottos des Grossen: Ein Rückblick nach tausend Jahren," *Historische Zeitschrift* 195 (1962): 553–5.

42 Helmut Beumann, "Laurentius und Mauritius: Zu den missionspolitischen Folgen des Ungarnsieges Ottos des Grossen," in Helmut Beumann, ed., *Festschrift für Walter Schlesinger*, Mitteldeutsche Forschungen 74, 2 vols. (Cologne, 1974), 2:238–75.

43 See Ernst-Dieter Hehl, "Merseburg – eine Bistumsgründung unter Vorbehalt: Gelübde, Kirchenrecht und politischer Spielraum im 10. Jahrhundert," *Frühmittelalterliche Studien* 31 (1997): 96–119.

light the suppression of this bishopric in 981 must have been seen to threaten this stability. Consequently, not only did the coronation of Kunigunde in 1002 occur in Paderborn on Saint Lawrence's feast, but the royal pair also made a vow there to restore the bishopric of Merseburg.[44] The gifts made by Henry in October 1021 in connection with the consecration of the Merseburg cathedral express, respectively, the hope that the realm would in return be strengthened.[45] Such a thought was recorded at the very beginning of Henry's reign in the *arenga* of a diploma for the monastery of Saint John: Through his actions the realm that had been entrusted to him would continue to exist.[46]

All of the named saints, Maurice and Lawrence, Emmeram and Ulrich, were guarantors for the undivided continuance of this realm and its people, and they obligated the king – the new Moses – to follow this program. Moreover, I find it worthy to note that it was precisely these particular victory-bringing saints who were incorporated into the programmatic picture of the Regensburg gospel book, for they not only had a special significance for the East Frankish kingdom but also were bishops.

With all of this, the analysis of the Regensburg gospel book's ruler miniature is still not exhausted. I also would like to point out that the idea of *paterna successio* (claim to paternal succession) found emphasis not only in the inscription framing the picture[47] but also in that, for the first time, a ruler was depicted with the holy lance, the symbol of rulership that was traced back to Henry I.[48]

These observations make it clear that Henry II defined and anchored his kingship in an entirely new way, using a liturgical-sacral foundation. Although this conclusion is certainly not surprising, I do believe that we must pay more attention to the new elements and the consequences of

---

44 Georg Heinrich Pertz, ed., *Annales Quedlinburgenses, MGH SS* 3 (Hannover, 1839), s.a. 1002, p. 78, ll. 37–9.

45 *MGH DD H II* 449–51: "Si venerabilia ecclesiarum dei loca alicuius doni commodo ditare ac sublimare studuerimus, nobis id regnique nostri statui profuturum esse minime dubitamus."

46 *MGH DH II* 3: "Si ad hoc sumus intenti et desiderio pleni, ut proprietates ecclesiarum dei de die in diem adaugmentemus, regnum ad hoc nobis commissum diutius prolongari et in futuro cum electis anime nostrae remunerari procul dubio scimus."

47 Inscription: "Behold the pious King Henry is crowned by divine disposition and anointed and he is elevated into the vault of heaven by the lineage of his paternal ancestors" ("Ecce coronatur divinitus atque beatur / Rex pius Heinricus proavorum stirpe polosus"), *Monumenta Germaniae Historica, Poetae latini* 5.2, ed. Karl Strecker (Dublin, 1939), 434. See Weinfurter, "Sakralkönigtum," 84–7; Weinfurter, "Der Anspruch," 125.

48 Weinfurter, "Der Anspruch," 127–8; Eduard Hlawitschka, *Vom Frankenreich zur Formierung der europäischen Staaten- und Völkergemeinschaft: 804-1046* (Darmstadt, 1986), 208–10, provides a summary of the research on the Holy Lance.

this shift in thought: An electoral procedure was no longer necessary, at least not as a constitutive act, for this conception of kingship. God himself entrusted the new king with his people, just as the section of the Mosaic laws dealing with kingship had established this as a legitimation for the king.[49] This explains why, in fact, in 1002 no election by the magnates of the realm took place. Only the royal consecration mattered for Henry II and his supporters.[50] The opposition recognized this clearly and it is why Duke Hermann II of Swabia strove so desperately to block Henry's procession to Mainz, the place of consecration.[51] With the anointing and coronation on June 7 in Mainz, everything had been decided for Henry II. All that followed counted only toward the recognition of his kingship by his competitors, their adherents, and various groups in the realm.

No less important was the new alliance that, as a consequence of the new idea of kingship, arose between the king and the bishops of the realm, with the archbishop of Mainz at their head. It is not at all the case, as the studies of Ernst-Dieter Hehl have recently made clear, that a long developmental process of the symbiosis between kingship and church had reached a new high point under Henry II – as previous scholars have believed.[52] One must consider much more that Otto III, in concert with Pope Gregory V, had tried to destroy the jurisdictional prominence of Archbishop Willigis of Mainz in the royal church, that is, the canonically defined preeminence of the archbishop of Mainz; and he had thereby attempted to break up the closed system of the royal church. The new alliance under Henry II, which once again placed the archbishop of Mainz at the pinnacle of the royal church, thus meant a radical about-face in the relationship of kingship and the royal church, indeed one tending toward the closed order of the church in the East Frankish kingdom.[53] The people whom God had entrusted to the king were thereby bound to the renewed and strengthened unity of the royal church, a process that was made evident ceremonially in the Dortmund prayer confraternity of

---

49 *Deuteronomium* 17:15: "eum constitues, quem dominus deus tuus elegerit."
50 See Fried, *Der Weg*, 607; Weinfurter, "Der Anspruch," 131–2.
51 Thietmar, *Chronicon* 5.11, pp. 232, 234.
52 Ernst-Dieter Hehl, "Herrscher, Kirche und Kirchenrecht im spätottonischen Reich," in Bernd Schneidmüller and Stefan Weinfurter, eds., *Otto III. – Heinrich II.: Eine Wende?* Mittelalter-Forschungen 1 (Sigmaringen, 1997), 169–203; Hehl, "Merseburg"; Ernst-Dieter Hehl, "Der widerspenstige Bischof: Bischöfliche Zustimmung und bischöflicher Protest in der ottonischen Reichskirche," in Gerd Althoff and Ernst Schubert, eds., *Herrschaftsrepräsentation im ottonischen Sachsen*, Vorträge und Forschungen 46 (Sigmaringen, 1998), 295–344.
53 Stefan Weinfurter, "Otto III. und Heinrich II. im Vergleich: Ein Resümee," in Schneidmüller and Weinfurter, eds., *Otto III. – Heinrich II.*, 387–413.

1005.[54] As Thietmar reports,[55] Henry, together with his episcopal colleagues, the *coepiscopi*, had with common consent created a completely
new institution (*nova institutio*),[56] namely, a prayer confraternity spanning
the realm's northern half, for the good of the church and in order to end
the conflicts brewing in that realm.[57] It was precisely the novelty of this
institution that received such emphasis because it was borne by a liturgically and ritually anchored display of the new unity between the king
and the royal church.

Other new or changed forms of ritual royal presentation also appeared.
Henry's preference for episcopal cities in his itinerary – long noted by
scholars – would at most have had only a secondary reason in considerations of hospitality. As Thomas Zotz has shown, Henry II celebrated the
high church feasts together with the bishops with new regularity and
established Pentecost as a key event in ecclesiastical-royal presentation.[58]
As no ruler before him had done, Henry not only regularly attended
the great church consecrations of his day (such as at Quedlinburg,
Gandersheim, Nienburg, and Merseburg), but also determined dates and
sequences of events, such as the Quedlinburg *Annals* report,[59] and stayed
close to clerical circles even during liturgical functions that were off limits
to laymen.[60]

The changes that can be detected in Henry's behavior toward secular
magnates have often been discussed.[61] I need only recall the radical limita-

---

54 Thietmar, *Chronicon* 6.18, pp. 294–7; see Joachim Wollasch, "Geschichtliche Hintergründe der
   Dortmunder Versammlung des Jahres 1005," *Westfalen* 58 (1980): 55–69.
55 Thietmar, *Chronicon* 6.18, p. 294.   56 Ibid.
57 One might conjecture similar occurrences for the southern half of the realm. Possibly the entries
   in the Trent Diptych might be related to these; see Gerd Althoff, "Gebetsgedenken für Teilnehmer
   an Italienzügen: Ein bisher unbeachtetes Trienter Diptychon," *Frühmittelalterliche Studien* 16 (1982):
   129–42. See also Gerd Althoff, *Adels- und Königsfamilien im Spiegel ihrer Memorialüberlieferung: Studien
   zum Totengedenken der Billunger und Ottonen*, Münstersche Mittelalter-Schriften 47 (Munich, 1984),
   244.
58 Thomas Zotz, "Präsenz und Repräsentation: Beobachtungen zur königlichen Herrschaftspraxis
   im hohen und späten Mittelalter," in Alf Lüdtke, ed., *Herrschaft als soziale Praxis: Historische und
   sozial-anthropologische Studien*, Veröffentlichungen des Max-Planck-Instituts für Geschichte 91
   (Göttingen, 1991), 168–94; Thomas Zotz, "Die Gegenwart des Königs: Zur Herrschaftspraxis
   Ottos III. und Heinrichs II.," in Schneidmüller and Weinfurter, eds., *Otto III. – Heinrich II.*,
   349–86.
59 *Annales Quedlinburgenses*, MGH SS 3, s.a. 1021, p. 86, l. 40: "ipso iubente." Likewise, Frutolf von
   Michelsberg, *Chronica*, ed. Franz-Josef Schmale and Irene Schmale-Ott, Ausgewählte Quellen zur
   deutschen Geschichte 15 (Darmstadt, 1972), 52: "ipso presidente ac disponente."
60 See Karl Josef Benz, *Untersuchungen zur politischen Bedeutung der Kirchweihe unter Teilnahme der
   deutschen Herrscher im hohen Mittelalter: Ein Beitrag zum Studium des Verhältnisses zwischen weltlicher
   Macht und kirchlicher Wirklichkeit unter Otto III. und Heinrich II.*, Regensburger Historische
   Forschungen 4 (Kallmünz, 1975), 92–220.
61 Keller, "Reichsstruktur," 100–4; Stefan Weinfurter, "Die Zentralisierung der Herrschaftsgewalt im
   Reich durch Kaiser Heinrich II.," *Historisches Jahrbuch* 106 (1986): 241–97.

tion on ducal authority in Swabia[62] and Bavaria,[63] and the measures Henry
took to establish himself in place of the dukes as an authority equally able
to impose peace, in Swabia in 1004 (the *pax* for *tota Alemannia*) and in
Saxony in 1012 (*mutua pax*).[64] Henry's conduct in the prosecution of feuds
– Gerd Althoff has recently pointed this out – appears as a decisive change
in contrast to the normal model of conflict resolution under the Ottonians.[65] Henry's manner of proceeding was marked by hardness and lack of
pity, by rejection of compromise, and the refusal of mercy without regard
to his opponent's submission. Brun of Querfurt's sharp criticism of Henry
in his letter of 1008 is instructive: "Oh that you were only merciful and
would win your people to you, not always with violence, but also with
mercy, and that you would find its affection."[66] Here both the novelty and
differentness of the king's mode of behavior were addressed. A number
of other sources also make clear just how intensely people in these years
discussed the changes in the king's exercise of leadership.[67]

From no other period do we have so many texts that put forth the
ruler as the guardian, even as the "creator," of the law. Henry is called
iusticie amator (lover of justice),[68] or *auctor iustitiae* (author of justice),[69] or
even *iura dans* (one who gives the laws).[70] The second ruler portrait contained in the Regensburg gospel book bears the inscription *nam ditione
tua sunt omnia iura subacta* (all law is subject to your power).[71] We should

---

62 Thomas Zotz, *Der Breisgau und das alemannische Herzogtum: Zur Verfassungs- und Besitzgeschichte im
    10. und beginnenden 11. Jahrhundert*, Vorträge und Forschungen, Sonderband 15 (Sigmaringen,
    1974), 166–207; Helmut Maurer, *Der Herzog von Schwaben: Grundlagen, Wirkungen und Wesen seiner
    Herrschaft in ottonischer, salischer und staufischer Zeit* (Sigmaringen, 1978), 163–5.
63 Wilhelm Störmer, "Heinrichs II. Schenkungen"; Wilhelm Störmer, "Kaiser Heinrich II., Kaiserin
    Kunigunde und das Herzogtum Bayern," *Zeitschrift für Bayerische Landesgeschichte* 60 (1997):
    437–63.
64 Reinhold Kaiser, "Selbsthilfe und Gewaltenmonopol. Königliche Friedenswahrung in Deutsch-
    land und Frankreich im Mittelalter," *Frühmittelalterliche Studien* 17 (1983): 65–6.
65 Gerd Althoff, "Otto III. und Heinrich II. in Konflikten," in Schneidmüller and Weinfurter, eds.,
    Otto III. – Heinrich II., 77–94.
66 Jadwiga Karwasinska, ed., *Brunonis Querfurtensis epistola ad Henricum regem*, Monumenta Poloniae
    Historica, n.s. 4, 3 (Warsaw, 1973), 103: "ut etiam sis misericors et non semper cum potestate, sed
    etiam cum misericordia populum tibi concilies et acceptabilem prepares."
67 See Fried's summary in *Der Weg*, 623: "Heinrich war ein König, der konfrontierte, nicht befriedete,
    der Gräben aufriss, nicht zuschüttete. Er bediente sich aller Mittel, von der List über den Verrat
    bis zur nackten Gewalt und mit besonderer Vorliebe des kanonischen Rechts."
68 Auguste Molinier, ed., *Historiens de France, Obituaires* 12 (Paris, 1906), 192.
69 Thietmar, *Chronicon* 5.27, p. 253.
70 Brun of Querfurt, *Passio sancti Adelberti episcopi et martyris*, ed. Jadwiga Karwasinska, Monumenta
    Poloniae Historica n.s. 4, 2 (Warsaw, 1969), 3: "quem longe lateque iura dantem hodie tremunt
    populi, Heinrico regi accessit proximus nepos" (cf. Ernst Voigt, *Brun von Querfurt* [Stuttgart, 1907],
    334).
71 *MGH Poetae latini* 5.2, p. 435, l. 5. Also worth noting is the tenet found in Egbert of Liège's
    Fecunda Ratis, ed. Ernst Voigt (Halle, 1889), p. 56, v. 243: "Rex, ubi uult, solet inuitas discindere
    leges," and the gloss on it: "Rex, in quam partem uoluerit, per uim legem conuertit."

not misunderstand such formulations: In no way did the king see himself as a lawgiver. He did, however, claim the right to see that the law of God was respected. He was not only the guardian of the law but also saw himself invested with the duty of implementing it.

This belief was expressed in another ruler miniature of Henry II, as far as I know once again for the first time in the history of the East Frankish-German kingship. It is found in the Codex Ottobonianus lat. 74, the gospel book that was made in Regensburg probably around 1024 and may have been given by the emperor to the monastery of Monte Cassino (see Figure 1.2).[72] The famous image shows Henry enthroned in the center of a quatrefoil or Greek cross. The dove of the Holy Spirit

---

72 See Weinfurter, "Sakralkönigtum," 96–101; Kuder, "Die Handschriften," 34; Ulrike Surmann, "Evangeliar Kaiser Heinrichs II.," *Biblioteca Apostolica Vaticana: Liturgie und Andacht im Mittelalter* (Stuttgart, 1992), 92–5. Of fundamental importance is Hagen Keller, "Das Bildnis Kaiser Heinrichs im Regensburger Evangeliar aus Montecassino (Bibl. Vat., Ottob. lat. 74): Zugleich ein Beitrag zu Wipos 'Tetralogus,'" *Frühmittelalterliche Studien* 30 (1996): 173–214. Keller attributes the picture to Emperor Henry III. He justifies this primarily in that the rulership ideas as they are developed in Wipo's *Tetralogus* correspond with the rulership concept of the picture. One readily follows the very subtle and keen argumentation. Nevertheless, I still am inclined to hold firm to the attribution of the picture to Henry II for the following reasons: (1) The rulership concept or program of Henry II is very similar to that of Henry III. The preservation of justice and peace holds a central importance for both. Let me give one example. In the *Pericopes Book* of Henry II (Munich, Staatsbibliothek, Clm 4452), at the end of the manuscript, one finds a section with a compilation of masses, in which the theme of the "unjust judge" is addressed. For this treatment, the example from the Gospel *Luke* 18:1–15 is brought into play.

There it is made clear how the "just judge" had to act, and naturally the ruler ought to orient himself to that example. (2) The inscription of the middle medallion of the picture in the Montecassino Evangelary (Vatican Library, Ottob. lat. 74) reads as follows: "Henry shines on the paternally inherited throne of dominion, Emperor and Augustus worthy through the distinction of the imperial robe" ("Imperii solio fulget Heinricus avito / Caesar et augustus trabeali munere dignus," *MGH Poetae latini* 5.2, p. 438). The derivation of his rulership from his paternal ancestors had a fundamental legitimizing significance for Henry II; see Weinfurter, "Der Anspruch." The dedication inscription to the ruler portrait of Henry II's *Pericopes Book* (Munich Clm 4452, fol. 1v) very correspondingly reads: "Greatest King Henry, shining exultantly in the splendor of the faith, prosperously enjoys the dominion inherited from his great grandfather" ("*Rex Heinricus ovans, fidei splendore coruscans/Maximus imperio, fruitur quo prosper avito,*" *MGH Poetae latini* 5.2, p. 433). On the other hand, this relationship to the "paternal ancestors" did not play any legitimizing role at all for Henry III, and moreover, it is not emphasized anywhere else in the sources. (3) The tradition that prevailed in Montecassino around 1100 connected the Evangelary with Henry II, who, according to tradition, is said to have given it to the monastery; see Herbert Bloch, *Monte Cassino in the Middle Ages*, 3 vols. (Rome, 1986), 1: 19–20. As the reason for the gift, it is reported that Henry II had doubted that St. Benedict lay buried in the monastery. Consequently, through a miracle of St. Benedict he was taught a better way of thinking and bestowed precious gifts on the monastery. In the case, however, that the evangelary had been given by Henry III, then Henry III must have been replaced in the local tradition by Henry II. Yet, what would have been the reason for that? As a proof that the relics of St. Benedict were in Monte Cassino, the authority of Henry III would have been no less powerful around 1100 than that of Henry II. Nevertheless, there is an argument that one has to recognize for the attribution to Henry III. In the uppermost medallion it states: "Spiritus alme deus regem benedicito clemens." The designation *rex* for Emperor Henry II around 1022 is very unusual and difficult to explain. This entire problem requires further discussion.

Figure 1.2   Miniature of Henry II in the Gospel book of Monte Cassino. Vatican Library, Codex Ottobonianus lat. 74, fol. 193v. Reproduced by permission.

descends on Henry, who occupies the position of the Pantocrator. His priestlike rank is underlined by the golden stole that he wears over his robe. This was probably copied from the Byzantine *loros* but also corresponds to the band worn by a deacon and recalls the girdle of the high

priest in the Old Testament.[73] Is the idea of the new Moses here present?
It would then be expanded to incorporate the type of the high priest,
the type of Aaron.[74]

Henry appears in God's place as the administrator of the law. Around
him are personifications of the four virtues of a ruler. In the lower corners
one finds masculine figures: *lex* (law of God) on the left, depicted as a
cleric with an opened book containing the law of God and *ius* (customary law) on the right as an elderly layman who knows the old law. In
the lower medallion a tyrant kneels; an executioner stands before him
with a drawn sword looking up at the emperor, from whom they both
await the deciding signal: execution or mercy, naturally not as capricious
judgment but as a decision made with consideration of wisdom, clever
reflection, justice, and piety, and with exact knowledge of the law and the
laws of God. The power to adjudicate, however – and the entire composition points to this – should lie with the ruler alone: All law is subject
to his power.[75]

At this point one can see the level of importance the "instrument" of
pardon from the king's hand developed.[76] At the moment when he did
not grant the royal *gratia* (grace) according to the received rules but rather
made it dependent on the principles of his conception of rulership, the
right to pardon became a powerful tool of an entirely new quality. By
means of the exercise of *gratia*, the way to the power of adjudication lay
open to the king[77] – provided that his conception of rulership was able
to win acceptance.[78]

The foregoing considerations and views show well enough the central
concern here: the question of how the seemingly affirmatively constructed
ritual and ceremonial structure present in the interactions of rulers, on
the one hand, and conceptions of royal rule, on the other, interact. Or,
to express it in more general terms, the question of the interaction
between established orders and mentally conceived orders.[79] Hagen Keller
recently investigated this question with respect to investiture.[80] The ritual
ceremony that effected investiture changed little over centuries. However,
the inner meaning of investiture was subject to far-reaching changes –

---

73 *Exodus* 28:7–8.   74 See *Exodus* 28, 39.
75 See note 70 to this chapter.
76 On this, see Gerd Althoff, "Huld: Überlegungen zu einem Zentralbegriff der mittelalterlichen
   Herrschaftsordnung," *Frühmittelalterliche Studien* 25 (1991): 259–82.
77 Ibid., 264: "Den Entzug der Huld verfügte und verantwortete der Herr offenbar allein."
78 See ibid., 271.
79 See Assmann, *Das kulturelle Gedächtnis*, 78–83, 142–3.
80 Keller, "Die Investitur."

particularly when we consider the investiture of bishops – varying according to conceptions that were associated with feudal obligations.

My observations of Henry II as an example point in the same direction. His execution of rulership was guided, it seems to me, by an idea that had its origin in the functional definition of the kingship. To strengthen the unity and peace of the realm and to further its integration and overcome its gentile-based structure required an intensification of royal authority. Henry and his aides blazed new paths here and strengthened the sacral legitimization of kingship through the idea of a "kingship of Moses," the task of which was to establish a theocratic order among the people entrusted to him by God. I place a high value on the effectiveness of this concept, marked as it was by a consciousness of having a personal duty to fulfill and of bearing a great and personal responsibility to God.[81] Henry's repeated and marked claim to a very personal power of adjudication must have had its origin here. This legitimation of rulership led in turn to new forms of royal presentation and to actions that moved away from the received patterns of behavior, particularly in the pursuit of conflict. Henry saw himself as empowered, better yet obligated, to go against the established "rules of the game" in order to fulfill the commission he had received.

We know what results this justification of action brought: The conflicts with the magnates of the realm increased in their intensity,[82] the struggles with the Ezzonids, the Conradines, Salians, Welfs, and Billungs stretched out over years and decades, and even among his own kin, the Luxemburgers, Henry met with resistance.[83] The high nobility defended its own "rules of the game."

But as surprising as it may seem, the real problem facing this kingship did not lie in the conflicts with the high nobility but rather in those with the bishops and in those between the bishops, for the king had to solve these in order to maintain peace. The episcopate of the realm constituted a group standing apart from the king, even though he was their *simpnista*, their colleague, and had the rank of a Levite.[84] But the decisive factor was that in the law of the Church this group had its own system of rules.[85] This system of rules was, however, more tightly organized than the "rules of behavior" of the nobility. It guaranteed the legal position of the bishops in general as well as that of each individual bishop. Conflicts within this

---

81 The idea of personal responsibility is especially pronounced in *MGH DD H II* 99 and 504; see also John W. Bernhardt, "Der Herrscher im Spiegel der Urkunden: Otto III. und Heinrich II. im Vergleich," in Schneidmüller and Weinfurter, eds., *Otto III. – Heinrich II.*
82 Althoff, "Der König im Konflikt."
83 See Weinfurter, "Die Zentralisierung," 273–84.
84 Thietmar, *Chronicon* 6.38, p. 321.   85 See Hehl, "Der widerspenstige Bischof."

group could, in principle, only be resolved by means of ecclesiastical law or by a synodal decision – and perhaps not even then![86] Unresolvable conflicts threatened the entire system. Above all, the canonical principle that the alteration of a bishopric was impossible without the consent of the bishop affected by the change could be used to advantage by both parties in a fight, as was the case in the Gandersheim conflict.[87]

It must have been extremely explosive for the bishops when they were expected to deny this key episcopal right – what one might call the fundamental episcopal right – to one of their colleagues. For then the entire system of the royal-episcopal church was in danger.

But such was exactly the issue at stake when we began our study. When Henry II sought to obtain approval at the synod of Frankfurt for the establishment of the diocese of Bamberg in 1007, the bishop of Würzburg, whose diocese would be affected by the new foundation, did not consent. His representative, his chaplain Berengar, touched the heart of the problem with this argument: If the bishops voted for the establishment of Bamberg, they would thereby create a fundamental precedent that would endanger the legal position of every other bishop.[88] It absolutely and logically followed, argued Berengar, that the assembly of bishops had to decide against the king! And now we understand: This situation was the single most important test for Henry's theory of authority as it presents itself to us and for the new legitimation he gave his actions.

With this in mind, the significance of Henry's action of humility becomes clear: By throwing himself on the ground and humbling himself, the king made it clear that he was prepared to risk and vindicate the entire principle of authority behind his kingship. He gave the bishops the alternative of choosing between their own system of rules or the new forms used to legitimize royal policy and action. The decision for or against Bamberg fundamentally was a decision for or against the authority – in turn derived from biblical and patristic norms – of the representative of the heavenly king to adjudicate.

---

86 In this regard and according to pseudo-isidorian tradition, one reads in the *Decretum* of Bishop Burchard of Worms: "Ut episcopi a solo deo sint diiudicandi" (*Decretum* 1.133).

87 Hans Goetting, *Das Bistum Hildesheim 3: Die Hildesheimer Bischöfe von 815 bis 1221 (1227)*, Germania Sacra n.s. 20 (Berlin, 1984), 183–4; Heinz Wolter, *Die Synoden im Reichsgebiet und in Reichsitalien von 916 bis 1056* (Paderborn, 1988), 182–210; Knut Görich, "Der Gandersheimer Streit zur Zeit Ottos III.: Ein Konflikt um die Metropolitanrechte des Erzbischofs Willigis von Mainz," *Zeitschrift für Rechtsgeschichte, kan. Abt.* 79 (1993): 56–94; Stephanie Coué, *Hagiographie im Kontext: Schreibanlass und Funktion von Bischofsviten aus dem 11. und vom Anfang des 12. Jahrhunderts*, Arbeiten zur Frühmittelalterforschung 24 (Berlin, 1997), 41–61; Hehl, "Der widerspenstige Bischof."

88 Thietmar, *Chronicon* 6.32, p. 312: "et obsecrat cunctos presentes per Christi amorem, ne talia fieri absente eo futurum sibi in exemplum paterentur."

The argumentation used at the synod of Frankfurt is by chance reported to us in a letter that one of those in attendance at the synod, Bishop Arnold of Halberstadt, wrote shortly thereafter to the bishop of Würzburg.[89] He goes over in detail the arguments put forth at the synod. The letter reaches its rhetorical height with the words:

It is not I personally who wishes to convince you . . . rather the Apostle should step forward. That chosen one, the teacher of the nations, should speak for me. . . . He says: "Each soul is subject to a higher authority. There is of course no authority apart from God. Every authority is established by God. He who sets himself against authority, acts contrary to God's order. He who opposes Him, will stand condemned before the court." Now you see why I warn you . . . much less I, but the Apostle, and what is more not only he, but through him God Himself: Do not set yourself against the decrees of God, lest at the end of time you be damned. For it leads without exception to damnation, if one places himself above that order that the authorities raised above us.[90]

In the end, as we see, the divine command that the king had authority to adjudicate was placed above the ecclesiastical law that the bishopric was immutable.[91] This argumentation led the members of the synod finally to decide against one of their number. The synod gave in, as would never again occur in a comparable case. The new, infinitely increased *auctoritas* of the king had had its way. The self-humiliation of Henry at Bamberg, which is without precedent and may only with difficulty be regarded as a premeditated theatrical performance, allowed Henry not only to break the impasse blocking the foundation of his bishopric but, much more than that, it brought victory to his conception of rulership and order and thereby represented the high point of his authority.

89 Philipp Jaffé, ed., *Monumenta Bambergensia*, Bibliotheca rerum Germanicarum 5 (Berlin, 1869), *Ep. Bambergens.* no. 2, pp. 472–9. Concerning the dating, see von Guttenberg, *Die Regesten*, no. 75 (beginning of 1008, before May 7).

90 *Monumenta Bambergensia*, p. 476: "Absit a me, ut, nisi desipiam, huiusmodi tibi persuadeam; magis, si ullo modo sciam, in haec ipsa te ducere velim. Procedat apostolus; loquatur pro me ille vas electionis, doctor gentium. Ecce doctor noster; non enim ex Iudeis, sed ex gentibus nos. Quid ait apostolus? 'Omnis anima,' inquit, 'potestatibus sublimioribus subdita sit. Non est enim potestas nisi a Deo. Quae autem sunt, a Deo ordinata sunt. Itaque, qui resistit potestati, Dei ordinationi resistit. Qui autem resistunt, ipsi sibi damnationem adquirunt.' Ecce, quid hortor; ecce, in qua duco; immo non ego, sed apostolus; immo non ille, sed per illum Deus: ut Dei ordinationi non resistas nec ipse tibi damnationem assumas. Fortassis hoc est damnationem sibi assumere: ea, quae a sublimioribus iniunguntur, supersedere."

91 Disobedience to ruler appears as disobedience to God and therefore as treason: "Difficile est, reum esse maiestatis" (p. 474). Cf. Thietmar, *Chronicon* 5.32, p. 256: "Quibus reciproco, non ullam in hoc seculo esse dominationem, nisi a deo, et qui se contra eam erigat, divinae maiestatis offensam incurrat."

2

King Henry II of Germany

Royal Self-Representation and Historical Memory

JOHN W. BERNHARDT

INTRODUCTION

I would like to examine a few examples taken from the reign of Henry II of Germany that illustrate the interaction of royal self-representation, or imagination, if you will, and historical memory, especially as it came to be recorded. Throughout, one will see that rituals of various sorts played an important role in these examples as it did throughout the early Middle Ages. In particular, I address three topics: aspects of how Henry imagined and represented his claims to rulership, aspects of how Henry imagined and represented himself to be the master of the church, and one manuscript portrait of Henry II that provides a visual example of the intersection of royal self-representation and historical memory.

SELF-REPRESENTATION AND RITUAL IN THE
LEGITIMIZATION OF HENRY II'S RULERSHIP

In January 1002 Otto III died suddenly in Italy without an heir and without having made arrangements for succession. This event caused much discussion among the powerful about the succession, and three main candidates emerged for the German throne: Duke Henry of Bavaria, Count Ekkehard of Meissen, and Duke Hermann of Swabia.[1] Of these three, Duke Henry of Bavaria succeeded in making the strongest claim to succeed Otto III on the basis of heredity and his closeness (*Königsnähe*)

---

1 Johann Friedrich Böhmer, *Regesta Imperii 2 (Sächsisches Haus 919–1024)/4: Die Regesten des Kaiserreiches unter Heinrich II. 1002–1024*, ed. Theodor Graff, new ed. (Vienna, 1971), no. 1483dd. (hereafter *BG* 1483dd). The election of 1002 has spawned a huge literature. For a thorough overview that cites all previous literature and analyzes much of it, see Armin Wolf, "*Quasi hereditatem inter filios*: Zur Kontroverse über das Königswahlrecht im Jahre 1002 und die Genealogie der Konradiner," *Zeitschrift der Savigny-Stiftung für Rechtsgeschichte Germanistische Abteilung* 112 (1995): 64–157.

to the previous ruler.[2] To further fortify his position, however, he took the initiative to meet the entourage bearing Otto III's body from Italy to Aachen at Polling, in southern Bavaria, accompanied it to Augsburg and Neuburg, and seized the *regalia*, the symbols of royal office, including the Holy Lance, which Archbishop Heribert had sent ahead and Henry had to acquire through intimidation.[3] Duke Henry thereby demonstrated emphatically his intention to put forth a claim to the throne. Nevertheless, a large group of the nobility either openly opposed him or did not show much initial support of his candidacy.[4] By June 1002, however, Henry managed to have himself elected, anointed, and crowned king at Mainz by a small but influential group of nobles and churchmen. Thereafter, he still had to force Duke Hermann of Swabia into submission and final recognition on the battlefield. Then, through the ritual repetition of ceremonial, constitutive acts, Henry had to take possession of the realm physically and have his election and kingship publicly acclaimed and formally recognized by the peoples of the several duchies of the realm.[5]

On January 15, 1003, Henry issued a remarkable royal charter for the bishopric of Strasbourg,[6] which praised and rewarded Bishop Werner of Strasbourg for his loyal support and punished their common foe, Duke Hermann of Swabia, who not only had taken up arms against Henry's candidacy but also had attacked and plundered Strasbourg.[7] Hermann was forced to concede to Bishop Werner control of Strasbourg, its profitable market, and the ducal convent of Saint Stephan. What makes this charter so remarkable, however, appears in the *narratio*, which Henry II may well have dictated himself.[8] Here we see how Henry II wanted to represent

---

2 Wolf, "*Quasi hereditatem*," and Stefan Weinfurter, "Der Anspruch Heinrichs II. auf die Königsherrschaft 1002," in Joachim Dahlhaus and Armin Kohnle, eds., *Papstgeschichte und Landesgeschichte: Festschrift für Hermann Jakobs zum 65. Geburtstag* (Cologne, 1995), 121–34.

3 He took Archbishop Heribert hostage until his brother, Bishop Henry of Würzburg, delivered the Holy Lance. See Thietmar, *Chronicon*, ed. Robert Holtzmann, in *Monumenta Germaniae Historica, Scriptores rerum Germanicarum* n.s. 9 (Berlin, 1935), bk. 4, cc. 50–1 (hereafter Thietmar 4.50–1, *MGH SrG*); *BG* 1483gg; on the importance of the Holy Lance as a rulership symbol to Henry II, see Reinhard Schneider, "Die Königserhebung Heinrichs II. im Jahre 1002," *Deutsches Archiv* 28 (1972): 76–80, and Weinfurter, "Der Anspruch," 127–8.

4 Thietmar 4.50–1, 54, *MGH SrG*.

5 For these events, see Thietmar, bk. 5; and for their interpretation, see Schneider, "Die Königserhebung," 96–104. Cf. Walter Schlesinger, "Die sogenannte Nachwahl Heinrichs II. in Merseburg," in Friedrich Prinz, Franz-Josef Schmale, and Ferdinand Seibt, eds., *Geschichte in der Gesellschaft: Festschrift für Karl Bosl zum 65. Geburtstag* (Stuttgart, 1974), 362–9.

6 *Monumenta Germaniae Historica, Diplomata regum et imperatorum Germaniae 3: Heinrici II. et Arduini Diplomata*, ed. Harry Bresslau, Hermann Bloch, and Robert Holtzmann (Hannover, 1900–3; reprint, Munich, 1980), no. 34 (hereafter *MGH DH II* 34).

7 Thietmar 5.12, *MGH SrG*.

8 Hartmut Hoffmann, "Eigendiktat in den Urkunden Ottos III. und Heinrichs II.," *Deutsches Archiv* 44 (1988): 414–16.

himself. He stressed his close friendship with Otto III since their youth and his consanguinity with him, and stated that these things convinced Werner to support him; whereby, with God directing, the people and the princes granted him, by election and by hereditary right, the succession to the realm without any division.

Stefan Weinfurter recently demonstrated in two erudite articles how the *narratio* (or narration of the specific motives for issuance) of this charter provides clues as to how Henry saw his claim to the throne and, perhaps more importantly, how Henry systematically developed a programmatic conceptual legitimization of his rulership.[9] This program or set of ideas included his closeness or *Königsnähe* to Otto III, his hereditary claim stretching back in the agnatic line to his great-grandfather, King Henry I, and an emphasis on a divinely ordained kingdom that granted the king undiminished royal power. Weinfurter shows how this program made extensive use of models drawn from the coronation *ordo* (rite) of Mainz to sacralize Henry II's notion of kingship – conceived on the basis of Christ-centered kingship and of Old Testament models, especially of Moses – and shows that the ruler portraits of Henry II in the Regensburg Evangelary (see Figure 2.1) and the *Pericopes Book* gave visual form and liturgical confirmation to these ideas.[10] Moreover, these ideas also became part of the written historical memory as reflected in such literary sources as the *Vita Mathilda posterior*, Thietmar's *Chronicle*, Adalbold's *Vita Heinrici* and Wolfher's *Vita Godehardi*.[11] Thus, Henry II solidly established his kingship on an ecclesiastical-liturgical foundation rooted firmly in both the Old and the New Testaments and based on Carolingian models of a sacral, fully integrative, and all-encompassing royal dominion.[12]

When one examines the charters of Henry II, further evidence emerges

---

9 Weinfurter, "Der Anspruch" and "Sakralkönigtum und Herrschaftsbegründung um die Jahrhundertwende: Die Kaiser Otto III. und Heinrich II. in ihren Bildern," both in Helmut Altrichter, ed., *Bilder erzählen Geschichte*, Rombach Historiae 6 (Freiburg im Breisgau, 1995), 84–103.

10 Cyrille Vogel and Reinhard Elze, eds., *Le Pontifical Romano-Germanique du Dixième Siècle*, 3 vols., *Studi e Testi* 226–7, 269 (Vatican City, 1963–72), 1:246–61; see also Carl Erdmann, *Forschungen zur politischen Ideenwelt des Frühmittelalters: Aus dem Nachlass des Verfassers*, ed. Friedrich Baethgen (Berlin, 1951), 54–70. One finds these ruler portraits in the *Regensburg Sacramentary* (Munich, Staatsbibliothek Clm 4456, ff. 11ʳ, 11ᵛ) and the *Pericopes Book* (Munich, Staatsbibliothek Clm 4452, f. 2ʳ).

11 E.g., *Vita Mathildis reginae posterior*, ed. Bernd Schütte, in *MGH SrG* 66 (Hannover, 1994), c. 20; Thietmar 5.2–3, *MGH SrG*; Adalbold, *Vita Heinrici*, ed. Hans van Rij, in *Nederlandse Historische Bronnen* 3 (Amsterdam, 1983), cc. 1, 5, pp. 48, 50 (hereafter Adalbold c. 5); Wolfher, *Vita Godehardi Episcopi prior*, ed. Georg H. Pertz, in *Monumenta Germaniae Historica, Scriptores* (hereafter *MGH SS*) 11 (Hannover, 1854), c. 13.

12 Stefan Weinfurter, "Zur 'Funktion' des ottonischen und salischen Königtums," in Michael Borgolte, ed. *Mittelalterforschung nach der Wende 1989*, supplement to *Historische Zeitschrift* n.s. 20 (Munich, 1995), 350–5.

Figure 2.1 Coronation picture of Henry II in the Regensburg Cathedral sacramentary. Staatsbibliothek München (clm 4456), fol. 11r. Reproduced by permission.

supporting Henry II's emphasis on ideas taken from the coronation *ordo* of Mainz, such as his divine appointment and his high sense of obligation that resulted from the charges placed on him by it.[13] The *arengae*, or

13 See, e.g., Vogel and Elze, *Le Pontifical*, §7, pp. 248–9, §11, p. 251, and §19, p. 256.

preambles providing the general purpose and reasons, of Henry's charters display a generous use of notions of preordained or at least divinely conceded kingship. This contrasts, for example, with far fewer similar expressions in the *arengae* of Henry II's predecessor, Otto III, or even in those of Otto I.[14] In reference to accession to the throne or to God-granted duties, the *arengae* employ such words as *commitere* (to commit), *concedere* (to concede), *evehere* (to elevate), *promovere* (to promote), *provehere* (to exult), and *perducere* (to guide).[15] For example, we read: "Among all the things, which we undertake in ruling and which we hold committed to us by the king of kings";[16] or "We, who the providence of divine disposition has promoted to the supreme height of the realm to rule";[17] or "We, who by the concession of divine piety, sit on the throne of the realm";[18] or finally, "Because the providence of divine disposition exulted us to rule the kingdom of the whole realm with the apostolic blessing."[19]

These represent only a few examples of the use of these notions. More specifically, the *arenga* of a charter granted to Paderborn in 1013 contains a direct reference to the coronation *ordo* and the obligations imposed by it: "The *ordo* of our royal promotion demands that we enrich the churches of Christ and that we dutifully and with indulgence provide relief for the needs of their servants."[20] Finally, the *arenga* of a charter for the prebend of the canonical chapter of Saint Adalbert at Aachen demonstrates clearly that Henry II took his divinely conceded charges seriously. Here the *arenga* reads: "We know that, in the house of God, we are the highest givers of copious gifts; if we dispense [them] faithfully, we will be blessed and will enter into the joy of the Lord and we will have his good things; [but] if we dispense [them] unfaithfully, we will be cast down into Hell, and we will be tortured [there] until [we have paid] to the last

---

14 See John W. Bernhardt, "Der Herrscher im Spiegel der Urkunden: Otto III. und Heinrich II. im Vergleich," in Bernd Schneidmüller and Stefan Weinfurter, eds., *Otto III – Heinrich II. Eine Wende?*, Mittelalter-Forschung 1 (Sigmaringen, 1997), 342–3; and Ronald Neumann, "Die Arengen der Urkunden Ottos des Grossen," *Archiv für Diplomatik* 24 (1978): 292–358.

15 *MGH DH II* 100, 269, 223, 263, 307, 225; cf. Vogel and Elze, *Le Pontifical*, §§3, 5, p. 247.

16 *MGH DH II* 100: "Inter omnia, que regenda suscepimus et nobis a rege regum commissa tenemus."

17 *MGH DH II* 263: "nos, quos divinae dispositionis providentia ad summum rei publice culmen regendum promovit."

18 *MGH DH II* 269: "Nos, qui divinae pietatis concessu in solio regni sedemus."

19 *MGH DH II* 307: "Quoniam divinae dispositionis providentia nos ad regendam totius rei publicae monarchiam apostolica benedictione provexit."

20 *MGH DH II* 264: "Aecclesias Christi ampliare servorumque eius necessitatibus pie ac clementer subvenire regalis promocionis ordo deposcit." One finds this *arenga* used again in DH II 342, also for Paderborn, in which *imperialis* replaces *regalis* since the charter was issued after Henry's imperial coronation in 1014.

penny."[21] Thus, in his charters, Henry II represents himself as fully in accord with the highly sacralized notion of rulership that Stefan Weinfurter found visually and liturgically expressed in his ruler portraits.[22]

Before leaving the subject of Henry II's succession to the throne, one further example – Duke and King Henry's ritual assumption of the role of heir and presumptive successor in rituals regarding Otto III's burial – conforms nicely to the theme of this volume. Weinfurter has stressed that Henry II's hereditary link to his great-grandfather, King Henry I, played a stronger role in forming his hereditary consciousness than his collateral relationship to Otto III.[23] Nonetheless, Henry's role in Otto III's burial rites provides an interesting and instructive historiographical perspective, and also offers another example of how Henry represented himself or wanted to be seen and remembered. Our account of this incident comes primarily from Thietmar of Merseburg's *Chronicle*, but with significant additions from Adalbold's *Vita Heinrici*, which itself depends largely on Thietmar.[24] Thietmar reports that a tearful Duke Henry met the procession transporting Otto III's body at Polling, where Henry made pressing entreaties concerning his candidacy to a mostly unreceptive audience and then, as previously mentioned, took the opportunity to seize the *regalia*. Henry accompanied the party to Augsburg, where he had Otto III's entrails buried next to the chapel of Saint Ulrich in the basilica of Saint Afra and then granted the church a memorial gift of 100 *mansi*, or units of manorial holdings, from his personal property for Otto's salvation. Henry then proceeded with the party to Neuburg on the Danube, where he took his leave reluctantly, personally saying farewell to the individual members of the group and instructing his brother-in-law, Henry of Luxembourg, to accompany the body to Aachen.[25]

Although Adalbold confuses the chronology of the procession – placing the arrival in Neuburg prior to that of Augsburg (or quite possibly attributing events that happened at Polling to Neuburg) – he generally

---

21 *MGH DH II* 99: "In domo dei largiflua summos dispensatores nos esse scimus; si fideliter dispensaverimus, beati erimus et in gaudium domini intrantes bona ipsius possidebimus, si infideliter, in tortorium detrudemur et usque ad novissimum quadrantem torquebimur." On this last phrase, "et usque ad novissimum quadrantem torquebimur," see Tertullian, *De Oratione* 7.2, and Matthew 5.26.

22 Weinfurter, "Sakralkönigtum," 79, 85–6. 23 Weinfurter, "Der Anspruch," 126–8, 132–3.

24 Thietmar 4.50–1, *MGH SrG*; Adalbold, cc. 3–4, pp. 48, 50. Lothar Bornscheuer, *Miseriae Regum: Untersuchungen zum Krisen- und Todesgedanken in den herrschaftstheologischen Vorstellungen der ottonisch-salischen Zeit*, Arbeiten zur Frühmittelalterforschung 4 (Berlin, 1968), 122–40, remains basic and essential for the interpretation of Adalbold; on Adalbold's dependence on Thietmar's *Chronicle*, see Bornscheuer, 122–4, who cites the older literature.

25 Thietmar 4.50–1, *MGH SrG*.

offers an similar account of events similar to that of Thietmar;[26] but Adalbold significantly sharpens the emphasis on Henry's role as heir by adding noteworthy details. For instance, in chapter three Adalbold states that when Henry met the procession bearing the body, "he [Henry] treated the body of his lord and relative (*corpus senioris et consanguinei*) with fitting veneration, gave the whole army a worthy reception, and then led it [the funeral procession] through his land as deemed appropriate."[27] Adalbold appears to be using ideas expressed in Henry's charter granted in 1003 to Bishop Werner of Strasbourg, which describes Otto and Henry's relationship to him as one of lord and of relative, both through his parents and through broader familial relations.[28] Moreover, Adalbold adds that Henry carried Otto's casket on his shoulders into Neuburg (or Polling?), demonstrating piety and a debt of human sympathy.[29]

The bearing of the casket represents another ritual act of the deceased's presumptive heir and heightens Henry's public representation as Otto's heir and thus the successor to the throne. For example, a later source, Wipo, tells us that Henry III acted as pallbearer for his father, Conrad II.[30] Moreover, we know from Saint Arnold of Emmeram that as duke, Henry had taken part in similar ritual acts, such as when he symbolically carried the body of Saint Ramwold on his shoulders during the saint's funeral.[31] Finally, in chapter four, Adalbold offers a shortened version of Thietmar's chapter 51 – that is, the burial of Otto's entrails in Saint Afra at Augsburg and Henry's personal gift of a memorial endowment for Otto III – and merely a single sentence about the burial of Otto's body in Aachen. Adalbold completely omits the elaborate funeral events detailed by Thietmar in chapter 53, that is, the arrangements orchestrated by

---

26 This is the judgment of Georg Waitz, who edited the *Monumenta Germaniae Historica* edition of this text. See Adalbold, *Vita Heinrici II imperatoris*, ed. Georg Waitz, in *MGH SS* 4 (Hannover, 1841; reprint, Stuttgart, 1982), 684n41.

27 Adalbold c. 3, pp. 48, 50: "*corpus senioris et consanguinei sui* qua decuit veneration suscepit; totum exercitum qua debuit liberalitate recepit, per terram suam qua oportuit commoditate conduxit" (emphasis added).

28 *MGH DH II* 34: "qualiter divae memoriae *senior noster* et antecessor tercius Otto. . . . Post tanti itaque imperatoris ab hac vita discessum vetus inter nos a pueris propagata familiaritas et ea que cum tali caesar *nobis erat parentele et consanguinitatis affinitas*" (emphasis added).

29 Adalbold, c. 3, p. 50: "Tandem Nuiveborg perveniens, ipse suis humeris corpus imperatoris in civitatem subvexit, pietatis exemplum et humanitatis exhibens debitum." On Henry II's understanding of *humanitas* or human sympathy, see Bornscheuer, *Miseriae Regum*, 131–6.

30 Wipo, *Gesta Chuonradi*, in *Wiponis Opera*, 3d ed., ed. Harry Bresslau, in *MGH SrG* 61 (Hannover, 1915; reprint, 1977), 58–9.

31 Arnold, *Ex libris de s. Emmeramo*, ed. Georg Waitz, in *MGH SS* 4 (Hannover, 1841; reprint, 1982) 543–74, bk. 2, c.39, p. 568: "ad funus pii abbatis [St. Ramwold] . . . ipse princeps [Duke Henry IV] propriis humeris non erubuit feretrum portare, necnon accuratius sepulturam parare."

Archbishop Heribert for the burial of Otto's body – a kind of counter-ritual – which began in Cologne and concluded with the interment in Aachen.[32] Obviously, Adalbold wanted to emphasize Henry's role in Otto's burial, effectively downplaying that of Archbishop Heribert and Henry's opponents. Thus, in Adalbold's report, Henry played the ritual role of next of kin by personally bearing the body into town and the role of hereditary heir apparent to the throne by ensuring a proper burial and endowing a suitable and lasting memorial remembrance of the departed.[33] Henry thereby publicly and demonstratively exhibited his status as Otto's heir. Adalbold took Thietmar's account and placed the emphasis on Henry's role, specifically adding crucial details of ritual to portray Henry as Otto's heir.

Thietmar reports in chapter 53 that later, during Easter Week, Archbishop Heribert stage-managed the elaborate burial of Otto's corpse. The body was displayed in a stational-type procession at various churches in Cologne and then carried ceremoniously to Aachen for burial on Easter Sunday in the basilica of Saint Mary.[34] Although many of Henry's opponents participated in these events, he himself did not. Nevertheless, Henry's appearance in Aachen to celebrate the anniversary of Otto's death one year later, shortly after he had issued his famous charter for Strasbourg at Diedenhofen, now as the crowned and anointed king, left little doubt about the identity of Otto's heir.[35] Moreover, it took Henry three and one-half years to make a memorial grant to the burial site of Otto III's body, the basilica and collegiate chapter of Saint Mary. On July 6, 1005, he bestowed the gift on behalf of the salvation of Charlemagne and especially of Otto III, of Henry's parents and ancestors, and of Henry himself.[36] This grant concluded the burial and memorial arrangements of Otto's heir and successor. Thus, in addition to programmatically emphasizing his hereditary right on the agnate side from the Heinrician line, Henry also successfully played the ritual role of next of kin to Otto III and presumptive successor to the throne. What Thietmar had implied, Adalbold made explicit in the historical memory.

---

32 For an analysis of the ritual of both burials, the entrails and the body, as an element of Thietmar's historical method and style, see David A. Warner, "Thietmar of Merseberg on Rituals of Kingship," *Viator: Medieval and Renaissance Studies* 25 (1995): 69–73.
33 Bornscheuer, *Miseriae Regum*, 130–1.
34 Thietmar 4.53, *MGH SrG*; see Warner, "Thietmar of Merseburg," 69–73.
35 Thietmar 5.28, *MGH SrG*; Adalbold c. 20: "Colloquio potenter habito Aquisgrani ire decrevit, ut ibi et anniversarium imperatoris debita devotione recoleret. . . . Ibi commemoratione consanguinei et senioris sui devotissime habita."
36 *MGH H II* 98.

HENRY II AS ADVOCATE AND MASTER OF THE ROYAL CHURCH

After becoming king, Henry quickly developed his concept of a divinely ordained kingship with undiminished royal power in both the secular and the ecclesiastical spheres. With regard to Henry II's policies and actions in the ecclesiastical sphere, scholars have called attention to a whole range of elements: Henry II's foundation of churches and monasteries; his calling of and participation in church synods and councils; his enrichment and empowerment of royal churches, yet his imposition of more direct royal control over them; his systematization of the *servitium regis* or material obligations of bishoprics and monasteries; his expansion of the sacral space of royal churches and increased stays in places having such space; and finally, his general piety.[37] In this context, some aspects of and specific events in Henry's relationship to the church enable one to compare how Henry II represented himself through word and action in a dual role – that is, as a strong advocate of the royal church and yet its master – with how the sources as the conveyors of historical memory report events or respond to royal actions.

Henry II's charters often employed a language that mirrored his governmental policies and his personal concepts of rulership. As Stefan Weinfurter has observed: "According to Henry II's ruling notions, the church, realm, and people had been handed over to him by God."[38] An examination of the *arengae* of Henry II's charters confirms this assertion, for they are characterized throughout by ecclesiastical and liturgical ideas of rulership. In fact, it appears as if his *arengae* also formed part of a programmatic notion of ruling as they strongly emphasize the idea of a pre-ordained and divinely mandated kingship. For example, at least fourteen *arengae* speak of rulership as a mandate of God.[39] Three deal with the

---

37 A selection from the vast literature on these topics includes the sections on Henry II in Theodor Schieffer, "Heinrich II. und Konrad II.," *Deutsches Archiv* 8 (1951): 384–437; Karl J. Benz, *Untersuchungen zur politischen Bedeutung der Kirchweihe unter Teilnahme der deutschen Herrscher im hohen Mittelalter: Ein Beitrag zum Studium des Verhältnisses zwischen weltlicher Macht und kirchlicher Wirklichkeit unter Otto III. und Heinrich II.*, Regensburger historische Forschungen 4 (Kallmünz, 1975); Gerhard Streich, *Burg und Kirche während des deutschen Mittelalters: Untersuchungen zur Sakraltopographie von Pfalzen, Burgen und Herrensitzen*, 2 vols., Vorträge und Forschungen, Sonderband 29.1–2 (Sigmaringen, 1984); John W. Bernhardt, *Itinerant Kingship and Royal Monasteries in Early Medieval Germany, c. 936–1075*, Cambridge Studies in Medieval Life and Thought, 4th ser. vol. 21 (Cambridge, 1993); and Hartmut Hoffmann, *Mönchskönig und "rex idiota": Studien zur Kirchenpolitik Heinrichs II. und Konrads II.*, MGH Studien und Texte 8 (Hannover, 1993).
38 Weinfurter, "Der Anspruch," 133: "so waren auch Heinrich II., seiner Herrscheridee zufolge, Kirche, Reich und Volk von Gott in die Hände gelegt worden."
39 *MGH DDH II* 100, 223, 225, 260, 263, 265b, 269, 281, 283, 307, 352, 433, 486, 504. Some examples include *MGH DH II* 100: "Inter omnia, que regenda suscepimus et nobis a rege regum

obligations of the ruler to God,[40] and at least seven are concerned with the obligations of the king to protect and promote the church.[41] Six *arengae* contain special requests for monasteries to pray for the king and the realm,[42] and one mentions a connection between the income of a monastery and its ability to pray for king and realm.[43] At least five *arengae* link service with gifts.[44] Likewise, in five *arengae* we find a direct mention of or an allusion to the Biblical metaphor, "Cui plus committitur, plus ab eo exigitur" (to whom much is entrusted, from them much is demanded).[45] Interestingly, in a charter for Fulda containing this metaphor, the idea refers to the abbot; but in an earlier charter for the collegiate church of Saint Mary in Aachen containing the same metaphor, it refers specifically to the king.[46] In these two charters, one for a monastery and the other for a house of canons, the quotation almost certainly derives directly from the Benedictine *Rule*.[47] All of this speaks emphatically to Henry's self-representation as a pious and divinely ordained supporter of the church.

Moreover, Henry's enrichment and empowerment of royal churches, of both episcopal and monastic foundation, did not come without significant increases in royal dominion over these institutions. This domin-

commissa tenemus"; DH II 263: "nos, quos divinae dispositionis providentia ad summum rei publice culmen regendum promovit"; *MGH DH II* 269: "Nos, qui divinae pietatis concessu in solio regni sedemus"; and *MGH DH II* 307: "Quoniam divinae dispositionis providentia nos ad regendam totius rei publicae monarchiam apostolica benedictione provexit."

40 *MGH DDH II* 99, 100, 504.

41 *MGH DDH II* 84, 172, 210, 223, 290, 304, 504.

42 *MGH DDH II* 53, 297, 354, 356, 398, 441.   43 *MGH DH II* 356.

44 *MGH DDH II* 34, 95, 244, 268, 274. If one searches further in the charters for this kind of connection, one finds many mentions, e.g., *MGH DDH II* 328, 350, 367, 422, 484.

45 *MGH DDH II* 102, 263, 433, 504, 509. For the identification of the quote, see Hartmut Hoffmann, *Buchkunst und Königtum im ottonischen und frühsalischen Reich*, 2 vols., Monumenta Germaniae Historica, Schriften 30.1–2 (Stuttgart, 1986), 1:24–5n40, and Hoffmann, "Eigendiktat," 416n42.

46 Cf. *MGH DH II* 509: "Quoniam nostrum est de bonis nobis divinitus collatis precipue sanctas ditare ecclesias, eidem devotioni, licet perpauca munera, pia tamen nostra prestare est voluntas in domino, qui dat premia pro bona voluntate [end of the arenga]. . . . Oportet, ut in ecclesiis multe sint facultates et maxime in Fuldensi, quia 'cui plus committitur, plus ab eo exigitur'; multa enim debet dare servicia et Romane et regali curie," with *MGH DDH II* 433: "Quia divine pietatis munificentia hucusque nobis propicia quamvis inmeriti regni et imperii fasces accepimus, dignum et utile atque anime nostre profuturum iudicamus, illud adtendentes: 'Cui plus committitur, ab eo plus exigitur,' ut ei, a quo et per quem regnamus, in ecclesiis restaurandis et sublimandis et in Christi fidelibus ministris adiuvandis et consolandis fideliter studeamus deservire."

47 *Benedicti Regula*, ed. altera, Rudolph Hanslik, *CSEL* 75 (Vienna, 1977), II.30, p. 26. Hoffmann, *Buchkunst*, 1:24n40, indicated that this quote derived from Isidor, Synonyma 2.89, PL 83.865, where he talks about the rights and obligations of kings, or from Augustine, Epistolae 194.24, CSEL 57.195.9, not *Luke* 12.48, but later, "Eigendiktat," 416n42, indicated the possibility of a derivation from the Benedictine *Rule*, which in these two charters would be the most plausible derivation.

ion likewise appears linked to Henry's overall concept of prerogatives and obligations of governance under an anointed Christian king. The language of the charters instructs us here also. Many charters granting properties or sovereign rights to royal churches often contain references to the increased stability of the realm as the desired result of the grant.[48] Others contain allusions or direct statements to the effect that in return for these gifts, the king expected more prayers to be said for himself and the realm or they required "prompter and more devoted service" from these prelates and their institutions.[49] Such statements occur frequently and typically in royal charters. A striking characteristic of Henry's charters for royal churches and a notable diffference from the charters of previous rulers, however, concerns instances of direct exercise of royal dominion. In charters concerning the election rights of bishoprics and royal monasteries, for example, Henry often places stipulations on the right of ecclesiastical congregations to exercise a free election of their bishop or abbot,[50] or alternately, he insists on the royal prerogative of investiture, the constitutive act of office.[51] Phrases such as "the king's choice however taking precedence," or "saving the royal or imperial consent," or "with like consent of the king" appear frequently inserted specifically to limit previously granted rights of free elections by the will of the king.[52] In other instances, when the king was confirming pre-existing rights, he apparently directed the royal chancery to use an older charter for their model that did not contain a clause granting the free right of election.[53] Thus, as royal favor and governmental service increased, so did royal dominion, and this corresponds directly to the ways in which we have seen that the king represented himself and his concepts of rulership. As a consequence

---

48 *MGH DDH II* 53, 199, 253, 331, 398, 418, 430, 441, 444.
49 *MGH DDH II* 53, 244, 268, 274, 297, 314, 320, 336, 356, 483.
50 *MGH DDH II* 50, 189, 256 (episcopal). *MGH DDH II* 53, 76, 97, 354, 369, 429 (monastic).
51 *MGH DDH II* 43, 44, 369.
52 *MGH DH II* 76: "abbatis inter se eligendi licentium habent praeposita tamem in omnibus regia electione"; *MGH DDH II* 189, 354, 429: "salvo (tamen) regis vel imperatoris consensu"; *MGH DDH II* 50, 97, 256: "aequo (tamen) regis consensu."
53 *MGH DDH II* 12, 45 (see the introductions to both). Henry II granted five election privileges to bishoprics. One confirmed the right, one left a previous election right totally out of the confirmation of privileges, and three subjected the election privilege to royal consent. For monasteries, the picture is even more dramatic. Of thirty-five election privileges for monasteries, eighteen went to royal institutions, seven to convents, and eleven to monasteries. Among the seven convents, we find six outright grants or confirmations and only one that contains a royal limitation of the right. Of the eleven to royal monasteries, however, we find one previous election right (Corvey) totally left out, six subjected to various royal limitations, two that totally lost their royal status, and only two granted without question. Among those on which some kind of limitation was imposed we find Nienburg, Ellwangen, St. Gall, Echternach, Reichenau, Fulda, and Corvey, some of the oldest, most prestigious, and most powerful royal monasteries.

of his God-given office, the king could exercise total authority in his realm, a dominion of undiminished power in all areas, both secular and ecclesiastical.[54]

The sources report little about Henry II limiting monastic election rights or controlling elections, except when an abbot was deposed in a reform intervention, which under Henry II primarily meant the reimposition of the Benedictine *Rule* on a community that had drifted away from it.[55] However, the sources frequently report instances in which the king intervened in or put aside an episcopal election. For instance, both the *Annals* of Quedlinburg and Thietmar (and later Adam of Bremen) report that, in 1013, Henry II overturned the archiepiscopal election at Hamburg-Bremen.[56] Although Thietmar offers the more detailed account, the entry in *Annals* of Quedlinburg contains a biting criticism of the king written in rhymed prose,[57] which is a particular characteristic of these Annals when they advance strong criticism.[58] Otto, the unanimous nominee of the cathedral chapter – and according to the *Annals* and Thietmar also the designated choice of the previous archbishop – appeared with clergy and laymen in Magdeburg, where Henry was celebrating the feast of the purification of the Virgin Mary, to seek the king's grace to complete the election by granting the royal investiture and sanctioning episcopal consecration. Henry had other ideas, however; he rejected the chapter's nominee, Otto, and imposed on them his own choice, his chaplain Unwan. As a consolation, the king took Otto into his service.[59] This example is indicative of Henry's exercise of the royal prerogative in ecclesiastical affairs, but it is not all that surprising if one considers Henry's charter for Hamburg in May 1003. In that diploma Henry had confirmed Hamburg's election right but had specifically limited that right by making it contingent on the royal consent.[60] Here we see Henry's limitation in

---

54 The notion finds explicit expression in the *arenga* to DH II 486: "Quoniam divine dignationis clementia ad regnendum totius rei publicae statum nos provexit suae immense pietatis magnificentia, ante omnia ad hoc laborare debemus." On Henry's expanded notion of royal authority, see Stefan Weinfurter's chapter in this book.

55 Hoffmann, *Mönchskönig*, 34.

56 *Annales Quedlinburgenses*, ed. George H. Pertz, in *MGH SS* 3 (Hannover, 1839) 22–90, anno 1013, p. 81 (hereafter *Ann. Qued.* a.); Thietmar 6.89, *MGH SrG*; Adam of Bremen, *Gesta Hamburgensis Ecclesiae Pontificum*, 3d. ed., ed. Bernhard Schmeidler, in *MGH SrG* 2 (Hannover, 1917; reprint, 1977), bk. 2, cc. 28–9, pp. 89–90.

57 *Ann. Qued.* a. 1013, p. 81: "Sed regis animus immitis, et habendi misera sitis, renuit supplicantium preces, contemnendo flentium voces."

58 See Robert Holtzmann, "Die Quedlinburger Annalen," *Sachsen und Anhalt* 1 (1925): 110–14.

59 *Ann. Qued.* a. 1013, p. 81; Thietmar 6.88–9, *MGH SrG*.

60 DH II 50: "Donamus quoque Hammaburgensis . . . ecclesiae . . . clericis potestatem eligendi inter se sive aliunde . . . episcopum, aequo tamen regis consensu."

action, that is, the withholding of his consent, and we read the resulting outcry of the *Annals* of Quedlinburg against him.

However, it also should be mentioned here that the tone of the Quedlinburg *Annals* becomes much more favorable to Henry II after the author of the *Annals* returned to writing around 1020, following a four-year hiatus. Robert Holtzmann attributed this to Henry II's successful treaty with Boleslav Chobry and Henry's close later relationship with the reform party.[61] Yet, Gerd Althoff observed that the peak of historical writing in Quedlinburg occurred exactly when its fortunes began to ebb early in Henry's reign and especially after the spring of 1013, when Henry abandoned the traditional Ottonian custom of the king celebrating Easter at Quedlinburg when in Saxony or nearby. Thus, Quedlinburg used historical writing in an attempt to establish its importance and to ensure continued royal support. This occasioned open criticism of the ruler and his policies early in his reign and especially sharp criticism in 1013;[62] but once Henry II began to expand the power of its abbess (1014) or favor Quedlinburg with significant grants or a special royal visit (1021), thus restoring some of its royal favor and access (*Königsnähe*), a more favorable tone regarding the king emerged.[63] These observations are especially interesting in light of what the *Annals* report about the episcopal elections in 1023. Whereas the entry for 1013 openly and harshly criticized Henry for not honoring the elected nominee of the chapter at Hamburg-Bremen, the report for the year 1023 recounts the deaths of many bishops and states that all those bishoprics affected sent emissaries to the king in Bamberg, where he, in council with his most trusted advisers, made all the necessary replacements.[64] Except for expressing that those sent were anxious about the appointments, the Quedlinburg annalist now seems to accept fully – and with little comment – the fact that the king would make the episcopal appointments and makes no mention whatsoever of chapter elections.

The case of the restoration of the bishopric of Merseburg, which combines information about Henry II's intervention in an episcopal election at Magdeburg, his imposition of a new bishop for Merseburg, and his performance of a ritual act in regard to these events, demands closer

---

61 Holtzmann, "Die Quedlinburger Annalen," 102–3, 110–16, 124–5.
62 Gerd Althoff, "Gandersheim und Quedlinburg: Ottonische Frauenklöster als Herrschafts- und Überlieferungszentren," *Frühmittelalterliche Studien* 25 (1991): 135–7, 142–4; see also note 57 to this chapter.
63 Althoff, "Gandersheim und Quedlinburg," 142–4.
64 *Ann. Qued.* a. 1023, p. 89.

examination. Here the historical memory is more vivid precisely because of Thietmar's closeness to the situation; but as we will see, even Thietmar, arguably our best single source for Henry II's reign, was not always an unbiased observer of events when he had pragmatic interests at stake.[65] The chronology of these events is quite important so I will deal with the three elements – the episcopal election at Magdeburg, the restoration of Merseburg, and Henry's performance of a ritual action and the historical memory of it – in their chronological rather than topical order.

In book 5, chapter 39, Thietmar tells us that Henry II had sent Archbishop Willigis of Mainz to convince Archbishop Giselher of Magdeburg, who was deathly ill at the time, to return and take up his former see, that is, Merseburg.[66] Emperor Otto II had decided to abandon the bishopric of Merseburg in 981, and its bishop, Giselher, had craftily managed to get himself appointed archbishop of Magdeburg.[67] Henry's demand was probably motivated both by politics and by his genuinely pious concern for the salvation of Giselher's soul as he approached death.[68] Apparently, Otto III had decided on the restoration of Merseburg as a bishopric, but he had not been able to complete it before his death, due largely to Archbishop Giselher's delaying tactics. For Giselher this would have been a great demotion in status and an admission of wrongdoing. However, Giselher's death at Trebra, reported by Thietmar in the same chapter, offered Henry II his chance to complete the restoration. Thietmar's next chapter, forty, describes three days, January 28–30, 1004, during which much happened.[69] The king piously accompanied Giselher's body to Magdeburg and sent his chaplain, Wigbert, ahead to arrange with the cathedral chapter the election of the candidate he had in mind, Tagino.

Meanwhile, back in Magdeburg, the provost of the cathedral chapter, Walthard, called the chapter together, told them of Giselher's death and of the imminent arrival of the king, and urged them to elect a successor quickly in order to protect their traditional election right. The chapter, of course, chose Walthard. The funeral procession bearing Giselher's corpse went first to the monastery of Saint John at Berge and then on the following day proceeded ceremoniously to the Magdeburg cathedral of Saint

65 On the characteristics and value of Thietmar's *Chronicle*, see Werner Goez, *Gestalten des Hochmittelalters: Personengeschichtliche Essays in allgemeinhistorischem Kontext* (Darmstadt, 1983), 70–83; Karl Leyser, *The Ascent of Latin Europe* (Oxford, 1986), 19–24; and Robert E. Lerner, "Thietmar von Merseburg (975–1018)," in Joseph R. Strayer, ed., *Dictionary of the Middle Ages*, 13 vols. (New York, 1989), 12:27–8.

66 Thietmar 5.39, *MGH SrG*.   67 Ibid., 3.12–14.

68 Hoffmann, *Mönchskönig*, 107–8.   69 Thietmar 5.40, *MGH SrG*.

Maurice. Then, in chapter 41, we are told that the king sent Bishop Arnulf of Halberstadt to the members of the chapter and the vassals of the church to present the king's position.[70] Walthard, as spokesman of the chapter, told Bishop Arnulf that they did not know what the king had in mind, but if possible, they would like to exercise their election right; otherwise they feared great damage to their church and thus asked the king's understanding. Finally, the king called Walthard to him, made many promises to him, and obtained his and the chapter's assent to the election of the king's candidate, his chaplain Tagino. Immediately thereafter, the king called everyone together, invested Tagino ad hoc with Bishop Arnulf of Halberstadt's staff, installed him on the episcopal throne, and then concluded Giselher's funeral services. Thus, on January 30, 1004, Tagino stood as a bishop-elect who had received the royal investiture.[71] Once again, Henry had exercised his divinely ordained authority to intervene and order the churches in his realm.[72]

In the last chapter (c. 44) of book five, which describes the events of February 2–6, 1004, Thietmar tells us that Henry II traveled to Merseburg to restore it, that Tagino was elevated from bishop-elect of Magdeburg to bishop through the consecration, and that the king negotiated the necessary property exchanges for the restoration of the bishopric of Merseburg.[73] Thietmar begins book six in the same time-frame. In chapter 1, he tells us that Henry gave the bishopric of Merseburg to his chaplain, Wigbert, using Tagino's staff, thereby erasing the blemish of his (Henry's) ancestors, that Wigbert was enthroned and anointed on the same day by Tagino, and that all the bishops who had participated in the division of Merseburg were in attendance and in agreement.[74] Significantly, both Magdeburg and Merseburg had received a bishop who came from the royal chapel. This is another indication of the increasing royal control of churches.[75]

Finally, after Thietmar inserts a short interlude in chapter 2 and describes a military campaign, he reports in chapter 3 that Henry decided to go on an Italian campaign, and before doing so he visited Magdeburg

---

70 Ibid., 5.41, *MGH SrG.*

71 On this legal status, see Robert L. Benson, *The Bishop Elect: A Study in Medieval Ecclesiastical Office* (Princeton, N.J., 1968), 3–10.

72 One also finds the notion of a royal obligation to order the churches of the realm expressed explicitly in the *arengae* of Henry's charters. See, e.g., DDH II 352, 439.

73 Thietmar 5.44, *MGH SrG.*   74 Ibid., 6.1, *MGH SrG.*

75 On the increasing number of royal chaplains who became bishops under Henry II, see Josef Fleckenstein, *Die Hofkapelle der deutschen Könige, 2: Die Hofkapelle im Rahmen der ottonisch-salischen Reichskirche*, MGH Schriften 16.2 (Stuttgart, 1966), 208–21.

to pray to Saint Maurice for his intervention with God and for his bless-ing of the expedition.[76] This ends Thietmar's account of these events, although he later dutifully records all of the continuing difficulties that the cathedral chapter of Magdeburg experienced in maintaining its right to elect the archbishop. This is not surprising considering that Thietmar followed Wigbert as bishop of Merseburg and had a compelling interest in episcopal elections.

What, however, did Thietmar not tell us and why? The answer to this question offers us some insights on the creation of historical memory. David Warner recently discussed this incident in great detail, and I would like to relate some of his ideas to this question of historical memory.[77] Although Thietmar informs us that, after restoring Merseburg, Henry II visited Magdeburg to obtain Saint Maurice's aid for his Italian campaign, Thietmar does not tell us that on this visit to Magdeburg the king granted Magdeburg additional relics of Saint Maurice from his chapel. Nor does he relate that Henry, garbed as a penitent and ritually playing that role, carried those relics on the thirty-day anniversary of Giselher's death in a solemn procession from the monastery of Berge to the cathedral of Saint Maurice. These details are provided by two twelfth-century sources, the *Gesta* of the archbishops of Magdeburg and the *Annals* of Magdeburg,[78] and the *Gesta* at least usually drew quite heavily on Thietmar.[79] We also have a contempo-rary charter of Henry II, dated February 25, 1004, that records property grants to compensate Magdeburg for its losses in the restoration of Merse-burg and that specifically mentions Henry's gift of Saint Maurice's relics.[80] In this instance, the king appears to be enacting a ritual resolution of con-flict.[81] As the cathedral chapter at Magdeburg had feared, the restoration of Merseburg came at great cost to Magdeburg in terms of lost property holdings, that is, those restored to Merseburg, and in terms of damage to the cathedral chapter's election right. One also might add that Tagino's incipient status in his new archbishopric probably sustained some damage

---

76 Ibid., 6.3, *MGH SrG.*

77 David A. Warner, "Henry II at Magdeburg: Kingship, Ritual and the Cult of Saints," *Early Medieval History* 3 (1994): 133–66.

78 *Gesta archiepiscoporum Magdeburgensium*, ed. Wilhelm. Schum, in *MGH SS* 14 (Hannover, 1883; reprint, Stuttgart, 1988), c. 15, p. 393; *Annales Magdeburgenses*, ed. Georg H. Pertz, in *MGH SS* 16 (Hannover, 1859), a. 1004, p. 163.

79 Warner, "Henry II at Magdeburg," 145–9.

80 DH II 63: "Sed ne per nos eadem sacri archiepiscopii sedes quasi inminuta damnum pati videretur . . . contulimus pariter cum quadam parte reliquiarum sancti Mauricii, que nobiscum erant reposite."

81 Warner, "Henry II at Magdeburg," 160–6.

due to his support of the king in the restoration of Merseburg, which from the Magdeburg viewpoint countered the interests of his new see. Thus, once the restoration of Merseburg had been accomplished, Henry II set out to compensate the injured parties, soothe egos, and facilitate future relations. For Magdeburg, this took the form of new grants of property and a gift of relics, solemnly and humbly presented.[82] Thus, as Warner has written, "Henry's procession with the relics of Saint Maurice reaffirmed his relations with an important and influential community of clerics and provided a symbolic conclusion to a divisive dispute."[83] Yet Thietmar, a witness to these events and usually a highly reliable source, records none of these events. Why? For Thietmar, who began writing his *Chronicle* after he had become bishop of Merseburg in 1009, the issue of Henry's piety and its relation to Magdeburg's compensation was too potentially dangerous to the interests of his own bishopric, Merseburg, and to his attempts and those of his successors to recover all of Merseburg's properties, many of which Magdeburg still retained. Thus, Warner argues that Thietmar manipulated some of the facts, or just did not report them, in the interest of his own diocese.[84]

Here we find an instance when several, even competing, historical memories exist. The authors of the accounts emerging from both Merseburg and Magdeburg had strong local interests. Thietmar, who generally wrote positively about Henry II and had good information on his actions in this instance appears to have suppressed mention of the king's ritual performance because the implications of that action may have conflicted with the interests of his own bishopric. His immediate and local interest outweighed his bond to the king. The *Gesta* of the archbishops of Magdeburg and the *Annals* of Magdeburg, however, although they normally drew heavily from Thietmar, nevertheless dutifully reported the king's ritual self-representation, not only because it apparently happened, but also for the same reason that Thietmar omitted mention of it – it was in the best interests of their community to do so.

Other aspects of royal domination in the ecclesiastical sphere under Henry II also provide information about Henry's royal self-representation and historical memory. Henry attempted to reassert royal claims to gov-

---

82 The words used in the charter also imply this; see note 80 to this chapter. Merely the granting of a royal charter was considered a solemn act of ruler self-representation; see Heinrich Fichtenau, *Arenga: Spätantike und Mittelalter im Spiegel von Urkundenformeln*, Mitteilungen des Instituts für österreichische Geschichtsforschung, Sonderband 18 (Vienna, 1957), 19–30, 62.
83 Warner, "Henry II at Magdeburg," 165.   84 Ibid., 162.

erning rights over the higher churches of the realm, the bishoprics, and the royal monasteries, and at the same time to increase systematically their overall service to the realm. He supported and furthered the monastic reform movement that emanated originally from Gorze in Lotharingia and then from Saint Maximin in Trier. This monastic reform initiated a stricter and different monastic custumal (*consuetudo*), called for more orderly estate management and improved economy with monastic lands, and often was initiated by the king with the cooperation of royal bishops. Sometimes these reform measures included the secularization of some monastic property or the granting of smaller or economically or politically weaker ecclesiastical foundations.[85] We find the conceptualization behind such actions clearly and dramatically enunciated in the *arenga* of a royal charter of 1013–1014 for the bishopric of Strasbourg, in which the king granted the monastery of Schwarzach to the bishopric.[86] The *arenga* demands to be quoted in full:

Because the form of the human body was created from the rational order of the omnipotent God, in such a way that whatever lesser members (*membra*) are subject to the head (*caput*) and are governed by it just as if under some military commander, we do not think that it is incongruous to this model to place certain smaller churches in our realm beneath the greater ones, and we have judged that it in no way counters the will of the king of kings, who knew how to set apart the celestial and earthly domain with a miraculous ordering.[87]

This *arenga* provides us with an image that illuminates Henry's personal conception of rulership and his understanding of the role and duties of

---

85 See Bernhardt, *Itinerant Kingship*, 70–5, 120–2, 212–16, 247–52, with citations to wider literature. Royal legal status refers to a group of churches and monasteries that enjoyed the special royal protection (beyond the king's general duty to protect all churches in the realm) and thereby a higher legal status. These churches stood in the special protection ("ecclesias . . . sub nostrae tuicionis munimine defendendas") of the king and by extension under direct jurisdiction of the king and the realm ("in ius proprietatem nostri publici iuris aut fisci"). Royal monasteries, which formed a subgroup within the larger class of the royal churches, had several fundamental characteristics. These included: their inalienability from the possession of the realm; the king's right to full disposition over the royal monasteries, including their performance of various mandatory services (*servitia*); the royal immunity from public legal jurisdiction; a royal proprietary right to the monastery based on the royal protection; the monastic community's right freely to elect its own abbot or abbess, conditional upon the king's right to approve and to invest the candidate; and, the monastery's obligation to appoint a lay advocate to administer the monastery's jurisdiction, represent it in the secular world, and exercise the king's rights within the monastery.

86 *MGH DH II* 277.

87 Ibid.: "Cum ex rationabili ordine omnipotentis dei corporis humani forma eo modo sit condita, ut quelibet minora membra capiti sint subiecta et ab eo veluti sub quodam duce regantur, non incongruum putavimus ad hanc imitationem quasdam minores ecclesias in regno nostro subdere maioribus et id voluntati regis regum nihil obstare arbitrati sumus, qui celestes atque terrenos principatus miro ordine novit distingere."

the royal churches in the realm.[88] The image of the head and the members working together for the good of the whole body is an idea taken from antiquity. Here Henry has taken this organological form and projected it onto the realm to clarify his own political theory of governance.[89] Henry, the king, is the head to whom the larger churches, that is, bishoprics and powerful royal monasteries, and the smaller churches and monasteries are subjected. The whole, the realm, can maintain a healthy existence only when all of the members work together in a proper ordering; but this does not imply equal rank. The king, empowered and ordained by God, functions in the earthly realm as the head of the royal church and can alter the tasks and functions of the member churches with regard to the well-being of the whole.[90] Already in 1941, Robert Holtzmann exclaimed: "This is one of those *arengae* in which the king himself speaks to us, not a chancery scribe with a gift for words," and Hartmut Hoffmann has further substantiated this claim.[91]

The appearance of this *arenga* at the end of 1013 coincides with other royal actions in the monastic arena. Henry II granted the monastery of Schwarzach to Strasbourg, forcibly reformed the great royal monastery of Fulda, and imposed royal reform measures on Corvey in the following year, and later on Stavelot-Malmèdy.[92] Indeed, if one looks at later years, Henry's use of the head-body concept can be seen as programmatic. In 1015 and 1017 respectively, the king granted the increasingly impoverished royal monastery of Memleben to the powerful royal monastery Hersfeld and the trouble-plagued royal monastery of Helmarshausen to the bishopric of Paderborn.[93] In both cases, economically and politically

---

88 Hubertus Seibert, "Libertas und Reichsabtei: Zur Klosterpolitik der salischen Herrscher," in Stefan Weinfurter, ed., *Die Salier und das Reich 2: Die Reichskirche in der Salierzeit* (Sigmaringen, 1991), 509–10.

89 On this concept, see Tilman Struve, *Die Entwicklung der organologischen Staatsauffassung im Mittelalter*, Monographien zur Geschichte des Mittelalters 16 (Stuttgart, 1978), who, however, does not mention this charter of Henry II.

90 Seibert, "Libertas und Reichsabtei," 509–10, discusses the classical head-body-members terminology in reference to the *arenga* in DH II 277 for the bishop of Strasbourg. Although I generally follow his analysis, I have expanded the concept. To my knowledge no one has noticed or remarked that the *arenga* of Henry II's charter of March 20, 1019, for the bishopric of Paderborn (DH II 403) also contains an allusion to a similar head and body metaphor. In this charter Henry granted to Paderborn the convent of canonesses, Schildesche, which thereby lost its independent, royal status. On Schildesche, see Hermann Bannasch, *Das Bistum Paderborn unter den Bischöfen Rethar und Meinwerk 983–1036*, Studien und Quellen zur Westfälischen Geschichte 12 (Paderborn, 1972), 43–6, 180–1, 217.

91 Robert Holtzmann, *Geschichte der sächsischen Kaiserzeit (900–1024)*, 3d. rev. ed. (Munich, 1955), 482; and Hoffmann, "Eigendiktat," 418.

92 Bernhardt, *Itinerant Kingship*, 111, 123–5.

93 *MGH DDH II* 331, 371. On the two events, see ibid., 215–16, 250–2.

weaker monasteries, unable to provide adequate service to the king, were placed under the dominion of more powerful institutions, regardless of the fact that they had earlier been granted the freedom or *libertas* of royal status. Obviously, the legal ruling contained in the *Weistum* of Frankfurt in 951 – which stated that no abbey possessing the right to elect its own abbot or abbess could be given into the ownership (*in proprium*) of a monastery or anyone else, but that abbeys lacking a privilege of free election granted by the king could be annexed to another monastery that stood under royal protection – did not constrain these actions that Henry II took as "head" of the church and realm to regulate the individual "members" of the church body.[94]

Memleben had lost most of its incomes and possessions in the East during the Slavic uprising of 983 and the conflicts on the eastern frontier thereafter.[95] Although the *arenga* of the charter of February 5, 1015, granting Memleben to Hersfeld contains only general platitudes about ensuring the king's personal salvation and the stability of the realm by bestowing gifts to churches, we learn a bit more from the *narratio*.[96] We read that Abbot Arnolf of Hersfeld, with his entire congregation of monks and the monastery's retainers (*milites*), personally petitioned the king to issue the charter. It further informs us that Henry intended to relieve the desperate impoverishment of the monastery by granting it to the much richer Hersfeld.[97] It failed to mention, however, that Henry had previously impoverished it further through a series of interrelated property transactions.[98] Regardless, although the charter's *narratio* expressed the

---

94 *Monumenta Germaniae Historica, Constitutiones et acta publica imperatorum et regum 1: Constitutiones et acta publica imperatorum et regum inde ab a. DCCCCXI usque ad. a. MCXCVII (911–1197)*, ed., Ludwig Weiland (Hannover, 1893; reprint, 1963), no. 8, p. 17. This was also the case once again in 1017, when Henry granted the royal monastery of Helmarshausen to Bishop Meinwerk of Paderborn. On the Frankfurt *Weistum* and royal policy, see Bernhardt, *Itinerant Kingship*, 73–5n133.

95 See Wolfgang H. Fritze, "Der slawische Aufstand von 983: Eine Schicksalswende in der Geschichte Europas," in Eckart Henning and Walter Vogel, eds., *Festschrift der Landesgeschichtlichen Vereinigung für die Mark Brandenburg zu ihrem hundertjährigen Bestehen 1884–1984* (Berlin, 1984), 9–55; on Memleben's role as a missionary monastery for the Slavic lands, especially Poland, see Johannes Fried, "Theophanu und die Slawen: Bemerkungen zur Ostpolitik der Kaiserin," in Anton von Euw and Peter Schreiner, eds., *Kaiserin Theophanu: Begegnung des Ostens und Westens um die Wende des ersten Jahrtausends*, 2 vols. (Cologne, 1991), 2:361–70.

96 Hans Weirich, ed., *Urkundenbuch der Reichsabtei Hersfeld*, Veröffentlichung der Historischen Kommission für Hessen und Waldeck 19 (Marburg, 1936), no. 82 (*MGH DH II 331*).

97 Ibid.: "qualiter nos divini amoris instinctu pro remedio animae nostrae cuiusdam abbatiae Mimeleua dictae inopiam considerantes fratrumque ibi deo famulantium penuriam inspicientes hoc modo eis providere decrevimus, ut eandem abbatiam Heroluesueldensi abbatiae tradamus, ea videlicet ratione, uti ex Arnoldi eiusdem abbatiae abbatis suorumque successorum industria ac eiusdem abbatiae copia iam dictorum fratrum relevetur inopia."

98 Bernhardt, *Itinerant Kingship*, 247–51.

king's intentions only in the noblest terms, it did have a basis in fact and cannot be dismissed merely as empty rhetoric.[99]

Henry II's dissolution of the Memleben monastery also appears to have had another dimension: Henry's action effectively dismantled the Ottonian *memoria* concept.[100] Both Henry I and Otto I had died at Memleben, and Otto's entrails were buried there in the church of Saint Mary.[101] Either under Otto I, perhaps as early as 942,[102] but certainly after Otto I's death, Memleben became a site of Ottonian *memoria* or commemoration for the dead king(s).[103] The *memoria* is known primarily from the charters and from the ruins of a huge church (ca. 266 × 92 feet) having three naves and a double apse, possibly intended to have two crypts and to be used as sacral space for the *memoria*.[104] This monumental building project seems to have been interrupted and abandoned before completion. The abandonment of this building project, in addition to the dissolution of the royal monastery, appears connected to Merseburg's reestablishment as a bishopric and its rise to become Henry's main center

---

99 As does Hans Patze, *Die Entstehung der Landesherrschaft in Thüringen* (Cologne, 1962), 1:85. In contrast, Hans Peter Wehlt, *Reichsabtei und König* (Göttingen, 1970), 178, overemphasizes the importance that the monastery's weakened economic state played in the overall process. Hoffmann, "Eigendiktat," 399–420, demonstrates clearly that in the *arengae* of Henry II's charters one often hears a true echo of the king himself, not merely formulaic rhetoric.

100 I thank Johannes Fried for the suggestion to investigate this area.

101 Thietmar 1.18, 2.43, *MGH SrG*.

102 On the early dating of a church in Memleben and the likelihood of a *memoria* established by Otto I for his father, see Ernst Schubert, "Zur Datierung der ottonischen Kirche zu Memleben," in Karl-Heinz Otto and Joachim Hermann, eds., *Siedlung, Burg und Stadt*, Deutsche Akademie der Wissenschaften zu Berlin, Schriften der Sektion für Vor- und Frühgeschichte 25 (Berlin, 1969), 520–4; Gerhard Leopold and Ernst Schubert, "Otto III. und die Sachsen: Die ottonische Kirche in Memleben: Geschichte und Gestalt," in Euw and Schreiner, eds., *Kaiserin Theophanu*, 2:377–80; and Gerhard Streich, *Burg und Kirche während des deutschen Mittelalters: Untersuchungen zur Sakraltopographie von Pfalzen, Burgen und Herrensitzen*, 2 vols., Vorträge und Forschungen, Sonderband no. 29, vols. 1–2 (Sigmaringen, 1984), 1:165–8, 401–2.

103 Schubert, Leopold and Schubert, and Streich (previous note) suggest, with good reasoning but unfortunately no source witnesses, that both the *memoria* of Henry I and Otto I were kept in Memleben. Fried, "Theophanu und die Slawen," 363–4, and Joachim Ehlers, "Otto II. und Kloster Memleben," *Sachsen und Anhalt* 18 (1994): 51–2, 55–60, both reject Schubert's idea of an early church at Memleben and see Otto II and Theophanu as founders of church and monastery. Fried also discounts the notion of a *memoria* for Henry I at Memleben, considers the *memoria* only for Otto I, Otto II and Theophanu, and suggests the idea that Memleben may have been intended as a gravesite for Otto II, and Theophanu. Ehlers likewise rejects a *memoria* for Henry I at Memleben, or believes that it was abandoned (58, 62), and sees the creation of a special *memoria* at Memleben for Otto I and the founding couple as spiritual compensation for dissolution of the bishopric of Merseburg (62, 71–6).

104 *Monumenta Germaniae Historica, Diplomata regum et imperatorum Germaniae 2.1: Ottonis II. Diplomata*, ed. Theodor Sickel (Hannover, 1888; reprint, Munich 1980) nos. 191, 194–6 (hereafter *MGH DO II*), and *Papsturkunden 896–1046*, ed. Harald Zimmermann, 3 vols., 2d. rev. ed., Österreichische Akademie der Wissenschaften, Phil.-Hist. Kl., Denkschriften 174, 177, 198 (Vienna, 1988–9), 1:521–2, no. 265. On the archaeology of the church, see Leopold and Schubert, "Otto III. und die Sachsen," 379–82.

of royal representation in Saxony, as well as to Henry's creation of his own centers of *memoria* to commemorate the noble dead and to pray for the living members of the family.[105] Beginning in 1013, Henry altered the Ottonian custom of celebrating the high feast of Easter at Quedlinburg when present in Saxony. Instead of Quedlinburg, Henry's favored residence in Saxony, Merseburg, became his preferred Easter residence. He held the Easter feast there in 1015, 1019, 1021, and 1023.[106] A similar shifting of tradition occurred in 1017, when Henry also had the preservation and observance of the *memoria* of the entire Liudolfing/Ottonian family, thereafter to include himself and his wife, Kunigunde, transferred from its former center at Quedlinburg to Merseburg.[107] In addition, when one examines the property transactions occurring among Memleben, Hersfeld, and Bamberg around the time of the dissolution of Memleben as a royal monastery, one finds that these transactions ultimately benefitted Bamberg, which likewise was a *memoria* foundation of Henry II and his intended burial site.[108]

But what do other sources say about the granting of Memleben to Hersfeld? With the exception of Thietmar of Merseburg, who mentions it almost as an aside (although one evincing genuine sadness), there is no mention of the dissolution of the royal monastery or the Ottonian *memoria* that was celebrated there. Notwithstanding that Thietmar, as bishop of Merseburg, would benefit from Memleben's dissolution in terms of tithe incomes and less competition in the area, his report of the suppression nevertheless contains strong language. He bewails the fact that Memleben had to exchange its constitutional freedom (*libertas*) for servitude (*servitudo*).[109] Yet, to my knowledge, no other contemporary source reported on this revocation of the *libertas* of a significant royal monastery. Memleben's dissolution appears to have been one part of a series of

---

105 See Hoffmann, *Mönchskönig*, 104–5.

106 Gerald Beyreuther, "Die Osterfeier als Akt königlicher Repräsentanz und Herrschaftsausübung unter Heinrich II. (1002–1024)," in Detlef Altenburg, Jörg Jarnut, and Hans-Hugo Steinhoff, eds., *Feste und Feiern im Mittelalter: Paderborner Symposium des Mediävistenverbandes* (Sigmaringen, 1991), 250–3, who cites the older literature.

107 Gerd Althoff, *Adels- und Königsfamilien im Spiegel ihrer Memorialüberlieferung: Studien zum Totengedenken der Billunger und Ottonen*, Münstersche Mittelalter–Schriften 47 (Munich, 1984), 193–200, and Gerd Althoff, "Beobachtungen zum liudolfingisch-ottonischen Gedenkwesen," in Karl Schmid and Joachim Wollasch, eds., *Memoria: Der geschichtliche Zeugniswert des liturgischen Gedenkens im Mittelalter*, Münstersche Mittelalter-Schriften 48 (Munich, 1984), 657–8, 661.

108 *MGH DDH II* 329–30, 332ab, 334, 335ab. See Hoffmann, *Mönchskönig*, 92, 101, 200–1.

109 Thietmar 7.31, *MGH SrG*: "Notandum quoque est et non absque singultu gravi proferendum, quod monasterium in Miminlevo consitutum a libertate diu corroborata in servitutem redactum est. Deposito namque eiusdem coenobii abbate Reinoldo dispersisque late confratribus hiis Heresfeldensi aecclesiae eiusque tunc provisori Arnoldo illud subditum est."

ecclesiastical and political adjustments on the eastern frontier, and it likewise was linked to an enhanced self-consciousness in the ruler, which
found expression in the creation by Henry II of new centers for the
celebration of high feasts and for the *memoria* of the Liudolfing/Otton-
ian family.[110] Moreover, the process was expedited by the new affinity
between Hersfeld and the king resulting from the royally initiated reform
of the monastery (1005–1012) by Henry's friend and confidant, Godehard, and the subsequent election of Godehard's student, Arnolf, to
succeed him as abbot of Hersfeld.

The case of Helmarshausen and Paderborn offers a second example
of a lesser church being granted to a greater one. Helmarshausen, first
established in 997, found itself plunged into a long and bitter struggle
over its independence with the powerful relatives of its founders, the
Eckhardingers, because they had effectively disinherited their family in
favor of the monastery.[111] This struggle with Eckhard's family sapped
much of the monastery's energy and assets and effectively closed off a
source of valuable property grants for the newly endowed foundation.
Moreover, even though it had attained royal status, active royal support in
the form of royal property grants was not forthcoming.[112] Consequently,
according to the *Vita Meinwerci*, in 1017, after an assembly of princes had
adjudged the monastery's royal status against the claims of Eckhard's heirs,
Henry II, on the counsel and intervention of the assembled princes and
bishops, granted Helmarshausen as a proprietary monastery to Bishop
Meinwerk of Paderborn and his bishopric.[113] The *arenga* of the grant,
which turns to canon law and emphasizes episcopal control over monasteries, and the beginning of the *narratio*, which speaks of a shifting of royal
burdens to bishops, are highly original and interesting:

---

110 On Memleben's role in Ottonian eastern policy, see Fried, "Theophanu und die Slawen," 365–70,
and on Henry's adjustments on the eastern frontier, which demonstrate a new "border or frontier" consciousness, see Bernhardt, *Itinerant Kingship*, 41–3, 249–52, and Hoffmann, *Mönchskönig*,
102–8.

111 On the history of the monastery of Helmarshausen, see Hermann Jakobs, "Helmarshausen," in
Germania Pontifica, vol. 5: *Paderborn* (forthcoming), 270–95. I thank Professor Jakobs for allowing me to read his contribution when it was still in manuscript form. For an overview of the
monastery's early history, see Bernhardt, *Itinerant Kingship*, 212–15, and also Bannasch, *Das Bistum
Paderborn*, 110–14, who view events in the broad perspective of royal politics and where the
older and specialized literature is cited.

112 *Monumenta Germaniae Historica, Diplomata regum et imperatorum Germaniae 2.2: Ottonis III. Diplomata*, ed. Theodor Sickel (Hannover, 1893; reprint, Munich, 1980), no. 256. Paul Kehr, "Die
älteren Urkunden für Helmarshausen," *Neues Archiv* 49 (1932): 86–114, offers the best edition
of the Helmarshausen charters (*MGH DO III* 256-kehr 1).

113 *Vita Meinwerci episcopi Patherbrunnensis (Das Leben des Bischofs Meinwerk von Paderborn)*, ed. Franz
Tenckhoff, in *MGH SrG* 59 (Hannover, 1921; reprint, 1983), c. 144, p. 76.

The statutes of the canons, which have been established not by the mouth of men but through the spirit of God, order that bishops visit the cloisters of monks frequently, and if they find something there outside of the rule, let them root [it] out and correct [it]. Vigilantly contemplating these things and lightening our burdens in the course of this life by imposing them on the bishops, we . . . (and into the *narratio*).[114]

Here once again, the king, or *caput*, quite in accordance with the organological *arenga* (DH II 277), withdrew the *libertas* of a smaller or lesser church and granted it to a greater one. In this instance the king dissolved the independence of the monastery and made it an episcopal proprietary monastery. However, in the charter granting Helmarshausen to Paderborn, neither the *arenga* nor the *narratio* stated anything about Helmarshausen's economic poverty or its struggles with the heirs of the founder. Instead, the *arenga* appealed to canon law and emphasized the bishop's general dominion over and oversight of diocesan monasteries. The appeal in this *arenga* also appears connected to Meinwerk's activity in the reform of the royal monastery Corvey.[115] When Henry II issued his first charter to Corvey in 1002 confirming its rights, the charter left out the monastery's right to elect their abbot and contained a stipulation regarding the *servitium* and accommodation owed to the bishop during his yearly visits to the monasteries of his diocese.[116] Then, in 1009, when Meinwerk, as the newly elected bishop, attempted to visit Corvey to make corrections there and thus to claim his right of visitation, he was thrown out of the monastery.[117] Thus, Corvey's treatment of Meinwerk was not only a violation of his rights as stated in Henry's charter of 1002 for Corvey but also a violation of canon law. This event finds an echo later in the *arenga* for Helmarshausen.[118] Moreover, the canonistic prescriptions in the *arenga* about bishops' power of oversight and the theological sense that lay behind it can be found in the *Decretum* of Burchard of Worms, which Henry II often used as a support for his ecclesiastical policies.[119]

---

114 *MGH DH II* 371: "Canonum statuta non ore hominum, sed spiritu dei condita precipiunt, ut episcopi frequenter claustra monachorum visitent, et, si qua extra regulam illic invenerint, abscidant et corrigant. Hec vigilanter interius contemplantes et in huius vite itinere onera nostra episcopis inponendo levigantes."

115 See Wilhelm Stüwer, "Corvey und Lorsch: Ein Beitrag zu ihren Beziehungen im 11. Jahrhundert/Liuthar und Ebergis, Bischöfe von Minden," in Friedrich Knöpp, ed., *Die Reichsabtei Lorsch: Festschrift zum Gedenken an ihre Stiftung 764*, 2 vols. (Darmstadt, 1973–7), 1:270–3, 289–90.

116 *MGH DH II* 12: "Episcopis vero, quibus servitium et mansionatica debent, tempore circuitus sui secundum scripta sua singulis annis persolvant." See also note 53 to this chapter.

117 *Vita Meinwerci*, c. 145, pp. 76–7.

118 Stüwer, "Corvey und Lorsch," 272–3.

119 Burchard, *Dekret*, Migne PL 140 Lib. LXVI, LXVII, Sp. 805D–806AB, e.g., for the general sense, LXVII, S. 806B: "Abbates pro humilitate religionis in episcoporum postestate consistant."

We find out about the economic woes of Helmarshausen and its political troubles with the founder's heirs only from the two other sources
reporting the event, the *Vita Meinwerci* and *Translatio s. Modoaldi*. These,
however, provide merely a narrative account of events; we hear no voices
of dissent regarding the king's action, although the *Translatio* does try to
defend the monastery's independence from the bishop of Paderborn and
represents the bishop's position merely as one of protection.[120] This, of
course, does not agree with the stipulations in Henry's grant to Meinwerk. Essentially, Helmarshausen was too poor to supply the king a
servitium, held marginal value for the realm, and was granted away. The
traditio to the bishop of Paderborn probably provided the best possible
way out of the exhausting struggle for all parties involved.[121] Moreover,
it corresponds nicely with all the ideas expressed in the *arenga*, especially
that of the increasing imposition of royal cares or burdens on bishops.
This pertained particularly to bishops such as Meinwerk, whom Henry
was in the process of systematically strengthening, and who like the abbot
of Fulda were strong proponents of Henry's measures toward monastic
reform.[122]

Thus, Henry II systematically increased his royal dominion over all
spheres of the realm, announced his political and religious ideology
through the language in his charters, and formulated a theoretical concept
regarding his authority over the royal church. As *caput,* he personally and
actively intervened in problems concerning the *membra*. He strengthened
bishops and increased their duties; imposed monastic reform on powerful royal monasteries; and sanctioned the granting of smaller and economically weaker churches and monasteries – with total disregard of their
royal *libertas* – to more powerful royal churches. This idea corresponded
to the new conception of rulership that Henry II had been developing
since the beginning of his reign. Royal authority should be total and
undiminished, the royal church should be controlled yet granted political
muscle, and weaker members of the church (*membra*) should be subordinated hierarchically to the stronger, with the king as the head (*caput*) of
both the church and the government. Although these ideas found little
dissent in the historical memory, their execution brought intensified

---

120 The *Translatio s. Modoaldi*, produced after the Hirsau reform, emphasized Helmarshausen's
original independence in an attempt to withdraw it from its proprietary status to the bishop
of Paderborn. I thank Professor Jakobs for his private comments on the later history of
Helmarshausen. See Jakobs, "Helmarshausen," 270–95.
121 See Bernhardt, *Itinerant Kingship*, 212–15, and Bannasch, *Das Bistum Paderborn*, 110–14.
122 See *Vita Meinwerci* c. 145, pp. 76–7; Stüwer, "Corvey und Lorsch," 270–3, 289–90; and Bernhardt, *Itinerant Kingship*, 123–4, 198.

conflict with the magnates of the realm and caused the prelates of the realm to reconsider fundamentally the concept of royal authority.[123]

VATICAN, OTTOBONIANUS LAT. 74

In conclusion, I would like to suggest and demonstrate a final connection between royal self-representation, ritual, and historical memory. I want to consider briefly a famous portrait of Henry II, which depicts the king and emperor in his capacity as judge (see Figure 2.2). This ruler portrait appears in a gospel book that was made in Regensburg around 1022, which, according to the medieval tradition of the monastery of Monte Cassino, Emperor Henry II gave to the monastery.[124] In terms of

---

123 See Weinfurter's essay (Chapter 1) in this book.
124 From an art historical perspective, see Ulrich Kuder, "Evangeliar Heinrichs II. aus Montecassino," in Michael Brandt and Arne Eggebrecht, eds., *Bernward von Hildesheim und das Zeitalter der Ottonen: Katalog der Austellung Hildesheim 1993*, 2 vols. (Hildesheim, 1993), 2:94–6; idem, "Die Handschriften," in Florentine Mütherich and Karl Dachs, eds., *Regensburg Buchmalerei: Von frühkarolingischer Zeit bis zum Ausgang des Mittelalters*, Bayerische Staatsbibliothek, Ausstellungskataloge 39 (Munich, 1987), 34; Ulrike Surmann, "Evangeliar Kaiser Heinrichs II.," in Joachim M. Plotzek et al., eds., *Biblioteca Apostolica Vaticana: Liturgie und Andacht im Mittelalter* (Stuttgart, 1992), 92–5; and Susanne Künzel, *Denkmale der Herrschaftstheologie Kaiser Heinrichs II.*, Schriften aus dem Institut für Kunstgeschichte der Universität München 43 (Munich, 1989), 36–52. Recently, Hagen Keller, "Das Bildnis Kaiser Heinrichs im Regensburger Evangeliar aus Montecassino (Bibl. Vat., Ottob. lat. 74): Zugleich ein Beitrag zu Wipos 'Tetralogus,'" *Frühmittelalterliche Studien* 30 (1996): 173–214, in a well-argued and erudite article, has attempted to attribute the ruler portrait and the commissioning of the manuscript to Henry III. He bases this on an iconographical construct of rulership ideas in the portrait that have similarities to those expressed in Wipo's *Tetralogus*. His arguments have not convinced me to abandon the attribution of the picture to Henry II for numerous reasons. Since Weinfurter, in his chapter in this book (note 72), has enumerated several objections to Keller's attribution with which I fully agree, I do not repeat them here. I add, however, some additional reservations of my own, while still recognizing that the question should be discussed further: First, Keller (pp. 176–7) to a certain degree begins his whole inquiry based on a suggested later paleographical dating of the hand in the manuscript by Hoffmann, *Buchkunst*, 1:300–1. As knowledgeable as Hoffmann is with these manuscripts, the dating of hands when we have no autograph is inexact at best, and even skilled paleographers as Hoffmann rarely can date closer than within about thirty years at best. Hence, the later dating is not compelling. Second, in his section about the judgment of the tyrant (pp. 185–8), Keller draws an example from Wipo which he claims suits as well to the picture as the trial of Pandulf IV (which I discuss momentarily).
Yet Keller's example contains no idea of regulating the harshness of a judgment that is key to the picture (*discernant leges pietas iustitia mites*) and that fits exactly to the situation of Pandulf IV and Henry II as known from Leo of Ostia's *Chronicle of Monte Cassino*. Third, Keller's emphasis on the importance of ideas found in the coronation *ordo* (189–90, 208) fits just as well, probably better, to Henry II since Weinfurter, "Der Anspruch" and "Authority and Legitimation" has demonstrated that Henry II used the coronation *ordo* as the conceptual basis for his kingship. Fourth, although Keller (212–13) acknowledges that the medieval tradition of Monte Cassino does not agree with his attribution, he downplays this very substantial problem. He provides no plausible reason why a "false identification of the royal portrait" may have occurred at Monte Cassino, and he prefers an iconographical construct of rulership ideas represented in the picture to the equally valid and very real historical possibility, based on Leo of Ostia and the Monte

Figure 2.2   Miniature of Henry II in the Gospel book of Monte Cassino. Vatican Library, Codex Ottobonianus lat. 74, fol. 193v. Reproduced by permission.

Cassino tradition, that Henry II granted the monastery a precious evangelary and that the portrait therein may represent other events recounted in the same tradition. Finally, I merely want to point out that the designation *rex* for Emperor Henry II, which Weinfurter (again, see his chapter in this book, note 72), sees as problematic, has a parallel in Thietmar 7.54, *MGH SrG*, where Thietmar in 1016–17 refers to Henry in the same chapter as emperor and king.

historical memory, the portrait in the gospel book is particularly interesting because it has been associated with a specific action of the ruler.[125] The figure cringing at Henry II's feet is commonly identified as Pandulf IV, the Prince of Capua who was sentenced to death by an imperial tribunal in 1022 and spared by the emperor's clemency.[126] The portrait, which appears in the manuscript before the Gospel of John, depicts the emperor sitting in the central medallion of a quadriform cross and enthroned in majesty.[127] The virtues of wisdom and prudence appear in the medallions at his sides, and the holy spirit descends bearing divine wisdom in the medallion above his head. Justice and piety stand above his shoulders in the upper corners, and in the lower corners law (*lex*) and right (*ius*) stand at his command.[128] The medallion beneath his feet depicts an impending execution. As the executioner prepares to draw his sword, the kneeling prisoner raises his arms, and both figures gaze upward at the ruler. The significance of the scene is suggested by an inscription: "Law and justice condemn the tyrant at the emperor's nod."[129] Overall, the

125 Herbert Bloch, "Monte Cassino, Byzantium and the West in the Earlier Middle Ages," *Dumbarton Oaks Papers* 3 (1946): 177–87, and Herbert Bloch, *Monte Cassino in the Middle Ages*, 3 vols. (Rome, 1986), 1:15–30. Because the latter is based on the former and is more current, I cite exclusively from it.

126 Leo of Ostia, *Chronica Monasterii Casinensis*, ed. Hartmut Hoffmann, in *MGH SS* 34 (Hannover, 1980), bk.2 c. 40 (hereafter Leo of Ostia, 2.40). Bloch, *Monte Cassino*, 15–16, 27–8. Keller, "Das Bildnis Kaiser Heinrichs," 185–6n60, recognizes the general acceptance of this attribution, but himself rejects the idea of a historical attribution to the miniature, as does Kuder, "Evangeliar Heinrichs II.," 96. On the other hand, Joachim Ott, "Vom Zeichencharakter der Herrscherkrone. Krönungszeremoniell und Krönungsbild im Mittelalter: Der *Mainzer Ordo* und das *Sakramentar Heinrichs II.*," in Jörg Jochen Berns and Thomas Rahn, eds., *Zeremoniell als höfische Ästhetik in Spätmittelalter und Früher Neuzeit* (Tübingen, 1995), 569, makes a general warning against not considering historical events in considering the motivations behind illuminated manuscripts.

127 On the technical difficulties regarding the placement of the portrait, see Bloch, *Monte Cassino*, 23–4, who follows Augusto Campana, "Per il 'Textus Evangeli' donato da Enrico II a Montecassino (Vat. Ottob. lat. 74)," in *La Bibliofilia: Rivista di storia del libro e delle arti grafiche di bibliografia ed erudizione* 60 (1958): 34–47, who both see the royal portrait as being inserted and not as part of the original placement, possibly out of a sudden change in the intended purpose of the manuscript. Künzel, *Denkmale der Herrschaftstheologie*, 46–52, offers an art-historical and iconographical interpretation and explanation of why the ruler portrait may indeed have been specifically intended for this placement, even if it was inserted later.

128 In addition to the Antependium of Basel, which Henry II donated, Henry II is also associated with the virtues of rulership in a poem from Tegernsee. See Joachim Wollasch, "Bemerkungen zur Goldenen Altartafel von Basel," in Christel Meier and Uwe Ruberg, eds., *Text und Bild: Aspekte des Zusammenwirkens zweier Künste in Mittelalter und früher Neuzeit* (Wiesbaden, 1980), 383–407, and Froumund, *Codex Epistolarum Tegernseensium (Die Tegernseer Briefsammlung)*, ed. Karl Strecker, in *Monumenta Germaniae Historica, Epistolae Selectae* 3 (Berlin, 1925; reprint, Munich, 1964), no. 38, p. 117: "Ecce tuum nomen virtutis predocet omen,/Quam bene cesareo conveniens titulo./Cuius de numero consistit sillaba quadro,/Quadre virtutis innuit et speciem."

129 "Caesaris ad nutum dampnant lex iusque tyrannum." Bloch, *Monte Cassino*, 28, makes the significant observation that Abbot Desiderius (1058–71) of Monte Cassino as well as Leo of Ostia repeatedly employ the word *tyrannus* in reference to Pandulf IV.

portrait employs the abstract and universal vocabulary of Christian kingship.[130] The king passes judgment, but his authority to judge comes from
God, as the dove hovering in the medallion over his head suggests.

I believe that there is good reason to accept the argument that the
figure in the portrait represents Prince Pandulf. Following Pandulf's trial,
Henry visited Monte Cassino,[131] and the local tradition relates that he
personally intervened in an abbatial election and experienced a miraculous cure through the intercession of Saint Benedict.[132] The *arenga* of the
charter that he granted to Monte Cassino on the occasion mentions
Henry's special veneration for Saint Benedict and may indeed refer to this
cure.[133] According to the local tradition, the monarch showed his grati-
tude by giving the community a deluxe copy of the gospels.[134] Herbert
Bloch has argued that this specific Gospel book, which was made in
Regensburg, and another manuscript containing two of his portraits,[135]
came to Monte Cassino soon after Henry's visit and that the portrait was
added specifically to enhance its appropriateness in regard to the occasion.[136] Thus, if the execution scene in Henry's portrait is in fact a reference to Pandulf's trial, the general iconographical context with reference
to the virtues of kings becomes in addition a monument to a specific
historical moment and a spectacular act of clemency.

Pandulf's trial occurred during a military campaign against the Byzantine Greeks, whose influence in southern Italy had enjoyed a resurgence
in the latter part of the tenth century. Though nominally allies of the
Ottonians, the princes of Capua and Salerno had acknowledged Byzantine overlordship. Aside from disloyalty, Pandulf was implicated in the
death of one of the leaders of an anti-Byzantine conspiracy who had connections with Henry II and was a protégé of Pope Benedict VIII. Indeed,

---

130 See Robert Deshman, "*Christus rex et magi reges*: Kingship and Christology in Ottonian and
Anglo-Saxon Art (Taf. XII–XXIII)," *Frühmittelalterliche Studien* 10 (1976): 381–90, and Stefan
Weinfurter, "Sakralkönigtum," 96–101.

131 *MGH DH II* 474.   132 Leo of Ostia, 2.42–3.

133 *MGH DH II* 474: "Quamvis communiter loca deo ubique dicata cottidie in melius proficere
nostra ope adhibita velimus, singulariter tamen et quasi specialius ceteris locum, in quo vener-
abilis patris nostri sanctissimi Benedicti corpus fovetur, pollere admodum cupimus, quippe quem
a primo aetatis flore semper maxime dileximus cuiusque intercessione piissima hactenus et in
regno roborati et in infirmitate sepius positi misericorditer relevati sumus" (see also Bloch, *Monte
Cassino*, 17n1).

134 Leo of Ostia, 2.43, 249; and Bloch, *Monte Cassino*, 17–22.

135 *Regensburg Sacramentary* (Munich, Staatsbibliothek Clm 4456, ff. 11ʳ, 11ᵛ).

136 Bloch, *Monte Cassino*, 19–25. Bloch (25n3), citing older literature, makes some insightful comments on medieval portraiture and its connection to reality, which I find more convincing than
those of Keller, "Das Bildnis Kaiser Heinrichs," 210, who believes that the round-bearded figure
in the Monte Cassino Evangelary can still be Henry III regardless of the fact that Henry III
almost always is depicted with a long, pointed beard and Henry II with a round beard.

Benedict had entreated the emperor to undertake the campaign and accompanied him on it.[137] According to the account compiled by Leo of Ostia in his *Chronicle*,[138] Henry II had Pandulf brought before a tribunal that heard many bitter accusations against him and then condemned him to death. At this point, Archbishop Pilgrim of Cologne intervened and convinced the emperor to spare Pandulf. Leo notes that he felt the penalty was too harsh and that he was confident others would support him. Thus, rather than being put to death, Pandulf was taken off to Germany in chains and imprisoned there. His principality was then transferred to another member of the Capuan dynasty.[139]

Pilgrim played the key ritual role of mediator on this occasion. In fact, his contribution began prior to the trial. Henry originally sent the archbishop to capture both Pandulf and his brother, Abbot Atenulf of Monte Cassino. The abbot managed to escape, but Pilgrim caught up to the prince in his capital city of Capua. Rather than resist, the prince voluntarily exited the city and met with Pilgrim. Leo states that he minimized his guilt but promised to do justice before the emperor for the things of which he had been accused. The issue of the trial and its outcome may have been discussed as well. Thus, Pandulf probably knew the rules of the game beforehand and accepted shame and a period of imprisonment as better than the alternative. Thus, the lower medallion of the picture of Henry II represents not only an impending execution but also a ritual of submission.[140]

Henry had good reason to deal leniently with Pandulf. The Capuan dynasty occupied a dominant position in the region, and cooperation with the Ottonians went back to Otto I. Henry II would not have wished to offend this family too deeply if he wanted to retain influence in the area. This indeed might explain his decision to leave the principality intact and in the hands of Pandulf's family. Pandulf was released by Conrad II after Henry II died. Moreover, the ease with which he again assumed his former position suggests that his allies and supporters expected his return.[141]

Thus, this magnificent portrait, splendid and rich in meaning, appears to offer a point where historical memory, ritual, and ruler self-representation join in a single image. One might say we have an example

---

137 Leo of Ostia, 2.39, 42. See also Bloch, *Monte Cassino*, 12–14, and Warner, "Thietmar of Merseburg," 60.
138 Leo of Ostia, 2.40.   139 Leo of Ostia, 2.41; *MGH DH II* 483.
140 Ibid., 2.40. On the interpretation of the ritual implications of this passage, see Warner, "Thietmar of Merseburg," 60–3.
141 Ibid., 61–2.

of art imitating history rather than the reverse. For Henry II's contemporaries and the following generation the image offers a poignant historical memory of Pandulf's treachery, his ritual submission, trial, and judgment, and the memory of Emperor Henry II's magnanimous display of leniency by commuting Pandulf's sentence of death. This audience might include those who witnessed the trial as well as the monks of Monte Cassino, whose former abbot, Pandulf's brother, had taken part in the conspiracy and on whom – some perhaps partisans – Henry had imposed a new abbot in the interests of the realm. For these immediate audiences, the portrait may have served as a warning concerning the treatment of rebels and the inescapability of imperial authority.[142] For later viewers not cognizant of the earlier historical events, the portrait presents the ideal concept of the all-powerful Christian emperor, Henry, aided by the virtues of justice, piety, wisdom, and prudence, and ultimately guided by the Holy Spirit of God, sitting as judge of life and death over doers of evil.[143]

142 On the question of audience and of immediate and transposed messages, see Bloch, *Monte Cassino*, 16–17, 28; Warner, "Thietmar of Merseburg," 63; and Künzel, *Denkmale der Herrschafts-theologie*, 41, 45.

143 Künzel, *Denkmale der Herrschaftstheologie*, 36–52, provides the most thorough examination of the interplay between the historical and the ideal interpretations of this ruler portrait.

3

The Variability of Rituals in the Middle Ages

GERD ALTHOFF

Rituals are a subject of interest for many disciplines. History, and especially medieval studies, cannot claim to play a leading part in the investigation of rituals. Yet despite – or perhaps because of – the many disciplines conducting research into ritual, there is no common understanding of what exactly constitutes the essence of ritual.

Any attempt to define ritual by bringing together the various opinions of scholars in behavioral, ethnic, religious, social-psychological, or other studies on the constitutive elements of ritual is bound to fail.[1] Therefore, all that will be done here is to identify some of the commonly accepted building blocks for such a definition: We talk about rituals when actions, or rather chains of actions, of a complex nature are repeated by actors in certain circumstances in the same or similar ways, and, if this happens deliberately, with the conscious goal of familiarity. In the minds of both actors and spectators, an ideal type of ritual exists that takes on a material form that is easily recognized in its various concrete manifestations.[2] Actors and spectators act in the consciousness of being bound to

---

1 On the different approaches, see, e.g., Niklas Luhmann, *Funktion der Religion* (Frankfurt am Main, 1977); Ernst Cassirer, *Philosophie der symbolischen Formen*, 3 vols. (Darmstadt, 1954), vol. 3; Ernst Cassirer, *Wesen und Wirkung des Symbolbegriffs* (Darmstadt, 1956); Edmund R. Leach, "Ritual," in David L. Sills, ed., *International Encyclopedia of the Social Sciences*, 19 vols. (New York, 1968), 13:520–6; Edmund R. Leach, "The Structure of Symbolism," in J. S. LaFontaine, ed., *The Interpretation of Ritual: Essays in Honour of A. I. Richards* (London, 1972), 239–75; Maurice Halbwachs, *Das kollektive Gedächtnis* (Stuttgart, 1967); Arnold van Gennep, *Übergangsriten* (Frankfurt am Main, 1986); French ed.: *Rites de passage: Etude systematique des rites de la porte et du seuil* . . . (Paris, 1909); Irenäus Eibl-Eibesfeldt, *Die Biologie des menschlichen Verhaltens: Grundriss der Humanethologie* (Munich, 1984); Wolfgang Braungart, *Ritual und Literatur*, Konzepte der Sprach- und Literaturwissenschaft no. 53 (Tübingen, 1996); see also Iwar Werlen, *Ritual und Sprache: Zum Verhältnis von Sprechen und Handeln in Ritualen* (Tübingen, 1984); and notes 2 through 7 to this chapter.
2 Cf. Gerhard Wolf, "Inszenierte Wirklichkeit und literarisierte Aufführung: Bedingungen und Funktion der 'performance' in Spiel- und Chroniktexten des Spätmittelalters," in Jan-Dirk Müller, ed., *"Aufführung" und "Schrift" im Mittelalter und Früher Neuzeit*, Germanistische Symposien Berichtsbände 17 (Stuttgart, 1996), 381–405; and Braungart, *Ritual und Literatur*, 216ff.

a given scheme, which does not, however, prevent the ritual from having the desired effect. Many other supposed characteristics of ritual must be qualified with the restriction "most of the time" or "often." For example, rituals are usually arranged ceremoniously; they frequently serve to acknowledge the social order, and often they serve the purpose of commemoration or confirmation – or both. One could continue in this vein, but to define the notion of ritual precisely is not my intent in this chapter. It is neither possible nor necessary to delimit ritual vis-à-vis related phenomena such as rite, custom, ceremony, or habit. To be conscious of the fluid boundaries between these notions is surely a more adequate approach to the subject.

The difficulty in defining ritual undoubtedly has to do with the fact that we use the term to describe phenomena from very different areas. Crudely typologized, there is on the one hand the vast religious-cultural domain: Religion is usually dominated by ritual.[3] On the other hand, there is a multitude of rituals in the secular sphere, for example, in public communication.[4] Rituals occur in politics, law, and the everyday intercourse of people and groups.[5] Rituals resist being rooted out. They constantly reconstitute themselves anew, and even groups or movements that

3 On ritual and religion, see Emile Durkheim, *Die elementaren Formen des religiösen Lebens* (Frankfurt am Main, 1981); French ed.: *Les formes élémentaires de la vie religieuse: Le systeme totémique en Australie* (Paris, 1912); see also Marcel Mauss, *Oeuvres*, vol. 1: *Les fonctions sociales du sacré: Présentation de Victor Karady* (Paris, 1968); for a different approach, see Maurice Halbwachs, *Das Gedächtnis und seine sozialen Bedingungen*, Soziologische Texte no. 34 (Berlin, 1966); French ed.: *Les cadres sociaux de la mémoire* (Paris, 1925), 279ff.; Esther Goody, "Religion and Ritual: The Definitional Problem," *British Journal of Sociology* 12 (1961): 142–64.

4 On the notion of ritual in social anthropology, see Max Gluckman, *Politics, Law and Ritual in Tribal Society* (Oxford, 1965); A. R. Radcliff-Brown, *Structure and Function in Primitive Society* (London, 1952); Edmund R. Leach, *Kultur und Kommunikation* (Frankfurt am Main, 1978); English ed.: *Culture and Communication: The Logic by which Symbols Are Connected: An Introduction to the Use of Structuralist Analysis in Social Anthropology* (Cambridge, 1976); Victor Turner, *Das Ritual: Struktur und Antistruktur*, Theorie und Gesellschaft 10 (Frankfurt am Main, 1989); English ed.: *The Ritual Process: Structure and Anti-Structure* (London, 1969).

5 On the notion of ritual in policy, see Marc Abélès and Werner Rossade, eds., *Politique Symbolique en Europe: Symbolische Politik in Europa*, Beiträge zur politischen Wissenschaft, vol. 69 (Berlin, 1993); Thomas Meyer, *Die Inszenierung des Scheins: Voraussetzungen und Folgen symbolischer Politik: Essay-Montage* (Frankfurt am Main, 1992); Murray J. Edelman, *Politik als Ritual: Die symbolische Funktion staatlicher Institutionen und politischen Handelns*, Campus Studium: Kritische Sozialwissenschaft no. 512 (Frankfurt am Main, 1976); English ed.: *The Symbolic Use of Politics* (Urbana, Ill., 1964); Sean Wilentz, ed., *Rites of Power: Symbolism, Ritual, and Politics Since the Middle Ages* (Philadelphia, 1985); and David I. Kertzer, *Ritual, Politics, and Power* (London, 1988). On the notion of ritual in social psychology, see Erving Goffman, *Verhalten in sozialen Situationen: Strukturen und Regeln der Interaktion im öffentlichen Raum* (Gütersloh, 1971); English ed.: *Behaviour in Public Places: Notes on the Social Organization of Gatherings* (New York, 1969); Erving Goffman, *Interaktionsrituale: Über Verhalten in direkter Kommunikation* (Frankfurt am Main, 1971); English ed.: *Interaction Rituals: Essays in Face-to-Face Behavior* (Chicago, 1967).

have set out under the banner of antiritualism soon create their own forms of ritual communication.[6]

Connected with the various domains where rituals occur are the various opinions held by different scholars and disciplines concerning the possibility of variation in ritual. Scholars starting from religious-cultural rituals, and those who explain ritual by appeal to the instinctive behavior of men and animals, emphasize the compulsion toward the exact fulfillment of ritual acts. They speak of "sacral ritual rigidity," of the "compulsion to repeat," and so forth, and thus perpetuate the conception that in archaic societies dominated by magic-religious beliefs, rituals, through their structural permanence, constitute a "given" to which men are subject and by which they are even subjugated.[7]

This may indeed apply to ritual in the practice of religion. But I wish to demonstrate that this concept does not adequately describe rituals of public communication in the Middle Ages. The actors on medieval political stages did not carry out established rituals in a servile way but rather used the given rituals in a utilitarian-rational way. They varied, mixed, or updated them in keeping with the given situation or even invented new rituals if there was no suitable pre-existing ritual language at their disposal.

At this point it must be stressed that medieval public communication was ritual and demonstrative, a fact that has not been sufficiently considered by medieval scholars.[8] Public interactions involving secular and

---

6 Cf. Hans-Georg Soeffner, "Rituale des Antiritualismus – Materialien für Ausseralltägliches," in Hans Ulrich Gumbrecht and K. Ludwig Pfeiffer, eds., *Materialität der Kommunikation* (Frankfurt am Main, 1988), 519–46; see also in Hans-Georg Soeffner, *Die Ordnung der Rituale: Die Auslegung des Alltags* (Frankfurt am Main, 1992), 102–30; English ed.: *The Order of Rituals: The Interpretation of Everyday Life* (New Brunswick, N.J., 1997).

7 See, e.g., Erich Neumann, "Zur psychologischen Bedeutung des Ritus," *Eranos-Jahrbuch*, vol. 19: *Mensch und Ritus* (1950): 97ff.; Niklas Luhmann, *Legitimation durch Verfahren*, Soziologische Texte 66 (Darmstadt, 1975); Durkheim, *Die elementaren Formen des religiösen Lebens*, 60; Jan Assmann, *Das kulturelle Gedächtnis: Schrift, Erinnerung und politische Identität in frühen Hochkulturen* (Munich, 1992); Ingolf U. Dalferth, "Mythos, Ritual, Dogmatik: Strukturen der religiösen Textwelt," *Evangelische Theologie* 47 (1987): 283–4; Eugene G. D'Aquili, Charles D. Laughlin, and John McManus, *The Spectrum of Ritual: A Biogenetic Structural Analysis* (New York, 1979); on medieval rituals, see Karl Leyser, "Ritual, Zeremonie und Gestik: Das ottonische Reich," *Frühmittelalterliche Studien* 27 (1993): 25–6.

8 Important insights can already be found in Heinrich Fichtenau, *Lebensordnungen des 10. Jahrhunderts: Studien über Denkart und Existenz im einstigen Karolingerreich*, Monographien zur Geschichte des Mittelalters, vol. 30, pt. 1 (Stuttgart, 1984), 50ff.; in general, see Bernd Thum, "Öffentlichkeit und Kommunikation im Mittelalter. Zur Herstellung von Öffentlichkeit im Bezugsfeld elementarer Kommunikationsformen im 13. Jahrhundert," in Hedda Ragotzky and Horst Wenzel, eds., *Höfische Repräsentation: Das Zeremoniell und die Zeichen* (Tübingen, 1990), 65–87; and the essays by Karl Leyser, Gerd Althoff, Hagen Keller, Dagmar Hupper, and Jan-Dirk Müller, in *Frühmittelalterliche Studien* 27 (1993): 1–146, with further literature. See also Gerd Althoff, ed., *Formen*

clerical magnates – but not only these – consisted for the most part of ritual-demonstrative actions that acknowledged the existing order and expressed the status and honor of the participants.[9] In this manner the maintenance of mutual good relations was ensured, for example, by means of appropriate greetings, honors, or appropriate forms of leave-taking.[10] There also were signs used to give sufficiently early warning of a deterioration in relations or of a threatened disturbance of the social order. Escalations of conflict were ritualized. Changes and innovations in the social order also were announced by such actions, for example, by the ritual of investiture or by rituals for ending conflict and making peace.[11] The new situation was expressed in a very demonstrative way, through actions such as taking a common meal, doing homage, or presenting gifts.[12] The spoken word was not lacking in this ritual communication, but the actions alone sufficed to establish an obligation and guarantee appropriate behavior in the future.[13] The public quality of such actions was essential because the spectators assumed the role of witnesses and thereby made the action "legally binding" – this being a favorite, although anachronistic, notion of German medievalists.[14]

und Funktionen öffentlicher Kommunikation im Mittelalter: Vorträge und Forschungen (forthcoming). Of doubtful value is Werner Faulstich, *Medien und Öffentlichkeiten im Mittelalter: 800–1400*, Die Geschichte der Medien 2 (Göttingen, 1996).

9 On status, see Fichtenau, *Lebensordnungen des 10. Jahrhunderts*, 11ff.

10 Cf. Horst Fuhrmann, "'Willkommen und Abschied': Über Begrüssungs- und Abschiedsrituale im Mittelalter," in Wilfried Hartmann, ed., *Mittelalter: Annäherung an eine fremde Zeit*, Schriftenreihe der Universität Regensburg, n.s. 19 (Regensburg, 1993), 111–39; see also Horst Fuhrmann, *Überall ist Mittelalter: Von der Gegenwart einer vergangenen Zeit* (Munich, 1996), 17–39.

11 On investiture as a ritual of law, see Hagen Keller, "Die Investitur: Ein Beitrag zum Problem der 'Staatssymbolik' im Hochmittelalter," *Frühmittelalterliche Studien* 27 (1993): 55ff.

12 On the common meal, see Karl Hauck, "Rituelle Speisegemeinschaft im 10. und 11. Jahrhundert," *Studium Generale* 3 (1950): 611–21; Joachim Bumke, *Höfische Kultur: Literatur und Gesellschaft im hohen Mittelalter*, 2 vols. (Munich, 1986), 1:276ff.; English ed.: *Courtly Culture: Literature and Society in the High Middle Ages* (Berkeley, Calif., 1991); Detlef Altenburg et al., eds., *Feste und Feiern im Mittelalter*, Paderborner Symposion des Mediävistenverbandes (Sigmaringen, 1991); Gerd Althoff, "Der frieden-, bündnis- und gemeinschaftsstiftende Charakter des Mahles im früheren Mittelalter," in Irmgard Bitsch, Trude Ehlert, and Xenia von Ertzdorff, eds., *Essen und Trinken in Mittelalter und Neuzeit* (Sigmaringen, 1987), 13–25; and Gerd Althoff, *Verwandte, Freunde und Getreue: Zum politischen Stellenwert der Gruppenbindungen im früheren Mittelalter* (Darmstadt, 1990), 203ff., with further literature.

13 On the theory of medieval gestures, see Jean-Claude Schmitt, ed., *Gestures*, History and Anthropology series, vol. 1, pt. 1 (London, 1984), and Schmitt, *La raison du gestes: Pour une histoire des gestes en Occident (IIIe-XIIIe siècle)* (Paris, 1989); German ed.: *Die Logik der Gesten*.

14 On the importance and function of audience, see Thum, "Öffentlichkeit und Kommunikation," 75ff.; Donald A. Bullough, "Games People Played: Drama and Ritual as Propaganda in Medieval Europe," *Transactions of the Royal Historical Society*, 5th ser., 24 (1974): 97–122; J. J. Nelson, "Ritual and Reality in the Early Medieval Ordines," in Derek Baker, ed., *The Materials, Sources, and Methods of Ecclesiastical History*, Studies in church History, no. 11 (London, 1975), 47–50; and David A. Warner, "Henry II at Magdeburg: Kingship, Ritual, and the Cult of Saints," *Early Medieval Europe* 3 (1994): 140–1n27.

These ritual forms of communication among the leading strata, as attested throughout the Middle Ages, provide an excellent starting point for research on continuity and change in ritual because descriptions of such rituals by various authors have survived.[15] In contrast to oral societies, whose rituals ethnologists describe on the basis of fieldwork, the semi-oral society of the Middle Ages has provided us with descriptions of ritual behavior over the centuries, snapshots that can and must be compared.[16] In this manner we can obtain criteria for determining whether an action was usual or unusual, as in conforming with custom or altering it; we can observe innovations in old rituals; and we can see rituals appear and disappear. From this ability to compare across the centuries – one not available to ethnologists – comes my estimation of the highly rational attitude displayed by medieval people toward their secular or semisecular rituals.

I carried out such a comparison some time ago for the ritual of the *deditio*, which represented a common way to amicably settle disputes in the Middle Ages.[17] The ritual was used both by individual persons and by larger groups, such as castle garrisons, townsfolk, and members of a clan. The same basic elements of this ritual come up repeatedly. The supplicant had to wear clothes similar to those of a penitent and had to walk barefoot.[18] The core of the ritual was prostration before the former opponent, accompanied by words of self-accusation and surrender. In most cases the supplicant received the lord's pardon, was raised from the floor, and was often honored by a kiss of peace.[19] These elements of the ritual

15 See, e.g., David A. Warner, "Thietmar of Merseburg on Rituals of Kingship," *Viator: Medieval and Renaissance Studies* 26 (1995): 53–76.

16 Numerous examples of ritual behavior are found in medieval literature; see Dietmar Peil, *Die Gebärde bei Chrétien, Hartmann und Wolfram: Erec – Iwain – Parzival*, Medium Aevum 28 (Munich, 1975); Martin J. Schubert, *Zur Theorie des Gebarens im Mittelalter: Analyse von nichtsprachlicher Äusserung in mittelhochdeutscher Epik: Rolandslied, Eneasroman, Tristan*, Kölner Germanistische Studien 31 (Cologne, 1991); Harald Haferland, *Höfische Interaktion: Interpretationen zur höfischen Epik und Didaktik um 1200*, Forschungen zur Geschichte der älteren deutschen Literatur 10 (Munich, 1989); and Gert Kaiser and Jan-Dirk Müller, *Höfische Literatur, Hofgesellschaft, höfische Lebensformen um 1200*, Studia humaniora 6 (Düsseldorf, 1986).

17 Cf. Gerd Althoff, "Das Privileg der deditio: Formen gütlicher Konfliktbeendigung in der mittelalterlichen Adelsgesellschaft," in Gerd Althoff, *Spielregeln der Politik im Mittelalter: Kommunikation in Frieden und Fehde* (Darmstadt, 1997), 99–125; see also Otto Gerhard Oexle and Werner Paravicini, eds., *Nobilitas: Funktion und Repräsentation des Adels in Alteuropa*, Veröffentlichungen des Max-Planck-Instituts für Geschichte 133 (Göttingen, 1997), with additional literature.

18 See, in general, Gabriele Raudszus, *Die Zeichensprache der Kleidung: Untersuchungen zur Symbolik des Gewandes in der deutschen Epik des Mittelalters* (Hildesheim, 1985), 132ff., 217ff.

19 Cf. Klaus Schreiner, "'Er küsse mich mit dem Kuss seines Mundes' (Osculetur me osculo oris sui, Cant 1,1): Metaphorik, kommunikative und herrschaftliche Funktion einer symbolischen Handlung," in Ragotzky and Wenzel, eds., *Höfische Repräsentation*, 89–132; and Fichtenau, *Lebensordnungen des 10. Jahrhunderts*, 57ff.

can be shown to have been for centuries the constitutive forms for the public, amicable settlement of disputes.[20]

Nevertheless, individual cases show that the execution and arrangement of the ritual were not characterized by a rigid compulsion to repeat; the ritual could be modified appropriately, according to the individual situation. There were honorable or less severe forms of the ritual, and the details of its execution were debated beforehand, as we know for certain in some cases. The purpose of these debates is made plain, for example, by the seemingly minor detail that the citizens of Milan in 1158, before their own *deditio*, offered to give Barbarossa 5,000 silver marks if he allowed them to carry out the ritual while wearing their shoes. Barbarossa refused.[21] Only when one expects the possibility of such situation-specific variations in ritual can one see particularities in individual ritual descriptions, as I will now demonstrate with the following example.

An exceedingly original deviation from the basic form of the *deditio* was conceived in 1008 in Milan.[22] Archbishop Arnulf of Milan had refused to consecrate bishop Alderich of Asti, whom Henry II had newly invested. Alderich had been meant to replace one of Arduin's followers in Asti, who fled to Milan. Alderich received his consecration, which had been refused by Arnulf, from the pope in Rome. This infuriated Arnulf

---

20 For individual examples, see Althoff, *Das Privileg der deditio*, 99ff.; Gerd Althoff, "Königsherrschaft und Konfliktbewältigung im 10. und 11. Jahrhundert," *Frühmittelalterliche Studien* 23 (1989): 265–90, and again Althoff, *Spielregeln der Politik im Mittelalter*, 32ff., 49ff.; Gerd Althoff, "Demonstration und Inszenierung: Spielregeln der Kommunikation in mittelalterlicher Öffentlichkeit," *Frühmittelalterliche Studien* 27 (1993): 27–50; Althoff, *Spielregeln der Politik im Mittelalter*, 240ff.; Althoff, "Empörung, Tränen, Zerknirschung: 'Emotionen' in der öffentlichen Kommunikation des Mittelalters," *Frühmittelalterliche Studien* 30 (1996): 60–79, again in Althoff, *Spielregeln der Politik im Mittelalter*, 268ff.; Althoff, "Genugtuung (satisfactio): Zur Eigenart gütlicher Konfliktbeilegung im Mittelalter," in Joachim Heinzle, ed., *Modernes Mittelalter* (Frankfurt am Main, 1994), 252ff.; Althoff, "Konfliktverhalten und Rechtsbewusstsein: Die Welfen im 12. Jahrhundert," *Frühmittelalterliche Studien* 26 (1992): 331–52; again in Althoff, *Spielregeln der Politik im Mittelalter*, 70ff.

21 Cf. Wilhelm Wattenbach, ed., *Vincentii Pragensis annales, Monumenta Germaniae Historica, Scriptores*, vol. 17 (Hannover, 1861), 654–83, 1158, 674–5: "Post hec duodecim Mediolanensium consules electi, gladios suos super colla sua ferentes, nudis pedibus – licet enim plurimam offerent pecuniam quod eis calciatis hanc satisfactionem facere liceret, nullomodo tamen obtinere potuerunt – suo ordine progrediuntur, coram tot et tantis principibus imperatori suo sedenti pro tribunali super colla sua nudos offerunt gladios." See also Thomas Zotz, "Präsenz und Repräsentation: Beobachtungen zur königlichen Herrschaftspraxis im hohen und späten Mittelalter," in Alf Lüdtke, ed., *Herrschaft als soziale Praxis*, Veröffentlichungen des Max-Planck-Instituts für Geschichte, vol. 91 (Göttingen, 1991), 181.

22 Cf. Claudia Zey, ed., Arnulf von Mailand, *Liber gestorum recentium, Monumenta Germaniae Historica, Scriptores rerum Germanicarum* 67 (Hannover, 1994), 1:18–20, 141ff.; see also Siegfried Hirsch, *Jahrbücher des Deutschen Reichs unter Heinrich II. (1002–1024)*, Jahrbücher der Deutschen Geschichte 2 (Berlin, 1864), 370–1.

to such an extent that he not only excommunicated Alderich at a synod but also besieged Alderich and his brother, the margrave Manfred of Susa, in Asti.[23] The conflict was settled amicably; the *pacis conditio* (conditions for re-establishing peace) that the bishop and the margrave had to fulfill was as follows: They went together to Milan and dismounted their horses three miles from the city. They then walked barefoot, the bishop carrying a book and the margrave a dog.[24] At the doors of Saint Ambrosius' church they confessed their misdeeds. Bishop Alderich then placed his staff of office and his ring on the altar of the church. Manfred, on the other hand, presented the church with a huge amount of money, which was used to make a crucifix. After this, the two marched on, still barefoot, to the middle of the city, where they were received in peace by the archbishop and the people in front of the cathedral.[25] What was original about this settlement of the conflict was, first, the simultaneous reparation offered by the brothers in ways appropriate to their respective stations, and second, the processionlike march that spread out their penance over several locations.[26]

The following examples come from the medieval ritual of the king's election and coronation, an arena where ritual behavior of a special nature can be observed. Despite the fixation on custom, however, and despite all the *ordines* (orders of ceremony) that were meant to ensure proper behavior, descriptions of acts without precedent in the tradition can be found, acts that were adapted to the ceremony according to the given situation. To these belong the hitherto unjustly neglected events Wipo mentions in his account of the election of Conrad II. While the newly raised king was on his way to the cathedral of Mainz, where his consecration was to take place, the following happened:

---

23 On the synod in the summer of 1008, see Heinz Wolter, *Die Synoden im Reichsgebiet und in Reichsitalien von 916 bis 1056*, Konziliengeschichte, Reihe A: Darstellungen (Paderborn, 1988), 253ff.; and Roland Pauler, *Das Regnum Italiae in ottonischer Zeit: Markgrafen, Grafen und Bischöfe als politische Kräfte*, Bibliothek des Deutschen Historischen Instituts in Rom 54 (Tübingen, 1982), 15–16.

24 Cf. Arnulf von Mailand, *Liber gestorum recentium*, 1:19, 142: "Hec autem fuit pacis conditio, quod venientes Mediolanum tertio ab urbe miliario nudis incedendo vestigiis episcopus codicem, marchio canem baiulans." On the *Hundetragen*, see Bernd Schwenk, "Das Hundetragen: Ein Rechtsbrauch im Mittelalter," *Historisches Jahrbuch* 110 (1990): 301–2.

25 Cf. Arnulf von Mailand, *Liber gestorum recentium*, 1:19, 142–3: "ante fores ecclesie beati Ambrosii reatus proprios devotissime sunt confessi. Preterea episcopus virgam et anulum suscepti pontificatus supra sancti confessoris altare deposuit, que postea largiente archiepiscopo pie resumpsit. Frater vero illius Mainfredus marchio donavit ecclesie auri talenta quamplurima, unde producta est crux illa pulcherima, que usque hodie precipuis tantum geritur in diebus. Deinde nudis sicut venerant pedibus per medium civitatis ad ecclesiam maiorem sancte Theototos usque deveniunt, ab archiepiscopo et clero cunctoque recepti in pace populo."

26 On comparable royal processions, see David A. Warner, *Henry II at Magdeburg*, 141ff.

While the king made his entry, three people with special grievances approached him. The first was a peasant of the Mainz church, the second an orphan, the third a widow. Because the king wanted to listen to their requests, some princes sought to distract him by pointing out that he should not delay his consecration and that he should hear the holy office on time. But like a real vicar of Christ, he replied piously with his gaze on the bishops: "If the office of king is my duty, and a man faithful to himself must not put off what it is possible for him to do, then it seems to me more important to do my duty than to let others tell me what to do." With these words, he stood still where the unhappy people had approached him and paused to render justice. No sooner had he continued on than someone stepped before him claiming that he had been innocently thrust into misery. The king took his hand, led him in the view of everyone up to his throne, and conscientiously entrusted the poor man's case to one of his princes. Thus blessed his reign began.[27]

Wipo then underlines his praise of Conrad's royal virtues with a number of quotations from the Bible.[28]

As I have already pointed out elsewhere, to imagine here that four desperate people had no other way out of their misery than confiding in the king is not realistic.[29] Wipo describes here a *mise-en-scene* that presented Conrad II with the opportunity to demonstrate effectively certain royal virtues, namely, *clementia* (mercy) and *iustitia* (justice).[30] For an unknown reason, the rituals of pleading for mercy, justice, and forgiveness were added to the ceremony of coronation, thus giving Conrad the opportunity to demonstrate *clementia* and *iustitia*. I do not want to spend much time speculating about who staged the scene or what the motives were. It is conceivable that experiences with Conrad's predecessor made

27 Harry Bresslau, ed., *Wiponis Gesta Chuonradi II imperatoris*, in Wiponis Opera, Monumenta Germaniae Historica Scriptores rerum Germanicarum, vol. 61, 3d ed. (Hannover, 1915), cap. 5, pp. 26–7: "In ipsa processione regis tres venerunt ante illum cum singulis querimoniis. Unus erat colonus ecclesiae Moguntinensis, alter pupillus fuit et quaedam vidua. Dum rex eorum causas audire coepisset, quidam de principus suis avertebant eum dicentes, ne consecrationis suae aliquam moram faceret et mature divina officia audiret; respiciens ad episcopos, ut vicarius Christi, christianissime respondebat:'Si meum est regimini insistere et id viri constantis est nequaquam differre, quod apte fieri valet, rectius mihi videtur facere, quod debeo, quam, quid faciendum sit, audire, ab alio . . .' Haec dicens in eadem statione moratus, ubi primum occurrerant illi calamitosi, Passibus immotis legem praefecerat illis. Hinc paululum procedens, venit ante illum quidam dicens, se expulsum esse patria omnino sine culpa, quem rex per brachium apprehendens super omnes circumstantes attraxit usque ad solium suum ibique causam miseri cuidam principum suorum diligenter commendavit. Felix initium regnandi cernitur esse."

28 *Wiponis Gesta Chuonradi*, cap. 5, p. 27: "per semitam iustitiae incedebat, quando regium honorem petebat. Poterat dicere cum psalmista: 'Pes meus stetit in via recta.' Firmavit se per gratiae bonum, priusquam conscenderet iudicialem thronum. . . . scriptum est enim: 'Honor regis iudicium diligit.'"

29 See Gerd Althoff, "Demonstration und Inszenierung," 233ff.

30 On the staging character, see also Ulrich Reuling, *Die Kur in Deutschland und Frankreich: Untersuchungen zur Entwicklung des rechtsförmlichen Wahlaktes bei der Königserhebung im 11. und 12. Jahrhundert*, Veröffentlichungen des Max-Planck-Instituts für Geschichte, vol. 64 (Göttingen, 1979), 33–4.

it appear advisable to put the king more explicitly under an obligation to perform the kingly virtues than was customary. It also could be conceivable that the staging was thought necessary because Conrad had lived for many years as an ordinary member of noble society, without concrete prospects for succession to the kingship. In any case, the scene confronted him with his new duties; with his agreement to the request he promised similar behavior in the future.

Another famous example of a serious change in the coronation *ordines* is the refusal by Henry I to accept anointment in Fritzlar in 919.[31] In this case, a new and adequate understanding of the event presents itself only if the scene is understood as having been staged and carried out by the mutual consent of the main actors, that is, the archbishop of Mainz, Heriger, and the new king. Their goal was to express Henry's wish to be a different king than his anointed predecessors. Here, too, the ritual was changed in a significant manner, by beginning it but then presenting the new king with the opportunity to explain why he wanted to do without it.

A third example from the arena of royal coronation must be discussed in this context, but it is more difficult to understand. At Frederick Barbarossa's coronation, a ministerial is reported to have thrown himself at the feet of the king in the church and to have pleaded for pardon for previous offenses. He was refused the pardon, which Otto von Freising explained by saying that even on such a day, Barbarossa was not to be diverted from the *rigor iustitiae* (inflexibility of justice).[32]

---

31 Paul Hirsch with Hans-Eberhard Lohmann, eds., *Widukindi monachi Corbeiensis Rerum Gestarum Saxonicarum libri tres*, Monumenta Germaniae Historica Scriptores rerum Germanicarum, vol. 60, 5th ed. (Hannover, 1935), 1:26, 39: "Cumque ei offerretur unctio cum diademate a summo pontifice, qui eo tempore Hirigerus erat, non sprevit, nec tamen suscepit: 'Satis,' inquiens, 'michi est, ut pre maioribus meis rex dicar et designer, divina annuente gratia ac vestra pietate; penes meliores vero nobis unctio et diadema sit: tanto honore nos indignos arbitramur"; and Robert Holtzmann, ed., *Thietmari Merseburgensis episcopi Chronicon, Monumenta Germaniae Historica, Scriptores rerum Germanicarum*, n.s. 9, 2d ed. (Berlin, 1955), 1:5, 9; see Gerd Althoff and Hagen Keller, *Heinrich I. und Otto der Grosse: Neubeginn auf karolingischem Erbe*, Persönlichkeit und Geschichte 122–3 (Göttingen, 1985), 56ff.; and Johannes Fried, "Die Königserhebung Heinrichs I.: Erinnerung, Mündlichkeit und Traditionsbildung im 10. Jahrhundert," in Michael Borgolte, ed., *Mittelalterforschung nach der Wende 1989*, supplement to *Historische Zeitschrift*, n.s. 20 (Munich, 1995), 302ff.

32 Otto von Freising and Rahewin, *Die Taten Friedrichs oder richtiger Cronica*, ed. Franz-Josef Schmale, Freiherr vom Stein-Gedächtnisausgabe 17 (Darmstadt, 1965), 2:3, 286–7: "Nec pretereundum estimo, quod, dum finito unctionis sacramento diadema sibi imponeretur, quidam de ministris eius, qui pro quibusdam excessibus gravibus a gratia sua adhuc privati sequestratus fuerat, circa mediam ecclesiam ad pedes ipsius se proiecit, sperans ob presentis diei alacritatem eius se animum a rigore iustitie emollire posse. Ipse vero mentem in priori severitate retinens et tamquam fixus manens constantie sue omnibus nobis non parvum dedit indicium, dicens non ex odio, sed iustitie intuitu illum a gratia sua exculsum fuisse"; see also Gerd Althoff, "Ira regis: Prolegomena

It is not easy to comprehend this event. One can assume, of course, that the ministerial knew about the custom of demonstratively forgiving in precisely such a situation. According to this explanation, then, he tried to force the king by his prostration into a fait accompli and failed. Such attempts are known in other cases as well. It is also conceivable, however, that the whole scene was staged and represented a deliberate turning away from old ritual forms by which the obligation for *clementia* was accepted. According to this interpretation, the ritual was changed deliberately, in order to express in a demonstrative way a new hierarchy of royal virtues, namely, the pre-eminence of *iustitia* over *clementia*. Both possibilities are left open to discussion without one of them being favored over the other.

In the preceding examples, rituals were changed or supplemented in order to adjust them to a given situation. Now I would like to present cases in which the situation was so special that we could almost say a new ritual had been invented, had the elements used in these cases not been well-known ones that simply were combined in a new original way.

In the middle of the tenth century, a serious conflict between the abbot and some of the monks of Saint Gall brought a dire crisis to the monastery.[33] The mediator in this crisis, Bishop Ulrich of Augsburg, hindered the making of peace because he allowed himself to be seduced into most unusual behavior. At the reception a monk gave the gospel for the kiss of peace only to the bishop and not to the Abbot Craloh, who was accompanying the bishop. Ulrich ran after the monk and seized him by the hair, whereupon the monk hurled the Holy Book at Ulrich and vanished in a fury.[34] This was no good beginning for negotiations concerning the arrangement of peace, though negotiations were started

to a History of Royal Anger," in Barbara Rosenwein, ed., *Anger's Past: The Social Uses of an Emotion in the Middle Ages* (Ithaca, N.Y., 1998); and Althoff, *Konfliktverhalten und Rechtsbewusstsein,* 65n25.

33 Hermann Kamp recently analyzed the conflict in Spoleto, because he is an extremely good example for the line of work of a mediator, here Bishop Ulrich of Augsburg. See Hermann Kamp, "Vermittler in Konflikten des hohen Mittelalters," in *La Giustizia nell'alto medioevo II (secoli IX–XI),* Settimane di studio del Centro italiano di studi sull'alto Medioevo, vol. 44 (Spoleto, 1997). On the function of mediators generally, see Torstein Eckhoff, "The Mediator, the Judge, and the Administrator in Conflict-Resolution, *Acta sociologica* 10 (1967): 148–72; and Simon Roberts, *Order and Dispute: An Introduction to Legal Anthropology* (New York, 1979); German ed.: *Ordnung und Konflikt: Eine Einführung in die Rechtsethnologie* (Stuttgart, 1981), 72ff., 172ff.

34 Hans F. Haefele, ed., *Ekkehardi casus sancti Galli,* Freiherr vom Stein-Gedächtnisausgabe, vol. 10 (Darmstadt, 1980), cap. 74, p. 152: "Suscipitur episcopus. Victor ewangelium optulit ipsi. Quod ub ille osculatur, Victor revertitur. At episcopus currax post illum veniens, a capillo hominem capiens regiravit. At ille ewangelium in episcopum reiciens furibundus abscessit." See also Althoff, *Demonstration und Inszenierung,* 251–2.

nevertheless. The most important point was reached when the ritual to express the reconciliation of the abbot and the monks was discussed. According to Ekkehard of Saint Gall, they took council about "how to reconcile the whole body with the head and the head with the whole body."[35] Two mediators, Bishop Ulrich and a wise layman, in addition to the abbot Craloh and four chosen monks of Saint Gall, were involved in this council. "It was decided to place the father, in order to present him to the sons, on Saint Benedict's chair, whose picture was drawn there. He was guided in at the bishop's hand, took his seat, and remained thus for a while. Finally he rose and, weeping, fell to his knees; but with him the bishop and all the brothers fell to their knees. It was obvious that the Holy Spirit accomplished his deed. After they had all kissed one another, the concord in the house was perfect."[36]

Ekkehard's description is a good example of the manner in which medieval authors depicted such events. On the one hand, Ekkehard clearly states that a council about how to carry out a reconciliation took place and that a decision was made. On the other hand, he ascribes the success to the work of the Holy Spirit. The simultaneous falling to their knees of the abbot, the brothers, and the mediator, who also had a reason to make reparations because of his behavior at the reception, expresses the difficult situation in such a way that its successful resolution was not owed to the Holy Spirit alone. Everybody's falling to their knees was, like the abbot's taking of his seat, the subject of the council and of the decision. Thus, the fact was expressed that every side had reason to give satisfaction to the other side and to ask for forgiveness. A careful analysis of the course of events shows that the abbot took his seat, and furthermore remained on his seat for some time, thus having his claim to the seat acknowledged by everyone present. Only thereafter did the mutual asking for forgiveness and the granting of it by the kiss of peace take place.

As a whole this ritual is an original invention; however, a number of known ritual acts were used in a sort of building-block fashion, such as the taking of the seat, the falling to the knees as a gesture for forgiveness, and the kiss of peace. Otherwise, there would have been no chance for the ritual's message to have been recognized. The quality of

---

35 Haefele, ed., *Ekkehardi casus sancti Galli*, cap. 76, p. 160: "Conferuntur consilia, qualiter totum corpus capiti et caput corpori restituatur."

36 Ibid., cap. 76, p. 160: "Stat consilium patrem filiis oblatum in sancti Benedicti, cuius imago appicta sedebat, ponere solium. Inducitur manu episcopi locatusque parumper residet. Tandemque assurgens lacrimando in veniam corruit; sed et episcopo secum ruente fratres omnes econtra ruebant. Erat facietenus videre spiritum sanctum opus suum ibimet agere. Osculatis singulis unanimitas in domo solidatur."

the solution is a result of the careful juxtaposition of the single elements, in particular of the simultaneous fall to the knees by which joint guilt was made clear.

The obligations imposed by participation in the described ritual acts are shown by the behavior of one monk, who was a bitter enemy of the abbot: "Victor, with raging heart, could not bear this sight. When he had to look at the abbot on the seat, he jumped up wildly and left the chapter house as if he wanted to run away from the monastery. But the bishop fetched him, soothed him, and led him back to the abbot's favor."[37] The peace did not hold long; regardless, the monk's behavior shows that participation in the ritual meant consent, an insight that is crucial in order to understand behavior in and with respect to rituals in general. When viewed from this perspective, being absent becomes one of the most important forms of expression in medieval political communication. By staying away, magnates refused their participation in ritual acts that demonstratively and publicly expressed consent, whether at the court or at judicial hearings. The quick departure of some persons or groups thus is easily explained, when rising dissent rendered participation in ritual acts more difficult or even hindered it.

In spite of these models for behavior, rituals could fail if the participants did not engage in them or if they deliberately courted failure. This happened, for example, when Ekkehard of Meissen and his episcopal and ducal companions took over a festive dinner already in progress and snatched the food away from the royal ladies and their followers. Other examples include failed feasts of reconciliation at which participants were poisoned or murdered, and the famous scene at Canossa when Pope Gregory VII agreed to participate, but only after long hesitation; at least that is what he claimed afterward. In order to disrupt the course of a ritual, however, one needed to be in a position of strength. Similarly, to see who designed rituals and dominated their enactment gives insight into the distribution of power.

The following example of an original use of the arsenal of ritual expressions also comes from Ekkehard of Saint Gall. It is contained in his description of the conflict between Bishop Salomo of Constance and the so-called Swabian ambassadors Erchanger and Berthold. According to Ekkehard, after his capture, the bishop was compelled to perform the following ritual: "the bishop was led to a nearby hiding place. There he was

---

37 Ibid., cap. 76, p. 160: "Non tulit hanc speciem furiato pectore Victor. Abbatem quippe in sede sua cum vidisset, turbidus exiliit et quasi loco cessurus capituli domo exivit. Quem tamen episcopus, prout potuit, revocatum delinivit et in abbatis gratiam reductum ad tempus compescuit."

told to dismount, and he sat down while the others stepped aside and consulted about what to do with him. Liutfrid proposed that they should either tear out his eyes or cut off his right hand. But the more sensible among the warriors warned that they should not rage further against the Lord's anointed; it would be better if he remained unhurt. Finally, the brothers decided to bring him to the Thietpoldsburg, where Erchanger's wife Berta was staying at the time. A cheap nag was saddled for the man of God; swineherds saw the group and came to stare. When Berthold saw them, he said: 'bow to those, Godforsaken, and lick their feet so that they beg mercy for you.' Seeing the hopelessness of his position, he did as he was told."[38]

At first sight this seems to have been an arbitrary, barbarian act designed to dishonor and humiliate. Although it surely was meant to humiliate the bishop, it turns out on closer examination of the context to have been a calculated use of a known ritual in a new situation. The bishop's capture, however, was based on a series of past events: In the course of their long-running dispute, the bishop, meeting the counts by chance, complained of their crimes. This angered the counts, whereupon the bishop replied: "Truly, you should remember for all time that you once were in the deepest trouble with King Arnulf because of me, trouble that I could only rescue you from by the most extreme effort."[39] This very sentence caused the conflict to escalate – as Ekkehard points out: "Immediately Liutfrid, the counts' nephew, a most rebellious young man, said, 'This most wicked of monks boasts about the wrong you suffered for his sake, my uncles, and you leave him alive?' And he pulled his sword and would have struck down the bishop, if the counts had not stopped him."[40]

Ekkehard also describes the event Bishop Salomo was referring to when he taunted the counts. "The king – at that time Arnulf – ordered

38 Ibid., cap. 17–18, pp. 46–8: "Ducitur episcopus in diverticulum quoddam propinquum, ubi descendere iussus sedit, usque dum illi in partem cedentes, quid de eo facturi sint, tractent. . . . Suadet Luitfridus, ut ei aut oculos eruant aut dexteram abscidant. Militum autem pars sanior, ne quid amplius in christum Domini insanirent, omnimodis flagitat; sed et incolomem relinqui optimum fore aiebant. Stat tandem fratribus consilium, ut in Thietpoldispurch, ubi Perhta, uxor Erchingeri, tunc agebat, duceretur. . . . Sternitur viro Dei vilior interea equus. Porcarii autem cum viderent turbam, ad spectandum accurrunt. Quibus visis Perhtolt: 'Inclinare coram istis,' inquit, 'Dei maledicte, et, ut tibi veniam precentur, pedes eis lambe!' Ille vero, quoniam vim sciebat, quod issus est fecerat." See also the introduction to Althoff, *Spielregeln der Politik im Mittelalter,* 16.
39 *Ekkehardi casus sancti Galli,* cap. 17, p. 46: " 'Enimvero,' ait, 'cum mei causa in eis aliquando angustiis coram rege Arnolfo fueritis, unde egerrime ego ipse vos eripui, iam eius articuli semper liceat recordari.' "
40 Ibid., cap. 17, p. 46: "Ilico Luitfridus, sororis amborum filius, iuvenis pertinacissimus: 'Gloriaturne,' inquit, 'monachorum sceleratissimus iniuriarum pro se vobis inlatarum, o avunculi, et vivere eum patimini?' Extractoque gladio, nisi ab ambobus premeretur, episcopum occidisset."

the bishop and the ambassadors to come to court in Mainz under a flag of truce. There a public trial took place; after the counts had been found guilty of a capital crime, they were imprisoned in Ingelheim until a sentence of exile or death could be carried out. Fearing that he might be the cause of their violent death, Salomo, together with Bishop Hatto, strove for their release. In secret, they both went to the king to plead. They moved the king's heart and reconciled him with those enemies; these had to humiliate themselves before Salomo in public and make peace. Then, with his help, they were re-established in their former positions."[41]

In other words, Salomo had pleaded with the king to show mercy to the ambassadors, and they had had to humiliate themselves in public in return, probably by a prostration. This Salomo had called to mind by his remark at his chance meeting with the counts. The remark apparently was too much and caused the escalation of the conflict. This shows that the *deditio* was considered shameful. By his forced prostration in front of the swineherds, Salomo had to replay the scene with the roles reversed; Salomo thereby undid the counts' prostration and re-established their honor. Ethnologists, among others, know the process of inverting a ritual to undo something done earlier.[42] This is precisely the process described by Ekkehard. One of the counts demonstrated his inventiveness in the language of rituals in a rather drastic way. This did him little good, however; it must be brought to mind that the counts were put to death not much later by the king for their conflict with Bishop Salomo.

A final point: Quotation belongs among the original uses of ritual language. Quotations from the Bible in particular can be seen in medieval rituals designed to communicate the meaning contained in biblical scenes. In this arena as well, medieval people acted according to the situation and in original fashion.

A few examples will serve to illustrate this. According to Liutprand of Cremona, when Otto the Great was unable to help his troops, he fell to his knees and prayed in front of nails from Christ's cross that were incorporated in the Holy lance. His men were hard-pressed on the other side

---

41 Ibid., cap. 12, pp. 36–8: "Iubentur a rege, tunc quidem Arnoldo, episcopus et ipsi sup panno pacis ad aulam Magontie venire. Ubi causa publice peracta, rei maiestatis lege pronuntiati ipsi illi in Ingilinheim truduntur, usque dum exilio aut morte punirentur. Egit tandem Salomon cum Hattone episcopo, anxius, ne cedis illorum ipse quidem causa foret, ut eos liberaret. Adeunt suplices ambo secreto imperium. Cor regis molliunt, hostes illos in gratiam reducunt; coram omnibus Salamoni suplices facti pacificantur, potestati pristine ipso iuvante restituuntur."

42 Cf. Barbara A. Babcock, ed., *The Reversible World: Symbolic Inversion in Art and Society* (Ithaca, N.Y., 1978).

of the Rhine, in what is known as the Battle of Birken. It is told explicitly that Otto was imitating Moses and his actions in the battle against the Amalekites – and that he succeeded, as Moses did.[43] Louis the Pious and his son Lothar staged their meeting in Worms in 839 by imitating the parable of the lost son, thus demonstrating their mutual preparedness for reconciliation.[44] The citizens of Troja in Southern Italy, besieged by Henry II, sent their children in a procession to the emperor to achieve a favorable end to the siege. The children succeeded only after they had carried out two processions.[45] Bishop Ulrich of Augsburg had infants placed around him on the floor while he prayed for the rescue of the city from the Hungarians. Their cries stressed the urgency of his prayers.[46] The words of the innocent children whose pleas are more easily listened to is made very clear in these last two cases.

It is not clear which model from the Bible or elsewhere Barbarossa used to demonstrate his readiness to reconcile himself with Pope Alexander III in Venice in 1177.[47] Rather than refer to the prostration and kissing of the feet in front of Saint Mark's cathedral recently noted by Klaus Schreiner, I would prefer to focus on Barbarossa's behavior a day later, during the celebration of High Mass by the pope.[48] First, he cleared the way to the church for the pope and the cardinals and even expelled the laymen from the choir, where he attended mass with the priests. When the pope began to preach from the pulpit, Barbarossa placed himself under the pulpit and listened attentively. The pope, coincidentally, showed consideration and had the sermon translated into German.[49] More important than this information about Barbarossa's knowledge of Latin is the fact

43 Joseph Becker, ed., *Liudprandi Antapodosis*, Monumenta Germaniae Historica Scriptores rerum Germanicarum, vol. 41, 3d ed. (Hannover, 1915), 1–158, IV, cap. 24, pp. 117–18.
44 Ernst Müller, ed., *Nithardi Historiarum libri IIII*, *Monumenta Germaniae Historica, Scriptores rerum Germanicarum*, vol. 44, 3d ed. (Hannover, 1907), 1:6–7, 10–11; see Althoff, *Das Privileg der deditio*, 118–19n36.
45 Cf. Hirsch, *Jahrbücher des Deutschen Reichs unter Heinrich II.*, 3:202.
46 *Ekkehard casus sancti Galli*, cap. 60, p. 132: "Nam imminente irruptionis illorum iam facili introitu, infantulos urbis universos ab uberibus matrum raptos circa se coram altaribus nuda terra iactari iusserat, vagitibusque illorum lacrimas cum eiulatibus miscens infestissimos illos alter Ezechias abegerat hostes." See also Althoff, "Demonstration und Inszenierung," 251.
47 See Gerd Althoff, "Friedrich Barbarossa als Schauspieler: Ein Beitrag zum Verständnis des Friedens von Venedig (1177)," in Trude Ehlert, ed., *Chevaliers errants, Demoiselles et l'Autre – Höfische und nachhöfische Literatur im europäischen Mittelalter: Festschrift für Xenja von Ertzdorff zum 65. Geburtstag* (Göppingen, 1998).
48 Cf. Schreiner, "Er küsse mich mit dem Kuss seines Mundes," 115–16.
49 C. A. Garufi, ed., *Romuald von Salerno, Chronik*, Raccolta degli Storici Italiani 7, pt. 1 (Città di Castello, 1937), 285: "Cumque dicto euangelio papa ascendisset pulpitum, ut alloqueretur populum, imperator accedens propius, cepit uerba eius attentius auscultare. Cuius deuotionem papa diligenter attendens, uerba, que ipse litteratorie proferebat, fecit per patriarcham Aquileie in lingua Teotonica euidenter exponi."

that Barbarossa demonstrated, in the manner described, his intent to obey the pope in the future. Perhaps Barbarossa quoted something in this case, or perhaps he invented an original way to demonstrate his new relationship with Alexander by means of his behavior.

In summary, I would like to point out once more what I believe to be important. The omnipresence of rituals and ritual behavior is an essential feature of communication in the Middle Ages. Through rituals and ritual acts, a wide range of information was conveyed to the public; the obligations and claims expressed in ritual were thus publicly acknowledged.[50] Ritual behavior had the same function and created the same obligations as an oath or a written treaty. The ritual often accompanied these forms of communication, its function, however, being more than merely ornamental. In order to fulfill its function, the meaning of a ritual in public communication had to be unambiguous and easily understandable.[51] This separates the rituals described here from, for example, occult-religious rituals, for which the exact opposite can often be true. Consequently, a limited stock of gestures and modes of behavior, the sense of which was unmistakable to the experienced eye, was used constantly in medieval ritual communication. Nonetheless, the impression of rigidity and slavish execution of given patterns of behavior does not do justice to the vivacity of the communication practiced in this manner. Medieval actors handled the stock of stereotypical gestures and actions in a masterly fashion and produced new meanings, especially in exceptional situations, by building with the available bricks and by transferring rituals from one field to another, thus inventing specific ritual expressions for special situations.

These public stagings required clarification beforehand, which we usually learn nothing about. How detailed this clarification had to be is an interesting but hitherto largely unsolved question. I mentioned above that it was the subject of negotiation whether a *deditio* was to be performed with shoes or without, but does this mean that every detail had to be fixed? When the same citizens of Milan who negotiated the shoes threw their crosses into the chamber of the Empress Beatrix, thus asking for her mediation, did they act according to a script, did they use some freedom in arranging the ritual, or did they even act completely sponta-

---

50 Cf. Bernd Thum, "Öffentlich-Machen, Öffentlichkeit, Recht: Zu den Grundlagen und Verfahren der politischen Publizistik im Spätmittelalter," *Zeitschrift für Literaturwissenschaft und Linguistik* 37 (1980): 12–69.

51 On the consent-forming character of rituals, see Klaus Schreiner, "Er küsse mich mit dem Kuss seines Mundes," 129.

neously in an otherwise fixed frame of action?[52] These questions sketch out lines of inquiry worth pursuing.

Some reflections on the question of whether the described scenes took place or not should be added, which might be applied to other examples as well. It may be doubtful that the authors describe the scenes as they happened, although it is not possible to prove this one way or the other. Nevertheless, the stories told by medieval authors can be used in our questions about the forms and functions of public communication because the authors telling these stories had to consider the common rules and customs governing behavior if they wanted their contemporaries to believe them. Perhaps authors could trespass on this rule or the other, perhaps they could illustrate a point by exaggeration or play with some of the rules, but only to such an extent that contemporaries could see through it. On the whole, the description had to correspond to the usual practices of communication. These stories can be used for the investigation of these practices – but not for the history of events.

In order to obtain an adequate understanding of the contents of medieval rituals, we have to strive to regain the point of view from which medieval contemporaries looked at rituals. This is a necessary first step, after which we should of course add our own evaluation.

---

52 Georg Waitz, ed., *Chronica regia Coloniensis, Monumenta Germaniae Historica, Scriptores rerum Germanicarum* 18 (Hannover, 1880), a. 1162, p. 111: "Illi autem spe misericordiae cruces, quas tenebant in manibus, per cancellos in caminatam imperatricis proiciebant, cum ante conspectum eius introitum non haberent."

4

Rebels and Rituals

From Demonstrations of Enmity to Criminal Justice

HANNA VOLLRATH

Medieval kings faced many problems. The most persistent ones were the relations with the people they somewhat euphemistically called their "faithful ones" – *fideles* – the great princes or barons on whose consent the kings' capacity to act depended. The greater part of medieval historical writing deals with the feuds of these great men with each other, lesser nobles, or their kings. We, and in fact royal-minded contemporaries, call the last rebellions. The term *rebellion* carries the notion that feuding with the king was something quite different from regular noble warfare, that it was, indeed, illegitimate, a notion that the kings and their ecclesiastical propaganda staffs tried to drive home in many ways. Because they were the ones who put their ideas into writing, it is predominantly their views we read. The nobles who made war on their kings thought quite differently about it and claimed – justly or unjustly – that they were defending their rights against a king turned tyrant. How did the kings deal with these formidable rebels? They tried to fight them, to be sure, but it is generally believed that the kings also tried to make use of their supreme judicial authority and make the nobles account for their deeds in the royal law courts.

Heinrich Mitteis analyzed a number of notorious trials of mighty nobles dating from the tenth to the twelfth centuries and argued that procedurally they all ended in verdicts for *contumacia*, that is, verdicts for not having appeared in court.[1] Mitteis assumed that all these noble defendants preferred not to stand trial, either because in headstrong defiance they refused to accept the king's justice or because they knew their defense to be hopeless, thus admitting their guilt.[2] In Mitteis's view, this amounted

---

1 Heinrich Mitteis, *Politische Prozesse des früheren Mittelalters in Deutschland und Frankreich* (Heidelberg, 1926; reprint, Darmstadt, 1974).
2 "Sie sind Kontumazialverfahren, Verfahren, die sich ganz oder in ihrem entscheidenden Teile auf schuldhafte Säumnis des Beklagten gründen. Und das ist zweifellos kein Zufall. Denn fast stets liegt

to sabotaging justice, and he thought that the way governments reacted to this kind of sabotage reveals much about their strength. In the High Middle Ages, royal government responded by having the defendants convicted for not appearing in court.

Heinrich Mitteis was a legal historian whose approach was heavily criticized by Otto Brunner in the 1930s and 1940s for dividing the totality of life into separate disciplines (*Trennungsdenken*). Brunner called for *Verfassungsgeschichte*, by which he meant that historians should content themselves with describing the mechanisms of social activity at a given time and with accepting as legal that which was regarded as such in a particular society. This meant accepting feuds as a medieval legal procedure and renouncing a perception that defined law and justice as means in the hands of public powers to subject human action to norms basically rooted in moral values. As such, Brunner's approach included the rejection of the idea that basic moral values should be considered valid for all humankind. Otto Brunner's concept of "descriptive constitutional history," as posited against "normative legal history," has in turn been criticized for dissolving the idea of justice into all kinds of contingencies.[3] Nevertheless, the way back to a pre-Brunnerian legal history seems to be barred to us. It is widely accepted in contemporary German historiography that medieval law cannot adequately be treated as a virtually separate entity operating according to its own timeless rules, but must be treated as part of medieval society.[4]

Although Mitteis's approach to dealing with trials by analyzing their procedures is outmoded, his treatise on political trials still serves as a starting point for historians who deal with any of the trials he analyzed. Con-

---

dieselbe eindeutig bestimmte psychologische Kausalität vor: Der Angeklagte wird sich nicht stellen wollen, sei es, dass er in trotzigem Übermut das Recht verweigert und es auf eine Machtprobe ankommen lassen will, sei es, dass ihm die Verteidigung von vornherein aussichtslos erscheint, dass er durch sein Fernbleiben ein Schuldbekenntnis ablegt" (Mitteis, *Politische Prozesse*, 9–10). The inherent assumption that trials will always do justice and that the defendant can depend on this shows that for Mitteis it is unthinkable that judicial powers will not be committed to this end; it betrays an authoritarian (or liberal?) trait in Mitteis's thinking.

3 In writing for English-speaking readers, it would probably be best to cite the introduction to the English edition of *Land und Herrschaft*, which explains Brunner's criticism of legal historians like Mitteis. The citation is Otto Brunner, *Land and Lordship: Structures of Governance in Medieval Austria*, trans. Howard Kaminsky and James Van Horn Melton (Philadelphia, 1992), xiii–lxi. Otto Gerhard Oexle, "Sozialgeschichte – Begriffsgeschichte – Wissenschaftsgeschichte: Anmerkungen zum Werk Otto Brunners," *Vierteljahrsschrift für Sozial- und Wirtschaftsgeschichte* (hereafter *VSWG*) 71 (1984): 305–41.

4 See Karl Kroeschell, "Verfassungsgeschichte und Rechtsgeschichte des Mittelalters: Gegenstand und Begriffe der Verfassungsgeschichtsschreibung," *Der Staat* 6 (1983): 47–77.

sequently, a number of his basic assumptions have never been questioned. One of these is that trials quite regularly ended with verdicts for *contumacia* (contempt of court due to nonappearance). The concept of a verdict for *contumacia* is meaningful only within a framework in which trials are authoritative pronouncements of the law by judges in law courts, a paradigm derived from modern states. During the last twenty years or so, however, quite a different paradigm has emerged for the earlier Middle Ages. If we understand "political trials" to mean trials that used judicial means to serve political ends, it is evident that a change of paradigm in the system as a whole will affect our understanding of the political trials.[5] In this chapter I reconsider the widely accepted notion that noble defendants usually ignored the summons to court and were then convicted of *contumacia*, in light of recent research on the functioning of the medieval legal system.

Whereas *contumacia* seems to play a rather prominent role in modern scholarship on the Middle Ages, it is conspicuously absent in the works of medieval historians, who neither employed the word nor mentioned the fact that the crime of the defendant consisted in not having answered a summons to court. Even more surprising is the fact that they hardly mention the trials at all. Nor do the medieval authors, even those who are openly hostile to the defendants, mention headstrong defiance or fear of the outcome as Mitteis does. Medieval historians rarely mention that the accused did not appear in court; it is Heinrich Mitteis who assumed that this was the rule. It is even more striking that not even the very rare documentary evidence concerning trials refers to *contumacia* or uses the term. The one notable exception is the *Gelnhäuser Urkunde* of 1180, a charter of Frederick Barbarossa in favor of the archbishop of Cologne, the *narratio* (summary history of the case) of which consists of an account of the proceedings against Henry the Lion.[6] It is this charter, which in many points is anything but clear and which consequently has given rise to never-ending scholarly debates, that states with uncontroversial clarity

---

5 Although Mitteis still dominates in a way the German discussions on political trials, his *definition* of what political trials were has to my knowledge never been discussed. He defines "political trials" – which, as he points out, is no established category in legal systematizations – as trials that had exceptionally important *results* in the constitutional development of a country: "Politische Prozesse sind also im Mittelalter solche, die unmittelbar auf die Fortentwicklung der Verfassung eingewirkt haben" (Mitteis, *Politische Prozesse*, 7). Taking the political trials in the totalitarian systems of our own century into account, I find this definition unacceptable.
6 *Monumenta Germaniae Historica* (hereafter *MGH*), *Diplomata regum et imperatorum Germaniae: Die Urkunden der deutschen Könige und Kaiser*, Charters of Frederick Barbarossa, no. 795.

that Henry the Lion, although called to the emperor's court, neither
appeared nor sent a representative and was therefore sentenced as a *contumax*.[7] Mitteis apparently considered the procedure employed in this trial
at the end of the twelfth century to be typical of the Middle Ages in
general and therefore felt free to assume its application even in those
political trials where the contemporary sources neither mention the fact
nor the term *contumacia*. Counter to this, I argue that *contumacia* as a clearly
defined offense was the product of the legal changes of the twelfth
century and that trials in the earlier Middle Ages functioned within
a social and legal framework that did not allow for an offense called
contumacia.

It is from two starting points that our understanding of early medieval
law and court procedures has been challenged. One approach examines
how conflicts were dealt with in the earlier Middle Ages, whereas the
other asks how law courts functioned in that particular society. Frederick
Cheyette was one of the first, to my knowledge, to challenge the assumption that in prestate Europe conflicts were settled the same way as in societies organized as states, namely, by authoritative courts in accordance with
objective criteria. The French material he examined revealed instead that
up to the middle of the thirteenth century, conflicts were settled by arbitration and compromise, if not violence.[8] Further research has substantiated Cheyette's supposition and has uncovered a rich arsenal of devices
people employed to settle conflicts and to reestablish peace between conflicting parties.[9] Mediators were important, and the term *internuntii* (mes-
sengers) reveals their function: They had to breach the gap that separated
the conflicting parties and negotiate the conditions both sides would
accept for the reestablishment of peace.[10] It is sometimes mentioned that

---

7 For the interpretive and legal aspects of the charter, see Gerhard Theuerkauf, "Der Prozess gegen
  Heinrich den Löwen: Über Landrecht und Lehnrecht im hohen Mittelalter," in Wolf-Dieter
  Mohrmann, ed., *Heinrich der Löwe* (Göttingen, 1980), 217–48; Karl Heinemeyer, "Der Prozess
  Heinrichs des Löwen," *Blätter für deutsche Landesgeschichte* 117 (1981): 1–60; Karl Heinemeyer,
  "Kaiser und Reichsfürst: Die Absetzung Heinrichs des Löwen durch Friedrich Barbarossa," *Macht
  und Recht: Grosse Prozesse in der Geschichte* (Munich, 1990), 59–79.
8 Frederic L. Cheyette, "Suum Cuique tribuere," *French Historical Studies* 6 (1970): 287–99.
9 A brilliant analysis with a discussion of the work that appeared since Cheyette's seminal paper
  and with rich exemplary material from southern France is Patrick J. Geary, "Living with Conflicts in Stateless France: A Typology of Conflict Management Mechanisms, 1050–1200," in Patrick
  J. Geary, *Living with the Dead in the Middle Ages* (Ithaca, N.Y., 1994), 125–60; see also Patrick J.
  Geary, "Extra-Judicial Means of Conflict Resolution," in *La Giustizia nell'alto medioevo (secoli
  V–VIII)* (Spoleto, 1995), 575–85; and the essays by Gerd Althoff referred to throughout this
  chapter.
10 Gerd Althoff, *Verwandte, Freunde und Getreue* (Darmstadt, 1990), 195–203; Gerd Althoff, "Konfliktverhalten und Rechtsbewusstsein: Die Welfen in der Mitte des 12. Jahrhunderts," *Frühmittelalterliche Studien* 26 (1992): 331–52; Gerd Althoff, "Genugtuung (*satisfactio*): Zur Eigenart gütlicher

mediators received a portion of the sums that were paid to settle conflicts, and it can be assumed that they could quite regularly expect notable remuneration if their mission ended successfully.

In post-Carolingian times courts came to operate according to the same principle: They did not authoritatively pronounce verdicts but provided forums for arbitration. It could be the court of an office-holder, such as a count or a duke, but as the courts of other eminent personages of a district were sought as well, people might sometimes have chosen a count's or duke's court less for their public qualities than for the social authority of their owners.[11] Basically, it was in the litigants' best interest – and hence required their ingenuity – to find means and ways to achieve their ends, whether through violence or peaceful means; and it was also for them to decide when one approach or the other was preferred.[12] Social pressure was undoubtedly exercised to reach compromises in order to avoid or end violence.[13] Although litigations over property had a different quality than those that we would call criminal cases, they both had to be solved in a society that lacked regular means of enforcing the law. It is more important to realize, however, that conflicts were not perceived as the deeds of individual perpetrators but as a matter of extended groups of people bound to the initial litigant or culprit by all sorts of personal ties. It was these groups that had to be appeased, at least as long as they stood by the incriminated member and refused to isolate him. Under these circumstances it does not make sense to take a conflict out of its

Konfliktbeilegung im Mittelalter," in Joachim Heinzle, ed., *Modernes Mittelalter* (Frankfurt am Main, 1994), 247–65. It can be assumed that recourse to mediators was only taken in conflicts between important persons with wide-ranging activities, as litigants on the peasant level could hardly avoid seeing each other and the other side's friends and helpers daily in their everyday activities; Patrick J. Geary rightly notes that on the local level conflicts were a matter for the whole community; Geary, "Living with Conflicts," 137–8.

11 Wendy Davies, *Small Worlds: The Village Community in Early Medieval Brittany* (London, 1988), 154ff.; Wendy Davies, "People and Places in Dispute in Ninth-Century Brittany," in Paul Fouracre and Wendy Davies, eds., *The Settlement of Disputes in Early Medieval Europe* (Cambridge, 1986), 65–84. As far as the time of transformation of the Carolingian *mallus publicus* into courts of arbitration of a more private character is concerned, there were regional differences. Carolingian court procedure survived in the Mâconnais until the middle of the tenth century: Georges Duby, *La société aux XIe et XIIe siècles dans la région mâconnaise* (Paris, 1971), 89–134. François-Louis Ganshof observed that from the eleventh to the beginning of the thirteenth century, the duke of Burgundy's court had no regulated appearance; the duke sometimes had his wife or children with him and there were no official assessors on the bench. "Etude sur l'administration de justice dans la région bourgouinionne de la fin du Xe au début du XIIe siècle," *Revue historique* 135 (1920): 193–218.

12 Timothy Reuter, "Unruhestiftung, Fehde, Rebellion, Widerstand: Gewalt und Frieden in der Politik der Salierzeit," in Stefan Weinfurter, ed., *Die Salier und das Reich*, 3 vols. (Sigmaringen, 1991), 3:297–325.

13 See the telling example in Paul R. Hyams, "Feud in Medieval England," *Haskins Society Journal* 3 (1991): 1–21.

social context and treat it as a "case" in court. If courts were convened and judgments pronounced at all, they were just one element in a whole range of measures that were employed to resolve a controversy. If peace and amity were to return to the disputing parties, a solution had to be found that all were ready to accept as "just." It was this acceptance that assured that the peace would last. The solution might be pronounced as a judgment in court, but litigations were ended without court participation as well.

For the purpose of my own arguments, it is important to note that in prestate medieval Europe, just as in other stateless societies, judgments summed up all the endeavors that had been undertaken to reestablish peace and made them public.[14] Although in cases of noble rebellions they sometimes *looked* like legal pronouncements, particularly when they demanded unconditional surrender, it nevertheless was clearly understood that the surrendering party could depend on the "generosity" of the other and expect the accepted rules and negotiated conditions to be kept in return.[15]

All the work referred to above deals with conflict resolution, that is, it investigates the means and mechanisms that were at people's disposal to reach concord in case of conflict. In these cases judgments pronounced the results of the negotiations to reestablish peace. By definition, cases such as this would never end in verdicts for *contumacia*. But there were judgments that had the opposite function, namely, to demonstrate that all endeavors to reestablish peace had broken down, that a compromise had not been reached.[16] It is in cases such as this that Mitteis assumed that the defendants had not appeared and were therefore sentenced for their contumacy. Here, I analyze two cases where Mitteis assumed verdicts for *contumacia*, namely, the trial of Margrave Ekbert of Meissen in 1089 and the trial of King John of England in 1202. I then compare the results of these analyses with the procedure followed in the case of Henry the Lion in 1180.

---

14 Medievalists have come to appreciate and consult works in social anthropology on conflict resolution in order to enhance their understanding of the phenomenon in medieval society. One of the most widely read surveys in legal anthropology nowadays is Simon Roberts, *Order and Dispute: An Introduction to Legal Anthropology* (Oxford, 1979), a German translation of which was published in Stuttgart in 1981; see also John L. Comaroff and Simon Roberts, eds., *Rules and Processes: The Cultural Logic of Dispute in an African Context* (Chicago, 1981).

15 Gerd Althoff has presented a lot of exemplary source material with which he analyzes the manifold mechanisms of conflict resolution in the High Middle Ages; see note 10 to this chapter.

16 I have analyzed one such case already, namely, the judgment pronounced by Conrad III and his court against Duke Henry the Proud in 1138: "Fürstenurteile im staufisch-welfischen Konflikt von 1138 bis zum Privilegium Minus: Recht und Gericht in der oralen Rechtswelt des früheren Mittelalters," in Karl Kroeschell and Albrecht Cordes, eds., *Funktion und Form: Quellen- und Methodenprobleme der mittelalterlichen Rechtsgeschichte* (Berlin, 1996), 39–62.

Margrave Ekbert II of Meissen was a kinsman of King Henry IV but nevertheless played a prominent role in the Saxon uprisings against the king in the 1070s and 1080s.[17] The conflict between king and margrave ended in Ekbert's deposition and dispossession. A portion of his possessions was given to the bishop of Utrecht, and it is in three royal donation charters to this bishop that we are given an extensive account of the trials that played a role in the undoing of the margrave.[18] Numbers 386 and 388 are dated February and April 1086, respectively; no. 402, dated February 1, 1089, is the most comprehensive. It contains the renewed confirmation of the donation of the Frisian county to the bishop of Utrecht. It had been given to the bishop after Ekbert's revolt in 1086 but had been returned to Ekbert after his reconciliation with the king, only to be taken away by the latter permanently after Ekbert's subsequent rebellion. Ekbert II was a member of the *Brunonen*, a Saxon noble family; his family's possessions lay in Brunswick and Lüneburg. Ekbert's father, Ekbert I, was made margrave of Meissen in 1067 on the death of Margrave Otto of Meissen-Orlamünde, whose daughter Gertrud was married to the young Ekbert. The margraviate of Meissen was situated in the most southeastern part of Saxony, where most of Ekbert's possessions were located, whereas the Frisian county was situated in the most northwestern part of the kingdom. Although the county must have been of considerable value to the bishop of Utrecht, its practical value for Ekbert is hard to estimate. Given its geographical situation, it can only have been a minor possession.[19] By contrast, Ekbert's Saxon possessions were vital to him and guaranteed his status as a prince.

Because Ekbert was a prominent prince with powerful family connections, his consecutive rebellions attracted the attention of contemporary historians, too. But it is the charters that concentrate on what we

17 See Karl Leyser, "The Crisis of Medieval Germany," *Communications and Power in Medieval Europe,* vol. 2: *The Gregorian Revolution and Beyond,* ed. Timothy Reuter (London, 1994), 21–49. For an introduction to the Salian kings' clashes with the papacy and noble opponents and the interrelationship of the two fields of conflict, see Horst Fuhrmann, *Germany in the High Middle Ages, ca. 1050–1250* (Cambridge, 1986), and Alfred Haverkamp, *Medieval Germany, 1056–1273* (Oxford, 1988). A cogent analysis of the Saxon wars in particular was given by the late Karl Leyser, "The Crisis of Medieval Germany," Raleigh Lecture 1983, *Proceedings of the British Academy* 69 (Oxford, 1983), 409–43.

18 *MGH,* Charters of Henry IV, nos. 386, 388, 402. The charters have not survived in the original, but in the *Liber donationum* of the church of Utrecht written at the end of the twelfth century. The editor assumes that the royal clerks who wrote the charters drew on some kind of written documentation of the trial.

19 The Brunonen had family interests in Frisia, however, as Brun, the brother of Ekbert I, had been margrave there; on his death the margraviate was given to his brother, who left it to his son. Already after Ekbert's first rebellion another Frisian county called Staveren was given to the bishop of Utrecht (*MGH,* Charters of Henry IV, no. 301).

would call the legal side of the matter. With their clerical propaganda staffs, kings had never officially abandoned the Carolingian theory that "the honor of the king loves just judgment" (*honor regis iudicium diligit*), which, in fact, became part of the royal liturgy.[20] Solemn charters were formulated according to this theory. In this particular case, the bishop of Utrecht's possessory rights depended on the fact that Ekbert's dispossession had been just. It was in the bishop's interest, therefore, that the charters recorded everything that would convince contemporaries of the justness of his cause. In the charter, we find a circumstantial account of what was undertaken to settle the conflict. I therefore base my analysis more on the charters than on the historical narratives.

Ekbert had been very young – *adhuc puer* – when he had first lent his counsel and aid to the rebelling Saxons in their endeavor to depose and murder the king.[21] On this, the king must have withdrawn his grace with the implication that Ekbert was banned from his presence because when Ekbert asked to be restored to royal grace, he expressly needed permission to appear before the king.[22] The conditions of the reconciliation, which had been agreed to by both sides in advance, followed a well-known pattern. Ekbert humbled himself before the king, the latter put aside any thought of revenge, received him back, and "embraced him like a son restoring by his grace what Ekbert had forfeited by law."[23] All this was certainly enacted publicly. In view of the fact that the banning of a prominent prince from the royal court could have disastrous consequences if a ruler proceeded imprudently, a ruler would make sure that he had the support of

20 See Hagen Keller, "Die Idee der Gerechtigkeit und die Praxis königlicher Rechtswahrung im Reich der Ottonen," in *La Giustizia nell'alto medioevo (secoli IX–XI)*, 2 vols. (Spoleto, 1997), 1:91–131; several other papers, published in the companion volume, *La Giustizia nell'alto medioevo* (secoli V–VIII) (Spoleto, 1995), postulate that, even in Carolingian times, royal insistence that conflicts be solved in public courts rather than through "private" negotiation was theory and program rather than social reality.
21 Ekbert's case has received some attention. The last one to deal with the legal and ritual implications was Gerd Althoff, "Königsherrschaft und Konfliktbewältigung im 10. und 11. Jahrhundert," *Frühmittelalterliche Studien* 23 (1989): 284–86. For Ekbert's position and role in Saxon politics, see Heinz Stoob, "Über den Schwerpunktwechsel in der niederdeutschen Adelsführung während des Kampfes gegen die salischen Herrscher," in Dieter Berg and Hans-Werner Goetz, eds., *Ecclesia et regnum: Festschrift für Franz-Josef Schmale* (Bochum, 1989), 121–37; and Wolfgang Giese, "Reichsstrukturprobleme unter den Saliern – der Adel in Ostsachsen," in Stefan Weinfurter, ed., *Die Salier und das Reich*, 3 vols. (Sigmaringen, 1991), 1:273–308. Both Ekbert and his father are accorded an entry by Ernst Karf in Robert Auty et al., eds., *Lexikon des Mittelalters*, 19 vols. (Munich, 1986ff), 3:1761–2.
22 *MGH H IV* 388: "gratiam nostram requirentem data venia ad nos benigne recepimus."
23 For Althoff, the concept of grace, its withdrawal, and restitution was central to rulership in premodern time. See Gerd Althoff, "Huld: Überlegungen zu einem Zentralbegriff der mittelalterlichen Herrschaftsordnung," *Frühmittelalterliche Studien* 25 (1991): 259–82.

his other men.[24] The pronouncement of the ban and the ceremony of reconciliation both were rituals. Ritual was a "language" with agreed on meanings, but this did not make it inflexible to the point of becoming a rigid mechanism. The essence of rituals seems to lie in the fact that they were performed by persons in the presence of a knowledgeable audience. "The audience . . . decided whether the king's refusal to grant mercy to a suppliant rebel was justice, tyranny, or an astute exercise of power, his offering of that mercy weakness, cunning, or prudence."[25]

These very ideas are expressed in the commentary by Pope Gregory VII on the ritual humiliation of the German king, Henry IV, at Canossa in 1077. The king had been banned by the pope, and the German princes threatened Henry with the election of a rival king should he fail to have the ban lifted. Contrary to what the princes had expected and hoped for, Henry went to Italy and succeeded in having the ban reversed through a ritual of humiliation, the particulars of which had been negotiated in advance.[26] The pope felt obliged to justify his actions in a letter to the German princes. He described the king begging pardon barefoot and in woolen clothes – the garb of penitence – for three days before the doors of the strong castle of Canossa, and "he ceased not with many tears to beseech the apostolic help and comfort until all who were present or who had heard the story were so moved by pity and compassion that they pleaded his cause with prayers and tears. All marveled at our unwonted severity, and some even cried out that we were showing, not the seriousness of apostolic authority (*apostolice severitatis gravitatem*), but rather the cruelty of a savage tyrant (*tyrannice feritatis crudelitatem*)."[27] Although

---

24 Whereas Jürgen Weitzel, *Dinggenossenschaft und Recht: Untersuchungen zum Rechtsverständnis im fränkisch-deutschen Mittelalter*, 2 vols. (Cologne, 1985), 2:1170ff., believes that the withdrawal of grace required a legal procedure, Gerd Althoff, "Huld," 263–4, sees the ruler acting alone on his own responsibility. I do not think that this alternative does justice to the intricate texture of medieval society. Although there were, on the one hand, rather rigid formalities, there was a lot of freedom on the other in the choice of the means to achieve highly valued ends. The end to achieve in such a case was consent – *consensus*. The way a ruler assured himself of noble consent depended very much on the situation and on the people involved. See the brilliant analysis of a king's scope of action by G. C. Holt, *Magna Carta*, 2d ed. (Cambridge, 1992), chap. 4: "Custom and Law," 75–122; See also Susan Reynolds' characterization of early medieval law as "consultive legislation," *Kingdoms and Communities in Western Europe, 900–1300* (Oxford, 1984), 21.

25 Geoffrey Koziol, *Begging Pardon and Favor: Ritual and Political Order in Early Medieval France* (Ithaca, N.Y., 1992), 311.

26 See Harald Zimmermann, *Der Canossa-Gang von 1077: Wirkungen und Wirklichkeit* (Mainz, 1975), 37ff.

27 See *The Correspondence of Pope Gregory VII: Selected Letters from the Registrum*, trans. Ephraim Emerton, Records of Civilization: Sources and Studies, vol. 14 (New York, 1932), 112. *Das Register Gregors VII.*, ed. Erich Caspar, in *MGH, Epistolae Selectae*, 5 vols. (Berlin, 1916–52), 2, no. IV, 12:312–14.

medieval theory did not bind papal authority to the consent of his followers, and although Gregory VII was a pope who insisted on the sovereignty of his God-given position, he knew that the impression of cruelty
and tyranny on his side would compromise the acceptance he needed to
be regarded as the "rightful" pope.[28]

All medieval rulers had to take into account that they were dealing
with "persons," or the concept of *persona*, meaning the whole status, everything a man (or a woman) had and owned. This status encompassed not
only material inheritance and immaterial rights but also a person's rank,
honor, and prestige, which were derived from his or her membership in
a noble clan and the resulting "friendship" with other nobles and their
families. This concept of personhood makes it inconceivable that every
rebel wishing to regain a ruler's favor was subjected to an identical ritual
of humiliation. We must think of the appropriate traditional elements of
ritual being selected from a range of possibilities and being negotiated to
fit the overall social situation rather than of fixed patterns of conduct.
"Rituals and symbols are part of social discourse," as Geoffrey Koziol
rightly observes.[29] In this respect, the term *rules of the game* (*Spielregeln*),
used by some German scholars to characterize the acting out of rituals,
is misleading because it ignores the social integration and hence the variability of ritualized performances. In Ekbert's case, his being banned from
the royal presence and the ritual humiliation by which he regained the
king's favor had to be such as not to allow his mighty relatives and friends
to perceive the proceedings as harmful to the honor of the extended
family – the honor on which the clan's social standing depended.

Ekbert's second rebellion took place in 1085. According to the royal
charter, Ekbert showed himself on this occasion to be exceptionally mean
and cruel. The king convened the "princes of Saxony and Thuringia" at
his court to declare Ekbert a devastator of the realm and a persecutor of
its lord king and to have them adjudicate all Ekbert's possessions to the
king. Henry confirmed "their just judgment," and, having received
Ekbert's possessions, gave his county in Frisia to the church of Utrecht
and confirmed the donation with a royal charter.

The narrative sources tell an altogether different story, though without
really contradicting the king's version, which was laid down in his donation charters to Utrecht. Although some of these historical accounts are

---

28 Theoretically, this was incompatible with the claim of the church to act according to God's
   mandate alone; in practice its officials were part of the type of communal activities so brilliantly
   analyzed by Susan Reynolds in *Kingdoms and Communities*.
29 *Begging Pardon*, 303.

unquestionably hostile to Henry IV while others are dedicated to the king's cause, and although Frutolf of Michelsberg in his chronicle more or less tries to give an unbiased story, they all give a basically similar account.[30] After having held a royal court in Mainz at Easter, where he had replaced the Gregorian bishops by clerics from his own side, the king went to Saxony, which he found so peaceful that he sent his army home. Some time later, however, the Saxons renewed their hostility, formed a conspiracy, forced the king and the bishops nominated by him to the Saxon sees to flee the country, and recalled their Gregorian bishops. Subsequently, King Henry returned to ravage Saxony but withdrew because it was the beginning of Lent. None of the narrative sources supplies dates and none makes any mention of a court proceeding against Ekbert or of his dispossession.

In combining the dates suggested by Frutolf's annalistic scheme with the other evidence, it is possible, however, to arrive at a somewhat coherent story. Frutolf mentions the king ravaging Saxony as his first entry for the year 1086. The donation charter to Utrecht is dated February 7, 1086, and lists Wechmar in Thuringia as the place where the charter to Utrecht was issued "mox ut in Eggebertum fuerat iudicium pronunciatum" (soon after the verdict against Ekbert was given).[31] The *Liber de unitate ecclesiae conservanda* relates that the king traversed both provinces, namely, Saxony and Thuringia, with his army and then retreated because Lent was drawing near (*propter instantem quadragesimam*) after having made peace according to the conditions that the princes from both sides judged right and proper (*composita pace iuxta conditiones, quas principes utrimque aequas et utiles judicassent*). Here, then, is a *iudicium principum*, which must have been pronounced just before February 18, the beginning of Lent, whereas, according to the charter, the judgment against Ekbert was pronounced just before February 7. Obviously both relate to the same event, and what looks contradictory at first glance really is not: The charter gives only that part of the story relevant to its cause, that is, the donation to Utrecht, which presupposes Ekbert's dispossession. It fails to mention that Ekbert's dispossession was part of a larger peace settlement negotiated by the nobles from both sides, which apparently treated other issues as well. It

---

30 Prominent anti-Henrician historians who mention the Ekbert case are the twelfth-century *Annalista Saxo* (who writes from a decidedly pro-Saxon point of view using contemporary eleventh-century material now lost) and *Bernold of Constance*, whereas the author of the *Liber de unitate ecclesiae conservanda* and the *Augsburg Annals* takes the king's side.

31 In a charter dated Regensburg April 3, 1086, the Frisian county of Ijsselgau was given to Utrecht as well. *MGH*, Charters of Henry IV, no. 388. The greater part of the *narratio* was taken over from Henry IV's charter no. 386.

might have included the killings a year before in a feud in which Ekbert's brother-in-law had been killed; Ekbert had then besieged the town of Hildesheim, putting its bishop in chains and having one of the hostages beheaded.[32] The latter incident seems to have involved dissension within the Saxon party, which would explain why Saxon nobles had agreed to Ekbert's punishment as part of the peace settlement. Because the charter is concerned only with that part of Ekbert's possessions that were conferred to Utrecht, it is not known whether any of his Saxon possessions were given away as well. It rather looks as if the king had retained the bulk of Ekbert's family possessions for the time being.

Once again, Ekbert sought reconciliation through humiliation, and therafter, all his possessions were returned to him. Ekbert's allegiance lasted until 1088. In the course of the renewed Saxon fighting he turned once more against the king. This was his third rebellion. The judgment of the princes of the royal court was proscription, but even now, after his third breach of allegiance, Ekbert was not summoned like a culprit (*citatione vocatus*). Rather, the royal charter maintains that Ekbert was declared an outlaw for taking flight and refusing to give satisfaction neither for right nor for mercy (*nec pro iustitia nec pro misericordia satisfacere volens*). Apparently, the king had tried again to come to terms with Ekbert by negotiation, offering him different ways in which this could be done: either "pro iustitia" – by justice, that is, by terms pronounced by a law court – or "pro misericordia" – by mercy, which would mean an unconditional submission to the king. But Ekbert, so the king said, had accepted neither. Because it was the third time Ekbert had rebelled, we can assume that a renewal of peace and concord would have cost him dearly; he could not have expected the loving reception of a lost son with the restitution of all his possessions as before. Still, it was only after Ekbert had definitely refused any kind of negotiated peace that he was proscribed. The wording

---

32 The *Liber* mentions a feud following the debate at Gerstungen in January 1085 about the justice of the king's cause, in which nobles from both sides participated and in which the bishop of Utrecht incidentally had defended the king's side. As the Saxons could not agree on just how to assess the outcome, a fight ensued among them. *MGH, Libelli de lite* 2:235. The pro-Henrician author describes it as a dissension within the opposing party, which would explain why Saxon nobles would agree to a punishment of Ekbert as part of a peace settlement. The fact that *Lampert of Hersfeld* and Brun in his *Book on the Saxon War* are both hostile to King Henry while being critical of Ekbert at the same time equally reveals the deep-set animosities within the Saxon party. It should warn us not to perceive the Saxons as a monolithic block of "friends" united in *amicitia* against the king. Eleventh-century Saxons appear as a lot of people very much given to outbreaks of violence in all kinds of causes. Modern historiography tends to isolate the rebellions against the king. In calling them "Saxon Wars," it creates the impression of two well-defined camps opposing each other. The outbreak after Gerstungen shows that this was not the case.

of the charter makes it very clear that the pronouncement of proscription not only defined Ekbert's new status as an outlaw but at the same time was directed at the princes who had participated in the law court. They all are named: Siegfried, who had pronounced the judgment that Ekbert should be prosecuted as a public enemy of the realm and of his lord king; Henry, who had judged that Ekbert should lose the margraviate and all his possessions; and the other lay and ecclesiastical nobles who are named individually in the charter as those who had endorsed the verdict. The prosecution of Ekbert was a public duty; with their participation in the verdict the princes first and foremost bound themselves to fulfil that duty.

In a way Ekbert was being punished for nonappearance, but in quite a different way than Mitteis thought. Mitteis had modern criminal procedures in mind: An action deemed a crime demands the institution of criminal proceedings, and the defendant is summoned to appear in court. If he does not do so, he is guilty of contempt. Ekbert's nonappearance was of a quite different nature, however. It was not linked to a summons that he had ignored but rather to his refusal to accept an invitation to negotiate peace. The verdict of the royal court was the public pronouncement of the view that Ekbert was an enemy of the king because he had refused all invitations to negotiate peace. His presence at the pronouncement would not have made sense. If a formal summons was part of the ritual pronouncement of enmity, then the defendant certainly was not expected to appear. Given the nature of early medieval law courts as forums for arbitration, a summons to stand one's trial must have been regarded as part of the declaration of enmity. To implement the verdict, some of Ekbert's castles were besieged. This was not a punishment in the modern sense but was done, so the king maintains, "rather to win him back than to alienate him further from us."

The king and his court figure as judges in criminal cases, but the way they dealt with this matter is incompatible with the modern notion of criminal procedure, in which summons, verdict, and penalty are basic, inseparable elements. Cases like Ekbert's were a recurring phenomenon in the Middle Ages, whenever a crown vassal became the enemy of his king. Because the very essence of a feudal kingdom depended on the allegiance of its constituent noble clans, it had to be a king's chief concern not to arouse the nobility's sympathy for his enemy by allowing that noble to appear as a victim of royal severity. This was the background for Henry IV's insistence that he had repeatedly tried to win Ekbert back by peaceful as well as warlike means. We should keep in mind, though, that our most eloquent sources, the charters, give the king's version of the conflict. We may assume that the king tried by his actions to leave the same impression he so elaborately enunciated in writing, namely, that his mind was set on peace and not on war. By citing the biblical parable of the prodigal son, he enacted a ritual of peace just as the solemn condemnation of Ekbert was a ritual of enmity.

The condemnation of John Lackland by the court of King Philip II of France, although separated by more than a century from the Ekbert trial, can be compared to the latter because it followed the same traditional pattern. John had inherited from his brother and predecessor Richard Lionheart the quarrels with the French king, Philip Augustus, over the Angevin kings' vast continental fiefs, which he managed to settle in May 1200 with the Treaty of Le Goulet.[33] In the same year a conflict broke out between John and one of his most formidable Aquitanian vassals, Hugh of Lusignan. The main cause was John's marriage to Isabelle, the heiress presumptive to the county of Angoulême, which took place in August 1200. Isabelle had been engaged to Hugh, and she was already living in the Lusignan household from which King John, Hugh's feudal lord, abducted her with the consent of her father to marry her himself. Whatever John's motives might have been, the Lusignans had every right to expect compensation, which John, however, appears to have refused.[34] The Lusignan clan initiated a feud, whereon John summoned them to his Poitevin court with the intention to sort out "right" and "wrong "by way of judicial combat. The Lusignans denied the court's competence and appealed to the French king, who held a judicial curia in Melun on April 28, 1202. This time it was John's turn to deny the court's competence and not appear.

Thereupon the court of the French king pronounced the judgment that John had forfeited Poitou and Aquitaine, which he held from Philip. The narrative sources are anything but clear as to the course of events

33 The newest book on King John is Ralph V. Turner, *King John* (London, 1994). A circumstantial report of the French King's actions with minute reference to the written evidence is given by Alexander Cartellieri, *Philipp II. August, König von Frankreich*, 5 vols. (Leipzig, 1899–1922). The dispossession of John Lackland is treated in vol. 4. For an overview of Philip's relations with the Plantagenets, see Jacques Boussard, "Philippe Auguste et les Plantagenêts," in Robert-Henri Bautier, ed., *La France de Philippe Auguste: Le temps de Mutations* (Paris, 1982), 263–87. From an English perspective, see Frank Barlow, *The Feudal Kingdom of England, 1042–1216*, 4th ed. (London, 1988), and still with rich details Maurice Powicke, *The Loss of Normandy, 1189–1204* (1913; reprint, Manchester, 1960); W. L. Warren, *King John* (London, 1961), 263–4, discusses the evidence in appendix A.

34 William Chester Jordan, "Isabelle d'Angoulême, By the Grace of God, Queen," *Revue belge de philologie et d'histoire* 69 (1991): 821–52, starts his report on Isabelle's altogether stormy carreer with a discussion of the possible motives of John's marriage to her.

and the legal implications of the different actions. It is generally accepted that the most reliable account is that given by Pope Innocent III, an eminent jurist and hence well versed in precise legal language. He wrote a letter to King John dated October 31, 1203, which is said to be based on an account given to the pope by the French court.[35] As a source it comes close to the intention and to the background of the charters in the Ekbert case. In both cases the documentary evidence presented the view of one side, namely, that of the royal lord of the respective defendant; and in both cases the sources presenting the royal position were carefully drafted as to the judicial implications of the terms employed. In John's case it has to be taken into account that Innocent's letter was written more than a year after the two kings had broken off relations and that the pope thus was aware of the events that followed. Philip had immediately started a war against John and had been very successful. In his letter, the pope maintained that Philip had tried for more than a year to make John settle the dispute peacefully, "begging and expecting satisfaction" (*satisfactionem expetens et expectans*).[36] Again, just as in the Ekbert case, the king presents himself as a model *rex pacificus* (peace-loving king), eager to avoid violence by promoting peace.

The further course of events is given in the following sentences. For my argument, the sequence of events is important, so I present them in full, adding numbers to indicate when I feel something new is beginning. After the sentence is quoted, the papal letter continues:

Cumque, communicato cum baronibus et hominibus suis consilio	Finally, taking council with his barons and followers
1) certum tibi terminum statuisset, ut in eius presentia	he appointed for you a definite day to appear before him and

35 *Selected Letters of Pope Innocent III Concerning England*, ed. C. R. Cheney and W. H. Semple (London, 1953), no. 20:60–2. The letter to John is one in a series of letters, with which the Pope tried to influence the conflict between the two kings. For an overview, see C. R. Cheney and M. G. Cheney, *The Letters of Pope Innocent III (1198–1216) Concerning England and Wales: A Calendar* (Oxford, 1967).

36 *Selected Letters*, 61. The pope mentions two disputes for which Philip is said to have demanded that satisfaction be given: One concerned the church of St. Martin at Tours, a man of which had been killed by John's followers. The church was situated in Angevin territory but was bound to the king of France by receiving its temporalities from him. According to the pope, Philip had demanded numerous times that John give satisfaction to the abbey. Other charges regarded some of John's secular vassals who are said to have complained to the king of France, John's lord, of having been deprived of castles and lands by John. Although the pope does not name them, it is generally assumed that the pope is referring here to John's feud with the Lusignans over the abduction of Isabelle of Angoulême.

comparares, quod ius dictaret sine retractatione facturus.	to fulfill without evasion what justice prescribed,
2) licet esses ligius homo eius nec ivisti tamen ad diem statutum nec misisti aliquem responsalem, sed mandatum eius penitus contempsisti.	But, though you were his liege, you neither went on the day appointed nor sent a representative, in fact you completely ignored his command.
3) Consequenter vero personaliter te convenit, et super hiis commonuit viva voce, cum non haberet in votisut faceret tibi guerram, si talem te circa eum qualem tenebaris ex debito exhiberes.	Subsequently he met you personally and by word of mouth reminded you of these matters — for he had no desire to go to war with you, if only you adopted toward him the attitude which was required by your liege duty.
4) Verum, cum nec sic satisfacere voluisses, licet te de baronum et hominum suorum consilio diffidasset, mota tamen guerra,	But although even then you would not give satisfaction, and he defied you with the counsel of his barons and followers and made war on you,
5) ad te quatuor ex militibus suis misit, volens certificari per eos, si velles ea que in ipsum commiseras, emendare.	he sent four of his knights to you wishing to ascertain through them whether you consented to put right the wrongs you had committed against him.[37]

The first sentence is usually understood to mean that John had been summoned to appear in Philip's court to stand trial and that the formal *diffidatio* (defiance) mentioned in sentence no. 4 was pronounced at this very date as an answer to his failure to appear. If the *diffidatio* is understood

---

37 I follow the translation given by Cheney in his edition of the *Selected Letters* except for the translation of no. 4, where I propose a slight though I feel significant emendation, as is pointed out in note 39 to this chapter.

this way, the subsequent interview of the two kings becomes indeed "improbable," as Cheney maintains.[38] A close reading suggests a somewhat different meaning, however. At first Philip had demanded satisfaction from John by sending numerous envoys to him. When John did not comply, he demanded to see him personally. Such a demand certainly carried more weight than an invitation that an addressee might or might not accept. It was a command (*mandatum*) of a lord to his man, a command to appear in order to settle a dispute. John was not summoned as a manifest criminal but as a man who could be certain that his lord would take his extraordinary position into consideration. In view of the long series of disputes over ceremonial precedence between the kings of France and their royal Angevin vassals, the question that really mattered was probably whether John would appear at all. When John did not comply, Philip arranged for a personal interview, assuring him that he had no intention of waging war on him "if only John lived up to his obligations toward his lord." For Philip, John's obligations included giving satisfaction, which John again refused to do. As a consequence, Philip declared all bonds of fidelity broken ("defied him") and started the war.[39]

There is a confirmation of this reading in the report of July 1202, wherein Philip gave notice of his contract with Arthur, John's nephew, whom he enfeoffed with Anjou, Maine, and Touraine, which hitherto were held by John. The date of reference is "the day we defied John, king of England, because of the privations he inflicted on us in this last war in which we besieged Boutavant."[40] Whatever the privations (*interceptiones*) refer to, they certainly do not mean contumacy, that is, John's not having answered Philip's summons to come to court. Ralph of Coggeshall, the contemporary English historian who wrote his hostile account of John in circa 1220, is the only English chronicler to mention explicitly French

38 *Selected Letters*, 61–2n4, understands the passage as follows: "John, having failed to appear in the court of his peers at Paris (Apr. 28, 1202), was condemned for contumacy, and the King of France formally broke off the feudal contract, or 'defied' him (cf. *Recueil des Actes de Philippe Auguste* II, 293). There is no confirmation of Philip's improbable statement that he had met John after his contumacy (they had met on Mar 25, 1202), or of his more likely story of the four knights." The text referred to by Cheney is Philip's report on his contract with Arthur in July 1202, which is discussed subsequently.

39 As for the time sequence, the *voluisses* and the *diffidasset* are clearly on the same level. It is very improbable, therefore, that the pope would have understood the *diffidatio* as having taken place *before* the interview and its outcome. Also, Philip's assurance that it was not his intention to make war on John (sentence 3) does not make sense if war had already started, as it did as a consequence of the *diffidatio* (sentence 4).

40 Original: "eo die quo nos diffiduciavimus Johannem regem Anglie pro interceptionibus quas nobis fecerat de hoc ultima guerra de qua nos obsedimus Botavant," cited according to Henri-François Delaborde et al., eds., *Recueil des Actes de Philippe Auguste, roi de France*, 4 vols. (Paris, 1843), 2 no. 723:292–3.

court proceedings. He relates the dispossession of John to an even broader range of faults: "Finally, the court of the French king judged that the king of England should be deprived of all the lands which he and his forefathers had held from the kings of France because they (!) had for a long time denied almost all services due from these lands and because they did not want to obey their Lord in almost anything."[41] For Ralph, then, it was the inappropriate behavior of *all* the Angevins that deserved punishment; it culminated in John, but only because he continued the ways of his predecessors. He was punished as the representative of a clan, not only as an individual.

The sequence of events given in the papal letter, based on information from the French court, thus would have been this: Philip demanded satisfaction from John through "diplomatic channels." When this failed, he demanded to see him at his court, but John did not appear. Philip then arranged a personal interview at a "neutral" place, telling John that he had no intention of waging war on him but that he would if John continued to refuse satisfaction. John did just that, and Philip defied him and started the war but nevertheless sent four knights to John because he wanted to know for sure whether these last steps showing his determination had not made John change his mind.

The whole procedure is strikingly similar to that in the Ekbert case. In both instances the respective lords claimed to have sought peaceful reconciliation by trying to persuade the defendants to negotiate peace and give satisfaction. Both admit to having failed in this because neither Ekbert nor John was willing to enter into negotiations. The decision that Ekbert was to be "prosecuted as a public enemy of the realm and of his lord emperor" corresponds to King Philip's *diffidatio* "with the counsel of his barons and men." Both declared that all peaceful means to arrive at a settlement had failed, and they had been forced to resort to hostile measures. In both cases it was a ritual declaration of enmity. Both lords started actions of war accordingly, and both maintained that these were just other means to arrive at a settlement – King Henry by saying so directly in his charter and King Philip saying so indirectly by sending envoys to John.

Unlike the charters concerning Ekbert, the pope used the word *contumacy* in a later passage in his letter. After relating that Philip had made John's men his allies only after his many efforts at a peaceful settlement

---

41 Radulphi de Coggeshall, *Chronicon Anglicanum*, ed. Joseph Stevenson, Rolls Series (London, 1875), 136.

had failed, Innocent continued: "He (Philip) admits that he received homage from some of them (John's men). This, he maintains, must be ascribed to your own contumacy – though he is still ready, if you so request, to grant you full justice in his own court, but only after receiving an adequate guarantee that you will abide by the judgment of the court."[42] The term *contumacia* might mean John's failure to appear in court, but it does not have to. It is rather unlikely that it does because the pope went out of his way to enumerate the many steps Philip had undertaken to come to terms with John, and it is the failure of *all* of them that puts the blame at John's door. If the pope had felt that by not appearing in Philip's court John had committed a specific crime that incurred a specific punishment, which was the legal justification for Philip's going to war, it is strange that a jurist such as Innocent would not have said so at the appropriate place in his arguments.

His use of the word *contumacy* seems to be more in line with the broader sense of the word in Roman times, where it covered any type of disobedient behavior toward a magistrate. With the magistrates gone and the authority of public offices extremely diminished, the term *contumacia* acquired an even broader definition. In the *Lex Baiuvariorum*, for example, it reads: "If a duke, in regard to the duchy to which the king ordained him, is so audacious (*audax*) or *contumax* or stimulated by levity (*levitate stimulus*) or impudent (*protervus*) or proud (*elatus*) or arrogant (*superbus*) or rebellious (*rebellus*), that he shows contempt for the order of the king, he shall lose the grant of the duchy, and he shall further know that he shall lose any hope of eternal rest and salvation."[43] Although a duke is described here as having offended royal authority, the offense is not defined as a breach of a particular obligation but rather as a general misdemeanor that covers all actions or behavior. A duke would be considered contumacious if he had not "adopted toward (his lord) the attitude that was required by (his) liege duty," to use King Philip's words. This attitude required that a subordinate come when his lord demanded his presence, but throughout the earlier Middle Ages the failure to do so

---

42 Original: "a quibusdam recepisse hominia se fatetur, quod contumacie tue asserit imputandum, licet adhuc paratus existat in curia sua, si petieris, tibi iustitie plenitudinem exhibere, sufficienti tamen cautione recepta, quod iudicio curie acquiescas."

43 The Bavarian laws have been translated into English. Theodore John Rivers, *Laws of the Alamans and Bavarians* (Philadelphia, 1977). For the Latin text, see *Lex Baiuvariorum*, ed. Karl August Eckhardt, Germanenrechte II, 2 (Weimar 1934), 8a, 96. For another striking example, see Fredegar, *Chronicorum Liber Quartus cum Continuationibus*, ed. John Michael Wallace-Hadrill, (London, 1960), c. 38, 108–9, where Aistulf, the Lombard king, is reported to have sworn "never again to rebel against Pepin and the Frankish nobility – "ut numquam . . . rebellis contumax esse non debeat."

was not a legally defined offense followed by a legally defined punishment, as is best shown by the fact that a disobedient duke was not only supposed to incur the loss of his duchy but also his soul's salvation.

The legal situation is quite different in the *Gelnhäuser Urkunde*, the *narratio* of which reports the condemnation of Henry the Lion. Here the terms *contumacia* and *contumax* occupy central places in the report about the trial. The case began with charges (*querimonia*) by the princes and other nobles, whereupon the emperor summoned Henry to his presence (*citatione vocatus maiestati nostre presentari*). When the defendant failed to appear (*contempserit*), the princes gave a verdict of proscription for contumacy (*et pro hac contumacia . . . proscriptionis nostre inciderit sentenciam*). Because Henry did not cease his action, he was again summoned and, because (*eo quod*) he did not come nor send a representative, he was judged a *contumax*.[44] Here there is no doubt that contumacy is a clearly defined offense: the offense of not having answered a summons to the royal law court. There is no indication that the emperor had tried to bring about a negotiated peace, and the procedure does resemble a modern criminal proceeding.[45]

Besides the charter, the most comprehensive historical report of Henry's trial is by Arnold of Lübeck, who openly sided with him.[46] Arnold relates that it was Duke Henry who complained to Frederick Barbarossa about acts of violence committed against him by the archbishop of Cologne. The emperor called both litigants, so Arnold says, to a royal curia – *eis curiam indixit apud Wormatiam*. This might look at first glance like a traditional invitation to negotiate peace, but it really was not because the duke found himself summoned to answer charges – *ducem tamen precipue ad audientiam citavit, illuc responsurum querimoniis*. Arnold continued: "When the duke realized this, he refused to come," being offended, so we may add, by being placed in the position of a common criminal instead of being treated as an eminent noble and kinsman of the emperor.

---

44 For the historical context, see Karl Jordan, *Heinrich der Löwe* (Munich, 1980), also available in English as *Henry the Lion: A Biography*, trans. P. S. Falla (Oxford, 1986). Odilo Engels, "Zur Entmachtung Heinrichs des Löwen," *Münchener Historische Studien, Abt. Bayerische Geschichte: Festschrift Andreas Kraus* (Kallmünz, 1982), 45–59, and Odilo Engels, "Friedrich Barbarossa und die Welfen," in Rainer Gehl, ed., *Welf VI* (Sigmaringen, 1994), 59–74. Stefan Weinfurter, "Die Entmachtung Heinrichs des Löwen," in Jochen Luckhardt and Franz Niehoff, eds., *Heinrich der Löwe und seine Zeit*, catalog of the Braunschweig exhibition in 1995, vol. 2 (Munich, 1995), 180–9, questions the view that Frederick Barbarossa was foremost in bringing about the dispossession of the duke.

45 This understanding of *contumacia* was also known in English law with its elaborate judicial system; see J. C. Holt, *Magna Carta*, 109.

46 *Arnoldi Chronica Slavorum*, ed. J. M. Lappenberg, in *MGH SS* 21, 1868, Lib. II, chap. 10, 47–9.

It becomes apparent that this was indeed what Arnold meant to say by comparing the terms used by him with those used in Frederick's *Landfrieden* (territorial peace), proclaimed the very same year that the proceedings against Henry the Lion began.[47] It states that if malfactors who are legitimately summoned (*legitime citati*) three times (*ad ternas inducias*) and fail to appear, they are to be punished by proscription. I have argued elsewhere that Frederick's German *Landfrieden* are not to be understood as acts of legislation in the modern sense of the word but as solemn pronouncements of what people had learned to regard as criminal breaches of the peace.[48] In this they stand in the tradition of the Peace-of-God movement, which had been trying to establish that certain acts of violence hitherto regarded as legitimate elements of a feud were criminal.[49] It helped thereby to re-establish the difference between civil and criminal justice, meaning that certain acts of violence were crimes that could not be settled by arbitration but rather deserved punishment. The prevalence of negotiated compensations had blurred this difference in the earlier Middle Ages and, with it, the precision of judicial vocabulary. If self-help and arbitration were to be superseded by judicial trials in law courts, a precision of legal terminology that previously had not been needed and that had not been taught for centuries was indispensable. The study of Roman law, which was resumed at the end of the eleventh century, could provide adequate means to overcome this deficiency.[50] This revival coincided with the Investiture Conflict, which brought the reenforcement of ecclesiastical norms with the development of canon law.[51]

47 *MGH*, Charters of Frederick Barbarossa, no. 774.
48 Hanna Vollrath, "Die deutschen königlichen Landfrieden und die Rechtsprechung," in *La Giustizia nell'alto medioevo*, 1:591–630; see also Hanna Vollrath, "Politische Ordnungsvorstellung und politisches Handeln im Vergleich: Philipp II. August von Frankreich und Friedrich Barbarossa im Konflikt mit ihren mächtigsten Fürsten," in Joseph Canning and Otto Gerhard Oexle, eds., *Political Thought and the Realities of Power in the Middle Ages* (Göttingen, 1998), 33–51.
49 See Thomas Head and Richard Landes, eds., *The Peace of God: Social Violence and Religious Response in France Around the year 1000* (Ithaca, N.Y., 1992). There are two recent overviews of the scholarly debate on the Peace-of-God movement and the *Landfrieden*: F. S. Paxton, "History, Historians, and the Peace of God," Head and Landes, eds., *Peace of God*, ibid., 21–40, and Elmar Wadle, "Gottesfrieden und Landfrieden als Gegenstand der Forschung nach 1950," in Karl Kroeschell and Albrecht Cordes, eds., *Funktion und Form: Quellen- und Methodenprobleme der mittelalterlichen Rechtsgeschichte* (Berlin, 1996), 63–91.
50 Eltjo H. J. Schrage, *Utrumque Ius*, trans. from Dutch (Berlin, 1992); Gerhard Otte, "Logische Einteilungstechniken bei den Glossatoren des römischen Rechts," in Johannes Fried, ed., *Dialektik und Rhetorik im früheren und hohen Mittelalter: Rezeption, Überlieferung und gesellschaftliche Wirkung antiker Gelehrsamkeit* (Munich, 1997), 157–69.
51 Johannes Fried underscored Stephen Kuttner's hypothesis that the eminent English canonist, Gerard Pucelle, was teaching around 1180 at the cathedral school of Cologne. See Johannes Fried, "Gerard Pucelle und Köln," *Zeitschrift für Rechtsgeschichte: Kanonistische Abteilung* 68 (1982): 125–35; whereas Stefan Weinfurter has shown that it was the influence of the Cologne chancery that

Ecclesiastical legislation and the renewed regularity of church councils show that the Roman church led the way in the reassessment of law and justice, taking up or merging with the ideas developed by French ecclesiastics in the Peace-of-God movement. The German *Landfrieden* were a response to the same challenge. Although they were certainly directed against feuding nobles, it is very unlikely that great princes such as Henry the Lion were imagined as the addressees. The legal terminology of the *Gelnhäuser Urkunde* as well as of Arnold of Lübeck that corresponds to that of the *Landfrieden* shows that this is exactly what was done.

In view of all of this, Frederick's summoning the duke to answer criminal charges must be seen as an outright provocation that left no room for the traditional rituals of noble society. It also marks an attempt to reinforce the notion of the kingdom as a legal community with a common law, where trespassers were prosecuted as criminals irrespective of their social rank. At the end of the twelfth century this was more an idea than a living reality in the European kingdoms. The fact that Henry the Lion was sentenced in that way certainly does not mean that it was more of a reality in Germany than elsewhere. The trial of Henry the Lion was a political trial. A certain political constellation – namely, the fact that Henry the Lion had isolated himself from his peers through all sorts of actions that were deemed inappropriate – allowed his enemies to find means that would undo him. They found them by applying rules that had been developing in other contexts for more than two centuries. No contemporary would have expected that from here on, all similar cases would be dealt with in the same fashion. Hence, the proceedings lacked the predictability that is essential if law is to perform its function in society.[52]

---

makes itself felt in the terminology of the *Gelnhäuser Urkunde*: "Erzbischof Philipp von Köln und der Sturz Heinrichs des Löwen," in Hanna Vollrath and Stefan Weinfurter, eds., *Köln: Stadt und Bistum in Kirche und Reich des Mittelalters: Festschrift für O. Engels* (Cologne, 1993). For the reception of Bolognese jurisprudence in Germany, see Johannes Fried, "Die Rezeption bologneser Wissenschaft in Deutschland während des 12. Jahrhundert," *Viator: Medieval and Renaissance Studies* 21 (1990): 136ff.

52 Rosalyn Higgins, ed., *International Law and the Avoidance, Containment, and Resolution of Disputes*, Académie de Droit International, Recueil des Cours (Dordrecht, 1993), 32.

5

Oblivion Between Orality and Textuality in the Tenth Century

PATRICK J. GEARY

In a recent book, I attempted to examine the means by which European communities transmitted and redefined their remembered pasts in the tenth and eleventh centuries.[1] I argued that the period of roughly 950 to 1050 saw a great amount of "creative forgetting" as individuals and communities, both lay and secular, readjusted their sense of a relationship to the past, creating a new and more useful memory through a process of transmission, adaptation, and suppression. In that study I concentrated primarily on written traditions and examined how a wide spectrum of texts were restructured and transformed in the process of creating a useful past.

A number of scholars have criticized my work, and rightly so, for not having explored in more detail the specific issues of orality in the context of remembering. The position I took in the book was that, in the period I studied, the relationship between orality and literacy was a complex one. The rememberers moved between the two worlds with great facility: Oral tradition might be called on to validate or interpret written tradition, and written tradition might incorporate much that had been oral. Thus, I saw orality and literacy so deeply intertwined that I did not believe it necessary to devote a separate discussion to oral transmission of the past. I still think that this is essentially correct, but I recognize that I could have provided more concentrated attention to the issues of explicitly oral transmission within what Ursula Schaefer and others term vocality, taking into account the work of Hanna Vollrath, Horst Wenzel, and others who have examined the parameters of orality in medieval society.[2] What I would

---

1 Patrick J. Geary, *Phantoms of Remembrance: Memory and Oblivion at the End of the First Millennium* (Princeton, N.J., 1994).
2 Horst Wenzel, *Hören und Sehen, Schrift und Bild: Kultur und Gedächtnis im Mittelalter* (Munich, 1995).

111

like to do here is to make up for this deficit by exploring in more detail how some of the theoretical reflections on orality and vocality can be applied to understanding the relationship between memory and imagination in the tenth and eleventh centuries.

"Quod loquimur transit, quod scribimus permanet," announced Gregory the Great. If he invented this dictum himself, he must have been very proud of it: He uses it at least three times in varying contexts.[3] However, the apparent opposition that it suggests is not as clear in the Middle Ages or in the present as an earlier tradition of scholarship would have wanted us to believe. As Vollrath has pointed out, the culture of the Middle Ages never was purely oral, being exactly that period when a largely oral culture, that is, Germanic (and, one might add, Celtic and Slavic) combined with the Christian literary culture of late antiquity.[4] This much is widely accepted by scholars. Orality and literacy no longer are approached as dichotomous or mutually exclusive categories belonging to different social orders or cultural spheres. However, arguments, often heated, develop when one asks to what extent, in different periods and in different regions of Europe, populations continued to function largely within the parameters of oral culture and what influences these oral modes of thought and reflection might have had on how people perceived and represented their worlds. In terms of the actual extent of literacy, or at least the integration of the written word into society, one can distinguish a broad spectrum of positions, from the "maximalist" position of Rosamund McKitterick, who believes that lay literacy already was widespread not only in the heavily Romance regions of southern Europe but also in the zones of Germanic settlement in Alemannia and the Rhineland,[5] to that of Michael Richter, equally convinced of the overwhelming predominance of orality as the principal mode of communication and recording not only in the Celtic world he knows well but throughout western Europe.[6]

3 *Moralia in Job* XXXIII, *Patrologia latina* (hereafter *PL*), ed. Jacques Paul Migne (Paris, 1841–64), 76:672; *Moralia* XI, 45; *Enarrationes in Psalmos* XLIV, 6. Cited by Michael Richter, *The Formation of the Medieval West: Studies in the Oral Culture of the Barbarians* (Dublin, 1994), 81, who declares these words to be "either trivial or misleading." The phrase was repeated frequently in the Middle Ages, especially by Taio of Caesaraugustus (*PL* 80:735) and Odo of Cluny (*PL* 133:231).

4 Hanna Vollrath, "Das Mittelalter in der Typik oraler Gesellschaften," *Historische Zeitschrift* 233 (1981): 587. See also Ursula Schaefer, *Vokalität: Altenglische Dichtungen zwischen Mündlichkeit und Schriftlichkeit* (Tübingen, 1992), who also cites Vollrath, "Das Mittelalter," 14.

5 Rosamund McKitterick, *The Carolingians and the Written Word* (Cambridge, 1989).

6 See especially Richter, *Formation of the Medieval West*, and his *The Oral Tradition in the Early Medieval West*, Typologie des Sources du moyen âge occidental, fasc. 71 (Turnhout, 1994).

Of course, it is not sufficient simply to argue how widely ordinary people came into contact with the written word or indeed whether a special category of singers (bards, scops, troubadours) were charged with transmitting an alternative past. A related area of debate is the effect of oral and written modes of understanding on the processing of information. American, British, Canadian, and German scholars, drawing on the traditions of ethnographic studies, are exploring the different processes of oral and written perception. Peter Koch and Wolf Oesterreicher, for example, urge that we distinguish between different relationships of texts to orality. Koch would describe the simple notation of the spoken word as *Verschriftung*, that is, the transference from phonetic to graphic medium, while reserving the term *Verschriftlichung* for the more complex conceptual process by which textualization creates a qualitative difference between that which is oral and that which is written.[7]

Vollrath has recently explored a different but perhaps related problem regarding the use of texts to show how the parameters of the early investiture debate may have been in large part complicated by the emergence of a new way of dealing with texts. Even within clerical circles long accustomed to the use of written evidence, she suggests that in the course of the eleventh century one can discern a very gradual development of a new way of using texts, of analyzing them abstractly for their meaning, a meaning that might be in contrast to contemporary practice. In an insightful analysis of how Frutolf of Michelsberg and Odo of Ostia each interpreted the Pseudo-Isidorian decretal that states, "No one deprived of his belongings or ousted from his episcopal see by force or terror can be accused, summoned, judged, and sentenced unless full legal restitution has been made allowing him to enjoy his rights freely and peacefully," she shows how very differently contemporaries might approach a text. She argues that one mode, which would become identified with abstract, historically differentiated interpretation, stands in contrast to a traditional way of using texts derived from oral modes of perception in which dissidence between text and contemporary practice were minimized or ignored. However, Vollrath points out that although one may see individuals using texts in an abstract way, the transition is

---

7 Peter Koch, "Distanz im Dictamen. Zur Schriftlichkeit und Pragmatik mittelalterlicher Brief- und Redemodelle in Italien," Habilitation, University of Freiburg, 1987, 94, cited by Schaefer, *Vokalität*, 17n24; Wulf Oesterreicher, "Verschriftung und Verschriftlichung im Kontexte medialer und konzeptioneller Schriftlichkeit," in Ursula Schaefer, ed., *Schriftlichkeit im frühen Mittelalter* (Tübingen, 1993), 267–92.

hardly uniform or linear across even the most educated and literate strata of medieval society.[8]

Other scholars explicitly reject a comparatist approach to medieval orality and textuality. Writing in the same volume as Vollrath, Alois Wolf refuses any attempt to understand medieval transmission through comparison with traditions in contemporary nonliterate societies. He states baldly: "Theories based upon isolated observations of exotic material cut off from the singular historical context can give only a limited number of elementary, even banal, insights and fail to explain the unique situations in medieval Europe."[9] Unfortunately, Wolf's refusal to approach his subject comparatively makes the task he sets, namely, to "explain the unique situations in medieval Europe," impossible. By excluding a comparative perspective, he is unable to determine what is indeed unique about the medieval case.

However, as Vollrath herself points out, if there is indeed a shift between two modes of reasoning, the shift is extremely difficult to establish within any tight chronological structure. In fact, the two persist together for centuries.[10] Nor is it entirely clear that the two modes of reasoning she so correctly identifies need be connected with either orality or literacy. The different mental approaches to texts that she so correctly observes can be recognized in other disputes over texts even centuries later.

Thus, while I am unwilling to dismiss the rich tradition of ethnographic studies as insignificant for medieval historians, I also am hesitant to argue that varying ways of dealing with texts should be placed in an evolutionary pattern. However, I do not intend to settle any of these areas of debate here. What I would like to do is much less ambitious: to reflect on the different ways that one can see oral tradition not as a separate culture but as an integral part of the culture that is accessible to us through the written evidence of the past.

Obviously, one cannot study a purely oral tradition unless either its content or the evidence of its existence has been textualized. We thus are always faced with the necessity of studying the interface between orality and textuality and arguing about what other spheres of orality may have existed. Because we cannot hope to listen to the oral tradition itself, we

8 Hanna Vollrath, "Oral Modes of Perception in Eleventh-Century Chronicles," in A. N. Doane and Carol Braun Pasternack, eds., *Vox intexta: Orality and Textuality in the Middle Ages* (Madison, Wis., 1991), 102–111.

9 Alois Wolf, "Medieval Heroic Traditions and Their Transitions from Orality to Literacy," in Doane and Pasternack, eds., *Vox intexta*, 68.

10 Vollrath, "Oral Modes of Perception," 111.

can only do one of three things. First, we can consider traditions that may have been oral but that now have been textualized. The process is, of course, fraught with difficulties – in an age before tape recorders or even a practical shorthand system, transcription of oral material not only fails to represent fully what was said, but, as we are well aware, textual transmission is a fundamentally different form of transmission and transforms the content along with the form. An orally transmitted story not only loses the formal structure of orality, but its context and social value are changed by the process of recording it. The performance context, so vital to the deep appreciation of the material, is irretrievably lost. As Ursula Schaefer has argued concerning early medieval poetry, "Early medieval poetic discourse was . . . taken as indexical, as pointing to the receivers' lifeworld. . . . For a contemporary audience, the meaning of the discourse was supposed to be found not in the text but in the context."[11] Such a judgment may not sit well with Deridaian poststructuralists, but it accords well with an understanding of medieval culture essentially as a culture of memory in which listening to texts is intended to key memory, not to provide the listeners with new information.

Often, too, one moves from vernacular to Latin and from one social register (peasant, lay aristocrat) to another (cleric). Thus, we are never studying orality per se or indeed simple *Verschriftung* when we find bits of material brought from one register to the other. Rather, we are dealing with *Verschriftlichung*, the conceptual transformation of the oral record.

The second possibility is to look for the evidence of oral performance within texts. Written texts in the Middle Ages were created and performed orally; thus, most texts have an essentially oral character – they were vocalized at the time that they were transcribed and were intended to be vocalized in their reading, whether for an individual reading aloud to him- or herself, or as a performance for others.[12] As a result, if we have no direct contact with pure orality from the Middle Ages, we have abundant evidence of vocality, of performance of texts, at every turn. This is a different orality from that which most people are interested in because it is the orality of a literate minority, even if they, through reading, reach a much wider audience.

The third possibility is to look for descriptions of the encounter between literate and oral modes in medieval texts; that is to say, to listen to how literate authors describe their interaction with those for whom

---

11 Ursula Schaefer, "Hearing from Books: The Rise of Fictionality in Old English Poetry," in Doane and Pasternack, eds., *Vox intexta*, 121.
12 See Schaefer, *Vokalität*.

the text is always mediated. This approach too is problematic because the presentation of the encounter is entirely in the hands of the literate party. The extent to which his or her construction of the nonliterate party (or at least the party who is providing access to oral modes of communication and transmission) will be constructed to a great extent from assumptions, literary topoi, and values that pertain to the literate world. Moreover, as Franz Bäuml has argued concerning literature, "In referring to the oral tradition, the written text fictionalizes it. Since the one is given a role to play within the other, since oral formulae in the garb of writing refer to 'orality' within the written tradition, the oral tradition becomes an implicit fictional 'character' of literacy."[13] Nevertheless, at the level of representation of vocality, examination of such descriptions provides a vital if partial entry into the world of medieval orality.

Between the ninth and twelfth centuries, two types of texts provide us with the best evidence in which to observe both explicit representations of vocality and the literate authors' need to incorporate material from the oral world. These are accounts of miracles and legal testimony. Although at first view hagiography and legal texts might seem to be at opposite poles of medieval discourse, the two are extremely similar in certain ways. In both cases, the literate world must rely to some extent on input from a world outside of the literate sphere. The establishment of the validity and significance of the cult of saints is predicated on the testimony of those to whom the posthumous power of the saint was manifest. Thus, oral testimony, whether from *literati* or from *rustici*, must be integrated as such into the text. In disputes both within and outside of the legal system, written evidence, for a variety of reasons, often requires validation, interpretation, augmentation, or opposition that only can come from oral tradition. Thus, in both the demonstration of the power of saints and in the termination of disputes, oral testimony is important to the outcome. Not that one can assume any more accuracy in such a report than in any other form of reporting, of course, but there is at least a possibility of looking with some depth into the process of crossing the line between oral and written in such cases. I will examine only one of these two categories here, that of legal disputes in which orality and textuality work in complicated and interesting ways.

Because my argument is that orality is essential to the functioning of written law and evidence, I draw my examples from the regions in which

13 Franz Bäuml, "Medieval Texts and the Two Theories of Oral-Formulaic Composition: A Proposal for a Third Theory," *New Literary History* 16 (1984–5): 43. Cited by Schaefer, *Vokalität*, 115–16n49.

it is widely accepted that written law and documentary evidence continued to play a major role in the settlement of disputes – lower Aquitaine
and Provence – regions where scholars have recently wanted to argue that
high levels of literacy survived, and along with them, the tradition of
Roman law.[14] I examine a number of *placita* here to see the spectrum of
interaction between written and oral proof and argumentation. The result
is to suggest that neither oral nor written testimony was unambiguously
superior, nor did the much-celebrated permanence of the written word,
even in this area, enjoy clear advantage over the spoken past.

Let us begin with a fairly straightforward account of a dispute held
before Aagilardus, bishop of Nîmes, in 898.[15] The bishop's advocate,
Joshua, accused one Rostagnus of having recently seized a church and its
estates that had been donated to the cathedral by bishop Christianus some
time during the first half of the ninth century and which the cathedral
had held for over thirty years. Joshua stated that he could prove this
donation with the "cartul[a] donationis quem ego in manu mea teneo."
Rostagnus was asked whether he could provide counterevidence, and he
replied that he could produce a certain Aimardus as an *auctoritas* to
demonstrate his right to the property. He was given forty days to produce
Aimardus. At the end of this time the court met in the Arena of Nîmes.
Rostagnus stated that he was unable to produce Aimardus as his *auctoritas*. The judges asked Rostagnus if he had *scripturas aut ullum inditium veritatis* by which he could defend his position. He said that he could not,
and the property was returned to the church.

One can never assume that the reports of such cases reproduce exact
speech or indeed that they are faithful summaries of what actually
occurred. They tend to be highly formulaic and often hide as much as
they reveal. However, we see in this apparently straightforward decision
that Rostagnus had been offered the possibility of producing an *auctoritas*
in the nature of a person to counter a charter of donation. What might
have happened had he done so we cannot know, but clearly the court
held out the possibility, however theoretical, that the validity of the charter

14 Among the scholars who have emphasized the strong continuity of Roman legal traditions in
the Midi, see Marie-Louise Carlin, *La pénétration du droit romain dans les actes de la pratique provençale
(XIe–XIIIe siècle)* (Paris, 1967); Jean-Pierre Poly, *La Provence et la société féodale 879–1166: Contribution à l'étude des structures dites féodales dans le Midi* (Paris, 1976); Elizabeth Magnou-Nortier, *La
société laïque et l'église dans la province ecclésiastique de Narbonne* (Toulouse, 1974). See, however, the
important corrective brought to the question by Jeffrey A. Bowman, "Do Neo-Romans Curse?
Law, Land, and Ritual in the Midi (900–1100)," *Viator: Medieval and Renaissance Studies* 28 (1997):
1–32.
15 Eugène Germer-Durant, ed., *Cartulaire du Chapitre de l'église cathédrale Notre Dame de Nîmes*
(Nîmes, 1874), no. VIII, 16–18.

was not *prima facie* evidence but was prepared to hear oral testimony that might nullify it in order to reach a judgment.

A few years later, the situation was reversed. At a court meeting in 902 the advocate of the bishop claimed that one Anselmus had unjustly seized another property belonging to the cathedral. When the judges examined Anselmus, he replied that he had a *scriptura* that proved his right. The text was then read out loud before the assembly. However, for reasons not stated, the judges found it "inofficiosa, non bona." Anselmus was asked if he had "alias scripturas aut ullum indicium veritatis." When he could produce neither written evidence nor testimony, the decision was awarded to the bishop.[16]

Similarly, at Elne in 1000, the canons of the church claimed that on his deathbed one of their members, Auriolus, had donated a property to them. However, because he died shortly thereafter, he had been unable to confirm the donation in writing. His granddaughter and her husband disputed this donation and appeared in court with a *scriptura donationis*, by which they claimed Auriolus had transferred the property to her. The judge had the charter read aloud and found it "mendacem atque falsissimam et contra lege," lacking the proper subscription and clearly adulterated. Deprived of their written evidence, the husband was asked if he was willing to prove by undergoing an ordeal that he was not a conscious participant in the fraud. Initially, he agreed but then, through intermediaries, announced his willingness to cede the property to the church.[17]

Thus, texts might carry the day, but they also could be judged forged or at least irregular. Oral testimony might be accepted, or it might be unavailable. But what if neither side could produce written evidence? In 921 the church of Saint André de Costebalen disputed the payment of the tithes of a series of village churches with the church of Saint Martin le Quart. The former claimed before Bishop Ucbertus of Nîmes that the allod of the Le Luc church had been sold to men from Le Luc, who had granted the tithe to Saint Martin but that at the time of the consecration of Saint André, Bishop Christian (808–858) had granted these tithes to Saint André. They claimed that they had enjoyed these rights for thirty years and more, that is, beyond the Roman period for reclamations.

Neither side could produce documentary evidence for their positions, and both were reporting events that had transpired more than sixty years

---

16 Nîmes, IX, 19–20.
17 Cl. Devic and J. Vaissete, *Histoire générale de Languedoc avec des notes et les pieces justificatives*, 15 vols. in 17 (Toulouse, 1872–92) (hereafter HGL), 5:1, cols. 338–9.

previously. The bishop therefore sent his *missi* to circumambulate the boundaries of the allod and to investigate the situation. These *missi* convoked the "vicini comanentes" that is, the inhabitants of the villas involved in the dispute. They were then ordered to swear "through God the Father all-powerful and Jesus Christ his son" that they would tell the truth. The testimony revealed that Saint André had more right to the tithes than Saint Martin.

The testimony did not end the dispute, however. The two men who held the property continued to direct the tithes to the church of Saint Martin, and again Ansemirus, the priest representing Saint André, appeared before the bishop. This time Bishop Ucbertus himself went to the site, circumambulated it, and then constrained the inhabitants of the village of Quart to swear to the truth of the matter. They gave the same testimony as before. Following this second on-site investigation, Ansemirus was ordered to appear with his witnesses before the bishop the following Thursday. Here, he produced his *testimonia*, that is, a new list of inhabitants of one of the disputed villages who swore a solemn oath that the tithe belonged to Saint André.

In this case we see the importance of physical circumambulation of the disputed property and especially of the oral testimony of the inhabitants of the villages under dispute. This testimony was essential but valid only under oath and had to be extracted from a series of witnesses in different venues. Moreover, the oral testimony itself had to be textualized: The document in which this dispute was recorded is not so much in the tradition of Carolingian *placita* as it is written evidence of the last series of oaths. It concluded with a detailed statement of the testimony sworn by the witnesses and is in the first person plural: "sic est veritas sicut hunc sacramentum juramus; eaque scimus recte et fideliter juramus," and is followed first by the signs of those taking the oath and only then by Bishop Ucbertus and others as witnesses to the oath. The document thus produced is much more than simply the *Verschriftung* of the oral oath: It is a transformation, a *Verschriftlichung*, in order to produce something that is qualitatively different from the oath itself. At the same time the narrative of the process by which it was extracted, like the other *placitum* records, creates, in Bäuml's words, an implicit fictional "character" of literacy.[18]

Gregory the Great and others may have praised the permanence of the written word, but of course not everything that is written endures. In

18 Bäuml, "Medieval Texts," 43.

928, Bishop Ucbertus and his advocate Ictor appeared before an assembly to declare that he had lost a certain *scriptura* in which one Adalardus and his wife had donated a half of a villa in Trabuc to the cathedral. He explained that he had given the document to the priest Lambertus (the reason is not stated – was it a mortgage?), who had died before he could return it. The bishop appealed to Fredolo, termed *missus* or *actor vel defensator*, to acknowledge the validity of the donation in the absence of the charter.

Again, oral testimony was essential. Ictor produced five witnesses who swore that they had "seen and heard" the reading of this donation. After providing this testimony before the court, they then entered the church of Saint Steven near the committal palace and swore the truth of their testimony on the altar. Two documents relate these events: One is the formal *plantura* or *appensa* produced by the court in the Roman law tradition of replacement of lost or destroyed titles subscribed by Fredolo and his judges; the second is the statement of the oath subscribed by those who swore it and then witnessed by the court.

In this case as in others, oral testimony was essential in establishing what had taken place. Moreover, the witnesses not only testified to having seen the document but also to having heard it read. Again and again, the formulaic descriptions of the presentation of written evidence in tenth- and eleventh-century *placita* indicate that the evidence was vocalized: At Elne, the judge determined that the charter presented was invalid after it had been exhibited in his presence and then "predictus judex audivit eam legentem et relegentem";[19] at a *placitum* held in Narbonne in 955, Bishop Udalgarius judged on the validity of a deathbed donation only after he had seen and heard it, "vidit et audivit."[20] Seeing and hearing, as Horst Wenzel has argued in other contexts, was an essential part of the process of determining cases.[21]

There could be much more to the process of juxtaposing written and oral testimony than determining whether one was to be accepted over the other. Participants in disputes could be aware of the possibility that texts might preserve a past that no longer corresponded to a present. Even at the level of humble disputes over land, the kind of recognition of the inability of texts to maintain contact with the dynamics of change was always possible. This is the conclusion one must draw from a lengthy document generated on behalf of the monastery of Saint Victor of Marseilles

19 HGL V: 339.   20 HGL V: 222.
21 Horst Wenzel, *Hören und Sehen, Schrift und Bild: Kultur und Gedächtnis im Mittelalter* (Munich, 1995).

in the last quarter of the eleventh century. It is a record, prepared by the prior of the monastery, of a long-standing dispute between the monastery and certain knights over rights to property in the villa of Chaudols. It is a fascinating and complex affair that I have discussed at length elsewhere.[22] For our purposes, I want to return to it to emphasize the relationship between text and oral testimony of the past.

The dispute arose over a manse that the monks claimed had been donated to Saint Victor a generation previously. The donation had been made and duly recorded in a charter preserved by the monastery. Neither side disputed the validity of the charter or the donation. However, the charter specifically described the property donated as that manse cultivated by Benedict Pela, the peasant who worked the land.[23] However, by the 1070s, when the dispute was under way, this very title had become an obstacle to the monks' pursuit of their claims. The reason, according to the prior, was that "long after the death of Benedict Pela, his two successors had divided the manse into two parts. One was called Salamus and the other Ferreng. After this division, the names of the manses also changed: One part is called Salamuns, the other Ferreng."[24] Thus, when the dispute was presented before Count Isnoard of Gap, the charter was duly brought forth and read out loud to the assembly, but the knights argued that the charter could not be used to demonstrate that the property described in the document was the same as that in dispute. Written evidence, because of its very permanence, was an inadequate means of determining the proper resolution to the conflict.

The result was that the various tribunals and bodies of arbitration had to resort to local memory. Who could remember what the original manse of Benedict Pela was? Whose testimony could be considered acceptable to both parties? Who could force local residents acceptable to both sides to swear to the truth of the matter? These issues, which required oral, performative, ritualized statements before the local community and representatives of the opposing forces, became the crux of the conflict, a conflict that continued for decades.

In each of these cases, we see the complexities of orality and textuality within the most practical, mundane aspects of life. Texts in the Roman tradition continue to be extremely important, at times decisive. But this

22 Patrick J. Geary, "Living with Conflicts in Stateless France: A Typology of Conflict Management Mechanisms, 1050–1200," in Patrick J. Geary, *Living with the Dead in the Middle Ages* (Ithaca, N.Y., 1994), 125–60.
23 Benjamin Guérard, ed., *Cartulaire de l'abbaye de Saint-Victor de Marseille*, 2 vols. (Paris, 1857), 2: 555–64, no. 1089.
24 Ibid., 556.

written evidence never "speaks for itself." It first must be vocalized so that the sounds it carries are once more heard by the judge and his advisers. It then must be confronted by oral memory, which might be a memory of the creation of the written text or a memory of events not mentioned in the text, or a memory of what transpired after the text was created. Finally, the oral memory itself, whether of events or indeed of the presentation and vocalization of written texts, must be "fictionalized," that is, placed into a narrative structure that is the formal presentation of the court procedure. In the legal context, then, oral memory and written memory functioned together, at times at odds, at times in concert. Texts needed contexts for interpretation and validation, but these contexts were oral and performative. When speaking of oral tradition, one is not necessarily speaking of a different content parallel to or even in opposition to the written tradition. Oral tradition can just as well mean a tradition of how written texts are to be evaluated; it can be less a fixed content than the hermeneutic apparatus of these texts.

By the same token, in the complex world of human conflict and dispute resolution, oral testimony from those who have lived experience, from the *vicini* and the *comanentes*, can carry more weight than a text. It may be that "quod loquimur transit, quod scribimus permanet," but it is equally true that "Littera occidit, spiritus autem vivificat" (II Cor. III, 6).

6

Text and Ritual in Ninth-Century Political Culture

Rome, 864

PHILIPPE BUC

By the reigns of Charlemagne's grandsons, the ritual repertoire we have come to associate with the monarchy of the high Middle Ages was well established.[1] Its emergence owed much to competition, first to the eighth-century need to affirm a new dynasty, second to rivalry with the Roman Empire in the East, and third to the intrafamilial struggles that exploded in the 830s.[2] For these reasons, the second half of the ninth century provides a wonderful window through which to observe the workings of a specific political culture and, especially, its rituals. Competing entities – Carolingian subkingdoms but also the Republic of Saint Peter – strove for autonomy as well as for the satellization or absorption of one another. At the same time they spoke in the language of power that a now waning

---

1 This essay is an abridged version of a part of chapter 2 in *The Dangers of Ritual: Between Early Medieval Texts and Social Scientific Theory* (Princeton, N.J., 2001), to which I refer the reader for further materials. I thank Patrick J. Geary, Igor Gorevich, Tom Head, Mayke de Jong, Janet Nelson, and Amy Remensnyder for comments on this and other versions. Gallicisms remain my responsibility.
2 General historiographical introduction in Richard Sullivan, "The Carolingian Age: Reflections on its Place in the History of the Middle Ages," *Speculum* 64 (1989): 267–306. Good master narratives in Rosamund McKitterick, ed., *New Cambridge Medieval History*, vol. 2: *c. 700–c. 900* (Cambridge, 1995), 110–69 (articles by Janet Nelson and Johannes Fried). For the Byzantine horizon, see Michael McCormick, "Byzantium and the West, 700–900," in ibid., 349–80 (and the appended bibliography), with Nikolaus Staubach, "Graecae Gloriae: Die Rezeption des Griechischen als Element spätkarolingisch-frühottonischer Hofkultur," in Anton von Euw and Peter Schreiner, eds., *Kaiserin Theophanu: Begegnung des Ostens und Westens um die Wende des ersten Jahrtausends*, 2 vols. (Cologne, 1991), 1:343–67. Janet Nelson, "Kingship and Royal Government," in McKitterick, ed., *New Cambridge Medieval History*, 428–9, and Janet Nelson, "Carolingian Royal Ritual," in David Cannadine and Simon Price, eds., *Rituals of Royalty: Power and Ceremonial in Traditional Societies* (Cambridge, 1987), 137–80, deal with Carolingian rituals. Karl Leyser, "Ritual, Ceremony and Gesture: Ottonian Germany," in Karl Leyser, ed., *Communications and Power in Medieval Europe*, 2 vols. (London, 1994), 1:189–91, discusses a number of anthropological models.

Carolingian unity had made uniform. Each entity produced a historiography that argued its ruler's superiority but at the same time was interested in and informed about its neighbors. Convergent and divergent, the contents of the so-called *Annals of Fulda, Annals of Saint Bertin, Liber pontificalis,* and papal epistolary registers are quite revelatory. But what exactly do they reveal? Not necessarily what actually happened.[3] I shall not embark on such a difficult quest here, but rather focus on the role of rituals, especially "bad rituals," in written narratives. Such a focus, I argue, can lead us to tangible realities in ninth-century political culture.

If we take ninth-century texts as good indicators of events, rituals were omnipresent. According to Robert Bartlett, in the ninth century the Carolingians generalized ordeals by fire and water.[4] The coronation received its first surviving codification in ordines.[5] In what seems to have been a première for the dynasty, Charles the Bald (d. 877) personally transferred relics, carrying them on his shoulders in Soissons (841) and Auxerre (859) – deeds that parallel a similar gesture of piety attributed to Theodosius I in the *Life of Ambrose* rewritten in that period.[6] Kings tearfully worshipped before saints' shrines – thus Odo in 895 "went to Saint Vaast's body and, prostrating himself on the soil before the saint's tomb, prayed most devotedly and cried most abundantly" before hearing a mass of thanksgiving to God.[7] They also adopted the monastic and clerical practice of personally washing the feet of chosen poor on Maundy Thursday – as attested by a diploma for the abbey of Saint-Denis drawn up for Charles the Bald in 851.[8] We meet in Andrew of Bergamo's short history the first

---

3 See the discussion in Timothy Reuter, "Pre-Gregorian Mentalities," *Journal of Ecclesiastical History* 45, no. 3 (1994): 470–4.

4 Robert Bartlett, *Trial by Fire and Water: The Medieval Judicial Ordeal* (Oxford, 1986), 9–12.

5 Richard A. Jackson, "Who Wrote Hincmar's Ordines?" *Viator: Medieval and Renaissance Studies* 25 (1994): 31–52, and Richard A. Jackson, ed., *Ordines coronationis Franciae I: Texts and Ordines for the Coronation of Frankish and French Kings and Queens in the Middle Ages* (Philadelphia, 1995).

6 For Charles at Saint-Médard de Soissons (right after the Battle of Fontenoy) who *beatorum corpora propriis humeribus cum omni veneratione transtulit,* see Nithard, *Historia 3.2,* ed. Philippe Lauer (Paris, 1926), 86–8n4; for Charles in Auxerre, see Heiric of Auxerre, *Miracula sancti Germani* 2.2.99–102, ed. L.-M. Duru, *Bibliothèque historique de l'Yonne,* 2 vols. (Auxerre-Paris, 1850–64), 2:167–8, or Patrologia Latina 124, 1254–5c.; for Theodosius, see *Vita Ambrosii* (BHL 377d), ed. Pierre Courcelle, *Recherches sur saint Ambroise: Vies anciennes, culture, iconographie* (Paris, 1973), 83; cf. Angelo Paredi, *Vita e Meriti di S. Ambrogio: Testo inedito del secolo nono illustrato con le minaiure del Salterio di Arnolfo,* Fontes Ambrosiani 37 (Milan, 1964), 11, who dates (on the strength of Bernard Bishoff's expertise) the ms St Gall Stiftbibliothek 569 to 860/880 and attributes it to a Milanese scriptorium and situates the text in the context of contemporary north-Italian ecclesiastical politics.

7 *Annales Vedastini* ad an. 895, ed. B. de Simpson, 76–7. See already the *Chronicle of Moissac* ad an. 800, ed. Georg Pertz, *Monumenta Germaniae Historica, Scriptores* (hereafter *MGH SS*) 1 (Hannover, 1826), 304:22–5, and the *Annales Laureshamenses* ad an. 800, *MGH SS* 1, 38.

8 D.Ch. II. 135 (Jan. 16, 851), ed. Georges Tessier, *Recueil des actes de Charles le Chauve,* 3 vols. (Paris, 1943), 1.357–9, here 358:13–27.

substantially developed account of a royal funeral since late Roman times, that of Emperor Louis II in 875. Like saints' translations, it involved rotating escorts of clergy (the ecclesiastical cortège changed whenever the procession crossed into a new diocese), psalm-singing, and tears. Just as Charles the Bald had taken pride in carrying on his own shoulders the saints worshipped at Saint-Médard de Soissons and Saint-Germain d'Auxerre, Andrew gloried in having been able to transport the emperor's body.[9]

Some of these rituals involving royalty (such as physical participation in transfers of relics or tearful prayers before the saints) look like full-fledged novelties in the Western half of the Christian world. However, one should not discount that here as in other domains the Carolingians managed to erase the achievements of their predecessors and rivals, the Merovingians, and the Lombards.[10] In surviving southern Italian hagiography, that is, outside the sphere of Frankish control, the Lombard prince of Salerno, Arechis, festively met processions that brought saints' relics into his city. On one occasion, dated to 760, the *princeps* (prince) may have carried in his arms the holy remnants; on another, dated to 768, he publicly and tearfully beseeched the relics while prostrate on the ground and having laid aside his princely *ornatus* (ornaments) for a hair shirt.[11] Hence, while competition may have fostered the development of a repertoire of rituals and the recording of individual occurrences, we should suspect that it could as well lead to the obfuscation of the enemy's own performances.

Thus envisaged, these public ceremonials were key elements in the political struggles of the ninth century – but not only through their smooth, hieratic, and consensual performance. Indeed, the existence of rituals opened up a possibility for the manipulation of rituals. In other words, if, as Gerd Althoff has argued, there existed "rules of the game" for political communications, actors in that game could seek strategically

9 Andreas of Bergamo, *Historia* 18, ed. Georg Waitz, in *MGH SS, Rerum Langobardicarum* (Hannover, 1878), 220–30 at 229:24–36. For royal funerary rituals of late antiquity and the Middle Ages, see Sabina MacCormack, *Art and Ceremony in Late Antiquity* (Berkeley, Calif., 1981), and vol. 31 of *Médiévales* (1996), which is devoted to "La mort des grands."

10 See the recent discussions in Felice Lifshitz, *The Norman Conquest of Pious Neustria: Historiographic Discourse and Saintly Relics 684–1090*, Studies and Texts, no. 122 (Toronto, 1995), 11–12; and Yitzak Hen, *Culture and Religion in Merovingian Gaul, A.D. 481–751* (Leiden, 1995), 197–205.

11 *Translatio duodecim martyrum* (BHL 2300) vv. 46–66, in Waitz, ed., *MGH SS, Rerum Langobardicarum*, 575:14–34: "Many, to be allowed to carry on their arms the fatherland's patrons / give their patrimony and promise all their future goods / through documents inscribed with [the names of] witnesses, as is customary in law. / Prince Arechis, desirous to surpass others' gifts, / as was right, bestows the city through written briefs, and gives villages, domains and estates in all the regions subjected to him"; *Translatio sancti Mercurii* (BHL 5938) vv. 92–102, in ibid., 580:17–27.

to twist them to their advantage.[12] Furthermore, performed to enhance
the symbolic capital of one group, rituals became targets for that group's
opponents. No wonder then that Carolingian sources depict smooth-
running rituals as often as disrupted or stage-managed rituals – "bad
rituals" in this chapter's shorthand.[13]

Like Roman civic rituals in late antiquity, medieval rituals provided
targets for the hostile pen as much as, if not more than, for hostile
actions.[14] The most basic form of hostility is (as stated previously) erasure.
But when depicted, rituals seldom are free of partisan coloring. Even if
one were to accept Althoff's insight that actual rituals served "communication" among the elite and thus functioned to reinforce the established
order, the written sources in which historians find rituals often can aim
at the obfuscation of the ritual act's original meaning and serve polemics
more than consensus.[15] A few examples of the polemical depiction of
rituals should suffice. Ordeals: Out of favor and accused of horrendous
sexual sins, King Lothar II's unfortunate queen, Theutberga, sent a representative to trial by water. He emerged victorious, and the king's
partisans sought ways to invalidate the outcome of the judgment. It
was, they argued, a *falsum iudicium* (falsified trial) as opposed to a *verifica
examinatio* (truth-telling ordeal).[16] Coronations: The same Lothar publicly
married and crowned his beloved Waldrada in 862. A nuptial blessing
(*benedictio*) became under Pope Nicholas I's irate pen a malediction
(*maledictio*).[17] Another opponent, Archbishop Hincmar of Reims, attacked
this coronation-wedding by recounting it in the same breath as another

---

12 See Gerd Althoff's chapter in this book, as well as his *Spielregeln der Politik im Mittelalter:
Kommunikation in Frieden und Fehde* (Darmstadt, 1997), with the criticisms in Leyser, "Ritual,
Ceremony," 213n130. Stephen White has developed a praxeological approach for a specific
ritual in his "Proposing the Ordeal and Avoiding It: Strategy and Power in Western French
Litigation, 1050–1110," in Thomas N. Bisson, ed., *Cultures of Power* (Philadelphia, 1995), 89–
123.

13 As Althoff, *Spielregeln*, 13, recognizes, mentioning "die Fälle . . . in denen Akte der Repräsentation
bewusst gestört wurden."

14 See Philippe Buc, "Martyre et ritualité dans l'Antiquité Tardive. Horizons de l'écriture médiévale
des rituels," *Annales* 48, no. 1 (1997): 63–92.

15 Althoff, *Spielregeln*, 2, 11–13.

16 Hincmar, *De divortio Lotharii interrogatio-responsio* 1, ed. Lehta Böhringer, in *MGH Concilia* 4, suppl.
1 (Berlin, 1992), 122:2, 123:28. See Karl Heidecker, *Kerk, huwelijk en politieke macht: de zaak Lothar-
ius II, 855–869* (Amsterdam, 1997), with German summary.

17 Nicolas I, *Ep.* 57, ed. Ernst Perels, in *Epistolae Kar. Aevi* 4.2.1 (*Monumenta Germaniae Historica,
Epistolae* 6.2.1 [Berlin, 1912]), 361:26–7. According to Cyrille Vogel, "Les rites de la célébration
du mariage: leur signification dans la formation du lien durant le Haut Moyen Age," *Il matrimo-
nio nella società altomedievale*, Centro italiano di studi sull'alto medioevo, Settimane 24, 2 vols.
(Spoleto, 1977), 1:431, the first ordo drawn specifically for a marriage is owed to Hincmar and
was composed for a queen, that is, *Judith's Ordo* of 856, published in Jackson, ed., *Ordines coronationis Franciae*, 73–9, interestingly called *Benedictio super reginam.*

consecration to which it stood as a polar opposite, that of Reims's *mater ecclesia.*[18] Funerals: The same Hincmar, having turned against his king's policies, joined the East-Frankish Fulda annalist in ridiculing Charles the Bald's 877 death train. Hincmar insisted on the body's stench and clumsy embalming.[19] We see here a pattern of invalidation of opponents' ritual through writing – one of the standard tools of Carolingian historiography since its inception. The best-known example of this Carolingian tactic may be the way in which the *Annales Laurissenses minores*, Einhardt, and others, disqualified the Merovingian kings by representing them as the puppets of the mayors of the palace in royal ritual.[20]

Texts invalidate rituals; rituals (or so it might seem at first glance) also invalidate texts. Historians of early medieval culture have long known that rituals can serve to validate writings. Putting a libel (*libellus*) on an altar constitutes a ritual, or part of a ritual;[21] conversely, the rituals that accompany this gesture confirm the text thus entrusted to the sacred.[22] Louis the Pious's multiple prostrations at Compiègne in 833 were both constitutive

---

18 *Annales Bertiniani* (hereafter *AB*) ad an. 862, ed. Félix Grat, Jeanne Vielliard, and Suzanne Clémencet (Paris, 1964), 93–4: "Hlotharius Waldradam concubinam, maleficis, ut ferebatur, artibus dementatus et ipsius pellicis pro qua uxorem suam Theotbergam abiecerat caeco amore inlectus, faventibus sibi Liutfrido, avunculo suo, et Vualtario, qui vel ob hoc maxime illi erant familiares, et, quod nefas est dictu, quibusdam etiam regni sui episcopis consentientibus, coronat et quasi in coniugem et reginam sibi, amicis dolentibus atque contradicentibus, copulat. Hincmarus Remorum episcopus, veniente Karolo rege in eandem civitatem, accitis conprovincialibus suis episcopis, matrem ecclesiam ipsius provinciae in honore sanctae Mariae sicut et antiqua fuerat sacrata, xv kalendas octobris [Sept. 17] venerabiliter dedicat." Hincmar's constancy in naming his supernatural spouse provides yet another contrast with Lothar's polygamy. For the intimate conceptual relationship between church, Mary, the archiepiscopal office, and the liturgical impression of "forms" of office, see Karl F. Morrison, " 'Unum ex Multis': Hincmar of Rheims' medical and aesthetic rationales for unification," *Nascità dell'Europa ed Europa Carolingia: un'equazione da verificare*, Centro Italiano di studi sull'alto medioevo, Settimane 27 (Spoleto, 1981), reprinted in his *Holiness and Politics in Early Medieval Thought* (London, 1985), 592, 596, 609.
19 *Annales Fuldenses* (hereafter *AF*) ad an. 877, ed. Friedrich Kurze, *Monumenta Germaniae Historica, Scriptores rerum Germanicarum in usum scholarum* 7 (Hannover, 1895), 90; Hincmar, *AB* ad an. 877, ed. Grat, Vielliard, and Clémencet, 216–17. See now Janet L. Nelson, "La mort de Charles le Chauve," *Médiévales* 31 (1996): 61–5, with whom I discussed these texts at a seminar at King's College, London, in Marcy 1995. I use these "bad funeral" narratives for a critique of functionalist interpretations in *Dangers of Ritual*.
20 *Dangers of Ritual*, chap. 3, analyzing on Einhardt, *Vita Karoli* 1, ed. Louis Halphen (Paris, 1923), 8–10, and on *Annales Laurissenses minores* ad an. 753 [750], *MGH SS* 1, 116:7–21.
21 The acts of the synod of Troyes of 878, in Johannes Dominicus Mansi, ed., *Sacrorum conciliorum amplissima collectio* 17 (Venice, 1772), 345–7, provide a good contemporary example of a series of different complaints laid down in individual *libelli*. See notes 29–30 to this chapter.
22 Cf. the *Liber pontificalis, Vita Hadrianis* I 41–42, ed. Louis Duchesne (hereafter *LP*), 3 vols. (Paris, 1955), 1:498:22–29, where writing and ritual actions blend inside Saint Peter's basilica in a narrative depicting and hallowing Charlemagne's 774 territorial donation. See also Geoffrey Koziol, *Begging Pardon and Favor: Ritual and Political Order in Early Medieval France* (Ithaca, N.Y., 1992), 68–70, 90. For the later period, see Michael Clanchy, *From Memory to Written Record: England, 1066–1307*, 2d ed. (Oxford, 1993), 254–60.

elements in his deposition and a visual subscription of his written confession.[23] One sees this as well with Queen Theutberga: Coerced admissions on vellum and imposed ritual forms lent one another authoritative force and commemorative power.[24] Hence, it should not be surprising that rituals can invalidate writings and vice-versa. A rich plurality of sources focusing on the events of 863–864 will provide us with a case in point.

The story's outline is well known: Archbishops Gunthar and Theutgaud had been active in helping their king, Lothar II, secure his wife Theutberga's untrue confession of incest and in proclaiming the divorce the king sought. All of this had taken place in four successive Lotharingian councils between 860 and 863. Having brought to Rome the latest conciliar decisions, which pope Nicholas I (r. 858–867) opposed, they were deposed in 863 during a synod presided over by the pope. Their deposition motivated Emperor Louis II in 864 to lead an expedition to Rome to seek redress.

Two accounts preserved with slight variations in both the *Annals of Fulda* and the *Annals of Saint Bertin* are critical to this story. They are in effect two rival interpretations of archbishops Gunthar and Theutgaud's depositions at the October 863 Roman Synod: One is the papal version of the synodal acts, the other the Lotharingian bishops' letter of protest, which also recounts the synod. One stratum of the *Annals of Fulda* ends in 865, before Lothar II's burial in Piacenza (869) closed the dispute in his enemies' favor. Consequently, this rendering of the events of 863–864 is less likely to have been contaminated by the knowledge of Lothar's ultimate failure. This redaction lays immediately side by side the two versions, whereas the parallel source, Hincmar's *Annals of Saint Bertin*, establishes a much clearer hierarchy by placing the two documents under two different years, 863 and 864.[25] The Fulda author does hint at a preference for the papal synodal acts over the bishops' version: He speaks of Nicholas I's *scripta* (epistle) but also of

---

23 See Mayke de Jong, "Power and Humility in Carolingian Society: The Public Penance of Louis the Pious," *Early Medieval Europe* 1, no. 1 (1992): 29–52, and Mayke de Jong, "What Was Public About Carolingian Public Penance?" *La giustizia nell'alto medioevo (secoli IX–XI)*, Centro italiano di studi sull'alto medioevo, Settimane 44, 2 vols. (Spoleto, 1997), 2:863–904.

24 Hincmar, *De divortio Lotharii*, 121:9–13. Hincmar discusses in *De divortio* 1–2 the relationship in general between legal forms and ritual forms as well as the validity of *libelli*.

25 *AF* ad an. 863, 57–8: "iuste quidem et canonice, ut scriptis suis ipse [papa] testatur; iniuste vero, sicut illi rescriptis et assertionibus firmare conantur." Horst Fuhrmann, "Eine im Original erhaltene Propagandaschrift des Erzbischofs Gunthar von Köln (865)," *Archiv für Diplomatik* 4 (1958): 51, gives a sense of the means by which such texts were diffused. On the *AF*, see Heinz Löwe, "Geschichtsschreibung der ausgehenden Karolingerzeit," *Deutsches Archiv für Erforschung des Mittelalters* 23 (1967): 1–30, reprinted in Heinz Löwe, *Von Cassiodor zu Dante: Ausgewählte Aufsätze zur Geschichtsschreibung und politischen Ideenwelt des Mittelalters* (Berlin, 1973), 183–8.

Theutgaud and Gunthar's *rescripta* (reply letter) and *assertiones* (declarations). But he still explicitly lets the reader compare and choose.

Both the papal and episcopal versions polemicized in terms of the perceived understanding of what was a "good council." As defined in early medieval formularies (*ordines de celebrando concilii*), a good council presupposed the Holy Spirit's presence, which was made ritually manifest by smooth ceremonial and unanimous consensus.[26] No wonder then that the Roman synod's minutes present Nicholas as the mediator or representative of "the Holy Spirit's judgment and Saint Peter's authority." They assimilate the Metz synod of 863, which, with the approval of corrupt papal legates, had recognized the earlier Lotharingian conciliar decisions, into the classic pseudocouncil, the "robbery of Ephesus." They condemn any bishops who might join Gunthar and Theutgaud in forming "a sedition, conjurations, or conspiracies."

The episcopal *libellus* answers the synodal acts within the terms of the same political culture. Nicholas, not the agentless consensus of all, had stage-managed the council. Could it be called a council at all? The pope had kept Gunthar and Theutgaud waiting for three weeks before summoning them without any hint of hostility. The doors had then been shut and blocked behind the unsuspecting pair, and a mixed crowd of clerics and laymen surrounded them. "In the manner of a conspiracy of bandits" (*more latrocinali conspiratione*): Inspired by a spirit of banditry rather than by the Holy Spirit, the assembly was not a council but a mob (*turba*).[27] The bishops had been separated from their servants and entourage, and the proceedings lacked all the features necessary to legal rites: There were no canonical examinations, not a single accuser or witness, no judicial debate or use of authoritative texts, nor a confession of the accused. This demonstrated the Holy Spirit's absence. Nicholas had acted tyrannically, "outside the consent of all." In other words, the unanimity constitutive of early medieval "good ritual" was wholly lacking. The pope had claimed that the Spirit spoke through him; the bishops accused him of having been possessed instead by fury.[28]

---

26 Cf. *Die Konzilsordines des Früh- und Hochmittelalters*, ed. Herbert Schneider, in *Monumenta Germaniae Historica, Ordines de celebrando concilio* (Hannover, 1996), 176–86. For "good conciliar ritual," see Roger Reynolds, "Rites and Signs of Conciliar Decision in the Early Middle Ages," *Segni e riti nella chiesa altomedievale occidentale*, Centro Italiano di studi sull'alto medioevo, Settimane 33 (Spoleto, 1987), 1:207–78.

27 *AF* ad an. 863, 61; cf. *AB* ad an. 863 and 864, ed. Grat, Vielliard, and Clémencet, 99–103, 107–10.

28 The pope's words (*AF* ad an. 863, 59, cf. *AB*, 100, 102): "cum Ephesino latrocinio . . . in perpetuum damnandam nec vocari sinodum" . . . and . . . "si cum his coniuncti seditionem, coniurationes vel conspirationes fecerint . . ." seem to be countered by the bishops' . . . "facta more latrocinali conspiratione" (*AF*, 61; cf. *AB* 864, 109). Similarly, the papal "spiritus sancti iudicio et

Nicholas had turned the Lotharingian synods into conspiracies. The bishops' retort invoked the same themes previously discussed. They attempted to invalidate their trial by presenting it as canonically incorrect and by painting it as a disorderly and improper ritual. The structure of Hincmar's narrative, however, sought to invalidate their written protest. His *Annals of Saint Bertin* color Gunthar and Theutgaud's letter of protest by sandwiching it between two episodes, each involving a "bad ritual."

According to the *Annals of Saint Bertin*, Gunthar's response to his deposition was not limited to the redaction of a protest. Emperor Louis II (Lothar's brother) had transmitted the two bishops to the 863 Roman synod under his safekeeping (*fiducia*); Gunthar convinced Louis that in stripping them of their dignity, the pope had insulted him. The emperor flared into anger and resolved to force Nicholas to recant his decision. In 864 Louis entered Rome. Once there, his warriors encountered a penitential procession on Saint Peter's steps. It was a ritual of opposition insofar as it bemoaned the emperor's lack of respect for papal authority. The troops dispersed it by force, breaking crosses and banners, and killed a man in the process. God's vengeance struck: Louis fell ill and was forced to accept the papal verdict.

The second episode directly concerns the episcopal complaint. Gunthar had entrusted his brother Hilduin with a mission, to place the episcopal *libellus* on Peter's grave should Nicholas not accept it:

Hilduin, in armor and with Gunthar's men, entered without any reverence Saint Peter's church and sought to throw that diabolical writ . . . on Saint Peter's body. The guardians prevented him from doing so, and both he and his accomplices began to strike these same guardians with blows, to the point that one of them was killed. Then Hilduin threw that writ on Saint Peter's body, and he and those who had come with him, protecting themselves with drawn swords, exited the church.[29]

The audience of the Annals is supposed to understand that Gunthar sought to ritually appeal the pope's judgment to the Apostle's or to validate his

beati Petri per nos auctoritate" (cf. *AB* 863, 101) is inverted into (cf. *AB* 864, 109) "nullaque . . . auctoritatum probatione . . . extra omnium omnino consensum tuo solius arbitrio et tyrannico furore" (let us recall that both Holy Spirit and furor possess their vessel).

29 *AB* 864, ed. Grat, Vielliard, and Clémencet, 111. Cf. also Nicolas I, *Ep.* 53, to Louis the German's bishops, dated from much after the fact, i.e., 31 x 867, ed. Ernst Perels, *Epistolae Kar. Aevi* 4.2.1 (*Monumenta Germaniae Historica, Epistolae* 6.2.1 [Berlin, 1912]), 340–51, recounts all of Theutgaud and Gunthar's evil deeds, including "qualiter nos tyrannice penes sanctum Petrum positos afflixerint, oppresserint et quibus potuerint malis fatigaverint, adeo ut homines eorum adita sancti Petri violaverint et in ecclesia ipsius sanguinem fuderint. Qualiter etiam ibidem nobis matitunales hymnos celebrantibus illi noctu post tribunal ecclesiae ipsius cum complicibus et fautoribus suis contra Calcedonense concilium coniuraverint" (346:3–11). The *LP* does not document this crisis, which may mean that Nicholas in fact lost.

letter to the bishops with Peter's approval.[30] Hincmar (or his source) invalidated his move – and therefore the Lotharingian *libellus* – by turning the archbishop's ritual of protest into a bloody desecration of Peter's shrine.

Thus, Hincmar framed the archbishops' written protest between two stories, one suggesting disrespect for liturgy, the other an attempt to coerce Saint Peter. Narratives involving ritual and violence envelop and counter (or so Hincmar hoped) a narrative that also itself claimed that liturgical forms had been manipulated.

However, it was not so much bad rituals as *texts* about bad rituals that invalidated the archbishops' written protest. The bad rituals themselves may never have happened. For if the attack on the procession seems at first sight confirmed by two other sources, the specifics of this apparent convergence make it impossible to recover what actually transpired in Rome in 864. What can be salvaged is why Hincmar and others crafted their stories as they did and why they chose to configure them as they did. Let us look again at the *Annals of Saint Bertin* for 864, this time in detail, before moving to the parallel accounts: Rumor had reached Rome that the emperor intended to force, violently if necessary, the Lotharingian archbishops' reinstatement.

Hearing this, the pope imposed on himself and on the Romans a general fast with litanies, so that God through the apostles' intercession might give the aforesaid emperor good intentions and reverence toward the divine cult and the apostolic see's authority.[31] But as the emperor had reached Rome and was taking lodging near Saint Peter's basilica,[32] the Roman clergy and people, celebrating the fast with crosses and litanies, went to blessed Peter's memoria. When they began to ascend the steps before Saint Peter's basilica, the emperor's men threw them flat to the ground and beat them with many blows. Their crosses and banners broken, those who could escape took flight.[33]

---

30 Pope Stephen III first "consecrated" a protest letter before sending it to Charlemagne (770–1), *Codex Carolinus* 45, ed. Wilhelm Gundlach, *Monumenta Germaniae Historica, Epistolae*, 563:33–5. See as well the late tenth-century protest Aymo bishop of Valence deposed on Saint Stephen's altar in Arles, Jules Marion, ed., *Cartulaires de l'église cathédrale de Grenoble, dits cartulaires de Saint-Hugues* (Paris, 1869), 59–61.

31 See Hincmar's own *Libellus expostulationis* 28, ed. Wilfried Hartmann, *Die Konzilien der karolingischen Teilreiche 860–874* (*Monumenta Germaniae Historica, Concilia* 4 [Hannover, 1998]), 467:24–7, for what he himself thought such litanies involved: "Audivimus namque, quia sanctae memoriae Nicolaus papa, sancta romana ecclesia in afflictione posita, . . . in ieiunio et fletu ac planctu, in cinere et cilicio laetanias indixerit."

32 The place is identified as an old Carolingian palace by Carlrichard Brühl, "Die Kaiserpfalz bei St. Peter und die Pfalz Ottos III. auf dem Palatin," reworked in Carlrichard Brühl, *Aus Mittelalter und Diplomatik: Gesammelte Aufsätze*, 2 vols. (Berlin, 1989), 2:3–31, at 2:7, citing the *Libellus de imperatoria potestate*, in Giuseppe Zucchetti, ed., *Il Chronicon di Benedetto monaco di S. Andrea del Soratee e il Libellus de imperatoria potestate in urbe Roma*, Fonti per la storia d'Italia 55 (Rome, 1920), 204:1.

33 *AB* ad an. 864, ed. Grat, Vielliard, and Clémencet, 106. As Herbert Zielinski remarks, the account is highly crafted – Böhmer-Zielinski, *Regesta Imperii* 1.3.1: *Die Karolinger im Regnum Italiae 840–887(888)* (Cologne, 1991), Louis II, no. 215, 91.

In the affray, a man in Louis's service broke the wondrous cross Empress Helena had given the Apostle and threw it in the mud. Nicholas locked himself in Saint Peter's basilica and fasted for two days, triggering God's vengeance: The cross-breaker died, and the emperor fell ill with fevers. Louis then sought an understanding with the pope: It was agreed that the two deposed bishops would return to Francia without being restored to their rank.

According to Hincmar, the affray takes place on the steps of Saint Peter's. However, in a Beneventine source, Erchempert's *History of the Lombards*, written at some distance from Rome and 864, it is Louis II's reception in Rome (and not a chance encounter with a penitential procession) that provides the setting for violence: "According to the age-old custom, a sacerdotal procession dressed in pure white came to encounter him (*obvium ei*), but he, spurning the fear of God, had the clergy beaten with sticks and the crosses and all the consecrated mysteries trampled underfoot."[34]

Matters reach a yet higher degree of complexity when still another text is considered. While using the same structural elements as Hincmar and Erchempert, the late ninth-century *Libellus de imperatoria potestate in urbe Roma* (Booklet concerning imperial rights in the city of Rome) casts the event in a totally different light.[35] Is it actually the same event? The affray occurs somewhere on the road between Saint Paul and the imperial palace near Saint Peter's. The archbishop who causes trouble is not Gunthar of Cologne, who is entirely absent from this narrative. Instead, the conflict between the royal and papal offices is triggered by Nicholas's jealousy of the influence John, the archbishop of Ravenna, enjoys with the emperor, and by Nicholas's attempts to unjustly depose this favorite imperial councilor.[36] Louis hardens his power over Rome and journeys

---

34 Erchempert, *Historia Langobardorum Beneventanorum* 37, ed. Georg Waitz, *MGH SS, Rerum Lango-*
    bardicarum, 231–64, at 248:33–40: "Cur autem iam dicto augusto supradictum opprobrium domino
    permittente Beneventani inferre quiverint, de multis duo inferam: primum quia veniens quodam
    tempore Romam, ut duos episcopos condempnatos ad pristinam reduceret dignitatem, et dum
    nollet ei consentiret [sic] Nicolaus papa, vir deo plenus, secundum antiquum morem obvium ei
    venit candidatum sacerdotalem agmen; at ille, spreto timore dei, fustibus clerum caedi fecit, cruces
    vero omniaque sacrata ministeria pedibus calcari, Romamque pene miliari spatio depredatus est
    vicariumque beati Petri quasi vile mancipium ab officio suo ministerii, nisi dominus restitisset,
    privare voluit."
35 For various hypotheses on the *Libellus's* date of composition, see Wilhelm Wattenbach, *Deutsch-*
    lands Geschichtsquellen im Mittelalter: Vorzeit und Karolinger: Die Karolinger vom Vertrag von Verdun bis
    zum Herrschaftsantritt der Herrscher aus dem sächsischen Hause: Italien und das Papsttum, ed. Heinz
    Löwe (Weimar, 1963), 425–6 (according to Löwe from the tenth century's first decade).
36 The *Vita Nicolai* 50, LP, ed. Duchesne, 2:160–1, does not in the least allude to any version of the
    864 events but lumps together Gunthar, Theutgaud, and John as plotters against the pope.

to the city with the archbishop. There, the citizens, great and small, organize an honorific entry. Upset, the pope reacts:

As all his [Nicholas's] ambushes against the royal dignity were held for nothing, he ordered monks and virgins consecrated to God from Rome's monasteries to celebrate, as if under the pretext of religion, daily litanies that ambulated around the walls [*per circuitum murorum*], and to sing masses against princes who behave evilly.[37]

Needless to say, this striking recuperation of a liturgy of supplication normally used against pagans could hardly please the warriors in Louis's entourage:

When they heard this, the king's magnates humbly approached the pope and asked him in a friendly manner to forbid such things. But since they were unable to obtain anything from him, they went back, mournful. But one day, as some warriors of the said prince had gone to Saint Paul and were coming back, it happened that they encountered these litanies. Impelled by the Ancient Enemy, the warriors lapsed into fury, and, because they were faithful to their lord, took vengeance against these people [i.e., the monks and the consecrated virgins], striking them and beating them with the sticks they carried in their hands. The others fled and threw away the crosses and the icons they carried . . . and many were broken.[38]

The aftermath, according to the *Libellus de imperatoria potestate*, mirrors in negative the events reported in the *Annals of Saint Bertin*. The emperor is moved to anger and the pope to meekness. Nicholas has to go to Louis and beg pardon for his partisans. The salient structural parallels and oppositions between these texts can be summarized as follows:

Hincmar:	. . . . . .	procession attacked
Erchempert:	*occursus* attacked	. . . .
Libellus:	*occursus*	procession attacked

37 See Michael McCormick, "Liturgie et guerre des Carolingiens à la première croisade," *'Militia Christi' e Crociata nei secoli XI–XIII*, Miscellanea del Centro di studi medioevali no. 13 (Milan, 1992), 220–33. *Laetaniae* ranged from procession or station to any supplicatory ritual; see Walahfrid Strabo, *De exordiis et incrementis rerum ecclesiasticarum* 29, *Monumenta Germaniae Historica, Capitularia* 2.2 (Hannover, 1893), 514:4–6: "Notandum autem laetanias non tantum dici illam recitationem nominum, qua sancti in adiutorium vocantur infirmitatis humanae, sed etiam cuncta quae supplicationibus [var.: in supplicationibus] fiunt orationes [var.: rogationes]." Cf. Dom F. Cabrol, "Litanies," *Dictionnaire d'Archéologie Chrétienne et de Liturgie*, ed. Fernand Cabrol, 15 vols. (Paris, 1907–53), 9:2, 1540–7. The closest parallel in the Roman tradition is *Vita Stephani* II 10–11, LP, ed. Duchesne, 1.442:17–443:8, where the pope, whom King Aistulf besieged in Rome, organized elaborate processional litanies against his opponent.
38 *Libellus*, 204:1–15.

So what, if anything, really happened? The texts offer three alternative versions. One might be tempted to search for the actual event behind these texts, which would mean creating yet another alternative narrative.[39] Had Louis been greeted by a respectful and conventional (*secundum antiquum morem*) processional reception (*occursus*) that he had then furiously assailed (Erchempert)? Had the emperor chanced upon a penitential liturgy which, bemoaning publicly his hostile intentions, triggered his men's violence (Hincmar)? Or was the aggressive atmosphere at least as much due to the pope as to the Carolingian, insofar as Nicholas had intended from the beginning to confront the emperor liturgically (the *Libellus*)? Did a relatively orderly advent into Rome lead to a few scuffles that the Carolingian's enemies later blew out of proportion (the truth behind Erchempert)? Did Nicholas try to counterbalance a positive *adventus* with his monastic processions (the truth behind the *Libellus*)? Or did Nicholas stage on purpose a quasi-clamor within the imperial lodging's immediate surroundings, which he knew would provoke Louis's faithful (the truth behind a synthesis of Hincmar and the *Libellus*)? Or did he orchestrate a highly ambiguous *occursus* that served both to honor the imperial office and to criticize this specific emperor's policy (one of the truths arrived at through a conflation of the three texts)?

Rather than attempt to reconstruct the events of 864, one should concentrate on why the three authors crafted their accounts as they did. To do so, one should focus on Roman topography and the ceremonial forms traditionally attached to Roman places. The locus of the affray, Saint Peter's steps, happened to be the all-important final station in a monarch's entry into Rome. The steps had played this role in the seminal year 800 for Charlemagne's *adventus*, providing a precedent for later Carolingian rulers. According to the Regensburg continuation of the *Annals of Fulda*, in the year 896, a victorious Arnulf was honorably received (*susceptus*) at the Milvian Bridge "by the whole Roman senate as well as the Greek scholae with banners and crosses," then received in turn by the pope "in the place called Saint Peter's steps" before being crowned and named Augustus (896).[40] Conversely, if we trust Hincmar's quill, Pope Hadrian

---

39 See, e.g., Robert Parisot's collage in *Le royaume de Lorraine sous les Carolingiens* (Paris, 1898; reprint, Geneva, 1975), 241–2, 245. It in the main follows the *Libellus* up to the immediate aftermath of the affray, then adopts the *AB*'s narrative line and posits a change of attitude once the imperial side learns that Helena's cross has been broken.

40 The *AF, Continuatio Ratisponensis* ad an. 896, ed. Friedrich Kurze, *Annales Fuldenses*, 128, note that Saint Peter's steps constitute "a place." According to the *Vita Leonis III* 19, LP, ed. Duchesne, 2:6:17–24, Leo III was also received at the Milvian Bridge when he returned – triumphantly with Charlemagne's backing – to Rome.

II signaled his disapproval of Lothar II by not granting him a festive reception when he reached Saint Peter's (869).[41] It is not accidental, then, that Hincmar and the *Libellus* situated the confrontation at Saint Peter's steps or in its neighborhood, the expected and highly meaningful point of arrival for the imperial advent.

All three texts contain at least one processional ritual (either an *occursus* or litanies or both) that ninth-century political culture utilized to convey friendship. All three texts share the knowledge or the assumption that such a ceremonial event took place. Whether it occurred or not is unclear, but it was *expected* to occur. A procession provided medieval political culture with a recognizable way to gauge the relationship between two parties, qualitatively (by detailing the nature of the train and its trappings) and quantitatively (by evaluating the length an *occursus* traveled to meet its recipient). The past – in texts and memory – had supplied various models that themselves could become the basis of meaningful variation. The ambient political culture's assumptions and commonplaces concerning what could and should happen can be recovered from the ninth-century sources. This, more than what actually happened (*was eigentlich gewesen ist*), constitutes the harvest of an examination of Carolingian rituals. These expectations shaped the horizons of the three authors who spoke about Louis II and Nicholas I. For these assumptions, Charlemagne's reception in 800 loomed large, at least in Frankish memory: an *occursus* twelve miles from Rome led by the pope in person, a meal on that spot, and on the next day, as Leo waited on Saint Peter's steps, another *occursus*, which involved the sending of the city's banners to meet the king and the stationing of groups of citizens and foreigners on the way.[42]

In text and probably in action, processions were instruments to measure the respective power of two parties in a political relationship.[43] No wonder

---

41 *AB* ad an. 869, ed. Grat, Vielliard, and Clémencet, 155: "Ubi nullum clericum obvium habuit, sed tantum ipse usque ad sepulchrum sancti Petri cum suis pervenit, indeque solarium secus ecclesiam beati Petri mansionem habiturus intravit, quem nec etiam scopa mundatum invenit."

42 *Annales regni Francorum* ad an. 800, ed. Friedrich Kurze, in *Monumenta Germaniae Historica, Scriptores in usum scholarum* 6 (Hannover, 1895), 110–12. See also Otto II's during Christmas week 967, *Continuatio Reginonis*, ed. Friedrich Kurze, in *Reginonis abbatis Prumiensis Chronicon cum continuatione Treverensi*, in *Monumenta Germaniae Historica, Scriptores rerum Germanicarum in usum scholarum* 47 (Hannover, 1890), 179. Papal sources document other variants, which I cannot detail here, but, e.g., see the *LP*, 1.429:18–430:5, reception of Zachary (741–52), for which the exarch of Ravenna travels fifty miles. See also Josef Déer, "Die Vorrechte des Kaisers in Rom (772–800)," *Schweizer Beiträge zur Allgemeinen Geschichte* 15 (1957): 42–5, drawing on the *LP*, 1.378 n.15, 1.343, 1.372, 1.496–7.

43 See the remarks on processions and order in Bernhard Jussen, "Über 'Bischofsherrschaften' und die Prozeduren politisch-sozialer Umordnung in Gallien zwischen 'Antike' und 'Mittelalter,'" *Historische Zeitschrift* 260 (1995): 673–718.

then that, to the puzzlement of later historians, two sources recounting what seems to be the same event can diverge radically, as in the case of the meeting at the palace of Ponthion (754) between Pippin II and Stephen II (752–757). In the *Liber pontificalis*, Pippin sent his son Charles, with some magnates, to meet the pope one hundred miles outside the palace, then went himself with his wife, other children, and magnates, three miles out of the palace, descended from his horse, prostrated himself before the pope, and served as his groom for part of the way. In the *Chronicle of Aniane*, Pippin did not participate in the *occursus* and did not act as groom. Rather, it was the pope who prostrated himself on the meeting's second day, "together with his clergy, clad in sack-cloth, and covered with ashes" (*una cum clero suo aspersus cinere et indutus cilicio in terra prostratus*), to beg for help against the Lombards.[44] This divergence indicates that the papal and Frankish protagonists disagreed as to who was the leading element in their alliance.

In extreme cases when a political relationship was breaking down, processions, being measuring instruments, were expected to break down as well. Short of this, a hint of violence underlined in narratives the righteousness of one party. A tension within a ritual in a text has a narrative role and modalities. Where it leads to open conflict, as in the 864 texts, it is used to convey the radical moral or providential superiority of one side over another.[45] Contained, it reveals right order. Such is the case in what is, structurally speaking, the closest parallel to our 864 textual cluster: the description in the *Liber pontificalis* of Sergius II's 844 reception of King Louis II for his coronation. Despite initial Frankish depredations outside of Rome, all the magistrates (*universi iudices*) went out to meet the king nine miles outside of Rome with banners (*signa*) and hymns of praise (*laudes*). Then, one mile from the city, Louis and his enlarged escort encountered another train: the different corps (*scholae*) of the militia, including the Greeks, who sang imperial lauds and brought out crosses. Sergius himself, surrounded by his clergy, waited on Saint Peter's steps.[46] It is at this point that the papal biographer injected the

---

44 *Vita Stephani* II 25, LP, ed. Duchesne, 1.447:10–15 and *Chronicle of Aniane* ad an. 754, *MGH SS* 1, 292:43–293:9, with Thomas F. X. Noble, *The Republic of St. Peter: The Birth of the Papal State, 680–825* (Philadelphia, 1984), 80. See also the readings in Heinrich Fichtenau, *Lebensordnungen des 10. Jahrhunderts*, 2 vols., Monographien zur Geschichte des Mittelalters 30 (Stuttgart, 1984), 1:50, and Koziol, *Begging*, 309–10.

45 See Buc, "Martyre et ritualité," 75–7.

46 *Vita Sergii* II 9–10, LP, ed. Duchesne, 2.88:5–15. The closest ceremonial is Hadrian I's 774 reception of Charlemagne, *Vita Hadriani* 35, LP, 1.496:27–497:20, in which the respective distances were thirty miles and one mile.

ritual's description with a second element of tension to highlight right order: The *Liber pontificalis* sought to enshrine in the proceedings (and therefore to make normative) the king's recognition of Sergius II's election, which had taken place without royal consent.

In recounting the ceremony as it did, the *Liber* also sought to legitimize the papal position on two other issues: Sergius refused to reinstate Ebbo, the deposed archbishop of Reims, and Sergius did not want Rome's magnates to swear an oath of fidelity to Louis. For the faction whose views the *Vita Sergii* reflects, these were critical signs of liberty from Carolingian power.[47] The narrative argued for the necessity of this liberty through the symbolic irruption of the miraculous: the ritual became tense and almost turned "bad." Indeed, after Louis had taken his host's right hand, and after both had entered Saint Peter's atrium, a demon seized a Frankish warrior in the royal retinue. The pope reacted, ordering the church's doors to be closed. If later ordines indicate anything about ninth-century understanding of Saint Peter's liturgical space, the silver gates beyond the atrium led to the locus of imperial consecration and provided a station in that ritual.[48] Louis had to assure Sergius "that he had come there with neither malignity in his spirit nor any wickedness nor evil guile" before Sergius opened the doors again and they stepped into Saint Peter's proper to worship.[49] The warrior's possession symbolically suggested that the potentially badly intentioned Frankish king (recall that his army had plundered and raged in the Roman countryside) was constantly in danger of being seized himself by fury; the doors' closure signified the church's sovereign means against any such hostility: a denial of access to the king-making liturgy. Within the economy of the narrative describing Louis's ritualized reception, this overcoming of a crisis inspired by the Devil ultimately highlighted the right order. But in the 864 texts the

---

47 *Vita Sergii II* 15–16, *LP*, ed. Duchesne, 2.90:11–21. Cf. ibid., 18, 2.91:2–4, after Louis II's departure for Pavia: "Tunc vero leti omnes . . . senatus populusque romanus ingenti peste liberati et iugo tirannice immanitatis redempti, sanctissimum Sergium praesulem velut salutis auctorem ac restitutorem pacis venerabant."

48 See the earliest surviving Ordo, a Roman Ordo in the Mainz Pontifical (before 960), Reinhard Elze, ed., *Die Ordines für die Weihe und Krönung des Kaisers und der Kaiserin*, Fontes Iuris Germanici in usum scholarum 9 (Hannover, 1960), 2–3. The ceremony moves from *ante portam argenteam* (2:12) and finishes *ante confessionem beati Petri* (2:20). Interestingly, the best guide to the 844 ceremony is the *Ordo of Censius II*, ed. Elze, 35–47, from the twelfth-century Roman curia, a text that greatly subordinates the emperor to the papacy.

49 *Vita Sergii II* 11, *LP*, ed. Duchesne, 2.88:19–31. Cf. Gregory of Tours, *Vita Patrum* 17.2, ed. Bruno Krusch and Wilhelm Arndt, in *Monumenta Germaniae Historica, Scriptores rerum Merovingicarum* 1 (Hannover, 1885), 729:25–28. On the atrium and its role in processions as a space in which to incorporate the laity, see most recently Kristin Mary Sazama, "The Assertion of Monastic Spiritual and Temporal Authority in the Romanesque Sculpture of Sainte-Madeleine at Vézelay," Ph.D. diss., Northwestern University, 1995, 32–4, 82–95.

demon triumphed, and the rituals turned "bad," dramatizing the bad relationship between the heads of *regnum* and *sacerdotium*.

Given the precedents provided by this political culture, an assessment of the relationship between Nicholas and Louis II in 864 had a strong probability of crystallizing in this space, on the road to Rome's walls or near Saint Peter's basilica, and around a processional ritual. There may have been a real procession, then; or there may have been merely, independently of any actual event, a "first-story" or "Ur-narrative" involving a procession because a procession provided the best means to quantify and qualify their political relationship.

Rival interpretations soon surrounded the fact or the fiction: Hincmar's, which demonstrated the righteousness of the papal stance against the Lotharingians; Erchempert's, which placed within providential history the death of a ruler who had sided against Benevento; and the *Libellus*, which hinted at the evilness of autocratic popes with the aim of justifying a balance of power more in favor of royal *potestas*. Because all these authors shared the understanding that the relationship between Louis and Nicholas was shot through with political tensions almost beyond repair, the three stories all featured disrupted processions. Here, as in many other cases, the real or imaginary ritual's interpretation weighed more than its actuality.

The more a political culture attributes importance to rituals, the less one can trust its textual production to depict a ritual event as it actually happened, or even to depict an actual event. Rituals are just too momentous not to be the objects of complex writing strategies or even invention. Is the historian thereby hopelessly denied access to the past? No. In the quest for propagandistic efficacy, the medieval historiographer had to draw on the most meaningful forms available in the political culture to which he belonged. These narrative proclivities are an indirect but trustworthy index of what agents in the political game measured and valued – and therefore of the horizons of their actual action.[50]

---

50 In this sense I agree with Althoff that the historian can reconstruct early medieval political culture, but I am wary of his work's implicit optimism as to our access to specific, individual ritual events. See Gerd Althoff, "Königsherrschaft und Konfliktbewältigung im 10. und 11. Jahrhundert," in Althoff, *Spielregeln*, 21–56; a problem eloquently raised by Reuter, "Mentalities," 469n12, 471–4. We can describe with some degree of safety to forms of behavior but not to how specific individuals acted at a specific point in time and place. When we try to reconstruct political trends based on an author's (or set of ideologically like-minded authors') description of a series of ritual events, we risk creating an optical illusion or being the victims of authorial ideology. Exemplary of the more cautious approach here advocated is David A. Warner, "Thietmar of Merseburg on Rituals of Kingship," *Viator: Medieval and Renaissance Studies* 26 (1995): 53–76.

7

The Concept of Time in the Historiography of the Eleventh and Twelfth Centuries

HANS-WERNER GOETZ

Concepts of the past (*Geschichtsbild*) and historical consciousness (*Geschichtsbewusstsein*) are central elements in a modern, increasingly anthropological historiography. To a large extent they are shaped by contemporary interests, thus "creating" the actuality of history, the "presence of the past," which can be observed most clearly in historiographical sources because they were consciously written to "represent" the past and link it with the present.[1] In this activity, time or, better yet, the way an author deals with time naturally becomes a decisive factor. To illustrate some characteristic features of the historiographical consciousness of time in the eleventh and twelfth centuries, I shall concentrate entirely on this aspect. More precisely, I should like to point out a (seeming) discrepancy in the concepts of time of the chroniclers: On the one hand, we observe a strong tendency to "place" historical facts in the right chronological order and attribute them to their exact date. On the other, temporal changes – the differences in times and epochs – were often neglected by unceremonious comparisons of events from distinctly different centuries or eras.

To illuminate and perhaps explain these features, I first consider the importance of "time" to a medieval chronicler, and, more specifically, I try to show why a conscious concept of time was an essential element in every historiographical work. Second, I examine the manner and methods of how facts were dated and placed in a temporal framework. Third, this practice is explored in light of certain cases where epochal

---

1 See Hans-Werner Goetz, "Die Gegenwart der Vergangenheit im früh- und hochmittelalterlichen Geschichtsbewusstsein," *Historische Zeitschrift* 255 (1992): 61–97. For an epistemological foundation of this perspective, see Hans-Werner Goetz, "Einführung," in Hans-Werner Goetz, ed., *Hochmittelalterliches Geschichtsbewusstsein im Spiegel nichthistoriographischer Quellen* (Berlin, 1998), 9–16.

differences were neglected. And fourth, I attempt to explain this apparent inconsistency by understanding the underlying concepts of the past that were characteristic of these centuries.[2]

HISTORICAL FACT AND HISTORICAL TIME AS THE ESSENTIAL FEATURES IN CONSTRUCTING HISTORY

A historical consciousness is defined by three major elements: a consciousness of a historic nature of the world, a conception of history, and a (specific) interest in history. If the first element includes at the same time a consciousness of the mutability of history itself and of the historic authenticity of individual events, the second element covers a mental act of organizing the amorphous mass of historical information and knowledge into a systematic process, and the third element closely combines past and present (and sometimes also the future), then we may conclude that there exists an inevitable coherence between "time" and "history": History is what happens, placed in a temporal frame. Consequently, a historical consciousness is inconceivable without a (conscious) concept of time.[3] Time, in turn, is a natural condition of human life, whereas its representation – that is, the way time is dealt with by historians – and its measurement and the perception of it – that is, how it is experienced – are social and historical categories and therefore subject to change.[4]

---

2 These ideas are integrated into a broader context of historical "imaginations" in Hans-Werner Goetz, *Geschichtsschreibung und Geschichtsbewusstsein im hohen Mittelalter*, Orbis mediaevalis 1 (Berlin, 1999).

3 On the historiographical concept of time in the high Middle Ages, see Hans-Werner Goetz, "Die Zeit als Ordnungsfaktor in der hochmittelalterlichen Geschichtsschreibung," in Peter Dilg, Gundolf Keil, and Dietz-Rüdiger Moser, eds., *Rhythmus und Saisonalität: Kongressakten des 5. Symposiums des Mediävistenverbandes in Göttingen, 1993* (Sigmaringen, 1995), 63–74; and Hans-Werner Goetz, "Zeitbewusstsein und Zeitkonzeptionen in der hochmittelalterlichen Geschichtsschreibung," in Trude Ehlert, ed., *Zeitkonzeptionen – Zeiterfahrung – Zeitmessung: Stationen ihres Wandels vom Mittelalter bis zur Moderne* (Paderborn, 1997), 12–32.

4 See Jean Leclercq, "Zeiterfahrung und Zeitbegriff im Spätmittelalter," in Albert Zimmermann, ed., *Antiqui und Moderni: Traditionsbewusstsein und Fortschrittsbewusstsein im späten Mittelalter*, Miscellanea Mediaevalia 9 (Berlin, 1974), 1–20; Rudolf Wendorff, *Zeit und Kultur: Geschichte des Zeitbewusstseins in Europa*, 2d ed. (Wiesbaden, 1980); Jacques Le Goff, "Zeit der Kirche und Zeit des Händlers im Mittelalter," in Claudia Honegger, ed., *Schrift und Materie der Geschichte: Vorschläge zur systematischen Aneignung historischer Prozesse* (Frankfurt am Main, 1977), 393–414 (Jacques Le Goff, "Au Moyen Âge: Temps de l'Église et temps du marchand," in Jacques Le Goff, *Pour un autre Moyen Âge: Temps, travail et culture en Occident: 18 essais* [Paris, 1977], 46–65); Aaron Gurjewitsch, *Das Weltbild des mittelalterlichen Menschen* (Munich, 1980), 98–187; Anna-Dorothee von den Brincken, "Hodie tot anni sunt – Grosse Zeiträume im Geschichtsdenken der frühen und hohen Scholastik," in Albert Zimmermann, ed., *Mensura: Mass, Zahl, Zahlensymbolik im Mittelalter*, Miscellanea Mediaevalia 16, pt. 1 (Berlin, 1983), 1:192–211; Hans-Ulrich Grimm, "'Zeit' als 'Beziehungssymbol': Die soziale Genese des bürgerlichen Zeitbewusstseins im Mittelalter," *Geschichte in Wissenschaft und Unterricht* 37 (1986): 199–221; Giles Constable, "Past and Present in the Eleventh and Twelfth Centuries:

The close relationships between time and history are reflected best in historiographical texts that, according to Franz-Josef Schmale, are a "reflection of discourses with the past" by virtue of the authors' intentions.[5] A consciousness of history or a concept of the past is presupposed in historiography. By informing present and future readers about the past (a standard phrase in historiographical prologues), it links all three temporal levels through its representation and function. In the conceptions of medieval historiographers, time and history or time and historical writing are connected in a fourfold manner:

In the first instance, there is a *terminological coherence*. Whereas the medieval term for history (*historia*), in the famous definition given by Isidore of Sevilla (*historia est narratio rerum gestarum*), referred to the historical "fact" – and, against differing opinions, the wording clearly proves that *historia* here does not mean "history" but rather "historiography" – the Latin "chronicle" (*chronica*) is derived directly from the Greek term for time ($\chi\rho o \nu o \varsigma$).

Second, terminological coherence coincides with a *coherence in substance*: Historiography links the present to the past with an intellectual "representation" of the past through narrative. Seen from the angle of a theology of history, "time" is an inextinguishable condition of earthly (that is, "temporal") life because it is directly connected with creation and the essence of having been created by the Creator. Thus, it is opposed to eternity, which, as God's "time," is timeless and unmoving. "Earthly time," Honorius Augustudunensis wrote in the early twelfth century, "is a shadow of eternity; it has begun with the world and will end with the world."[6]

Third, and even more important in our context, is a *methodological relationship*: Time is a necessary constituent element of historiography. In the prologue of his chronicle, Hugh of Saint Victor named three

Perceptions of Time and Change," in *L'Europa dei secoli XI e XII fra novità e tradizione: Sviluppi di una cultura, Atti della X° Settimana internazionale di studio (Mendola, 1986)*, Pubblicazioni dell'Università Cattolica del Sacro Cuore, Miscellanea del Centro di studi medioevali 12 (Milan, 1989), 135–70; Arno Borst, *Computus: Zeit und Zahl in der Geschichte Europas* (Berlin, 1990); Gertrud Bodmann, *Jahreszahlen und Weltalter: Zeit- und Raumvorstellungen im Mittelalter* (Frankfurt am Main, 1992); Gerhard Dohrn-Van Rossum, *Die Geschichte der Stunde: Uhren und moderne Zeitordnung* (Munich, 1992). A summary of the state of research is now given, though without any new evidence, by Werner Sulzgruber, *Zeiterfahrung und Zeitordnung vom frühen Mittelalter bis ins 16. Jahrhundert* (Hamburg, 1995).

5 Franz-Josef Schmale, *Funktion und Formen mittelalterlicher Geschichtsschreibung: Eine Einführung* (Darmstadt, 1985), 55ff.

6 Honorius Augustudunensis, *Imago mundi* 2,3, ed. Valerie I. J. Flint, *Archives d'histoire doctrinale et littéraire du moyen âge* 49 (1983): 92: "Tempus autem mundi est umbra evi: Hoc cum mundo incipit et cum mundo desinet."

particular "circumstances" of historical facts (*de tribus maximis circumstan-tiis gestorum*):[7] "The knowledge of facts particularly depends on three aspects: the persons (*personae*) by whom they have been done, the places (*loca*) where they have been done, and the times (*tempora*) when they have been done."[8] If we add the action (*negotium*), a historical narrative was determined by these four elements.[9] Explanations in other historio-graphical prologues show that such a concept was more than mere theory.[10] Therefore, it should not be surprising that place, time, and history form not only the contents of famous medieval encyclopedias, such as the *Imago mundi* of Honorius Augustudunensis, but that some chronicles start with "time tables" or even with theoretical discussions on time. (Bede the Venerable's "chronicle" actually was part of the author's treatise on time.) The chronicle of Marianus Scottus was not only preceded by tables for the calculation of Easter, but, moreover, the complete first book was devoted to various computations.[11] Bernold of Saint Blasien likewise pref-aced his chronicle with calculations of time.

Finally, the last criterion coincides with the medieval *concept of histori-ography as a genre*, which also is based on time: Isidore's definition, which has been quoted previously, reveals that historiography was seen as a par-ticular literary genre, distinct from others due to its subject (the *res gestae*) and its function: "Historiography is the narration of facts for the purpose of historical knowledge" (*Historia est narratio rei gestae, per quam ea, quae in praeterito facta sunt, dinoscuntur*).[12] Therefore, not every text dealing with historical matters can be classified as historiographical. Otto of Freising, for example, complained that his "sequence of facts" (*series rerum gestarum*),

---

7 This title has been given to the prologue of Hugh's chronicle; see *Speculum* 18 (1943): 484–93.

8 Ibid., 491, l.16–18: "Tria igitur sunt, in quibus praecipue cognitio pendet rerum gestarum, id est personae, a quibus res gestae sunt, loca, in quibus gestae sunt, et tempora, quando gestae sunt."

9 Hugh of Saint Victor, *Didascalicon* 6,3, ed. Charles Henry Buttimer (Washington, D.C., 1939), 113–4: "Sic nimirum in doctrina fieri oportet, ut videlicet prius historiam discas et rerum ges-tarum veritatem a principio repetens usque ad finem quid gestum sit, quando gestum sit, ubi gestum sit, et a quibus gestum sit, diligenter memoriae commendes. Haec enim quattuor prae-cipue in historia requirenda sunt, persona, negotium, tempus et locus."

10 The authors intended to write down at what time and by which persons the monastery took its origin, as we can read, for example, in the "Historia monasterii Salemitani" prol., ed. Georg Waitz, in *Monumenta Germaniae Historica, Scriptores* (hereafter *MGH SS*), 24, p. 643: "vel quando vel a quibus personis hoc cenobium initiatum sit." In Josef A. Giefel, ed., *Historia monasterii Marchthe-lanensis* Württembergische Geschichtsquellen 4 (Stuttgart, 1891), 5, an attempt was made to describe, by which persons, under which bishop, and at what time the church (Marchthal) had been founded and given land: "sollicitus fui scire volentibus scriptis propalare et successorum nos-trorum memorie commendare, a quibus personis vel sub quibus prelatis et quo tempore predicta ecclesia fundata, dotata, prediis nobilitata et aucmentata exstiterit."

11 Marianus Scottus, *Chronicon*, *MGH SS* 5. For these parts, we still lack a critical edition; see, however, the titles of the single chapters, *MGH SS* 5, p. 495.

12 Isidor of Sevilla, *Etymologiae sive Origines* 1, 41, ed. W. M. Lindsay (Oxford, 1912).

by reason of all the misery in the world resembled a tragedy;[13] Geoffrey of Viterbo wrote that *historiae* and the characters of kings and emperors were better subject matter than fables;[14] and the author of the *Deeds of Archbishop Albero of Trier* feared that he had to acquire the quality of his ancient models in order either to depict the glorious deeds of his heroes in elaborate poetry or to discuss matter-of-factly all the details with the mind of an historian, thus representing them in a way that enabled the reader to "realize" them (as if the reader had them before his eyes).[15] All these authors actually acknowledged historiography as a proper genre, although their definitions certainly applied standards different from ours.

According to the contemporary perceptions of that time, there were five particular criteria that delimited historiography from other genres:

1. By its subject, the *res gestae*, from which the author had to choose those that were worth remembering (*memorabilia gesta*), historiography was distinct from "scientific" literature, particularly from the higher, nonliteral interpretations (senses) of medieval exegesis;[16]
2. By claiming to recollect the truth (the real facts), it was distinguished from fiction;
3. By its examination of the past and, especially, the "origins" (*origines*), it was separated from the prophecies about the future (which nevertheless were also regarded);[17]
4. By its intention to hand down the *res gestae* of the past to posterity (*memoriae commendare*),[18] it was constituted as historiography;
5. By its specific manner of representation, the chronological order, it acquired its proper character.

---

13 Otto of Freising, *Chronicle*, letter of devotion, ed. Adolf Hofmeister, in *Monumenta Germaniae Historica, Scriptores rerum Germanicarum* (hereafter *MGH SSrG*), 1912, 2–3.
14 Geoffrey of Viterbo, *Speculum regum* prol., ed. Georg Waitz, in *MGH SS* 22, p. 22: "si placet, in puerorum scolis facias lectitari; cum sit honestius istorias et naturas regum et imperatorum, quibus mundus instruitur et ornatur, animo pueri legentis imprimere, quam fabulas Choridonis vel pecudes Melibei memorie commendare."
15 Balderich, *Gesta Alberonis archiepiscopi* 16, ed. Georg Waitz, in *MGH SS* 8, p. 252: "Quod si singulorum hinc inde facta virorum inclita et in Martiis congressionibus varios belli eventus et nunc horum nunc illorum cedentium vel inpellentium diversas fortunas poetica vellem arte simulare, vel secundum hystoricorum peritiam, singula callida narratione renovando, tanquam ea ante oculos videas fieri, tibi, o lector, representem: aut oneri, quod verum est, succumberem, aut non impar Virgilio vel Stacio, Tito Livio vel Iosepho invenirer." For connections between *historia* and *fabula*, see Peter G. Bietenholz, *Historia and Fabula: Myths and Legends in Historical Thought from Antiquity to the Modern Age*, Brill's Studies in Intellectual History, vol. 59 (Leiden, 1994).
16 See Benoît Lacroix, *L'historien au moyen âge* (Montréal, 1971), 19ff.
17 Cf. Otto of Freising, *Chronicle* 8 prol., 392: "Sic Daniel ab historica narratione ordiens profundissima visione opus suum terminavit."
18 For this frequent motive, see, e.g., *Gesta Cnutonis regis* prol., ed. G. H. Pertz, in *MGH SSrG* 1865, 1: "memoriam rerum gestarum . . . litteris meis posteritati mandare." The ancestors (*maiores*), according to Berthold of Zwiefalten, *Chronik* prol., ed. Luitpold Wallach, Erich König, and Karl

These criteria centered on the elements "fact" (*gesta*) and "time" (*tempus*), which Gert Melville has rightly described as the two typical historiographical elements of all narrative literature.[19] In medieval perception, chronicles were *series rerum gestarum* and, consequently, *series temporum* (sequence of time). Historiography ordinarily was a diachronical narrative of facts. This is explicitly confirmed by Hugh of Saint Victor when he writes: "You will find the order of time in the sequence of events" (*In serie gestorum ordo temporis invenitur*).[20] The author of the Annals of Pöhlde criticized that the successors of Eusebe (Jerome) had neglected to put in order (*ordinare*) the sequence of time.[21] Lampert of Hersfeld recorded the events in a temporal order (*eo quo gesta sunt ordine et tempore*),[22] the Annals of Hildesheim conceived themselves even as a "book on the order of times" (*Liber de ordine temporum*),[23] and Heimo of Bamberg styled the continuous sequence of years from the beginning of the world to the present time as the subject matter of his chronicle.[24] "The correct order of narrating" (*legitimus narrationis ordo*), Arnulf of Milan wrote, "descends from top to bottom" (*a superioribus ad inferiora descendit*).[25] The chronological order of a historical narrative was so self-evident that this could be characterized as a historical (*ordo historicus*) or even as a natural order (*ordo naturalis*).[26]

Historiography and historical consciousness were determined by time and historical fact as two unseparably coherent elements. Sigebert of Gembloux therefore could classify "the sequence of time and events" (*con-*

Otto Müller, Schwäbische Chroniken der Stauferzeit 2 (1941; reprint, Sigmaringen, 1978), 136, which legitimized and defined historiography, had invented the art (*ars*) of recording what was worth to be remembered by writing it down and handing it down to posterity ("omnia literis comprehensa notarentur sicque in posteros transmitterentur").

19 Gert Melville, "System und Diachronie: Untersuchungen zur theoretischen Grundlegung geschichtsschreiberischer Praxis im Mittelalter," *Historisches Jahrbuch* 95 (1975): 33–67, 308–41.

20 Hugh of Saint Victor, *De vanitate mundi* 2, ed. Jacques Paul Migne, in *Patrologia latina* 176, col. 717 (Paris, 1841–64).

21 Annales Palidenses prol., ed. Georg Heinrich Pertz, in *MGH SS* 16, 51, l.35ss: "Sed attendendum de his quae postea descripta sunt, quosdam ordinare cupientes seriem temporum minus diligenter considerasse, a quibus operis sui viam debuerant assumsisse."

22 Lampert of Hersfeld, *Annales* a. 1072, ed. Oswald Holder-Egger, *MGH SSrG* 1894, 247.

23 *MGH SS* 3, 22.

24 Heimo, *De decurso temporum libri*, ed. Philipp Jaffé, Bibliotheca rerum Germanicarum 5 (Berlin, 1869), 543: "Est autem materia huius libri continuus annorum decursus de principio mundi usque ad nostrum tempus."

25 Arnulf of Milan, *Liber gestarum recentium* (*Gesta archiepiscoporum Mediolanensium*), 1, prol., ed. Claudia Zey, in *MGH SSrG* 67, 1994, 118.

26 See Marie Schulz, *Die Lehre von der historischen Methode bei den Geschichtsschreibern des Mittelalters (VI.–XIII. Jahrhundert)*, Abhandlungen zur mittleren und neueren Geschichte 13 (Berlin, 1909), 98–107; Lacroix, *L'historien au moyen âge*, 84–97; Bernard Guenée, *Histoire et Culture historique dans l'Occident médiéval* (Paris, 1980), 21–2.

sequentia temporum et rerum gestarum) as the subject matter of his chronicle.[27] The installation of historical events in their temporal and chronological frame in a way became the most genuine task of medieval historiography.

The relevance of time in historical writing and its methodological criteria were determined by two factors: a critical element, resulting from the claim for truth, and a narrative element that emerged from the determination of *historia* as *narratio rerum gestarum*, a narration of "facts." The historiographer's task to arrange events according to their time and date had to be preceded by a critical examination, particularly of the temporal aspect. The chroniclers indicated chronological uncertainties[28] and strove to standardize or even improve the chronological system used in their sources: Hermann of Reichenau transferred the incarnation era (the "Anno Domini" era) back to the first centuries after Christ's birth, whereas his sources still used the Roman dating system, an innovation henceforth adopted by other authors. Marianus Scottus and Heimo of Bamberg corrected the exact date of Christ's incarnation by twenty-two or thirty-three years, respectively,[29] because, as Marianus wrote, Christ's resurrection could not have occurred (according to Bede) on March 27 but rather on March 25.[30] Corresponding adjustments of the traditional dating systems were made by Sigebert of Gembloux, who likewise pointed out that the lunisolar cycle of 532 years, "invented" by Dionysius Exiguus and on which the Easter calculations of the Middle Ages were based, did not conform with the biblical report of the day of Christ's death (at age 33), which, in accordance with the lunisolar conditions, fell in the year 13.[31] Consequently,

---

27 Sigebert of Gembloux, *Catalogus de viris illustribus* 172, ed. Robert Witte, Lateinische Sprache und Literatur des Mittelalters 1 (Frankfurt am Main, 1974), 105.

28 See Adam of Bremen, *Gesta Hammaburgensis ecclesiae pontificum* 1, 17, ed. Bernhard Schmeidler, in *MGH SSrG* 1917, 24; 1, 24, 30–31; 1, 28, 34.

29 On Heimo, see Anna-Dorothee von den Brincken, "Die Welt- und Inkarnationsära bei Heimo von St. Jakob. Kritik an der christlichen Zeitrechnung durch Bamberger Komputisten in der ersten Hälfte des 12. Jahrhunderts," *Deutsches Archiv* 16 (1960): 155–94; on Marianus Scotus, see Anna-Dorothee von den Brincken, "Marianus Scottus: Unter besonderer Berücksichtigung der nicht veröffentlichten Teile seiner Chronik," *Deutsches Archiv* 17 (1961): 197ff., 208ff.

30 See von den Brincken, "Marianus."

31 Sigebert of Gembloux, *Chronicle* a. 532, ed. Ludwig Conrad Bethmann, *MGH SS* 6, 316: "Hoc anno expletus est a Christi nativitate magnus annus annorum 532. Ab hoc etiam anno Dyonisius abbas orditur ciclum suum ciclorum quinque decennovennalium. Et quia secundus annus operis huius concordare debet in ratione compoti primo anno nativitatis Christi, debet 35ᵘˢ annus cycli Dyonisii concordare in ratione compoti 33° anno nati Christi, scilicet ut 16ᵐᵃ luna Aprilis

this cycle of 532 years should not begin at year one but twenty-one years earlier.[32]

Marianus also corrected the date of creation with the somewhat unreasonable argument that the year of creation must have been the first year of an indiction: In the final analysis the chronology was meticulously checked and at the same time submitted to unhistorical chronological systems determined by theological beliefs. The indiction was considered to be a "natural" or divine institution, whereas its late-antique origin as a Roman tax cycle of fifteen years had long been forgotten. This fact alone, however, can explain its relevance to the medieval chronology (in charters, for example), although its calculation caused difficulties and many mistakes in practical use.

Inconsistencies in the sequence of office holders were caused by solely considering their years in office. Chroniclers such as Hugh of Flavigny or Hugh of Saint Victor therefore not only registered the years of the popes' pontificates but also the months and days, and Frutolf of Michelsberg debated in his writings whether the Emperor Decius had governed for more than one year (as was handed down by some sources).[33] Chronological calculations such as these did not serve to verify the truth of the historical reports that had been handed down but rather first and foremost served to examine the congruity and correctness of the historical dates that formed the center of historical interest. It is significant when Frutolf of Michelsberg assures us that the discrepancies regarding the successors of Saint Peter did not concern the existence of the papacy in the early church but rather the sequence and term of office of the early

occurrat 9. Kal. Aprilis in 5. feria; passio Christi 8. Kal. Aprilis in 6. feria, resurrectio 6. Kal. Aprilis in dominica die. Sed quia non ita occurrit, sed luna 14[ma] Aprilis occurrit eo anno 12. Kal. Aprilis in 1. feria, dominica vero dies paschae in 5. Kal. Aprilis, ideo improbatur, qui repugnat euangelicae veritati." Ibid., a. 1063, 361: "Hoc anno finitus magnus ciclus annorum 532, continens ciclos decennovennales 28, qui ad omnem rationem paschalis compoti omnino utilis, ab evo in evum in semet ipsum sine errore revolvitur. Sed hoc in eo reprehensibile esse videtur, quod annis dominicae incarnationis ei inconsiderate prescriptis, discordat a veritate euangelii in anno dominicae passionis, preferens 14. lunam Aprilis eo anno in prima feria fuisse; quod omnino falsum est, quia secundum fidem euangelii eo anno luna 14. Aprilis fuit in 5. feria, et in 6. feria luna 15. Dominus passus est."

32 Ibid., a. 1076, 363: "Hoc anno, qui est 13. annus primi decennovennalis cicli in repetito magno anno Dionisii, duobus magnis annis a passione Domini revolutis, omnia quae ad cursum solis et lunae spectant, anno dominicae passionis concordant. Unde apparet, quod Dionisius non recte annos Domini ciclo suo annexuit. Quia enim ab anno Domini 532. ciclum suum orditus est, nimirum intendit, Christum fuisse natum anno secundo prioris magni anni; ac per hoc hic annus anno dominicae passionis concordans, debuisset esse magni cicli annus non 13. sed 33., quia is fuit annus passionis Domini. Et per hanc consequentiam solaris et lunaris cursus, concordantem euangelicae veritati, Dionisius posuit nativitatem Christi viginti uno annis tardius quam debuit."

33 Frutolf of Michelsberg, *Chronicle* a. 254, ed. Georg Waitz, in *MGH SS* 6, 108.

alleged popes.[34] Through all the debates mentioned, however, the calculations gained much more importance than they would have acquired as auxiliary scientific activities: They touched the core of the medieval concept of time and the past.

Critical examination was inevitably followed by verbal representation. From the beginning it had been a major concern of Christian historiographers to attribute facts to their corresponding dates or times and place them correctly within the continuous chronology. The oldest Christian universal histories had been developed for the simple purpose of satisfying the demand to integrate the biblical history (which was not at all clear in its temporal exactness) into the ancient chronology, which was precise but indebted to various eras, and to establish a concurrence between the two traditions. Eusebe of Caesarea had solved this task by creating a synoptical representation of the various chronologies, and Jerome passed this solution on to the Latin Occident. Medieval historiographers did not content themselves with this solution: Calculating time remained a key issue.[35] Bernard Guenée has spoken of a downright "computistic fever."[36]

Structuring the historical material in a temporal system was essential for any historiographical activity, although there were many ways to accomplish this goal. The most obvious examples are the annals with their annual reports, which, as they developed from the Easter tables, became a link in the evolution of the calculation of time. Most chronicles retained the annalistic form, although a division into chapters and books was also determined by temporal factors. Many episcopal or monastic chronicles were subdivided into chapters that were devoted to one bishop or monk each, and Marianus Scottus, at least according to his table of contents, attempted to arrange his universal chronicle in such a way that granted each emperor just one chapter. A division into books created a division into temporal caesuras and "periodizations": Andreas of Marchiennes described the history of the three *genealogiae*, that is, the three dynasties, of French history (the Merovingians, the Carolingians, and the Capetians) in three books.[37] In a later version of his adaptation of the universal chronicle of Frutolf of Michelsberg, Ekkehard of Aura divided Frutolf's

---

34 Ibid., a. 46, 99: "De successione vero pontificum Romanorum et ordine et temporibus eorum iam inde a principio et deinceps in plurimis diversa sentiuntur a diversis."

35 See Anna-Dorothee von den Brincken, "Weltären," *Archiv für Kulturgeschichte* 39 (1957): 133–49; von den Brincken, "Hodie tot anni sunt."

36 Guenée, *Histoire*, 152.

37 Partly edited by Georg Waitz, *MGH SS* 26, 204–15; cf. the "epilogs" of the three books, ibid., 205–6.

linearly written chronicle into five books that in their external appearance already displayed the historical cuts he thought important: the foundation of Rome, the birth of Christ, the empire of Charlemagne, and Henry V's accession to the throne as the beginning of contemporary history.[38] Thus, Ekkehard – in addition to Christ as the center of salvational history – used the new formations of political power as his reference points. Otto of Freising composed his chronicle, which also was based on Frutolf, but, for reasons that lay in his theological concept of history, concluded each book with a radical political change in history or even a kind of disaster indicating the transitoriness (*mutabilitas*) of the world.[39]

Two chronological systems dominated the yearly report entries in the chronicles of the high Middle Ages: the incarnation era and the registering of reigns and pontificates. It was the intention of numerous chroniclers to establish a factual as well as a narrative unity of these elements, and they not infrequently attempted to "translate" this into a visual system. A few examples illustrate this point:

Hermann of Reichenau developed his own special temporal and chronological dating system in which, up to the Emperor Valens (that is, to the end of Hermann's main source, the chronicle of Jerome) he recorded the years A.D. (the incarnation era) in the left margin and the reign of the Roman emperors in the right margin (see Figure 7.1). He resumed the system with the Frankish *maiores domus* (Charles Martel, 714) and continued with it up to Henry II. At the accession of each emperor to the throne, Hermann recorded the duration of the reign in years, months, and days in the right margin.

Frutolf of Michelsberg, in the pre-Christian era, even presented his whole chronicle as a set of parallel timetables in which separate columns recorded the reigns of the kings or emperors of the great realms. Bibli-

---

38 Ekkehard of Aura, *Recensio* III, prol., ed. Franz-Josef Schmale, Freiherr vom Stein–Gedächtnisausgabe 17 (Darmstadt, 1972), 268.

39 Otto of Freising, *Chronicle* 1 prol., 10. The first book covered the events until the transfer of power (*translatio regni*) from Babylon to the Medes, the second began with the origins of Rome and ended with Caesar's fall, the third extended from the birth of Christ and the reign of Augustus up to Diocletianus, the fourth from Constantine (the first Christian Emperor) and the transfer of power to the Greeks by the foundation of Constantinople, the new capital, up to Odoacer and Chlovis, the fifth from Theoderic to Charlemagne (the *translatio* to the Franks) and the following divisions of the empire, the sixth from Lothar I to the Investiture Contest (the excommunication of Henry IV), the seventh, finally, from the First Crusade to the disorders of the present. The number of seven "historical" books followed the example of Orosius who had written "Seven Books against the Heathens"; it corresponded with the seven days (the cosmic week). The caesuras in the historical development, however, that meanwhile had progressed by 700 years, had changed. Moreover, Otto added an eighth book about the end of times and eternity. This structure is unique in the history of medieval historiography.

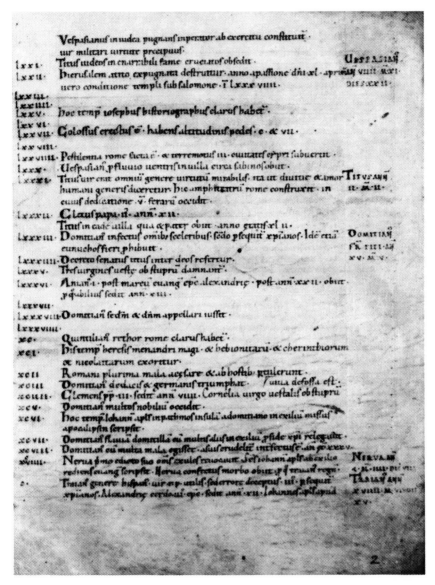

Figure 7.1 Hermann of Reichenau, Chronicle. Badische Landesbibliothek, Karlsruhe, Aug. 175, fol. 2^r. Reproduced by permission.

cal history was granted the first column. The columns formed a structural frame in which changes of reigns or important events were added in the margins or, in the case of longer entries, by interrupting the tables in favor of written text (see Figure 7.2). This system (as the primary

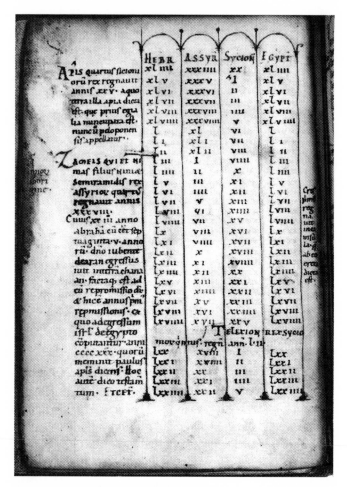

Figure 7.2   Frutolf of Michelsberg, Chronicle. Thüringer Universitäts- und Landesbibliothek, Jena, Bose q. 19, fol. 7ᵛ. Reproduced by permission.

structural frame) was continued even if there were no events recorded at
all. The kings of the great realms were enumerated. In Christian times
(after 428) Frutolf arranged his accounts strictly according to the incarnation years, with the year of the reign added in the left (recto pages) or
the right margin (verso pages) respectively. Every fifteen years he recorded
the beginning of a new indiction (see Figure 7.3).[40]

40 The reigns of the emperors since Augustus were omitted only occasionally when Frutolf lacked
      precise information (e.g., a. 364–77). With the imperial coronation of Charlemagne, the reigns of
      the Byzantine emperors were dropped.

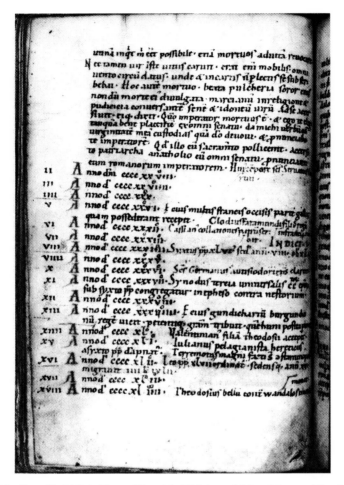

Figure 7.3   Frutolf of Michelsberg, Chronicle. Thüringer Universitäts- und Landesbibliothek, Jena, Bose q. 19, fol. 87ᵛ. Reproduced by permission.

Sigebert of Gembloux, who continued the chronicle of Jerome, solved the task of organizing dates and times similarly by recording the reigns of kings of various kingdoms in up to nine synoptical dating columns (*lineae*) (see Figure 7.4). Through this arrangement he illustrated (according to his own words) the contemporaneousness of kingdoms (*contemporalitas regnorum*).[41] Unlike Frutolf, however, he began each annual report

41 Sigebert of Gembloux, *Chronicle* prol., 300: "Dicturi aliquid iuvante Deo de contemporalitate regnorum, primum pauca dicamus de origine singularum gentium; quatenus sequi poterimus vestigia maiorum, directi per semitas historiarum. Ponemus in prima linea regnum Romanorum,

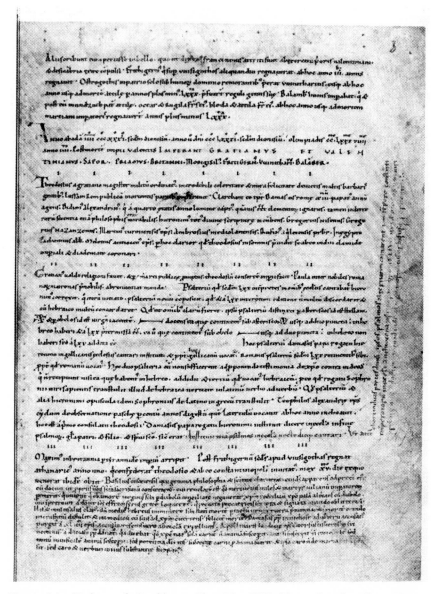

Figure 7.4 Sigebert of Gembloux, Chronicle. Bibliothèque Royale Albert Ier, ms 18239–40, fol. 3^r. Reproduced by permission.

in secunda Persarum, in tertia Francorum, in quarta Wandalorum, in quinta Anglorum, in sexta Langobardorum, in septima Wisigotharum, in octava Ostrogotharum, in nona Hunorum." See Anna-Dorothee von den Brincken, "Contemporalitas Regnorum: Beobachtungen zum Versuch des Sigebert von Gembloux, die Chronik des Hieronymus fortzusetzen," in Dieter Berg and Hans-

with such a "dating line," and he maintained this system through the Christian era up to his present. Altogether he traced twelve kingdoms, which, however, did not all exist simultaneously – only Romans and Franks served as an uninterrupted dating system throughout the chronicle, despite dynastic changes. Thus, through the timetables, the most relevant kingdoms of each epoch jump out at the reader. Moreover, the sequence of kingdoms changed occasionally, for at the same time it symbolized an "order" of the realms (*ordo regnorum*). For example, such an alteration of the order was caused by the imperial coronation of Charlemagne: Henceforth the Roman Empire was placed before the Greek Empire of Byzantium.[42] All in all, this system created a unique conceptual presentation of time and space by the way in which rules and reigns were coordinated.

The unpublished chronicle of Hugh of Saint Victor (preserved mainly in the Bibliothèque Nationale in Paris in various manuscripts from the twelfth century)[43] includes a synoptical list of popes and emperors that in four columns records the years of incarnation, the indiction, the names of popes and emperors, and the (individual) years of their pontificate or reign.

These examples should suffice to illustrate how carefully the chroniclers not only recorded the historical facts but also provided a visual system of their "temporalization" by "placing" the facts into their corresponding "time" in a clearly arranged layout. At least in some chronicles these temporal systems even seemed to be the primary element through which the events were attributed to their corresponding dates.

DETACHING EVENTS, OR NEGLECTING TIME

Chroniclers' endeavors to place the historical events in their precise historical time are juxtaposed by a somewhat contrasting process that detached the same events from their chronology and transferred them (intellectually) to the present or future. This detachment of events from a temporal frame originates in the perception of time and history. On the

---

Werner Goetz, eds., *Historiographia mediaevalis: Studien zur Geschichtsschreibung und Quellenkunde des Mittelalters: Festschrift Franz-Josef Schmale* (Darmstadt, 1988), 199–211; Anna-Dorothee von den Brincken, *Studien zur lateinischen Weltchronistik bis in das Zeitalter Ottos von Freising* (Düsseldorf, 1957), 182ff.

42 Sigebert, *Chronicle* a. 801, 336: "Immutato ordine regnorum, immutandus est etiam ordo titulorum; quia abhinc sub uno comprehendum est regnum Francorum et Romanorum, et Constantinopolitanum regnum distinguendum est a regno Romanorum."

43 Paris, Bibliothèque Nationale (herafter BN), ms lat. 15009; see also Paris, BN, ms lat. 14872.

one hand, history meant (constant) change, a continuously progressing development toward the end of all history. For Honorius Augustudunensis, the *vicissitudo rerum* resembled a rope that stretched across the whole world from east to west, and through the daily coiling, the rope would finally be used up.[44] The theoretical basis for this statement lay in the theology of history and resulted in a belief in the natural changeability and transitoriness of history as such, because all earthly things were ruled by time. The theory of the *mutabilitas mundi* reached its most developed expression in the works of Otto of Freising.[45] Particularly for Otto, this concept included a perception of caesuras (and, consequently, of chronological periodizations). These were formed either in the events of the history of salvation, such as the birth of Christ or the Christianization of the Roman Empire, or in the succession of the four great kingdoms of the world (Babylonians – Medes/Persians – Greeks – Romans) and the medieval "translations of power" or, more precisely, the "translations of imperial power" (*translationes imperii*) within the Roman Empire to new peoples and dynasties (Greeks, Franks, "Italians," and Germans): "Since the times of Constantine the Great, the son of Helena, up to that time," Frutolf of Michelsberg wrote regarding Charlemagne's imperial coronation, "the Roman Empire remained in Constantinople and was held by the Emperors of the Greeks; it was only through Charles that it was transferred to the kings or emperors of the Franks."[46] For the medieval chroniclers, historical change was primarily a cycle of political rise and fall, the growth and decay of regents and kingdoms.

Yet, despite all incongruencies, this development was seen as a continuum. Actually, the theory of "translations" offers a good example of this seeming contradiction because it integrated the shifts in power into the continuity of the Roman Empire. Characteristic of this logic, the medieval emperors were repeatedly included in the enumeration of the ancient Roman Empire, although in differing counting systems.[47] By this proce-

---

44 Honorius Augustudunensis, *Imago mundi* 2,3, 92: "Veluti si funis ab oriente in occidentem extenderetur qui cottidie plicando collectus, tandem totus absumeretur."

45 For details of Otto's concept of history, see Hans-Werner Goetz, *Das Geschichtsbild Ottos von Freising: Ein Beitrag zur historischen Vorstellungswelt und zur Geschichte des 12. Jahrhunderts*, Archiv für Kulturgeschichte, supplement no. 19 (Cologne, 1994); on the *mutabilitas*, see ibid., 86–94, 307–8.

46 Frutolf of Michelsberg, *Chronicle* a. 800, 169: "Hucusque Romanum imperium a temporibus Constantini Magni, Helenae filii, apud Constantinopolim in Grecorum imperatoribus mansit, ex hoc iam ad reges immo ad imperatores Francorum per Karolum transiit." Hugh of Saint Victor, in his tables of the emperors in his chronicle (Paris, BN, ms lat. 15009), pursued the East Roman emperors up to Michael; they were followed by lists of the reigns of the West Roman emperors and the Frankish kings.

47 For Adam of Bremen, *Gesta* 3,1, 142, Conrad II was the 90th ruler since Augustus; for Frutolf, who, in favor of the continuity of the Frankish-German empire, included into his counting even

dure, the high medieval emperor was seen as the immediate successor of Augustus, the founder of the Roman Empire. This view prevented the start of the modern, unending discussion of the fall of the Roman Empire and the transition from Antiquity to the Middle Ages (the "modern age" of those times).

The tendency to link the present time with the period of the Roman Empire and to emphasize a continuity indicates a characteristic feature of the concept (or consciousness) of history in the high Middle Ages that seems to contradict the tendency to determine and record precise historic dates. On the one hand, the authors acknowledged and noted change and development, and they distinguished between epochs or phases in history; on the other hand, their perceptions of the events leave the amazing impression of a certain "timelessness" that ignored a real difference in the epochal character insofar as this went beyond the political succession of power, reign, and kingdoms. On the contrary, it allowed events that were long past to be applied directly to the present. (In the fifth century Orosius had adopted this method in order to prove his theory of a continuous amelioration of the Christian faith.)[48] It was no doubt important for the chroniclers to attribute the factual events to a certain date, but in substance they might at any time detach this event from its chronological context and transfer its contents to the present or to a level that was independent of time.

Evidence of this phenomenon can be drawn from various sources. In pictorial representations, historical figures were dressed in contemporary clothes and furnished with the medieval insignia of power: throne, scepter, crown, and orb. In the famous series of illuminations in the Jena manuscript of Otto of Freising's chronicle,[49] Augustus, Charlemagne, and Otto I are not only represented but also equipped in a confusingly similar manner (see Figures 7.5a–c). Augustus does not wear a diadem but rather a crown; not a toga, but rather a medieval coronation coat "buttoned" by a fibula; and, in medieval fashion, he also carries a scepter. The artist (or the author, Otto himself) was certainly interested in the historical

---

kings who never received the imperial title (such as Louis the Child), Conrad II was only the 85th emperor; for his continuator, Ekkehard of Aura, Henry V was even the 72th emperor, whereas Otto of Freising counted him as the 92nd emperor.

48 See Hans-Werner Goetz, *Die Geschichtstheologie des Orosius*, Impulse der Forschung 32 (Darmstadt, 1980), 29ff.

49 See Walther Lammers, "Ein universales Geschichtsbild der Stauferzeit in Miniaturen: Der Bilderzyklus zur Chronik Ottos von Freising im Jenenser Codex Bose q. 6," (1963), in Walther Lammers, *Vestigia mediaevalia: Ausgewählte Aufsätze zur mittelalterlichen Historiographie, Landes- und Kirchengeschichte*, Frankfurter Historische Abhandlungen 19 (Wiesbaden, 1979), 45–87.

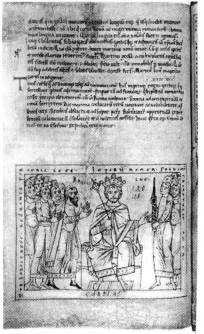

a

b

c

Figure 7.5 Otto of Freising, Chronicle. Thüringer Universitäts- und Landesbibliothek, Jena, Bose q. 6, 38b (Augustus), 67b (Charlemagne), 78b (Otto I). Reproduced by permission.

personalities, but not in their historical being (and their historical relevance), meaning that all three embodied the same ideal of imperial rule. The Middle Ages were not characterized by a historical or individual, but by a typological representation.[50] The pictorial uniformity, however, was not a sign of negligence, but rather an expression of a figurative concept of the past that at the same time symbolized and superceded epochal differences. The sequence of illuminations representing these three emperors was actually meant to illustrate the aforementioned correlation between the medieval and Roman empires and to make Charlemagne and Otto appear visually as immediate successors of Augustus, the founder of the Roman Empire. Thus, they were placed in the decisive line of historical tradition. At the same time, these same illuminations signified change in history by symbolizing three important transfers of power to the Romans (Augustus), the Franks (Charlemagne), and the Germans (Otto). By the similarity of the three – historically distinct – rulers (who were further distinguished not only by the *tituli* but also by certain physical attributes), we recognize at the same time a reflection of change and continuity, of progress and coherence of history, of placing events in their temporal frame while at the same time detaching them from it.

Correspondingly, the popular high Middle Age miniature portraits in genealogical trees, such as the tree of the Salian emperors in the chronicles of Frutolf and Ekkehard in the Berlin manuscript (see Figure 7.6),[51] of the lineage of the Welfs in the *Historia Welforum*,[52] or of the Ottonian and Salian rulers in the chronicle of St. Pantaleon in Cologne (see Figure 7.7),[53] which were intended to illustrate the continuity of the family, distinguished between men and women or between different officeholders (emperors, kings, or dukes) by use of recognizable crowns or other symbols. "Individual" distinctions, however, were reduced to a few superficialities, such as hair color or beard shape. The Salians in the medallions of the Liber Aureus of Trier[54] varied in their facial expressions and in the way they bore their heads, yet they represented a significant similarity in

---

50 See also strictly in this sense Sverre Bagge, "The Individual in Medieval Historiography," in Janet Coleman, ed., *The Individual in Political Theory and Practice* (Oxford, 1996), 35–7, who denies that the medieval historiography was the prominent place for the much-debated "discovery of the individual" in the twelfth century.

51 Latinus fol. 295, fol. 80ᵛ. Illustration in *Das Reich der Salier 1024–1125: Katalog zur Ausstellung im Historischen Museum der Pfalz in Speyer* (Speyer, 1992) 421–3.

52 Weingarten manuscript. Illustration in *Heinrich der Löwe und seine Zeit: Herrschaft und Repräsentation der Welfen 1125–1235* (Munich, 1995), 64.

53 Wolfenbüttel manuscript. Illustration in Nora Gädeke, *Zeugnisse bildlicher Darstellung der Nachkommenschaft Heinrichs I.*, Arbeiten zur Frühmittelalterforschung 22 (Berlin, 1992), table 7.

54 Illustration in ibid., table 11.

Figure 7.6   Ekkehard of Aura, Chronicle. Staatsbibliothek Berlin, ms lat. fol. 295, fol. 81ᵛ. Reproduced by permission.

Figure 7.7 Chronicle of Saint Pantaleon, Cologne. Herzog August Bibliothek, Wolfen-büttel, Codex Guelf 74.3, Aug. 2°, fol. 114ᵛ (p. 226). Reproduced by permission.

function. The Cambridge manuscript of the so-called imperial chronicle (*Kaiserchronik*)[55] comprises a sequence of illustrations of the sixteen German emperors and kings from Charlemagne to Henry IV. The illuminations display the sovereigns in a standardized representation, facing forward, seated on a throne, and dressed in full coronation robe.[56] Through their chronological order, however, and their being placed next to the corresponding historical narrative, these seemingly "timeless" representations of rulers were again placed in their correct time.

This typical method of presentation in miniatures also is seen in the written representation in chronicles. This phenomenon can be observed in the technique of medieval historiographers who carelessly described events of the present with the wording of their ancient sources, referring to completely different situations (a method that has been widely discussed). At the same time, such a procedure demonstrates the use of ancient authors as ideal models. Describing the deeds of Archbishop Albero of Trier, as Albero's anonymous biographer complained, would be a subject worthy of a Homer, if only Homer were adequate to this subject.[57] Again, the model function of the ancient authors was complemented by a self-consciousness that was based on the present. The contemporary author, the biographer continued, had to be an equivalent of a Statius, Titus Livius, or Josephus to give an account of Albero's deeds.[58] Such an attitude explains why medieval authors tended to follow their precursors word by word and why they inserted significant quotations or verses from ancient authors into their descriptions of later or contemporary events or persons. A typological way of thinking enabled the chroniclers to detect (or even construct) a correlation of events that was widely separated in place and time. This construction, however, was not made haphazardly but, on the contrary, completely consciously. "For a similar reason," the same author commented on the fact that Count Louis I, the "speaker" of the laymen who laid claim to the secular administration of the bishopric for himself, violently resisted the election of the new archbishop in 1132: "The Frankish king Childeric had been deprived of his power, which, under the consent of Pope Hadrian, fell to the very person to whom he himself had delegated the administration of the realm,

---

55 Cambridge, Corpus Christi College, ms fol. 373; see *Heinrich der Löwe*, 299–300.
56 See Claudia A. Meier, "Chronikillustrationen im hohen Mittelalter: Zur Entstehung des Ereignisbildes im Bild-Text-Bezug," in Goetz, ed., *Hochmittelalterliches Geschichtsbewusstsein*, 357–75.
57 *Gesta Alberonis archiepiscopi* 16, ed. Georg Waitz, *MGH SS* 8, 252: "Quis enim dictis equare possit fortia facta huius viri Alberonis . . . ? Haec viribus Homeri sufficiens esset materia, si tamen ipse materiae sufficeret."
58 Ibid., 252.

namely to the *maior domus* Pippin."[59] (Differently from 751, however, the new archbishop soon succeeded to keep his vassal within bounds.)

A similar, well-known example illustrates this process. Certain peoples continued to exist through the centuries, although they may have adopted new names. To mention only one of innumerable examples: for Peter of Montecassino, Soliman (Kilidsch Arslan), the sultan of Iconium, was "king of the Huns whom we now call Turks."[60] Avars, Hungarians, and finally Turks remained Huns not only because of their Asian origins but, moreover, because they could still be described by the same characteristic features that the ancient authors had attributed to this ancient people. Following this reasoning, the Hungarian historiography began with an extraordinarily exhaustive representation of the early history of the Huns.[61] Frutolf of Michelsberg was acquainted with Skyths as early as in the time of King Minos, and he associated them with the *Geti*, who, in their turn, were traditionally identified with the Goths.[62] Up to the thirteenth century, even the Spanish history was written as a "history of the (Visi-)Goths."[63]

Regarding the past with the eyes of the present to such a degree easily leads to anachronisms: Charlemagne was not only presented as a martial Frankish emperor but also as a knight and a crusader.[64] In the account of Caesar's (ostensible) conquest of "Germany" in the *Chronicon Ebersheimense*,[65] the Roman camps (*castella*) became medieval castles, the legionaries (*milites*) turned into knights, the magistrates into ministerials, and the Germanic peoples became Germans. The author of the *Historia Welforum* antedated the court officials (*Hausämter*) to the early times of Roman history.[66] In the same vein, earlier times were used as a model

---

59 Ibid., 12, 250: "Ob similem quoque causam Hildericus rex Francorum a regno depositus est, et ei, cui ipse commiserat regendum, datum est, Pipino scilicet maiori domus, domino papa Adriano approbante."

60 *Chronicon monasterii Casinensis* 4,11, ed. Hartmut Hoffmann, in *MGH SS* 34 (1980), 478, l. 23–4: "Soliman rex Unnorum, quos nunc Turcos vocamus."

61 See Norbert Kersken, *Geschichtsschreibung im Europa der "nationes": Nationalgeschichtliche Gesamtdarstellungen im Mittelalter*, Münstersche Historische Forschungen 8 (Cologne, 1995), 696ff.

62 Frutolf, *Chronicle* 43: "Hi autem fuerunt, qui Getae vel Gothi dicti sunt, et huc modo hocque tempore primum de Scythia exierunt."

63 See Kersken, *Geschichtsschreibung*, 76. It may be attributed to the same appeal to old peoples when the Danes were referred to as *Daci* in some chronicles, such as Sven Aggesen.

64 See Hans Rall, *Zeitgeschichtliche Züge im Vergangenheitsbild mittelalterlicher, namentlich mittellateinischer Schriftsteller*, Historische Studien 322 (Berlin, 1937; reprint, Vaduz, 1965), 189ff.

65 *Chronicon Ebersheimense* 2, ed. Ludwig Weiland, in *MGH SS* 23, 432.

66 *Historia Welforum* 1, ed. Erich König, Schwäbische Chroniken der Stauferzeit 1 (1938; reprint, Sigmaringen, 1978) 4: "Domum quoque suam regio more ordinaverant, ita ut quaeque officia curiae (id est ministeria dapiferi, pincernae, marscalci, camerarii, signiferi) per comites vel eis aequipollentes regerentur." By emphasizing that these court offices were (ostensibly) held by counts, the author expresses his *Zeitkritik* against the contemporary ministerials.

for a political demi–renaissance, as seen in the reestablishment of the Senate in Rome (1143–1149),[67] which remained, however, completely rooted in the present. The action was leveled at the papal power over the town, and the historical connection to Antiquity was never seriously meant as a revival of Roman republican conditions. On the contrary, the Romans hurried to offer Conrad III the imperial crown (though now from their own hands instead of the pope's). Consequently, this demonstration served exclusively for political purposes.

Historical development was primarily perceived as chronological, an ever-progressing process. Historical changes were seen in political rise and decline or in change of rulership, possibly complemented by spatial displacement of the centers of power, and historical events were installed in their precise temporal frame. But these changes were not estimated, interpreted, or explained according to their respective historical situations, as structural changes, changes in contemporary attitudes, or even in the historical conditions. Owing to a linear concept of time, the authors recognized an irretrievability of history, but they did not acknowledge a thorough alteration through the coming of new epochs. Therefore, they completely lacked any sense of "alternative pasts"[68] or of the historical peculiarity of each epoch. The twelfth century, Janet Coleman states, was not simply concerned with "the pastness of the past"[69] but with "a timeless edification."[70]

The medieval concept of the past thus was determined by an extremely peculiar, ambiguous mixture of belief in historical progression on the one hand and its consistency on the other, of an epochal change and at the same time a continuity of times and historical situations. In the final analysis, it lacked a sense of the truly historical character of the past. Owing to the chronological arrangement, this understanding cannot be classified as being truly timeless, but in various regards it nevertheless lacked a sense of epochal peculiarity. The past was perceived as a (temporal) development corresponding to the *saeculum*, the earthly time, with an unchanging character and essence. Thus, the widespread tendency to

---

67 See Robert L. Benson, "Political Renovatio: Two Models from Roman Antiquity," in Robert L. Benson and Giles Constable, eds., *Renaissance and Renewal in the Twelfth Century* (Oxford, 1982), 339–86. More reluctantly, see Ingrid Baumgärtner, "Rombeherrschung und Romerneuerung: Die römische Kommune im 12. Jahrhundert," *Quellen und Forschungen aus italienischen Archiven und Bibliotheken* 69 (1989): 27–79.

68 See Patrick J. Geary, *Phantoms of Remembrance: Memory and Oblivion at the End of the First Millennium* (Princeton, N.J., 1994), 132.

69 Janet Coleman, *Ancient and Medieval Memories: Studies in the Reconstruction of the Past* (Cambridge, 1992), 294.

70 Ibid., 324.

order historical events according to their respective time was in no way seen as contradictory to the opposing tendency to detach the subject matter of the same events from their chronological order. The pictorial representations and the theory of "translations" prove that these two apparently juxtaposed approaches were not perceived as a contradiction. How then, we should ask in a fourth and last section, can we explain such thinking that to us seems contradictory?

PLACING HISTORICAL EVENTS IN AND DETACHING THEM FROM THEIR TEMPORAL FRAMEWORKS: COMPLEMENTARY ELEMENTS IN THE MEDIEVAL CONCEPT OF THE PAST

The explanation of this seemingly ambiguous concept of time has to be searched for in the specifically medieval concept of the past. On the one hand, the inseparable coherence of time and events required a chronological "temporalization" of the latter, a verification of the temporal systems, and a parallelization (or synopsis) of contemporaneous events in different spaces and realms. Not only was it incontestable that history followed a temporal progression, but this feature even was a decisive part of its essence and a presupposition of the doctrine of salvation that looked ahead toward the end, that is, redemption. History was an ever-progressing development. Such a view did not lead the chroniclers to ignore ruptures in history or the origins of a historical development, both of which actually were central to almost all historical thinking: the beginning of the world in universal chronicles and of one's own institution in the *Gesta episcoporum* and the *Gesta abbatum*. These origins, however, were favorably dated back to the remote dawn of history, thus creating a continuity that was as long lasting as possible. According to the *Gesta Treverorum*, Trier had been founded by Trebetas, a son of the first Assyrian king Ninus, precisely 1,250 years before the foundation of Rome! The genetic perspective, the teleological representation of history from the beginning to the present time, required a temporal succession and at the same time emphasized the inherent links with the present.

Actually, these links between past and present were responsible for the detachment of facts from their "correct" temporal place. The perception of the past did not have an end in itself, neither in the Middle Ages nor nowadays. The lucid, partly synoptical chronological dating system was meant for further exemplary usage and should provide historical information for any arising problem. Thus, chronological-genetic and exemplary concepts of the past complemented each other: The former located historical events into their precise time, and the latter detached them from it. The view of the past was intended to emphasize genetic coherence; however, it did not pursue this aim (like nowadays) in order to survey the formation of the present but rather to investigate the temporal position of the present in the course of the universal and salvational history. Moreover, it was a didactic tool that illuminated examples of correct behavior. Thus, like today, it served for a better recognition of the present; this was not achieved by contrasting but rather by typological comparison. This attitude arose because the past was perceived as being fairly "present" or, better, modern. No one doubted that distinct historical times were comparable and similar to each other. Therefore, the chroniclers felt completely entitled to dissolve the difference in substance between former and present times and to confront past and present directly while neglecting the historical changes in between and forgetting about or ignoring distinct structures.[71] Consequently, typological comparisons always were permissible; biblical conditions from the Old Testament were applied to solve current questions: The example of Saul and Samuel served as a model solution for the investiture problem, although in those remote, pre-Christian times there existed neither bishops nor investitures. The intention, however, was not to establish the historical origins of these institutions, but rather the (original and therefore ideal) relationship between *regnum* and *sacerdotium*, secular and spiritual powers. We may conclude, therefore, that a "detemporalization" (detaching events from their temporal position) was the medieval way of "representing" the past.

Regarding the medieval concept of the past, a deeper justification for this method may be found in the Christian belief of the sense and end of all historical events (history itself), which reveals a substantial difference to our way of thinking: Time was an essential part of earthly existence, yet at the same time it was a symbol of the eternal world. The belief in a comparability and thus in a potential "detemporalization" of historical events was based on the conviction that all history was God's revelation of the process of salvation. History did not only occur according to God's providence but also revealed his intention. Therefore, it had sense and meaning. Events of the past, as they had been handed down, had not come to pass by chance but with specific objectives. Consequently, it contained a message for mankind that had to be investigated and interpreted. Whenever the medieval historian discovered similarities

---

71 Cf. Amos Funkenstein, *Heilsplan und natürliche Entwicklung: Formen der Gegenwartsbestimmung im Geschichtsdenken des hohen Mittelalters* (Munich, 1965), 71: The questions remained the same.

in the actions or in the conditions between single events, he was convinced that he had discerned the divine plan and message in them.

It is true that various traditions mingled in this manner of thinking. Historiographical thinking was combined with the theological needs of history. Yet it remains significant that these different traditions were inseparably linked with one another instead of one element being disposed of: Symbolic and typological comparisons did not result in the renunciation of a temporal framework that, on the contrary, was even emphasized by this comparison. History was a "sequence of time," the importance of which lay in a constant re-presentation, not in a representation of the past as such, but of a certain past that was relevant for the present. In regard to this aspect at least, and notwithstanding changes in attitudes, methods, intentions, and convictions, we may discover certain parallels to our modern historical thinking.

8

Constructing the Past by Means of the Present

Historiographical Foundations of Medieval Institutions, Dynasties, Peoples, and Communities

BERND SCHNEIDMÜLLER

Most educated people share the belief that history teaches us lessons – that the historical past leads to the present and somehow extends into the future. The persistence of this belief is such that historians, as a professional group, benefit from sustained employment and positions of rank in many high cultures. The historian's desire to elucidate the present, or even to unearth behavioral models for the future, results in a constant evolution of the questions that historians pose on the past. In our century, the historian's desire for contemporary relevance has played a role in the growth of social history. More recently, it has contributed to the popularity of research projects on the environment and on gender roles. In using the past to explain the present, however, academic historians rarely achieve consensus in their conclusions, and they generally prognosticate future developments with no greater degree of success than the average person.

Of course, no one would contest that our present relates in a real sense to our past. However, the historian who researches the history of historiography or the development of an historical consciousness in a past society is soon forced to recognize a countervailing fact. In any period contemporary needs and yearnings determine why and how we explore the historical record. In reconstructing the past from the present we discover that the boundaries separating historical research from pure construction are not easily defined. Describing long-term developments in a few sentences or images inevitably embroils the historian in a process of

This chapter is an enlarged and translated version of a German paper read at the Heidelberg conference. For advice and help in preparing the American text, I am grateful to Pegatha Taylor (Berkeley), Philippe Buc (Stanford), and Klaus van Eickels (Bamberg).

abstraction and reduction. The resulting *mise en scène* necessarily aims at the present and, at the same time, stems from it. Naturally, every historian displays personal tendencies: One has a great love for detail, the next shows instead a feel for the spirit of the times. Some historians take a critical stance toward the textual traditions shaping their sources, and others prefer simple storytelling. Some have a talent for assembling detailed facts, while others are preoccupied with isolating large structures and processes. The extent to which these conceptualizations and their forms of presentation win credit in the academic and public spheres depends largely on their compatibility with the sources, against which or without which history cannot be written.

This chapter is designed to contribute to an understanding of this imaginative process. I shall discuss four independent examples from the central and later Middle Ages in order to address two points: To what ends and in which ways did our predecessors conceptualize history? More detailed explorations of these particular cases have already appeared in print. I do not intend to discuss the reliability of the sources in detail, nor shall I provide an overall analysis of the individual texts. Rather, my purpose is to assess aims and forms of historiographical efforts that served the creation and maintenance of an historical consciousness in different social groups.

I have chosen the following examples: (1) an institution – the Capetian monarchy at a point of transition from the central to the later Middle Ages; (2) a dynasty – the Welfs, emerging territorial princes in Northern Germany; (3) a people – the Frisians, who were in a process of social evolution over the course of the thirteenth century; (4) a social group – the elites in the cities of northern Germany who were searching for an historical orientation at the end of the Middle Ages. The extant sources that testify to the birth of these different historical perspectives belong to dissimilar periods and literary types. My goal – to assess the close interdependence between historical writing and its contemporary sociopolitical context – is the only unifying element among them. When approached as a form of *mise en scène* that the historian constructs out of the past, our sources will reveal how closely any "history of the imagination" is and ought to be bound up with social history.

ON THE ROAD TO A *RECTA LINEA ARBORIS GENEALOGIAE REGUM FRANCORUM*

A longing for continuity and a harmonization of its dynastic history is characteristic of French historiography in the central medieval period.

This provides a counterpoint to the many breaks and discontinuities in the history of the Frankish, West Frankish, and French kingdoms of the eighth to the eleventh centuries.[1] As of the eleventh century, an attempt was made to construct an orderly succession of three ruling families in the *regnum Francorum* (Frankish kingdom). The attempt originated in the spiritual centers of the royally controlled region of Francia.[2] At the beginning of the thirteenth century, either the Capetian court[3] or the royal monastery of St. Denis took over the project.[4] Oddly enough, it has only recently been realized – thanks to the work of American, French, and German scholars – that these historiographical compilations are of great value as forerunners of the *Grandes chroniques*.[5] These texts, written first in Latin and later in Old French, do not contain any new information; thus they were neglected by historians who were only interested in facts. They do, however, provide rich material for the history of ideas because the reports taken from other sources were

1 Karl Ferdinand Werner, *Histoire de France*, vol. 1: *Les origines (avant l'an mil)* (Paris, 1984); Jean Dunbabin, *France in the Making* (Oxford, 1985); Carlrichard Brühl, *Deutschland – Frankreich: Die Geburt zweier Völker* (Cologne, 1990); Janet L. Nelson, "The Frankish Kingdoms, 814–898: The West," in Rosamond McKitterick, ed., *The New Cambridge History*, vol. 2: *c. 700–c. 900* (Cambridge, 1995), 110–41.

2 For the royal domaine, see William Mendel Newman, *Le domaine royal sous les premiers Capétiens (987–1180)* (Paris, 1937). The most important spiritual centers were Fleury, Reims, Saint-Denis, and Tours; see Alexandre Vidier, *L'historiographie à Saint-Benoît-sur-Loire et les miracles de Saint Benoît* (Paris, 1965); Robert-Henri Bautier, "La place de l'abbaye de Fleury-sur-Loire dans l'historiographie française du IXe au XIIe siècle," *Études Ligériennes d'histoire et d'archéologie médiévale* (Auxerre, 1975), 25–33; Michel Sot, *Un historien et son église au Xe siècle: Flodoard de Reims* (Paris, 1993); Anne Lombard-Jourdan, *Montjoie et Saint Denis! Le Centre de la Gaule aux origines de Paris et de Saint-Denis* (Paris, 1989); Tom Waldman, "Saint-Denis et les premiers Capétiens," in Dominique Iogna-Prat and Jean-Charles Picard, eds., *Religion et culture autour de l'an mil: Royaume capétien et Lotharingie* (Paris, 1990), 191–7; Sharon Farmer, *Communities of Saint Martin: Legend and Ritual in Medieval Tours* (Ithaca and London, 1991).

3 Bernd Schneidmüller, *Nomen patriae: Die Entstehung Frankreichs in der politisch-geographischen Terminologie (10.–13. Jahrhundert)* (Sigmaringen, 1987), 167–90.

4 Gabrielle Spiegel, *The Chronicle Tradition of Saint-Denis: A Survey* (Brookline, Mass., 1978); Donatella Nebbiai-Dalla Guarda, *La bibliothèque de l'abbaye de Saint-Denis en France du IXe au XVIIIe siècle* (Paris, 1985).

5 Jules Viard, ed., *Grandes chroniques de France*, 10 vols. (Paris, 1920–53). On forerunners recently identified: Pierre Botineau, "L'histoire de France en français de Charlemagne à Philippe Auguste: La compilation du manuscrit 624 du fonds de la Reine à la Bibliothèque Vaticane," *Romania* 90 (1969): 79–99; Bernd Schneidmüller, "Ein Geschichtskompendium des frühen 13. Jahrhunderts aus Saint-Denis (Vat. Reg. Lat. 550) als Vorläufer der Grandes Chroniques," *Quellen und Forschungen aus italienischen Archiven und Bibliotheken* 67 (1987): 447–61; Gabrielle M. Spiegel, "Social Change and Literary Language: The Textualization of the Past in Thirteenth-Century Old French Historiography," *Journal of Medieval and Renaissance Studies* 17 (1987): 129–48; Gabrielle M. Spiegel, "Moral imagination and the rise of the bureaucratic state: images of government in the "Chronique des Rois de France," Chantilly, MS. 869," *Journal of Medieval and Renaissance Studies* 18 (1988): 157–73; Gillette Labory, "Essai d'une histoire nationale au XIIIe siècle: La chronique de l'anonyme de Chantilly-Vatican," *Bibliothèque de l'École des Chartes* 148 (1990): 301–54.

ordered and composed in a completely new way and thus acquired new meaning.[6]

The first step in the creation of an indigenous tradition in France focusing on the unique history of the realm consisted of promoting the image of a smooth transition between the three genealogical lines of the Merovingians, Carolingians, and Capetians. This endeavor got under way in the first half of the eleventh century. The notion subsequently passed into the French historical consciousness of the modern period, under the rubric of the three dynasties of kings of France (*trois races des rois de France*). The early medieval centuries also bequeathed to the French a flexible notion of Frankish-French continuity from its Trojan beginnings up to the Capetians.[7] By ordering the kings' graves in St. Denis, Louis IX created in the thirteenth century a monumental visual counterpart[8] to the many royal genealogical texts compiled in parchment codices.[9] The Merovingian-Carolingian and the Capetian tombs were laid out in two rows. The graves of Philip II Augustus and Louis VIII created a unifying link between the *genealogiae* (families) of two former enemies, the Carolingians and the Capetians.[10] At the same time these graves marked biologically the "return of the governance of the Franks to the line of Charlemagne" (*reditus regni Francorum ad stirpem Karoli Magni*).[11]

The idea of the three *genealogiae* of the *reges Francorum* (kings of the Franks), which postulates two dynastic caesurae in 751 and 987, is found

---

6 The necessity of studying these historiographical compilations as prerequisite for a better knowledge of historiographical production is underscored by Gert Melville, "Spätmittelalterliche Geschichtskompendien – eine Aufgabenstellung," *Römische Historische Mitteilungen* 22 (1980): 51–104; Bernard Guenée, "L'historien et la compilation au XIIIe siècle," *Journal des savants* (1985): 119–35.

7 Maria Klippel, "Die Darstellung der Fränkischen Trojanersage in Geschichtsschreibung und Dichtung vom Mittelalter bis zur Renaissance in Frankreich," Ph.D. diss., University of Marburg, 1936; Colette Beaune, *Naissance de la nation France* (Paris, 1985), 19–54.

8 Alain Erlande-Brandenburg, *Le roi est mort: Études sur les funérailles, les sépultures et les tombeaux des rois de France jusqu'à la fin du XIIIe siècle* (Geneva, 1975); Joachim Ehlers, "Kontinuität und Tradition als Grundlage mittelalterlicher Nationsbildung in Frankreich," in Helmut Beumann, ed., *Beiträge zur Bildung der französischen Nation im Früh- und Hochmittelalter* (Sigmaringen, 1983), 32–5.

9 Thorough studies in the textual traditions of these genealogical lists and their enlarged historiographical versions, as well as of their place in the manuscripts, are missing. For Aegidius Parisiensis (Giles of Paris) and his Genealogia regum Francorum cf. Andrew W. Lewis, "Dynastic Structures and Capetian Throne Right: The Views of Giles of Paris," *Traditio* 33 (1977): 225–52; Gert Melville, "Geschichte in graphischer Gestalt: Beobachtungen zu einer spätmittelalterlichen Darstellungsweise," in Hans Patze, ed., *Geschichtsschreibung und Geschichtsbewusstsein im späten Mittelalter* (Sigmaringen, 1987), 57–154.

10 For a reconstruction, see Ehlers, "Kontinuität und Tradition," 33.

11 Karl Ferdinand Werner, "Die Legitimität der Kapetinger und die Entstehung des 'Reditus regni Francorum ad stirpem Karoli,'" *Die Welt als Geschichte* 12 (1952): 203–25; Gabrielle M. Spiegel, "The 'Reditus regni ad stirpem Karoli Magni': a new look," *French Historical Studies* 7 (1971): 145–74.

first in the *Historia Francorum Senonensis*.[12] In this form it became a source
for later, more ambitious renderings of the continuities in the Frankish
royal tradition. Andreas of Marchiennes broadened the scope of this doctrine by spreading the claim that the Capetian kingdom had Carolingian
roots.[13] The Capetian court then adopted these ideas in the thirteenth
century. The luxury manuscripts of the French kings' genealogical trees
(*arbores genealogiae*) brought the process to a close in the fourteenth
century. The *arbores*, which were prepared serially for purposes of propaganda in the workshops of Bernard Gui,[14] traced the lineage of the French
kings from their Trojan origins to the current ruler.[15] The genealogical
trees were not intended to provide visual renditions of French history in
all its variety; instead, they helped to construct a genealogy of French rule,
a "direct line of the genealogical tree of the kings of France" (*recta linea
arboris genealogiae regum Francorum*).

Admittedly, anyone acquainted with the history of the West Franks in
the ninth and tenth centuries knows of the long-standing rivalry between
the two claimants to the throne, the Carolingians and the Capetians. Their
competition for the French crown was punctuated by breaks, forward
leaps, and coincidences.[16] Three hundred years later, however, the victory
of a dynastic principle smoothed over these confusing multiplicities: The
French discovered something akin to a genealogical leitmotif in the dis-
ruptions of their past. The construction of the *recta linea arboris genealogiae*
came in response to the requirements that the central medieval system of
dynastic accession and the monarchy as an institution placed on the concrete person of the king.[17] In central medieval France, no one regretted

12 "Historia Francorum Senonensis," ed. Georg Waitz, in *Monumenta Germaniae Historica, Scriptores* 9
(Hannover, 1851), 364–9. See Joachim Ehlers, "Die 'Historia Francorum Senonensis' und der
Aufstieg des Hauses Capet," *Journal of Medieval History* 4 (1978): 1–25.

13 Karl Ferdinand Werner, "Andreas von Marchiennes und die Geschichtsschreibung von Anchin und
Marchiennes in der zweiten Hälfte des 12. Jahrhunderts," *Deutsches Archiv* 9 (1952): 402–63.

14 Léopold Delisle, "Notice sur les manuscrits de Bernard Gui," *Notices et extraits des manuscrits de la
Bibliothèque Nationale* 27 (1879): 169–455; A. Thomas, "Bernard Gui, frère précheur," *Histoire littéraire de la France* 35 (1921): 139–232.

15 *Bernard Gui et son monde* (Toulouse, 1981); Bernard Guenée, *Entre l'église et l'état: Quatre vies de
prélats français à la fin du moyen âge (XIIIe–XVe siècle)* (Paris, 1987), 49–85. The genealogical production of the scriptorium of Bernard Gui is analyzed by Gert Melville, "Vorfahren und
Vorgänger: Spätmittelalterliche Genealogien als dynastische Legitimation zur Herrschaft," in Peter
Johannes Schuler, ed., *Die Familie als sozialer und historischer Verband* (Sigmaringen, 1987), 203–309.

16 Cf. Bernd Schneidmüller, *Karolingische Tradition und frühes französisches Königtum: Untersuchungen zur
Herrschaftslegitimation der westfränkisch-französischen Monarchie im 10. Jahrhundert* (Wiesbaden, 1979).

17 Percy Ernst Schramm, *Der König von Frankreich: Das Wesen der Monarchie vom 9. zum 16. Jahrhundert*, 2d ed., 2 vols. (Darmstadt, 1960); Bernd Schneidmüller, "Herrscher über Land oder Leute?:
Der kapetingische Herrschertitel in der Zeit Philipps II. August und seiner Nachfolger
(1180–1270)," in Herwig Wolfram and Anton Scharer, eds., *Intitulatio III: Lateinische Herrschertitel
und Herrschertitulaturen vom 7. bis zum 13. Jahrhundert* (Vienna, 1988), 131–62.

the historiographical distortions that were necessary for the invention of a direct dynastic line. No one condemned these distortions as falsifications; rather, they were viewed as part of a proper ordering, proper, that is, from the vantage point of the thirteenth and fourteenth centuries. Ultimately, the view of reality came to shape reality.[18]

The authors of the *recta linea* consistently excluded Hugh Capet from their lists of kings, which suggests that the texts also were part of an attempt to circumvent the real biological roots of the ruling Capetians.[19] What possible explanations exist for this tactic? Picturesque historical trivia, such as the claim that Hugh may have been the son of a Paris butcher, provide the least enticing answers.[20] Far more relevant is an issue recently raised and disputed by German medievalists: Can an historiographical tradition offer insights into the historical consciousness of princes or kings? Or must our texts be read exclusively as the products of their (clerical) authors and of the institutions from which they came?[21]

In contrast to the historiographical products of the Welfish court, the *recta linea* is a sufficiently well-defined corpus that it can be used reliably to answer this question. We are well informed about the use of luxury genealogical manuscripts at the French court in the fourteenth century.[22] The uniquely rich trove of registry books from the royal chancery provides even clearer evidence at the start of the thirteenth century.

---

18 For the relation between reality and the views of reality in the middle ages, cf. the works of Georges Duby, reviewed by Otto Gerhard Oexle, "Die 'Wirklichkeit' und das 'Wissen': Ein Blick auf das sozialgeschichtliche Oeuvre von Georges Duby," *Historische Zeitschrift* 232 (1981): 61–91. Otto Gerhard Oexle, "Deutungsschemata der sozialen Wirklichkeit im frühen und hohen Mittelalter: Ein Beitrag zur Geschichte des Wissens," in František Graus, ed., *Mentalitäten im Mittelalter: Methodische und inhaltliche Probleme* (Sigmaringen, 1987), 65–117.

19 Examples: Biblioteca Apostolica Vaticana, cod. Reg. lat. 518, fol. 78^{r-v} (*Hugo Capet obtentor regni*); Paris, Bibliothèque Nationale (hereafter BN), lat. 4975, fol. 121^{r-v}; Paris, Bibliothèque Nationale, lat. 4976, fol. 148^{r-v}; Paris, BN, ms lat. 4988, fol. 53^{v}–54^{r}; Paris, BN, ms lat. 5988, fol. 10^{r-v}; Paris, BN, ms lat. 5929, fol. 10^{r-v}; Paris, BN, ms lat. n.a. 1171, fol. 142^{v}–143^{r}. However, one may also recognize the existence of other genealogical manuscripts that show an appreciation of Hugh's role as founder of the Capetian dynasty. See the *rotuli* in Paris, Bibliothèque Sainte-Geneviève, mss 522–3.

20 Piera Alessandra Maccioni, "Une note sur Hugues Capet: Sa chanson de geste et l'historiographie médiévale anglaise," in Dominique Iogna-Prat and Jean-Charles Picard, eds., *Religion et culture autour de l'an mil: Royaume capétien et Lotharingie* (Paris, 1990), 227–9. For Hugh Capet as founder of the Capetian dynasty, see Michel Parisse and Xavier Barral I. Altet, eds., *Le roi de France et son royaume autour de l'an mil* (Paris, 1992); Bernd Schneidmüller, "1000 Jahre Frankreich? Forschungen zum Herrschaftsantritt Hugo Capets 987," *Francia* 21, no. 1 (1994): 227–44.

21 See note 34 to this chapter.

22 Mario Schiff, "Oeuvres de Bernard Gui offertes à Philippe de Valois," *Bibliothèque de l'École des chartes* 57 (1896): 637–9.

These registry books now are accessible in a new edition by John Baldwin.[23]

Lists of rulers and their regnal years appear in the two French royal chancery registers C and E from the period of Philip II.[24] They accompany a variety of other administrative texts. It is conceivable that they were designed to help the reader keep track of the many kings' names that appear elsewhere in the books. No one as yet has systematically collected and analyzed these lists within the framework of a broader knowledge of the sources. Therefore, the lists of the Capetian chancery registers cannot be identified with particular textual traditions.[25] The lists have various unusual characteristics – most relevant for our purposes is the simple fact that they were placed in a chancery register. It sheds light on a complicated process in which the clerics working in the immediate circles of the Capetian rulers encoded their diplomatic, administrative, eschatological, geographical, and historical knowledge in a textual format.

The 1992 edition of the royal registers divides the various personal names in the texts into the categories of popes, emperors, and kings, a format that is quite misleading in the case of the list *Nomina regum Francorum qui venerunt de Troia* (names of king of the Franks/the French who came from Troia).[26] The scribes of the two registers naturally placed the names of the Frankish and French kings before the list of the Roman emperors beginning with Julius Caesar and running up to 813.[27]

23 John W. Baldwin (avec le concours de Françoise Gasparri, Michel Nortier et Elisabeth Lalou, sous la direction de Robert-Henri Bautier), ed., *Les registres de Philippe Auguste*, vol. 1: *Texte* (Paris, 1992); cf. my review in *Francia* 23, no. 1 (1996): 300–2.

24 Register C: Paris, Archives Nationales, JJ 7 (compiled 1212, with additions to 1220), fol. 144ᵛ; 2d list fol. 145ʳ. Register E: Paris, Archives Nationales, JJ 26 (compiled 1220, with additions to 1276), fol. 304ʳ. Cf. John W. Baldwin, *The Government of Philip Augustus: Foundations of French Royal Power in the Middle Ages* (Berkeley, Calif., 1986).

25 Elizabeth A. R. Brown, "La notion de la légitimité et la prophétie à la cour de Philippe Auguste," in Robert-Henri Bautier, ed., *La France de Philippe Auguste: Le temps des mutations* (Paris, 1982), 83n30, suggests a similarity with the lists of French kings attributed to Hugh of St.-Victor, but in fact textual dependencies on lists organized elsewhere cannot be proved: Hugh of St.-Victor, *Liber de tribus maximis circumstantiis gestorum*, Paris Bibiliothèque Nationale, lat. 15009, fol. 24ʳ–26ᵛ; cf. Joachim Ehlers, *Hugo von St. Viktor: Studien zum Geschichtsdenken und zur Geschichtsschreibung des 12. Jahrhunderts* (Wiesbaden, 1973), 97–102.

26 *Les registres de Philippe Auguste*, 345–7 (popes), 349–50 (Roman emperors), 350–2 (kings of France).

27 Paris, Archives Nationales, JJ 7, fol. 144ᵛ; JJ 26, fol. 304ʳ. The *translatio imperii* in the time of Eirene and Charlemagne is mentioned: "Hyrenee sola X./ Sub hoc tempore imperium Romanum ad reges Francorum translatum est Karolo Magno, filio Pepini regis, primo imperatore facto. In Constantinopoli vero regnum Grecorum permansit et post Hyreneem Nicephorus imperium arripuit./ Nicephorus VIII./ Michael II." (*Les registres de Philippe Auguste*, 350). Illustrations of the manuscript evidence are given in Bernd Schneidmüller, "Die Gegenwart der Vorgänger: Geschichtsbewusstsein in den westfränkisch-französischen Herrscherurkunden des Hochmittelalters," in Hans-Werner Goetz, ed., *Hochmittelalterliches Geschichtsbewusstsein im Spiegel nichthistoriographischer Quellen* (Berlin, 1998), 217–35.

The Robertine ancestry of King Philip II Augustus seems to have been a particular sore point for the compilers of this list. They eliminated from their text all the Robertine kings who had disrupted the continuity of the Carolingian line before 987. Over a hundred years prior to Bernard Gui's *recta linea arboris genealogiae*, therefore, clerics within the French king's entourage seem to have been responsible for the first "codification" of an administrative royal tradition. In the registry books they traced the Carolingians down to Charles of Lower Lorraine, the uncle of the last ruling Carolingian, Louis V. Not a word was spoken of the Robertine King Odo (888–898); the disqualifier *alienus* (strange) appeared next to Robert I (922–923), who was Hugh Capet's own grandfather, and next to Raoul of Burgundy (923–936).[28] One of the lists of rulers found in Register C blots out Robert and Raoul altogether. It admittedly includes King Odo, but it refers to him exclusively as a regent acting for the legitimate Carolingian ruler Charles III (893–898 to 923–929) – *tamquam ballivus*; the first Capetian ruler, Hugh (987–996), was then supposedly *electus a baronibus* (chosen by the nobles).[29]

From the perspective of the thirteenth century, and above all in light of the Capetian principles of dynastic succession, the ellipses of West Frankish rulership in the ninth and tenth centuries were part of a history that was capable of being corrected.[30] Indeed, it stood in need of correction. When these lists were being compiled, the administrative tradition of the court – the historical primacy that was accorded to the tenure of royal office – proved a stronger influence than the memory of family lineages. This was the case in thirteenth-century France because the office and the institution of the monarchy had acquired by that point greater importance than the person of the monarch himself.[31]

In order that the French monarchy would remain durable, it seemed necessary that someone compose an orderly history of the monarchy as an institution. For the Capetians of the central Middle Ages, this meant abandoning their forefathers in favor of those who had preceded them in the office of king, going all the way back to a Trojan prehistory. It is impossible to explain the reasons why the French royal registers constructed such a history if one focuses exclusively on the surviving primary sources or on the historical realities of the ninth and tenth centuries. The

28 *Les registres de Philippe Auguste*, 351.   29 Ibid., 352.
30 Andrew W. Lewis, *Royal Succession in Capetian France: Studies in Familial Order and the State* (Cambridge, Mass., 1981).
31 Cf. Schramm, *Der König von Frankreich*; Ferdinand Lot, Robert Fawtier, *Histoire des institutions françaises au moyen âge*, vol. 2: *Institutions royales* (Paris, 1958).

political context of the thirteenth and fourteenth centuries is the only factor that makes sense of this development.

TRANSFERRING DYNASTIC ROOTS: THE WELFS AND THE CREATION OF THEIR SAXON GENEAOLOGY

We now shift the topic from the administrative *memoria* (memory) of the French monarchy to the historiography of a noble house in the medieval *imperium* (empire). A body of research already exists that has analyzed the development of a self-conscious dynastic identity between the twelfth and fifteenth centuries among the Welfs.[32] The Welfs were the first noble house of the Empire to attract the interest of historiographers.[33] A lively debate currently rages as to whether the Welfish histories of the central Middle Ages were a history of a noble house or were more an institutionally oriented endeavor.[34] Historians have often discussed the monuments of the various Welfish genealogical conceptions.[35] For this reason I shall not review here the problems in dating and interpreting the details of their production.

I shall instead focus on two works from the second half of the twelfth century, the Welfish genealogical tree from the Swabian Benedictine house of Weingarten,[36] and the coronation portrait of Henry the Lion and

32 See Hans Patze, "Die Welfen in der mittelalterlichen Geschichte Europas," *Blätter für deutsche Landesgeschichte* 117 (1981): 139–66; Bernd Schneidmüller, "Landesherrschaft, welfische Identität und sächsische Geschichte," in Peter Moraw, ed., *Regionale Identität und soziale Gruppen im deutschen Mittelalter* (Berlin, 1992), 65–101.

33 Erich König, ed., *Historia Welforum*, 2d ed. (Sigmaringen, 1978). See Karl Schmid, "Welfisches Selbstverständnis," in *Adel und Kirche: Festschrift Gerd Tellenbach* (Freiburg im Breisgau, 1968), 389–416.

34 Gerd Althoff, "Anlässe zur schriftlichen Fixierung adligen Selbstverständnisses," *Zeitschrift für die Geschichte des Oberrheins* 134 (1986): 34–46; Otto Gerhard Oexle, "Welfische Memoria: Zugleich ein Beitrag über adlige Hausüberlieferung und die Kriterien ihrer Erforschung," in Bernd Schneidmüller, ed., *Die Welfen und ihr Braunschweiger Hof im hohen Mittelalter* (Wiesbaden, 1995), 61–94.

35 Otto Gerhard Oexle, "Die 'sächsische Welfenquelle' als Zeugnis der welfischen Hausüberlieferung," *Deutsches Archiv* 24 (1968): 435–97; Otto Gerhard Oexle, "Adliges Selbstverständnis und seine Verknüpfung mit dem liturgischen Gedenken: Das Beispiel der Welfen," *Zeitschrift für die Geschichte des Oberrheins* 134 (1986): 47–75; Michel Parisse, "Exercice et perte du pouvoir d'un prince: Henri le Lion," *Les princes et le pouvoir au moyen âge* (Paris, 1993), 69–90; Otto Gerhard Oexle, "Die Memoria Heinrichs des Löwen," in Dieter Geuenich and Otto Gerhard Oexle, eds., *Memoria in der Gesellschaft des Mittelalters* (Göttingen, 1994), 128–77; Bernd Schneidmüller, "Grosse Herzöge, oft Kaisern widerstehend?: Die Welfen im hochmittelalterlichen Europa," in Jochen Luckhardt and Franz Niehoff, eds., *Heinrich der Löwe und seine Zeit: Herrschaft und Repräsentation der Welfen 1125–1235: Katalog der Ausstellung Braunschweig 1995*, 3 vols. (Munich, 1995), 2:49–61; Joachim Ehlers, *Heinrich der Löwe* (Göttingen, 1997); Joachim Ehlers and Dietrich Kötzsche, eds., *Der Welfenschatz und sein Umkreis* (Mainz, 1998).

36 Fulda, Hessische Landesbibliothek, Cod. D 11, fol. 13ᵛ; facsimile in Jochen Luckhardt and Franz Niehoff, eds., *Heinrich der Löwe und seine Zeit*, 1:63. Cf. Otto Gerhard Oexle, "Welfische und staufische Hausüberlieferung in der Handschrift Fulda D 11 aus Weingarten," in Artur Brall, ed., *Von der Klosterbibliothek zur Landesbibliothek* (Stuttgart, 1978), 203–31.

Mathilda in the Helmarshausen Gospels.[37] Two late medieval sources that
have only recently come to light provide some complementary information. The first consists of a genealogical compilation incorporating the
most important noble houses of Saxony and of the Empire. It was first
assembled as a *stemma* in the middle of the thirteenth century[38] and about
half a century later was enlarged and illuminated in Braunschweig.[39] The
second is a table of kings and princes from the middle of the fifteenth
century, painted in color on two pages.[40] These documents reflect the
constantly changing construction of a dynastic or institutional past, of
genealogy and prosopography.

Once again, the selection of materials for these *stemmata* is only understandable with reference to the needs and interests felt in the period of
their composition. In order to take these into account, the compilers,
artists, and scribes did not resort to genealogical fictions.[41] Rather, they
sought out the appropriate lines and branches of succession in a much
larger body of factual material.

The Weingarten genealogical tree focuses on the Staufer heirs of the
Welfish patrimony (*patrimonium*). From the viewer's perspective, the male
branch of the tree made a turn to the left and came to a halt at Welf VII
and Henry the Lion. This line did not appear to have any future because
Henry the Lion was represented without wife or children. As a result, it
was possible for the genealogist to place another figure at the center of
the tree, a descendant from the female line. The label on the unfinished
medallion (*Fridericus imperator*) indicates that the man portrayed was
Frederick I Barbarossa, a grandson, via his mother Judith, of the Welfish
duke Henry the Black of Bavaria. The intention was that the viewer draw
the conclusion that the history of the Welfish founders of Weingarten was

---

37 Wolfenbüttel, Herzog August Bibliothek, Cod. Guelf. 105 Noviss. 2° = München, Bayerische
   Staatsbibliothek, Clm 30055, fol. 171ᵛ; facsimile in *Das Evangeliar Heinrichs des Löwen und das mittelalterliche Herrscherbild* (Munich, 1986), plate 29. Cf. Dietrich Kötzsche, ed., *Das Evangeliar Heinrichs des Löwen: Kommentar zum Faksimile* (Frankfurt am Main, 1989); Jochen Luckhardt and Franz
   Niehoff, eds., *Heinrich der Löwe und seine Zeit*, 1:206–10.
38 "Annales Stadenses," ed. I. M. Lappenberg, in *Monumenta Germaniae Historica, Scriptores* 16 (Hannover, 1859), 329; facsimile of the only extant medieval manuscript in Jochen Luckhardt and
   Franz Niehoff, eds., *Heinrich der Löwe und seine Zeit*, 1:72. See Klaus Nass, "Zur Cronica Saxonum
   und verwandten Braunschweiger Werken," *Deutsches Archiv* 49 (1993): 557–82.
39 Wolfenbüttel, Niedersächsisches Staatsarchiv, VII B Hs 129, fol. 47ᵛ; facsimile in Jochen Luckhardt
   and Franz Niehoff, eds., *Heinrich der Löwe und seine Zeit*, 1:73.
40 Wolfenbüttel, Herzog August Bibliothek, Cod. Guelf. Weissenburg A, fol. 11ᵛ–12ʳ; facsimile in
   Jochen Luckhardt and Franz Niehoff, eds., *Heinrich der Löwe und seine Zeit*, 3:111.
41 See examples in Gerd Althoff, "Genealogische und andere Fiktionen in mittelalterlicher Historiographie," in *Fälschungen im Mittelalter: Internationaler Kongress der Monumenta Germaniae Historica,
   München, 16.–19. September 1986*, 6 vols. (Hannover, 1988–90), 1:417–41.

fulfilled mainly in Barbarossa: The adjacent recto in the manuscript is taken up by the famous picture grouping together the Staufer emperor Frederick I and his two sons, King Henry (subsequently Emperor Henry VI) and Duke Frederick of Swabia: *in medio prolis residet pater imperialis.*[42]

The coronation image in the Helmarshausen Gospels joins together the community of saints with the ducal pair and their forefathers selected chiefly on the ground of their imperial and royal extraction. A heavenly coronation connects the one sphere with the other.[43] It has been argued that the selection of a coronation image demonstrates that Henry the Lion and his wife had a self-conscious conception of themselves as secular rulers.[44] However, the coronation also has been interpreted as an accession to the crown of eternal life.[45]

Both interpretations are critical when it comes to deciding whether to date the Gospels to the 1170s (before the duke's fall from power in 1180) or to the 1180s. Nonetheless, critics have challenged these two interpretations for a long time. It is a modern invention to differentiate clearly between power and religion, and between the earthly and heavenly realms – whether the composers of the tables were conscious of such a distinction is moot. A twelfth-century audience was capable of seeing both: the crowned ducal couple in its unique political position in the Empire on the one hand and the pious donors yearning for the reward of eternal life on the other.

---

42 Fulda, Hessische Landesbibliothek, Cod. D 11, fol. 14ʳ; facsimile in Jochen Luckhardt and Franz Niehoff, eds., *Heinrich der Löwe und seine Zeit*, 1:69.

43 An example of a coronation with the crown of eternal life is given by Wolfgang Milde, "Christus verheisst das Reich des Lebens. Krönungsdarstellungen von Schreibern und Stiftern," in Bernd Schneidmüller, ed., *Die Welfen und ihr Braunschweiger Hof im hohen Mittelalter* (Wiesbaden, 1995), 279–96 (second half of the twelfth century; lost manuscript: Douai, Bibliothèque municipale, ms. 257): a monk-scribe crowned by the crown of eternal life (facsimile, p. 286).

44 Johannes Fried, "Königsgedanken Heinrichs des Löwen," *Archiv für Kulturgeschichte* 55 (1973): 312–51; Hermann Jakobs, "Dynastische Verheissung: Die Krönung Heinrichs des Löwen und Mathildes im Helmarshausener Evangeliar," in Jan Assmann and Dietrich Harth, eds., *Kultur und Konflikt* (Frankfurt am Main, 1990), 215–59; Martin Möhle, "Die Krypta als Herrscherkapelle: Die Krypta des Braunschweiger Domes, ihr Patrozinium und das Evangeliar Heinrichs des Löwen," *Archiv für Kulturgeschichte* 73 (1991): 1–24.

45 Reiner Haussherr, "Zur Datierung des Helmarshausener Evangeliars Heinrichs des Löwen," *Zeitschrift des Deutschen Vereins für Kunstwissenschaft* 34 (1980): 3–15; Ursula Nilgen, "Theologisches Konzept und Bildorganisation im Evangeliar Heinrichs des Löwen," *Zeitschrift für Kunstgeschichte* 52 (1989): 301–33. See the controversy between Johannes Fried, "'Das goldglänzende Buch': Heinrich der Löwe, sein Evangeliar, sein Selbstverständnis. Bemerkungen zu einer Neuerscheinung," *Göttingische Gelehrte Anzeigen* 242 (1990): 34–79; and Otto Gerhard Oexle, "Zur Kritik neuer Forschungen über das Evangeliar Heinrichs des Löwen," *Göttingische Gelehrte Anzeigen* 245 (1993): 70–109; Otto Gerhard Oexle, "Lignage et parenté, politique et religion dans la noblesse du XIIᵉ s.: L'évangeliare de Henri le Lion," *Cahiers de civilisation médiévale* 36 (1993): 339–54.

The chronicle of Albert of Stade was one of the first works in Saxony to bring the enracination process of the Welfs in their new *patria* (fatherland) up to date by incorporating into the genealogy the results of the protracted conflict between the Welfs and the Staufers, the Saxon predecessors of the Welf ducal house. At this point, Albert introduced into the genealogical tradition Duke Otto the Child of Braunschweig-Lüneburg (d. 1252) and his wife Mechthild/Mathilde with their many progeny. They were represented as the descendants of the Billung dukes of Saxony from whom the famous lines of the Welfs, Ascanians, and Staufers issued. An enlarged compilation of the Welfish Saxon ascendants was produced in the collegial foundation of St. Blasius/Braunschweig around 1300 as a continuation of Albert's chronicle.[46]

Finally, anonymous scribes collected the Saxon princely families over a period of more than 700 years into two prosopographic tables extant from the middle of the fifteenth century. The tables begin with Widukind, run through the Ottonian emperors, and end with the Braunschweiger Welfs of the late Middle Ages. In this instance, the compilers consistently avoided a genealogical ordering of the material. They stressed instead the continuity in the office of ruler of Saxony.[47]

Above and beyond the disagreements over the details of these sources, one thing remains uncontested: The reconstruction of Welfish genealogies served as a showcase for contemporary claims and desires. It also is clear that the purpose behind these legitimizing strategies varied. The Welfs' genealogical tree in the Weingartner codex took into account the change in incumbents to the *patrimonium*. The Braunschweiger coronation image, on the other hand, pointed to the royal status of the ducal house and associated the Welfish genealogy with a pious donation.

The Welfish ideology of rule and the historical knowledge attached to the Welfs were formalized and transmitted in writing and images while still in the process of evolution. This is particularly the case if we look beyond the more famous sources of the twelfth century, monuments of a central medieval memorial culture, to the lesser-known late medieval *stemmata*. The late medieval sources are no less relevant to the topic of construction of the past by means of the present.

46 See notes 38–9 to this chapter. See also Bernd Schneidmüller, "Billunger – Welfen – Askanier: Eine genealogische Bildtafel aus dem Braunschweiger Blasius-Stift und das hochadlige Familienbewusstsein in Sachsen um 1300," *Archiv für Kulturgeschichte* 69 (1987): 30–61.
47 See note 40 to this chapter. Cf. Bernd Schneidmüller, "Reichsnähe – Königsferne: Goslar, Braunschweig und das Reich im späten Mittelalter," *Niedersächsisches Jahrbuch für Landesgeschichte* 64 (1992): 45–8.

The Welfs' history was altered by their defeat at the hands of their Staufer rivals. The change in their fortunes prompted new historical and genealogical reconstructions of their past. King Philip II Augustus's victory over the Welfish emperor Otto IV at Bouvines in 1214 prepared the way for this defeat. The political marginalization of the Welfs in the 1220s also was a contributing factor, as was the establishment of the duchy of Braunschweig in 1235 by Emperor Frederick II.[48]

This creation of the new duchy marked the Welfs' abandonment of their southern German homeland and the definitive restriction of their princely power to Saxony. In response to this geopolitical narrowing, the late-medieval sources concentrated exclusively on the Saxon ancestors of the Welfs, although the authors certainly were aware that the dynasty had once enjoyed ascendancy throughout Europe.

This phenomenon is first observable in the territorially and genealogically oriented historical writings of the last quarter of the thirteenth century.[49] The Braunschweig foundation of St. Blasius, a spiritual and cultic center, lost interest in the roots of the Welfish family.[50] The members of its scriptorium focused instead on the history of the ducal office, on the rule of the land and on those who ruled. Admittedly, certain genealogical continuities in the ducal office were still noted, but these were guaranteed by the princesses, daughters of various Saxon noble families, rather than by the princesses' Welfish husbands.

The famous prologue to the *Sachsenspiegel* provided the most plausible explanation for the contradictory fact that the Welfs came from Swabia but ruled in Saxony. It drew a distinction between descent and place of birth: "Those of Brunswick [and other lines] are all Swabians" (*De van Brunswik . . . dit sint alle Swavee*). But then: "The dukes of Lüneburg and

48 Ludwig Weiland, ed., *Monumenta Germaniae Historica, Constitutiones* 2 (Hannover, 1896), 263–5. See Erich Klingelhöfer, *Die Reichsgesetze von 1220, 1231/32 und 1235: Ihr Werden und ihre Wirkung im deutschen Staat Friedrichs II.* (Weimar, 1955); Egon Boshof, "Die Entstehung des Herzogtums Braunschweig-Lüneburg," in Wolf-Dieter Mohrmann, ed., *Heinrich der Löwe* (Göttingen, 1980), 249–74; Hans Patze and Karl-Heinz Ahrens, "Die Begründung des Herzogtums Braunschweig im Jahre 1235 und die 'Braunschweigische Reimchronik,'" *Blätter für deutsche Landesgeschichte* 122 (1986): 67–89.

49 Hans Patze, "Adel und Stifterchronik: Frühformen territorialer Geschichtsschreibung im hochmittelalterlichen Reich," *Blätter für deutsche Landesgeschichte* 100 (1964): 8–81; 101 (1965): 67–128; Schneidmüller, "Landesherrschaft."

50 Ernst Döll, *Die Kollegiatstifte St. Blasius und St. Cyriacus zu Braunschweig* (Braunschweig, 1967); Bernd Schneidmüller, "Welfische Kollegiatstifte und Stadtentstehung im hochmittelalterlichen Braunschweig," *Rat und Verfassung im mittelalterlichen Braunschweig* (Braunschweig, 1986), 253–315; Arno Weinmann, *Braunschweig als landesherrliche Residenz im Mittelalter* (Braunschweig, 1991); Bernd Schneidmüller, "Burg – Stadt – Vaterland: Braunschweig und die Welfen im hohen Mittelalter," in Johannes Fried and Otto Gerhard Oexle, eds., *Heinrich der Löwe: Diskussionen und Perspektiven* (forthcoming).

their family are born Saxons" (*De hertoge van Luneborch unde sin geslechte sin geborne Sassen*).[51]

The innate reality of birth was matched by the new conceptualization of Welfish history, which supplied the dynasty with a Saxon past. The St. Blasius table from 1300, just like the two office holders' tables from the middle of the fifteenth century, inscribed the Welfs into a line of Saxon continuity at the expense of their southern German history. I am currently working with various manuscripts in the Wolfenbüttel collection from the richer genealogical literature of the sixteenth and seventeenth centuries in order to follow up on this practice of weaving together the Immedings, Billungs, Liudolfings, and Welfs as a means of praising Saxon continuity.

Around 1700 Gottfried Wilhelm Leibniz and his assistants rolled back the horizons of the Welfs' history beyond Saxony, to include the whole of Europe. Once again, contemporary aspirations were the deciding factor. Because a ninth electoral principality had been created in the Empire and a German line had ascended to the throne of England, a new public version of history needed to be written. This past was modeled on the present in order to serve new and different purposes. The authors no longer swore to the enracination of the Welfish house in the Saxon earth since time immemorial. Instead, they gloried in the diverse *Origines Guelficae* (Welfish origins) in England, Flanders, and Italy.[52] The Europeanization of the Welfs' identity as a noble line came to replace the practice of Saxon regionalism, but not because the historiographers of the eighteenth century were more ingenious than their predecessors. Rather, they widened their range of vision, because that was what was expected.

In any case, the evolving historical consciousness of this noble house consistently oriented itself during the twelfth to the eighteenth centuries toward the reality of rulership and the fulfillment of specific aspirations. A new present repeatedly forced a return to the past. The Welfish histo-

---

51 "Sachsenspiegel. Landrecht," ed. Karl August Eckhardt, in *Monumenta Germaniae Historica: Fontes iuris Germanici antiqui*, n. s. 1, pt. 1 (Göttingen, 1955), 53–4.
52 Armin Reese, *Die Rolle der Historie beim Aufstieg des Welfenhauses 1680–1714* (Hildesheim, 1967); Horst Eckert, *Gottfried Wilhelm Leibniz' Scriptores Rerum Brunsvicensium: Entstehung und historiographische Bedeutung* (Frankfurt am Main, 1971); G. Scheel, "Leibniz und die deutsche Geschichtswissenschaft um 1700," in Karl Hammer and Jürgen Voss, eds., *Historische Forschung im 18. Jahrhundert: Organisation – Zielsetzung – Ergebnisse* (Bonn, 1976), 82–101; Armin Reese, "Heinrich der Löwe als Argument: Zur dynastischen Historiographie der Welfen im 17. und 18. Jahrhundert," in Jochen Luckhardt and Franz Niehoff, eds., *Heinrich der Löwe und seine Zeit*, 3:41–7; Gerd van den Heuvel, " 'Dess NiederSächsischen Vaterlandes Antiquitäten': Barockhistorie und landesgeschichtliche Forschung bei Leibniz und seinen Zeitgenossen," *Niedersächsisches Jahrbuch für Landesgeschichte* 68 (1996): 19–41.

riographers did not intend to bring the past to life in the form of fiction. Instead, they sought to isolate segments or selected passages from the historical continuum that were relevant to the present – a process only comprehensible with reference to contemporary needs.

The next case study demands of the researcher a certain degree of sensitivity because it is more difficult to identify the groups interested in constructing a special past for themselves. We find our group of writers working in Frisia at the turn from the central to the late Middle Ages. In the process of assigning transtemporal attributes and rights to their own people, these authors assisted the birth of a Frisian historical consciousness. Here again they transferred social and political realities or corresponding postulates onto the past in order to provide historical reasons ready for use in contemporary arguments.

THE ETERNAL FREEDOM OF THE FRISIAN PEOPLE

In the history of Western freedom, Frisian *libertas* enjoys a particular status.[53] It was largely defined as the right to possess property and to remain independent from outside rule. In the thirteenth century this freedom was constructed as an innate characteristic of the Frisians as a people. The Emperor Charlemagne was thought to have been the first to endow it with legal authority. Up until today, the doctrine of the free and noble Frisians has been influential in maintaining a self-conscious regional identity on the peripheries of several nation-states. Frisian identity is thought to rest on particular qualities of the people; according to popular opinion, these qualities developed out of an unending battle with the sea and found expression in Frisian speech and culture. They also were mirrored in the stylized rendering of an ideal past.[54]

The most important elements of Frisian identity have been reiterated constantly throughout Frisian historiography and seem to have survived the passage of time, from the murky dawn of history up until the present day. It is precisely this longevity that arouses suspicion: It calls for a

---

53 Johannes Fried, "Über den Universalismus der Freiheit im Mittelalter," *Historische Zeitschrift* 240 (1985): 313–61; Johannes Fried, ed., *Die abendländische Freiheit vom 10. zum 14. Jahrhundert: Der Wirkungszusammenhang von Idee und Wirklichkeit im europäischen Vergleich* (Sigmaringen, 1991).

54 Heinrich Schmidt, "Studien zur Geschichte der friesischen Freiheit im Mittelalter," *Jahrbuch der Gesellschaft für bildende Kunst und vaterländische Altertümer zu Emden* 43 (1963): 5–78; Oebele Vries, *Het Heilige Roomse Rijk en de Friese vrijheid* (Leeuwarden, 1986); Bernd Schneidmüller, "Friesen – Welfen – Braunschweiger: Träger regionaler Identität im 13. Jahrhundert," in Rainer Babel and Jean-Marie Moeglin, eds., *Identité nationale et conscience régionale en France et en Allemagne du moyen âge à l'époque moderne* (Sigmaringen, 1997), 305–24.

critical assessment of sources and dating, the transmission and origins of which have yet to be the subject of proper research.

The key legal texts, which are our main source in this context, generally are dated to the eleventh century.[55] Although they vary greatly from region to region in their extant form, these texts deserve to be read together because of a shared core of ideas. Yet the manuscript transmission on its own would suggest that these texts were more likely composed in the late twelfth and thirteenth centuries.[56] In order to explain this discrepancy, scholars have postulated a temporal gap between the initial creation of a self-conscious political and legal ideology in Frisia and its full encoding in written works. This point will prove important when it comes to identifying the boundaries within which Frisian freedoms first developed.

As far as we can see, the Frisian communities (*communitates terre*, frequently just called *terre* or *universitates*) emerged as organized communities in the thirteenth century only.[57] The members of these groups, which had just completed the process of formation, looked to the past for a source of social and legal legitimation. Thirteenth-century observers thought that their autonomy was ancient. In fact, it does not seem to have predated the fall of the Brunonian counts in the late eleventh century, and it probably only became fully real after Duke Henry the Lion ceased to rule in Saxony in 1180.[58] Only at that point did the Frisians invoke for the first time as a legal precedent a grant supposedly made to them by Charlemagne. They hoped in this way to defend their freedoms and to provide them with the hallowed patina of age. We should not be misled by the fact that various written sources have survived from this period, all of which tell the story of Charlemagne's grant. Many recent

---

55 Karl Freiherr von Richthofen, *Friesische Rechtsquellen* (Berlin, 1840). The Old-Frisian texts are edited with a German translation by Wybren Jan Buma and Wilhelm Ebel, eds., *Altfriesische Rechtsquellen*, 9 vols. (Göttingen, 1963–77).

56 See Gerhard Köbler, "Friesisches Recht," *Lexikon des Mittelalters* 4 (1989): 978 f. A description of manuscripts is given by Jelle Hoekstra, *Die gemeinfriesischen siebzehn Küren* (Assen, 1940), 27 sqq.; but the dates remain contested; see N. E. Algra, *De tekstfiliatie van de 17 keuren en de 24 landrechten: Een voorbereidend onderzoek* (Grins, 1966); Willi Krogmann, "Die friesische Vorstufe des 'Vetus Ius Frisicum' (17 Küren, 24 Landrechte, allgemeine Busstaxen)," *Zeitschrift der Savigny-Stiftung für Rechtsgeschichte: Germanistische Abteilung* 89 (1972): 33–77; 90 (1973): 31–72.

57 Heinrich Schmidt, "Zum Aufstieg der hochmittelalterlichen Landesgemeinden im östlichen Friesland," *Res Frisicae: Beiträge zur ostfriesischen Verfassungs-, Sozial- und Kulturgeschichte* (Aurich, 1978), 11–27. Special regional developments are studied by Almuth Salomon, *Geschichte des Harlingerlandes bis 1600* (Aurich, 1965); Hajo van Lengen, *Geschichte des Emsigerlandes vom frühen 13. bis zum späten 15. Jahrhundert*, 2 vols. (Aurich, 1973); Wilfried Ehbrecht, *Landesherrschaft und Klosterwesen im ostfriesischen Fivelgo (970–1290)* (Münster, 1974); Albrecht Graf Finck von Finckenstein, *Die Geschichte Butjadingens und des Stadlandes bis 1514* (Oldenburg, 1975).

58 Heinrich Schmidt, *Politische Geschichte Ostfrieslands* (Leer, 1975).

studies have been published on the relationship between orality and textuality in the Middle Ages, on the resilience of oral traditions and the process of their preservation in written texts. They show us that we should not, without very good reason, assign too great an age or reliability to this particular tradition before it existed in textual form. Rather, the Frisian texts encourage us to pose questions about the concrete circumstances in which the historical materials were first collected. What was the purpose of these texts – in other words, their "place in the world"?

We discover that the Frisians were convinced of the age-old liberty of their people and that they testified to it in the middle of the thirteenth century in their legal texts and in a forged charter of liberties, supposedly granted by Charlemagne.[59] This conviction, however, stemmed from the political context of the twelfth and thirteenth centuries. The use of the forgery and the encoding of corresponding legal texts reflect royal and ducal attempts to assert authority over the Frisians; it also came in response to changes in social structure within the Frisian *communitates terre*.

The Frisian elites within the *communitates terre*, who consisted of the *consules* or *redjeven*, were responsible for propagating these historical constructs. It would be misleading to think of the *consules* and *redjeven* as an oligarchy of peasants. As a social group, they were not defined by the fact that they were agricultural landowners but rather by a common desire to gain access to a knightly way of life.[60] Out of their geographical and political multiplicity a historical consciousness crystallized that was in no sense homogeneous. It did, however, rest on a particular core of traditions.

The Latin version of the seventh Frisian *Küre* (sentence of law) based the first of these traditional rights of the people on Charlemagne's gift (*Hec est prima petitio et Karoli regis concessio. omnibus frisonibus, quod vniuersi rebus propriis utantur. Quam diu non demeruerunt possidere*). Having agreed to convert to Christianity and to be subject to the king from the South, the Frisians had supposedly bought their *nobilitas* (nobility) and *libertas* (freedom) with a tax (*huslotha*). According to the tenth *Küre*, the king had demanded that the Frisians provide him with armies as far as Hitzacker and to the Sinkfal; they finally saw their duties reduced to accompanying

---

59 Robert Folz, *Le souvenir et la légende de Charlemagne dans l'Empire germanique médiévale* (Paris, 1950), 172–6, 334–40. On uses of Charlemagne in contemporary France, cf. Amy G. Remensnyder, *Remembering Kings Past: Monastic Foundation Legends in Medieval Southern France* (Ithaca and London, 1995).

60 Cf. Heinrich Schmidt, "Adel und Bauern im friesischen Mittelalter," *Niedersächsisches Jahrbuch für Landesgeschichte* 45 (1973): 45–95.

a Frankish host as far east as the Weser and as far west as the Flie, so that they might protect their land against the waves and against the pagan army.[61] Freedom in this instance came as a token of imperial favor, bought at the price of protecting the coast and turning away the Normans. This privilege and duty applied not only to the *asega* – those versed in the law – but rather to the entire Frisian community.[62]

The idea of a fundamental Frisian freedom also underwent noticeable changes, an indication that an evolution was occurring in the imagined world of Frisian politics. The *Magnusküren*, which were composed later than the seventeen common Frisian *Küren*, are an example. They are usually dated to the twelfth century, although it is possible that they owe their wording to the process by which Frisian oral law was codified in the thirteenth century. According to the *Magnusküren*, the special status of the Frisians – *that Fresan fri heran were* – derived from a victory that the *nakeda Fresan* won for Charlemagne at the gates of Rome, under the bannerman Magnus.[63] In the thirteenth century, Magnus apparently was a figure capable of playing the role of prototype for the Frisian fighter. In this tradition, the Frisian warriors refused to be paid in gold. Instead, they received from the king the confirmation of their freedom in the form of seven *Küren*. Charlemagne also decreed that the wooden necklace, worn by the Frisians as a sign of servitude, be abolished. According to the later seventeen general Frisian *Küren*, specific regulations were codified. These included the freedom from all forms of taxation duty other than the *riochte huslada* and church tithes, as well as limited military duty between the Weser and Flie, to extend as far as the flood tide and back with the ebb.[64] Although the *Magnusküren* do not introduce new stipulations, they give a new quality to the Frisian liberties by demanding their confirmation by papal and royal charter.

The gift of freedom, freedom bought, freedom fought for, a freedom resting on the authority of the pope and the king, the freedom stylized in historiographical narratives as an innate characteristic of the people –

---

61 Jelle Hoekstra, *De eerste en de tweede Hunsinger codex* (The Hague, 1950), 110, 112.

62 Heinrich Schmidt, "Friesische Freiheitsüberlieferungen im hohen Mittelalter," *Festschrift für Hermann Heimpel*, 3 vols. (Göttingen, 1972), 3:524; Willi Krogmann, "Asega," *Handwörterbuch zur deutschen Rechtsgeschichte* 1 (1971): 239–42.

63 Text in P. Sipma, *Fon alra Fresena fridome* (Snits, 1947), 158–60. Cf. Schmidt, "Friesische Freiheitsüberlieferungen," 525–7.

64 "That se nene hera fordera an herefferd ne volde folgia, than aster ti ther wiser and wester ti ther fle up mittha flode and wth mittha ebba, truch that se thine ower wariad deis and nachtis with thine nordkoning and thine wilda witzingis ses flod mit tha fif wepnum, mit suerde, mit scilde, mit spada, and mit forca, and mit etkeres orda" (Magnusküren, no. 5: Sipma, *Fon alra Fresena fridome*, 159).

it is within these parameters that multiple conceptions of Frisian liberty evolved over the course of the central Middle Ages.[65] Only rarely are the images of Frisian freedom univalent, either politically or socially. They instead tend to promote numerous conceptual variations on the basic theme of independence.

The existence of different social strata within Frisia partly accounts for this type of pluralism, but other factors were at work as well. By all appearances it also was related to the open structure of the *communitates terre*, which coexisted side by side but were not bound to one another. It is true that the Frisians also lived in a state of warfare with the sea. In the minds of thirteenth-century chroniclers this relationship with the sea translated into a particular covenant with God. The historiographers Emo, who wrote in the monastery of Floridus Hortus (Wittewierum) and discussed the vices and virtues of Frisia,[66] and Menko, who found an explanation for the land's floods in the Frisians' refusal to pay tithes,[67] composed some reflections on the frequent floodings that indicate as much. Nonetheless, this state of affairs did not lead to the development of a common policy within Frisia, nor to any meaningful political activity directed outward. Admittedly, the Frisians enforced a promise to defend their *tota Frisia* and to maintain the unity of the seven coastal provinces, but in decisive conflicts with other powers, this intention proved an empty

65 Hans van Rij, ed., *Quedam narracio de Groninghe, de Thrente, de Covordia et de diversis aliis sub diversis episcopis Traiectensibus* (Hilversum, 1989), written after Sept. 29, 1232, gives an example of the voluntariness of Frisian military activities: "Et post pauca dies belli contra Drentones indicitur, ad quem nostri Frisones tamquam veri peregrini et sue ecclesie Traiectensis specialissimi defensores, non ex iure, cum sint homines liberi et ab omni iugo servitutis vel cuiuslibet prementis dominii exuti, ex mera et pia compassione et propter indulgenciam predicatam episcopo parati evocantur per suos plebanos, per decanos, per monachos et viros religiosos et per abbates" (Quedam narracio, p. 78). Cf. M. P. van Buijtenen, "De grondslag van de Friese vrijheid," Ph.D. diss., University of Amsterdam, 1953.

66 "Pro violentia vero Frisie oppressione per subitam maris diruptionem multas secum causas pertractabat, que licet multis religiosorum conventibus sit insignis, qui pio affectu pro ea indesinenter supplicant, quia tamen numerosa hominum multitudine est elata et libertate, que res est inestimabilis, pauperum et divitum ditissima, animalium quoque copia, pascuis et fructuum fertilitate opulenta et iocunda, forsitan in oculis Altissimi pro tot et tantis bonis rea arguitur ingratitudinis et convincitur iudicio diluvii, famis et pestilentiae, ne innoxia sibi videatur, sed ut reatum suum cognoscat et abhominationes suas et precipue illorum qui deberent esse sal terre, saporem sapientie et lucem scientie in salsuginem et tenebras convertunt. Unde posita est terra in salsuginem a malicia inhabitantium in ea"; Emo, "Chronicon," ed. Ludwig Weiland, in *Monumenta Germaniae Historica, Scriptores* 23 (Hannover, 1874), 491.

67 "Credibile autem est, quod quia sola inter omnes nationes christianorum Frisia decimas et primicias non solvit, plagam occeani tollere, quod Deo denegatur, secundum quod in psalmo dicitur: 'Posuit terram fructiferam in salsuginem a malitia habitantium in ea' (Ps. 106, 34) . . . Et sic sepe in Frisia, quod non datur Christo, tollit occeanus"; Menko, "Chronicon," ed. Ludwig Weiland, in *Monumenta Germaniae Historica, Scriptores* 23 (Hannover, 1874), 552. For the historiography of Emo and Menko, see H. P. H. Jansen and A. Janse, *Kroniek van het klooster Bloemhof te Wittewierum* (Hilversum, 1991).

formula.[68] For a short period in the first half of the thirteenth century,[69] as well as in the 1320s,[70] it seems that the East Frisians in Upstalsboom[71] discovered supracommunal forms of communities. The inspiration for these leagues apparently came from central medieval forms of communalism, however, rather than from the early stages of an ancient Frisian history.[72]

In the thirteenth century the self-identity of the Frisians also was affected by the need to focus foreign policy on the definition of Frisia's borders. The withdrawal of a royal presence, the disappearance of an expansive ducal power in Saxony, the late crusader movement sponsored by the French crown, and the development of a coastal trade which transcended political borders were the grounds for Frisian independence and for the tighter communal association of rural oligarchies. The reason that the Frisian mixture of independence and communalism acquired value had less to do with the availability of models from earlier periods. Rather, the Frisians of the thirteenth century developed European contacts and discovered historical defenses for their autonomy and way of life by looking to their own contemporary situation.

The Frisians' reliance on the precedent of Charlemagne's gift even played a role in practical politics. This was the case in various Frisian-French economic transactions from the late thirteenth century and in communal business conducted in the 1330s. According to the *consules* of Ostergo and Wangerland, Charlemagne, ancestor (*attavus*) of the French king Philip III, had defined Frisian freedom in such a way that it remained

---

68 For the symbolism of this number until the fifteenth century, see Heinrich Schmidt, "Stammes-bewusstsein, bäuerliche Landesgemeinde und politische Identität im mittelalterlichen Friesland," in Peter Moraw, ed., *Regionale Identität und soziale Gruppen im deutschen Mittelalter* (Berlin, 1992), 19–20.

69 Emo gives his report for 1222: "Contremuit tota terra propter iuratos, quos universitas Frisonum de more vetustissimo creaverunt apud Upstellesbome"; Emo, *Monumenta Germaniae Historica, Scriptores* 23:495–6; see also 505, 513.

70 For diplomatic sources, see Ernst Friedlaender, ed., *Ostfriesisches Urkundenbuch*, 2 vols. (Emden, 1878), 1: nos. 50, 51, 53; a third volume followed much later: Heinrich Reimers et al., eds., *Ostfriesisches Urkundenbuch: Ergänzende Regesten und Urkunden zu Bd. I und II, 854–1500*, Quellen zur Geschichte Ostfrieslands 10 (Aurich, 1975): nos. 90–3. Cf. Hendrik Derk Meijering, *De willekeuren van de Opstalsboom (1323): Een filologisch-historische monografie* (Groningen, 1974).

71 The sources for the Upstalsboom, along with many hypotheses, are collected by Georg Sello, "Vom Upstalsbom und vom Totius-Frisiae-Siegel," *Jahrbuch der Gesellschaft für bildende Kunst und vaterländische Altertümer zu Emden* 21 (1925): 65–137.

72 B. H. Slicher van Bath, "Universitas," in B. H. Slicher van Bath, *Herschreven historie: Schetsen en studien op het gebied der middeleeuwse geschiedenis* (Leiden, 1949), 281–304; Heinz Stoob, "Landausbau und Gemeindebildung an der Nordseeküste im Mittelalter," in Konstanzer Arbeitskreis für mittelalterliche Geschichte, ed., *Die Anfänge der Landgemeinde und ihr Wesen*, 2 vols., Vorträge und Forschungen 7–8 (Constance, 1964), 1:365–422; Wilhelm Ebel, "Zur Rechtsgeschichte der Landgemeinde in Ostfriesland," ibid., 305–24.

independent from the German king and all other powers (*rex Allimannie* and all *potestates cuiuslibet nationis*).[73] Roughly fifty years later, according to materials extant in the Archives Nationales in Paris, Philip VI took up this text again.[74] In 1337, styling himself the follower of the great Carolingian ruler, he flatteringly identified the Frisians with the French as free persons (*Franci, qui apud nos "liberi" interpretantur*).[75]

In Frisia proper, the tradition of Carolingian freedom went back further. At a court held in Aachen in 1248, King William of Holland granted his Frisian warriors as a reward for their support "all the rights, freedoms, and privileges our predecessor of sainted memory, Emperor Charlemagne, conceded to all Frisians" (*omnia iura, libertates et privilegia concessa Frisonibus universis a Karolo magno imperatore, antecessore nostro sancte memorie*).[76] The editor of William's charters has defended the authenticity of this document, an original of which was still extant in the seventeenth century. He has rejected an earlier supposition that the famous forgery of Charlemagne's diploma to the Frisians was created on the occasion of King William's gift in 1248.[77] Instead, he deems it more likely that William's authentic charter encouraged the fabrication of the Carolingian forgery at a later date.[78] A thorough study of the transmission of this forgery, which is only extant in unsatisfactory printed editions, is a *desideratum*: Some light may then be shed on the whole problem.[79]

Nonetheless, it is possible to identify and define the basic content of this diploma, even if the circumstances surrounding its creation – a mixture of a Frisian mythology of freedom and the knightly aspirations of a rising upper class – are ultimately unrecoverable. According to the forgery attributed to Charlemagne, the Frisians' bravery had won them *libertas*, both through their warfare against the Saxons and when they fought before the gates of Rome. This freedom expressed itself in

---

73 Fritz Kern, ed., *Acta Imperii, Angliae et Franciae ab a. 1267 ad a. 1313* (Tübingen, 1911), no. 1.

74 Cf. P. J. Blok, "Oorkonden betrekkelijk Friesland en zijne verhouding tot Frankrijk in de 13e en 14e eeuw," *De vrije Fries* 19 (1900): 317–33.

75 Fritz Kern, "Analekten zur Geschichte des 13. und 14. Jahrhunderts V: Frankreich und die Friesen," *Mitteilungen des Instituts für österreichische Geschichtsforschung* 31 (1910): 83.

76 Dieter Hägermann and Jaap G. Kruisheer, eds., *Monumenta Germaniae Historica, Diplomata regum et imperatorum Germaniae* 18, pt. 1 (Hannover, 1989), no. 48.

77 Dieter Hägermann, *Studien zum Urkundenwesen Wilhelms von Holland* (Cologne, 1987), 111–26.

78 Dieter Hägermann, "Die Urkundenfälschungen auf Karl den Grossen: Eine Übersicht," *Fälschungen im Mittelalter*, 6 vols. (Hannover, 1988–1990), 3: 433–43; 440–1.

79 For an insufficient edition, see Engelbert Mühlbacher, ed., *Monumenta Germaniae Historica, Diplomatum Karolinorum* 1 (Hannover, 1906), no. 269. A parallel printing of three extant manuscripts exists in Karl Freiherr von Richthofen, *Untersuchungen über friesische Rechtsgeschichte*, 4 vols. (Berlin, 1882), 2, pt. 1: 165–213. Cf. the critique of Friedrich Bock, "Friesland und das Reich," *Jahrbuch der Gesellschaft für bildende Kunst und vaterländische Altertümer zu Emden* 33 (1953): 33–4.

the absence of taxes or other duties, as well as in the Frisians' independence from outside rule. The Frisians also had the right to elect their
own *consules*.

In one respect the forgery reached far beyond any contemporary social
reality: It claimed that the *consules* were allowed to elect a *potestas Frisie*,
who was to be lord over Frisia as a whole and entitled to elevate those
who were willing and able to the status of knight, *more militum regni
Francie*.[80] In this way, the military elite of Frisia acquired the trappings of
the knightly order. Its members aspired to adorn their shields with the
imperial coat of arms, and they dreamed of a *podestà*, of an Italian-style
potentate, to survey the foggy shores of the North Sea.

This propagandistic activity marked the beginning of a process
whereby some magnates came to dominate in Frisia over the course of
the fourteenth and fifteenth centuries. Rather than a uniform development, this process arose out of overlapping commitments to lordship
and communal rule, and it ultimately led to the feudalization of East
Frisia.[81] The Frisians nonetheless continued to be lauded for their freedom
and nobility.[82]

URBAN ELITES OUT OF ROYAL GRACE

In order to complete this survey of the social-historical forces at work in
the constitution of an historical imagination, we must conclude with a
look at the conceptualization of the past in late-medieval cities in the
north of the Empire. Again I shall focus on how certain elites, in this case
the burghers, constructed their history in order to stabilize their self-
identity as a social group. It is possible to list only a small number of
examples and to acknowledge regretfully here that one cannot give a
broader overview of urban historical writing in relation to the history of
mentalities and textual forms.[83] I shall limit myself to analyzing a few
instances that hitherto have rarely been noticed and that reveal how the

---

80 Engelbert Mühlbacher, ed., *Diplomatum Karolinorum*, no. 269.
81 Willem van Iterson, "Feudalisierungsversuche im westerlauwerschen Friesland," *Zeitschrift der
    Savigny-Stiftung für Rechtsgeschichte: Germanistische Abteilung* 79 (1962): 72–103; Vries, *Het Heilige
    Roomse Rijk*.
82 Oebele Vries, "De aldfryske pearformule *fry ende freesk*," *Us Wurk* 35 (1986): 75–84.
83 Cf. Heinrich Schmidt, *Die deutschen Städtechroniken als Spiegel des bürgerlichen Selbstverständnisses im
    Spätmittelalter* (Göttingen, 1958); Johannes Bernhard Menke, "Geschichtsschreibung und Politik in
    deutschen Städten des Spätmittelalters: Die Entstehung deutscher Geschichtsprosa in Köln, Braun-
    schweig, Lübeck, Mainz und Magdeburg," *Jahrbuch des Kölnischen Geschichtsvereins* 33 (1958): 1–84;
    34–5 (1960): 85–194; Joachim Ehlers, "Historiographie, Geschichtsbild und Stadtverfassung im
    spätmittelalterlichen Braunschweig," *Rat und Verfassung im mittelalterlichen Braunschweig* (Braun-

late-medieval urban elites in northern Germany envisaged the creation of an urban patriciate as an act of royal favor.

To claim that a king or prince took the initiative in founding one's city is as common a tactic in medieval town chronicles as the attempt to ascribe to one's own commune a high degree of antiquity and distinguished origins. The foundation of Magdeburg by Julius Caesar and the creation of Braunschweig at the behest of the Ottonians, Brunonians, or Welfs should suffice to illustrate the point. In this context, however, it is more important to note that urban historiography was subject to a general process by which urban society increasingly split into strata. When the patriciate emerged as an authority endowed with a God-given right to rule, urban chroniclers, when describing the origins of their city as a social body, no longer focused exclusively on the emancipation of the city dwellers from their lords in the central Middle Ages.[84]

In the twelfth and thirteenth centuries city dwellers fought for their autonomy and an independent communalism against kings, princes, and bishops. Yet late-medieval city chroniclers did not stress these struggles nor underline the genuine achievement of the burghers. They were far more interested in explaining the royal acts of favor that had fostered the development of their cities. They integrated the community of burghers into the history of the realm and thereby helped to create a regional identity. Moreover, they avoided a conceptual division between the sphere of the citizen and the feudal world of lords and knights. This type of urban historical consciousness was not oriented toward dissent between the commune and the lords of the town. Instead, it underscored a basic level of consent between all actors as to the overall importance of urban growth.[85]

The chroniclers of the more important Saxon cities – and these cities alone shall be taken as exemplary here – went a decisive step further. They attributed to royalty – that is, to the influence of Henry I – not only the creation of their cities but also of their patriciates. A famous passage in Widukind of Corvey recounts the early Ottonians' projects to provide Saxony with an extensive system of fortified castles.[86] His late

---

schweig, 1986), 99–134; Rolf Sprandel, *Chronisten als Zeitzeugen: Forschungen zur spätmittel-alterlichen Geschichtsschreibung in Deutschland* (Cologne, 1994).

84 Eberhard Isenmann, *Die deutsche Stadt im Spätmittelalter 1250–1500* (Stuttgart 1988), 131–3.

85 Schneidmüller, "Reichsnähe – Königsferne," 1–52; Schneidmüller, "Friesen."

86 Widukind of Corvey, *Res gestae Saxonicae*, ed. Hans-Eberhard Lohmann and Paul Hirsch, 5th ed. (Hannover, 1935), 48–9: "Igitur Heinricus rex, accepta pace ab Ungariis ad novem annos, quanta prudentia vigilaverit in munienda patria et in expugnando barbaras nationes, supra nostram est virtutem edicere, licet omnimodis non oporteat taceri. Et primum quidem ex agrariis militibus

medieval borrowers transformed Widukind's tenth-century narrative into an account of the creation of the first urban elites.

The *Chronecken der Sassen* reported in 1492 that Henry I had granted freedom and noble status to the keepers of his castles and named them *borgere* (castle dwellers).[87] This act was supposed to have produced the first patrician families, town dwellers who defended themselves by fighting like knights in Henry's castles and who led a knightly lifestyle. It was thanks to them and to their loyalty that the duchy of Braunschweig came into being. In this narrative the city of Braunschweig grew to be the mirror and the crown of the whole land.[88]

The late medieval urban chronicler was no longer interested in his city as a countertype to the feudal world. Rather, he viewed it as an environment in which the urban elite adopted and developed knightly habits. The economic and political ascent of cities, which found their place in the structure of the late medieval empire, corresponded to their acculturation into the feudal world. It reflected the desire of the citizens to take part in tournaments and other aspects of the knightly way of life.[89]

A century before the Braunschweig chronicle, the Magdeburg chronicler had already attributed the foundation of Magdeburg and its subsequent rank as a city to the castle-building projects of Henry I. The

nonum quemque eligens in urbibus habitare fecit, ut ceteris confamiliaribus suis octo habitacula extrueret, frugum omnium tertiam partem exciperet servaretque. Caeteri vero octo seminarent et meterent frugesque colligerent nono et suis eas locis reconderent. Concilia et omnes conventus atque convivia in urbibus voluit celebrari; in quibus extruendis die noctuque operam dabant, quatinus in pace discerent, quid contra hostes in necessitate facere debuissent. Vilia aut nulla extra urbes fuere moenia."

87 Henry I: "vnde gaff se fry vnde eddel dat se borger scholden hete(n) dar van sunt de schlechte in den steden gekomen de sick in dussen stucken meyst bewiseden in vechten vnde in striden dat heldem do vor rittermatsche menne vnde heten de eddlinghe der borger"; *Chronecken der Sassen* (Mainz, 1492), fol. 54ᵛ. Cf. Karl Stackmann, "Die Stadt in der norddeutschen Welt- und Landeschronistik des 13. bis 16. Jahrhundert," in Josef Fleckenstein and Karl Stackmann, eds., *Über Bürger, Stadt und städtische Literatur im Spätmittelalter: Bericht über Kolloquien der Kommission zur Erforschung der Kultur des Spätmittelalters 1975–1977* (Göttingen, 1980), 301.

88 Hermen Bote, one of the most famous historiographers of late-medieval Northern Germany, gave the following comment on the foundation of Braunschweig in 861: "unde is van daghe to daghe, van jaren to jaren beter, starcker, mechtiger geworden, unde is eyne kronen unde eyn speygel des landes to Sassen unde der fürsten to Brunswick unde Lüneborch"; Gerhard Cordes, *Auswahl aus den Werken von Hermann Bote* (Wolfenbüttel and Hannover, 1948), 14. Cf. Herbert Blume and Werner Wunderlich, eds., *Hermen Bote: Bilanz und Perspektiven der Forschung* (Göppingen, 1982); Detlev Schöttker and Werner Wunderlich, eds., *Hermen Bote: Braunschweiger Autor zwischen Mittelalter und Neuzeit* (Wiesbaden, 1987); Herbert Blume and Eberhard Rohse, eds., *Hermann Bote: Städtisch-hansischer Autor in Braunschweig 1488–1988: Beiträge zum Braunschweiger Bote-Kolloquium 1988* (Tübingen, 1991).

89 For the example of Braunschweig cf. Schneidmüller, "Reichsnähe – Königsferne"; for tournaments in late medieval towns, see Thomas Zotz, "Adel, Bürgertum und Turnier in deutschen Städten vom 13. bis 15. Jahrhundert," in Josef Fleckenstein, ed., *Das ritterliche Turnier im Mittelalter* (Göttingen 1985), 450–99.

Magdeburg historian expanded on Widukind's text in order to praise the creation of his own town: Henry supposedly granted the cities the right of *Heerschild*, which resulted in the integration of Magdeburg into the feudal order of the Empire. According to the chronicle, the citizens owed it to the "emperor" Henry that various feasts and tournaments took place in their town; consequently, their leading representatives had the chance to practice bearing arms in the knightly fashion.[90]

The nineteenth-century bourgeois school of medieval studies, which sought the medieval origins of its own emancipation as a class, preferred to treat such sources as fables. In fact, our sources reflect a progressive assimilation in the late Middle Ages of the world of the patriciate into that of the knights. The communal elites exploited history as a method of argumentation, exactly as the Frisian oligarchy had done, by claiming that their own nobility and knightly status was a product of royal favor.

In the late Middle Ages, historical figures such as Charlemagne and Henry I became the founders of a particular integrative process. They were thought to have granted communes a place in the feudal order of the empire. These foundations must be conceived as realities and desires projected onto the past by the rural communes or urban patriciates. The chroniclers whose works we have reviewed did not simply resort to composing fiction; they extended the scope of historical reality, to their own credit and fame.

CONCLUSION

These windows onto the construction of the past with a view to the present are designed to challenge the comfortable self-image that posi-

---

90 Karl Janicke, ed., *Die Magdeburger Schöppenchronik* (Leipzig, 1869), 43: "Bi keiser Hinrikes tiden, do de Ungeren dit land so sere anvochten, do satte keiser Hinrik dat de negende man ut den dorpen scholde in de stede teen und bevesten und bewaren, und dat men neine hochtide und tavernen scholde hebben wenne in den steden, und de keiser hadde einen vrede nomen mit den Ungeren to negen jaren. dar binnen satte he dat men torneie scholde maken in den steden, uppe dat sik de lude und borgere an den wapen oveden, und satte dat dat de eldeste broder scholde in dat here varen, und satte dat dat hereweide scholde vallen up den negesten swertmach. dat wart do recht. To voren was dat nicht wenn slicht erve, dat alle gut vel up den negesten mach. nu seggen vele, lude und borgere, de in den steden sitten, enhebben des herschildes nicht. disse enweten nicht dat dat hereweide allererst dorch der stede willen gesat is und dat se sik an ridderschap schollen oven; und dat se ok van ridderart sin. dat os schinbar dar an, dat se hereweide geven und nemen . . . dit recht satte koning Karl van den ridderen, und keiser Hinrik de satte dit dat de borger under sik hereweide geven und nemen scholden und des herschildes bruken. hir ut neme ik disse rede: we herweide let, de het den herschild. de borger geven und nemen herweide, dar umme hebben se de herschilt, to dem minsten den sevenden." Cf. Bernd Schneidmüller, "'Dem Heiligen Römischen Reich zu Ehren': Sächsische Städte und das Reich im späten Mittelalter," in Matthias Puhle, ed., *Hanse − Städte − Bünde: Die sächsischen Städte zwischen Elbe und Weser um 1500*, 2 vols. (Magdeburg, 1996), 1:45–61.

tivism enjoys in medieval studies. Since the nineteenth century at least, the positivist school has insisted that a rigid distinction exists between reality and fiction. The role of the historian supposedly is to act as judge, sorting out more reliable primary sources from weaker ones. This approach is wholly appropriate, as long as it is kept in mind that it constitutes only one of many possible methods of historical research – its use is particularly defensible in the case of diplomatics. In general, however, this method does more to inform the public about the modern historical observer than about his medieval sources. It nonetheless is not left up to the discretion of the historian to treat the tradition as arbitrarily as he or she sees fit. However, it is important to understand that the form of reality described within the traditional epistemological framework of medieval studies cannot be subordinated to a single constitutive reality. It ought instead to take a position alongside its constitutive model. Historical research and knowledge must be able to encompass a plurality of meanings.

The Capetian yearning for a direct, dynastic line of kings; the Welfs' yearning to establish roots in their own land; the Frisian yearning for Charlemagne, for his freedom and knightly order; and finally the urban yearning for a historically valid place within the world of knights – none of these are "true" in the sense of the diplomatic *discrimen veri ac falsi*. Yet the practice of staging history by means of the present is as much a part of the medieval reality as the remaining diplomatic sources that we celebrate as monuments of the age. By getting a sense of the agility and flexibility with which medieval chroniclers drew a contemporary argument out of the past, we may become more sensitive to our own working methods. We ought then to assess with greater equanimity the relative merit that today's efforts will enjoy in the eyes of posterity.

9

Topographies of Memory

Center and Periphery in High Medieval France

AMY G. REMENSNYDER

In the eleventh century, the Gascon abbey of Saint Sever made for itself a richly illustrated Beatus commentary on the Book of Apocalypse.[1] A map of the world occupies two facing folios of the commentary. On it, three locations are immediately distinguishable from the plethora of tiny schematic buildings: Rome, Jerusalem, and Saint Sever.[2] Of these three sacred places, the last is particularly highlighted, painted with more vivid shades of color and given an architectural design different from any other on the map. In this visual homology, Saint Sever is the most significant of these sacred centers of Christendom. This map thus projects an image of the world as the abbey imagined it – a world constructed around symbolic centers, of which the monastery itself is the most important.[3]

As this eleventh-century topography demonstrates with such visual eloquence, people can read, describe, and of course shape their physical surroundings to endow them with meaning.[4] Furthermore, as the map shows, the process of the imposition of significance on place can be intricately bound up with statements about identity – in this case, the identity of the monastic community but in others, the identity of the

---

1 This chapter represents a reformulation of some of the main ideas in Amy G. Remensnyder, *Remembering Kings Past: Monastic Foundation Legends in Medieval Southern France* (Ithaca, N.Y., 1995).
2 Paris, Bibliothèque Nationale, ms lat. 8878, ff. 45^{bis}v–45ter. See the color reproduction in *Saint-Sever: Millénaire de l'abbaye: Colloque international 25, 26 et 27 mai 1985* (Mont-de-Marsan, 1986), 8–9. On this map, see François Dainville, "La *Gallia* dans la mappemonde de Saint-Sever," *Actes du 93e Congrès National des Sociétés Savants (Tours 1968)* (Paris, 1970), 391–404.
3 On how maps often serve such interests, see Denis Wood with John Fels, *The Power of Maps* (New York, 1992), 48–69.
4 A point emphasized in different ways by the many recent studies in cultural and social geography; see, for example, the essays collected in James Duncan and David Ley, eds., *Place/Culture/Representation* (London, 1993), and in Patricia Yaeger, ed., *The Geography of Identity* (Ann Arbor, Mich., 1996).

nation-state or of the individual. Such statements can be made verbally as well as visually, as the same Beatus manuscript demonstrates. Later in the eleventh century, a charter containing a legend about Saint Sever's origins as a monastic community was copied onto the first of the folios, which had been left blank at the end of the Beatus manuscript.[5] This legend implicitly orders space in terms of the abbey. For example, the text characterizes the physical site of the abbey as differentiated from the surrounding secular space: Count Guillaume-Sanche builds the monastery over the tomb of the martyr Severus as a shrine to this saint and as a thanksgiving offering for the saint's aid in battle. The monastery was then intrinsically sacred space, necessarily a focal point of the landscape – as it was in the map. Furthermore, the legend's description of Guillaume-Sanche's generous grant of various estates to the abbey plots territory in relation to the abbey. The legend and the Beatus map thus conceive of space in the same fashion: as organized around a symbolic center, the monastery.

This legend orders space – but it also commemorates the abbey's origins. These two dimensions are complementary, for the process of the imposition of significance on places often intersects with the processes of memory and commemoration. Place can become the framework and repository for the social and cultural memory of groups as well as of individuals.[6] This conjunction of place, centering, and the process of remembering characterizes the way that medieval monasteries often narrated their beginnings as communities. As at Saint Sever, these narrations often took the form not of sober histories but of foundation legends.[7] I define

5 For an edition of the fabulous foundation charter copied in the *Beatus* (Paris, Bibliothèque Nationale [hereafter BN], ms lat. 8878), see "Documents transcrits à la fin du *Beatus*," in *Saint-Sever: Millénaire de l'abbaye: Colloque international 25, 26 et 27 mai 1985* (Mont-de-Marsan, 1986), 114–16. For a discussion of this document, see Charles Higounet and Jean-Bernard Marquette, "Les origines de l'abbaye de Saint-Sever: Révision critique," in *Saint-Sever*, 27–37.

6 For examples of group memories structured by place, see Maurice Halbwachs, *La Topographie légendaire des évangiles en Terre Sainte*, 2d ed. (Paris, 1971), 144–8; and Susan Slyomovics, "The Memory of Place: Rebuilding the Pre-1948 Palestinian Village," *Diaspora* 2 (1994): 157–68.

7 For studies of medieval foundation legends, see Sharon Farmer, *Communities of Saint Martin: Legend and Ritual in Medieval Tours* (Ithaca, N.Y., 1991), 151–86; Antonia Gransden, "The Growth of the Glastonbury Traditions and Legends," *Journal of Ecclesiastical History* 27 (1976): 337–58; Thomas Head, "Hrotsvit's Primordia and the Historical Traditions of Monastic Communities," in Katharina M. Wilson, ed., *Hrotsvit of Gandersheim: Rara Avis in Saxonia?* Medieval and Renaissance Monograph Series, 7 (Ann Arbor, Mich., 1987), 143–64; Dominique Iogna-Prat, "La geste des origines dans l'historiographie clunisienne des XIe–XIIe siècles," *Revue Bénédictine* 102 (1992): 135–91; Penelope Johnson, "Pious Legends and Historical Realities: The Legends of La Trinité Vendôme, Bonport, and Holyrood," *Revue Bénédictine* 91 (1981): 184–93; Jörg Kastner, *Historiae fundationum monasteriorum: Frühformen monastischer Institutionsgeschichtsschreibung im Mittelalter*, Münchener Beiträge zur Mediävistik und Renaissance-Forschung 18 (Munich, 1974); Hans Patze, "Adel und Stifterchronik: Frühformen territorialer Geschichtsschreibung im hochmittelalterlichen Reich,"

legend not as a fixed formal genre but rather as any form of reflection on a monastery's beginnings as a community. Legends thus could take the shape of discrete narrative texts, but they also could appear as charters, royal diplomas, hagiography, reliquaries, sculpture, and even architectural design. Furthermore, legends evolved over time, acquiring new layers. One community's legend could consist of, say, a *vita*, a series of forged charters, and a reliquary, all spread perhaps over two centuries.

These legends represent what I call the "imaginative memory" of each monastery.[8] I use the term *imaginative* to evoke the creative flair of the legends and their often fantastic transformations of reality. But if these legends are so fantastic, why put them in the category of "memory" rather than that of "fiction" or "forgery"?[9] Memory is the appropriate term because the members of monastic communities believed in these images of their past, just as we in the twentieth century believe what we remember, no matter how fantastic it might be, as the recent furor over memories of childhood sexual abuse during Satanic rituals has shown.[10] We can call monasteries communities of memory, then, for more reasons than their liturgical commemoration of the dead.[11]

Among the many characteristics of monastic imaginative memory was a focus on space. In their legends, monasteries created themselves as places of special significance, ordering space symbolically or even physically around them, much like the Saint Sever map. Whether implicitly or explicitly, legends thus described the landscape in terms of a center and

---

Blätter für deutsche Landesgeschichte 100 (1964): 8–81; 101 (1965): 67–128; Remensnyder, *Remembering Kings Past*.

8 For further discussion of the term *imaginative memory*, see Remensnyder, *Remembering Kings Past*, 1–3.

9 For a detailed consideration of forgery, see the articles in *Fälschungen im Mittelalter: Internationaler Kongress der Monumenta Germaniae Historica, München, 16.–19. September 1986*, 5 vols., MGH Schriften 33.1–5 (Hannover, 1988).

10 On memory and belief, see James Fentress and Chris Wickham, *Social Memory* (Oxford, 1992); Elizabeth F. Loftus, "The Reality of Repressed Memories," *American Psychologist* 48 (May 1993): 518–37. For discussion of legends and belief, see Walter Goffart, *The Le Mans Forgeries: A Chapter from the History of Church Property in the Ninth Century* (Cambridge, Mass., 1966), 248; and Roman Michalowski, "Il culto dei santi fondatori nei monasteri tedeschi dei secoli XI e XII: Proposte di ricerca," in Sofia Boesch Gajano and Lucia Sebastiani, eds., *Culto dei santi istituzioni e classi sociali in età preindustriale* (L'Aquila, 1984), 114–15. Raffaele Pettazzoni argues that myths about beginnings are often granted value as being true; see his "The Truth of Myth" in Alan Dundes, ed., *Sacred Narrative: Readings in the Theory of Myth* (Berkeley, Calif., 1984), 99–103.

11 On monasteries and liturgical *memoria*, see Megan McLaughlin, *Consorting with Saints: Prayer for the Dead in Early Medieval France* (Ithaca, N.Y., 1994); and the many studies of Otto Gerhard Oexle, including: "Memoria und Memorialüberlieferung im früheren Mittelalter," *Frühmittelalterliche Studien* 10 (1976): 70–95; "Die Gegenwart der Toten," in Herman Braet and Werner Verbeke, eds., *Death in the Middle Ages* (Louvain, 1983), 19–77. On abbeys' liturgical commemoration of founders, see Christine Sauer, *Fundatio und Memoria: Stifter und Klostergründer im Bild 1100 bis 1350* (Göttingen, 1993), 149–60.

its periphery. The relationship between center and periphery – whether of actual physical geography, political relations, economic structures, or culture and values – has been the subject of much scholarly discussion. Many scholars use this conceptual framework to describe what they see as real relations between a dominant core and a subjugated or subordinate periphery.[12] More recently, however, scholars have begun to explore how images of center and periphery also can be constructions, social fictions produced by self-proclaimed centers – fictions that are potent but that can mask much more complex realities.[13] In other words, we need to understand center and periphery in terms of representations, both the heuristic representations of modern scholarship and the representations created by the subjects of scholarly inquiry.

Here I have defined coherent temporal and spatial parameters in order to explore how, through their legends, a certain set of monasteries constructed themselves as centers. I have chosen to look at the foundation legends elaborated by forty-one monasteries located in the old Carolingian Aquitaine and its march – roughly the area south of the Loire, west of the Rhône, and east of the Pyrenees.[14] I begin my study with the emergence of the legends in the late tenth century and end in the mid-thirteenth century. One further parameter: With the exception of one abbey, Notre Dame de la Règle of Limoges, these were male communities. This focus on male houses is not a product of deliberate choice on my part, for I selected monasteries according to a very simple principle, that is, by incorporating every abbey in this region for which I could find a legend. Nor would this paucity of legends from women's communities seem to reflect differences between male and female monastic culture.

12 See examples: Peter Alter, *Nationalismus* (Frankfurt am Main, 1985), 27–28; and Clifford Geertz, "Centers, Kings, and Charisma: Reflections on the Symbolics of Power," in Clifford Geertz, *Local Knowledge: Further Essays in Interpretive Anthropology* (New York, 1983), 121–46; Edward Shils, *Center and Periphery: Essays in Macrosociology* (Chicago, 1975), 3–16. See also the summary (and critique) of center/periphery theories in John Agnew, "Representing Space: Space, Scale and Culture in Social Science," in Duncan and Ley, eds., *Place / Culture / Representation*, 256–61.

13 See, for example, Arjun Appadurai, "Theory in Anthropology: Center and Periphery," *Comparative Studies in Society and History* 28 (1986): 356–61; Saskia Sassen, "Identity in the Global City: Economic and Cultural Encasements," in Patricia Yaeger, ed., *The Geography of Identity* (Ann Arbor, Mich., 1996), 131–51. For a critique of "the myth of the center," see A. P. Cohen, *The Symbolic Construction of Community* (London, 1985), 36–7.

14 The monastic communities include: Alet, Aniane, Brantôme, Charroux, Clairvaux d'Aveyron, Conques, Figeac, Gaillaguet, Gellone (also known as Saint-Guilhem-le-Désert), Gerri, Issoire, Joncels, La Règle, La Réole, La Sauve-Majeure, Lagrasse, Laguenne, Langogne, Maillezais, Menat, Moissac, Mozac, Perse, Psalmodi, Rocamadour, Saint-Chaffre, Saint-Genou, Saint-Germier, Saint-Gilles, Saint-Jean d'Angely, Saint-Martial of Limoges, Saint-Michel-de-Cuxa, Saint-Polycarpe, Saint-Savin of Lavedan, Saint-Sever, Sainte-Enimie, Sarlat, Sorde, Sorèze, Uzerche, Vabres.

Female monasteries in other regions created such legends.[15] The lack of legends from female abbeys seems to relate rather to the small number of Benedictine monasteries for women that existed in southwestern France during this period.[16]

The topographies of meaning created by these legends illuminate medieval notions of what constituted a "center." Equally, they also suggest a reconsideration of the way that modern historians have used the concept of center and periphery to understand certain aspects of the political culture of Capetian France. These monasteries were located in an area that modern historians of medieval France have often seen as part of the political periphery in this period. For, from the mid-tenth to the mid-thirteenth century, the Frankish and then the French kings rarely ventured into this area, distant from their sphere of power north of the Loire. Despite the occasional forays of Louis VI and Louis VII into this region, it was really only in the mid-thirteenth century that this slice of southern France was effectively integrated into the Capetian realm. From the perspective of royal power, this region was then peripheral. But the monasteries of this area remembered themselves as centers, and often did so by invoking images of royal power.

A. CENTERS AND PERIPHERIES: THE LEGENDS

Centers can be created with symbolic language, as in the case of the Saint Sever map. The language can be that of the sacred, for the vocabulary of the sacred and the vocabulary of the center often overlap; centers are sacred and the sacred is central.[17] In their legends, southern French monasteries could employ this symbolic nexus to endow themselves with

---

15 See, for example, the foundation legend of Gandersheim: Hrotsvit of Gandersheim, *Primordia coenobii Gandeshemensis*, in Helene Homeyer, ed., *Opera* (Munich, 1970), 440–72.

16 For example, most female communities in Languedoc were founded only after 1100, and the vast majority only in the thirteenth and fourteenth centuries. Furthermore, Benedictine houses made up only 21 percent of the total female communities extant in Languedoc between the eleventh and the fourteenth centuries. Here I draw on Pierre-Roger Gaussin, "Les communautés féminines dans l'espace Languedocien de la fin du XIe à la fin du XIVe s." in *La femme dans la vie religieuse du Languedoc: XIIIe–XIVe s*, Cahiers de Fanjeaux, 23 (Toulouse, 1988), 299–332; and Elisabeth Magnou-Nortier, "Formes féminines de vie consacrée dans les pays du Midi jusqu'au début du XIIe siècle" in ibid., 193–5.

17 For example, in medieval thought, Jerusalem was a sacred center; see Jerome, *Commentarium in Hiezechielem Libri XIV*, II.v in *S. Hieronymi presbyteri opera*, Corpus Christianorum, 75 (Turnholt, 1964), 55–7. I am grateful to Philippe Buc for this reference. On the general phenomenon of the sacred and the center, see Mircea Eliade, *The Sacred and the Profane: The Nature of Religion*, trans. Willard R. Trask (New York, 1959), 36–46; and Shils, *Center and Periphery*, 3, 8.

the status of a center.[18] Proclaiming that the abbey was from its inception a sacred place touched by the hand of God, the legends emphasized
the symbolic centrality of the abbey's location.[19] This theophany, or irruption of the divine, was expressed through various motifs of revelation of
the sacred site.

For example, a twelfth-century layer of the legend from the abbey of
Mozac relates that one Christmas Eve, an abbot of this apparently dilapi-
dated monastery had a vision.[20] He saw a snow-white deer that entered
the abbey's graveyard and drew a shape in the snow with its hooves and
antlers. Later the abbot had another vision confirming and amplifying the
first. In this vision he met King Pippin the Short and told the king of
his vision of the deer. Pippin responded by saying that he too had had a
vision. According to the royal vision, Saint Austremonius, the patron saint
of Mozac, led Pippin to the monastery and showed him the deer's tracks
in the snow. The saint informed Pippin that these were the tracks of a
"holy angel" and told the king that he should restore the abbey. Later,
the text specifies, the visions were realized: Pippin came to the abbey and
ordered that a church be built on the exact site demarcated by the still
visible tracks of the deer.

In this legend the sacredness of the site is assured by the interlocking
visions implying that Mozac's refoundation is an expression of God's will.
Furthermore, the deer itself is a heavenly messenger. Not only does
Austremonius call it an angel, but its snowy-white color is typical of
heavenly inhabitants. Indeed, the deer may be intended as even more
than an angel – it may symbolize Christ himself. Ever since the late second
century the deer was considered an allegorical representation of Christ.[21]
The vision's timing, Christmas Eve, reinforces the possible Christological
overtones: The monastery's rebirth is made parallel to Christ's birth.

---

18 This construction was a feature of most medieval monastic legends, not just those in southern
    France; see the studies cited in note 7 to this chapter.
19 On the creation of the center through theophany, see Eliade, *Sacred and Profane*, 21–2.
20 The vision text is edited by Bruno Krusch in his "Reise nach Frankreich im Frühjahr und
    Sommer 1892. Fortsetzung und Schluss. 3. Aufzeichnung des Abtes Lamfred von Mozac über
    König Pippins Beziehungen zu seinem Kloster," *Neues Archiv der Gesellschaft für ältere deutsche
    Geschichtskunde* 19 (1894): 24–5.
21 This allegorical interpretation appears in the *Physiologus* (see, for example, the facsimile of the
    lovely ninth-century Bern Physiologus, *Physiologus Bernensis*, ed. Otto Homburger [Basel, 1964],
    ff. 17ʳ⁻ᵛ) and is taken up by later Christian authors; see Herbert Kolb, "Der Hirsch, der Schlangen
    frisst: Bermerkungen zum Verhältnis von Naturkunde und Theologie in der mittelalterlichen
    Literatur," in Ursula Hennig and Herbert Kolb, eds., *Mediaevalia litteraria: Festschrift für Helmut de
    Boor zum 80. Geburtstag* (Munich, 1971), 583–610; and Carl Pschmadt, *Die Sage von der verfolgten
    Hinde: Ihre Heimat und Wanderung, Bedeutung und Entwicklung mit besonderer Berücksichtigung ihrer
    Verwendung in der Literatur des Mittelalters* (Greifswald, 1911), 53–63.

Mozac's legend thus makes it clear that the monastery's site had been revealed as indubitably sacred. This same statement is made by the similar motifs used in legends from other monasteries. Visions, animals that are clearly heaven sent, holy hermits living in caves – these are among the favorite tropes for the revelation of the future monastery's sacred site.[22]

In all these ways, the legends fashion the site of the future monastery as a sacred center. The site becomes an incarnation of the verse from Genesis that forms a refrain in the central ritual of foundation, the abbey church's consecration: "How terrible is this place! It can be none other than God's dwelling and heaven's door" (Genesis 28.17).[23] The legends create the monastery as "this place" hedged with the sanctions of the divine, a prefiguration of the heavenly Paradise.

As they imaginatively remembered their community's origins, the monks thus emphasized the revelation of the sacred site, that is, the vertical connection between the monastery and heaven. But in their legends monasteries also recognized the horizontal or terrestrial dimension in which the communities existed. The monastery was a community of humans living in this world. Its position in this world, especially relative to its human neighbors, needed to be delineated. In their legendary descriptions of this physical and social topography, monastic communities often played very explicitly with the idea of centering.

The organization of space around the monastery as center can be quite literal, as the legend of Clairvaux d'Aveyron, a priory of the abbey of Conques, demonstrates. According to this legend (two narrative charters included in the twelfth-century cartulary of Conques), an English prince making a penitential pilgrimage "throughout the whole world" came to the Rouergue.[24] There he came across the ruins of a *monasterium* (monastery) formerly dedicated to Peter in a valley called Clairvaux. After praying among the ruins, he decided the church should be restored to its former state. He thus approached the *seniores* (lords) of the two castles perched on the opposing heights of Panat and Cassagnes above Clairvaux and persuaded them and all their followers to help him refound the monastery.[25] Here the liminal stranger mediates between the two *castra* (castles) located only two kilometers apart, as does the monastery whose refoundation he prompts. One charter implies that conflict between the

---

22 For detailed discussion of these motifs, see Remensnyder, *Remembering Kings Past*, 42–65.

23 On this ritual, see ibid., 30–8.

24 Gustave Desjardins, ed., *Cartulaire de l'abbaye de Conques en Rouergue* (Paris, 1879), 16–21 (nos. 14 and 15).

25 Ibid., 16 (no. 14).

two *castra* and its *milites* (knights) had caused the church's ruin;[26] its refoundation obviously created peace between them, as indicated by the conditions recorded in the charters to which both sets of *seniores* agreed.[27] The monastery's role as mediator thus mirrored its physical location as the center point between the two *castra*.

More often, however, the organization of the landscape around the sacred center of the monastery is a symbol of domination rather than of mediation. The act of describing a landscape can inherently be an act of taking possession, whether at the metaphoric or the literal level – and these legends are no exception, for the topographies detailed in the legends often function to express the abbey's acquisition of its landed property.[28] In these descriptions, the language of center and periphery is used as a thinly veiled assertion of lordship and thus power.

Often in the legends the actions of a saintly founder demarcate the abbey's lands, creating a centered and bounded physical space as charged as his or her body.[29] For example, in a rather humorously recounted episode of an eleventh-century version of the *vita* of Saint Gilles, King Flavius, ruler of the Goths, decided to endow the monastery he had just founded on the site of the saintly hermit's retreat.[30] To determine the amount of

---

26 "Antiquis enim diebus fuit fundatum quoddam monasterium in honore sancti Petri apostoli inter castra Panatensium et Cassaniensium, sed supercrescente zizania confractum et destructum diebus multis in magna egestate permansit" (Ibid., 19 [no. 15]).

27 Not only do both sets of *seniores* endow the monastery, but they agree that it will be the common burial place for the inhabitants. Furthermore, they agree no violence will be perpetrated on the abbey's territory. For an even more explicit example of a legend in which foundation of a monastery creates peace between two *castra*, see the eleventh-century(?) charter describing the ninth-century foundation of San Martin de Cercito in Antonio Ubieto Arteta, ed., *Cartulario de San Juan de la Peña*, Textos Medievales 6 (Valencia, 1962), 37–9 (no. 9). The establishment of such sanctuaries related in part to the attempts in this period to regulate violence and establish peace; see for example the fascinating evidence discussed by Pierre Bonnassie, "Les *sagreres* catalanes: La concentration de l'habitat dans le 'cercle de paix' des églises," in Michel Fixot and Elisabeth Zadora-Rio, eds., *L'environnement des églises et la topographie religieuse des campagnes médiévales* (Paris, 1994), 68–79. On eleventh-century efforts to create peace, see most recently the articles in Thomas Head and Richard Landes, eds., *The Peace of God: Religion and Violence in Tenth- and Eleventh-Century France* (Ithaca, N.Y., 1992).

28 For very different aspects of how the description of landscape relates to ownership and domination, see Nuala Ni Dhomhnaill, "Dinnsheanchas: The Naming of Holy Places," in Patricia Yaeger, ed., *The Geography of Identity* (Ann Arbor, Mich., 1996), 431; James Duncan and David Ley, "Introduction: Representing the Place of Culture," in Duncan and Ley, eds., *Place / Culture / Representation*, 1; Wood, *Power of Maps*, 115.

29 Cf. the case of Saint Leonard's delineation of Noblat's property in the early eleventh-century *Vita sancti Leonardi confessoris*; *AASS* Nov. 3:153. On this text, see Steven Sargent, "Religious Responses to Social Violence in Eleventh-Century Aquitaine," *Historical Reflections / Reflexions Historiques* 12 (1985): 219–40.

30 *Vita sancti Aegidii* in *Analecta Bollandiana* 8 (1889): 116. The episode is recounted in less dramatic terms in the versions of the *vita* in *AASS* Sept. 1:301–2, and in E. C. Jones, *Saint Gilles: Essai d'histoire littéraire* (Paris, 1914), 107.

property he would grant, the king proposed the following to Gilles. He, Flavius, would return to Nîmes. Gilles meanwhile should get up early the next morning and set out to meet the king. Flavius would then endow the monastery with as much land as Gilles had traversed. But the next morning, Gilles performed what seems to have been the full office of matins before setting out. As a result, he met the king a mere two miles from his cave. Flavius realized that this distance would hardly translate into sufficient land for the monastery and admonished Gilles to wake up earlier the next morning. Gilles did so and covered five miles. Flavius accordingly allotted the monastery the territory within this radius around Gilles's cave.

In this legend as in others, relations between the monastery and the surrounding landscape are ordered. In the process, generic, undefined space is defined and a world is created around the abbey. For, as in the case of Saint Gilles, the legendary delineation of monastic patrimony often organizes territory in a concentric fashion, making the abbey in question the symbolic focal point. The hierarchical nature of the relation between the resulting center and its periphery is underlined in the compendious and colorful legend of the abbey of Lagrasse, the mid-thirteenth-century *Gesta Karoli Magni ad Carcassonam et Narbonam.*[31] According to this narrative prose text, Charlemagne and his epic peers founded the monastery of Lagrasse. On the occasion of the abbey church's consecration, Charlemagne endowed Lagrasse with the land "around" (*circumquaque*) it for the distance a mule can walk in one day. He then ordered that all those people who lived within that circumference, no matter their social status (*qualitercumque fuerit dignitatis*), be subject (*submissi*) to the abbey and that all owed homage and fealty to the abbot.[32]

More subtle statements of domination were made by legends that spin a web of lines radiating from the monastery, thus connecting center and other topographical points. The motif is that of the founder's further foundations, the creation of ecclesiastical communities subordinate to the one that was established first. For example, in the third version of the *vita* of Saint Austremonius, a text from the second half of the eleventh century composed at Issoire, a monastery claiming this saint as founder, the saint establishes not only this abbey but also a series of churches and chapels in its vicinity.[33] Although Austremonius does not explicitly grant them to

---

31 F. E. Schneegans, ed., *Gesta Karoli Magni ad Carcassonam et Narbonam* (Romanische Bibliothek, 15; Halle: 1898). On the dating of this text, see Remensnyder, *Remembering Kings Past*, 317.

32 Schneegans, ed., *Gesta Karoli Magni*, 98.

33 *Vita tertia sancti Austremonii*; *AASS* Nov. 1: 69, 70, 73. On the dating and composition of this text, see Pierre-François Fournier, "Saint Austremoine, premier évêque de Clermont," *Bulletin historique et scientifique de l'Auvergne* 89 (1979): 456–64.

Issoire, his actions trace connections between his foundations, primary and secondary. Furthermore, other sources reveal that at least some of these churches were Issoire's priories.[34]

In an interesting twist on this motif, churches might be built for family members of a saintly founder. Here kinship becomes the metaphor for the inclusion of these churches in the circle of dependencies of the monastery. The *vita* of Meneleus recounts how this saint fled from marriage and established a monastery, Menat. But, unable to live without him, the saint's female relatives (including his rejected wife) searched desperately for him. When they finally discovered him at Menat, Savinianus, one of Meneleus's male companions, suggested that a *cella* be built for the women (the site was then indicated by an angel).[35] The resulting church, Saint Mary of Lisseuil, located some six kilometers south of Menat, was one of this abbey's priories – although the *vita* does not say so.[36] But is this not implied in the episode? After all, the church that housed the saint's family surely belonged to the saint's monastery. And furthermore, does not the gender of Meneleus's relatives indicate, underline, and reinforce the subordinate status of their church?[37]

This process of organizing patrimonial space through further foundations can become the morphological principle of the entire legend, as it is in Lagrasse's *Gesta Karoli Magni*. The reader of this legend can hardly help but be struck by its remarkable focus on place. The legend abounds in place names, almost each of which the text highlights in terms of its relation to Lagrasse's foundation. The abbey's origins accordingly become a narrative trope for the description of space, and for centering that space on the monastery. And in this concentric characterization of space, these places often are explicitly asserted to be the abbey's own property and thus subject to its domination. Indeed, approximately half of the fifty-odd places mentioned in the legend represented churches or estates either that belonged to the abbey or that it was trying to claim when the *Gesta Karoli Magni* was composed.[38]

---

34 Cf. Fournier's identifications in "Saint Austremoine," 458–9.
35 *Vita Menelei abbatis Menatensis*; *MGH SSRM* 2:142.
36 On Lisseuil's status as a priory, see the editor's remark in *Vita Menelei*; *MGH SSRM* 2:142n6.
37 Cf. the case of Guillaume of Gellone's sisters who plead with their brother to allow them to enter the religious life with him; *Vita [S. Willelmi ducis]*; *AASS* May 6:813. Does this episode serve as the trope for the foundation of the community of nuns (over which the abbot held certain rights) at Gellone? Cf. G. Henschius's remarks in *AASS* May 6:814, note q and those of Mabillon in *AASSosB* 4.1:72.
38 Out of fifty-one places named in the legend, I have been able to find at least twenty-one claimed in the abbey's charters (authentic and forged) as its property. This documentation is too extensive to be included here.

This process of creating specific, centered space from generic space through the description of the abbey's origins is so marked that it almost can be diagrammed. As we have seen, Charlemagne grants to the abbey as much land as a mule can circumambulate in one day.[39] But Lagrasse's patrimony also comes into being through the actions of Charlemagne and the epic peers accompanying him. A series of chapels founded at the king's express command by his entourage of princes and prelates forms the first circle around Lagrasse.[40] The majority of those that I have been able to identify are within a few kilometers of the abbey. For example, on the "plain" of Mirailles (1.6 kilometers to the southwest of Lagrasse, now a large open patchwork of fields), Charlemagne dubs 3,000 of his knights and erects a large stone, declaring that this place should be known as *Petrafixa*.[41] Furthermore, Charlemagne fights one of his first battles on a rugged elevation a kilometer and a half southeast of Lagrasse; Turpin then declares that it should henceforth be called *Mons Bressorum* because among the thousands of Muslims captured there were seven hundred infants *in bressibus* (diapers? breeches?) whom he baptized.[42] Charlemagne approved this and constructed there a chapel dedicated to Saint Vincent. The king, his prelates, and princes founded further chapels that form a ring around Lagrasse.[43] And, as burial places for various fallen peers, they established another monastery, Saint Marie des Palais (modern Les Palais on the River Nielle, ten kilometers east of Lagrasse).[44]

When the heroes moved away from Lagrasse, they still traced out a landscape centered on the abbey. As Charlemagne progressed toward his epic battle at Narbonne, he founded a number of churches, some of which, we know from other sources, were dependencies of the abbey.[45] Roland and Ogier then separated from the main army to lay siege to Gerona. Ogier was killed in the battle, and Roland founded a monastery in honor of Saint Andrew as a fitting place for his companion's eternal rest.[46] Later, after a successful clash with Marsilius for the possession of Roussillon, Charlemagne buried all the fallen Christians at the new monastery.[47] This

---

39 See note 32 to this chapter.
40 Schneegans, ed., *Gesta Karoli Magni*, 28, 30, 32.
41 Ibid., 78. Given the nature of this elevated but flat site, today an open patchwork of vineyards and fields, one can see why the text would designate it as the gathering place for an army.
42 Ibid., 32. This site probably also is the one that the text refers to as *Ville Bercianis*. For example, both *Mons Bressorum* and *Ville Bercianis* appear in connection with *Rupe Gileria*, a place near Lagrasse that I have been unable to identify (54, 90). Furthermore, the text locates both *Mons Bressorum* and *Ville Bercianis* in the same place in relation to Lagrasse.
43 Ibid., 28, 30, 32.   44 Ibid., 30, 72.
45 Ibid., 102, 104.   46 Ibid., 48.
47 Ibid., 92.

epic necropolis is Saint André de Sorède, located on the gentle plain at the foot of the Pyrenees, approximately fifteen kilometers south of Perpignan.

The *Gesta Karoli Magni*'s narrative center, Lagrasse, thus also is its geographic center: The landscape demarcated and named by the king and his epic peers was almost always defined in relation to the abbey itself and its patrimony. Charlemagne or one of his peers granted to the abbey a number of the places thus described by the legend; and many of these places, such as Saint André de Sorède and Saint Marie des Palais, were in fact among the abbey's properties by the time of the legend's composition.[48] Even in those cases where the legend does not specify that the places delineated by Charlemagne and his companions belong to the abbey, other sources do. For example, by the tenth century, Lagrasse had acquired estates at *Mons Bressorum* (modern day Ville Bresses, a gentle hill some one-and-a-half kilometers to the south of the abbey), and by at least the thirteenth century it had a priory at Mirailles.[49] In any case, the legend implicitly endows Lagrasse with all the space it defines. This world is constructed through the abbey's origins and hence relates back to Lagrasse. A map is created with the abbey at its center. And, as is implied by this privileged location, the abbey dominates the area defined as its periphery.

B. CENTERS AND CENTERS: FOUNDERS

In the legends, the language of the sacred and the language of space create topographies describing the abbey as the center to which the periphery is subjugated. These landscapes are delineated through a series of motifs, many of which involve, as we have seen, the actions of the figures cast in the role of founder. Charlemagne, with his epic peers at Lagrasse and Gilles at Saint Gilles, demarcated the sacred space centered on the abbey, which became its own.

But it was not merely the actions of Gilles, Charlemagne, and the other founders imaginatively remembered by southern French monasteries that endowed the abbey with the status of center. The identity of the founders

---

48 Lagrasse held Saint-André de Sorède by the early twelfth century; see the charters of donation in *Gallia Christiana*, 2d ed., 16 vols. (Paris, 1715–1865), 6: instrumenta 484–5. For its possession of Sainte-Marie, see Abbé Sabarthès, *Dictionnaire topographique du Département de l'Aude comprenant les noms de lieu anciens et modernes* (Paris, 1912), 288.

49 In 959 the archbishop of Narbonne sold to Lagrasse the church he and his canons held at *Villa Berciano*; *Gallia Christiana* 6, instr. 19–20. For Mirailles, see the bull of Gregory IX in Paris, BN, ms Doat 66, f. 232ᵛ.

favored by southern French monasteries was itself crucial. Unlike abbeys from other parts of Europe, in their legends these monasteries did not often choose to celebrate local nobles as their founders, even in cases where an aristocrat actually had established the abbey.[50] Rather, the founders celebrated in southern French legends generally embodied sources of authority that eclipsed the local. Hence these figures themselves represented symbolic centers.[51] Either a local figure might be transformed into an embodiment of the larger authority, or a personage who originally represented this authority could be shaped to also become part of the local landscape. In either case, through their founders the abbeys came to participate in and enjoy the qualities of the larger authority. The nature of the legendary founders popular among southern monasteries thus heightened the centering effect of the topographies created by imaginative memory.

Southern abbeys might draw the connection between their origins and such authority through figures representing the primordial layer of Christianity, typically "apostles" who had known Christ (or his mother) or who had been entrusted by Saint Peter or an early pope with an evangelical mission to Gaul. The authority thus tapped was that of the apostles' chief heir, the pope, although popes themselves, whether past or present, hardly ever appeared in the role of legendary founder.[52]

For example, three mid- to late eleventh-century *vitae* recount how Severus, patron saint of Saint Sever, born somewhere in Asia Minor, converts to Christianity under Julian the Apostate.[53] After a brief spell as a hermit, he turns to the apostolic duty of preaching, unsuccessfully attempting to convert the Vandals. Eventually he and six companions arrive in Rome, where they spend a year "under the patronage of the apostles" and the tutelage of a Pope Eugenius. An angel then appears to Severus and tells him to make his way to Gascony, the region he is predestined to convert to Christianity.[54] There he constructs various churches

---

50 Abbeys in Germany and northern France, for example, often chose to celebrate aristocratic founders. On the German legends, see Patze, "Adel und Stifterchronik," 8–81; 101 (1965): 67–128. For northern French legends, see Farmer, *Communities of Saint Martin*, 79–88; and Léon Mirot, ed., *La chronique de Morigny (1095–1152)* (Paris, 1912). On the often deliberate occlusion of noble founders in southern French legends, see Remensnyder, *Remembering Kings Past*, 93, 103–6.

51 See Shils's remarks about the relation between figures of authority and the "center" in his *Center and Periphery*, 8.

52 For a detailed discussion of the legends celebrating apostles, see Remensnyder, *Remembering Kings Past*, 95–100.

53 *Prima vita sancti severi martyris*; *Secunda vita sancti Severi metrice scripta*; *Vita tertia sancti Severi martyris*; *AASS* Nov. 1:220–233. I follow the text of the *Vita tertia* for the most part here.

54 *Vita tertia sancti Severi martyris*; *AASS* Nov. 1:229.

and preaches with much success. Martyrdom at the hands of invading barbarians crowns his apostolic career. Saint Sever's patron, sent by Peter's heir, the pope, thus becomes the apostle of Gascony, lauded as such in a panegyric at the close of the final version of the *vita*.[55]

Whether or not the saint in question was made into a member of the living Christ's own circle of disciples, the apostolic claims placed the church that bore the saint's name and enshrined his (or, rarely, her) relics in contact with the primordial layer of Christianity. Other patron saints, one of the original twelve apostles for example, or the Virgin, or Mary Magdalene could and did have this meaning. But in the cases of local saints endowed with an apostolic function, the dynamic of the patron-church relationship is particular. The church, through its relics, becomes coterminous with and embodies both the local introduction of Christianity and the integration of the region into the larger entity of the church. It thus becomes itself a center from which Christianity emanated and creates for itself a connection with the authority represented by the apostles and their imitators. The charisma of the apostles as representatives of the center reinforced the monastery's claim to centrality.

The charisma possessed by representatives of another sort of center, however, outshone the apostles in monastic imaginative memory. The most favored founders in these legends were royal − kings, not queens, for in their legends, these abbeys tended either to ignore queens or to place them in the shadow of male figures.[56] Approximately three-quarters of the over forty ecclesiastical communities I studied chose to associate a male royal founder with their imaginatively remembered origins.

This extraordinary development of the royal image in these legends − not a trait of medieval monastic legends in general − reveals the ways that these abbeys constructed themselves as centers. It also makes us question how modern historians have implicitly used the lens of center and periphery to understand the production of the royal past in Capetian France. When considering this aspect of the royal image, historians have tended to focus on the activity of the monarchs and their circles. The argument, grossly oversimplified, runs as follows: Between the eleventh and thirteenth centuries, the intimates of the Capetian kings, that is, writers from

---

55 *Prima vita sancti Severi martyris*; *AASS* Nov. 1:225–6. Not only is Severus presented as the apostle of Gascony, but he is also implicitly made into the heir and successor of Saturninus, the bishop who, according to Gregory of Tours, had been sent to convert Toulouse. Here the Christianization of Gascony is genealogically linked with that of the rest of Gaul; *Vita tertia sancti Severi martyris*; *AASS* Nov. 1:229–30.

56 On queens in these legends, see Remensnyder, *Remembering Kings Past*, 100–1.

northern French ecclesiastical establishments (such as Fleury and Saint Denis) traditionally associated with the Frankish kings, wrought Charlemagne and other past rulers into symbols of monarchy. This helped engender a "nation" and a "national consciousness" centered on the Capetian kings.[57] With few exceptions, medieval historians thus have tended to look at how the political center produces an image of itself, an approach that could be called centrist.[58] By analytically privileging the king and his circles, this approach accepts the perspective that it purports to explain: that the monarch is the generative symbolic center and all else is peripheral. But what about the vibrant portraits of kings past created in the legends of southern French monasteries located not within the royal orbit but at its periphery?[59]

In these legends the most popular royal founders were three Frankish rulers of the past: Clovis, Pippin the Short, and, most favored of all, Charlemagne, who figured in some way in approximately half the legends considered here.[60] This selection is in and of itself significant, for it reveals

57 The bibliography on this question is vast; see among others Colette Beaune, *Naissance de la nation France* (Paris, 1985); Joachim Ehlers, "Kontinuität und Tradition als Grundlage mittelalterlicher Nationsbildung in Frankreich," in Helmut Beumann, ed., *Beiträge zur Bildung der französischen Nation im Früh- und Hochmittelalter* (Sigmaringen, 1983), 16–47; Bernd Schneidmüller, *Nomen patriae: Die Entstehung Frankreichs in der politisch-geographischen Terminologie (10.–13. Jahrhundert)* (Sigmaringen, 1987); Percy E. Schramm, *Der König von Frankreich*, 2 vols. (Weimar, 1939); Karl Ferdinand Werner, "Die Legitimität der Kapetinger und die Entstehung des *Reditus regni francorum ad stirpem Karoli*," *Die Welt als Geschichte* 12 (1952): 203–25. See also Jacques Le Goff's summary and overview in his *Histoire de la France: L'Etat et les pouvoirs* (Paris, 1989), 58–60.

58 Some exceptions include Paul Freedman, "Cowardice, Heroism and the Legendary Origins of Catalonia," *Past and Present* (1988): 3–28; Julia Smith, who argues that the experience of provinces is as important as that of the central government for an understanding of empire; see her *Province and Empire: Brittany and the Carolingians* (Cambridge, 1992); and Gabrielle M. Spiegel, who shows how an image of the king was produced and manipulated by the aristocracy; see her *Romancing the Past: The Rise of Vernacular Prose Historiography in Thirteenth-Century France* (Berkeley, Calif., 1993). In his magisterial treatment of the "memory and legend" of Charlemagne in the medieval German realm (*Le souvenir et la légende de Charlemagne dans l'Empire germanique médiéval* [Paris, 1950]), Robert Folz does not ignore local traditions and indeed grants them their importance; nonetheless, the core of his argument is Charlemagne's shifting role in imperial ideology.

59 For a consideration of a different kind of creation of the political center by the so-called periphery, see Peter Sahlins, *Boundaries: The Making of France and Spain in the Pyrenees* (Berkeley, Calif., 1990).

60 Legends in which Clovis appears as founder: Figeac, Saint-Léonard of Noblat (a house of canons), Moissac, Saint-Germier, Sainte-Marie of Auch (the cathedral church); on these legends, see Remensnyder, *Remembering Kings Past*, 117–31. Legends in which Pippin the Short appears as (re)founder: Saint-Pierre of Uzerche, Figeac, Sorèze, Mozac, Notre Dame de la Règle, Saint-Quintin of Gaillaguet, Saint-Pierre of Joncels, Conques, Saint-Michel of Cuxa, Saint-Yrieix de la Perche (a house of canons); on these legends, see Remensnyder, *Remembering Kings Past*, 132–49. Charlemagne as (re)founder: Aniane, Brantôme, Charroux, Conques, Gerri, Lagrasse, Psalmodi, La Réole, Saint-Polycarpe, Saint-Michel of Cuxa, Saint-Savin of Lavedan, Sarlat, Sorde, Vabres (also the cathedral of Narbonne). Monasteries founded by members of Charlemagne's entourage: Alet, Gellone, Perse. Monasteries in whose legend Charlemagne played a significant role: Moissac, Saint-Gilles (also the house of canons of Saint-Yrieix de la Perche). On the Charlemagne legends, see Remensnyder, *Remembering Kings Past*, 150–201.

that these abbeys did *not* imaginatively remember themselves as part of a political periphery. These three monarchs all had worked to bring south-western France under the political control of the Frankish monarchy. Invoking these kings as legendary founders, the southern monasteries not only made the absent political center imaginatively present but also proclaimed themselves part of the larger integrated realm. Rulers such as Charles the Bald, glorious perhaps but a king of the north, and those such as the Pippins of Aquitaine or those would-be kings, Hunald and Waïfre, who represented the south as a separate subkingdom, were rejected or effaced in monastic imaginative memory in favor of these three kings who had incorporated (even violently) the south into a larger realm.[61]

Like the apostolic saints, Clovis, Pippin the Short, and Charlemagne permitted an imaginative exchange in which, on the one hand, the monastery became part of the political entity represented by the monarch and, on the other, the monarch's symbolic role as center communicated itself to the monastery. Thus, the relationship was not envisaged as one between a political center and its periphery but rather as one between two centers. In fact, in their legends the monks tended to shape the royal center in function of the monastery as center. For example, southern French monastic imaginative memory transformed Pippin the Short from his historical role as destroyer of churches south of the Loire into benevolent founder.[62] But perhaps the most relevant aspect of this monastic remembrance of kings past is the way in which the legends placed hints of halos – or even entire nimbuses – over these royal heads. This unofficial sanctification of royal founders occurred in many ways in the legends, a complex and fascinating process I have explored elsewhere.[63] It is the result of this process, most particularly in the case of Charlemagne, that interests me here. For the saintly Charlemagne created by these legends poses a challenge to the centrist framework of modern historians.

Scholars have argued that Charlemagne was officially made a saint by various monarchs seeking to legitimate their own reigns. They point to Charlemagne's canonization in Germany in 1165 at Frederick Barbarossa's

---

61 On Charlemagne the Bald seen as a ruler of the north, see Schneidmüller, *Nomen patriae*, 140–208. Southern French abbeys did not completely ignore Charles the Bald's prestige. A number of them (including Charroux and Lagrasse) in the tenth and eleventh centuries forged or interpolated diplomas in his name; cf. Jean Dufour, "Etat et comparaison des actes faux ou falsifiés, intitulés au nom des Carolingiens (840–987)," in *Fälschungen im Mittelalter*, 4:171–80, 205–8. On the occlusion of the Pippins of Aquitaine and the elision of Hunald and Waïfre, see Remensnyder, *Remembering Kings Past*, 134, 138–9, 143–6.

62 See ibid., 132–49.   63 Ibid., 89–92, 108–211.

behest and to Charles V's importation of the German cult to Paris in the mid-fourteenth century.[64] In other words, the historiography implies that it is to royal circles that we should look for the production of the image of the saintly king – yet another example of the assumption that the royal center necessarily created itself.

How then are we to understand the Saint Charlemagne who emerged in monastic legends south of the Loire? This Saint Charlemagne is perhaps best captured in the abbey of Lagrasse's legend, the *Gesta Karoli Magni*. This rich mid-thirteenth-century text relates how, on their way to Spain, Charlemagne and his epic peers stopped off to wrest Narbonne from the Muslims.[65] In a nearby valley they found seven hermits living in huts surrounding an oratory dedicated to the Virgin. Recognizing that the valley was a place chosen by God, Charlemagne decided to found a monastery there. The hermits, having fulfilled their function of revealing the sanctity of the site, were conveniently eliminated by the swords of the Muslims. As we have seen, the role of tracing the charged lines that demarcate the sacred space of the abbey thus devolved to Charlemagne and his companions.[66] Here Charlemagne and his companions usurp a role assigned to saints such as Gilles or Austremonius in earlier legends, that is, the physical delineation and organization of monastic space. Now it is Charlemagne's steps, not those of a saint as in earlier legends, that have the power to create sacred boundaries.[67] But how can Charlemagne's steps trace such lines if he himself has not become sanctifying and therefore saintly?

Lagrasse's legend thus represents the culmination of a process already incipient in twelfth-century legends invoking Charlemagne: This monarch had become the legitimizing and sanctifying principle structuring the monastery's image of its origins. For example, in the late twelfth-century layer of the abbey of Sorde's legend, Charlemagne founded the monastery and then "he, with the archbishop of Reims, Turpin, sealed the sacred altars with his own hand (*propria manu sigillavit*)."[68] Charlemagne's role as

64 On the German canonization, see Folz, *Le souvenir et la légende*, 159–234. For Charles V and the cult, see Robert Folz, "Aspects du culte liturgique de Saint Charlemagne en France," in Wolfgang Braufels *et al.*, eds., *Karl der Grosse: Lebenswerk und Nachleben*, 5 vols. (Düsseldorf, 1965–68), 4:77–99.

65 Schneegans, ed., *Gesta Karoli Magni*.   66 See notes 38–49 to this chapter.

67 On saints and earlier legends, see Remensnyder, *Remembering Kings Past*, 116–7, 121–2, 202.

68 *Monumenta Germaniae Historica, Diplomata Karolinorum*, 1:567–8. On the dating of this text, see Remensnyder, *Remembering Kings Past*, 326. In the last entry in the abbey's thirteenth-century cartulary there is a garbled reference to this legendary consecration, although here Pope Leo rather than Charlemagne aids Turpin: "[M]iloleo fuit patre Stampensis inter italiam et apuliam, ubi est sanctus angelus matre vero petragoricensis de sancto asterio [et] de sancto leone. In

a sanctifier of space is underlined in no uncertain terms, for here he usurps what was an episcopal prerogative: the rite of consecration.[69] But by the thirteenth century, as Lagrasse's legend shows, Charlemagne did not have to officiate at a ritual in order to consecrate the landscape. No mediation was necessary; Charlemagne's mere presence had become sanctifying.

In the process, Charlemagne himself was crowned with a halo visible perhaps not to modern historians focusing on developments in the Capetian center but certainly to our southern monks. By the thirteenth century there is evidence of liturgical commemoration of this king in at least one southern abbey: Gellone, an abbey that celebrated as its founder Charlemagne's epic peer, Guillaume.[70] In a martyrology of this period from Gellone, Charlemagne appears on January 28, his feast day.[71] He even may have been commemorated at this abbey in the eleventh century.[72] And by 1351 at Lagrasse, masses were celebrated daily in honor of Charlemagne, styled "founder" of the monastery. At some point before the seventeenth century, apparently with papal dispensation, these *suffragia* gave way to *cultus* (veneration).[73] By the sixteenth century at least Charlemagne figured in the abbey's liturgical calendar.[74] It should not be surprising, then, that by the fourteenth century an observer might explicitly call Lagrasse's Charlemagne a saint; when Charles V confirmed Lagrasse's privileges in 1376, he not only mentioned the abbey's miraculous consecra-

consecratione sordensis ecclesie fuerunt hi apostolicus miloleo Turpinus Remensis archiepiscopus"; Paul Raymond, ed., *Cartulaire de l'abbaye de Saint-Jean de Sorde* (Paris, 1872), 158 (no. 184) (with some minor changes as per my transcription from the manuscript, Paris, BN, ms lat. n.a. 182, f. 50v).

69 On the episcopal right to consecration, Remensnyder, *Remembering Kings Past*, 36–8.

70 On Gellone's legend, see ibid., 168–70, 188–93, 276–84.

71 "V febr. . . . Item in gallis apud aquisgrani palacium transitus domini karoli piissimi imperatoris," Montpellier, Bibliothèque Municipale, ms 13, f. 3ᵛ. For a consideration of Charlemagne in earlier necrologies (limited by the availability of editions of such sources), see Bernd Schneidmüller, *Karolingische Tradition und frühes französisches Königtum: Untersuchungen zur Herrschaftslegitimation der westfränkisch-französischen Monarchie im 10. Jahrhundert* (Wiesbaden, 1979), 15–23. On the importance of liturgical celebrations of kings as potential indications of cult, see Robert Folz, *Les saints rois du Moyen Age en Occident (VIe–XIIIe siècles)*, Subsidia Hagiographica 68 (Brussels, 1984), 173–5.

72 In the late seventeenth century, Dom Estiennot copied entries for Charlemagne from a martyrology of Gellone that he dated as eleventh-century; Paris, BN, ms lat. 12733, 394, 397.

73 In 1677, Dom Jean Trichaud copied the section relevant to Charlemagne of the *Rotulus Moysis* of 1351 containing the customs of the monastery and then remarked: "Desiit tandem mos ille ut licuit (probante suprema divi petri sede) non amplius suffragia sed cultum religisissimo imperatori adhibere . . ."; cf. his *Chronicon seu historia regalis Abbatiae Beatae Mariae de Crassa*; Paris, BN, ms lat. 12857, pp. 124–5. For a more complete copy of the *Rotulus Moysis*, see Alphonse Mahul, ed., *Cartulaire de l'ancien diocèse et de l'arrondissement administratif de Carcassonne*, 7 vols. (1857–82), 2:331ff.

74 Charlemagne's *obit* appears in a printed breviary of 1523; Mahul, ed., *Cartulaire de l'ancien diocèse*, 2:437.

tion described in its legend but also referred to its founder as "Saint Charlemagne."[75] Here Charles V speaks, not the abbey, and it was he who had introduced Charlemagne's cult in Paris.[76] But in this privilege, he uses the language of Lagrasse's legend, a legend that presented a Charlemagne with saintly traits.

This image of Charlemagne's sanctity did not remain hidden behind the walls of the monasteries that had created it. The cult of exactly this Saint Charlemagne – the one created by Lagrasse's legend and the memory of other southern French monasteries – was officially proclaimed in the diocese of Girona in 1345, a Catalonian city that had many links with these abbeys. Of course, at approximately the same time, north of the Loire, Charles V imported Charlemagne's cult from Germany to Paris. But this chronological coincidence was nothing more than that – coincidence. The liturgical office that was used to celebrate Charlemagne in Girona bears no resemblance whatsoever to the Office of Charlemagne composed at Aachen, used in Germany, and brought by Charles V to Paris.[77] Instead, the Office of Girona presents a king remarkably similar to the Charlemagne of Lagrasse's legend.[78] Charlemagne's salient characteristic in this office is that he founds local churches in conjunction with his epic expeditions against the Muslims. The resemblance between this office used in the public celebration of the king at Girona and Lagrasse's legend is not accidental. The Office has as its main source Lagrasse's legend, which in turn drew on other southern monastic legends.[79]

These monastic legends, then, were the source of Charlemagne's public face as a saint in southern France. Monastic imaginative memory, not royal initiative, determined how people in that region would see this saintly king of the past. The political "periphery" could create an image of the political center that did not depend on that center's image of itself. Nor was this sanctification (which also affected Clovis and Pippin the Short) the result of the abbeys' recognition of the "sacral" character of kings, if such inherent sacrality really was a royal property. Charlemagne did not acquire a halo because he was a king. Rather, Charlemagne became

---

75 This privilege (dated at Senlis, 1376) is edited in Mahul, ed., *Cartulaire de l'ancien diocèse*, 2:351.
76 See note 64 to this chapter.
77 On the importation of the Office of Aachen for use in Paris, see Folz, "Aspects du culte liturgique."
78 On this text and the introduction of the cult to Girona, see Jules Coulet, *Etude sur l'Office de Girone en l'honneur de Saint Charlemagne*, Publications de la Société pour l'étude des langues romanes 20 (Montpellier, 1907). The text is edited on 57–9.
79 Ibid., 138–58.

sanctified because he was remembered as a founder, because he was embraced in the sacred moment of the origins of a monastic community. The king was rendered saintly so that he could reinforce the abbey's nature as sacred center.

This process of sanctification was not specific to royal founders, nor was it limited to southern French abbeys.[80] For when they did not choose as their founders figures who were already saints, monastic communities tended to invest founders who were not originally saints with an aura of saintliness. This process of sanctification appears quite clearly in, for example, sources from the eleventh through the twelfth century relating to one of the few nobles celebrated in southern French monastic legends: Calminius, the (perhaps nonexistent) aristocrat claimed as legendary founder by three ecclesiastical communities (Laguenne, Mozac, and Saint Chaffre).[81] The eleventh-century sources do not depict Calminius as anything but an ordinary mortal, but by the middle of the twelfth century Mozac had composed a *vita* celebrating him in no uncertain terms as a saint.[82] Furthermore, in the last years of the twelfth century the abbot of Mozac commissioned a gorgeous reliquary for "Saint" Calminius that also ascribes to his wife Namadia the title of *beata*.[83] And by the thirteenth century, Calminius was commemorated as a confessor in the official liturgy for the diocese of Tulle.[84]

There thus was a complex structural connection between the role of founder and sanctity. Some historians have explained such sanctifications as the result of the ways in which the liturgical commemoration of dead founders could so easily overlap with the cult of the special dead, that is, the saints.[85] But sometimes liturgical commemoration happened only after the process of sanctification was well under way, as in the case of the kings in southern French legends. The connection between the role of founder and acquired sanctity is more fundamental. In legend, founders participated in the process of the revelation of the sacred center. Hence, they needed to be sanctifying themselves in some way. Animals who were

---

80 On such sanctifications of founders of monasteries elsewhere in Europe, see Michalowski, "Culto dei santi fondatori," 105–40; Sauer, *Fundatio und Memoria*, 183–208.

81 For detailed discussion of the legends relating to Calminius, see Remensnyder, *Remembering Kings Past*, 55, 104–6, 114.

82 *Vita S. Calminii confessoris*; *AASS* Aug. 3:760–1.

83 The dating of the reliquary is somewhat problematic; see Marie-Madeleine Gauthier (who argues that the reliquary was begun under Peter III, abbot from ca. 1168–1181, and completed ca. 1197), *Emaux du moyen âge occidental* (Fribourg, 1972), 333–5.

84 Paris, BN, ms lat. 1257, f. 69vb (thirteenth century); Paris, Bibliothèque Nationale, ms n.a. Latin 1872, f. 186v (fifteenth century).

85 Oexle, "Die Gegenwart der Toten," 30; Sauer, *Fundatio und Memoria*, 149–60.

really Christ in disguise (such as the deer in Mozac's legend) intrinsically possessed this quality, as did saints. Their presence alone could consecrate the site and designate it as a sacred center. But what about founders who were not saints to begin with? Over time, they could and did acquire the traits implicit in their role as agents who reveal sacred space.

Because Charlemagne and other kings of the past were claimed as founders by southern French abbeys with increasing frequency, they necessarily acquired the aura of sanctity. Fashioning themselves as sacred centers, these monasteries tailored an image of the absent royal center according to their own needs. Of course these needs could be functional as well as representational – abbeys might use their illustrious royal (or apostolic) origins as effective bulwarks in situations of tension or conflict. Imagined as a commanding sanctifying presence, the legendary king could be invoked in the face of those powers who actively sought to dominate the abbey and to diminish its liberty. Other aspects of the legendary production of the abbey as center could be read in this functional sense as well. As a sacred center, the abbey was in the category of that which could not be violated without divine retribution. This image – like that of the abbey as center dominating its patrimony – also could be used in various sorts of conflicts.[86]

In whatever ways abbeys appealed to these images, in their legends they mapped landscapes of which they were the center. The topographies created by monastic imaginative memory could describe the symbolic as well as the physical disposition of space around the abbey. Among the means used to express the abbey's position in relation to the larger world was the symbolic appropriation of the charisma of figures representing other centers: apostles and monarchs. These monasteries located in a region outside the sphere of the effective power of the monarch thus invoked exactly that absent royal center in their legends. But they did so in service of their self-image. Appealing to the charisma of other centers, abbeys imaginatively maintained themselves as the privileged center. While legends characterized the abbey in terms of its relation to these figures, the inverse also was true: Monasteries imaginatively remembered kings and apostles in terms of their relation to the abbey.

The flamboyant prologue of Lagrasse's legend makes this point through the trope of memory itself:

---

86 For the functional aspects of legends as discussed in this paragraph, see Remensnyder, *Remembering Kings Past*, 209–88.

The most Christian man beloved by God, the glorious king of the Franks and emperor Charles, while he was building this monastery, wished that the construction and consecration of the monastery of the blessed and glorious Virgin, Lagrasse, and the battles which he did in the taking of Narbonne should not be consigned completely to oblivion. And so he ordered . . . a writer by the name of Filomena . . . to write down the whole account (*ystoriam*).[87]

The prologue thus proclaims the legend and the events it relates as royal and epic, as consequently is Lagrasse itself. Furthermore, this text is quintessentially royal because it was originally written at Charlemagne's express command. It is Charlemagne's own official history, recounting events that the king himself wished to be remembered and not forgotten.[88] Charlemagne's will to commemorate his deeds confounds itself with Lagrasse's own desire to preserve its past, for, as the prologue immediately continues:

This account, written in ancient style letters (*antiquata litteratura*) and generally in very bad condition (*destructa*) was found in the aforesaid monastery's book repository. I, the Paduan, at the urging and request of Abbot Bernard and the whole community wrote and translated (*conposui . . . translatare*) this account with the help of Mary, the blessed mother of God, beginning at the beginning of that narrative.[89]

Lagrasse's legend thus is Charlemagne's memory of his deeds. Here royal memory cannot be distinguished from monastic imaginative memory. The two centers become one and all else is peripheral.

---

87 Schneegans, ed., *Gesta Karoli Magni*, 4, 6.
88 After the death of Ogier "of Normandy," Charlemagne orders that this event be recorded in the *ystoria*; ibid., 48. Once again, the *Gesta Karoli Magni* emphasizes that it is Charlemagne's own official history and that these are events he does not wish to be forgotten.
89 Ibid., 4, 6.

10

Challenging the Culture of Memoria

Dead Men, Oblivion, and the "Faithless Widow" in the Middle Ages

BERNHARD JUSSEN

Medieval people, according to current scholarly consensus, retained a presence among the living even after death; they continued to participate in social interactions and possessed rights of their own.[1] Those scholars who, during the past three decades, have popularized this theory under the heading of *memoria* (memory) aim at a "total" survey of medieval society, just as earlier scholars had aimed at a similar totality through now "classic" research on gift exchange.[2] Now that this enterprise, which has increasingly been taking form since the early 1960s, has gained wide acceptance, this may be an appropriate time to examine the outlines of this medieval "culture of *memoria*." Did medieval people really have no problem accepting the presence of the dead among the living? The title of this chapter hints at the answer: At times they had quite severe problems with the presence of the dead, and these problems manifested themselves in some remarkable ways, including in one of the most popular motifs of medieval narrative – the story of the "faithless widow."

Some recent studies have emphasized the prominent role of women within the system of *memoria*. It is striking, however, that the sources referred to in these works deal almost exclusively with exemplary specimens of the social category "widow."[3] Most of the sources cited mention

Pamela Selwyn translated this chapter from German.

1 A more detailed interpretation is found in Bernhard Jussen, *Der Name der Witwe: Erkundungen zur Semantik der mittelalterlichen Busskultur* (Göttingen, 2000).

2 For more on this perspective with its various areas of research, on its place within the intellectual framework of historical cultural studies, and on the literature in the field, see Otto Gerhard Oexle, "Memoria als Kultur," in Otto Gerhard Oexle, ed., *Memoria als Kultur* (Göttingen, 1995), 9–78.

3 Cf. Patrick Corbet, *Les saints ottoniens: Sainteté dynastique, sainteté royale et sainteté féminine autour de l'an Mil* (Sigmaringen, 1986); Patrick J. Geary, *Phantoms of Remembrance: Memory and Oblivion at the End of the First Millennium* (Princeton, N.J., 1994), chap. 2.

only subliminally, if at all, the no less common and often virtually expected option of a second marriage. The chronicler Thietmar of Merseburg (d. 1018), to name just one example, had the Duke Ernst of Swabia (d. 1015), who was on his deathbed, utter the request that his wife "preserve her *honor* and not forget me." The meaning of this request may need to be deciphered for us, but it was plain enough to contemporaries. The duke was quite unambiguously asking his wife not to remarry.[4]

The problem is familiar enough: Survival and kinship strategies often demanded remarriage, although Christian definitions of social roles offered no positive concept of a second marriage or *digamia*. Christianity offered only one model to the surviving wife, and that was widowhood (*viduitas*). This option was conceived of exclusively within the context of *memoria*: *Viduitas* meant mourning and lamentation as a way of life. According to church doctrine, there was only one way that the woman could, as Thietmar put it, "preserve her *honor*" by "not forgetting" through *memoria* as a way of life, as a permanent *vidua*.

All the same, most widows remarried. Should we then read the request of the dying Swabian duke to his wife as a symbol of a lasting conflict – remembrance versus remarriage? Must this conflict not have been revived with each death in the enigma of the surviving wife caught between *viduitas* and *digamia*? Didn't each remarriage represent a challenge to the culture of *memoria*? The scholarship on *memoria* has had nothing to say on this subject. Does this contradiction thus have only theoretical reality in retrospect but no connection to reality in the Middle Ages?

It did have a medieval reality. This contradiction between the concept of *memoria* and the logic of kinship, between the content of sermons and the exigencies of survival, between the demands of the dead and the requirements of life was repeatedly articulated in a very popular literary form. My examination of this contradiction is divided into five sections: (1) I shall begin by introducing the narrative form of this conflict, the story of the "faithless widow" (of Ephesus). I also shall provide a critique of the usual interpretations of this motif, which is generally viewed in quite a different manner from the one I propose here. (2) I then will situate the motif within the medieval narrative classifications. Finally, I will interpret the central aspects of the story, namely: (3) remarriage as the execution of the dead husband; (4) the widow as exemplary

---

4 Thietmar of Merseburg, *Chronicon* 7,14, ed. Robert Holtzmann, *Monumenta Germaniae Historica, Scriptores Rerum Germanicarum* 9 (Berlin, 1935), 414: "queso, commendate et uxorem meam, ut honorem suum servet et mei non obliviscatur, ammonete."

woman; and (5) the widow as the embodiment of an assault on gender relations.

SIMPLY A LECHEROUS FEMALE? THE STORY OF THE "FAITHLESS WIDOW"

The popularity within the Christian tradition of exemplary Biblical widow figures (Judith, Hannah, and so forth) was, if we are to believe literary scholars, greatly overshadowed by that of a figure of a widow whose representations predated Christianity and formed the subject of countless manuscripts into the sixteenth century: the "faithless widow" (of Ephesus). The occidental versions of this narrative motif were based on two first-century versions: the *Satyricon* of Petronius and Fables of Aesop of Phaedrus. The tale is considered "perhaps the most popular of all stories" (Jacobs) and "one of the best-loved motifs of world literature" (Huber).[5] Throughout the entire Middle Ages, no other exemplary widow could compare to the prominence of this story about a newly widowed woman who allowed a passing stranger "to have his way with her" on her husband's grave.[6]

The basic framework was always borrowed from the ancient motif, although the details changed constantly: A man dies, and his wife laments him loudly and vows not to leave his graveside. Yet she becomes "ever more yielding" (Phaedrus) to the first strange man who passes by, and in many versions "they celebrated their nuptials" (Petronius) on the grave (or in the mausoleum).[7] But the stranger turns out to be a sentry who is supposed to be guarding a hanged man (in antiquity, a crucified man) near the grave. And while the stranger is comforting the widow on the grave (or in the mausoleum), the hanged (or crucified) man's cadaver is stolen. The sentry, who may have to pay with his life (or sometimes only his property), becomes afraid, but the widow saves the day with a brilliant idea: The two of them remove her husband's corpse from the grave and hang it from the gallows (or on the cross).

It is not immediately clear why this fable should have been so widely disseminated in the Middle Ages. If I seek to show that the issue at stake

---

5 Jacobs's much-cited phrase can be found in Joseph Jacobs, *The Fables of Aesop*, 2 vols. (London, 1889), 1:13; Gerlinde Huber, *Das Motiv der "Witwe von Ephesus" in lateinischen Texten der Antike und des Mittelalters* (Tübingen, 1990), 7.

6 This is Marie de France's version, quoted in note 27 to this chapter.

7 Petronius, *Satyricon 112*, ed. Konrad Müller (Stuttgart, 1995), 119–20: "iacuerunt ergo una non tantum illa nocte qua nuptias fecerunt, sed postero etiam ac tertio die"; Phaedrus is cited in note 25 to this chapter.

here is that of "remembrance versus remarriage," I must begin with a critique of the usual interpretations of the story.

Modern interpretations seem fixated on the sexual content of the motif. The story's dissemination from Greco-Roman antiquity through the Near East to India and China must have contributed to the lack of attention to the historically and culturally specific meanings of the various narratives. Scholars seem to agree that this is an example of a transcultural "archetypal embodiment of deeply rooted male attitudes toward women and female sexuality."[8]

The fact that the lesson embedded in this extremely widespread story always seems fixed should arouse our suspicions. After all, it is a commonplace that the meaning lies not in the motif itself but in the social relations within which the motif circulates. The two imperial Roman authors lived in a completely different world from that of the medieval authors. When Petronius wrote his satire, the permanently celibate "widow" was an unknown concept; since Octavian, imperial laws were designed to compel widows to remarry.[9] The medieval versions, by contrast, come from a time when women who survived their husbands were presented, in the specifically Christian concept of "widow's estate," with the ideal of lifelong celibacy. Can such a fundamental reconceptualization of the protagonist have left no mark on the "most popular of all stories"?

So far as I can tell, no one has yet tried to read the narrative modifications that one finds in the story's many versions as signs of specific cultural constellations. The interpretations are so fixated on the sexual that they are even blind to the disappearance of sexual elements from the story: From the thirteenth century onward the sex scene on the grave is absent from the most widely disseminated versions. Instead, the widow is negotiating a new marriage with the stranger. This offers an essential key to the interpretation of the Christian occidental versions. The following section will be devoted to taking a closer look at this shift.

8 Heather M. Arden, "Grief, Widowhood, and Women's Sexuality in Medieval French Literature," in Louise Mirrer, ed., *Upon My Husband's Death: Widows in the Literature and Histories of Medieval Europe* (Ann Arbor, Mich., 1992), 306.
9 On this legislation, see Susan Treggiari, *Roman Marriage: Iusti Coniuges from the Time of Cicero to the Time of Ulpian* (Oxford, 1991); Angelika Mette-Dittmann, *Die Ehegesetze des Augustus: Eine Untersuchung im Rahmen der Gesellschaftspolitik des Princeps* (Stuttgart, 1991); on the "invention" of the widow as a social category around 400, see the sketch in Jussen, *Der Name der Witwe*, chap. 4; for a short version in English, see Bernhard Jussen, "On church Organization and the Definition of an Estate: The Idea of Widowhood in Late Antique and Early Medieval Christianity," *Tel Aviver Jahrbuch für deutsche Geschichte*, vol. 22: *Zur Sozial- und Begriffsgeschichte des Mittelalters* (1993): 25–42.

THE "FAITHLESS WIDOW" IN MEDIEVAL NARRATIVE:
NEGOTIATING A CULTURAL DILEMMA

In using the motif of the "faithless widow," medieval authors were continually addressing, with shifts of emphasis, a dilemma within the structures of society. At stake was an aporia in the concept of the community of the living and dead, the widow's particular role as a wanderer between these two groups, and her role in mourning and remembering the dead. In all epochs and in all cultures a woman who had survived her husband was at the center of the narrative. It was, however, only in a society measured by Christian standards, in which the penitent widow had become a paradigmatic figure, that the culturally nonspecific motif was directed at a central conflict: the conflict between the living and the dead. This conflict was played out in the figure of the widow.

I demonstrate this using a particularly detailed Latin version of the "faithless widow." It survives in the most widely disseminated Latin version of the *Story of the Seven Sages*, the so-called version "H." The *Story of the Seven Sages* is a narrative cycle that circulated in the west from the late twelfth century onward and has survived in more than ten languages and a number of different versions.[10] The "faithless widow" is more or less similar in nearly all versions of the Seven Sages. Version "H" is particularly interesting because it systematically transferred the antique material into a Christian life-world, thereby providing a thoroughly culturally specific interpretation of feminine cunning and faithlessness. I shall now turn my attention to the three detailed scenes in version "H."[11] In this version, the first two scenes develop the conflict by contrasting two opposing life choices for widows as two competing notions of good. Reduced to the shorthand terms "beauty" and "turtledove," they signify an existential dilemma for the individual woman and conflicting social expectations in society. The third scene offers an unusually brutal narrative solution to the conflict.

---

10 A particularly clear overview of the interdependence of various redactions and translations is presented in the introduction to Hans R. Runte, ed., *Li ystoire de la male marastre* (Tübingen, 1974), xviii (an edition of the French redaction M of the story of the Seven Sages); for a good discussion of difficult issues of dating, see Mary B. Speer, ed., *Le Roman des Sept Sages de Rome: A Critical Edition of the Two Verse Redactions of a Twelfth-Century Romance* (Lexington, Ky., 1989), 67–71 (an edition of the French redactions C and K).

11 The earliest manuscript dates from the year 1342 (Innsbruck, Universitätsbibliothek, Cod. lat. 310). It was edited by Georg Buchner, *Die historia septem Sapientium nach der Innsbrucker Handschrift v. J. 1342* (Erlangen, 1889; reprint, Amsterdam, 1970), 7–90.

Scene One: The Ideal Widow and the Advice of Kin

The first scene begins with the husband's sudden death. He has just enough time to send for a priest "so that he might bring with him the body of Christ" but to no avail because "he died before the priest arrived."[12] The medieval audience would have grasped the particular drama of the situation: The man died without the *viaticum* or the last rites. It thus was a potentially dangerous situation that recalled for the listeners a central expectation placed on the widow: She was to do penance in her husband's stead. And as all those who heard the story already knew from the many other versions, the tale now depicted the good widow – here, with a particular relish for detail: "She cried out, lamenting and sighing, and would not be comforted. Daily she wept: Alas, alas, whatever shall I do? Like a turtledove shall I remain henceforth!"[13]

Any glance at "real" life would show that this speech and the entire description of uninhibited lamentation were quite in keeping with the standards of female mourning behavior. The reference to the turtledove also was sufficient to evoke among the listeners a whole field of associations connected with the true Christian widow. Since the time of Ambrose, the turtledove had been considered an ideal widow because "after the loss of her mate she harbors a deep distaste for anything having to do with mating."[14] According to the bestiaries she became incapable of singing like other birds and took to sitting solitary and joyless on a bare branch, disappointed by life.

In the story, the continuation of the sad events also recalls traditional images: "When they had buried him, the widow (*domina*) repeatedly fell down on his grave. Her relations (*amici*) wanted to tear her away, but she vowed by God (*Deo vovit*) that she would never part from him. . . . When the dead man's relations saw this they built a small hut beside the grave. . . . Enclosed therein, they left her behind."[15]

---

12 *Sieben weise Meister*, Red. H, ed. Buchner, pp. 64–5: "Occulos apperuit et dixit: 'Celeriter michi sacerdotem querite! . . . Famuli hoc videntes unus post alium ad ecclesiam cucurrit pro sacerdote, ut secum Corpus Christi portaret; sed ecce tantum dolorem accepit, quod, antequam sacerdos venit, emisit spiritum: De cuius morte factus est planctus magnus in civitate.'"

13 Ibid., 65: "gemitus et suspiria emittebat nec consolari volebat set cottidie clamabat: 'Heu, michi heu! quid faciam ego? Ego sicut turtur de cetero ero.'"

14 Ambrosius of Milan, "Exameron 5,19,62/3," in Carolus Schenkl ed., *S. Ambrosii opera* 1 (Prague, 1897), 187–8: "fertur etenim turtur, ubi iugalis proprii fuerit amissione uiduata, pertaesum thalamos et nomen habere coniugii."

15 *Sieben weise Meister*, Red. H, ed. Buchner, p. 65: "Ipso sepulto domina semper super sepulcrum eius cecidit. Amici volebant eam ammovere, illa vero votum deo vovit quod nunquam de illo recederet. . . . Amici eius videntes hoc ultra sepulcrum eius parvam casam ei fecerunt, in qua omnia necessaria posuerunt: illa sic inclusa recesserunt."

In addition to the vow of loyalty and life as a recluse, the tale also cites her prostration on the grave and demonstrative hopelessness, likewise standard expressions of "real life" mourning behavior. It may suffice here to recall the famous illuminations to the funeral liturgy in the Sacramentary of Warmundus of Ivrea. In the combination of text and image, this manuscript from around the year 1000 illustrates the social division of labor in mourning rites. Hope was expressed in the spoken and sung text of the liturgy, hopelessness in the gestures of the woman. Seven illuminations depict the widow at the funeral rites with her dead husband; in three of them she tries to fling herself on the body, first onto the *cilicium* (f. 195v), then onto the coffin (f. 201v), and finally into the grave (f. 206v).[16]

These are the contexts to which the story refers. In a few key words (recluse, lament, turtledove, vow, the plunge into the grave) it cites the Christian occidental concept of "widow" as we also find it in ritual practice. But the man's relations are left to express a competing standard of proper behavior: "Oh dearest lady, what does it profit his soul that you should remain in this place? It would be better for you to return home and offer generous alms for his soul than to consume yourself in this place."[17] The relatives ask the widow to think of herself. Their voices represent the expectation of concern for her house and children, the expectations of those around her that she will become reintegrated into social life after a certain period of time. The moral dilemma is formulated in the juxtaposition between the widow's desire to join her husband in death and her relations' admonitions for self-preservation. The reference to the alms that would "consume" (*consumere*) the living less than would mourning at graveside places limits on the claims of the dead. The rights of the living are pitted against those of the dead, thus evoking the existential conflict toward which the story now moves.

Scene Two: A New Man

As in all versions of the "faithless widow" story, in the second scene there appears a new man who is guarding a hanged criminal near the cemetery. Like the relations of the deceased man, he too begins as an advocate of life. "My lady, you are beautiful, generous, slender and young, you

---

16 See the illustrations in Geary, *Phantoms of Remembrance*, 56–9 (plates 3–10).

17 *Sieben weise Meister*, Red. H, ed. Buchner, p. 65: "Dixeruntque amici: 'O domina karissima, quid prodest anime sue ut in isto loco maneas? Melius est tibi domum pergere, largas elemosynas pro anima sua perpetrare, quam in loco isto te ipsam consumere.'"

are rich. It would be better for you to remain at home offering rich alms
for the soul of your husband instead of staying alone here, consumed by
lamentations and sighs."[18] Here the model of the "turtledove," invoked by
the widow herself, is pitted against the logic of beauty, youth, and riches,
and staying alone against the scarcely oblique mention of the model of
remarriage. The story moves irresistibly toward a conflict that was as
routine as it was insurmountable.

How people dealt with this conflict after a "real life" death is well
known and scarcely surprising: They solved it ritually. The ritual sequence
called for the woman first to "die" along with her husband and then –
after a precisely defined time period – to return to life. In "real" life,
the conflict of values was elegantly clothed in a relatively standardized
ritual mourning process.[19] The story could only take on meaning,
however, by making the most of the aporia and testing the solutions
against extreme modes of behavior. And that brings us to the third scene
of the story.

Scene Three: Remarriage as the Execution of the Dead Man

As in all versions, matters in version H take a turn for the worse at the
moment when the stranger returns to the gallows. The hanged man's
corpse has been stolen and the soldier, fearing punishment, seeks the
widow's advice. In the Middle Ages, every listener or reader knew from
numerous other versions what advice the widow would give him; they
knew that the pair would now open the grave and place the dead husband
on the gallows in the convicted man's stead. What distinguishes the versions in the Seven Sages from the ancient texts and from much of the
medieval fable tradition is the marriage proposal that the widow ties to
her assistance. Scarcely has she made her offer of help when she begins
her proposal: "Would it please you to take me as your wife?"[20] After some
brief discussion and reflection the imperiled man consents to the proposal
and thus saves his skin.

What is important is that libido no longer plays any narrative role here.
The scene at the gallows no longer is the chilling climax of a sex scene,

---

18 Ibid., 66: "Miles dixit: 'Domina, tu pulchra, tu generosa, tu graciosa, iuvenis et dives es. Melius
   tibi esset in domo tua permanere, elemosynas largas pro anima mariti tui perpetrare, quam hic
   sola permanere et te ipsam per gemitus et suspiria consumere.'"
19 Bernhard Jussen, "*Dolor und Memoria*: Trauerriten, gemalte Trauer und soziale Ordnung im späten
   Mittelalter," in Oexle, ed., *Memoria als Kultur*, 207–53.
20 *Sieben weise Meister*, Red. H, ed. Buchner, p. 67: "Que ait: 'Numquid placet tibi me in uxorem
   habere?'"

as it was in Phaedrus and Petronius, but rather of a *marriage proposal*. The symbolism of the gallows is simple enough: The gallows stands for death without memory, the refusal of remembrance. What the tale expresses here in a particularly dramatic manner is a specific experience within Christian occidental culture: By rejecting the role of the eternally lamenting turtledove and remarrying, the surviving wife casts her dead husband into oblivion, of which the gallows was a terrible and omnipresent symbol. In literature, the very reaction to the death of a husband that was usually expected of women – remarriage – becomes a fearful deed, a deceitful execution "as a result of which," as the Innsbruck manuscript puts it, "the poor man cannot be remembered by succeeding generations."[21] By the way, the story of the "faithless widow" was by no means the only one that formulated this fateful connection between remarriage and oblivion.[22]

Now may be the moment to describe the difference between this Christian occidental constellation and its Roman counterpart more precisely. Both cultures conceived of themselves as communities encompassing both the living and the dead. In Roman society, however, in contrast to Christian occidental society, remembrance of the dead were bound up not with marriage but with the Roman concept of the agnatic family. Responsibility lay not with the surviving wife, but with the heir to the *patria potestas* and with the agnatic descendants. The widow had nothing to do with this.[23] Permanent widowhood was irrelevant to *memoria*; indeed it had even been forbidden since the time of Augustus.[24] The Roman tale thus did not deal with fundamental social institutions, such as the cult of the dead. It may be the case – as modern interpretations would have it – that its subject was indeed the image of woman. The whole point was that the widow and the sentry "celebrated their nuptials" (Petronius); to replace this with a proposal of marriage would have made no sense.

How different the Christian occidental versions are with their marriage proposal: Because mourning and remembering the dead no longer

---

21 The appendix to the usual story in the 1342 Innsbruck manuscript cod. lat. 310, in which this sentence is to be found, is absent from Buchner's edition; it is published in Huber, *Motiv*, 208: "carnalis voluptas, propter quam tantum homo miser non premeditatur de futuris."

22 For similar stories, see Mireille Othenin Girard, "Von dankbaren Toten zu Gespenstern: Wandel in den Vorstellungen der Wechselseitigkeit der Hilfeleistungen zwischen Lebenden und Verstorbenen," in Bernhard Jussen and Craig Koslofsky, eds., *Kulturelle Reformation: Sinnformationen im Umbruch 1400–1600* (Göttingen, 1999).

23 On the *pompa funebris*, see, e.g., Erich Bethe, *Ahnenkult und Familiengeschichte bei Römern und Griechen* (Munich, 1935), 30–1.

24 See note 9 to this chapter.

were the duty of the *paterfamilias* but rather of the widow, a key figure
in the social construction suddenly became the protagonist of the story.
For medieval listeners, the story was about the fundamental social and
religious institutions of their society – remembrance of the dead and
penitence by proxy, the institution of widowhood in its insoluble tension
with the institution of remarriage, the needs of the living versus those of
the dead.

In light of this interpretation, the meaning of those versions of the fifth
to fifteenth centuries in which the sexual scene on the grave (occasionally in the mausoleum) is not replaced by a proposal of marriage also
becomes clearer. For in these versions, too, strikingly little emphasis is
placed on the sexual element. Nearly all the narrators fall back on Phaedrus's austere ancient version in which the sexual scene is reduced to a
vague subordinate clause. Phaedrus limits the sexual content to the information that the mourning woman "became ever more yielding to the
stranger and was soon bound to him by closer ties."[25] The earliest
medieval treatment ("Romulus") is symptomatic of the entire tradition:
It allows for a sexual interpretation only in its reference to the widow as
the soldier's *amica*.[26] Another tradition was unambiguous but succinct.
Marie de France, for example, wrote: "The good woman looked at him.
She was well pleased and let him have his way."[27] In short, most versions
indicated only incidentally, if at all, that the widow's faithlessness had anything to do with her libido.

Naturally, modern scholars have noted this absence of a libidinous
element and have performed astounding feats of imagination in order to
ignore the implications. Thus, for example, the all-too-apparent offhand-
edness of the sexual references has been interpreted as the author's particular finesse in recounting a sexual tale. Now and then this paucity of
detail has even been deemed "progressive," part of a growing tendency to
avoid indecency, as if the medieval authors' purpose had been to supply
material for Elias's theory of civilization.[28] Undeterred by the absence of
sexual depictions, scholars persist in describing the "faithless widow" as

---

25 Phaedrus, *Fables*, ed. Alice Brenot (Paris, 1961), 97–8: "paulatim facta est aduenae submissior; mox
    artior devinxit animum copula."
26 Georg Thiele, ed., *Der lateinische Äsop des Romulus und die Prosafassungen des Phädrus* (Heidelberg,
    1910), 192: (recensio Gallicana) "dum illuc saepe ab amica vocatur"; 195 (recensio vetus) "et
    mulier non erubuit de officio suo."
27 Marie de France, Fable no. 25. "De vidua," ed. Karl Warnke (Halle, 1898), 112: "La prude femme
    l'esguarda; / grant joie fist, si otria / qu'ele fera sa volonté."
28 This is particularly the case in Dieter Beyerle, "Marie de France und die Witwe von Ephesus,"
    Romanistisches Jahrbuch 22 (1971): 92–3: "progressive" (*fortschrittlich*), or 94, 97, 99.

"simply another lecherous female who thinks only of finding a new outlet for her sexual needs."[29] For proponents of this widespread interpretation, the story titled "De cele qui se fist foutre sur la fosse de son mari" contains the true essence of the "faithless widow," "stripped of all nonessential elements" and reduced to the "central incident."[30] The fact that this supposedly "central incident" appears in most medieval versions either not at all or only very briefly does not appear to bother modern interpreters.

The error of these interpretations quite obviously lies in their failure to locate the protagonist within the social conceptions of the eras in which the tales were written down. Only when one takes such an approach does one notice that the tales told by Petronius in the first century and La Fontaine in the seventeenth century are similar but that the stories told in the intervening period used the same motif to address quite different issues. For Petronius the competing demands of life and death were not yet the topic of the story, and for La Fontaine, writing in the seventeenth century, they no longer were. The dead had ceased to have rights, and the story was of interest only because of its erotic dimension. "Better an upright churl," La Fontaine concluded, "than a buried emperor."[31] It was precisely this stance that many an author writing about the "faithless widow" after Petronius and before La Fontaine would have roundly rejected.

An initial, provisional appraisal thus takes us along quite another track from the usual interpretations: Medieval accounts of the "faithless widow" required no libidinous sequences, no recourse to the dangerous feminine, and no discussion of the gender order to help them explore the dimensions of the tensions between the remembrance of the dead and remarriage. The austere fable versions often limit themselves to the essentials: the dead man and the appearance of a living man, lamentation and the gallows.

It is all the more striking that practically all versions nevertheless end with some such perfunctory misogynist saying as "nothing good comes of women's doings."[32] Clearly, in the story of the "faithless widow" the problems of the relationship between the living and the dead have become entangled with the question of gender order. What, then, did these two

---

29 Arden, "Grief," 306.

30 Norris J. Lacy, "La Femme au Tombeau: Anonymous *fabliau* of the Thirteenth Century," Ph.D. diss., Indiana University, 1967, 51.

31 La Fontaine, *Contes* 15, 6, ed. Jean-Pierre Collinet (Paris, 1991), 394: "Mieux vaut Goujat debout qu'Empereur enterré."

32 "Gualterianae Fabulae 28. De malicia mulierum," in Léopold Hervieux, *Les Fabulistes Latins*, 2d. ed., 2 vols. (Paris, 1894), 2:391: "femineum nil bene finit opus."

things have to do with one another? At first glance the connection is by no means clear, and I shall have to take a little detour in order to interpret it.

Apparently the interconnection had something to do with the fact that the surviving wife united various stereotypes within herself: The widow was conceived of not only as a "turtledove" but also as an exemplary woman and the incarnation of an assault on the gender order. I shall begin by examining the widow as exemplary woman.

THE WIDOW AS EXEMPLARY WOMAN

It is significant that the tradition of the "faithless widow" is all but unrecognizable in that version in which the libido takes center stage: the *fabliau* "De cele qui se fist foutre sur la fosse de son mari." This version has more in common with a number of tales of widows with a clear erotic component – such as the Wife of Bath in Chaucer's *Canterbury Tales*, the "Old Woman" in Jean de Meung's *Romance of the Rose*, the "Widow" of Gauthier Le Leu, a handful of stories in the *Decameron* and some spectacular *fabliaux* – than it does with the "faithless widow."

The tale "De cele qui se fist foutre" began circulating in the thirteenth century. The episode involving the gallows was removed. It is no longer a sentry who embodies the arguments in favor of life but rather a lord and his servant who happen on the scene of mourning. They decide to put the female libido to the test. The lord hides, and the widow recounts her suffering to the servant, who replies with a sad story of his own: He, too, has just lost his beloved wife, and by his own fault: "En foutant, ma chère," he explains to the mourning widow. She reacts as expected: "Lord God," she says, overcome, "I have no talent for living. Dear Sir, come and deliver the world from me and kill me." She falls to the ground as if in a faint and lifts up her skirts. As is to be expected, this attempted killing ends in pleasure, and the man in his hiding place bursts out laughing, the point proven. If any further evidence were needed that this tale, unlike the other versions of the "faithless widow," is not about the relationship between the living and the dead, the final sentence supplies it. It is not faithlessness that is at issue here: "Thus did the lady comfort herself, who was consumed by such great pain."[33]

33 "Cele qui se fist foutre sur la fosse de son mari," in Willem Nooman and Nico van den Boogaard, eds., *Nouveau Recueil Complet des Fabliaux*, 5 vols. (Assen, 1986), 3:402: "Commant fait, Ceele arriere! / En fotant, doce amie chiere. / Deus, ja n'ai je talant de vivre: / Jantis hom, vien ça, si delivre / Lo siegle de moi, si me tue! / . . . A tant se laisse cheoir otre, / Ensi com s'ele

What ends here in roars of laughter is generally clearly marked as a danger for men. In the mid-thirteenth century, Gauthier Le Leu told the story of a widow who first heard out "kinswomen, cousins and neighbor women" who advised her to take a new husband "who was neither false nor lascivious." The widow, however, wished to "eat raw meat" and "to try out [a man] every night."[34] She describes her first husband as far too tame a specimen: "He treated me most generously/ he shod and clothed me/. . . . He had a very decent heart/ but he had nothing of the joys/ that good men have in bed./ For when my lord went to bed/ he turned his behind to me. /And so he slept the whole night through." Now that she was rich, though, she wanted to remain independent and live for pleasure. Gauthier's appeal to husbands in the final strophe to treat their defenseless wives with care "for she is beneath and you are on top" reads like an ironic commentary on the story he has just told.[35]

It is not particularly difficult to imagine why this uncontrollable "dark side" of women should have been explored particularly in stories about widows. Widows represented a constant challenge to the existing assignment of gender roles. At least in conceptual terms, the scope of wives and young girls was restricted by their husbands and fathers. Widows, by contrast, as Gauthier's tale shows, were considered free, dependent only on public opinion. Aspects of widowhood such as lone women's potentially precarious economic situation were dealt with in other stereotypes (for example, the stock pairing of "widows and orphans"). When it came to gender images, however, the alternatives for widows were extremely circumscribed and restricted to "free" versus "subject to control."

When Boccaccio writes in the *Decameron* of a good, chaste widow, he is precisely removing the element of freedom and subjecting the widow to male control: She lives in a house with her brothers and "desired to do nothing without her brothers' knowledge." But Boccaccio wants this

---

fust pasmee. / Et sil a sa robe levee / . . . Ensi la dame se conforte, / Qui or demenoit si grant dol."

34 Gauthier Le Leu, "La veuve," in Anatole de Montaiglon and Gaston Raynaud, eds., *Receuil général des fabliaux des XIIIe et XIVe siècles* (Paris, 1877), 2:200: "Dont commence li runemens, / Li conseil et li parlemens / Des parentes et des cousines, / Et des vechiens et des voisines; / Si li dient: . . . / Remarier? Male aventure! . . . / L'autres dist: Ma belle done, / Vos reprendereis un preudome / Ki ne sera faus ne lechieres"; 201: "Mais la dame est en autre point . . . / Ki desire à mangier char crue"; 202: "Ensi toute nuit estudie / Car ilh n'est ki li contredie."

35 Ibid., 205: "Il me faisoit mult de mes bons / Et de chaucher et de vestir; / . . . Il avoit mult le cuer honeste, / Mais ilh n'avoit point le delit / Ke li preudome ont en lor lit: / Car, cant mes sire astoit couchiés, / M'ert ses cus en mon sainch fichiés. / Là s'endormoit tote la nuit, / Si n'en avoi autre deduit; / Ce me devoit mult enuier"; on her wealth, 206: "Mais je sui riche femme à force"; on the final warning, 213: "Vos, ki les femmes despitiés, / Por Deu vos pri et por pitié, / Sovengne vos à icele hore / K'ele est desours et vos desore."

good widow to pretend to be bad, with "badness," in turn, being defined in terms of her freedom: "I have no husband to whom I must account for my nights," she says, feigning interest in an evil suitor before proceeding to feed a second stereotype with her request "that no one may ever hear of it."[36]

It is typical that secrecy – the undiscovered – plays a particular role in the stories. Neighbors exercise only incomplete control over the widowed woman, so that the fantasies apparently concentrated on her clandestine and undiscovered nights. In another story in the *Decameron*, a beautiful widow was actually expecting the margrave, who wanted to share a meal, a bath, and then "spend the night with her" – "secretly." The fact that the secret lover is hindered at the last minute by professional duties is no tragedy. A recently robbed merchant happens by and enjoys the night in his stead – just this once, of course, "so that no one might notice anything."[37]

Such tales transmit an image of the widow that – if we are to believe the scholarship in economic and social history – was actually (and throughout the Middle Ages) not far from the truth: Widows appeared in economic life, in the legal system, and in public more generally as persons who acted in their own right, often carrying on their husband's work.[38] They thus represented the greatest imaginable challenge to a society whose fabric was largely defined by relations among men. This, too, helps us to understand the story of the faithless widow.

ASSAULT ON THE GENDER ORDER

No one, in turn, better personified this assault by widows on the male sex than the "faithless widow" in the most widely disseminated and strictly christianized version, the Latin version "H." Between the theft of the hanged man's corpse and the hanging of the dead husband, the author has added a macabre sequence in which gender differences are expressly addressed as principles of social order. Scarcely has the widow suggested that her husband be placed on the gallows instead of the stolen thief, and the corpse been pulled from the grave, when the sentry speaks the leitmotif of the third scene: "Oh my lady, I am sorely afraid." The reason for his fear is the corpse's complete set of teeth, for the thief had been missing two. The sentry is reluctant to remove the teeth, but the widow has no

---

36 Boccaccio, *Decameron*, 8, 4, ed. Vittore Branca, 6th ed. (Milan, 1996), 657–62.
37 *Decameron* 2, 2, ibid., 96–103.
38 See, e.g., the contributions by Judith Bennett (village), Barbara Hanawalt (town), Harry Miskimin (court), and Cheryl Tallan (Jewish widows) in Louise Mirrer, ed., *Upon My Husband's Death*.

such qualms and knocks them out. The scene is repeated with a head wound, and then the game of fear and courage is pushed even further. The widow says, "Now be brave and string him up." The sentry replies, "I am still afraid." This time the reason is that the thief had been castrated. This final intensification of the mutilation is introduced by an explicit formulation of role expectations: "Never have I seen such a cowardly man. Still, it is a good thing that you should be saved. Quick, cut his testicles off and hang him up." Once again the soldier shies away from the deed and the episode culminates in the castration of the dead and much-lamented husband by his own widow.[39]

This role-playing allows us to see how the problem area of relations between the living and the dead is connected with that of the gender order. Just as in the first two scenes, so likewise in the last, the question of the rights of the dead takes center stage but this time with the roles reversed. The sentry, in the second scene the spokesman for life, now champions the rights of the dead man. The widow, who in the first part had placed her entire existence in the service of the dead, now represents the privileges of the living with the ultimate dramatic consistency: The dead man is treated as an object to be used in the service of the living. Here, as in the *Decameron* and many other tales about widows, we find a conceptualization of the surviving wife who returns to life after her husband's death as a menacing, castrating woman without a place in the gender order. The *relicta* who returns to the world of the living is a danger to all: to the dead, to the extent that remarriage is tantamount to execution; and to the living, to the extent that as a widow she confounds the orderly relations between the sexes and that as an experienced woman in a position to make comparisons, she threatens the masculinity of her next husband.

CONCLUSION: A HISTORICALLY SPECIFIC READING

Is, then, the story of the "faithless widow" a transcultural tale of the eternal feminine? This does not seem very plausible. What characterizes the medieval versions of the "faithless widow" is their transposition of the sexual profile well known from the version of Petronius onto a specifically occidental and Christian conflict surrounding the remembrance of

---

39 *Geschichte der sieben weisen Meister,* Version H, ed. Buchner, 67–8: "O domina, multum timeo. Latro, qui erat captus, duos dentes in superiori parte amisit' . . . At illa: 'Et ego pro amore tuo faciam' [etc] ait: 'Iam audacter eum in patibulo suspende!' . . . At illa: 'Tam timidum hominem nunquam vidi; tamen bonum est te esse securum. Succide testiculos eius cito, ut suspendatur.' . . . et sic salvatus est miles."

the dead and remarriage. The Christian interpretation of the surviving wife as a trustee of *memoria* was bound to change this "perhaps . . . most popular of all stories."[40] What in antiquity was an amusing story about the nature of woman, with few consequences for the construction of society, became in the Middle Ages a motif that touched a nerve within society's self-conception. Thus it was only logical for the particularly powerful narrative traditions to supplement the old motif with the widow's punishment. In the most severe case, the Latin version "H" of the *Seven Sages*, she is decapitated.[41] Apparently no author could imagine any other solution to the conflict of "the living versus the dead" and "remarriage versus remembrance" than an all-too-familiar attribution of guilt. The tale was an example to all "that no good comes of women's doings."[42]

It may be mere coincidence, but it is in any case quite fitting that the first treatment of the motif that does not attribute the dilemma to female nature was penned by a woman, Marie de France. In her version, the widow says, "The dead must deliver the living, of whom one expects aid." And then the author herself concludes, "And so we can see what trust the dead may place in the living. So false and deceitful is the world."[43] Marie's evaluation concentrated on the obvious site of the central tension, the conflict between the living and the dead. But in a world in which the dead possessed substantial rights and a woman who survived her husband could find a positive destiny only in the concept of the "widow" and only in the service of the dead, Marie's version remained a lone voice among depictions of the "faithless widow."

It is apparent, and scarcely surprising, that by the fifteenth century the story's popularity had already passed its zenith. As long as dead husbands had a claim on the services of their surviving widows and as long as the church remained the dominant producer of social concepts, this story expressed a fundamental conflict. Once the Reformers had dismissed this conflict lay people were only too happy to follow suit. In the sixteenth century, at least in Protestant regions, the dead were well and truly dead.[44]

---

40 Huber, *Das Motiv der "Witwe von Ephesus."*

41 *Sieben weise Meister*, Version "H," ed. Thiele, 68: "Gladium extraxit et uno ictu caput eius amputavit."

42 See note 32 to this chapter.

43 Marie de France, *De vidua*, ed. Warnke, 87: "La prude femme respundit: . . . 'Delivrer deit hum par le mort le vif dunt l'em atent cunfort.' Par iceste signefiance poum entendre quel creance deivent aveir li mort es vis. Tant est li munz fals e jolis."

44 Cf. Craig Koslofsky, *The Reformation of the Dead: Death and Ritual in Early Modern Germany, 1450–1700* (Basingstoke, U.K., 1999), chap. 2; and Craig Koslofsky, "Die Trennung der Lebenden von den Toten: Friedhofverlegungen und die Reformation in Leipzig, 1536," in Oexle, ed., *Memoria als Kultur*, 335–85.

In Catholic areas they may have maintained their rights for a while longer. Here, too, the career of the "faithless widow" ended at that moment when a diversity of discourses inherited the ecclesiastical power of definition. In the absence of the defining authority of the church, the correctness of the assertion that "an upright churl is better than a dead emperor," as La Fontaine put it, became all too apparent. Under the circumstances, the surviving wife, as an enigma evoking both the "turtledove" and the beauty, no longer was of interest.

In the Middle Ages, however, this enigma expressed the central and omnipresent challenge to the culture of *memoria*. As scholarship on *memoria* in recent decades has shown, notions of the presence of the dead among the living undoubtedly structured a good portion of thought and conduct in the Middle Ages. A number of institutions – widowhood, monastic communities, confraternities, and so forth – undoubtedly allowed the dead this presence among the living. But the self-evident practice of remarriage was not simply a game played on a different board. It was the constant reminder of a countermodel, a challenge to official social definitions and as such a continual topic of discussion – in one of the most widely disseminated stories of the Middle Ages.

11

Artistic and Literary Representations of Family Consciousness

JOHN B. FREED

Karl Schmid deepened our understanding of the German nobility's changing self-consciousness between the tenth and thirteenth centuries, most brilliantly, perhaps, in his article on the Welfs' rewriting of their dynastic history. Although critics have challenged and modified many of Schmid's specific points, it is clear that there was a change in family structure from amorphous sips composed of individuals who could claim kinship, whether agnatic or cognatic, with a powerful magnate to patrilineal dynasties that were often identified with the fortified center of the lineage's lordship, such as the Habsburgs.[1] This transformation was both a cause and a consequence of the process of territorialization and occurred, as the work of Georges Duby has made clear, at the expense of daughters and younger sons.[2]

In this chapter I look at three highly problematic and disparate artistic and literary texts that can be read as reflecting the tensions caused for

I wish to thank the Bayerisches Hauptstaatsarchiv in Munich for permission to reproduce the portrait of Count Sigiboto and the Landesdenkmalamt für Südtirol in Bolzano (Bozen) for permission to reproduce the Rodenegg frescoes. The photographs of the latter were made by Hubert Walder. I wish to thank my colleague, Professor Lawrence D. Walker, and the participants of the Heidelberg Conference for their helpful suggestions and criticisms.

1 Many of Karl Schmid's key articles can be found in his collected articles: *Gebetsgedenken und adliges Selbstverständnis im Mittelalter: Ausgewählte Beiträge: Festgabe zu seinem sechzigstem Geburtstag* (Sigmaringen, 1983). His piece on the Welfs, "Welfisches Selbstverständnis," was republished in that collection. For a discussion of Schmid's work, see John B. Freed, "Reflections on the Medieval German Nobility," *American Historical Review* 91 (1986): 560–6. See also Schmid's posthumous *Geblüt, Herrschaft, Geschlechterbewusstsein: Grundfragen zum Verständnis des Adels im Mittelalter*, edited and with an introduction to Schmid's work and its scholarly reception by Dieter Mertens and Thomas Zotz, Vorträge und Forschungen 44 (Sigmaringen, 1998).

2 See in particular Georges Duby's articles "Lineage, Nobility and Knighthood: The Mâconnais in the Twelfth Century – A Revision" and "Youth in Aristocratic Society: Northwestern France in the Twelfth Century," *The Chivalrous Society*, trans. Cynthia Postan (Berkeley, Calif., 1977), 59–80, 112–22. The best synthesis in English about the formation of the high-medieval German principalities is Benjamin Arnold, *Princes and Territories in Medieval Germany* (Cambridge, 1991).

and within noble or formerly noble families by the strengthening of princely authority. Each work was a response to a painful and troublesome past and an attempt to shape the lineage's future destiny. What the three pieces have in common is that each was produced by a man and/or woman who was or who perceived himself or herself as a loser or potential victim in the formation of the territorial principality. I focus primarily on the family portrait in the *Codex Falkensteinensis* that was drawn at the behest of Count Sigiboto IV of Falkenstein and that has aroused surprisingly little scholarly interest. I compare the portrait with two works that have inspired far more attention and that I have discussed in greater detail elsewhere: the Rodenegg frescoes, the oldest known Romanesque paintings with a secular theme, which were commissioned, I believe, by the noblewoman Mathilda of Hohenburg, the wife of Arnold III of Rodank, a ministerial of the bishop of Brixen; and the *Frauendienst* (Ladies' Service), the oldest European vernacular autobiography, composed by the Styrian ministerial, Ulrich of Liechtenstein.[3] The unique character of these three sources makes them inherently difficult to interpret, but I believe that these texts become more comprehensible by situating them in their familial context and that such contextualization in turn illuminates their creators' understanding of their own and their lineage's societal position.

Before leaving in 1166 on Frederick Barbarossa's ill-fated fourth Italian campaign, Count Sigiboto IV of Falkenstein commissioned a unique historical source, the *Codex Falkensteinensis*, the oldest extant family archive. Among its treasures are the only *Traditionsbuch* (collection of conveyances) and the oldest *Urbar* (manorial register) from a secular German lordship; two key texts about the *Hantgemal*, the Falkensteins' *predium libertatis* or earnest of free status (nos. 3, 131); Sigiboto's notorious so-called murder letter (no. 183); and a family portrait.[4] Max Kemmerich in his *Die frühmittelalterliche Portraitmalerei in Deutschland* (Early Medieval Portraiture in

3 Nicolò Rasmo, *Pitture murali in Alto Adige* (Bolzano, 1973), 9; and Timothy McFarland, "Ulrich von Liechtenstein and the Autobiographical Narrative Form," in Peter F. Ganz and Werner Schröder, eds. *Probleme mittelhochdeutscher Erzählformen: Marburger Colloquium, 1969* (Berlin, 1972), 195. I discuss the Rodenegg frescoes and the *Frauendienst* in John B. Freed, *Noble Bondsmen: Ministerial Marriages in the Archdiocese of Salzburg, 1100–1343* (Ithaca, N.Y., 1995), 218–66.

4 The most recent edition of the codex is Elisabeth Noichl, ed., *Codex Falkensteinensis: Die Rechtsaufzeichnungen der Grafen von Falkenstein*, Quellen und Erörterungen zur bayerischen Geschichte, n.s. 29 (Munich, 1978) (hereafter *CF*). The numbers in parentheses in the text refer to the entries in the Noichl edition. On the Falkensteins, see John B. Freed, *The Counts of Falkenstein: Noble Self-Consciousness in Twelfth-Century Germany*, Transactions of the American Philosophical Society, vol. 74/6 (Philadelphia, 1984). On the murder letter, see Patrick Geary and John B. Freed, "Literacy and Violence in Twelfth-Century Bavaria: The 'Murder Letter' of Count Sigiboto IV," *Viator: Medieval and Renaissance Studies* 25 (1994): 115–29.

Figure 11.1 Count Sigiboto IV of Falkenstein, Hildegard of Mödling, and Their Sons. Courtesy of the Bavarian State Archives, Munich. Reproduced by permission.

Germany) called this miniature "the first family portrait of which I know."[5] The portrait, which measures 12.3 by 16.2 centimeters, appears at the top of what was the first page of the manuscript when it was originally bound (see Figure 11.1). It shows Sigiboto, who is identified as "Lord Count Sigiboto" (Dominus Siboto comes), seated on a benchlike structure against a backdrop of stars with his wife Hildegard of Mödling and their two half-grown sons, Kuno and Sigiboto V. They hold across their laps a banner with Sigiboto's parting words: "Dic valeas patri, bene fili, dicite matri. Qui legis hec care, nostri petimus memorare. Hoc quidem cuncti, mage tu, carissime fili." Elisabeth Noichl, the most recent editor of the text, translated this difficult passage as: "Sag Lebewohl dem Vater, und Ihr, Söhne, befleissigt Euch einer ehrerbietigen Sprache gegenüber der Mutter. Lieber, der Du dies liest, gedenke, bitte, unser. Das mögen zwar alle (tun), in erster Linie aber Du, liebster Sohn." An idiomatic English translation is: "Sons, bid your father farewell and speak respect-

5 Cited by Noichl, *CF*, 30★.

fully to your mother. Dear one who reads this, we beseech you, remember us. All may do this, but especially you, dearest son."[6]

This portrait appears, at least at first glance, to be a visual representation of the patrilineal lineage that by the twelfth century had allegedly replaced the bilateral kinship groupings among the northern European nobility of the earlier Middle Ages. At the heart of this new family structure was a single dominant couple who, if we are to believe Sigiboto's words, were bound to each other and to their children by strong ties of affection but who, we know, actually favored their eldest son at the expense of his sisters and younger brothers.[7] Indeed, it is noteworthy that Sigiboto and/or the artist chose not to include the count's daughters in the portrait or in the genealogy that Sigiboto himself inserted into the codex after his return from Italy (no. 181). He later directed his sons to provide one of their sisters with a suitable dowry if he died before she married (no. 142) and required his son-in-law to designate his entire estate as the widow's dower of Sigiboto's daughter (no. 143). But the count also commanded that his daughters were to possess no share of the Austrian lands he had purchased from his niece (no. 171). At no time did Sigiboto deem it necessary to record the names of any of his daughters in the codex.

Understanding the portrait requires placing the miniature in its proper place within the manuscript. Beneath the portrait is the notice in which Sigiboto appointed his father-in-law, Kuno III of Mödling, as his sons' guardian were he to die on the expedition (no. 1). Before the codex was rebound in the sixteenth century, the facing page and its back (now f. 7-7′) contained the list of the count's fiefs (no. 2). After this came the first entry about the Falkensteins' *Hantgemal* (no. 3) (the second entry, no. 131, was added after the count's return) and on the reverse side of this page (now f. 2) was the notice about the endowment of Sigiboto's three Bavarian castles: Neuburg, Falkenstein, and Hartmannsberg (no. 4). The *Urbar* and *Traditionsbuch* followed. In other words, if a reader had opened the codex to the first page in 1166, he would have seen on the left side

---

6 Noichl, *CF*, 29★–33★. The portrait appears on f. 1′. The front side of this page (f. 1) was originally empty. Today it includes a number of entries and a title that was added by a thirteenth-century hand (37★). Noichl translated the inscription with the assistance of an expert in medieval Latin.

7 See David Herlihy, "The Making of the Medieval Family: Symmetry, Structure, and Sentiment," *Journal of Family History* 8 (1983): 116–30, and David Herlihy, *Medieval Households* (Cambridge, Mass., 1983), 112–30, saw the expression of sentiment within the family as a late-medieval phenomenon, a response to the breakdown in society caused by such events as the Black Death. Sigiboto's parting words suggest that the expression of such feelings may have existed earlier.

the portrait and Kuno of Mödling's appointment as guardian and on the right side the start of the list of the properties with which Sigiboto had been enfeoffed. Turning the page, the reader would have learned about the *Hantgemal* and then, turning the page once more, about the chapels' endowment. The initial manuscript, nearly half of the present codex, was the work of a single scribe (Noichl's F1), a canon of the Augustinian house of Herrenchiemsee who drafted the notices about Kuno's appointment and the *Hantgemal*, the list of fiefs, and the entire *Urbar*. He also copied the older conveyances into the codex and drew the miniatures but probably not the family portrait.[8]

The portrait and its inscription must be interpreted as part of this complex of materials. Two things, one temporal, the other eternal, weighed on Sigiboto's mind in the summer of 1166. The first was the fate of his young sons and his lands should he die on the expedition. For their protection, he appointed their maternal grandfather as their guardian, but whether Sigiboto realized that Kuno would be preoccupied with his own lordship or whether he did not fully trust a rival lord, the count circumscribed his father-in-law's authority. Five of Sigiboto's ministerials (*proprios viros*), one of whom, Otto of Hernstein, also was his first cousin, were to swear to Kuno in the presence of Sigiboto's other men that they would not permit their young lords to grant any fiefs from their revenues until they reached their majority. The count's other men were required to give their consent and aid the five ministerials in discharging their duties (no. 1).

As we have seen, the scribe listed the count's fiefs opposite the portrait. (It is the second-oldest extant German *Lehensverzeichnis*; the oldest is Werner of Bolanden's.) He had been enfeoffed by three dukes, two count-palatines, two margraves, seven counts, an archbishop, four bishops, and an abbot.[9] But Sigiboto's real concern was his Austrian domains, outside Vienna, which would have been difficult to manage under the best of circumstances either from his own Upper Bavarian castles or from Kuno's Mödling on the Inn in Upper Bavaria. The count admonished his ministerials, friends, and kinsmen (*proprios et amicos cognatosque* – as the case of Otto of Hernstein shows, it was possible for a man to fall into more than one category) to spare no amount of wealth and effort to secure for his sons four fiefs in particular. At stake were more than 400 hides situated near Tulln and St. Pölten in Lower Austria, which Sigiboto

---

8 Noichl, *CF*, 24*–26*, 32*, 36*–38*, 48*, 70*–71*.
9 Noichl, *CF*, 70*.

held from the bishop of Passau; another 400 hides, most of which were in Austria, held from the sons of the late Count Gebhard of Burghausen, who had died in 1163; nearly 400 hides with which Count Gebhard III of Sulzbach had enfeoffed him; and 100 hides that Otto VI of Wittelsbach, the count-palatine of Bavaria, had granted him. Sigiboto feared that the ministerials of Duke Heinrich Jasomirgott of Austria would be enfeoffed with these lands during his sons' minority and that the fiefs would be permanently lost. (The legal basis for such an action was, according to the entry itself, a feudal right known as *aneuel* that gave the lord use of a fief during the vassal's minority.)[10] Sigiboto was so worried about the possible loss of these four fiefs that after listing all his other holdings he once again warned, urged, and asked all his vassals (fideles suos) to give the highest priority to obtaining these fiefs for his sons (no. 2). The count's admonition reveals how a determined prince such as Heinrich Jasomirgott could use his ministerials as proxies to acquire the lands of weaker lords and how the Babenbergs consolidated their authority.

Sigiboto, however, had even greater reason to be concerned about his Austrian holdings and the future of his lineage. His paternal grandfather, Herrand I of Falkenstein, had built the eponymous castle of Hernstein (*Herrantestaine*) southwest of Vienna, on five royal hides that Emperor Henry II had given to Tegernsee in 1020. Herrand's father, Patto of Dilching, the advocate of the abbey in 1020, had presumably usurped this gift. The Falkensteins' title to Hernstein thus could be challenged at any time. In 1204 Duke Leopold VI confirmed the emperor's grant, although

---

10 The *Anfall* (in modern German *künftige Anfälle* are inheritances in reversion) was a problematic issue in the twelfth century, in part, seemingly, because there was some confusion about what the *Anfall* was. The issue was of concern to the Styrian ministerials in the *Georgenberger Handfeste* (the Georgenberg Compact), the privilege that Duke Otakar of Styria granted to his men in 1186 in anticipation of the Babenbergs' acquistion of the duchy. According to article 10 of the Compact, the Styrian ministerials were not to bear in the case of fiefs the imposition that was called in the vernacular *aneuelh* (the only German word in the Compact), but rather that those who had daughters would not be forbidden to bequeath their fief to their daughters. (In beneficiis nullam molestiam, que vulgo aneuelh vocatur, sustinere cogantur, sed etiam qui filios non habuerint, filiabus beneficium dimittere non prohibeantur.) Heinrich Fichtenau and Erich Zöllner, eds., *Urkundenbuch zur Geschichte der Babenberger in Österreich*, vol. 1: *Die Siegelurkunden der Babenberger bis 1215*, Publikationen des Instituts für Österreichische Geschichtsforschung, 3rd series (Vienna, 1950), 85–90, no. 65. Thus, the Compact would suggest that in Styria *Anfall* referred to the custom that the fief of a man who died without male issue escheated to the lord. This was obviously not true in Sigiboto's case. However, because Emperor Frederick II separated the clause about the *Anfall* from the right of daughters to inherit their fathers' fiefs when he confirmed the Compact in 1237, Karl Spreitzhofer (*Georgenberger Handfeste: Entstehung und Folgen der ersten Verfassungsurkunde der Steiermark*, Steiermärkisches Landesarchiv, n.s. 3 [Graz, 1986], 65), believes that the primary meaning of *Anfall* in the Compact was guardianship of a minor, i.e., Duke Otakar was protecting his ministerials from the abuse of the lord's right of guardianship, the issue that concerned Sigiboto as well.

there is no evidence that the hides had ever been in the monks' possession.[11] Still, the ducal confirmation indicates that Tegernsee had not forgotten its rights and raised the possibility that the Babenbergs, or more precisely the Kuenringer, the ducal ministerials who were the hereditary advocates for most of Tegernsee's possessions in Austria, could lay claim to Hernstein.[12] Let me stress, however, that there is no evidence that this was an issue in 1166.

Patto of Dilching, the advocate of Tegernsee, not only was the grandfather of Sigiboto's father; he also was the great-grandfather of Sigiboto's mother, the heiress Gertrude of Weyarn. Sigiboto's parents thus were first cousins once removed and had presumably contracted this flagrantly consanguineous union to reunite their Upper Bavarian and Austrian lordships.[13] The count was so embarrassed by his parents' marriage that he deliberately falsified his genealogy in the codex to conceal the truth (no. 181).[14]

Moreover, Sigiboto was not the sole owner of Hernstein or even the Upper Bavarian lands. Both his paternal uncle Wolfker and the count's younger brother, Herrand II, had inherited portions of the lineage's patrimony. After Herrand II's death around 1155, Sigiboto laid claim to some of his brother's men and properties. Wolfker and the count's friends and retainers had persuaded Sigiboto to drop his suit against Herrand's sons, and in return Wolfker, who was dead by 1158, had bequeathed his share of Hernstein to Sigiboto and his sons (nos. 114, 115). Shortly before his departure to Italy, Sigiboto and the older of his nephews, Sigiboto of Antwort (near the castle of Hartmannsberg in Upper Bavaria), had formally divided their alods, fiefs, and men and renounced all further claims to each other's share of the lineage's patrimony (no. 118). Perhaps significantly, this agreement was not included in the original collection prepared in 1166 because, as Noichl thinks, it brought Sigiboto no new acquisitions, or possibly, as I would suggest, because the count was not really ready to drop all his claims.[15] After his return from Italy, Sigiboto spent a quarter of a century systematically acquiring, piece by piece, all the possessions that had passed to his brother's widow, her second

---

11 Freed, *Counts of Falkenstein*, 22–8. The imperial charter is in Harry Bresslau, ed., *Die Urkunden Heinrichs II. und Arduins*, Monumenta Germaniae Historica, Diplomatum regum et imperatorum Germaniae 3 (Berlin, 1957), 431, no. 552. The ducal charter is in the *Urkundenbuch zur Geschichte der Babenberger*, 1:188–9, no. 145.

12 Folker Reichert, *Landesherrschaft, Adel und Vogtei: Zur Vorgeschichte des spätmittelalterlichen Ständestaates im Herzogtum Österreich*, Beihefte zum Archiv für Kulturgeschichte 23 (Cologne, 1985), 200–2.

13 Freed, *Counts of Falkenstein*, 22–30.   14 Ibid., 33–5.

15 Noichl, *CF*, 84, headnote to no. 118.

husband, his two nephews, their sister, and her children (nos. 135, 136, 148–52, 157–60, 171, 172).[16] Sigiboto's infamous so-called murder letter to Ortwin of Merkenstein, who may have been his kinsman, to get rid of or at least blind Rudolf of Piesting (no. 183) may have been written in conjunction with this family feud (both men lived in the vicinity of Hernstein).[17]

The legacy of Sigiboto's uncle Wolfker potentially may have been even more troublesome. Wolfker was the father of at least two sons: Otto of Hernstein, a Falkenstein retainer whom Sigiboto designated as one of Kuno of Mödling's five advisers (no. 1), and Lazarus of Falkenstein-Wolfratshausen (no. 115), a ministerial of the counts of Andechs-Wolfratshausen.[18] Both Franz Tyroller and Noichl identified Otto and Lazarus as the sons of a mésalliance but ventured no guess about their legitimacy or whether they had a common mother.[19] Both of Wolfker's sons held property that belonged to the Falkenstein patrimony. Otto sold to Sigiboto the property along the Panzenbach in Lower Austria (no. 125) that figured in the murder letter (no. 183), and Otto's toponym suggests that he may have been the burgrave of Hernstein. Sigiboto sub-enfeoffed Lazarus with an income of two pounds that he held from Count Berthold III of Andechs (no. 2); and at Wolfker's request the count had given a certain Hartlieb of Truchtlaching (in Upper Bavaria) to Lazarus (no. 115). These are the tidbits that a father might have conferred on a bastard, but it also may have been Falkenstein family policy, perhaps invoked for the first time in the case of Wolfker's marriage or marriages, to require a family member who married a ministerial to renounce his or her inheritance. At least we know that Sigiboto's granddaughter Adelaide did so later when she married the powerful Austrian ministerial, Henry of Kuenring.[20] Thus, it is possible that Otto of Hernstein and/or Lazarus

---

16 Freed, *Counts of Falkenstein,* 46–9.

17 Geary and Freed, "Literacy and Violence," 120–1.

18 For additional references to Lazarus, see Freed, *Counts of Falkenstein,* 30n63.

19 Noichl, *CF,* 3, headnote to no. 1; 5, headnote to no. 2; and Franz Tyroller, *Genealogie des altbayerischen Adels im Hochmittelalter,* Genealogische Tafeln zur mitteleuropäischen Geschichte 4 (Göttingen, 1962), 218, no. 11.

20 Josef von Zahn, *Geschichte von Hernstein in Nieder-Österreich und den damit vereinigten Gütern Starhemberg und Emmerberg,* in Moritz Alois Becker, ed., *Hernstein in Nieder-Österreich: Sein Gutsgebiet und das Land im weiteren Umkreise* 2/2 (Vienna, 1889), 441–3, no. 6: "that Lady Adelaide, sister of Lord Conrad, count of Neuburg, mother of Lady Euphemia of Pottendorf, renounced all the inheritance, which she would have obtained from her father's or mother's properties when she married an inferior, namely, a ministerial" (quod domina Alhedis soror domini C. comitis de Newenburch, mater domine O. de Potendorf, renunciauit omni hereditati, quam adeptura fuisset de bonis paternis siue maternis cum nupserit inferiori, videlicet ministeriali). Benjamin Arnold, *German Knighthood, 1050–1300* (Oxford, 1985), 171, discusses this case.

of Wolfratshausen were legitimate but were the offspring of a morganatic marriage or marriages. It is worth noting that I have never encountered any other man in twelfth-century Bavaria or Austria who was named Lazarus. He may have been given this unusual name to show that he was not a member of the lineage. It should be stressed that marriages between less powerful noblemen and ministerial women (*Dienstweiber*) were becoming increasingly common in the twelfth century and may have been deliberately encouraged by the princes to bring such men and their lordships under their control.[21]

If Sigiboto's cousins were legitimate, he may have feared that the Falkensteins' enemies might at some later date call into question his own and his sons' free status. The revelation of the servile origin of the Erembald clan that had led in 1127 to the murder of Count Charles the Good of Flanders offers an inkling about what may have been at stake. Sigiboto's response to this potential threat may have been the inclusion of the famous passage about the Falkensteins' *Hantgemal*, the token of their free birth, in a prominent place in the codex. He revealed to his descendants that they and his nephews, the sons of his brother – his ministerial cousins, it should be noted, were not included – shared with two other noble houses, the Haunsbergs, who lived north of Salzburg, and the Bruckbergs, whose castle was situated southwest of Landshut, a noble hide located in Geislbach, about fifty kilometers north of Falkenstein, as their common *Hantgemal* (no. 3). On August 4, 1168, after Sigiboto had returned, he procured a ruling from the count-palatine of Bavaria, Otto V of Wittelsbach, that this alod of freedom, the *predium libertatis*, belonged by perpetual right to him because Sigiboto appeared to be the senior member of his *generatio*, which can mean, of course, both generation and lineage (no. 131). This entry was recorded in the codex below the first one. Sigiboto's interest in his *Hantgemal* was not merely antiquarian; he was taking no chances that anyone could challenge the Falkensteins' status as free nobles. In short, Sigiboto did everything in his power to secure his sons' inheritance.

Like most medieval people facing death, Sigiboto also was concerned about his eternal well-being, as the inscription on the portrait shows. There is no evidence that he made extensive donations before his departure to any monasteries, not even to the Augustinian canons of Herrenchiemsee and Weyarn, where he was the advocate. But the *Traditionsbuch* of Herrenchiemsee is poorly edited, and Weyarn's own records

21 Freed, *Noble Bondsmen*, 44, 122n92, 184–94.

only start in the fourteenth century because the church and house burned down in 1236 and again in 1350.[22] Thus, we cannot exclude the possibility that Sigiboto made suitable arrangements in these two houses, in particular at Weyarn, which had been founded by his maternal grandfather in 1133, an event the then seven-year-old Sigiboto had witnessed.[23]

As far as we can now tell, the count focused his attention instead on the endowment of the chapels of his three Bavarian castles, where church services were to be conducted in perpetuity (no. 4). These arrangements were, it will be recalled, the fourth item in the original manuscript. The endowment of the lower altar in the chapel of Neuburg, which had been dedicated, according to another entry (no. 180), to the Virgin by the bishop of Freising on September 8, 1164, consisted of property in the village of Seeham. One of Sigiboto's own servile knights had challenged Weyarn's right to this property, and Sigiboto had settled this dispute and given the land to the canons, to whom he had committed the celebration of the divine office in the chapel. He had endowed the upper altar of Saint John the Baptist and Saint James in the same chapel with some property and serfs in Steingau. He had placed the monks of the Benedictine abbey of St. Peter am Madron, whose advocacy he had obtained in 1163, in charge of the chapel of Saint Leonard and Saint Giles in Falkenstein, to which he had given property in Durrhausen.[24] Finally, he had endowed the chapel of Saint James and Saint John the Evangelist in the castle of Hartmannsberg with property in Sonnering; the archbishop of Salzburg had consecrated this chapel in 1160 (no. 179). It should be noted that all these arrangements had occurred within a period of approximately six years preceding the commissioning of the codex and that Sigiboto made no comparable provisions for the disputed castle of Hernstein. He was chiefly concerned, it would appear, with his own and his immediate family's daily spiritual care at the seats of his lordship.

Let us turn our attention back to the inscription on the portrait. He asked whoever read the book to remember him. Whom did Sigiboto have in mind? Presumably, first of all, the canons of Herrenchiemsee who maintained the codex. This was, after all, their reciprocal obligation for his advocatorial protection. But if we define reading, as some charters did, as whoever seeing or *hearing* "read" the instrument, then Sigiboto may have had a larger circle in mind. It encompassed his father-in-law and the

---

22 Noichl, *CF*, 39*.
23 Willibald Hauthaler and Franz Martin, eds., *Salzburger Urkundenbuch*, 4 vols. (Salzburg, 1910–33), 2:234–6, no. 158. Sigiboto indicated he was seven when an eclipse of the sun occurred on August 2, 1133 (no. 181b).
24 Noichl, *CF*, 5, headnote to no. 2.

five retainers whom he had selected as Kuno's advisers and more broadly the "fideles suos" and the "proprios et amicos cognatosque" whom the count addressed below the miniature and on the page facing it. They were the ones meant to use the codex if he did not return.

But what special role did Sigiboto assign his son or sons in his remembrance? The inscription itself consists of two parts: The first, nearly indecipherable half, which Hildegard holds (*Dic valeas patri, bene fili, dicite matri* – "Sons, bid your father farewell and speak respectfully to your mother"), is written in majuscule; the second, Sigiboto's portion (*Qui legis hec care, nostri petimus memorare. Hoc quidem cuncti, mage tu, carissime fili* – "Dear one who reads this, we beseech you, remember us. All may do this, but especially you, dearest son"), is in minuscule.[25] Moreover, the portrait itself is bipolar: A vertical row of stars separates the couple; a cross, in line with the stars, divides the inscription; and the left side of the portrait is predominantly brown, whereas the right is mainly violet.[26] Above all, the parents are turned away from each other and, with fingers uplifted in gestures of instruction, seem to address different boys. Thus, Hildegard appears to be admonishing one son to say farewell to his father and to be nice to her, whereas Sigiboto commands the other boy to remember him.

Such an interpretation is not, however, without its problems. Although it makes perfect sense for a mother on the eve of her husband's departure on a dangerous undertaking to advise her son to bid goodbye to his father, the admonition to treat the mother with proper respect is more appropriate for the father. Moreover, there is the shift from the singular imperative (*Dic*) to the plural (*dicite*), which suggests that the first part of the inscription or at the very least the entreaty to be nice to the mother may have been addressed to both sons. In other words, the artist and/or scribe may have combined, somewhat clumsily, in the first half of the inscription the final words of instruction of both parents, that is, the shift from the singular to the plural imperative may have been an awkward device to indicate that both parents were speaking; or, alternatively, the whole first half of the inscription may have been Sigiboto's symbolic last words for both his sons. In the latter case, the tortured Latinity of the inscription, like that of the infamous murder letter, may have been quite literally Sigiboto's own words, the crude working Latin of a lay magnate.[27]

---

25 Noichl, *CF*, 29*n2.   26 Noichl, *CF*, 30*.

27 The text of the letter reads: "S(iboto) comes de Hademarperch O(rtwino) dilecto homini suo de Merchenstain salutem et omne bonum et quicquid amico. Mandatum istud, quod demandamus in secreto, si persolvitis in fide, omnia, quecumque cara sunt vobis, faciam vobis. Inimicum meum Rodolfum de Piesnich, qui multum infestavit me, si deponitis eum, ne fiat vobis et ei in

Whoever spoke the first words, the second half of the inscription, written in the singular, is clearly supposed to be Sigiboto's parting words to the son whom he faces, "tu carissime fili," and whom he singles out to remember him. The importance Sigiboto attached to this obligation may be reflected in the prominent place of the word *memorare* in the inscription. Although the boy on the right appears to be somewhat smaller than his brother (a realistic element in the portrait?), he was presumably Sigiboto's older son Kuno.[28] As Sigiboto's primary heir, Kuno was destined to obtain the greater part of the Falkensteins' lordships and would consequently have been in a better position financially than his younger brother to arrange for the proper commemoration of Sigiboto in the lineage's dynastic monasteries and other houses. The count's words assigning to Kuno a special memorial responsibility thus may have been Kuno's designation as Sigiboto's principal heir and, simultaneously, an admonition that the Falkenstein patrimony not be divided.

Conversely, Hildegard may have been bestowing to her younger son Sigiboto V her residual rights to Mödling. Interestingly enough, Sigiboto IV did lay an unsuccessful claim to Mödling in 1182–1183 after his father-in-law's death, even though Hildegard still had two living brothers (no. 163).[29] The placement of the portrait above Kuno of Mödling's appointment as the boys' guardian thus may also have been intended as a reminder to Kuno of his grandsons' potential rights to his domains.

What does this interpretation of the portrait tell us about Sigiboto's situation in 1166? He presented himself as the head of a patrilineal

---

carrinam, quecumque vultis, faciam vobis. Concedo vobis itaque bonum da der Panzinpach also er oueralbe in den Piesnic uellet unde dase da springet. Verbum istud et mandatum, ut fiat ante festum sancti Michaelis, videlicet ut privetur oculis, ne vos vel ipsum videat, ista omnia certa erunt vobis. Si autem ista non fiant nec possint fieri, rogo tamen, ut sint quasi in corde sculpta" (Noichl, *CF*, 163–4, no. 183). Given the Latin, the translation is problematic: S(iboto), count of Hartmannsberg, to O(rtwin) of Merkenstein, his cherished vassal, greetings and all that is good and proper for a friend. This mandate, which we ask you in secret, if you fulfill it faithfully, I will do all things that are dear to you. If you will get rid of my enemy Rudolf of Piesting, who has greatly troubled me, so that you do not incur a penance on his account I will do for you whatever you wish. I grant you the property along the Panzenbach from its source to where it flows into the Piesting. This order and mandate, which should be executed before the feast of St. Michael, that is, that he might be deprived of his eyes so that he cannot see you or himself, all of these things will undoubtedly be yours. If, however, these things are not and cannot be done, I ask you, nevertheless, that they remain as though engraved on your heart. See Geary and Freed, "Literacy and Violence," 115–9.

28 Kuno was never explicitly identified as the older brother, but several pieces of evidence indicate that he was. See Freed, *Counts of Falkenstein*, 31.

29 Sigiboto V was unable to acquire Mödling after the deaths of his two childless maternal uncles in the first decade of the thirteenth century. See Günther Flohrschütz, "Die Vögte von Mödling und ihr Gefolge," *Zeitschrift für bayerische Landesgeschichte* 38 (1975): 138–42.

lineage, but this was more a program for the future than a present reality. The breakup of the bilateral kindreds had occurred so recently in Bavaria that the Falkensteins still shared a common *Hantgemal* with the Haunsbergs and Bruckbergs. The inheritance of Patto of Dilching, the advocate of Tegernsee at the beginning of the eleventh century, had been divided among his Weyarn and Falkenstein descendants and reunited only by the embarrassing consanguineous marriage of Sigiboto's own parents. The count's father and paternal uncle Wolfker had shared their Austrian lordship, and Sigiboto and his younger brother Herrand II had done the same. In 1166 Hernstein was split between the count and his two nephews and niece, and was threatened by the rapacious ministerials of the duke of Austria. Wolfker's marriage or marriages, if they were such rather than extramarital unions, had called into doubt the Falkensteins' free status; and if Otto of Hernstein and Lazarus of Wolfrathausen had not been disinherited, one branch of the Falkensteins might have become like so many formerly free Austrian and Styrian nobles, Babenberg ministerials. Sigiboto had cause enough to be alarmed.

Sigiboto's response to this looming dynastic crisis was to commission the codex, a clerical tool usually wielded by those for whom the pen was mightier than the sword, in which he recorded his and his heirs' rights. In addition, he imposed a ruthless patrilineal strategy on his lineage. From Sigiboto's perspective his nameless daughters were a liability – unlike his niece Judith, they obtained no known share of the Falkenstein patrimony – and even Hildegard was an outsider, although he hoped to obtain Mödling through her. After his fortunate return from Italy, he spent a quarter of a century acquiring the lands that had passed to his brother's descendants, and the murder letter may tell us something about the tactics he employed. To prevent another ruinous fragmentation of the lineage's holdings, Sigiboto may have discouraged or even forbidden his sons to marry in his lifetime, a policy that may have been anticipated in the words, "tu, carissime fili," designating Kuno as his principal heir. As far as we know, the thirty-fiveish Kuno was a bachelor when he left on the Third Crusade, from which he never returned; and the count's surviving son Sigiboto V was approximately forty when he finally married in 1196 (no. 175). Ironically, this risky family strategy of limiting the number of sons who married, enunciated in the portrait, was a major cause in the lineage's extinction a generation later and the devolution of its patrimony to the Wittelsbachs and Habsburgs.[30]

30 Freed, *Counts of Falkenstein*, 58–67.

If Sigiboto felt endangered by the growing power of the dukes of Bavaria and Austria, then the Rodenegg frescoes and Ulrich of Liecht-enstein's *Frauendienst* can be interpreted as expressing the anxiety that noble or formerly noble families felt about territorialization and their mediatization by their former peers. The frescoes were painted around 1220 in the castle of Rodenegg (today Rodengo, Italy), outside of Brixen in South Tyrol, in a room approximately 7 meters long, 4.3 meters wide, and 3 meters high that has been identified as the lord's study or drink-ing chamber. The paintings show eleven scenes from Iwein's first cycle of adventures. These are: Iwein and the lord of the castle of Breziljan; Iwein's meeting with the wild man of the forest; Iwein pouring water at the fountain; Iwein and Askalon fighting with lances and swords; Iwein's final fatal blow as the portcullis falls at the gate of Askalon's castle; Askalon's death in the lap of his wife Laudine; Lunete, Laudine's maid, giving Iwein the magic ring that makes him invisible; Iwein watching the burial and mourning for Askalon; the fruitless search for Iwein; and Lunete presenting Iwein to the grieving Laudine. It is not known whether the artist worked directly from Hartmann von Aue's *Iwein*, which is cus-tomarily dated between 1199 and 1205, or relied on some oral version of the tale.[31]

The fascinating aspect of the frescoes, besides their early date and the insights that they may provide on how a lay audience understood the problematic story of a widow who married her husband's killer, is that the artist shifted the focus from the ostensible hero Iwein to Laudine. The central scene (Scene Seven), both in its placement in the room (it is the central scene on the wall opposite the door) and in the narra-tion of the story, shows Askalon's death in Laudine's lap (see Figure 11.2). This depiction of Laudine as the *Mater Dolorosa* separates Iwein's triumph over Askalon from his subsequent submission to Laudine. The cycle closes with Lunete presenting a kneeling Iwein to a grieving Laudine, who wears a crown (Scene Eleven; see Figure 11.3). There is no hint of the happy ending of the first part of the romance, Iwein's marriage to Laudine. In short, there is a distinctly feminine perspective to this narration of the Iwein tale: the sorrow caused by a knight's search for adventure.

---

31 James A. Rushing Jr., *Images of Adventure: Yvain in the Visual Arts* (Philadelphia, 1995), 30–90, argues, as he did in his Princeton dissertation, for an oral transmission of the story; but, as I pointed out in *Noble Bondsmen*, 225–6, the Rodanks were also in a geographical location and social position that would have enabled them to procure a copy of Hartmann's text at an early date.

Figure 11.2 Askalon's Death in Laudine's Lap. Courtesy of the Provincial Historical Monuments Office for South Tyrol, Bolzano. Reproduced by permission.

Figure 11.3   Lunete Presents Iwein to Laudine. Courtesy of the Provincial Historical Monuments Office for South Tyrol, Bolzano. Reproduced by permission.

Why may such a rendition of the romance have appealed to the lord and lady of Rodenegg in the first quarter of the thirteenth century, Arnold III of Rodank (1155/65–1221) and Mathilda of Hohenburg (d. ca. 1218–1224)? The Rodanks, who were first mentioned about 1090 and who may originally have been free episcopal vassals, were ministerials of the bishops of Brixen. Arnold's father had built Rodenegg in the 1140s and divided his lands with his younger brother, Arnold I, who had founded a cadet branch of the family at Schöneck, approximately eighteen kilometers from Rodenegg. Because both of Arnold I's sons died without an heir (one never returned from the Third Crusade), Arnold III, like Count Sigiboto, had by the 1190s reunited the entire Rodank patrimony. In the early 1190s Arnold married Mathilda, the daughter of the Bavarian nobleman Richer V of Hohenburg and Countess Mathilda of Peilstein and the widow of the Tyrolese nobleman Hugo III of Taufers, who had probably died on Barbarossa's crusade. Arnold's marriage to the granddaughter of a count was indicative of his status in society. The Rodanks reached the height of their power in 1200, when his first cousin Conrad of Rodank (as bishop 1200–1216) became the first ministerial to serve as prince-bishop of Brixen. It was upwardly mobile ministerial lineages such as the Rodanks, whose lifestyle and wealth were increasingly indistinguishable from that of free noble dynasties like the Falkensteins, whom Sigiboto feared.

It is hard to imagine that Arnold would have decorated his castle with this particular story if he had perceived Iwein as a murderer who had obtained his lordship through a criminal act. Rather, Iwein was an exemplary knight, the son of a king, who was presumably in some way a role model for Arnold or the guests whom he may have received in the room with the frescoes. Beyond that, viewers who were already familiar with some version of the Iwein story could easily have supplied the missing happy ending: Iwein's marriage to Laudine. Thus, the room with its emphasis on Laudine, who wears a crown, would have been a reminder of Arnold's own marriage to a noblewoman.

However, what if Mathilda as the mistress of the castle commissioned the frescoes, say, during one of Arnold's absences? The story of a defenseless widow who had married her husband's killer may have resonated with a noblewoman who had contracted a questionable second marriage to a ministerial, no matter how powerful. After all, Mathilda's position in the early 1190s after the death of her husband Hugo III of Taufers was a precarious one. She was the last Hohenburg and her son Hugo IV was a child. It is noteworthy that neither of Mathilda's husbands, unlike Sigiboto who named his older son Kuno after his father-in-law, gave one of their sons the distinctive *Leitname* or leading name of the Hohenburgs, Richer. Such a name was in itself often a claim to the mother's inheritance.[32] It is as if neither Hugo nor Arnold thought they had much hope of acquiring, let alone retaining, a lordship on the other side of the Alps, probably an accurate assessment of their position. In fact, we learn about Mathilda's family of origin from a 1214 document in which she and the children of her two marriages sold to Tegernsee for 100 marks their rights to the possessions that pertained to Hohenburg.[33] Moreover, Mathilda's noble son Hugo IV of Taufers, with his ministerial half-brothers, was a man teetering on the edge between noble and ministerial status. In 1225 Hugo surrendered his castles to the bishop of Brixen and received them back in fief. In return the bishop promised to defend and protect Hugo as if he were an episcopal ministerial. (*Plane nos fide data promisimus quod sepedictum Hvg[onem] in ivre suo tamquam ministerialem nostrum contra quemlibet defensabimus et*

---

32 Freed, *Noble Bondsmen*, 107–11.
33 Tyroller, *Genealogie des altbayerischen Adels*, 392, no. 24.

manutenebimus.)[34] Thus, the frescoes may have been Mathilda's explanation why she, like Laudine, had made such a socially dubious choice of a second husband and also may have been a reminder to Arnold of the deference he owed his noble-born wife.

The problem with such an interpretation of the frescoes is why Arnold III would have tolerated such a cycle in his castle. The answer may be a gendered one: Each spouse read the story differently. For Arnold the frescoes showed the story of an exemplary knight who married a queen; for Mathilda the cycle depicted the limited choices of a defenseless widow. Beyond that, Arnold, like Iwein, may toward the end of his life have been in a penitent mood. As the most powerful ministerial in the diocese, Arnold may have utilized the ministerials' electoral rights to secure his cousin's election after the previous bishop was elected archbishop of Salzburg (Eberhard II, 1200–1246) in defiance of the pope. Conrad of Rodank's election may have been even more scandalous because, as the son of Arnold's paternal uncle Reginbert, the provost of the cathedral chapter of Brixen, Conrad was in accordance with canon law illegitimate and ineligible to hold a high church office. Like Iwein, Arnold may have been pondering in old age the consequences of his actions. Thus, the Rodenegg frescoes may express the tensions that existed in a marriage between a noblewoman, the last representative of her lineage, and a ministerial, even one such as Arnold, whose family may have been of free ancestry and whose cousin was a bishop.[35]

If the portrait was commissioned by a man who feared for the future of his dynasty and the frescoes by a woman who was the last scion of her noble house, then Ulrich of Liechtenstein's *Frauendienst*, probably written in 1255, expresses the regrets and dreams of an influential ministerial whose family was of noble ancestry.[36] Ulrich's alleged autobiography has been extensively studied since the nineteenth century

---

34 Leo Santifaller and Heinrich Appelt, eds., *Die Urkunden der Brixner Hochstifts-Archive, 845–1295,* 2 vols. (Innsbruck, 1929–43), 2, pt. 1:661–63, no. 598. Hugo and his sons continued to be designated as nobles after 1225. See Freed, *Noble Bondsmen,* 43–4n63.

35 For further information on the frescoes, see Freed, *Noble Bondsmen,* 224–49.

36 The *Frauendienst* is still available for scholarly purposes only in a nineteenth-century edition: Reinhold Bechstein, ed., *Ulrich's von Liechtenstein Frauendienst,* 2 vols., Deutsche Dichtungen des Mittelalters 6, 7 (Leipzig, 1888). Franz Viktor Spechtler has published a new edition, *Ulrich von Liechtenstein Frauendienst,* Göppinger Arbeiten zur Germanistik 485 (Göppingen, 1987); but it is not, as he conceded in the preface, an annotated critical edition. J. W. Thomas published an English translation, *Ulrich von Liechtenstein's "Service of Ladies,"* University of North Carolina Studies in the Germanic Languages and Literatures, no. 63 (Chapel Hill, N.C., 1969), but it is so abridged as to be nearly useless.

because of its unprecedented mixture of lyric and narrative elements and supposed account of courtly life. Three incidents in particular have aroused the interest of historians: the Friesach tournament of 1224, an assembly of the princes of southeastern Germany, where Ulrich became the center of attention; the *Venusfahrt* (Venus tour) of 1227, when Ulrich dressed as Queen Venus jousted with hundreds of men on an adventure that took him from Mestre, near Venice, to the outskirts of Vienna; and the *Artusfahrt* (Arthur tour) of 1240, when, traveling through the Babenberg lands as King Arthur, Ulrich invited all who broke three spears with him to join his round table. These events were long treated by scholars as historical facts because of Ulrich's references to hundreds of specific places and men who can be independently identified. In reality, the *Frauendienst* is a carefully contrived piece of literature that deals with imaginary events. For example, there is no independent evidence that the princes of southeastern Germany, including the patriarch of Aquileia, the archbishop of Salzburg, and the dukes of Austria and Carinthia, assembled in Friesach for ten days in 1224. Most of the incidents in the "autobiography" are modeled after scenes that occur in earlier romances or are familiar motifs and themes in lyric poems. The obvious question is why Ulrich, the seneschal, marshal, and chief justiciar of the duchy of Styria who played a prominent role in Styrian politics for nearly half a century, chose to present himself as a madcap knight.

If nothing else, Ulrich demonstrated his knowledge of a great repertory of literary works, a hallmark of good breeding, that he either cited directly or alluded to. Such familiarity with the latest literary and cultural fashions was an assertion of Ulrich's claim to noble status. Beyond that, Heinz Dopsch argued that Ulrich knew that the Liechtensteins, who had entered the Styrian ministerialage in the mid-twelfth century, were the descendants of a great noble clan, the Traisen-Feistritz, whom the Otakare, the margraves of Styria, had eliminated when consolidating their power. In other words, Ulrich's ancestors had not escaped the fate that Sigiboto feared in 1166 might await his sons. The "autobiography" was a plea to remove the barriers that separated the great ministerial lineages, many of whom, such as the Liechtensteins, were of noble ancestry, from the few surviving families of comital and free noble status in the duchy. Ulrich's vision foreshadowed the Styrian *Herrenstand* or Estate of Lords, which formed a few decades later and which consisted of the few surviving noble dynasties and the most powerful ministerial families, such as the

Liechtensteins.[37] In Ulrich's imaginary world Duke Frederick II, the highest regional representative of the feudal order, could ask to serve Ulrich disguised as King Arthur. Unlike the Falkensteins, the Liechtensteins survived and prospered in the service of the Otakare and later the Babenbergs and Habsburgs, but at the cost of their status as free men.[38]

In conclusion, Sigiboto's family portrait, like the Rodenegg frescoes and the *Frauendienst*, is the product of a noble family that lost out in the process of the formation of the high-medieval German principality. The difference is that whereas Sigiboto feared for his sons' future, Mathilda of Hohenburg and Ulrich of Liechtenstein regretted a lost past.

---

37 Heinz Dopsch, "Der Dichter Ulrich von Liechtenstein und die Herkunft seiner Familie," in Herwig Ebner, ed., *Festschrift Friedrich Hausmann* (Graz, 1977), 93–118.
38 Freed, *Noble Bondsmen*, 249–65.

12

The Strange Pilgrimage of Odo of Deuil

BEATE SCHUSTER

Although Odo of Deuil's *De profectione Ludovici VII in Orientem*[1] constitutes the only detailed report of the Second Crusade that we possess, no comprehensive analysis of the text itself exists.[2] A consideration of the text's organizational structure has seemed unnecessary because the eyewitness perspective in which the events are presented attested to their authenticity.[3] Because Odo himself declares that he intends merely to inform his abbot, Suger, about the events, leaving to the abbot the task of writing a life of Louis VII,[4] it seemed possible to accept the events he presented as facts. Moreover, this monk of Saint Denis[5] and pupil of Suger seemed to fit easily into a historiographical tradition that has been characterized as Capetian propaganda.[6] Odo's biases therefore appeared easy to interpret. Consequently, the *De profectione* was classified as a second-rate student's work that reproduces a simplified version of Suger's concept of kingship.[7] In the context of this classification only Odo's nationalism was considered original.[8] It has been explained as a result of the crusade, where intercultural conflicts favored the development of a national

---

1 Unless otherwise specified, I quote from the American edition: Odo of Deuil, *De profectione Ludovici in Orientem: The Journey of Louis to the East*, ed. and trans. Victoria Gingerick Berry (New York, 1948). Because I do not think that Odo of Deuil was its author, I refer to the text as *De profectione*, abbreviated as *DP*.

2 Cf. Giles Constable, "The Second Crusade as Seen by Contemporaries," *Traditio* 9 (1953): 217–18.

3 Pascale Bourgain, "Odo von Deuil," in *Lexikon des Mittelalters*, 6 vols. (Zurich, 1980–93), 6:1359, Gilette Tyl-Labory, "Eudes de Deuil," in Geneviève Hasenohr and Michel Zink, eds., *Dictionnaire des Lettres Françaises: Le Moyen Age*, 2d ed. (Paris, 1992), 427.

4 *DP*, 2–3.

5 *DP*, xviff.; Eudes de Deuil, *La croisade de Louis VII, roi de France*, ed. Henri Waquet (Paris, 1949), 11.

6 Cf. Gabrielle Spiegel, "The Cult of Saint-Denis and Capetian Kingship," *Journal of Medieval History* 1 (1975): 43–69.

7 *DP*, xxix. Eudes de Deuil, *Croisade*, 11.

8 Tyl-Labory, "Eudes de Deuil," 427; Gabrielle Spiegel, *The Chronicle Tradition of Saint-Denis* (Brookline, Mass., 1978), 55.

consciousness.[9] Following this argument, we are confronted with a medieval text that illustrates how national identity came into being on crusade.

The hypothesis that the *De profectione* provides us with both a direct access to the events and with a crusader's reaction to them is seductive. However, if we compare the events included in the text to other historical writings on the Second Crusade, doubts arise. Although we would expect a crusader to respect his own version of personal experiences, the events Odo reports resemble in significant detail other, later historical accounts. The story about the pretender to the Hungarian throne can be retraced to a passage in Otto of Freising's *Gesta Frederici*, which precedes the account about the inundation of Chörobacchi, an event also covered by Odo. Like the *De profectione*, Otto reports that Lotharingians and Italians joined the French army and mentions the same names as those cited in the *De profectione*.[10] The description of the crossing of Greece corresponds to John Kinnamos' account,[11] whereas the circumstances of Conrad's defeat coincide closely with Geroh of Reichersberg's narrative in the *De Investigatione Antichristi*. This text also reports, as does the *De profectione*, that the pilgrims had to eat and to sell the flesh of their horses; that they protected themselves with the corpses of defeated crusaders; and that Bernard of Carinthie died at the spot where the French were defeated.[12] As for Bernard of Plötzkau, the Annals of Pöhlde portray him as a friend of the poor, as does the *De profectione*,[13] and the Annals of Magdeburg report his death during the retreat of the German army.[14] The disunity of the crusaders described in the *De profectione* seems to be inspired by John of Salisbury's *Historia Pontificalis*. Both texts name the bishop of Langres as the leader of the party that appealed to Frankish heroism; both relate that Conrad did not answer the message from Louis; and both mention Geoffrey of Rançon as leader of the vanguard on the

---

9 Veronika Epp, "*Importabiles Alemanni . . . omnia perturbant*: The Empire and the Germans as Reflected in Twelfth-Century Latin Crusaders' Reports," *Storia della Storiagraphia* 23 (1993): 22–3; cf. Ludwig Schmugge, "Über 'nationale' Vorurteile im Mittelalter," *Deutsches Archiv* 38 (1982): 439–59.

10 Otto of Freising und Rahewin, *Gesta Frederici seu rectius Cronica*, ed. Franz-Josef Schmale (Darmstadt, 1965), 191, 218–19; cf. *DP*, 34, 48, 50, 78.

11 *Ioannis Cinnami epitome rerum ab Ioanne et Alexio Comnenis gestarum*, ed. August Meinecke, in *Receuil des Historiens de la Croisade: Corpus scriptorum historiae Byzantinae*, 50 vols. (Bonn, 1828–97), 8:67–88; cf. *DP*, 42ff.

12 *Gerohi Reichersbergensis Libelli selecti de Investigatione Antichristi*, ed. Ernst Sackur, in *Libelli de lite imperatorum et pontificum saec. XI et XII conscripti*, 3 vols. (Hannover, 1891–97), 3:304–95, 376, 381; cf. *DP*, 112, 128, 134.

13 *Annales Palidenses auctore Theodoro monacho*, in *MGSS* 16:48–98, 83; cf. *DP*, 92.

14 *Annales Magdeburgenses*, in *MGSS* 16, 105–96, esp. 188; cf. *DP*, 92.

day of the defeat.[15] Finally, the close conformity between the description of the French defeat in the *De profectione* and William of Tyre's narrative already led the American editor to propose that they derived from a common source.[16]

How can we explain the fact that Odo considered the same events and details worthy of mention as did historiographers who wrote up to thirty years later in completely different surroundings? To appeal to the argument that these authors merely presented the "facts" as did the nineteenth-century historians no longer convinces, given modern insights into how individual perspectives and memories rework and distort reality. Furthermore, the fragmentary information that the annals and chronicles offer on the Second Crusade and the limited manuscript tradition of the *De profectione* renders the explanation unlikely that a wide diffusion of Odo's or another eyewitness's report led to this conformity.[17] If we were dealing with a modern text, we would conclude that the *De profectione* consisted of a sequentially arranged collage of events extracted from different sources about the Second Crusade, framed by the chronology and geography supplied by Louis VII's and Conrad's letters.[18] Is it possible to maintain such an assumption for the twelfth century?

Treating the *De profectione* as we might a modern text resolves the apparent discordancy between what has been considered a diary of a medieval "war correspondent" and what we know about the rhetoric, function, and intention of medieval historiography.[19] As Ann Caron Cioffi has shown, the fact that Odo's report is included in a letter resolves this apparent contradiction. The eyewitness narrative can be traced back to the epistolary style, and Odo's renouncing of literary ambitions corresponds perfectly with the topos of modesty that is common to historiographers.[20] Even the supposed proof of Odo's limited knowledge, the sentence "The flowers of France withered before they could bear fruit in Damas,"[21] can

---

15 *Ioannis Sarisberensis Historia pontificalis: John of Salisbury's Memoirs of a Papal Court*, ed. and trans. Marjorie Chibnall (London, 1956), 12, 54–5; cf. *DP*, 68, 78, 114.

16 *DP*, 92n. 17 *DP*, xxxii.

18 *Wibaldi epistolae*, in Philipp Jaffé, ed., *Bibliotheca rerum Germanicorum*, 6 vols. (Berlin, 1864–73), 1:126, 152–3; *Epistolae Sugerii abbatis S. Dionysii*, in Martin Bouquet, ed., *Recueil des Historiens des Gaules et de la France*, 24 vols. (Paris, 1738–1904; reprint, 1967–8), 15:487, 495–6. This collection is principally based on two medieval collections of Suger's letters.

19 As representative examples, see Franz-Josef Schmale, *Funktion und Formen mittelalterlicher Geschichtsschreibung: Eine Einführung* (Darmstadt, 1985); John O. Ward, "Some Principles of Rhetorical Historiography in the Twelfth Century," in Ernst Breisach, ed., *Classical Rhetoric and Medieval Historiography* (Kalamazoo, Mich., 1985): 103–66.

20 Caron Ann Cioffi, "The Epistolary Style of Odo of Deuil in his *De profectione Ludovici in Orientem*," *Mittellateinisches Jahrbuch* 23 (1988): 76–81, esp. 78.

21 "Marescunt flores Franciae antequam fructum faciant in Damasco" (*DP*, 118; cf. *DP*, xxii).

be understood as an a posteriori justification for why the defeat had been inevitable.[22]

Although this epistolary interpretation of the use of the eyewitness perspective in the *De profectione* is convincing, its rarity in the twelfth century[23] and the fact that it is an exception within the historiography of Saint Denis demands an explanation.[24] Why was the eyewitness perspective chosen for Odo's report, what did it transmit better than an authorial perspective, and what meanings did it convey to the reader? Moreover, a closer examination of the text suggests how Odo's naïveté in regard to the events undermines the credibility of the eyewitness perspective. As the following analysis shows, the eyewitness's simple interpretations contrast blatantly with the facts he reports. The moral framework he openly defends is contradicted by his own judgments, and even the biblical quotations he includes can be understood as critical comments on Odo's actions and point of view. This fundamental ambiguity in the text requires going beyond the epistolary assessment of the *De profectione*. Odo no longer can be regarded as the author of the account but as a narrator (a character based on a historical individual, that is, a creation of an unknown author). This literary use of a narrator was, according to Roger Dragonetti, quite common in twelfth-century literature and would have been familiar to medieval readers.[25]

Understanding Odo as a fictional narrator rather than as a historical author transforms our understanding of the text. The supposed direct access to the events and their perception by a crusader is necessarily mediated by the literary shaping of the unknown author. The nationalism apparent in the *De profectione* can be traced back to a medieval author who wanted to show with the help of this example that the crusades fostered nationalism. Finally, Odo's naïveté, which confirmed the prejudices of nineteenth- and twentieth-century readers toward medieval authors, can be considered as part of a literary strategy that permits an attentive and critical reader to distance him- or herself from a morally dubious narrator.

---

22 Cioffi, "Epistolary Style," 78; similarly: Hubert Glaser, "Wilhelm von Saint-Denis: ein Humanist aus der Umgebung des Abtes Suger und die Krise seiner Abtei 1151–1153," *Historisches Jahrbuch* 85 (1965): 312.

23 As far as I know, a consistent eyewitness perspective in the twelfth century appears only in crusade chronicles. The eyewitness reports of the First Crusade were thought to be authentic for a long time, but doubts of their authenticity have recently been expressed. See Jean Flori, *Pierre l'Ermite et la première croisade* (Paris, 1999), 33ff.

24 Spiegel, *Chronicle Tradition*, 54–5.

25 Roger Dragonetti, *Le mirage des sources: l'art du faux dans le roman médiéval* (Paris, 1987), 22–5, 39–44. I thank Amy G. Remensnyder for bringing this book to my attention.

In taking the person and perspective of Odo as the departure, as the literary construction and the medieval title *Epistola Odonis* suggest,[26] it is my intention to develop a new comprehension of the *De profectione*. Because the traditional approach, which treats historiography as a partial report of the facts, appears insufficient for a text such as the *De profectione*, my study is based on Karl Morrison's aesthetic understanding of twelfth-century historiography. With regard to the pictorial arts, he has theorized that the historiography of the twelfth century was less interested in facts than in converting the reader by appealing to his emotions.[27] This interaction between text and reader constitutes – according to Karl Morrison – a hermeneutic play.[28] Morrison's approach makes it possible to understand the eyewitness perspective as an offer to identify with the figure of the narrator, whereas the implicit contention of this perspective signals the reader to distance himself from this same figure. As I show in the first part of my article, the growing nationalism of the narrator functions within this interaction as a symptom of Odo's moral decline and is therefore meant to keep the reader at a distance. In the second part I suggest that this development of a nationalist outlook is part of a story of Odo's moral evolution that spans the time before, during, and after the crusade and that the reader must reconstruct. Finally, I argue that the *De profectione* implicitly critiques intellectual positions that were associated with Saint Denis.

THE SERPENT AND THE JUGGLER: THE TEMPTATION OF NATIONALISM

The way Odo designates Louis's, Conrad's, and Manuel's subjects reveals his project of exalting his group at the cost of others. Whereas he denies to the *Alemanni* and *Greci* their universal tradition by opposing them to the Romans and by restricting their origin to a part of their empire,[29] he lays an exclusive claim on the Carolingian heritage and on the crusade tradition by calling the French "Franks" and portraying them as the

---

26 *DP*, 2.
27 Karl Morrison, *History as Visual Art in the Twelfth-Century Renaissance* (Princeton, N.J., 1990), 37–8.
28 Ibid., 7.
29 The proverb "I fear the Greek even when they bear gifts" opposes the Greeks to Rome (*DP*, 26), as the praise of the German valor that had frightened Rome separates the German from Roman tradition (*DP*, 98). The term *rex Alemannus* restricts Conrad's realm to his possessions (Epp, "*Importabiles Alemanni*," 3); Odo also cuts off the Greeks from the territory on the other side of the Bosporus by creating the impression that the land is oppressed by Greek and Turkish invaders (*DP*, 86–88, 108).

"chosen people."[30] By reducing the two empires to the size of kingdoms Odo ascribes to their inhabitants a national character morally inferior to that of the French. He prides himself that he does not belong to the brutal, stupid, and impetuous German drunkards (*DP*, 42–8),[31] and that he does not resemble the effeminate and timid Greek lazybones who excel in cupidity and treachery.[32]

Odo uses national stereotypes even in situations where they contrast with appearances. For instance, he reports that the king suffered from Greek ruses after the crossing of the Bosporus, but he has to admit that the actions appeared to be inspired by vengeance. He solves this opposition by posing as a philosopher: "The man who knows a case partially makes a partial judgment, but the man who does not know the entire case cannot make a just judgment. Actually the Greeks could be injured and not appeased."[33] Because Odo illustrates by his use of the term "appeased" that his opponents were right, this sophism is hardly convincing. Such absurd interpretations would make the attentive reader laugh. The text thereby forces him to distance himself from a nationalistic interpretation of the events. Tropologically, such rhetorical slips illustrate that nationalists do not refrain from distorting the facts.

Such oppositions between the events and Odo's interpretation of them invite the reader to reflect on the reasons for and functions of national prejudices. These reasons become evident if he or she considers the context of the narrator's point of view. Odo's statement at the first encounter with the German army, "The Germans were unbearable even to us,"[34] and the fact that he blames them for the difficulties that the French experienced along the way to Constantinople (*DP*, 42–8) suggest an unconditional rejection of this group. After the German defeat, however, the narrator suddenly pities the fortune of his fellow crusaders, justifying their faults. Apart from some caustic remarks, he now praises their heroism (*DP*, 90ff.). How can this change be explained? Because Odo has just reported that

---

30 On several occasions, Odo affirms that the Franks followed the steps of the first crusaders (*DP*, 58, 130–1). He often refers to God's help or to his expectation of it (*DP*, 45, 108, 110–11, 112, 116). The allusion to Israel is evident when Odo insists on the facility with which the Franks ford rivers (*DP*, 30, 106). For the French ideology of the "chosen people," see Bernd Schneidmüller, "Frankenreich – Westfrankenreich – Frankreich: Konstanz und Wandel in der mittelalterlichen Nationenbildung," *Geschichte in Wissenschaft und Unterricht* 44 (1993): 760.

31 For the medieval prejudice of German impetuosity, see Ernst Dümmler, "Über den Furor Teutonicus," *Sitzungsberichte der preussischen Akademie der Wissenschaften, phil.-hist. Klasse* (Berlin, 1897), 112–26.

32 *DP*, 26, 42, 54–5, 60, 66–7, 82, 86–7, 90, 96–7, 104ff., 112–13.

33 "Ex parte iudicat qui rem novit ex parte, sed non potest facere rectum iudicium, qui causa ex integro non cognoscit. Illi enim offendi poterant non placari" (*DP*, 72).

34 *Nostri etiam importabiles erant Alemanni* (*DP*, 42).

the French were jealous of the German successes (*DP*, 72), the text suggests that the narrator himself must have been jealous.[35] This assumption seems confirmed because Odo stops denigrating the Germans as soon as he no longer fears their precedence. The ancient feeling of inferiority remains perceptible, however, in the malicious joy he takes in describing the misfortunes of the ancient rivals (*DP*, 98).[36]

Odo's rejection of the Greeks is more complex because it is grounded in a cultural conflict. The first confrontation with Byzantine courtesy intrigues the narrator. Pondering the differences, he remembers Virgil's "I fear the Greeks, even when they bear gifts" (*DP*, 24–5). Confusing antique rhetoric with proverbial truth, Odo from this point forward interprets Greek friendliness as treachery, and when the first conflicts arise he proudly claims to have foreseen and to have experienced it (*DP*, 56, 66–7, 71). The text challenges this certainty, which is based on a reception of a Roman tradition, by introducing events that are identical except for their biased interpretation. Although he refers to German barbarism as "pillage" and "plunder," Odo describes similar actions as "conquering the necessary," as "providing," and as "replenishing" when they are committed by his compatriots (*DP*, 40, 44, 78).[37] Passing quickly over French discord and desertion (*DP*, 24, 106), Odo revels in describing the Germans' scandalous disunity (*DP*, 50, 96). Stressing German aggressiveness, he always pretends that the French merely defended themselves (*DP*, 44, 52). Every tiny French advantage proves to be an indication of divine help (*DP*, 24, 106, 110–11), whereas he dismisses German successes as false rumors (*DP*, 50, 72, 90, 96).

The most significant example of the denigration of the Germans occurs in the account of an incident in Philippopolis:

Outside the walls of Philippopolis was located a fine settlement of Latins who sold a great many supplies to travelers. When the Germans had got settled in the tavern, by ill chance a juggler came in and, although ignorant of their language, nevertheless sat down, gave his money, and got a drink. After prolonged guzzling he took a snake, which he had charmed and kept in his inside pocket, and placed it in the top of a goblet that he had put on the floor, and thus, among people

35 Veronika Epp has recognized that rivalry plays an important role in Odo's portrayal of the Germans, but she misses the point in referring to noble aims and in supposing that Odo rediscovers with the German defeat his repressed feelings of solidarity (Epp, "*Importabiles Alemanni*," 4–5).

36 Odo always enjoyed pointing out the Germans' misfortunes (*DP*, 82–3, 90–6, 98–100).

37 The double meaning of the sentence, "Thus, by the same paths, but not with the same omens, we followed the Germans who had preceded us" (*Igitur eisdem vestigiis, sed non eisdem auspiciis, Alemannos subsequentur praecedentes*) (*DP*, 58) confirms that Odo interprets the same acts differently.

whose language and customs he did not know, he indulged in other juggler's pranks. As if they had seen an evil portent the Germans immediately rose up, seized the juggler, and tore him to bits; and they attributed the crime of one man to all, saying that the Greeks wished to poison them. The city was disturbed by the uproar in the outskirts, and with a group of men the governor came outside the city walls, unarmed but in haste, to calm the crowd. Agitated by wine and rage, however, the eyes of the Germans saw not the situation in regard to arms but the fact that to keep the peace people were rushing together from all sides. Angrily they rushed at those who were approaching, thinking that they came to wreak vengeance for the murder. In flight the Greeks now retreated to the city. Then, taking up their bows (for these are their weapons), they went forth again; they killed, wounded, and routed those whom they had fled, and only when all had been driven from the settlement did they stop. Many of the Germans were killed there, especially those who had taken refuge in inns and, in order to protect their money, in caves. When the survivors had recovered their spirits and taken up arms again, they rallied in order to avenge their own shame and the slaughter of their comrades, and they burned nearly everything outside the walls.[38]

In trying to prove German stupidity, Odo offers an analysis of the reasons for and dynamics of the conflicts between the crusaders and the resident population: Misunderstandings favored by the inability to communicate lead to suspicion and fear. Incomprehensible acts are then interpreted as proof of the group's animosity, and the situation will be misjudged as soon as one side feels menaced. When they resort to violence both parties are convinced that they must defend themselves, and the conflict finally degenerates into a murderous fight when revenge motivates their actions. Some profit from the situation by plundering, and innocent people are pillaged and killed.

The nationalistic bias of this interpretation is contradicted by another conflict between the crusaders and the resident population – this time

---

38 "Philippopolis extra muros nobilem burgum Latinorum habebat, qui supervenientibus necessaria abundanter pretio ministrabat. Ubi cum tabernis insedissent Alemanni malo auspicio adfuit ioculator qui, licet eorum linguam ignoraret, tamen sedit, symbolum dedit, bibit; et post longam ingurgationem serpentem quem praecantatum in sinu habebat extrahit et scypho terrae imposito superponit, et sic inter eos quorum mores et linguam nesciebat ceteris lusibus ioculatoriis sese frangit. Alemanni, quasi viso prodigio, ilico furore consurgunt, mimum rapiunt, et in frustra discerpunt; scelusque unius omnibus imputant, dicentes quod eos occidere Greci veneno volebant. Turbatur urbs tumultu suburbii, et dux cum turba suorum ut sedaret turbam foras inermis sed festinus egreditur. Turbatus autem a vino et furore, oculus Alemannorum non arma videt, sed cursum undique causa pacis. Accurrentibus occurrunt irati, putantes a se homicidii vindictam exigi. Illi autem fugientes in urbem recepti sunt. Tunc sumptis arcubus (haec enim sunt arma eorum), denuo exeunt; fugant quos fugerant, occidunt, vulnerant; expulsisque omnibus de suburbio cessant. Ibi multi Alemanni occisi sunt, et maxime in hospitiis et pro pecuniis suis in spelunci proiecti. Resumptis ergo animis et armis, ut vindicarent suam verecundiam et aliorum necem, redierunt et extra muros fere omnia combusserant" (*DP*, 42).

between the French and the population of Worms (*DP*, 22–3) – which resembles the conflict in Philippopolis so strongly that Odo's denigration of German impetuosity as well as his constant reproach of Greek treachery in French-Greek conflicts is refuted. The population in Worms reacts in the same way to the crusaders' violence as do the Greek citizens (*DP*, 22). They hesitate to provide the crusaders with essentials or may even deliberately provide them insufficiently in order to press them to continue on their way. As demand exceeds supply, prices skyrocket. The parallelism in the two episodes – which is reinforced by the similarity with another incident in Constantinople between the French army and the Greek population (*DP*, 67) – proves to the attentive reader that the violent acts of the crusaders constitute the core of all the problems along the way. The aggressions of the pilgrims provoke animosity and fear from which they themselves will suffer because they depend on supplies from the populace. When they try to take what they need by resorting to plundering (*DP*, 40, 96), they receive even less food (*DP*, 50, 72, 78), for the population begins to hide themselves and their goods (*DP*, 40, 114).

Because the Germans precede the French, Odo is right in considering that they suffered at the hands of the Germans (*DP*, 40, 44), but because the French commit the same acts of barbarism as the Germans, his accusation appears hypocritical (*DP*, 40, 46). In view of the crusaders' behavior, the Greeks' refusal to provide for them, as well as the Greeks' acts of revenge, appear comprehensible – a fact even Odo has to admit (*DP*, 54, 72). The experience with the Franks nevertheless cannot justify all the aggression, the plundering, and the killing of defenseless individuals or of smaller groups by the residents (*DP*, 46, 52–3, 74). Again, Odo is partially right, but he misses the point by insisting on Greek treachery, as if every abuse and violent act had been planned by the community. Odo resembles the Germans because he lets himself become blinded by his subjective impressions and attributes every misdeed to another national group.

For the reader familiar with the Old Testament, the crusaders' conduct finds another parallel: When they frighten the population, intimidate the kings, extort tributes along the way, pillage the countryside, kill innocents, and set the suburbs aflame, the pilgrims behave as Israel's heathen invaders did. Similarly, the Greek population reacts as the Hebrews did. Some of the cities try to appease the invaders with elaborate receptions with holy instruments; some citizens hide and are then killed; others defend themselves with bows and arrows, attacking the crusaders only when they are strategically vulnerable when outnumbered by the invaders.[39] These implicit references suggest that the text juxtaposes itself to Odo's nationalistic concept of the "chosen people." God seems always to be on the side of the oppressed, be they German, Greek, French, or heathen.

The text opposes Odo's emotional, nonrational nationalism with a more manipulative, premeditated form of nationalism, one that is attributed to a group associated with the bishop of Langres. They propose several times to attack the Greeks and attempt to convince the French nobles of such a plan by promising easy successes and by classifying the Greeks as heathen (*DP*, 68, 78). The nationalists do not prevail because a second group, "the wise," refute such arguments (*DP*, 70, 78–9). They insist on the Greeks' Christianity, remind the audience of the pope's command to fight against the heathens, and evoke the possible dangers of aggression. Both arguments are based more on convenience and pragmatism than on morality, and both groups try to convince by emotional appeals and by distorting the point of view of the opposition. The positions of the two groups, however, are tacitly grounded in a different concept of ethics that expresses itself in a different perception of reality. Whereas the aggressive party attributes a general value to their personal experience, "the wise" stress the limits of knowledge and demand that the audience consider the situation from the opposing point of view. Therefore, they are capable of questioning their own perspective out of respect for the other.

Odo sympathizes with the anti-Greek party (*DP*, 144). Each time they fail to convince the majority, he obstinately insists on the verisimilitude of their point of view, although he mitigates his anti-Greek statements in the wake of the disputes, as if the arguments of "the wise" had impressed him (*DP*, 72, 80). After the German defeat, however, the narrator definitively sides with the aggressive group. As if under the spell of a persecution complex, he from now on blames all obstacles on a Greek-Turkish conspiracy (*DP*, 116ff.). Finally, he even indulges in fantasies of murderous revenge (*DP*, 106, 112). At this point the character of the narrative begins to change: Now Odo clothes his ancient supposition of a Greek-Turkish arrangement in facts (*DP*, 110–11) and his resentment of the Greeks becomes open hatred. In Constantinople he had merely affirmed that the French considered killing a Greek a matter of no importance (*DP*, 56). Now he insinuates that defenseless inhabitants have been killed without trying to conceal the misdeed (*DP*, 114). As this example illustrates,

39 Cf. Idt, 1–7; I Mcc 1–3.

nationalism can justify murder. The implicit argument of the text resembles one of "the wise." Metaphorically speaking, the author points to the evil "fruits of nationalism" in order to denounce it.[40] According to the text, national stereotypes not only represent a danger for "scapegoats," they also blind the moral judgment of the nationalists and foster their moral vices. For in accusing others Odo overlooks his own faults, as if recognizing that the others have vices is proof of one's own virtue. Moreover, even his national self-critique illustrates his moral depravation because when he proudly invokes the French "stubborn arrogance," it merely serves to justify the repetition of one and the same fault (*DP*, 112).

The events prove that it is impossible to distinguish the three nations in regard to their morality. Wise and foolish men appear in all three camps (*DP*, 22, 44), and all three people represent more-or-less different aspects of a common heritage that Bernard of Clairvaux had attributed to the Romans.[41] The French, Greeks, and Germans taken together are arrogant, enjoy pomp, and have a natural tendency toward disorder and disunity. Pretending to obey, they prefer to dominate, and they insist on being consulted for every decision. They are impious, jealous of their neighbors, unpleasant to strangers, unthankful, and prone to flattery. In accusing the others all three are both right and wrong. Although if there is an element of truth in such reproaches, the global attribution of fault to another group is not only false but will also prevent an honest assessment of one's own faults.

The *De profectione* does not, however, deny the reality of "culture clash." The difficulty in understanding the other is constantly underlined by the importance of bilingual mediators (*DP*, 36, 42–3, 58, 100). When these mediators appear, tensions diminish and peace is easily reestablished (*DP*, 22, 52–3, 74–5). On the contrary, Odo, who lacks the ability to communicate through language, resorts to stereotypes inherited from Antiquity to explain differences. He adopts these easy explanations, even if they do not correspond to the actuality, because they serve to flatter. Only in regard to the Turks does he regain his lucidity. He describes a strange gesture – hairs plucked out and being thrown on the ground – as an ambivalent sign, admitting that it could not have any significance at all (*DP*, 126). Because this attitude seems possible only toward a group for which no inherited prejudices exist, it becomes evident that national

---

40 Cf. the allusion to Damas (*DP*, 118) and *DP*, 109; Mt. 12, 33.
41 Bernard of Clairvaux, *De consideratione*, in Henri Leclerq and Henri-Marie Rochais, eds., *Sancti Bernardi Opera*, 8 vols. (Rome, 1957–77), 3:451–2.

prejudices lead to error because they offer self-flattering, false explanations for cultural differences.

The reflections on nationalism in the *De profectione* are exemplified by
the metaphor of the snake. It appears not only in the anti-German
episode but also in a passage that describes the encounter of the French
ambassadors with the Greek emperor in his palace. The whole episode
playfully illustrates Bernard's assertion that Romans hate to wait in
antechambers.[42]

> They crossed early in the morning and were admitted to the palace by the
> doorkeepers, but they were not able to speak with the "idol." On that day the
> envoys had to solace each other; looking at pictures took the place of food, and
> at night the marble pavement was a substitute for a mattress or bed. On the fol-
> lowing day, however, after that impious man had risen at about the third hour,
> when at his summons they came into his presence without having eaten or slept,
> they carried out the aim of the embassy concerning both the reparation to his
> men and the complaints of ours; and with wise and gentle eloquence the bishop
> would have rendered the emperor tractable if that serpent could have been
> charmed by anyone; but deaf and swollen with poison as an adder, he had
> changed from the man whom they had seen before, or rather, the man stood
> revealed whom they had not known previously because he was hidden by a veil
> of deceit. Nevertheless, the bishop was insistent, and he prevailed in part; the
> army obtained a market, and a way of departure lay accessible to the pilgrims
> who had lost their goods. The emperor said that he would still confer with the
> king and would soon dispatch messengers. Then the bishop's own need forced
> him to withdraw before he should have to fast for a third day in the emperor's
> palace.[43]

As the Germans stared at the juggler's snake, Odo stares, in his account,
at the emperor, waiting for an attack. Both mistake a representation of
power for reality because they are disarmed by the culture with which
they are confronted. Frightened by exile, they misinterpret any Greek act
as a sign of animosity or contempt, even though the emperor proves his
intention to help the crusaders. The image of a snake can also be turned

---

42 Bernhard, *De consideratione*, 451–2.
43 "Satis mane transfretaverunt et aedituum gratia palatium intraverunt, sed loqui cum idolo
   nequiverunt. Illo die alter alteri pro solatio, intuitus picturam pro cibo, et instanti nocte, mar-
   moreum pavimentum pro culbrita vel lecto. Sequenti vero die, cum profanus ille circa tertiam
   surrexisset, vocati veniunt ante illum, sobrii et insomnes, suam legationem absolventes et de satis-
   factione suorum et de querela nostrorum; fecissetque eum episcopus satis tractabilem prudenti
   eloquentia et suavi, si posset serpens ille ab aliquo incantari; sed aspidis more surdus et veneno
   turgidus, mutatus est ab illo quem antea viderant, immo detectus quem doli tegmine prius non
   cognoverant. Tamen instat episcopus et ex parte praevalet; habet forum exercitus, et peregriniis
   suis rebus perditis patet egressus. Dicit ille se adhuc cum rege locuturum et cito nuntios prae-
   missurum. Urget episcopum regredi privata necessitas, ne cum eo faceret triduanum ieiunium"
   (*DP*, 76).

against Odo, however, as the reference to Psalm 57 suggests. Does he not resemble the snake, deaf and swollen with the poison of denigration? In this interpretation the role of the juggler falls to the manipulative nationalists, who can be held responsible for antique and modern prejudices. Although they will not succeed in imposing their plans on the crusaders, they will awaken and entertain negative feelings that contribute to the failure of the crusade by augmenting tensions between the nations. According to the *De profectione*, intercultural communication constituted the main difficulty along the way. If the crusaders had proven their humility by doubting their first impression of what they saw, they would have arrived at Jerusalem without having suffered hunger.

ODO'S CRUSADE: THE STORY OF A MORAL FAILURE

Although Odo, in regard to his nationalistic point of view, serves as a negative example, the author concedes attenuating circumstances to him by stressing the difficulty of the crusade and the evil influence exerted by his entourage. Because the narrator's point of view reflects his outlook, his contacts, and his experiences on the crusade, Odo's moral development in regard to the circumstances becomes accessible to a reader who is ready to reconstruct Odo's pilgrimage. Odo's justification of his intention to write a guide for future crusaders, "For never will there fail to be pilgrims to the Holy Sepulcher; and they will, I hope, be more cautious of our experience," therefore can also be understood as the expression of the text's intention to illustrate the moral dangers of a pilgrimage.[44]

The narrator's interest in the crossing of rivers, when the French pass through Germany, suggests that he belongs to the entourage of Alvisius of Arras, who was in charge of the organization of the crossings.[45] Under the influence of this diplomat, to whom negotiating with the Germans and the Greeks had been entrusted, Odo appears honest and still unbiased. He criticizes the behavior of his compatriots in Worms on the basis of the citizens' point of view, about which the mediator Alvisius may have informed him (*DP*, 22). The report of the first encounter with the Greek ambassadors in Regensburg remains equally balanced and is more observational than judgmental, although the Greeks'

---

44 "Nunquam deerunt sancti Sepulcri viatores; eruntque, si placet, de nostris eventibus cautiores" (*DP*, 28).
45 Even the indication of the distances correspond to Alvisius's speed. See Bernhard Kugler, *Studien zur Geschichte des Zweiten Kreuzzuges* (Stuttgart, 1866; reprint, Amsterdam, 1979), 135 (with the supposition that Odo thought of faster armies).

ceremonial submission intrigues Odo (*DP*, 28). Again Alvisius's diplomatic activity appears to have exposed his charge to the opposing point of view. When the bishop is sent ahead to Constantinople, however, he leaves his pupil behind.[46]

After he finds himself abandoned, Odo appears to have joined the nobles. For in Hungary, he already seems better informed than Louis about their plots, defending or at least covering them in his report of the incident with Boris.[47] At least from the Greek frontier onward, Odo adopts the narrative point of view of the van. Traveling faster on horseback, for they despise the throng,[48] his group hastens so far ahead that Odo knows more about Conrad's than about Louis's actions.[49] He generalizes his outlook when he accuses the Greeks of perjury and when he complains about the difficulties created by the preceding Germans. He and his friends are too far ahead to buy provisions on the markets established for the French, and when they, along with the Germans, try to buy provisions, a brawl ensues because they claim precedence over nonnobles. Even if Odo underlines the French bravery in this situation, they must have given in, because the outnumbered French subsequently keep their distance. Because the suspicious Greek population does not sell enough food to the unaccompanied knights, they live on plunder (*DP*, 40). Their difficulties in finding provisions arouse Odo's jealousy: He envies the Germans for their access to the market and their ability to pillage by surprise. Therefore, his ideological concept of a French-German rivalry has a materialistic and egocentric base, as do his reproaches to the Greeks. There is no Greek perjury, for his group could have waited for the throng, and there is no German impetuosity because the knights could have bought food together with the Germans, if they had renounced the privileges of their status.

When the German troops cross the Bosporus, Odo has just arrived in Constantinople, sent ahead by the bishop of Langres and the count of Warenne to buy provisions.[50] His group will be separated from their

46 Odo arrives in Philippopolis after the death of Alvisius because he relates (in the past perfect) that Alvisius "had died" (*obierat*) (*DP*, 44–5).
47 Odo's evasive remarks have disarmed the modern commentators who had difficulties identifying the "two princes" (cf. *DP*, 35n.). In my interpretation, Odo refers to French nobles.
48 "Nam quadam vice quidam nostrorum regiae multitudinis oppressionem vitantes et ideo praecurentes" (*DP*, 42).
49 The following analysis refers to *DP*, 40–8.
50 Odo's account is extremely evasive in regard to his group and its location because he tries to disguise the fact that he is far in advance of the king. In Regensburg he says that Alvisius, Bartholomeus the chancellor, Archibald of Bourbon, and "some others" had been sent ahead as envoys to the Greek emperor (*DP*, 28). Alvisius seems to have been replaced by Evrard of Barres,

Lotharingian companions when the Greeks force all Germans to cross (*DP*, 50–1). Because the French van refuses to follow, they are attacked by mercenaries (*DP*, 52–3), in all probability because the Greeks mistook them for undisciplined Germans. In any case, the Greek emperor appears not to have ordered the attack, for he is surprised when Louis's ambassadors inform him of the incident. Begging for pardon, he attempts to protect the French van by lodging them near the palace (*DP*, 52). Odo, however, does not forgive this humiliation and, when the Byzantine wealth awakens his jealousy (*DP*, 62–3), he gives vent to his anger and envy by reproaching the Greeks with heresy (*DP*, 54–5). From now on he sides with the anti-Greek party (cf. *DP*, 58, 64–5, 68–9). Disappointed that the proposal to attack Constantinople was outvoted twice, Odo can hardly restrain himself at the sight of the moneychangers' tables on the market on the other side of the Bosporus.[51] The fact that he accuses the Flemish of having seduced others to participate in the pillage and his resentment of Louis's punishment (illustrated by his furious reproach) suggests that he had also participated in the pillage (*DP*, 74–5).[52] In any case, the perspective of his account and its partiality permit the conclusion that he had been caught on one of the ships that rushed back to Constantinople.[53] There, he loses his equipment because the citizens pillage the French hostages in turn. From now on, Odo seems to depend on others for supplies. Because the anti-Greek party provides him with food "organized" by raids (*DP*, 78), he entirely adopts their point of view.[54] Murmuring against Louis,[55] the monk of Saint Denis calls those who venerate

the master of the temple, for Evrard negotiates along with the two others with the emperor in Constantinople (*DP*, 54). Although Odo calls Evrard of Breteuil, Manasses of Bulles, and Anselm, the seneschal of Flanders, "ambassadors" (*nuntii*), it appears doubtful that they belonged to the royal delegation. They are not admitted to the palace because they help to defend Odo's group when it is attacked by mercenaries (*DP*, 52–3). Odo's detailed knowledge of this incident suggests that he belongs to the entourage of the bishop of Langres (*DP*, 54). His laudatory characterization as "a man of wise intellect and saintly piety" (*prudens animo sacer religione*) (*DP*, 68) contrasts with the former, more distant "pious and spirited man" (*religiosus autem et animosus vir*) (*DP*, 26).

51 See "Sternunt gazas in littore; fulgent auro tabulae, vasisque argenteis quae in nostris emerant onustantur" (*DP*, 74).

52 The plunderers must have belonged to the entourage of the bishop of Langres because Louis tries to get hold of the stolen goods by permitting their return to the bishop.

53 Odo not only knows what happens on the other side of the Bosporus but also resents the spoliation of the prisoners. In addition, he takes the point of view of the other side in reporting "a way of departure lay accessible to the pilgrims" (*DP*, 76).

54 The change becomes evident in the two characterizations of Constantinople (*DP*, 62–6, 88).

55 Odo's group buys a ship to meet before the others, the newcomers who arrive from Italy (*DP*, 78; cf. 10). From now on, Odo will be informed about the emperor's war with Roger of Sicily (*DP*, 82). Already in Constantinople Odo had begun to complain about the delay with regard to the Germans (*DP*, 78–80).

the patron of his monastery heathen (*DP*, 72, 80, cf. 68). Odo remembers his monastery only when the emperor's defeat offers a possibility of
refilling his purse. Digging out some antiquated claims,[56] he complains to
Louis. When the king does not force Conrad to make restitution,[57] Odo
sulks, counting the losses as if he had only participated in the crusade to
enrich himself (*DP*, 104–5).

The narrator's morose mood only begins to change after the initial
skirmishes against the Turks. Proud of the Franks' valor, Odo rediscovers the ideal of the knight protecting the poor (*DP*, 94, 112), perhaps
because of Louis's example or simply because he is frightened and feels
the need for protection.[58] Be that as it may, from now on he presents
Louis's leadership in a more positive light (*DP*, 114). In the description
of the defeat against the Turks, he now assumes a royalist point of view
(*DP*, 114–24). Blaming Geoffrey of Rançon, Odo glorifies the king's
heroism and even accepts his engagement for the poor. In his enthusiasm
for Louis he praises – and in effect promotes – his deceased friends
as having been part of "a small but renowned royal escort."[59] Is it
Louis's heroism that makes Odo change his opinion? A closer examination of the events reveals that the narrator considerably exaggerates the
importance of the whole incident. The glorious defeat merely consisted
of a disorder caused by panic, and the knights appear to have been killed
because they refused to dismount. Odo was sent ahead to the van, so he
did not witness the scene. Therefore, Louis's heroism could be wishful
thinking (*DP*, 116).

Because Odo has lost his friends and must look for a new protector,
his praise of the king also has a material basis. As a "new pauper" he will
live at Louis's expense (*DP*, 112–13), but far from being grateful, his attitude still represents those of the knights, who are unwilling to spend more
money on an enterprise that does not serve their secular aims.[60] From

---

56 Cf. Franz Quarthal, "Die Geschichte der Fulradszelle in Esslingen nach der schriftlichen
   Überlieferung," in Günter P. Fehring and Barbara Scholkmann, eds., *Die Stadtkirche Dionysius in
   Esslingen a. N.: Archäologie und Baugeschichte*, vol. 1: *Die archäologische Untersuchung und ihre
   Ergebnisse* (Stuttgart, 1995), 483–510. I thank Klaus Graf for bringing this article to my attention.

57 Odo's account of the king's unlimited support appears hardly credible because there is no trace
   of any dissent with Conrad (*DP*, 102–3).

58 Odo's fear is suggested by his obsession with a Greek–Turkish conspiracy, his supposition that the
   Turks reassemble troops for revenge, and the attention he pays to the traces of Otto of Freising's
   defeat (*DP*, 111–12).

59 *DP*, 124; in contradiction with *DP*, 118, 122. In view of his friends' morality, it seems more prob-
   able that the king had preferred to keep them with him at the rear.

60 In the night of the defeat Odo pays nearly the same attention to material losses as to the number
   of knights missing (*DP*, 122). He admires the Templars only because they have saved their possessions (*DP*, 124).

now on Louis must finance the entire crusade from his own resources, compensating for the losses on the way and the high prices in Adalia. Even if Odo accuses the citizens of robbery (*DP*, 128, 132–3), he hardly suffers any privation, otherwise he would not have cited the price of hens, eggs, onions, garlic, and nuts as proof, without even mentioning bread (*DP*, 132–3). This omission, together with Odo's obsession with the declining number of horses, illustrates that he and the nobles are unwilling to renounce, even temporarily, their status (*DP*, 124–34). Therefore, Louis's proposal to continue on to Jerusalem by land and to send the poor by ship never had a chance (*DP*, 130). Finally, Louis continues by ship together with the nobles (*DP*, 134) in order to protect the citizens against an attack (*DP*, 134–5). Because the "new paupers" themselves urge him not to wait for them (*DP*, 136), they can possibly be considered hidden deserters.

Odo appears to have been among them, for the story continues after the king left Adalia.[61] And, because he is better informed about those who join the Turks, he also seems to have been among them (*DP*, 140). When he pities the fortune of those who denied their faith, Odo arouses suspicion in regard to his own attitude. Did he give up his Christian faith? In any case, the reason he gives for the decision to join the infidels – that the Turks had been more generous and an epidemic had ravaged the city – betray his lack of religious motivation, which had remained unaffected by the pilgrimage. Furthermore, this surprising end poses an essential question: If the Turks helped French crusaders in disregard of their religion, what had Odo and the crusaders to be afraid of?

Although the supposed end of Odo's pilgrimage illustrates the moral decline of the narrator, it also provides the reader with arguments to defend him. To try to survive is at least human, and because the youngsters play a prominent role in the end, he must be counted among them (*DP*, 138–9). The narrative betrays an inexperienced, naïve, and impetuous young man who has a penchant for adventures and whose instruction appears unfinished.[62] The *De profectione* can therefore be read as the story of a young man who participated in the crusade with the best of intentions but who was still too naïve to understand what was happening, too excited by the situation, and too weak to resist the temptations exerted by evildoers when he was abandoned by his spiritual mentor.

61 The American editor has suggested that he was informed by the count of Flanders, but the account continues even after his departure (*DP*, 138n.).
62 See Henri Waquet's assessment in his edition (Eudes of Deuil, *Croisade*, 12). The most conclusive hints are rhetoric counsels inserted in the account (*DP*, 32, 56).

Could Odo's inability to hide the truth, his tendency to accuse others, and his morose moods be interpreted as signs of a bad conscience?

The reader would be confronted with the ambiguity of external appearances if the account of Odo's development ended with his desertion to the Turks. The text, however, includes updated remarks that suggest a point of view after the crusade. The account of Odo's development thus continues.[63] The whole first chapter must have been written after the crusade because it abounds in references to events of the crusade: The evocation of the French-Norman alliance; the stress put on the Trinity; the refusal to mention the name of the Greek emperor; and the predictions of Greek treachery reflect the state of mind in which the narrator returned to France (*DP*, 6, 10, 14). When the narrator apologizes at the beginning of the second chapter:

Extreme garrulousness is always wearisome to a very busy man; and I fear that my account has run on too long without affording a breathing space. But please allow me this failing, father. I was engrossed in happy affairs, and, while writing the words connected with my native land and while remembering its affairs, unweariedly I recalled for too long a time what I had seen when a happy man; for pleasant events do not cause fatigue. Now, however, at this new beginning, I gird myself for difficult tasks, intending to enter strange countries in my description, just as we did in fact, and accordingly I shall bring to a swifter conclusion the hardships that ensued.[64]

he tries to hide the discrepancy between the elaborated rhetoric of the adult and the simple style of the adolescent. This lie proves that Odo has continued his negative moral career, although he has now perfected his instruction. His participation in the crusade was not merely a youthful sin but had laid the foundations for a lack of religious conviction as an adult.

The full sense of the reference to Odo's further moral evolution becomes clear only to readers who are informed about the historical Odo of Deuil. Close correspondences hint at an elaborate intertextuality between the *De profectione* and the *Apologetic Dialogue* — a text in which two monks of Saint Denis discuss Odo's merits and faults in regard to his

---

63 *DP*, 50, 82–3, 98, 118.
64 "Taediosa est semper longa loquacitas pluribus occupato; unde vereor ne nostra oratio nimis prolixe sine respiratione cucurrerit. Sed date quaeso mihi, pater, hanc noxam. Intereram laetis rebus et patriae meae nomina scribens et rerum reminiscens quod laetus videram sine taedio diutius recolebam; non enim cito afferunt iocunda laborem. Modo vero novo principio succingor ad aspera, intraturus exteras regiones, sicut actu fecimus sic sermone, et laboriosa deinceps citius terminabo" (*DP*, 20).

succession of Suger as abbot.[65] The information given about Odo's crusade in the *Apologetic Dialogue* not only confirms and elucidates the reader's reconstruction;[66] it also bridges the gap between the end of the *De profectione* and its beginning. After having joined the Turks, Odo returned to France by ship in Louis's company. On the way they were attacked by Greek ships and then liberated by Normans, an experience that explains Roger's praise and the even stronger anti-Greek tone of the first chapter (*DA*, 106ff.).[67] In addition, because the *Apologetic Dialogue* evokes Odo's occupations by alluding to his duties as recently elected abbot and to the disputes with which he was confronted,[68] the beginning of the second chapter, which generalizes the outlook of a busy man, suggests to the reader that Odo's rewriting of his early text is motivated by the reproaches of his adversaries. By unveiling his participation in Suger's historiographical project he wants to create the impression that he had always been faithful to Suger in order to refute the claim of his ingratitude (*DA*, 91–2). Here, Odo accomplishes the continuous degradation of his account's veracity: He has no scruples in creating the history that he needs by "rectifying" a document. However, his true feelings already become evident in the first chapter, when he describes the raising of the *Oriflamme* without mentioning Suger's name (*DP*, 16–17).

Because the advocate of Odo in the *Apologetic Dialogue*, the monk William, interprets Odo's staying with the infidels and his enrichment at Louis's expense as a sign of divine election (*DA*, esp. 108), the *De profectione* seems to side with his opponent Galfred, who reproaches Odo for not detaching himself from his social descent, the lower nobility (*DA*, 89–91, 98–100). However, even if the *De profectione* makes this reproach true when it attributes to Odo a penchant for noble friends and an identification with their perspective, it also corrects Galfred's point of view: The general reproach of ingratitude (*DA*, 91–2) is refuted, for the *De profectione* shows that Odo does not forget his deceased friends, whereas he

65 See "Le dialogue apologique du moine Guillaume, biographe de Suger," ed. André Wilmart, *Revue Mabillon* (1942): 102 (abbreviated as *DA*); for a more comprehensive interpretation of the text, see Glaser, "Wilhelm von Saint-Denis," 285–99.

66 According to the *Apologetic Dialogue*, Odo had indeed accompanied a bishop who had died on the crusade (*DA*, 102). The narrator's sensitivity to prices is explained by the restricted allocation attributed to him; and his idealization of the First Crusade as well as his interest in geography refer to the chronicle of the First Crusade he had taken with him (*DA*, 103).

67 Paul Magdalino has already supposed that the strong anti-Greek tone of the *De profectione* and the positive image of Roger reflected the political situation after the Second Crusade (Paul Magdalino, *The Empire of Manuel I Kommenos, 1143–1180* [Cambridge, 1993], 48).

68 *DA*, 82.

easily discards the instruction of Saint Denis. Therefore, Odo's moral imperfection is not due to a defect in his character but to a lack of both religious motivation and Christian morality, both of which can be attributed to his instruction at Saint Denis. This means that Odo's failure also stands for Suger's and Saint Denis's failure to put a young monk on the right track, and the fact that he succeeds Suger proves that his moral failure on the crusade had not only remained unpunished but was even rewarded by his career at Saint Denis.

Therefore, before and after the crusade Odo personifies all the negative qualities that he attributes to others: He represents the incarnation of Bernard's Roman, an ambitious, treacherous, flattering, and greedy courtier.[69] After the crusade he learned to hide perfectly his true intentions behind a religious ideology, and he used it to manipulate others.[70] Or, to go back to the image of the author: If the adder had been manipulated, it was still full of venom, and it enchanted others just as it had been enchanted by the juggler.

THE EVIL FRUITS: THE HIDDEN ARGUMENT OF THE *DE PROFECTIONE*

Karl Morrison's characterization of the mimetic and moral comprehension of history writing has provided an interpretative framework within which to analyze the *De profectione*. The preceding discussion has identified an alternate point of view hidden in the subtext and the construction of the figure of the narrator. Consequently, it is no longer possible to maintain the argument that the text represents Odo's point of view. The story of his moral decline revealed through a close reading of the text in conjunction with other accounts of the Second Crusade suggests that Odo is meant to provide an example of unworthy, negative behavior. The figure of the narrator was therefore constructed in order to bring disrepute on an intellectual position that was associated with the monastery in which Odo had been educated and where he was determined to become abbot. Through an allusion to the fruits of Damas based on Matthew 13, 33, Odo's moral decline is attributed to his education at Saint Denis. This symbolic reference forms a central argument of the *De profectione* in which negative morals – "the evil fruits" – are the conse-

---

69 Bernhard, *De consideratione*, 449–50.
70 Odo pretends that Manuel had promised everything demanded by the French in order to create the treachery he suspected before (*DP*, 10).

quences of the "evil tree," that is, the intellectual background. Following this argument and the negative view of Saint Denis that it projects, it is unlikely that the *De profectione* formed part of the historiography of Saint Denis.[71]

If we can establish the point of view of the narrator, that is, Odo, what can we deduce from an analysis of the text about the point of view of the author? The text criticizes a concept of group identity that confers on its members a moral superiority: Odo's nationalism permits him to elude self-criticism and to legitimate murders motivated by avarice. Furthermore, since the *Apologetic Dialogue* reports that Odo took a chronicle of the First Crusade with him (*DA*, 103), the nationalism attributed to Odo in the *De profectione* can be understood as a critique of the national outlook of the historiography of Saint Denis that had been inspired by the concept expressed in the crusade chronicles of the Franks as "the chosen people." The *De profectione* juxtaposes Odo's feeling of superiority with an implicit critique of the cultural heritage of the West. This critique is inspired by a passage in Bernhard of Clairvaux' *De consideratione*,[72] but the *De profectione* heightens its contrast with Odo's point of view, when the Turks are the only ones to disregard the religion of the poor in their donation of alms (*DP*, 140). Here, even the superiority of the Christians over the infidels, which is taken for granted both by Odo and Bernhard, is put into question.

This positive image of the infidels derives from an implicit critique of the crusade and Odo's crusade propaganda in the text. The *De profectione* reminds the reader of the outcome of the Second Crusade, which resulted in a harsh critique of its participants[73] and the pontiff's temporary suspension of his support for the enterprise.[74] The allusion to the "fruits of

---

71 These doubts are confirmed by the tradition of the *De profectione*. We possess only one manuscript, a copy made at the end of the twelfth century, probably in Clairvaux and inserted in a variant of the *Liber Sancti Iacobi* (DP, xxxiin., xxxvi; cf. Klaus Herbers, *Der Jakobuskult im 12. Jahrhundert und das Liber Sancti Iacobi: Studien über das Verhältnis zwischen Religion und Gesellschaft im hohen Mittelalter* [Wiesbaden, 1984]). At the beginning of the 1220s it was translated in French as part of a kind of vernacular version of the continuation of Aimon, which combines chronicles from Saint Germain und Saint Denis. Although the translator habitually indicates the provenance of his models, he omits any reference for the *De profectione* (Gilette Labory, "Essai d'une histoire nationale au XIIIème siècle: la chronique de l'anonyme de Chantilly-Vatican," *Bibliothèque de l'Ecole des Chartes* 148 (1990): 309). In spite of this integration into a model of the *Grandes Chroniques*, the *De profectione* is excluded in the final version (see Spiegel, *Chronicle Tradition*, 55). Even the modern destiny of the manuscript is mysterious. The national commission that had rediscovered the text in a regional archive did not deliver it to Paris, as they were supposed to for chronicles of national interest, but instead brought it to the library of the *Ecole de Médecine* in Montpellier, where it is still conserved.

72 Bernhard, *De consideratione*, 449–50.   73 Cf. Constable, "Second Crusade," esp. 275ff.

74 Christoph Tyerman, "Were There Any Crusades in the Twelfth Century?" *English Historical Review* 110 (1995): 559.

Damas" can therefore also be understood as a polemical jab at the shameful retreat of the crusaders. However, in contrast to Bernhard of Clairvaux, who in the *De consideratione* attributed its failure to the particular crusaders' moral imperfections,[75] the *De profectione* puts the entire crusade ideology into doubt. Eugene III's crusade bull *Quantum praedecessores* provides the basis for Odo's moral imperfection.[76] Odo's moral indifference toward the crusaders' forfeits corresponds with Eugene III's promise that the crusaders' sins will be pardoned (cf. *DP*, 118), his Frankish nationalism corresponds with the papal appeal to follow the example of the glorious Franks, and his obsession with the lost horses and weapons corresponds with the pope's recommendation to take care of their arms and horses. However, Odo's critique of Eugene proves that his conception of the crusade is not identical with that of the pontiff. Because the narrator is convinced that the unarmed poor impeded the progress of the war (*DP*, 94) and appears impatient because he can hardly wait for the first battle with the infidels (cf. *DP*, 73), it becomes evident that for him crusades constitute holy wars. This concept is opposed to the pilgrimage tradition, which justifies Eugene's restriction of the crusaders' luxury (*DP*, 94) and provides the foundation for the implicit moral point of view from which Odo is judged. Because both concepts were inextricably entwined during the twelfth-century crusades,[77] we can conclude that the *De profectione* deliberately puts into narrative form the internal contradiction of the crusade ideology.

If we take Saint Denis into consideration, a final ambiguity within the *De profectione* emerges, that is, the relationship between religion and the world. The attribution of Odo's moral weakness to his monastery can be considered an implicit criticism of the habitual close connection of worldly life and religion in Saint Denis. Because the founder of Saint Denis was Greek and because Odo shares the same concept of religion with Greeks, that is, the idea that God and his saints demand to be venerated by a sumptuous liturgy (*DP*, 68),[78] his criticism of Greeks can be understood by extension as an implicit critique of Saint Denis. Submission, perjury (*DP*, 58), lies justified by the Empire (*DP*, 56), craftiness (*DP*, 60), hypocrisy (*DP*, 68), and idolatry (*DP*, 76) can also be reproached in

---

75 Bernhard, *De consideratione*, 411–12.
76 For the latest edition, see Grosse Rolf, "Überlegungen zum Kreuzzugsaufruf Eugens III. von 1145/6 mit einer Neuedition von JL 8876," *Francia* 18 (1991): 85–92.
77 Tyerman, "Crusades," 567.
78 Erwin Panofsky derived Suger's religious and artistic concepts from Pseudo-Dionysian ideas. His critics have hinted at Suger's superficial understanding. See Lindy Grant, *Abbot Suger of St. Denis: Church and State in Early Twelfth-Century France* (London, 1998), 23ff.

the historiography of Saint Denis, which served the Capetians. And Odo's critique of the Greeks' lack of hospitality in the scene of the ambassador's reception in the Emperor's palace can also be taken as mirroring the critique possibly made by the poor of Saint Denis (*DP*, 76–7): The impressive new church does not offer a place to sleep, and the beautiful pictures on the walls do not appease their hunger. Inspired by the ideal of a religious detachment from the world, this critique is reminiscent of the controversy between Cistercians and Cluniacs in the twelfth century.[79] However, in concentrating on the charity toward the poor, this critique also embodies a contradiction between two essential Christian principles: the love of God and the love of one's fellow men. Therefore, the text deliberately contrasts two Christian obligations that are equally central and inextricably bound up in Christian tradition.

The deliberate opposition of contradictory concepts of nation, crusade, and Christianity suggests that the *De profectione* pleads for an intermediate position that takes both sides into consideration, according to the dialectic argumentation of Abelard's *Sic et non*. This supposition is confirmed if we take a third dimension of the criticism of the Greeks into consideration. Does not the author resemble a Greek? From a moral point of view a person who conceives a literary fiction is no less hypocritical, crafty, and deceitful than Odo. In addition, the author hides his criticism in a gift addressed to Saint Denis and to Suger (*DP*, 2). The parallel permits us to understand the criticism of the Greeks as a self-critical commentary on the creation of the *De profectione*.

For instance, the second chapter and the pilgrimage begin with the (already cited) words:

Extreme garrulousness is always wearisome to a very busy man; and I fear that my account has run on too long without affording a breathing space. But please allow me this failing, father. I was engrossed in happy affairs, and, while writing the words connected with my native land and while remembering its affairs, unweariedly I recalled for too long a time what I had seen when a happy man; for pleasant events do not cause fatigue. Now, however, at this new beginning, I gird myself for difficult tasks, intending to enter strange countries in my description, just as we did in fact, and accordingly I shall bring to a swifter conclusion the hardships that ensued. (*DP*, 20)

This passage can be interpreted as a message from the author addressed to the reader. He apologizes for intervening only after the first chapter

---

79 For the controversy between Cluny and Cîteaux, see Adriaan H. Bredero, *Bernard of Clairvaux: Between Cult and History* (Grand Rapids, Mich., 1996), 218ff.

by alluding to his "Greek" pleasure in hiding and deluding. Following this argument, the syntactically independent *sicut acu fecimus sic sermone* (just as we did in fact) attests to the moral dimension of the text because it draws a parallel between the acts of writing, listening, and crusading. The pilgrim entering a strange land is compared with the reading of an unknown text, and the author announces to the reader that his efforts in reading (*laborem* and *aspera*) will be compensated by *iocunda* ("pleasant" or rather "funny" events) as would the pilgrims' hardships. The beginning of the third chapter resumes this comparison and includes a warning in regard to "Greece," where the pilgrims and readers are about to enter: "Thus far we were engaged in play because we neither suffered injuries from men's will nor feared dangers arising from the cunning of crafty men. However, from the time we entered Bulgaria, a land belonging to the Greeks, our valor was put to the test and our emotions were aroused."[80] The author announces here that he will test the reader's virtue (the Latin "virtus" can either mean "valor" or "virtue") by arousing his "emotions" or, more specifically, by appealing to his "senses."

In regard to this challenge, the continuation of the text seems to be deceiving. Odo's exaggerations and obsessions that point to the narrator's impulsiveness, irascibility, simplicity, and audacity will only make the reader laugh.[81] The author's menace toward the reader's morality is a trick through which he captivates the reader's attention. The aforementioned metaphor of the snake serves as a parable of the author's manner of proceeding, which is justified in the metaphor as a juggler's prank (*DP*, 42). In opposition to appearances, the snake – Odo and his critic – have been enchanted by the juggler, that is, the author. Therefore, even if they appear dangerous to the spectators, that is, readers, because they are conceived in order to frighten them, they are in fact harmless. Only simple readers reproach the author for wanting to poison them. Furthermore, the image of the snake offers a key for the understanding of the oppositions within *De profectione*. That the juggler puts the snake on a goblet suggests that the text attributes Odo's and his critic's moral imperfections to their particular interpretation of the Eucharist.

Although the limitation of space here does not permit me to develop this argument, it is important to stress the significance of this interpreta-

---

80 "Hucusque lusimus, quia nec damna pertulimus ex malitia hominum nec pericula timuimus de astutia subdolorum. Ex quo autem intravimus terram Graecorum, et virtus laborem pertulit et sensus exercitium" (*DP*, 40).

81 For the comic dimension of such a character, see Philippe Ménard, *Le rire et le sourire dans le roman courtois en France au Moyen Age (1150–1250)* (Geneva, 1950), 149–50.

tion of the Eucharist for an understanding of both the crusade and pilgrimages. Indeed, a pilgrimage and a crusade only make sense if the continual presence of Christ on earth even after his death is considered possible. This means that pilgrims and crusaders share a realistic interpretation of the Eucharist. Using his habitual manner of proceeding, the author associates this position with negative moral consequences. Odo's and his opponent's lack of comprehension of each other appears to be founded on a confusion of appearances with reality. This implicit criticism of the simplicity and one-sidedness of the orthodox interpretation of the Eucharist changes Odo's simple sophism, "The man who knows a case partially makes a partial judgment, but the man who does not know the entire case cannot make a just judgment" (*DP*, 72) into a profound truth that can be considered as an expression of the author's point of view. He suggests that both interpretations of the Eucharist, the one as reality and the other as sign, are equally one-sided and do not capture a truth that appears to be inaccessible to human understanding. This position is associated in the *De profectione* with the moral superiority of "the wise." In an inversion of the habitual argument, the text characterizes this Neoplatonist point of view as a "good tree."

The allusion to the Eucharist therefore situates the *De profectione* within a larger theological debate of the twelfth century. If we consider the author to be a Neoplatonist, the fact that he pretends to be a monk at Saint Denis in the letter to Suger becomes spiritually true. His spiritual home is indeed Saint Denis because the abbey transmitted and translated the works of Pseudo-Denis,[82] and he can indeed consider Suger to be his father because this abbot of Saint Denis had recourse to Pseudo-Dionysian ideas before him. This intellectual position explains how the author can position himself beyond the oppositions he evokes in the text by pleading for a combination of both sides. He does not contest the existence of group identity or cultural difference but appears skeptical toward their positive or negative moral assessment.[83] Because good and evil individuals appear in all groups, moral attribution is reserved for individuals. As far as the relation between religion and world is concerned, he favors a compromise exemplified by Louis VII's visit to a leper colony and to Saint Denis before the crusade (*DP*, 16). Finally, the choice between the value of either the crusade or the pilgrimage is suspended

---

82 Cf. Martin Grabmann, *Mittelalterliches Geistesleben: Abhandlungen zur Geschichte der Scholastik und Mystik*, 3 vols. (Munich, 1926–56), 1:456.
83 Cf. the Lotharingians who associate with each other and the nostalgic look back at the *patria* at the beginning of the second chapter.

because the text ends at the point where the crusaders and pilgrims separate: at the frontier of the Holy Land. Even if the author appears skeptical toward both enterprises because of their moral dangers, the aforementioned sentence "For never will there fail to be pilgrims to the Holy Sepulcher; and they will, I hope, be the more cautious because of our experiences" (*DP*, 28–9) can be interpreted as a resignation to the fact that both pilgrimages and crusades will exist. Nevertheless, the text offers an alternative for youngsters who are attracted by the adventures of the journey, with the guarantee that the reader runs no serious moral risk. For the "pilgrimage to the Holy Sepulcher" can also be understood as a metaphor of human life, during the course of which we must resist temptations. In accordance with the fact that the author sought to put all certainties into question, the exact intentions of the *De profectione* are impossible to determine.

13

The Rhineland Massacres of Jews in the First Crusade

Memories Medieval and Modern

DAVID NIRENBERG

Nine hundred years ago, crusaders passing through the Rhineland on their way to Jerusalem attacked Jews in towns throughout the region surrounding Heidelberg. Many Jews were killed or converted to Christianity, and many took their own lives in order to avoid baptism. The events themselves occupy a significant place in modern Jewish historiography and are often presented as the first instance of an anti-Semitism that would henceforth never be forgotten and whose climax was the Holocaust. As Arno Mayer put it in his study of the "Final Solution": "The attack on the Jews [in 1096] set a disastrous precedent, depositing a fatal poison in the European psyche and imagination."[1] Moreover, some have seen the texts that a number of Jewish communities produced in the aftermath of the massacres as the vessels of a collective memory that gave Jews strength and allowed them to retain their identity throughout a history of tragedies; a collective memory that, in Alan Mintz's words, "summed up [for modern Jews] the past to be espoused or rejected."[2] The First

The author would like to thank Carl Caldwell, Jeremy Cohen, Jane Dailey, Susan Einbinder, Eva Haverkamp, Matthias Henze, Sara Lipton, Ussama Makdisi, Ivan Markus, Ricardo Nirenberg, and Michael Wyschogrod for their generous reading of earlier drafts of this chapter.

1 Arno Mayer, *Why Did the Heavens Not Darken? The "Final Solution" in History* (New York, 1988), 25. The title of the book is itself a quotation from a First Crusade chronicle. Cf. Cecil Roth, *A Short History of the Jewish People* (London, 1969), 185: "Take any realistic description of the position of world Jewry down to the close of the last century; take any indictment drawn up by an anti-Semite in our own times; take any contemporary analysis of the weakness of the Jewish position or the alleged shortcomings of the Jewish character; and in almost every instance it will be possible to trace the origin, if not actually to the crusades, to the currents which they stirred." My thanks to Jeremy Cohen for the latter reference.

2 Haim Hillel Ben Sasson, *A History of the Jewish People* (London, 1976), 414, on martyrdoms as a source of strength; Alan Mintz, *Ḥurban: Responses to Catastrophe in Hebrew Literature* (New York, 1984), x–xi.

Crusade massacres emerge in such scholarship as a focal point in a narrative of Jewish history that asserts the identity of past and present suffering, and that finds its coherence in a teleology of escalating persecution leading to the Holocaust and to Zionist redemption.

In this chapter I challenge both the teleology that binds the Holocaust to the First Crusade and the model of collective memory that underlies it. But my very choice of topic suggests a certain truth in Mintz's claim. I am a student of late medieval Spain (not of Germany or of the Crusades), yet I desire to approach Germany and the themes of this book through such a topic, so far from my own expertise. The reason, I suspect, is that the texts of the First Crusade and the historical narratives of identification they underwrite have so saturated my education (as they have that of many other Jews in the latter half of the twentieth century) that they seem to constitute a personal past as much as they do an object of academic inquiry. Today, for example, as the Neckar runs imperturbably past Heidelberg, where the discussions of memory, violence, and the writing of history that formed the basis of this essay collection first took place, those First Crusade sources that tell of the many Jews who were baptized or killed, or who had committed suicide in the waters of the Rhine and its tributaries come unbidden to my mind. Is an imagination too vivid that still sees the jerking limbs, the blood hurrying to an alien current? Even the landscape, it seems, conspires to blur the boundary between past and present, between history and memory.[3]

Why have these massacres become so indissolubly bound with modern Jewish identity and memory, and what are the consequences, historiographical and political, of this fusion? These are the questions with which this chapter is concerned. Their examination requires a three-tiered approach. I begin by describing and analyzing some of the texts produced by Jews in response to the massacres of 1096. The goal here is not so much to contribute to our historical understanding of the medieval Hebrew texts themselves (for which my knowledge of the language and the sources is insufficient) as to establish the sites at which the modern finds familiarity in the medieval. What is it about these texts that makes them seem so transparently relevant to the modern Jewish experience? Second, I trace parts of the reception history of the medieval texts in order to show how the peculiar model of memory they represent lost or

---

3 The question of the relationship between memory and history will be taken up again below. On the significance of river imagery in the First Crusade chronicles, see Israel Yuval, "Christliche Symbolik und jüdische Martyrologie zur Zeit der Kreuzzüge," in Alfred Haverkamp, ed., *Juden und Christen zur Zeit der Kreuzzüge* (Sigmaringen, 1999), 89–91.

found favor with later generations of "rememberers." The texts, in other words, do not constitute the collective memory of a transhistorical Jewish community but rather were drawn on by specific communities in particular situations.[4] Finally, I touch specifically on one modern model of memory, Freud's theory of trauma and the "return of the repressed," and examine its affinities with the study of the massacres of 1096 in order to suggest that the place of First Crusade texts within modern narratives of Jewish historical experience cannot be understood independently of certain models of memory forged in the anti-Semitic violence of the late nineteenth and early twentieth centuries. The analysis of trauma here is meant merely to be representative of a number of modern theorizations of memory and history that emphasize the repetition of the past in the present: models that have been particularly influential in representing Jewish history as a continuous response to violence.

There are a number of reasons for examining such continuities, although I confine myself to two of the most obvious. First, the memorialization of episodes of violence (beginning with the destruction of the First and Second Temples) came to occupy, and still occupies, a central but complex place in Jewish religion and culture, one that in my opinion remains insufficiently understood. Second, and more notorious, the magnitude of modern violence against Jews has lent a prima facie validity to even the most extreme invocations of teleology and historical continuity in explanations of violence against Jews. The Middle Ages often appear in these invocations as the origins of collective memories (remembered fantasies on the part of the persecutors, remembered sufferings on the part of the persecuted) through which the medieval becomes virtually continuous with the modern.[5]

---

4 Perhaps not surprisingly, one unintended result here will be yet another critique of Halbwachs' too stark distinction between memory and history. This is not the place to belabor the point, but I have profited from Yael Zerubavel, "The Death of Memory and the Memory of Death: Masada and the Holocaust as Historical Metaphors," *Representations* 45 (1994): 72–100.

5 Norman Cohn's *Warrant for Genocide*, written in the 1960s, provides a good example: "As I see it, the deadliest kind of antisemitism, the kind that results in massacre and attempted genocide, has little to do with real conflicts of interest between living people, or even with racial prejudice as such. At its heart lies the belief that Jews – all Jews everywhere – form a conspiratorial body set on ruining and then dominating the rest of mankind. And this belief is simply a modernized, secularized version of the popular medieval view" (*Warrant for Genocide: The Myth of the Jewish World-Conspiracy and the "Protocols of the Elders of Zion"* [New York, 1967], 16). A similar passage from the same work is quoted approvingly and expanded by Lionel Rothkrug, "Peasant and Jew: Fears of Pollution and German Collective Perceptions," *Historical Reflections / Réflexions Historiques* 10 (1983): 60. The tendency is particularly strong when writing of violence that occurred in any of the lands that would later become Germany. For a recent example, see Daniel J. Goldhagen, *Hitler's Willing Executioners: Ordinary Germans and the Holocaust* (New York, 1996). There have always been, of course, historians with the opposite view, e.g., Bernhard Blumenkranz, *Le Juif medieval au miroir de l'art Chretien* (Paris, 1966), 136.

The central question at issue here is far from being a monopoly of medievalists; it lies at the heart of much twentieth-century thought: How can collective myths, optimistically marked for extinction by the Enlightenment, erupt into World War or Holocaust in the modern age?[6] Already implicit within such a question, however, are certain assumptions about continuity and about the identification of the present with the past. The prevalence of these assumptions testifies to a peculiar truth in Jürgen Habermas's claim that "Auschwitz has changed the basis for the continuity of the conditions of life within history."[7] The sketchy history of the memories of 1096 that follows constitutes an exploration of a very small aspect of this change, perhaps so small as to remind one of the blind man mistaking the ear for the elephant. Nevertheless, it remains true that sometimes an elephant can be recognized by its ear.

MEDIEVAL MEMORIES OF 1096

The massacres of Jews in 1096 are a subchapter of a narrative well known to medievalists: the progress of the first crusaders toward the Holy Land. The path to Jerusalem took many crusading groups through the Rhineland, where they threatened numerous Jewish communities.[8] Most of these crusading groups were successfully bribed, passing into the East and into other histories without incident. But some chose to kill the Jews or to convert them by force. At Speyer, ten or eleven Jews died; at Worms, 800; in Mainz, 1,100 or more; other attacks occurred throughout the Moselle valley and further east, in Prague and Ratisbon.

These attacks are documented in Christian and Jewish sources, but the latter are most remarkable. They comprise a set of Hebrew chronicles (the so-called Mainz Anonymous, the chronicle attributed to Solomon bar Samson, and the chronicle of Eliezer bar Nathan) and a group of liturgical poems, prayers, and *Memorbücher* (books of memory).[9] The relation-

---

6 Halbwachs, Freud, Benjamin, Cassirer, Lévi-Strauss, Blumenberg, Braudel: All worked to some extent on this question, and all stressed, in their own way, the persistence of the past.

7 Jürgen Habermas, *Eine Art Schadensabwicklung* (Frankfurt am Main, 1987), 163.

8 A practice that they may have developed even earlier in their itinerary, e.g., at Rouen. See Guibert of Nogent, *Autobiographie*, ed. and trans. Edmond-René Labande (Paris, 1981) (*Recueil des historiens des Gaules et de la France*, 12:240); Mainz Anonymous, trans. in Shlomo Eidelberg, *The Jews and the Crusaders: The Hebrew Chronicles of the First and Second Crusades* (Madison, Wis., 1977), 99.

9 The edition of Abraham Meir Habermann, which includes many of the liturgical poems as well as the chronicles, has been utilized here: *Sefer gezerot Ashkenaz ve-tzarfat* (Jerusalem, 1945–6). A German translation by Seligmann Baer accompanies the earlier Adolf Neubauer and Moritz Stern, eds., *Hebräische Berichte über die Judenverfolgungen während der Kreuzzüge* (Berlin, 1892). It should be noted that Baer also edited the standard edition of the prayerbook for German Jews in the later nineteenth century. For ease of reference, all citations to the chronicles in the text are to the

ship between the sources is complex and unclear, their dating controversial: None is exactly contemporaneous with the events, and some clearly were written generations later.[10] The past twenty years have also witnessed a lively and productive debate that has called into question the longstanding consensus (still championed by Robert Chazan) that these texts can provide an accurate description of events or rendition of the ideology of the besieged Jews. Ivan Markus, for example, has emphasized the chronicles' narrative and representational strategies, whereas Jeremy Cohen has presented them as belated responses, influenced by survivor guilt and contact with Christian ideas.[11] My own sympathies are with the latter views, but for the purposes of this chapter the question is irrelevant, for we are interested here in understanding the resonance of these texts for later readers, particularly those of the twentieth century, and not in the history of the communities that produced them. That resonance, I argue, derives from the way First Crusade texts seem to relate violence and memory.

The memories of different groups saturate these texts. Crusaders, victims, even God, are all analyzed in terms of remembering, reenacting,

English translation of Eidelberg (cited in the previous note) unless otherwise indicated. The poems are also described in Avraham Grossman, "The Roots of Martyrdom in Early Ashkenaz" (Hebrew), in Isaiah Gafni and Aviezer Ravitzky, eds., *Sanctity in Life and Martyrdom: Studies in Memory of Amir Yekutiel* (Jerusalem, 1992), 99–130. In addition to the aformentioned, there are a number of collections of poems about persecution. See, e.g., Simon Bernfeld, *Sefer hademáot*, 3 vols. (Berlin, 1923–6). A number of related prayers and commentaries on prayers were collected in Abraham b. Azriel, *Sefer 'Arugat ha-Bosem*, ed. E. Urbach, 4 vols. (Jerusalem, 1939–63), e.g., 3:293, 323–32. Hebrew texts and English translations of some of the more famous can be found in T. Carmi, ed. and trans., *The Penguin Book of Hebrew Verse* (New York, 1981).

10 I am here summarizing a voluminous literature. See, among others, I. Sonne, "Nouvel examen des trois rélations hebraïques sur les persécutions de 1096," *Revue des Études Juives* (hereafter *REJ*) 96 (1933): 137–52; Yitzhak Baer, "The Persecution of 1096" (Hebrew), in M. D. Cassuto, ed., *Sefer Asaf* (Jerusalem, 1953), 126–40; and Anna Sapir Abulafia, "The Interrelationship between the Hebrew Chronicles of the First Crusade," *Journal of Semitic Studies* 27 (1982): 221–39. In addition, see the works of Robert Chazan mentioned in this chapter. We can look forward to the publication of a new edition of the chronicles, together with a stemma based on all the extant manuscripts, by Eva Haverkamp. See now her Ph.D. dissertation, "Hebräische Berichte über die Judenverfolgungen während des Ersten Kreuzzugs," University of Constance, 1998, 2 vols.

11 Jeremy Cohen, "The 'Persecutions of 1096' – From Martyrdom to Martyrology: the Sociocultural Context of the Hebrew Crusade Chronicles" (Hebrew), *Zion* 59 (1994): 169–208. Ivan Marcus was also skeptical about the chronicles' relationship to the ideology of the martyrs themselves. See his review of Chazan's *European Jewry and the First Crusade* in *Speculum* 64 (1989): 685–8; as well as his "From Politics to Martyrdom: Shifting Paradigms in the Hebrew Narratives of the 1096 Crusade Riots," *Prooftexts* 2 (1982): 40–52; and "History, Story, and Collective Memory: Narrativity in Early Ashkenazic Culture," *Prooftexts* 10 (1990): 365–88. Cf. Chazan's response to Marcus: "The Facticity of Medieval Narrative: A Case Study of the Hebrew First Crusade Narratives," *Association for Jewish Studies Review* 16 (1991): 31–56. I am most grateful to Jeremy Cohen for allowing me to read in draft his further contribution to the problem: "A 1096 Complex? Constructing the First Crusade in Jewish Historical Memory, Medieval and Modern."

and (at times) forgetting foundational acts of violence. The crusaders, for example, are presented as having exacted vengeance for a foundational act of violence, the Jews' killing of Christ: "Here, in our very midst, are the Jews – they whose forefathers murdered and crucified him for no reason. Let us first avenge ourselves on them and exterminate them from among the nations so that the name of Israel no longer will be remembered."[12] Even more marked is the symbolic repetition emphasized by Rabbi Ephraim of Bonn in his *Sefer Zekhirah* (Book of Remembrance), written in the wake of the Second Crusade, wherein he describes an attack by French crusaders on the revered Rabbi Jacob ben Meir of Ramerupt (Rabbenu Tam): "They inflicted five wounds on his head, saying: 'You are the leader of the Jews. So we shall take vengeance on you for the crucified one and wound you the way you inflicted the five wounds on our god.' "[13]

It is, however, with Jewish memory that this paper is primarily concerned, and there the massacres seem to have precipitated a massive rupture.[14] The rupture is most apparent in the unprecedented action the Jews took in order to avoid conversion or defilement at the hands of the crusading "sons of impurity": They sacrificed themselves. In the words of one chronicle, "They all cried out as one: 'Let us hasten and offer ourselves as a sacrifice before God. Anyone possessing a knife should examine it to see that it is not defective, and let him then proceed to slaughter us in sanctification of the Unique and Eternal one, then slaying himself.' "(31) The most dramatic of these sacrifices, and the most carefully detailed in the sources, were those of children by parents. The case of "Rachel, daughter of Isaac, son of Asher, and wife of Judah" (35) is one of those presented as exemplary: " 'Four children have I. Have no mercy on them either. . . . In my children, too, shall you sanctify the Holy Name of God.' A friend took the boy and slew him. . . . The mother spread her sleeves

---

12 Chronicle of Solomon bar Samson, 22. Cf. 26, and also Guibert of Nogent, *Autobiographie*, 12:240. See also Shelomo Dov Goitein, "Obadyah, a Norman Proselyte," *Journal of Jewish Studies* 4 (1953): 80–1.

13 Abraham Habermann, ed., *Sefer zekhirah, selihot ve-kinnot*, (Jerusalem, 1970), 121 (trans. Eidelberg, 130). I. Marcus points out that here Ephraim treats Rabbi Jacob as a "Jewish Christ figure": "Jews and Christians Imagining the Other in Medieval Europe," *Prooftexts* 15 (1995): 212. Marcus contrasts Jacob's title of "gedolan shel yisra'el" with Jesus' mock title "King of the Jews." It is ironic that, though in this Ashkenazic text the treatment of Rabbi Jacob serves to illustrate the darkness of the times, in the Sephardic Abraham ibn Daud's *Sefer ha-Qabbalah* (written in the mid-twelfth century, during the Almohade persecutions), Rabbi Jacob is presented as evidence that Jewish learning flourishes in Christian Europe, even if in al-Andalus it is being destroyed. See the edition of Gershon Cohen (Philadelphia, 1967), 66, ll. 322–3 of the Hebrew.

14 I say "seem" because the lack of Hebrew sources preceding the crusade makes the argument one from silence.

to receive the blood, according to the practice in the ancient Temple sacrificial rite." She herself sacrificed her two daughters once they had prepared the knife, and then drew her son Aaron out from under the box where he had hidden himself to avoid her and "slaughtered him before the Exalted and Lofty God" (36).[15]

In their narration of these episodes the surviving texts exhibit features that resonate strongly in the twentieth century, especially with responses to the Holocaust. First, they (at times) present the slaughters as an unprecedented shattering of the possibility of human understanding.[16] In the words of our texts, "What can we then say?" Second, they respond to this shock in protective ways. Specifically, they strive to repress devastation through repetition. Because the task of these texts is to find precedent for what is experienced in the present as unprecedented horror, they re-remember the past in such a way as to restore continuity and coherence by making the present seem less terribly new. Repression here is achieved by "return" or repetition in the past, in historical memory, and involves the relinking of present experience to previous traumas in sacred history so that they might once again become continuous with that history. Perhaps paradoxically, these two responses depend on one another. Although it has become customary to stress the confidence with which Rhineland Jews asserted precedent, coherence, and continuity in the face of disaster, the texts they produced are repeatedly marked by the intrusion of (ironic?) doubt about God's attentiveness to the violent sacrifices of his people.[17] This doubt nevertheless does not negate, and is not negated by, the assertion of continuity. Rather, one response draws nourishment from, and is always pregnant with, the other.

The unprecedented and the opaque are never far from the surface of our texts:

15 This version of the story of Rachel, taken from the Chronicle of Solomon bar Samson, is a conflation of the account in the Mainz Anonymous and one contained in a *piyyut* of Kalonymos ben Juda, as I. Sonne pointed out in his "Nouvel examen des trois rélations hebraïques sur les persécutions de 1096," 131–4. In "'Persecutions of 1096' – From Martyrdom to Martyrology," Jeremy Cohen suggested that Rachel's holding out her sleeves "in lieu of a chalice" (as the Hebrew has it) deliberately echoed Christian descriptions of Ecclesia standing beneath the cross catching Christ's blood.

16 Marcus, "From Politics to Martyrdom," 45; Mintz, *Hurban*, x–xi.

17 Simha Goldin's is the most recent piece to emphasize (too emphatically, in my opinion), the confidence of Jewish responses to violence in 1096. See his "The Socialization for *kiddush ha-Shem* Among Medieval Jews," *Journal of Medieval History* 23 (1997): 117–38. Others have highlighted passages of the chronicles that display traces of doubt and hesitation in the face of martyrdom. See Ivan Markus, "Une communauté pieuse et le doute: mourir por la Sanctification du Nom (Qiddouch ha-Chem) en Achkenaz (Europe du Nord) et l'histoire de rabbi Amnon de Mayence," *Annales HSS* 49 (1994), 1031–47; Jeremy Cohen, "The Hebrew Crusade Chronicles in their Christian Context," in Haverkamp, ed., *Juden und Christen*, 29.

Let the ears hearing this . . . be seared, for who has heard or seen the likes of it?
Inquire and seek: Was there ever such a mass sacrificial offering since the time
of Adam? Did it ever occur that there were one thousand and one hundred offerings on one single day – all of them comparable to the sacrifice of Isaac, the son
of Abraham? The earth trembled over just one offering that occurred on the
myrrh mountain – it is said: "Behold, the valiant ones cry without," and the
heavens are darkened. What have they [the martyrs] done? Why did the heavens
not darken and the stars not withhold their radiance, why did not the sun and
moon turn dark?[18]

Questions here are the symptoms of shattered understanding. "If God
suffers . . . anguish for the spilt blood of the wicked, how much more is
his mercy aroused for the spilt blood of the righteous?"[19] "No prophet
. . . was able to comprehend how the sin of the people . . . was deemed
so great as to cause the destruction of so many lives."(25) "But no! We
cannot question the ways. . . . What can we then say?"(133) And yet this
unutterable doubt had to be spoken, as Ephraim of Bonn put it in a
lament for those massacred at Blois in 1171: "Woe is me if I speak and
cast doubt on my Maker; woe is me if I do not speak, venting my sorrow."
In the rhetorical nature of these questions, in the danger that surrounds
their utterance, and in the silence of the divine interlocutor even distant
observers such as ourselves can sense the gap that suffering has opened
in the continuity of history.[20]

The Rhineland chroniclers and poets attempt to conceal that gap even
as they reveal it. One obvious way of doing so is by asserting continuity
with the ancient narratives of sacred history.[21] Such continuities are
explicit in allusions to biblical and (relatively few) Talmudic texts. They
are explicit as well in the chroniclers' evocation of ancient ritual practices, particularly those of the Temple cult. In our texts the martyrs speak
of themselves as sin offerings, check their knives for ritual imperfections,
recite the blessing for ritual slaughter, respond amen, hold out their sleeves
to catch the blood, as Rachel did "according to the practice in the ancient

---

18 Solomon bar Samson, 33. Cf. the Chronicle of Rabbi Eliezer Bar Nathan, 83. The same com-
    parison, and a similar question, were put forth in a threnody by R. Eliezer bar Joel ha-Levi. See
    Zunz, *Literaturgeschichte*, 327n1; Bernfeld, *Sefer ha-Demáot*, 1:209. The reference is to Isaiah 33:7,
    a verse associated with Isaac in Midrash Genesis Rabbah 56:6. Moses asks the same question of
    the sun in the Midrash on Lamentations, where the sun replies that he was violently forced to
    keep shining.
19 *Sefer Zekhirah*, 132, citing B. Sanhedrin 49a. Cf. Deut. 21:23.
20 Cf. Marcus, "From Politics to Martyrdom," 45. Ephraim's poem is translated in Carmi, *Hebrew
    Verse*, 384.
21 A strategy Marcus presents as primary: "From Politics to Martyrdom," 41: "The Jewish narrators
    are principally concerned with interpreting the meaning of those acts of unprecedented martyr-
    dom in traditionally acceptable modalities."

Temple sacrificial rite," and even sprinkle the synagogue walls with children's blood.[22]

The chroniclers' struggle to find exemplary precedents for the martyrs' deeds represents an assertion of continuity as well, as when they invoke the Talmudic Rabbi Akiva, who preferred to be martyred rather than stop teaching the Torah.[23] Yet, even as they assert these continuities the chroniclers and poets are aware that they mask an incommensurability. Rachel "died together with her four children, just as did that other righteous woman with her seven sons, and about them it is written: 'the mother of the sons rejoices'" (36). But in none of these earlier accounts did the mother herself wield the knife.[24] The central biblical precedent of the Akedah is equally unsatisfactory:[25] "[A]s Abraham did his son Isaac," they

---

22 David bar Meshullam, a leader of the Jewish community at Speyer who lived through the events of 1096 (he is recorded as a delegate from the community to the court of Henry IV in 1090), invoked the Temple even more explicitly: "Tender children and women gave/ themselves up to the binding, like/ choice lambs in the Chamber of the/ Hearth. . . . Yearling lambs without blemish were/ slaughtered like whole offerings,/ trapped and burnt like the sacrificial/ portions of shared offerings. They/ said to their mothers: "do not be/ moved by pity. Heaven has summoned/ us to be an offering by fire to the Lord." The translation is from Carmi, *Hebrew Verse*, 374–5. Cf. *Sefer Josippon*, David Flusser, ed., 2 vols. (Jerusalem, 1978–80), chap. 92: "There is no better sacrifice to our Lord in the Temple than our own flesh, and there is nothing better to spray in His Sanctuary . . . than our own blood."

23 For Akiva, see Berakhot 61b. Yet it is striking how uninterested the chroniclers are in finding halakhic precedents for the extreme actions they describe, and how few allusions to the Talmud they make. The most apposite precedent, that of the 400 youths who drowned themselves rather than be sexually defiled (B. Gittin, 57b), is never cited by the chroniclers, though it does seem to have influenced them, and is cited, for example, by Rabbi Jacob Tam in support of self-inflicted martyrdom: Tosafot to Avodah Zarah, 18a, s.v. ve-al yeḥabel ʿazmo. There were also rabbis who opposed such martyrdoms. See, for example, the Torah commentary in *Tosafot HaShalem*, J. Gellis, ed. (Jerusalem, 1982), 1:262. Modern scholars, on the other hand, have written a great deal about the precedents to these martyrdoms. See Spiegel, *The Last Trial: On the Legends and Lore of the Command to Abraham to Offer Isaac as a Sacrifice: The Akedah*, trans. Judah Goldin (Philadelphia, 1967); Chazan, *European Jewry and the First Crusade*, 116; Jonathan Katz, *Exclusiveness and Tolerance* (Oxford, 1961), 90ff.; Haym Soloveitchik, "Religious Law and Change: The Medieval Ashkenazic Example," *Association for Jewish Studies Review* 12 (1987): 205–21; Grossman, "Roots of Martyrdom." Important works on martyrdom in earlier periods include S. Lieberman, "Persecution of the Jewish Religion" (Hebrew), in the Hebrew volume of S. Lieberman, ed., *Salo Wittmayer Baron Jubilee Volume* (New York, 1974), 213–45; S. Lieberman, "The Martyrs of Caesarea," *Annuaire de l'Institut de Philologie et d'Histoire Orientales et Slaves* 7 (1939–44); Flusser, *Josippon*, 165–6.

24 The story is told in 2 Maccabees 7, but Maccabees was not the direct source for this allusion among medieval Jews. See Gershon Cohen, "The Story of Hannah and Her Seven Sons in Hebrew Literature" (Hebrew), in Moshe Davis, ed., *Mordecai M. Kaplan: Jubilee Volume on the Occasion of His Seventieth Birthday* (New York, 1953), 109–22. The chronicle's reference is to B. Gittin 57b, where the mother's comfort is confirmed by a voice from heaven.

25 As it had proved previously in the case of the mother and her seven sons. See B. Gittin 57b and Lamentations Rabbah, where the mother explicitly draws the comparison: "You built one altar and did not offer up your son, but I built seven altars and offered up my sons on them" (*Midrash Rabbah Lamentations*, trans. A. Cohen [London, 1939], xx). Cf. Yalkut, Lamentations, no. 1029: "Abraham, don't let your thoughts grow proud! . . . I on seven altars offered sacrifices!"

"bound their children in sacrifice," write the chroniclers.[26] But unlike the biblical Abraham, their hands were not stayed. Conventional readings of previous catastrophes do not suffice to contain pain within proof text. The Rhineland authors therefore perceive a need to reinterpret the past. In this sense, they have been "hurt" into a new historical consciousness.

This new consciousness demanded a transformation of the past and of the future. The transformation of the past is most evident in the sudden popularity of an obscure alternative reading of the Akedah: Abraham had not stayed his hand. He really had sacrificed Isaac, whom God then revived. The ram was introduced only to prevent Abraham from sacrificing his revived son a second time. This was a reading with ancient roots, but it flowered only now, in the need to find precedent for the unprecedented. I quote from a liturgical poem written by Rabbi Ephraim of Bonn and cited in Shalom Spiegel's brilliant treatment of this interpretive development:[27]

> [Abraham] made haste, he pinned him down with his knees,
> He made his two arms strong.
> With steady hands he slaughtered him according to the rite,
> Full right was the slaughter.
> Down upon him fell the resurrecting dew, and he revived.
> [The father] seized him [then] to slaughter him once more.
> Scripture, bear witness! Well-grounded is the fact:
> "And the Lord called Abraham, even a second time from heaven."

As Spiegel has shown (although he does not say so), Ephraim and his colleagues here have pieced together shards of a neglected textual heritage in order to produce a new memory of the past.[28] Through this rewriting

---

26 In this case Solomon bar Samson, 32. The verb ʿakdu, "bound," like the noun ʿakedah, both derive from the root ʿakad, "to bind," used to describe Abraham's binding of Isaac in Genesis 22. The allusion recurs frequently, though it is most extreme in the account of the sacrifice of Isaac, son of Meshullam of Worms, the first child to be sacrificed according to the Mainz Anonymous (103–4). See Spiegel, *The Last Trial*, 3–8, 26.

27 Spiegel's *Last Trial* surveys rabbinic interpretations on this issue. See esp. 28–37, 44–50. The following is translated on 148–9.

28 The extent to which this new memory may have been influenced by the contemporary Christian context has been a focus of polemic since at least the nineteenth century. Most recently, Israel Yuval, Ivan Markus, and Jeremy Cohen have all pointed to important instances of shared symbols and rituals, and all three have suggested (as have others) that the sharpening of Jewish-Christian polemic in the period forced Jews to reorient their traditions in order to confront Christian arguments. On the other hand, it is important to remember that many of the elements of this new memory had entered the Jewish textual tradition in the Second Temple and early rabbinic periods, even if they were more marginal in some periods than in others. On the sacrificial element, for example, see Jon Levenson, *The Death and Resurrection of the Beloved Son: the Transformation of Child Sacrifice in Judaism and Christianity* (New Haven, Conn., 1993).

Ephraim and his colleagues asserted identity and continuity with past sacrifices and past covenants even as they enacted and memorialized new ones.[29]

Although the interpretation of present sacrifices as the intensified repetition of ancient ones helped to explain these massacres within a traditional hermeneutic, it also posed some difficult problems of teleology. Where would this model of escalating repetition lead? Would the sacrifices be redemptive or merely an endlessly repeated suffering? The problem became especially acute when the crusaders' conquest of Jerusalem suggested that God had delayed His vengeance against them for their shedding of Jewish blood and when the recurrence of the attacks during the Second Crusade (1146) cast doubt on the redemptive nature of the earlier sacrifices. This doubt inspired Ephraim of Bonn's *Sefer Zekhirah* and is reflected in it:

We cried out to our God, saying: "Alas, Lord, God, not even fifty years, the number of years of a jubilee, have passed since our blood was shed in witness to the Oneness of Your Revered Name on the day of the great slaughter. Will you forsake us eternally, O Lord? Will You extend Your anger to all generations? Do not permit this suffering to recur." (122)[30]

Two possibilities are analytically distinguishable here, although they are empirically inseparable. The first is redemptive: The sacrifices would help God remember his covenant and the foundational 'Akedah that guaranteed it. The second is cyclical, even nihilistic: God would never remember and the sacrifices would be endlessly repeated.

For, of course, God's memory was very much at issue here. "[T]he verb *zakhar* appears . . . in the Bible no less than one hundred and sixty-nine

---

29 Spiegel, *Last Trial*, 137, alludes to just such a "rewriting" (my term, not his) in his discussion of the haggadic account of the song attributed to Isaac on the fire. I return to the issue of memorialization below. That the chroniclers thought of the sacrifices of 1096 as in some sense a new covenant is evident from passages such as this one from Solomon bar Samson: "May the blood of His devoted ones stand us in good stead and be an atonement for us and for our posterity after us, and our children's children eternally, like the 'Akedah of our Father Isaac when our Father Abraham bound him on the altar" (p. 49). Cf. the comparison made by Ephraim of Bonn between giving one's blood to the lord at circumcision, and sanctification of his name (p. 129). Again in his "'Akedah," Ephraim portrays Isaac's sacrifice as a circumcision writ large, an answer to Ishmael's boast of his adult circumcision, presumably more painful than Isaac's infant one. The reference is to B. Sanhedrin 89b and Targum Jonathan at Gen. 22:1.

30 The passage describes a war of memories. The past incites the crusaders ("Avenge the crucified one") to leave "no remnant or vestige . . . of Israel," to erase its memory, but God hears the Jews' commemorative appeal to jubilee and sends St. Bernard to save them. Bernard does so by insisting that Jews serve Christians as a mnemonic, "for in the Book of Psalms it is written of them: 'Slay them not, lest my people forget.'" Cf. Eliezer bar Nathan, 86, 90.

times, usually with either Israel or God as the subject, for memory is incumbent upon both" (cf. Psalm 44).[31] This divine memory was associated early on with human sacrifice, as when, in Tanḥuma vayyērāʾ 23, the rabbis write: "Whenever the children of Isaac sin and as a result come into distress, let there be remembered to their credit the Akedah of Isaac."[32] Elsewhere, God Himself acknowledges his debt: "The Holy One (blessed be He) said to Moses, 'I can be trusted to pay out the reward of Isaac, son of Abraham, who gave a quarter of [a *lōg* of] blood upon the altar.' "[33] Contemporaries such as Ephraim of Bonn (in his "ʿAkedah") invoke this tradition quite explicitly:

> Thus prayed the binder and the bound,
> That when their descendants commit a wrong
> This act be recalled to save them from disaster . . .
> O Righteous One, do us this grace! . . .
> Recall to our credit the many Akedahs,
> The saints, men and women, slain for Thy sake.

Recall. Remember. Credit: Nietzsche called this "a main clause of the oldest (unhappily also the most enduring) psychology on Earth" – that of sacrifice as stimulus to memory.[34] Here violence becomes a mnemonic for the divine.[35] What we should not forget, however, is that behind the human invocation of this mnemonic lies anxiety about God's memory. As David bar Meshullam put it in one of the earliest First Crusade poems, "O God, do not hush up the shedding of my blood": "Once, long ago,

---

31 Yosef H. Yerushalmi, *Zakhor: Jewish History and Jewish Memory* (Seattle, 1982), 5.

32 A number of rabbinic commentaries on Leviticus 26:39–42 ("they will make amends for their sin. Then will I remember my covenant with Jacob, and also my covenant with Isaac, and also my covenant with Abraham will I remember") are of particular interest here. See Spiegel, *Last Trial*, 41–2.

33 Mekhitta de Rabbi Shimon ben Yochai, in D. Hoffmann, *Mechilta de Rabbi Simon b. Jochai* (Frankfurt am Main, 1905), 4. The passage is cited by Jon Levenson, *Death and Resurrection of the Beloved Son*, 193. It continues with an invocation of Psalm 79:10–11: "Let the nations not say, 'Where is their God?' Before our eyes let it be known among the nations that You avenge the spilled blood of Your servant," a Psalm frequently cited in Jewish texts responding to violence.

34 *Genealogy of Morals* II.3.

35 For an ancient example, see Exodus 12:23, "and when He sees the blood upon the lintel." Cf. I Chron. 21:15, "And when He was about to destroy, the Lord beheld." Rabbinic interpretations conjoined these passages with the ʿAkedah and represented Isaac's blood as God's reminder. See, e.g., the *Mekhilta de-Rabbi Ishmael*, Bo, Pishaʾ 7 and 12. Cf. Seder Eliyahu R., 7, ed. Friedmann, 36; Lev. R. 2. Cf. B. Rosh ha-Shanah 16a, which associates the use of a ram's horn on Rosh ha-Shanah with God's remembering of the ʿAkedah, so that He might "account it to your credit"; and Pessikta R. 171b. (But contrast J. Rosh ha-Shanah, 59a.) These and other examples in Spiegel, *Last Trial*, 90–5, passim. To these add Targum Neofiti to Lev. 22:27; Leviticus rabbah 2:11; B. Berakot 16b. This Jewish anthropomorphizing of divine memory was noted by Muslim polemicists. See L. Strauss, "The Ways of Muslim Polemics," *Memorial Volume of the Rabbinical Seminary of Vienna* (Jerusalem, 1946), 188, no. 24.

we could rely upon the/ merit of Abraham's sacrifice at Mount/ Moriah, that it would safeguard us . . . / . . . / But now,/ one sacrifice follows another, they no longer can be counted."[36] Doubt about God's memory is everywhere marked in the sources, although rarely noted in modern commentaries. Hence, the gentle reminder from Isaiah, scattered like a refrain throughout the chronicles: "Wilt thou restrain Thyself for these things, O Lord?"[37] Less gentle the prodding vengeance in the Ashkenazic sabbath prayer:

May the Merciful Father . . . remember . . . the sacred communities that sacrificed themselves. . . . May He avenge the blood of his servants. . . . Why should the nations say: "where is their God?" Before our eyes let it be known among the nations that you avenge the spilled blood of your servants. (Psalm 79:10)[38]

The possibility that God has forgotten His people, that the massacres mark a break in God's memory, that human sacrifice cannot bring about divine recollection: This is the shattering possibility that our texts seek to repress even as they mark its intrusion.[39]

There are a number of ways to achieve repression and contain this doubt. One of these, the one most frequently stressed in modern scholarship, is simply to deny the novelty of the situation by resorting to conventional explanations about sin, punishment, atonement, and redemption.[40] Certain uses of allegory also constitute denial. When in Solomon bar Samson's chronicle Rabbi Moses ha-cohen exhorts his listeners to make the journey to a heavenly Jerusalem, he does so in evocative language: "Let us rise up and ascend to the house of the Lord" (*nakumah ve-n'aleh*). Through this reference to Genesis 35:3 (*ve-nakumah ve-n'aleh*), where Jacob commands his followers to ascend to Beth El to

---

36 The translation is from Carmi, *Hebrew Verse*, 374–5. Cf. the edition in Habermann, 71. The problem was accentuated by the explicit insistence, previously noted, that the First Crusade sacrifices took even greater courage than that of Isaac. Again, in the words of David bar Meshullam: "Bound on Mt. Moriah, his father bound him/ . . . /we, without being bound, are slaughtered for the sake of His love."

37 E.g., in that of Solomon Bar Samson, 33, 53. See Isaiah 64:11.

38 The prayer was known to Ephraim of Bonn. See Chazan, *European Jewry*, 145, citing R. Abraham ben Azriel, *Sefer 'Arugat ha-Bosem*, IV:49; *Seder 'Avodat Yisra'el*, ed. Seligmann Baer (Rödelheim, 1868), 233.

39 Modern commentators tend to ignore the role of doubt in First Crusade texts, preferring to stress the firm faith of the Rhineland Jews. In addition to Baer, Spiegel, and Goldin, whose views are cited elsewhere in this chapter, see Gershon Cohen, "Messianic Postures of Ashkenazim and Sephardim," *Leo Baeck Memorial Lecture* 9 (1976): 37.

40 E.g., Solomon bar Samson, 49; Eliezer bar Nathan, 82. The chronicles all close with a prayer for the redemption. Contemporary observers are presented as believing in the redemptive potential of the martyrdoms. Thus, Rabbi Meshullam assured the Jews of Speyer: "Now you need not fear, for his death [that of Meir Cohen] overweighs and atones for our transgressions" (see Solomon bar Samson, 71).

build the altar, and to the messianism of Jeremiah 31:5 ("Let us rise up and ascend to Zion, to the Lord our God"), his listeners are assured that the Jewish martyrs ascended to the true holy city despite the fact that the earthly one had fallen to the crusaders.[41]

More interesting for my purposes, however, is a form of repression and return that involves the simultaneous construction of the two related responses, redemptive and cyclical, that I referred to earlier. The first of these, redemptive teleology, creates a narrative that presents the shattering events themselves as signs that "values and wishes" are indeed being realized.[42] Some Rhineland authors, for example, present the mass suicides as atonement by the righteous for ancient collective guilt. According to this view it was the burden of every generation to atone for the ancient sins of Israel in proportion to its greatness; hence the old transgressions return with greatest force among the most pious.[43] The repetition and memorialization of sacrifices becomes crucial in such a model, and history becomes an account book chronicling the ongoing repayment of an ancient debt. Hence, in part, the renewed interest in memory evident in many of our Rhineland sources. The chronicles, of course, are all books of remembrance, even if only Ephraim's carries that name. The later *Memorbücher*, which commemorate Jewish martyrs, generally begin with the holy ones of 1096.[44] The liturgy too became a vehicle for memorialization as liturgical poems and prayers commemorating the Rhineland martyrs were incorporated into it. The circulation of these poems was often limited and local, but traces remain today in the dirges recited on

41 See Robert Chazan's "Jerusalem as Christian Symbol during the First Crusade: Jewish Awareness and Response," which he kindly allowed me to see in draft. See also the sensitive analysis in Marcus, "From Politics to Martyrdom," 49–51, where Mainz becomes the Temple in Jerusalem. For a sustained exploration of the theme, with important implications for an understanding of how Rhineland Jews transposed their topography into a sacral key, see now Israel Yuval, "Heilige Städte, heilige Gemeinden-Mainz als das Jerusalem Deutschlands," in Robert Jütte and Abraham Kustermann, eds., *Jüdische Gemeinden und Organisationsformen von der Antike bis zur Gegenwart*, (Wiesbaden, 1998), 91–101.

42 I am paraphrasing here from Dominick La Capra, *Representing the Holocaust: History, Theory, Trauma* (Ithaca, N.Y., 1994), 190–4. The analogy is deliberate, for, as I will suggest below, modern scholars often view the First Crusade material through the lens of (loosely) Freudian trauma.

43 See Solomon bar Samson, 22 (A. Habermann, *Sefer Gezerot*, 25). See also the penitential poem of Eliezer bar Nathan, "The Covenant and the Oath," in Habermann, 108; R. Joel bar Isaac ha-Levi's "'Akedah," 111–12; R. Baruch of Mainz, in Habermann, *Yediot ha-Makon le-Heker ha-Shirah* VI (Jerusalem, 1945), 121. For proof texts, see inter alia Psalm 11:5; Genesis Rabbah 32:3, 34:2.

44 E.g., see Siegmund Salfeld, *Das Martyrologium des Nürnberger Memorbuches*, Quellen zur Geschichte der Juden in Deutschland 3 (Berlin, 1898). Others are listed in the introduction, xvi–xxxix. See also Moritz Steinschneider, *Die Geschichtsliteratur der Juden* (Berlin, 1905), no. 24; Yerushalmi, *Zakhor*, 46; Chazan, *European Jewry*, 148.

the Ninth of Av and in the aforementioned remembrance of martyrs in the Ashkenazic Sabbath service.[45] These memorializations had multiple purposes: They were meant to preserve examples of appropriate heroism for communities constantly in need of them. They also were meant to inscribe the martyrs' sacrifices in a cycle of tragedies (such as those of the Ninth of Av, a date on which a number of disasters, including the fall of the Temple in Jerusalem, were thought to have occurred) and reiterate them liturgically each year, thus making present violence resonate with violence past and eternal. Perhaps most important, they were meant to remind God of the devotion of His people, to ensure that their payments of the ancient debts were duly noted, and even to prod God into a recollection of His covenant.

Redemptive teleology depended on anamnesis, on God's recollection, and many of the First Crusade texts were created in order to achieve such a recollection. Implicit in that task, however, was the possibility of its obverse, of God's amnesia. In the case of the Rhineland Jews, this took the form of the construction of history as a compulsory repetition of suffering wherein hope for redemption is illusory because God has indeed forgotten. The linkage between nihilism and forgetting already is present in the most foundational texts, as in the Deuteronomic injunction to memory: "Then beware lest you forget the Lord who brought you forth out of the land of Egypt, out of the house of bondage. . . . If you indeed forget the Lord your God . . . you shall utterly perish" (6:10–12, 8:11–19). This potential for oblivion provides an anxious background to many Jewish questions about God's silence in the face of catastrophe. Talmudic responses to the destruction of the Second Temple flirted with it. Referring to the Emperor Titus, destroyer of Jerusalem, Abba Hanan (in B. Gittin 56b) alluded to Psalm 89:9: " 'Who is like You, mighty in self-restraint?' You heard the blasphemy and insults of that wicked man, but You kept silent!" A student of Rabbi Ishmael's sharpened the sting of the allusion by playing on Exodus 15:11 ("Who is like You among the gods?"): Replacing *elim* (gods) with *illemim* (mute), he wrote, "Who is like You, O Lord, among the dumb?" In his poetic response to the Second Crusade, Isaac bar Shalom invokes these past reactions to catastrophe to raise the nihilistic stakes. He states that the Jews have kept their part of the bargain of memory and asks explicitly what it would take to jar God back into language and recollection:

45 Chazan, *European Jewry*, 145.

> There is none like You among the dumb,
> Keeping silent and being still in the face of those who aggrieve us.
> Our foes are many; they rise up against us,
> As they take council together to revile us.
> "Where is your King?" they taunt us.
> But we have not forgotten You nor deceived You.
> Do not keep silent![46]

This second response, like the first, emphasizes continuity and precedent. Again like the first, it treats the repetition of massacre and of commemoration as the building blocks of a coherent history. But here there is a hint of sacred parody, an "ironizing appropriation of the consecrated past or of constitutive texts that still manages to preserve their normative valence" but allows a hint of doubt about the telos, an undermining of the hope that suffering can bring about God's remembrance of His people and His promises.[47] Hence, these texts are pregnant with the possibility that massacre would eternally recur, that sacrifice would not bring about God's recollection. In the words of one Rhineland penitential prayer: "All exiles come to an end, only mine increases; all questions are answered, but my question returns ever to the place from which it came."[48]

THE MASSACRES IN PRE-HOLOCAUST MEMORY

This swaddling of the unthinkable in twin narratives of hope and despair (a process often referred to somewhat reductively in terms of art as "theodicy"), of course, is not unique to the First Crusade texts: Think, for example, of the much earlier reactions to the destruction of the Temples of Jerusalem. It is, however, this struggle to express and understand extreme suffering without shattering the traditional symbolic system that makes these sources resonate so strongly with twentieth-century sensibil-

---

46 Text and translation in Jakob Petuchowski, *Theology and Poetry: Studies in the Medieval Piyyut* (London, 1978), 71–83. The poem is anthologized in David Roskies, ed., *The Literature of Destruction: Jewish Responses to Catastrophe* (Philadelphia, 1989), 83–5. Cf. David bar Meshullam's "Oh God, do not hush up the shedding of my blood," ed. Habermann, 71. Cf. Also Mekilta, 42b (on Exod. 15:11).

47 Cf. Spiegel, *Last Trial*, 26, who claims that there is "not a hint," "not a whisper," that Rhineland Jews saw their experience as incommensurable with Abraham's, as Hannah had so vocally done before them. "You will never find that they protest." This is a strange claim, given much of the evidence already reviewed. Should this totalizing rejection of doubt by Spiegel itself be seen as part of the modern Jewish response to trauma discussed below? Spiegel's work was first published in 1950. The quote is from Sidra DeKoven Ezrahi, as cited without further reference in an unpublished comment by Gabrielle Spiegel. I have not been able to localize the precise reference.

48 Cited by Baer, *Galut*, 26.

ities. For the pious Jew, this struggle has always meant engaging the "unprecedented" through tradition in such a way as to preserve both its incomprehensibility and the possibility of a covenantal relationship with God. For the twentieth-century critic the problem is a related but slightly different one, of finding language with which to approach the Holocaust, an event so extreme that it calls into question the possibility of representation itself. It is this homology, I would argue, that has turned these chronicles from the early days of medieval German Jewish experience into "a site for the acting out of tensions generated by our own (essentially second generation) experience of the Holocaust."[49]

Before we take the affinity between such texts and modern responses to the Holocaust as evidence of a continuous Jewish attitude toward suffering and remembrance in the Diaspora, however, we should admit both that the First Crusade chronicles themselves have often been forgotten and that their attitude toward suffering has not always seemed so relevant or congenial. This should not be surprising, for no event, no matter how grave, commands its own future. The later massacres that devastated Iberian Jewry in 1391, for example, were larger by orders of magnitude than those of 1096 and had (arguably) a greater impact on the communities they devastated than those of the Rhineland. Whereas the events of 1096 had relatively little effect on the social and economic development of Ashkenazic Jewry, those of 1391 transformed the possibilities of Jewish existence in Iberia, leading directly to the expansion of the Inquisition's involvement in the *converso* question and to the expulsions of 1492. Yet thousands of pages are dedicated to 1096, whereas 1391 goes virtually unstudied.[50]

Granted, medieval Jews certainly did not engage in such a comparative calculus. Nevertheless, it would be a mistake to assume that these Ashkenazic chronicles and poetic texts that we are told "have provided the source material for the [modern] history of the persecution of the Jews" were always at the forefront of whatever we mean by Jewish collective memory. In fact, the chronicles we have discussed were both unusual and unpopular, judging from manuscript evidence. The Chronicle of bar Samson and the Mainz Anonymous each exist in only one

---

49 The quote is from a text delivered by Gabrielle Spiegel in her capacity as commentator on a panel comprised of Chazan, Cohen, and Markus. I am very grateful to her for providing me with a copy of these remarkable pages. On post-Holocaust questions of representation, see especially the essays in Saul Friedländer, ed., *Probing the Limits of Representation: Nazism and the "Final Solution"* (Cambridge, 1992), as well as the works cited below.

50 Except as a negative foil to 1096, as in Gershon Cohen, "Messianic Postures," 35–42.

manuscript (fifteenth and sixteenth century, respectively), that of Eliezer bar Nathan in a handful, only one of which is medieval (fourteenth century). Some of the poems and prayers achieved broad circulation and had an important impact on the piety of European Jews. Many other poems, however, were "recited only in those communities whose troubles they related," and the fast days introduced into local liturgical calendars to commemorate violence and sacrifice "were not widely observed or long preserved, any more than were the fasts undertaken by individual ascetics."[51]

There were, however, certain moments when the models of sacrifice and memory contained in First Crusade texts, and more specifically in the chronicles, came to seem relevant or useful to later generations. It is important to study these moments if we are to historicize Jewish memories of violence, but we should be careful not to conflate the reappearance of such texts in specific (and generally historical) textual traditions with their reemergence into something called "collective memory." Instead we might ask when, why, and for whom do the First Crusade chronicles become recognizable as a textual memory shared with the past?

Such questions are difficult to answer, first because they demand a very wide angle of historical vision across nearly a millennium, and second because they assume countless judgments about homology. For example, some later massacres, such as that at Blois in 1171 or at Troyes in 1288, did trigger the production of a commemorative literature, particularly in poetic form.[52] But this poetry is quite different in content from those memorializing the earlier events. The sanctifying martyrdom stressed in much of this later poetry consists not so much of ritual suicide but rather of suffering death at the hands of Christians.[53] Furthermore, the literature seems uninfluenced by the First Crusade chronicle tradition. More importantly, the literary responses to these later episodes tend not to treat

---

51 The three quotes are from Ismar Elbogen's *Jewish Liturgy: A Comprehensive History*, first published in German in 1913. I cite from the English translation by Raymond Scheindlin (Philadelphia, 1993), 180, 260. Clearly I am not convinced by Goldin's claim that "from the beginning of the twelfth century, the educational and socialization processes utilize these sources as a basis for internalizing . . . and creating a uniform, normative Jewish behavior of committing suicide" ("The Socialization for *kiddush ha-Shem*," 121). See also Joseph Dan, "The Problem of Qiddush ha-Shem in the Speculative Teaching of the German Hassidim" (Hebrew), in *Milhemet Kodesh u-Martirologiah* (Jerusalem, 1968), 121–9.

52 I am grateful to Susan Einbinder for allowing me to read in draft her essay "Medieval representations of martyrdom in prose and verse."

53 There are later examples of suicide for the sanctification of God's name (qiddush ha-Shem), but these are rare, and their positive valence is never so strong as the 1096 cases. See, for example, the apologetic tone of the responsum of Meir ben Baruch of Rothenburg, in his *Teshuvot, Pesakim, u-Minhagim*, I. Z. Cahana, ed. 3 vols. (Jerusalem, 1957–62), II, 54.

the violence they describe as unprecedented, unspeakable, or necessitating a struggle to reorder the relationship of the present with the past. For such a response, one must wait until the expulsions of Jews from Spain in 1492.

The expulsion of all Jews from the territories of Ferdinand and Isabella was seen as a blow of unprecedented proportions and seems to have prompted a turn to history, to the search for origins and for endings. As Tam Ibn Yahia put it in his introduction to a new (1510) edition of the Jewish historical classic *Yosippon*: "I, in the midst of exile, wallowing in the blood of the upheavals that are overtaking my people and nation, was roused to . . . print this book, . . . that has laid bare the source of the misfortunes of the House of Judah."[54] The result was a sixteenth-century Jewish "lachrymose school" of historiography, a school that had explicit affinities with the twelfth-century martyrographical movement. It too turned to past violence in order to create a narrative of cyclical, escalating tragedy ending in redemption. For the lachrymose school, Jewish history was a valley of tears, an itinerary marked by escalating sorrows whose end would be a tragedy so great that it would bring about redemption and return from exile. That the First Crusade chronicles were considered an outstanding monument in this valley is evident from Joseph ha-Kohen's extensive quotation from them in his history, titled "Valley of Tears" (*'Emeq ha-Bakha*). Their influence is detectable as well in his description of later events, such as the Iberian massacres of 1391. Joseph, a descendant of Sephardic exiles, underscored incidents of *qiddush ha-Shem* (sanctification of the divine name through suicide), claiming, for example, that many Jews killed their children during the massacres of 1391 or that a mother drowned herself and her daughters to avoid sexual intercourse with a Christian ship captain during the emigrations of 1492. Furthermore, he invoked these sacrifices as a supplement to divine memory, as when he wrote of the events of 1492: "We have not forgotten you nor betrayed your covenant. Now, Lord, do you not distance yourself. Make haste to save us. . . . For the love of your name!" Still, such influences should not be overemphasized. In his treatment of the events of 1096 the Sephardic chronicler Solomon Ibn Verga stresses the heroic *resistance* of the Rhineland Jews and mentions suicide only once; nor does he find "sanctification of the Name" in Iberia in 1391. Even under the black sun of double exile not all sixteenth-century Jewish historians found the First Crusade texts good to think with.[55]

54 In Hayim Hominer, ed., *Sefer Yosippon* (Jerusalem, 1965), 41, and quoted in Yerushalmi, *Zakhor*, 35. Sonne published a sixteenth-century Yiddish fragment of Solomon bar Samson in his "Nouvel examen des trois relations hebraïques sur les persécutions de 1096."

55 Joseph Ha-Cohen, *'Emeq ha-Bakha*, ed. Meir Letteris and Samuel Luzzatto (Cracow, 1895).

My point here is a simple, even an obvious one that does not require a deeper or more exhaustive survey of the reception history of First Crusade texts. There were clearly periods when the events of 1096 and the texts that commemorated them received little attention, while at other times these texts came to seem useful and relevant, that is, good to think with.[56] When First Crusade texts did seem important, there were still distinctions of genre: The poetic and liturgical texts seem to have had much more resonance than the chronicles and histories. And finally, even during these latter moments there were always many who, like Solomon Ibn Verga, preferred a different optic and would have sharply disagreed with Ben-Sasson's claim that these were the vessels of Jewish collective memory.

Such disagreement did not end with the birth of positivistic Jewish historiography in the nineteenth century. The practitioners of the new *Wissenschaft des Judentums* (Jewish Studies) were writing in the wake of Jewish "enlightenment" (*Haskalah*), emancipation, and assimilation. On the one hand, the First Crusade chronicles provided these authors with a rare historical source that could be fit between ancient and modern narratives in order to establish continuity between them. As Simon Schwarzfuchs put it, "these stories became history. . . . They also testified to the antiquity of Jewish settlement in Europe and transformed the Jews of the Rhine valley into Europeans. Overnight, the tragedy of the crusades became one of the high points in the entirety of Jewish history."[57] On the other hand, for many Enlightenment historians this was a history that had been, or should have been, left behind. Moritz Güdeman was typical in believing the memory of the First Crusade sacrifices to have been central to the survival of the Jewish people but pernicious in its influence on Judaism:

Everything that we now see and encounter among our people – the flight from the world, dejection of spirit, anxiety, petty-mindedness in matters of religion, superstition, and esotericisms – all these are products of that terrible time, which,

---

This is not the place to enter into a discussion of Sefardic responses to the persecutions of 1391, 1412–15, 1492, etc., though such an exploration is obviously of importance to my project.

56 There were other periods in which the First Crusade texts, particularly the piyyutim, became central, e.g., following the Chmielnicki massacres of 1648–49 in Poland. A fuller analysis would need to encompass these events and Jewish responses to them.

57 "The Place of the Crusades in Jewish History" (Hebrew), in Menahem Ben-Sasson et al., eds., *Culture and Society in Medieval Jewry: Studies Dedicated to the Memory of Haim Hillel Ben-Sasson* (Jerusalem, 1989), 266–7. I owe the quote to Jeremy Cohen's unpublished "A 1096 Complex?" 6–7. Cohen provides an overview of nineteenth-century historical attitudes toward the chronicles.

with repeated, periodic recurrences, has become deeply ensconced in their memory, never to be forgotten.[58]

It is in this context that we should understand Abraham Geiger's rather strained argument that the notion of merit accruing from human sacrifice so apparent in the First Crusade texts was an abomination that had entered Judaism only late and under the influence of Christianity. There was no collective, transhistorical guilt in Judaism, he claimed, no mediation of the individual's relationship with God and hence no notion that one person could be a "sin offering" for other people or other generations. In a liberal age confident of its progress, the Rhineland martyrs and their notions of sacrificial memory seemed at best a relic to be historicized.

THE HOLOCAUST AND THE FIRST CRUSADE

The events of the first half of the twentieth century, beginning with the Russian pogroms and the mounting German anti-Semitism that followed World War I and culminating in the Holocaust, shattered that confidence and transformed the First Crusade texts from vestigial archaism into living memory. Habermann's edition of the First Crusade texts, printed in Jerusalem in 1945–1946, clearly marks this transformation as it collapses the boundaries between the Middle Ages and the present, between prophecy and history, and adopts the language of its sources. In its opening words:

Our fathers were praised "because they cherished [times of] woe," and R. Simon ben Gamliel said: "we too cherish [times of] woe, but what are we to do, when we came to write them down we were not able" (Shabbat 13b). Israel's woes repeated over and over throughout the generations, and the later woes made them forget the earlier ones. Made them forget? That is unthinkable! Rather, they made them forget the need to record them or copy them down for the [later] generations, for surely there is nothing in this persecution but what was in the one before it, and one merely supplements the other. Indeed, it was a just decree from heaven, for those who were afflicted in those days, that weakened their will to write about purely historical things, and also dimmed their sense for historiography. (ix)

The historiographic effects of this transformation can be easily traced in the career of Fritz/Yitzhak Baer, a student of Heinrich Finke and

---

58 Moritz Güdeman, *Geschichte des Erziehungswesens und der Cultur der abendländischen Juden während des Mittelalters und der neueren Zeit*, 3 vols. (Warsaw, 1880–88; reprint, Amsterdam, 1966), 1:127–8. I again owe the quote to Jeremy Cohen, "A 1096 Complex?" 8.

Friedrich Meinecke at Freiburg and a founder of what is sometimes known as the "Jerusalem school" of Jewish history.[59] In his early work Baer set out to recover the Middle Ages as a formative period of Judaism. "There is nothing in our history," Baer wrote in 1930, "if we erase from its record one or two thousand years" [that is, the Middle Ages]. Baer adopted Leopold von Ranke's dictum that "every epoch is immediate to God" and applied it to a contextualized history of Judaism. In particular, Baer sought to reintegrate the history of Jews in medieval Christian Spain into a vibrant history of Judaism. Thus, in his early work on the Jews in medieval Spain, he argued against Heinrich Graetz's canonical view that this period was one of "increasing immiseration and decline" (*gesteigerten Elends und Verfalles*) for Jews. As he put it again in 1930, "We have been redeemed from the depths of collecting lists of authors and of persecutions and suffering."[60]

The late 1930s saw a sharp reversal. In a 1938 review of Salo Baron's antilachrymose *Social and Religious History of the Jews* Baer insisted, contra Baron, that "Jewish history in the Middle Ages was a relentless series of persecutions." But it is in *Galut* (exile), his somber meditation first published in National Socialist Berlin (1936), that we can clearly see the extent to which the focal points of Baer's historical consciousness have been realigned.[61] Baer's sense of rupture is evident from the title page, where for the first time there appeared his Hebrew name, Yitzhak, rather than the German Fritz. It is apparent, too, in his juxtapositioning of Spanish and German Jewry. The Spanish Jewish communities on which Baer had lavished his career and which he had previously upheld as exemplars of the vibrancy of medieval Judaism now represented a transhistorical example of the assimilationist betrayal of the Jewish spirit. It was their rationalist philosophical outlook and their materialism, Baer argued, that destroyed "the consciousness of Jewish unity." Baer's new heroes were the Rhineland martyrs of the First Crusade and their pietist successors, for in

---

59 The appearance of David N. Myers, *Re-Inventing the Jewish Past: European Jewish Intellectuals and the Zionist Return to History* (Oxford, 1995), has enabled me to amplify the reading of Baer I proposed in "Violence and the Persecution of Minorities in the Crown of Aragon: Jews, Lepers and Muslims before the Black Death," Ph.D. diss., Princeton University, 1992. See esp. 116–21 of Myers's study, on which I rely for many of the sources cited in this paragraph and the next.

60 For the quotes from Baer's 1930 Jerusalem lectures, see *Tkarim be-hakirat toldot Yisra'el: mavo litekufat yeme ha-benayim* (Jerusalem, 1930–31), 7, 15. His critique of Graetz is in *Die Juden im christlichen Spanien* (Berlin, 1936; reprint, London, 1970), 2:xxiv.

61 *Galut* (Berlin, 1936). I cite here from the English translation (New York, 1947; reprint, Lanham, Md., 1988).

their simple faith, he claimed, the essence of Judaism survived.[62] Finally, rupture is evident in Baer's shift from historical contextualization to redemptive teleology: "There is a power that lifts the Jewish people out of the realm of causal history." He commented again on this teleology in his *Israel Among the Nations*, this time with an emphasis on symbolic repetition and cyclicity: "Every episode in the long history of our people, every significant point in our historical existence, contains within it the secret of all previous and subsequent generations."[63]

For Baer (as for Habermann and many others), the First Crusade had become the significant past, "a momentous, catastrophic event" that presaged and helped to make sense of the present. Indeed, it is not too much of an exaggeration to say that these scholars saw themselves as fulfilling a role similar to that of Solomon bar Samson or Ephraim of Bonn. Responding in 1947 to a review of his book in the Catholic journal *Commonweal* that accused him of being anti-Christian, Baer replied (at the prompting of Hannah Arendt): "I wrote the book . . . out of the need to send . . . a word of comfort and emotional encouragement to my brethren, who saw before their eyes a terrifying death."[64] The book itself replicates tensions inherent in the First Crusade texts. For example, the chapter on "The Age of Crusades" closes with the penitential prayer I quoted earlier ("my question returns ever to the place from which it came"). The last chapter ("From the Ancient Faith to a new Historical Consciousness") echoes the prayer's nihilism: "The Galut [exile] has returned to its starting point." But then, like the Rhineland Jews, he confronts the unprecedented by marrying this cyclical nihilism to a redemptive narrative:

If we today can read each coming day's events in the ancient and dusty chronological tables, as though history were the ceaseless unrolling of a process

---

62 This was in some sense a reversal of nineteenth-century liberal assimilationist historiography, for whom the "Spanish period" was a model. See Maurice Kriegel, *Les Juifs à la fin du moyen âge dans l'Europe méditerranéenne* (Paris, 1979), 9. For the elaboration of Baer's views on the First Crusade massacres and the Rhineland pietists, see his "The Religious and Social Tendency of *Sefer Ḥasidim*" (Hebrew), *Zion* 3 (1938): 1–50; "The Persecution of 1096" (Hebrew), in M. D. Cassuto et al., eds., *Sefer Asaf* (Jerusalem, 1953), 126–40. For a lapidary statement of his view of Iberia as an assimilationist paradigm for which the sacrifice of the simple was the only antidote, see the last page of his *History of the Jews in Christian Spain*.

63 *Galut*, 120. *Yisra'el ba-'amim* (Jerusalem, 1955), 117. The latter formulation echoes Benjamin and Scholem, and may be Kabbalistic in origin. How curious that Baer never noted the Laplacean determinism inherent in the image, which seems to insist on causality rather than exclude it.

64 "Momentous catastrophic event" is from "The Persecution of 1096," 126. The 1947 response is discussed in Myers, *Re-Inventing the Jewish Past*, 119–20.

proclaimed once and for all in the Bible, then every Jew in every part of the Diaspora may recognize that there is a power that lifts the Jewish people out of the realm of all causal history. (120)

Galut is unusual in that at times it goes so far as to adopt the responses of the Rhineland Jews to the tragedies that beset them as its own. But it has distinguished company in discerning an affinity between Jewish responses to violence in the First Crusade and in the modern age. Shalom Spiegel's *The Last Trial*, a "commentary" on Ephraim of Bonn's "Akedah," was published to wide acclaim in Hebrew in 1950 and resonates strongly not only with the First Crusade texts but also with Freud's slightly earlier reconstruction of Jewish history in *Moses and Monotheism.*[65] It reconstructs Jewish responses to catastrophe by harkening back to ancient covenantal violences, in this case child sacrifices and their symbolic derivatives (castration, animal substitutes, etc.). It sees the memory of these violent events repressed but preserved as a type of archaic heritage: "[T]races . . . , age-old beliefs continued to nest in the thickets of the soul." And it sees the return of this repressed past in the midst of the massacres of the crusades, so that in a "fear-ridden" Ephraim of Bonn "there rose to the surface, from the hidden recesses of his soul," that dramatic reinterpretation of sacred history: "[The father] seized him [then] to slaughter him once more. Scripture, bear witness! Well-grounded is the fact."[66]

Spiegel's work differs from that of Baer, Dinur, Ben-Sasson and others in one important respect: He did not suggest an equivalence between First Crusade memories of violence and modern ones, nor did he ever valorize the responses he described or present them as crucial to the survival of Judaism in exile.[67] This has proved an unfashionable restraint. Most recent commentators tend to treat the First Crusade texts as representative of therapeutic, if not redemptive, transhistorical responses to trauma. Thus,

65 Spiegel's work first appeared as "The Legends of the Binding of Isaac: A Dirge on the Slaughter of Isaac and His Resurrection by R. Ephraim of Bonn," in *Alexander Marks Jubilee Volume* (New York, 1950), 471–547.

66 Although Spiegel never cites Freud, I am indirectly stressing the analogies between his work and Freud's (on which see below) in part because the parallels sharpen Freud's parapraxis about Abraham, as analyzed by Leonard Shengold, "A parapraxis of Freud in relation to Karl Abraham," *American Imago* 29 (1972): 123–59. The first quotation is on 77 (cf. 129), the second, from 138. Note that Spiegel, like Freud, attributes an important role to Christianity in stimulating this repression. See 82ff., 117.

67 See, for but one example from among many of the contrary approach, Haim Hillel Ben-Sasson's opinion in his contribution to the collaborative *A History of the Jewish People* (which he also edited): "martyrdom strengthened Jewry from within, enriched it spiritually, crystallized the concepts of 'honor' and 'heroism' among the Jews and *gave them the strength to face later trials*" (emphasis added). The work was first published in 1969. The quotation is on 414 of the English translation (London, 1976).

David Roskies argues that "Jewish collective memory has remained a vital resource, even in the modern era. Through their literature of destruction, Jews perceive the cyclical nature of violence and find some measure of comfort in the repeatability of the unprecedented."[68] Alan Mintz also sees in traumatic catastrophe the seeds of Jewish survival. For him, catastrophe is interesting not as destruction but as construction, the "reconstruction of [shattered] paradigms through interpretation" that he sees as "crucial to creative survival." The survival he has in mind is, of course, that of modern Jews, and for him the most useful paradigm for reconstruction is that of the Rhineland suicides: "From the retrospective vantage point of modern Hebrew literature, it was the vivid images of martyrdom on the Ashkenazic model which summed up the past to be espoused or rejected."[69] For Mintz and Roskies, as for Baer and many others, the assertion of a similarity between the First Crusade and the Holocaust is a prelude to a program of providing historical therapy for modern trauma; hence the emphasis on continuity of persecution and of experience, on what Roskies, surely aware of the psychoanalytic implications behind the paradox, calls "the repeatability of the unprecedented."[70]

TRAUMA, HISTORICAL MEMORY, AND THE IDENTITY OF THE PAST

The horrors of the early twentieth century transformed the relationship of Jewish historians to their past in such a way as to reveal to them a new identity between previous and present sufferings, an identity that turned the First Crusade texts into vital and therapeutic monuments of a collective Jewish historical memory. The theorizations of history and memory through which this identity was perceived, however, were themselves the product of the same transformations. One of the most influential of these theorizations, the Freudian concept of trauma, provides an important example because although medieval historians seldom turn explicitly to Freudian analysis, the vocabulary of trauma permeates, in a more-or-less technical sense, much modern commentary on Jewish responses to cata-

---

68 *The Literature of Destruction: Jewish Responses to Catastrophe* (Philadelphia, 1988), 4. Note that the equation of literature with collective memory is unexamined.

69 *Hurban*, x–xi. The First Crusade martyrdoms remain a flash point for debate. Witness the controversy stimulated by Israel Yuval, "Vengeance and Damnation, Blood and Defamation: From Jewish Martyrdom to Blood Libel Accusations" (Hebrew), *Zion* 58 (1993): 33–90. For a sample of the responses to this thesis, see the essays collected in *Zion* 59 (1994).

70 Cf. David Roskies, "Sholem Aleichem and Others: Laughing off the Trauma of History," *Prooftexts* 2 (1982): 53–77.

strophe and has been of tremendous importance in historical work on the Holocaust.[71] Violence is implicit in Freud's definition of traumas: "excitations from outside that are powerful enough to break through the protective shield [*Reizschutz*]." Traumatic events "provoke a disturbance . . . and . . . set in motion every possible defense."[72] These defenses seek to ensure the survival of the subject (whether an individual or a community) by restructuring an otherwise intolerable memory. The most basic defense is repression, a suppression of memory, but the repressed memory persists and manifests itself belatedly as repetitive intrusions into consciousness: the "return of the repressed."[73] This "return" is the most essential aspect of trauma: the repetition of the past in the present. The "return of the repressed" can be triggered by a "real repetition of the event," a retraumatization, but most often it takes the form of a "fixation," a "compulsion to repeat."[74] If these repetitions bring about recollection of the original suffering and heal memory of its traumatic excision, the process of repetition is called "working through." If, however, the repetition remains at the level of unconscious neuroses, it is called "acting out."[75] The role of the analyst is, of course, to encourage the more therapeutic route.[76]

---

71 The application of the concept of "trauma" in the historiography of modern Germany is extensive. For first hints, see Adorno's essay "Was bedeutet: Aufarbeitung der Vergangenheit" (1959), trans. and reprinted in Geoffrey H. Hartman, ed., *Bitburg in Moral and Political Perspective* (Bloomington, Ind., 1986), 114–30. For an influential psychohistorical study, Alexander and Margarete Mitscherlich, *The Inability to Mourn: Principles of Collective Behavior* (New York, 1975). There is an explosion of recent literature. See, e.g., Charles Maier, *The Unmasterable Past: History, Holocaust, and German National Identity* (Cambridge, Mass., 1988), 66, 139, 160–72; Saul Friedländer, *Memory, History, and the Extermination of the Jews of Europe* (Bloomington, Ind., 1993), 117–37; Dominick La Capra, *Representing the Holocaust: History, Theory, Trauma* (Ithaca, N.Y., 1994). For Holocaust survivor studies, see also Lawrence Langer, *Holocaust Testimonies: The Ruins of Memory* (New Haven, Conn., 1991). The approach has also been applied to film studies, most notably in Eric Santner, *Stranded Objects: Mourning, Memory, and Film in Postwar Germany* (Ithaca, N.Y., 1990). For its application to the film *Shoah*, see Koch, "Angel of Forgetfulness." See also Dominick La Capra, "Lanzmann's *Shoah*: 'Here There Is No Why,'" an unpublished paper presented at Rice University (1996) that inspired my approach in this chapter.

72 Sigmund Freud, *Beyond the Pleasure Principle*, in James Strachey, ed., *The Standard Edition of the Complete Psychological Works* (London, 1953–74), 18:29. See also "Introductory Lectures on Psychoanalysis (1916–17)," in ibid., 16:275. Trauma as a term has, however, been defined in a number of ways throughout the history of psychoanalysis. See Charles Figley, ed., *Trauma and Its Wake* 2 vols. (New York, 1985–6).

73 In *Moses and Monotheism* Freud gave the example of an accident victim, apparently unharmed, who after a period of "latency" develops "psychical" or "motor" symptoms, which Freud terms a "traumatic neurosis" (Strachey, ed., *Standard Edition*, 23:67–8).

74 *Moses and Monotheism*, 75, 95, 101.

75 *Ibid.*, 89. See especially Freud's "Remembering, Repeating, and Working-Through," *Standard Edition*, 12:150–54. This term has been frequently invoked in relation to the trauma of the Holocaust. An early example is Theodor Adorno, "Was bedeutet: Aufarbeitung der Vergangenheit" (1959). Most recently the distinction has become critical for Dominick La Capra and Saul Friedländer. References to their works are cited subsequently.

76 Thus, we might distinguish two levels of "survival." The repression and repetition of trauma is one; the reestablishment of a unity between this repetition and the originary event another,

In historical writing the concept of trauma has most often been applied to questions of violence against Jews. Freud himself did so most famously in his late work *Moses and Monotheism* (1939), where he applied the paradigm to a transhistorical collective, "the Jewish people." Freud located the foundational Jewish trauma in the slaying of the first Moses, itself a repetition of a prior trauma (the slaying of the founding father of *Totem and Taboo*) and a precursor of later ones, namely the slaying of Christ (in myth if not in reality) and the Christian hatred of Jews for their repression and denial of this triple deicide/parricide. Indeed, like Baer, Ben-Sasson, Roskies et al., Freud claimed that it was repeated trauma that "enabled the people of Israel to survive all the blows of fate" into their own day.[77] Freud's model of collective memory won few adherents, but the underlying analogy proved influential.[78] Just as a psychoanalyst uses the repetitive intrusions of the repressed into the conscious to work back to a trauma in a patient's past, so the psychohistorian looks for patterns of repetition in order to discover a foundational trauma or rupture. History becomes etiology, a search for the origins and progress of disease.[79]

Yet we should not forget the obvious: Freud's concerns, and in particular his model of the relationship between memory and violence (both in general and insofar as it applied to Jewish history), were very much the products of a particular time and place. Although the "Jewishness" of psychoanalysis has been a point of polemic since its inception, there is broad agreement (perhaps because Freud stated it explicitly) that Freud's view of Jewish history as the repeated return of a foundational trauma

---

"higher" one. This hierarchy is based on one of Freud's most problematic assumptions: that remembering the horrific is healthier than repressing it.

77 I say "in myth" because Freud himself did not believe that the Jews had killed Christ (*Moses and Monotheism*, p. 101). On Christian hatred of Jews being due to their repression of the deicide, see p. 90. It is almost too obvious to note that violence, and particularly family violence (the sacrifice, castration, or circumcision of sons by fathers, and the murder of fathers by sons), was intimately connected to foundational trauma in Freud's historical psychology. For the claim about survival, see 50–1.

78 Indeed, the model was outdated before it appeared. Freud seems to have formulated his "archaic heritage" (*Moses and Monotheism*, 98–102) in ignorance of Maurice Halbwach, *Les cadres sociaux de la mémoire* (1925). Freud also seems to have adhered to a Lamarckian view of psychological inheritance. See Sigmund Freud, *A Phylogenetic Fantasy: Overview of the Transference Neuroses*, ed. Ilse Grubrich-Simitis (Cambridge, Mass., 1987). To be fair, Freud himself never published the latter text, and in *Moses and Monotheism* he never claimed to be offering more than an analogy (70–2). See Yosef H. Yerushalmi, *Freud's Moses: Judaism Terminable and Interminable* (New Haven, Conn., 1991), 30. But cf. Sander L. Gilman's discussion of Freud's biological borrowings in *Freud, Race, and Gender* (Princeton, N.J., 1993).

79 The parallel importance of time, memory, and the past in history and psychoanalysis is often noted. Cf. Saul Friedländer, *History and Psychoanalysis: An Inquiry into the Possibilities and Limits of Psychohistory* (New York, 1978), 11.

was at least in part a response to mounting anti-Semitism and to the exile he himself experienced.[80]

Furthermore, the theory of trauma bears a strong family resemblance to a number of influential secular marriages of cyclicity and redemption put forward by other German-Jewish intellectuals living through the same events. Franz Rosenzweig's rejection of historicism, his turn to the idea of perpetual creation, revelation, and redemption, was one such cycle.[81] Walter Benjamin's theses on the philosophy of history, his dialectical messianism, and his distillation of history into focal points was another.[82] As a final example, this time drawn from an historian, consider Gershom Scholem's turn toward Lurianic Kabbalah. Lurianic Kabbalah was itself a "response by the Jews, albeit belated, to the series of traumatic events [surrounding] . . . their expulsion from Spain." It saw Jewish exile as an enacting of a trauma within the Godhead itself. In a sense it provided a mystical psychohistory, "a *biography* of God, recounting a catastrophe in the life of the Godhead and the slow, almost automatic overcoming of that catastrophe" through self-alienation.[83] This was the biography that Scholem rediscovered and rewrote in the middle decades of our century. Although for Freud the repressed returned only into the future, we might say that historians like Scholem and Baer (and Freud in the historical mode of *Moses and Monotheism*) were react-

---

80 On *Moses and Monotheism* as Freud's own response to trauma, see esp. Cathy Caruth, "Unclaimed Experience: Trauma and the Possibility of History," *Yale French Studies* 79 (1991): 188ff. Of course Freud applied the return of the repressed to Christian as well as to Jewish history, as in his analysis of German antisemitism (*Moses and Monotheism*, 54, 91–2), which he sees as a displaced "acting out" of the trauma of coerced baptism. Psychoanalysis was early on criticized as "Jewish science," as descriptive only of Jewish mentalities, and as a product of Jewish experience. There is a vast literature on the problem. See Gilman, *Freud, Race, and Gender*, 201–4, and his discussion of *Moses and Monotheism* on 181–5. An interesting but rarely quoted example of this "judaizing" critique is that of Sartre's draft script for John Huston's film "Freud" in *Le scénario Freud* (Paris, 1984). There Sartre expands Freud's self-analysis in "The Interpretation of Dreams" (Strachey, ed., *Standard Edition*, 4–5:197) in order to claim that the Oedipus complex stems from Freud's reaction to a violent antisemitic incident involving his father. Cf. G. Koch, "The Angel of Forgetfulness and the Black Box of Facticity: Trauma and Memory in Claude Lanzmann's Film *Shoah*," *History and Memory* 3 (1991): 119–34.

81 See *Der Stern der Erlösung* (Frankfurt am Main, 1921; reprint, The Hague, 1976). See also the commentary of Amos Funkenstein, "An Escape from History: Rosenzweig on the Destiny of Judaism," *History and Memory* 2 (1990): 117–35.

82 See esp. thesis no. 7, in *Illuminations*, where Benjamin brings together what he sees as a form of memory enjoined in the Torah with his dialectical messianism. Amos Funkenstein groups together Rosenzweig, Benjamin, and Scholem in "Gershom Scholem: Charisma, *Kairos*, and the Messianic Dialectic," *History and Memory* 4 (1992): 123–40. See, e.g., 135–6, where he talks of "three modes of messianism – that-which-has-always-been-eternally present (Rosenzweig), that-which-has-become-eternally-impossible (Benjamin), and that-which-has-now-become-possible (Scholem)."

83 Funkenstein, "Gershom Scholem," 131.

ing to the trauma of twentieth-century anti-Semitism by repeating it into the past.[84]

From this point of view it is easier to see why the First Crusade texts provide such an attractive site for the acting out of modern Jewish identities. To say this is not to imply either that Jews in the eleventh and twelfth centuries experienced catastrophe as Freudian trauma or that modern readers of medieval texts are suffering from it. My point is only that the explicit juxtaposition of First Crusade texts with the modern concepts and theorizations that condition their interpretation can help us to understand why these texts have become focal points for a historiography that asserts continuity in the experience of catastrophe. Such a juxtaposition can also help clarify certain aspects of a teleological tendency whose extreme form is a phylogenetic fantasy in which Jewish history becomes a search for the roots of Auschwitz: "For religion is linked with anti-Semitism, Genesis with genocide."[85] Finally, such a juxtaposition may tell us something about the modern concepts themselves, for as I suggested above, these sometimes reveal, in a secularized form, the influence of earlier ways of thinking about persecution and redemption.

One such concept that cannot be left unmentioned is, of course, Zionism. We have already seen how a scholar like Yitzhak Baer articulated his nationalist vision of a return to Zion through the exilic voice of the First Crusade texts. Baer and other historians argued for Zionism and against nonnationalist alternatives (which also had their historians) by emplotting Diaspora Jewish history as a cycle of repeated violence and persecution that was destined to be ended only by a redemptive return to a physical Jerusalem. Their vision of history as teleological process approached a form of secularized messianism, one that drew heavily on traditional theodicies and that often (as in the case of Baer) sought explicitly to transpose the sacrificial vocabulary of the Rhineland martyrologies into a nationalist key. In this sense, the identification of medieval and modern violences served to undergird a Zionist apologetic history, one whose academic power is still evident, for example, both in the neglect of medieval Sephardic history and in the extreme response of Israeli academics like Ezra Fleischer to Israel Yuval's revisionist article on the First Crusade martyrdoms.[86]

---

84 Of course these Jewish thinkers were heavily dependent on contemporary German philosophical thinking about, for example, eternal return. Nevertheless, it is their work that put the question of repetition, return, and continuity at the heart of the historiography we are interested in here.

85 Gavin Langmuir, *History, Religion, and Antisemitism* (Berkeley, Calif., 1990), viii.

86 Fleischer was responding to Yuval's 1993 article previously mentioned. He and others have accused Yuval, not only of faulty methodology, but also of promoting anti-Semitic and anti-Zionist slander.

But the consequences of this identification of past with present extend far beyond the bloodless realms of medieval historiography and into the world of political ideology. It facilitates, for example, the nationalization and secularization of religious models of martyrdom so as to promote, in the critical words of Yehuda Amichai, the sacrifice of the soldier/citizen "on the altar of the state."[87] Further, insofar as this model of history affirms the eternal status of the Diaspora Jew as victim, it can be used to arrogate moral impunity to the redeemed Jewish state.[88] It is no accident that, as Sidra Ezrahi points out, Israeli protest poetry in the wake of the Lebanese war ironically echoed marytrological literature. Her example is that of the poem "Yizkor," by Tzvi Atzmon, in which the Jewish nation, "exiled . . . persecuted . . . murdered . . . stoned . . . poisoned . . . burned . . . slaughtered . . . buried alive . . . gets up one morning, sees/ children shot while the sun was shining . . . Arab children."[89]

The mere possibility of such consequences reinforces the need for a genealogical understanding of violence and its memorialization that takes the difference between the past and present as seriously as it takes their kinship. This does not mean that we should abandon the study of sacrificial violence such as that of 1096. On the contrary, the simultaneous insistence on identity and difference inherent in sacrifice makes it a good parable for history and memory, for there is a continuum of identity and difference inherent in sacrifice just as there is in history itself.[90] At one

---

See his "Christian-Jewish Relations in the Middle Ages Distorted" (Hebrew), *Zion* 59 (1994): 267–316. Yuval's response is in the same volume: " 'The Lord will take Vengeance, Vengeance for His Temple': Historia sine ira et studio," 351–414.

87 *Pinkas patuah* (An Open Notebook) (Tel Aviv, 1979), 11: "al mizbeah hamedinah."

88 This does not mean that a critique of the teleological model of history necessarily constitutes an indictment of Zionism. Thus, while I agree with aspects of Amnon Raz-Krakotzkin's argument in "Exile within sovereignty: Toward a Critique of the 'Negation of Exile' in Israeli Culture" (Hebrew), *Teoriyah u-Vikoret* 4 (1993): 23–55), I also agree with Anita Shapira that such historiographic critiques do not tell us much about the moral valence of specific Zionist actions in the establishment of the state of Israel. See her "Politics and Collective Memory: The Debate over the 'New Historians' in Israel," *History and Memory* 7 (1995): 9–40.

89 "Revisioning the Past: the Changing Legacy of the Holocaust in Hebrew Literature," *Salmagundi* 68–9 (1985–6): 267. I have also benefited greatly from her *By Words Alone: The Holocaust in Literature* (Chicago, 1980), particularly chapter 5 on the legacy of Lamentations and chapter 6 on the covenantal context of Hebrew responses to the Holocaust.

90 At least this is the lesson I draw from Kierkegaard, whose historical distinction (made in *Repetition*) between premodern recollection and modern repetition ("recollection is the ethnical view of life, repetition the modern") should, I think, be linked to his meditation on the Akedah in *Fear and Trembling*. In the latter, he considered the repeatability of the Akedah. In the former, he posited a novel emphasis on repetition (which he opposed to hope and recollection) as a founding condition of modern metaphysics. The treatises were written concurrently and published simultaneously on October 16, 1843. The quote is from *Fear and Trembling/Repetition*, Howard and Edna Hong, ed. and trans., *Kierkegaard's Writings* (Princeton, N.J., 1983), 6:149; cf. 131–2.

extreme is the complete identification of sacrificer with sacrificed, an identification asserted by some of the martyrs of 1096 when they took their own lives. In the biblical Akedah, of course, it is a different principle that is proposed: that of substitutional identity. In place of himself, Abraham offers up what is most precious to him. The appearance of the ram takes substitution a step further. The ram can die for Isaac because the ram *is* Isaac, so much so that God swears to the equivalence.[91] And yet the ram is irreducibly *not* Isaac: In that miraculous and essential difference lies both Abraham's relief and ours.

91 In the words of Ephraim of Bonn: "I have accepted the sacrifice of your son; this is the word of the Lord – by My own self I swear it!" Translation from Carmi, *Hebrew Verse*, 382. Cf. Genesis Rabbah 56:9, where Abraham prays: "Master of the universe, regard it as though I had sacrificed my son Isaac first and only afterwards sacrificed this ram." In other traditions, God swears that the ram's ashes are Isaac's.

14

The Martyr, the Tomb, and the Matron

Constructing the (Masculine) "Past" as a Female Power Base

FELICE LIFSHITZ

The vitality of a culture or ideology depends upon its ability to channel the power of such mordant symbols as the corpse.[1]

THE FIGURE OF THE MARTYR AS AN HISTORICAL REPRESENTATION

This chapter discusses the gender dynamics surrounding one particular memorial practice: the cult of martyrs. Human decisions in the present are often influenced by beliefs concerning what has happened in the "past." Therefore, control over representations of the past can be a source of influence in society.[2] Furthermore, when the medium for representation of the past is the shrine tomb of a saint, the person who controls

Earlier versions of this chapter were presented before the American Historical Association (1995), at the University of Utrecht (1995), at the conference in Heidelberg, and at Florida International University (1996). Additional research was supported by the DAAD (1997) and the Humboldt Stiftung (1998) at the universities of Freiburg and Frankfurt. I would like to thank my hosts and their assistants: Johannes Fried, Gundula Grebner, Karl Weber, and Thomas Zotz. Kate Cooper provided initial bibliographical orientation in 1994, and the comments of Mayke de Jong, Giselle de Nie, Patrick J. Geary, Mitchell Hart, Richard Landes, Marco Mostert, Erika Rappaport, Beate Schuster, and Mark D. Szuchman have substantially improved my thinking about this essay. Philippe Buc and Jochen Martin read drafts of the chapter and provided incisive critiques. Finally, the comments of the anonymous readers for this book were extremely helpful.

1 Richard Huntington and Peter Metcalf, *Celebrations of Death: The Anthropology of Mortuary Ritual* (Cambridge, 1979), 211.

2 An excellent survey of the issues involved can be found in John R. Gillis, ed., *Commemorations: The Politics of National Identity* (Princeton, N.J., 1994); despite the exclusively "modern" focus of this volume, the essays are all nevertheless relevant to the period covered here. For "premodern" historical writing as commensurate with modern writing rather than as some separate, hopelessly theological historiography sui generis, see Ernst Breisach, "World History Sacred and Profane: The Case of Medieval Christian and Islamic World Chronicles," in Luther H. Martin, ed., *History, Historiography, and the History of Religions*, special issue of *Historical Reflections/Réflexions Historiques* 20 (1994): 337–56.

the monument (the place of memory) benefits from an additional source of power, in that holy corpses have been widely perceived as instrumental in the production of miracles.[3] Memorial practices connected with martyr cults involved construction in two senses: construction of the "past" in the guise of remembering it and construction of a physical shrine.

First, a few words about martyr cults in general. An indeterminate number of Christians were executed by Roman imperial authorities before the conversion of Emperor Constantine to Christianity early in the fourth century and his subsequent legalization of the new religion in 313.[4] Before the fourth century, Christians certainly cared about the fate of the remains of their executed relatives and friends, but (with extremely rare exceptions) neither established cults in their memory nor expected supernatural powers from them.[5] Yet, the fact that cults were eventually rendered to those "martyred" individuals tends to be treated by scholars as self-explanatory and even inevitable. Scholars have focused instead on explaining the roots of the act of martyrdom and the theological rationale for martyrdom;[6] meanwhile, general surveys of the veneration of saints skim over the development of martyr cults on the apparent assumption that little explanation or analysis is required.[7] An excellent sense of the inevitability normally ascribed to the development of elaborated martyr cults after the Constantinian conversion can be garnered from Hippolyte Delahaye, who considered the only change in martyr commemoration wrought by the legalization of

---

3 Two of the clearest available introductions to the subject of shrines as power bases are Peter Brown, *The Cult of the Saints: Its Rise and Function in Latin Christianity* (Chicago, 1981), and Benedicta Ward, *Miracles and the Medieval Mind: Theory, Record, and Event, 1000–1215* (Philadelphia, 1982).

4 For attempts to calculate a precise number, see Henri Grégoire, *Les persécutions dans l'empire romain*, 2d ed. (Brussels, 1964).

5 Evidence for this particular point was first assembled by Nicole Hermann-Mascard, *Les reliques des saints: Formation coutumière d'un droit*, Société d'Histoire du Droit, Collection d'Histoire Institutionelle et Sociale, no. 6 (Paris, 1975), 23–9; for a sophisticated and conveniently brief general sketch of the relations between saints and human communities through the fourth century, see Jochen Martin, "Die Macht der Heiligen," in *Christentum und Antike Gesellschaft* (Darmstadt, 1988), 440–74. Brigitte Beaujard has even recently insisted on the complete absence of any sort of saints' cults (to martyrs or nonmartyrs) in Gaul before the very end of the fourth century ("Victrice évêque de Rouen et le culte des saints en Gaule à la fin du IVe siècle," paper presented at the Colloque Internatonal: XVIe Centenaire de la Cathédrale Notre-Dame de Rouen, 396–1996, Dec. 1996, Rouen).

6 Hans von Campenhausen, *Die Idee des Martyriums in der alten Kirche* (Göttingen, 1936); Theofried Baumeister, *Die Anfänge der Theologie des Martyriums* (Munich, 1980); G. W. Bowersock, *Martyrdom and Rome* (Cambridge, 1995).

7 Arnold Angenendt, *Heilige und Reliquien: Die Geschichte ihres Kultes vom frühen Christentum bis zur Gegenwart* (Munich, 1994).

Christianity to have been the facilitation of a more public celebration of the illustrious dead.[8]

Despite the precedent of cults of the dead in antiquity, memorialization of the so-called martyrs was not inevitable. Although the practice of remembering persons who sacrificed themselves for a cause can be traced to numerous ancient non- and pre-Christian precedents, identifying the sources of martyr veneration does not answer the causal question of why that particular type of hero or heroine was chosen by some late-Roman Christians for cultural exploitation or how the memorialization of those martyrs functioned in late-Roman contexts. Furthermore, the fact that a theology of martyrdom was elaborated fairly early on by self-consciously Christian thinkers does not have to translate automatically from the realm of theory: To ascribe theological or cosmological significance to the act of self-sacrifice in imitation of Christ is not tantamount to establishing a cult of remembrance to the people who accomplished that act. To my knowledge, only Robert Markus and Philippe Buc have ever treated martyr cults as a contested feature of post-Constantinian historical consciousness, both in quite brilliant discussions concerning (respectively) the orthodox annexation of the past in the battle against the Donatists and the reading/remembering of the ritual execution of criminals under Roman law as Christian martyrdom.[9] This chapter continues that inquiry to cover other aspects of the commemorative dynamic, particularly by including a focus on gender politics.

Martyrs for the faith were not "natural" historical cult objects after the Constantinian conversion. Even the so-called protomartyr Stephen of Jerusalem, the major potential Greek bible model for martyr cults whose condemnation by the Sanhedrin and stoning by some Jews of Jerusalem is narrated in Acts 7, was the focus of no concerted historical memorialization until after the discovery of his body in 415.[10] In fact, only in

---

8 Hippolyte Delahaye, *Les passions des martyrs et les genres littéraires*, 2d ed., Subsidia Hagiographica 13B (Brussels, 1966), 133.

9 Robert Markus, *The End of Ancient Christianity* (Cambridge, 1990), 24, 86–100; Philippe Buc, "Martyre et ritualité dans l'Antiquité Tardive: Horizons de l'écriture médiévale des rituels," *Annales: E.S.C.* 48, no. 1 (1997): 63–92. The conclusions of the present chapter emphatically do not apply to the various North African churches (treated by Markus), where martyr commemoration clearly flourished from an early date and were so popular that, by the late fourth century, they apparently attracted not only Christians but Jews and non-Monotheists as well, a far cry from the contemporaneous conditions in Gaul or on the Italian peninsula; see Suzanne Poque, "Spectacles et festins offerts par Augustin d'Hippone pour les fêtes de martyrs," *Annales* 5 (1968): 103–5. A convenient guide to the sources is Maureen Tilly, trans., *Donatist Martyr Stories: The Church in Conflict in Roman North Africa* (Liverpool, 1996).

10 All the literary and documentary sources concerning the *inventio* are conveniently cataloged and discussed in Elizabeth A. Clark, "Claims on the Bones of Saint Stephen: The Partisans of Melania and Eudocia," *Church History* 51 (1982): 141–56. All of the − extremely scanty − visual evidence

the fourth century, when a consciousness of martyrdom as an historical act first developed, did memorializers realize that there must have been a chronologically *first* martyr; only then did the word "protomartyr" come into use in its current sense, and it was then applied to Jesus and Thecla as well as to Stephen[11] until Empresses Pulcheria and Eudocia (or perhaps the holy woman Melania the Younger) propelled Stephen's fame[12] beyond that of the female "martyr" Thecla. Furthermore, the prominence – indeed the dominance during the fourth century – of Thecla among the earliest commemorated "martyrs" itself thoroughly problematizes facile depictions of the beginnings of martyr remembrance; paradoxically, Thecla was, according to every known tradition, never in fact martyred at all but survived repeated attempts to execute her and died a peaceful death! Objects bearing Thecla's praying image between the lions who *refused to kill* her – such as glassware, oil lamps, and clay vials – were mass-produced as early as the fourth century.[13] The widespread popularity during the fourth century of a "martyr" who was not martyred, combined with the complete lack of any commemoration of the only later widely venerated "protomartyr" Stephen, indicates that martyr remembrance in the decades after the cessation of the persecutions did not develop in accordance with the preferred categories of twentieth-century scholarship.

We ourselves, fifty or so years after the end of World War II, are so surrounded by memorials to victims of persecution and have been so involved in remembrance of martyrs that it might seem "natural" for fourth-century Christians to have memorialized martyrs of the era before the Constantinian conversion and to have thereby depicted the era before it as one of persecution. But if such developments were "natural," there would be no place for history and no role for the historian – not now, and not in the fourth century.

An extremely high percentage of what is "known" about pre-Constantinian martyrs comes from the *Ecclesiastical History* by Bishop Eusebius of Caesarea,[14] whose plan in this monumental work was explic-

---

for the early memorialization of Stephen is cataloged and discussed by Eva Schurr, *Die Ikonographie der Heiligen: Eine Entwicklung ihrer Attribute von den Anfängen bis zum Achten Jahrhundert* (Dettelbach, 1997), 174–82. The virtual nonexistence of images for/to/of Stephen is the main theme of Schurr's discussion; none of the images that *do* exist present him as a "martyr" (rather than as a deacon) in any case.

11 Bowersock, *Martyrdom and Rome*, 75–7.

12 For the activities of Eudocia and Pulcheria, see Kenneth G. Holum, *Theodosian Empresses: Women and Imperial Dominion in Late Antiquity* (Berkeley, Calif., 1982), 103–11, 189, 196, 219; for the activities of those empresses and of Melania, see Clark, "Claims on the Bones."

13 Schurr, *Ikonographie*, 206–19.

14 Eusebius of Caesarea, *The History of the Church*, trans. G. A. Williamson and Andrew Louth (London, 1989).

itly to highlight three themes: proper apostolic succession in opposition to "heretics"; the calamities deservedly overwhelming the evil Jews; and the struggles of the Christian martyrs (beginning with Stephen), whose numbers he inflates well beyond his own evidence.[15] Eusebius's contribution, however, is not limited to inflating the numbers of martyrs but extends to his very interest in transmitting their memories at all. It is, in general, a sobering exercise to work through the manuscript evidence reported in Herbert Musurillo's classic collection of sources for "authentic" martyrs: Eight of the nine earliest Greek accounts of "authentic" martyred individuals or groups are attested primarily or solely through Eusebius.[16] Let us focus on the most important, most frequently cited, and supposedly earliest sources for pre-Constantinian martyr veneration.

The first (universally cited) evidence of martyrs specially remembered by Christian communities is the letter of the people of Smyrna (usually dated 155–167 C.E.) concerning the death of Polycarp. The report is transmitted by Eusebius, as well as in five manuscripts (dating from the ninth through the thirteenth centuries) whose texts are substantially identical to Eusebius's report. Although scholars tend to assume that Eusebius quoted an existing document, given the late date of the other manuscripts and the similarity of those manuscripts to Eusebius's version, the late manuscripts do not themselves constitute conclusive evidence of an independent transmission of the report; those manuscripts could just as easily have been derived from Eusebius, who "quotes" many other texts that are not considered by scholars to be authentic, such as the exchange of letters between Jesus Christ and Abgar.[17] In any case, recent linguistic analysis of the Polycarp letter has shown it to have been written no earlier than the late third century.[18]

The second (universally cited) "evidence" of martyrs being remembered by Christian communities is the report concerning the martyrs of Lyons and Vienne, for which Eusebius is the sole witness. In this case, it has recently been shown that Eusebius's "source," if he indeed had one, was itself a fictitious tableau and not a contemporary account and that, furthermore, Eusebius at the very least reworked his "source" rather than

---

15 Robert M. Grant (*Eusebius as Church Historian* [Oxford, 1980]), 26–7, 37, 124) underscores Eusebius's numerical exaggerations.

16 Herbert Musurillo, ed. and trans., *The Acts of the Christian Martyrs* (Oxford, 1972), xi–1.

17 Eusebius, *History of the Church*, 31–2.

18 Boudewijn Dehandschutter, "Hagiographie et histoire: A propos des actes et passions des martyrs," in M. Lamberigts and P. Van Deun, eds., *Martyrium in Multidisciplinary Perspective: Memorial Louis Reekmanns* (Leuven, 1995), 295–301.

merely quoting it.[19] Indeed, the blanket judgment of Boudewijn Dehand-schutter concerning all of the supposedly "authentic acts" of the martyrs published by Musurillo is that all represent later literary creations and that none goes back to an immediate desire to memorialize the period of persecutions or its hero(ine)s.[20] However, even if every single one of the extant, supposedly pre-Constantinian martyr accounts were both genuine and independent of Eusebius – which they are not – they would still amount only to a handful of texts for the entire Roman Empire, texts that, by Eusebius's own admission, had been ignored by other historians until he decided to incorporate them into his monumental history of "the church."[21]

The question here is not of denying the historicity or factuality of the events described by Eusebius, a perspective that is, for my purposes, irrel-evant; what is significant is that Eusebius was in a distinct minority in the decades immediately following the conversion, in that he considered it important to "remember" the persecutions and martydoms. Furthermore, despite his own attention to the martyrs of previous centuries, Eusebius betrays no knowledge of any active shrine cults to those very martyrs; indeed, he seems to exclude such cults from possibility![22]

Just as the early existence of literary monuments attesting to a lively interest in martyr remembrance no longer is taken for granted by liter-ary historians, so are the artistic monuments that were once considered evidence for early remembrance of martyrs being reinterpreted by art his-torians. For instance, eighteenth- and nineteenth-century scholars imme-diately submitted any images found in catacomb settings to a martyrial interpretation (when they did not outright lie about what they found in those catacombs), on the assumption that the remembrance of martyrs "naturally" must have been a thriving aspect of Christian practice from the earliest possible moment; by contrast, scenes once believed to depict martyrs being tortured are now seen as depictions of such mundane events as visits to dentists and optometrists.[23] Christian "collective memory"

19 W. L. Löhr, "Der Brief der Gemeinden von Lyons und Vienne: Eusebius h.e. v, 1–2 (4)," in Damaskenos Papandreu, eds., *Oecumenica et Patristica: Festschrift für Wilhelm Schneemelcher zum 75. Geburtstag* (Stuttgart, 1989), 135–49.
20 Dehandschutter, "Hagiographie et histoire." However, an argument has recently been made both for the authenticity and for the independence from Eusebius of the Greek account of the martyrdom of Pionius and his companions (Louis Robert, ed. and trans., *Le martyre de Pionios, prêtre de Smyrne* [mis au point et complété par G. W. Bowersock and C. P. Jones; Washington, D.C., 1994]).
21 Eusebius, *History of the Church*, 2.   22 Ibid., 122.
23 Fabrizio Bisconti, "Dentro e Intorno all'Iconografia Martiriale Romana: Dal 'Vuoto Figurative' all'Immaginario Devozionale," in Lamberigts and Van Deun, eds., *Martyrium in Multidisciplinary Perspective*, 247–53, 269–74.

(when judged by fourth-century pilgrimage accounts of the Holy Land) had no place for martyrs but was rooted in Jewish memories and connected with locales and personages of the Hebrew and Greek scriptures (particularly at their points of convergence).[24]

The argument was made long ago that even inhabitants of the city of Rome itself in the fourth century "knew" nothing about "their martyrs," with the possible exception of a few names and burial sites.[25] More recent research has raised questions about the degree of "certainty" that reigned concerning even these. When Bishop Damasus of Rome (366–384) decided to search the city's catacombs for martyrs, he had no idea where precisely within the miles of burial chambers to look, or for whom.[26] Having once decided where the true martyrs must have been, Damasus's interventions in the cemeteries of Rome were in fact massive; he marked a series of special graves by adding marble plaques to them, erecting more elaborate structures around them, or constructing hallways and staircases to (re)direct traffic through cemeterial areas to those graves. The overwhelming majority of Damasian selections correspond to no notable cultic hot spots; virtually all could have been random selections.[27] Furthermore, the content of the Damasian epigrams inscribed on the various plaques themselves betrays no knowledge concerning the figures commemorated. The empty monotony of the epitaphs has been variously interpreted as evidence of Damasus's lack of poetic talent and as part of his pastoral program to demonstrate the unity of the corps of the martyrs;[28] however, it also attests to a lack of current knowledge and thus of prior remembrance of the suddenly venerated figures.[29]

---

24 Maurice Halbwachs, *La topographie légendaire des évangiles en terre sainte: Etude de mémoire collective* (Paris, 1941), 61–2, 85–6, 175–7. Halbwachs places particular emphasis on the evidence supplied by the Bordeaux pilgrim of 333 ("Itinerarium a Burdigala Hierusalem usque et ab Heraclea per Aulonam et per urbem Romam Mediolanum usque," in Paul Geyer, ed., *Itinera Hierosolymitana Saeculi IV–VIII* [Prague, 1898]).

25 Albert Dufourcq, *Etude sur les Gesta Martyrum romains*, 4 vols. (Paris, 1900–10); a supplementary volume was later edited by François Dolbeau and published by the Ecole française de Rome in 1988.

26 Hermann-Mascard, *Les reliques des saints*, 127–8. For Damasus' commission to find and decorate martyr tombs, see E. Schäfer, *Die Bedeutung der Epigramme des Papstes Damasus' I. für die Geschichte der Heiligenverehrung* (Rome, 1932), and, now, Marianne Sagy, "Damasus and Roman Martyr Cults," Ph.D. diss., Princeton University, 1996.

27 The most recent comprehensive discussion of Damasus' activities argues that Damasus probably consecrated extant practices rather than innovating new ones, yet also consistently recognizes that a scrupulous treatment of the evidence does not permit us to push the importance of the various sites back beyond the pope's interventions (Jean Guyon, "Damase et l'Illustration des martyrs," in Lamberigts and Van Deun, eds., *Martyrium in Multidisciplinary Perspective*, 157–77).

28 Guyon, "Damase," 168–9.

29 The city of Rome may offer solid archeological evidence for local remembrance of one particular martyr, namely, Sebastian. See Elisabeth Jastrzebowska, *Untersuchungen zum christlichen Toten-*

At the very end of the fourth century, when memorialization of pre-Constantinian martyrs came to interest a wider range of people, the poet Prudentius lamented that no records of the martyrs survived for him to use; he suggested that a blasphemous soldier had deliberately destroyed records that must have existed.[30] Even the few examples of martyrial commemorative centers that Prudentius describes have recently been seen as poetic devices to aid the reader in the visualization of the martyrs' triumphs and not as actual descriptions of existing places.[31] In attempting to understand the development of martyr remembrance it should always be borne in mind that most Christians had not been martyred but rather had apostasized; until practically the end of the fourth century, commemoration of the victims of persecutions would have depended on actual survivors of those same persecutions, survivors who were probably struggling with their own psychological specters of guilt and self-hatred.[32] Apparently most people, Christians and non-Christians alike, were content to forget the sporadic persecutions.

The persecution of Christians before the Constantinian conversion had, in fact, been sporadic; despite the existence of anti-Christian legislation, that legislation remained largely unenforced, whereas churches had long been unofficially tolerated, and had become prosperous and powerful already in the third century, as well as possessed of large, recognizable *aulae ecclesiae* (places of assembly).[33] It therefore would have been possible and plausible to remember the pre-Constantinian situation as a period of religious toleration and calm, and it seems that many fourth-century Christians preferred to remember the past in that way.[34] The relative in-

---

mahl *aufgrund der Monumente des 3. und 4. Jahrhunderts unter der Basilika des Hl. Sebastian in Rom* (Frankfurt am Main, 1981). Unfortunately, the interpretation of archeological remains is extraordinarily problematic. A close reading of Hugo Brandenburg's *Roms frühchristliche Basiliken des 4. Jahrhunderts* (Munich, 1979), concerning the huge martyrial basilicas ostensibly erected around the Eternal City early in the fourth century, indicates not only that the dates of construction of the basilicas are open to question, but so also are their original purposes, which may well not have been martyrial or even Christian!

30 *Liber Peristephanon*, 1.73–7 in Prudentius, *Carmina*, ed. Maurice P. Cunningham (CCSL 126; Turnhout, 1966).

31 Bisconti, "Dentro e Intorno," 262–4.

32 Yoshiako Sato, "Martyrdom and Apostasy," in Harold W. Attridge and Goher Hata, eds., *Eusebius, Christianity, and Judaism* (Detroit, 1992), 619–34.

33 L. Michael White, *Building God's House in the Roman World: Architectural Adaptation Among Pagans, Jews, and Christians* (Baltimore, 1990), 111–39; W. H. C. Frend, *Martyrdom and Persecution in the Early Church: A Study of Conflict from the Maccabees to Donatus* (Oxford, 1965; reprint, Grand Rapids, Mich., 1981), 323–35; J. L. Creed, ed. and trans., Lactantius, *De mortibus persecutorum* (Oxford, 1984), xx–xxii.

34 The story of the "monumentalization" of martyrs' tombs is largely the story of the activities of Damasus of Rome, already discussed; otherwise, soundly attested basilicas or other sacred spaces dedicated to martyrs or constructed over martyr tombs are, for the fourth century, virtually non-

difference of most people to the memory of pre-Constantinian martyrs explains why there is so little overlap between the "historical" martyrs now recognized by scholars (such as Justin Martyr, ca. 165) and the figures who have been popularly venerated as martyrs as a result of later cultic inventions and promotions.[35]

The question must be asked of martyr cults as it is of other commemorative practices: Why would someone, after the Constantinian conversion, have wanted to keep alive the memory of the persecutions and embody the history of "church–state" relations in the figure of the martyr? The martyr image apparently functioned in different ways, depending on the circumstances of its utilization and its reception. In fact, the martyr was a successful embodiment of the past during the fourth century because it was multivalent, to use the language of semiotics. Martyrs were commemorated by a variety of individuals and groups, eventually including the imperial family itself, for a variety of reasons.

For Eusebius, a complicated but generally proimperial figure, remembering and writing about martyrs served multiple purposes, some of which were primarily theological.[36] For instance, the fact that people had been willing to die for Christ was, for Eusebius, a sign of Christ's immeasurable superiority over the prophets of old.[37] Eusebius's concerns were in many ways still apologetic, for Christianity at that time was hardly victorious over the other religions of the Roman Empire, including Judaism. Eusebius stimulated the commemoration of martyrs, a virtually

---

existent. For general surveys – which amount to discussions of Damasus – see Paul-Albert Février, "Martyre et sainteté," in Ecole Française de Rome, ed., *Les fonctions des saints dans le monde occidental (IIIe–XIIIe siècles)* (Rome, 1988); Victor Saxer, "Hagiographie et Archeologie des martyrs," and Louis Reekmans, "Récherches récentes dans les cryptes des martyrs romains," both in *Martyrium in Multidisciplinary Perspective*, 11–28, 31–70. The sole extant decorated martyr shrine which may date from the fourth century would have to be attributed to Ambrose of Milan, whose cultic orchestrations are the subject of the second half of this chapter; see Gilliam Mackie, "Symbolism and Purpose in an Early Christian Martyr Chapel: The Case of San Vittore in Ciel d'Oro, Milan," *Gesta* 34 (1995): 91–101.

35 For instance, one of the very earliest known extant genuine tomb epitaphs identifying a deceased person as a martyr is the funerary inscripton of Leucretia of Merida from the early sixth century. See E. Hübner, *Inscriptiones Hispaniae Christianae* (Paris, 1871), 19, no. 57, yet this "saint" does not appear in any of the historical martyrologies of the early Middle Ages, including the Iberian ones. See Jacques Dubois and Geneviève Renaud, eds., *Edition pratique des martyrologes de Bède, de l'Anonyme Lyonnais et de Florus*, IRHT Bibliographies, Colloques, Travaux Préparatoires (Paris, 1976) and Angel Fábrega Grau, ed., *Pasionario Hispánico*, Monumenta Hispaniae Sacra 6, 2 vols. (Madrid, 1955).

36 Glenn F. Chestnut, *The First Christian Histories: Eusebius, Socrates, Sozomen, Theodoret, and Evagrius*, 2d ed. (Macon, Ga., 1986), 77–83, 111–40, and Glenn F. Chestnut, "Eusebius: The History of Salvation from the Garden of Eden to the Rise of the Roman Empire," in Jacob Neusner, ed., *The Christian and Judaic Invention of History* (Atlanta, Ga., 1990), 77–101; see also Grant, *Eusebius*, 114–25, and Timothy D. Barnes, "The Constantinian Settlement," in Attridge and Hata, eds., *Eusebius, Christianity, and Judaism*, 437–42.

37 Eusebius, *History of the Church*, 11–12.

nonexistent practice at the time that he began writing; this was in part because such remembrance facilitated the expression of an anti-Jewish version of events. The bishop of Caesarea managed to depict centuries of martyrdom under the Roman Empire without blaming the empire or the ruling family for the bloodbaths. Imperial authorities (with the exception of the occasional demented emperor) were portrayed by Eusebius as Christian, as pro-Christian, or as restraining forces on anti-Christian violence, so that martyr remembrance never amounted to an indictment of Rome itself, the beloved Rome that Eusebius saw as a blessed political organism and an integral part of the Divine Plan.[38] Instead, Eusebius's martyrs were victims of evil imperial advisers, demons, idiosyncratic personal vendettas, vindictive local officials, popular mobs, and, above all, the plots of the bestial Jews.[39]

When Eusebius turned his attention to the role of the imperial courts themselves in the creation of martyrs, as he did in the closing books concerning the "Great Persecution," he presented the emperors as purgative instruments of the Divine Will, chastising Christians for the latters' own sins.[40] In some sense, therefore, those unfortunate persons who were actually martyred during the "Great Persecution" (to avoid casting aspersions perhaps, the historian only names three individuals) were themselves guilty and were only being properly punished! It is possible that personal anxieties influenced Eusebius's presentation of the recent "Great Persecution" as particularly providentially orchestrated; he himself had survived that persecution and was accused of having done so by cooperating with authorities.[41] The process of commemoration, rather than preserving the past, sometimes condemns to the past uncomfortable phenomena that the enshriner wishes either to forget or to remember only in limited, distorted ways.[42] Indeed, according to Friedrich Nietzsche, the very func-

38 Ibid., 80–2, 96, 112, 115–16, 151, 169–70, 198–9, 203, 206–7, 209, 226–8, 231, 250, 256–7.
39 At Polycarp's martyrdom, for instance, savage crowds "rushed to collect logs and faggots from workshops and public baths, the Jews as usual joining in with more enthusiasm than anyone" (Eusebius, *History of the Church*, 35–7, 58–61, 123–8, 133–4, 138–48, 169, 203, 208, 210–14; quotation on 121). Not only did the fact of having produced martyrs for Christ prove, for Eusebius, the truth of "orthodox" Christianity's claim of its founder's divinity, the fact that "heretical" Christians had not been "persecuted by the Jews or killed by the wicked . . . or whipped in Jewish synagogues or stoned" (162) was taken as invalidating the latters' truth claims.
40 Eusebius, *History of the Church*, 249, 257–8, 313, 318–19.
41 Grant, *Eusebius as Church Historian*, 123.
42 James E. Young, *The Texture of Memory: Holocaust Memorials and Meaning* (New Haven, Conn., 1993); Claudia Koonz, "Between Memory and Oblivion: Concentration Camps in German Memory," in Gillis, ed., *Commemorations*, 258–80. Thus, as is well known, Adolf Hitler intended to establish a museum of Jewish culture in Prague after the extermination of living Jews had been completed.

tion of the historian is forgetting,[43] and in his treatment of martyrs, Eusebius forgot at least as much as he remembered. Eusebius thus raised the profile of martyrs for the Christian faith when they might otherwise have been forgotten but also exercised preventive damage control lest the martyrs serve as rallying points against his beloved empire.

The polysemous martyr, in anti-imperial hands, could also function in a totally different manner from the complex Eusebian thematic. Lactantius, the only other early fourth-century historian (writing between 314 and 321) to discuss the period of persecutions, commemorated the tyrannical behavior of pre-Constantinian emperors who persecuted Christians. However, that persecution of Christians by Roman emperors formed but a small fraction of the Lactantian episodes describing the cruel butchery of Roman subjects-in-general by tyrannical rulers; more important, aside from the apostles Peter and Paul, not a single victim of state-sponsored religious persecution is remembered by name, let alone graced with a commemorative date, in Lactantius's narrative, indicating that he was unconcerned with memorializing the persecuted.[44] Lactantius wrote in the centuries-old aristocratic, prosenatorial, anti-imperial historiographical tradition that portrayed the emperors as bloodthirsty enemies of republican liberty.[45] The fact that the vast majority of the narrative is devoted to political and military history indicates that Lactantius was primarily interested in painting a negative portrait of the persecutors, a project for which the persecution of Christians was helpful but incidental.[46] Lactantius was not trying to foster the positive memory of "martyrs" (a term he does not use) but rather the negative memory of some particularly nasty emperors.[47]

Another function of martyr cults as historical representations probably was to help detach the loyalties of Christian citizens from (persecutory) Roman imperial power and to refocus those loyalties on alternative communities and leaders. An illuminating parallel may be found in a nineteenth-century politico–literary form: the historical romance novel. Historical romance novels played a central role in the creation of nationalist-patriotic consciousness during the nineteenth century in Europe, Latin America, and the United States; by grounding the fulfillment of

---

43 Hayden White, *Metahistory: The Historical Imagination in Nineteenth-Century Europe* (Baltimore, 1973), 350.

44 Lactantius, *De mortibus persecutorum*.   45 Creed, ed., Lactantius, p. lx.

46 As Creed writes: "No other Christian work from the period concerns itself so much with the purely political and secular events of its time" (xli).

47 *De mortibus persecutorum* I.7, ed. Creed, 4–5.

heterosexual desire in the framework of the nation-state, romance novelists (many of whom were politicians comparable to Eusebius) produced in their readers a passionate desire for and love of the nation-state.[48] Modern patriotism, according to Benedict Anderson, was constructed against a nonterritorialized "Christendom";[49] indeed, Delahaye long ago alluded to a certain symbolic equivalence between a Christian martyr and a "national" (gentile) foundation hero.[50] It therefore may not be going too far to suggest that martyr *passiones* (easily assimilable to ancient Greek romance novels, the literary form that they seem to have superseded),[51] in which the state executed some of its citizens – sometimes precisely because they did not desire to engage in procreative romance – contributed to detaching loyalties from the Roman Empire and funneling them toward other communities, such as the *ecclesia*. This political dimension surely was more than an unintended consequence of the shift during late antiquity from the Roman ideal of marital concord, with its concomitant obligation of procreation, to the Christian ideal of childless virginity, recently sketched by Kate Cooper.[52]

The final example concerns the city of Rome itself. Even there, the spur to martyr commemoration came only with the pontificate of Damasus, who also was – and surely not incidentally – the first bishop of Rome to try to establish the Roman bishopric as independent of the imperial court and as primatial in the Latin provinces.[53] The role of martyr commemoration in the creation of the Roman papacy, especially under Damasus, Leo I (440–461), and Gelasius (492–496) deserves a special study but is well beyond the scope of this chapter.[54] Clearly, one main target of the representation of the past embodied in the Damasian marble plaques – plastered as they were in large numbers all over, and particularly under, the city of Rome – was the imperial court. The repetitiveness of the inscriptions has already been noted. One of the most frequently repeated hemistichs in the bishop's repertoire involved praising

---

48 Doris Sommer, *Foundational Fictions: The National Romances of Latin America* (Berkeley, Calif., 1991); Benedict Anderson, *Imagined Communities: Reflections of the Origin and Spread of Nationalism*, 2d ed. (New York, 1991); Michel Foucault, *History of Sexuality: An Introduction*, trans. Robert Hurley (New York, 1980).

49 Anderson, *Imagined Communities*, 19.   50 Delahaye, *Passions*, 172.

51 Five ancient Greek romance novels dating from the first century B.C.E. to the sixth century C.E. are extant; see B. P. Reardon, ed., *Collected Ancient Greek Novels* (Berkeley, Calif., 1989).

52 Kate Cooper, *The Virgin and the Bride* (Cambridge, Mass., 1996).

53 Jochen Martin, *Spätantike und Völkerwanderung*, 2d ed. (Munich, 1990), 131.

54 Previous work on the subject took an entirely different approach; see, e.g., Michael Borgolte, *Petrusnachfolge und Kaiserimitation: Die Grablegen der Päpste, ihre Genese und Traditionsbildung* (Göttingen, 1989), and Michael Borgolte, "Papstgräber als 'Gedächtnisorte' der Kirche," *Historisches Jahrbuch* 112 (1992): 305–23.

the memorialized individual for having acted *contempto principe mundi* (with contempt for the prince of the world).[55] Previous scholarship has identified the *princeps* in question as the devil; however, it is hard to imagine a fourth-century Roman who would not also think of the imperial *princeps* when confronted with a reference to the prince of the world. Indeed, if late fourth-century martyrs were in fact being remembered for such activities as refusing imperial commands to sacrifice to the Roman deities, they would then literally have been celebrated as persons who acted bravely in contempt of the imperial *princeps*.

BISHOP AMBROSE AND THE MARTYR SHRINES OF FOURTH-CENTURY MILAN

Despite the importance of Eusebius and Damasus in disseminating the memory of Roman martyrs, it was not post-Constantinian male bishops who invented the tradition of venerating individuals said to have been killed by imperial authorities. After all, venerating a martyr to imperial tyranny in an imperially supported episcopal church could arouse "cognitive dissonance," whereas remembering such historical figures in an "unofficial" venue would have been much more logical and plausible.[56] In fact, a series of late-Roman women invented the practice, beginning in 295. Among the scholars who have discussed the practice of martyr memorialization during the fourth century, only Peter Brown has explicitly noticed the preponderance of women among early martyr commemorators.[57] Perhaps the greatest contribution of Brown's seminal work on the Christian cult of saints was to demonstrate that late-Roman bishops did not oppose the nascent martyr cults as "superstitious" and "pagan" but rather that they vigorously appropriated those pre-existent cults, wresting the control of martyr shrines from enterprising matrons at a time when such cults were still few and far between, and that the bishops then promoted the martyr cults with the greatest possible energy.

---

55 Guyon, "Damase," 169.
56 The likelihood of cognitive dissonance of course did not completely prevent the controlled instrumentalization of martyr cults by pro-imperial figures such as Eusebius.
57 Brown, *Cult of the Saints*; Martin Heinzelmann, *Translationsberichte und andere Quellen des Reliquienkultes*, Typologie des Sources du Moyen Age Occidental, no. 33 (Turnhout, 1979), names the two great innovators in practices connected to martyr relics as Lucilla of Carthage (20) and Asklepia of Salona (25). Hermann-Mascard likewise only names women as "unofficial" or "private" proprietors of relics (*Les reliques des saints*, 316).

Unfortunately, the episcopal appropriation of martyr cults was so successful that no clear evidence remains concerning how precisely the late-
Roman matrons utilized the image of the martyr. I would guess, however,
that fourth-century matrons were eager to remind their contemporaries of
the central and heroic roles played in early-Christian times by persons who
were not necessarily ecclesiastical office-holders. Furthermore, I suspect
that building a power base around (overwhelmingly male) figures from the
historical past permitted late-Roman matrons to divert attention from
their own persons and comportment and thus circumvent the potentially
paralyzing effects of both oxymoronic, bifurcated ideals of feminine behavior and misogynistic charges of stereotypically negative feminine traits.[58]
I argue that the martyr cults were the basis on which late-Roman matrons
retained some measure of status as religious leaders, even at a time when,
following the Constantinian conversion, their positions in the Nicene/
episcopal Roman church were being progressively restricted.

Let us turn to Milan in the time of Bishop Ambrose, the moment of
episcopal appropriation of martyr tombs.[59] In 385 Ambrose found himself
embroiled in a short-lived but fertile controversy with Monica, the
mother of Augustine, future bishop of Hippo. The conflict was made
famous by Augustine himself in his *Confessions*.[60] Ambrose had decided to
oppose the martyr commemorations (*refrigeria*) that were being held in
the cemeteries outside Milan, in the first known attempt to prevent what
seems to have become a regular rite among Christian women. According
to Augustine, Monica – theretofore a devotee of martyr commemorations
– easily capitulated before Ambrose's superior wisdom and agreed to
abandon the practice of memorializing martyrs by drinking wine at their
gravesites.[61] Nevertheless, I believe that it was Ambrose who was most

58 For some feminist analyses of the ways in which ideals of behavior created obstacles to women's
    attainment and exercise of authority, see R. Howard Bloch, *Medieval Misogyny and the Invention of
    Western Romantic Love* (Chicago, 1991), and Arlene W. Saxenhouse, "Introduction," Amy Richlin,
    "Julia's Jokes, Galla Placidia, and the Roman Use of Women as Political Icons," and Suzanne
    Dixon, "Conclusion: The Enduring Theme: Domineering Dowagers and Scheming Concubines,"
    all in Barbara Garlick, Suzanne Dixon, and Pauline Allen, eds., *Stereotypes of Women in Power: His-
    torical Perspectives and Revisionist Views*, Contributions in Women's Studies, no. 125 (New York,
    1992), 1–9, 65–91, 209–15.
59 For the precise locations of all the edifices and events connected with Ambrose's activities, see
    the discussion and series of clear maps and charts by Marco Sannazaro, "Considerazioni sulla
    topografia e le origini del cimeterio milanese ad martyres," *Aevum* 75 (1996): 81–111.
60 Augustine, *Confessiones* VI.2 (CC 27 or CSEL 33).
61 My interest in gender and commemoration of the dead around tombstones began quite suddenly
    in 1987 in a Jewish cemetery on Long Island, N.Y., during a dispute between my Polish-born
    mother and the rabbi officiating at the unveiling of my grandfather's tombstone. The dispute con-
    cerned whether it was licit for my mother to serve sponge cake and kosher wine to those in
    attendance at the ceremony, with the repast to be consumed on the newly unveiled memorial

enlightened by the controversy with Monica, an event that evidently caused the Milanese prelate to realize the importance some people placed on the commemoration of martyrs. He soon realized how useful the martyr could be as an historical image.

In 385 and 386 Ambrose (by that time a dedicated Nicene-Homoiousian Christian leader) also confronted more formidable enemies: the Gothic, Homoian (or "Arian") courtiers and bureaucrats at the Milanese imperial court[62] (and perhaps also the Empress Justina herself), who actively supported the Homoian Christian communities of Milan.[63] Suddenly, at the precise moment of his most heated conflict with the imperial court and immediately after his disagreement with Monica, Ambrose began removing corpses – which he identified as martyrs – from cemeteries; this after a lifetime of complete indifference to martyrs[64] and in contravention of a new imperial constitution expressly forbidding the exhumation and translation of corpses.[65]

June 17, 386, is the date of Ambrose's famous invention of the brothers Gervasius and Protasius. Ambrose suddenly accepted and began

stone. In the end, the rabbi stormed out and my mother performed the ritual; however, in 1993, at the unveiling of my grandmother's tombstone, my mother declined (to my great disappointment) to perform the ritual and permitted the rabbi to control the entire ceremony. Because I am a historian of the "Christian Middle Ages," I have been led to investigate versions of this controversy far removed from the episodes that sparked my initial curiosity. Nevertheless, I recount the incidents here in the hope that those more competent in twentieth-century U.S. history will consider a study of such contemporary practices.

62 Neil B. McLynn, *Ambrose of Milan: Church and Court in a Christian Capital* (Berkeley, Calif., 1994), 170–4.

63 An excellent and thorough recent discussion is found in Daniel H. Williams, *Ambrose of Milan and the End of the Nicene–Arian Conflicts* (Oxford, 1995).

64 Shortly before this cemetery transfer, which will be discussed subsequently, Ambrose began his career as a manipulator of dead bodies by moving the relics of some *apostles* of unknown provenance, perhaps Andrew, John, and Thomas, into the basilica Romana, a cemetery church in Milan. However, Ambrose never publicized his first corpse manipulation, nor do other contemporary commentators make very much of it. The short-lived attempt to establish bodies of apostles as an episcopal power base and as a focus of historical memory turned out to be a false start; Ambrose himself would wipe out the brief "apostolic" phase of the structure in 395, when he would invent the body of the martyr Nazarius from a local garden and, with all pomp and circumstance, move that corpse to the erstwhile basilica of the apostles, afterward known as S. Nazario. Finally, it may be that the transfer of the apostles' relics did not even happen until 395, immediately before the invention of Nazarius; in that case the invention of Gervasius and Protasius in 386 would mark Ambrose's first ever foray into cultic orchestration of any type. See Enrico Villa, "Il Culto agli Apostoli nell'Italia settentrionale alla fine del secolo IV," *Ambrosius* 33 (1957): 246–8; Ernst Dassmann, "Ambrosius und die Märtyrer," *Jahrbuch für Antike und Christentum* 18 (1975): 52–3; and McLynn, *Ambrose of Milan*, 227–35.

65 For the imperial legislation, including that of Theodosius in 386, see Hermann-Mascard, *Les reliques des saints*, 30–2. According to Hermann-Mascard, the Theosodian constitution (*Cod. Theod.* IX.17.7) technically only applied to the eastern provinces of the empire until the promulgation of the Theodosian Code in 439; the prohibition is treated as having been in force in Milan by Dassmann ("Ambrosius und die Märtyrer," 57), and by McLynn (*Ambrose of Milan*, 213).

to publicize the lives, passions, and deaths of these martyrs, whose bodies he had found in a Milanese cemetery (whence he removed them). In the early 390s, Ambrose then went to Bologna and found the corpses of Agricola and Vitalis in a Jewish cemetery. He then brought some of those relics to Florence, others he took home with him to Milan. Back at Milan in the mid-390s he discovered the bodies of the martyrs Nazarius and Celsus. Meanwhile, he undertook to distribute fragments of martyrs' bodies to other episcopal centers. Out of nowhere, and indeed after a lifetime of indifference to martyr cults and at the moment of his greatest battle against imperial authority, Ambrose suddenly began to dig up, with some regularity, evidence that the Roman Empire persecuted good, true Christians, and to disseminate that evidence throughout the Latin church.

Rudolf Schieffer has warned against reading Ambrose's relations with the imperial court through the lens of later "church–state" controversies, such as the Gregorian Reform movement of the late eleventh century. For instance, on the grounds that Ambrose was rooted in, and therefore would have accepted, the Roman tradition of imperial authority, Schieffer argues that the famous conflict between Ambrose and Theodosius should not be taken as an attempt on Ambrose's part to diminish imperial authority in any way and that Ambrose's claims to exercise penitential discipline over Theodosius were pastoral and individual, not political or ecclesiological.[66] I argue that Ambrose was able to look beyond the limited horizons of Roman governmental traditions. Ambrose was a man whose views evolved dramatically over time, even with regard to his stand on the Nicene-Arian question.[67] Certainly Ambrose began his *cursus honorum* rooted in Roman governmental traditions, but his conflict with Empress Justina in 385–386 would certainly have eroded his willingness to continue accepting the full range of "religious" authority traditionally attributed to the imperial court. The very fact that Ambrose invented Roman martyrs with such regularity during the late 380s and early 390s – precisely the time of his 390 conflict with Theodosius – indicates that he did intend to effect some diminution of imperial authority. No matter how much scholars may dispute the degree of straightness of the line "from Milan to Canossa," the current consensus holds that Ambrose did aim to locate the imperial family within "the church" rather

66 Rudolf Schieffer, "Von Mailand nach Canossa: Ein Beitrag zur Geschichte der christlichen Herrscherbusse von Theodosius d. Gr. bis zu Heinrich IV.," *Deutsches Archiv* 28 (1972): 333–70.
67 Williams, *Ambrose of Milan*.

than over it,[68] and martyrs surely helped in that regard. The image of the past that could so effortlessly be put forward through the figure of the martyr was precisely what Ambrose needed to help delegitimize imperial control over matters "ecclesiastical."

It has long been recognized that Ambrose's sudden interest in relics played a key role in his battles with the imperial court.[69] Indeed, Ambrose himself,[70] Augustine,[71] and Ambrose's biographer Paulinus[72] all tell us as much, but none of them say how the martyr image aided in Ambrose's power politics. The scholarly consensus is that the invention of Gervasius and Protasius helped Ambrose by validating his Homoiousian-Nicene position as "true" (as opposed to the Homoian-Arian position of the imperial court) simply by producing miracles for Ambrose. But if all Ambrose needed was miracles-in-general, he could have gotten them from numerous sources, from objects connected with Christ, the crucifixion, the apostles, the Virgin Mary, and so forth. He did not need to discover martyrs. Furthermore, as Ernst Dassmann has pointed out, it was Paulinus and the authors of later pseudo-Ambrosian works who emphasized and multiplied the miraculous events that supposedly surrounded the *inventio*; Ambrose himself made little of the miraculous.[73]

Ambrose appropriated a specific, content-laden historical image when he appropriated martyr cults, not just any miracle-producing relics.[74] A

---

68 Martin, *Spätantike und Völkerwanderung*, 211–12. For the most recent argument that the bishop of Milan fully intended to reshape imperial rulership in limiting, even subordinating ways, see Sarah Hamilton, "A New Model for Royal Penance? Helgaud of Fleury's *Life of Robert the Pious*," *Early Medieval Europe* 6 (1997): 189–200.

69 A partial listing of authors who have discussed how Ambrose profited politically in his anti-Arian struggle from his relic invention: Otto Seeck, *Geschichte des Untergangs der antiken Welt* (Stuttgart, 1922), 5:207 (who even went so far as to claim that Ambrose fabricated the discoveries in order to profit from them); Dassmann, "Ambrosius und die Märtyrer," 56; Vincenza Zangara, "L'Inventio dei corpi dei martiri Gervasio e Protasio: Testimonianze di Agostino su un fenomeno di religiosità popolare," *Augustinianum* 21 (1981): 119–33; and Williams, *Ambrose of Milan*, 9–10, 218–22.

70 Ambrose preached a number of anti-Arian/ anti-Justina/ anti-Jewish sermons in concert with his martyr corpse manipulations, and then sent a letter to his sister Marcellina describing his sermons and battles. These battles were battles against the practices of women, such as Monica and Justina. See Ambrose, Epistula 75 [22] (*Bibliotheca Hagiographica Latina* 3513) in *Sancti Ambrosii Epistulae* CSEL 82/3 (1982), 126–40.

71 Augustine (*Confessiones* IX.7) writes that God revealed the martyrs' relics to Ambrose in order to thwart the fury of a woman (Justina) and to prevent her from further persecuting the Catholic church. The bishop of Hippo also discussed the discovery of the relics in two later sermons on Stephen and on Gervasius and Protasius (Sermons 286 and 318 in PL 38 coll. 1297–1301 and 1437–40). Augustine was in Milan at the time of the invention of Gervasius and Protasius, but was not himself present at or an eyewitness to the events (Zangara, "L'Inventio dei corpi," 124).

72 Paulinus of Milan, *Vita di S. Ambrogio: Introduzione, testo critico e note*, ed. Michele Pellegrino, Verba Seniorum, n.s. 1 (Rome, 1961), chap. 32–3.

73 Dassmann, "Ambrosius und die Märtyrer," 59–61.

74 This does not mean that Ambrose treated martyrs exclusively as historical object lessons in how imperial power can run amok. On at least one occasion, he used the martyr Sebastian pastorally

concrete example: He presented the very opportunity to stand up to worldly powers, which martyrs such as Sebastian had enjoyed, as highly desirable at any time:

But God also suffered persecutors, that is, the powers of this world, to arise, but those who conquered in Christ did not vanish. Who at that time did not say, weak: "Lord, why have you given your people to a persecuting power?" Yet who today would deny that those who suffered are more blessed than those whom no tortures of the persecutors have vexed?[75]

Ambrose specifically and purposefully invoked the inspirational historical model of ancient martyrs who had resisted the "potestates saeculi" because they could be exploited in his own battles against those persecuting powers in 385 and 386. As he himself described it, the struggle in those years was to limit imperial "potestas"; witness his description of the basilica controversy:

I myself am being called on by counts and tribunes, so that a timely transfer of the basilica might take place; they are saying that the emperor is only making use of his own right, for all things are in his power. I answered, if he wanted something from me that was my own, this is, my landed property, my money, anything of mine of this sort, I would not refuse; indeed, all things that are mine belong to the poor. But those things that are divine are not subject to imperial power.[76]

Then, just as he was seeking to limit the "potestas" of worldly princes in some spheres, he suddenly discovered comrades-in-arms (his *propugnatores*, the martyrs Gervasius and Protasius, "not soldiers of the world but soldiers of Christ") who had actually stood up to worldly "potestas" in the past often enough to deserve to be called princes themselves: "Whom else ought we to consider as princes of the people if not the holy martyrs?"[77]

A consideration of the precise locations of the Ambrosian cemeterial inventions and interventions renders particularly clear the fact that the

---

as a symbol of courageous resistance to the myriad temptations in the average person's life (*PL* 15 col. 1497–1500).

75 Original: "Sed et persecutores Deus, id est, potestates saeculi est passus assurgere; ne decessent qui vincerent Christo. Quis tunc non dixit infirmus: Domine, cur dedisti plebem tuam in potestatem persequentium? Sed quis hodie neget beatiores illos esse qui passi sunt, quam illos quos nulla vexarunt supplicia persecutorum?" (PL 15 col. 1397).

76 Original: "Convenior ipse a comitibus et tribunis, ut basilicae fieret matura traditio, dicentibus imperatorem iuro suo uti, eo quod in potestate eius essent omnia. Respondi, si a me peteret, quod meum esset, id est, fundum meum, argentum meum, quidvis huiusmodi meum, me non refragaturum; quamquam omnia quae mei sunt, essent pauperum; verum ea quae sunt divina, imperatoriae potestati non esse subjecta" (Epistle XX, PL 16 coll. 996–7).

77 Epistle XXI, PL coll. 1021–2.

bishop not only was challenging imperial control of sacred spaces but also was simultaneously asserting episcopal control of politically key spaces. The previous sentence was cast in the vocabulary of late twentieth-century American English; full understanding of the fourth-century Milanese dynamic thus requires a clarifying statement: At the time there was no distinction between a sacred and a politically key space. Ambrose acted within and appropriated to himself an extended, interconnected area of western Milan and its adjacent extramural suburbs that already formed a sacro-political complex: the imperial palace, the circus/hippo-drome complete with imperial tribunal, and the cemetery *ad martyres*, with its multiple (often pre-Christian) structures and the imperial mausoleum. The importance of the precise location of Ambrose's invention of Gervasius and Protasius in 386, namely, within the heart of the imperial sacro-political complex of Milan, was underlined by Marco Sannazaro: Ambrose clearly intended to redefine an urban space theretofore marked by imperial ideology.[78] I would add that, in order for him to lay conceptual claim not only to the martyrial burial spot itself but also to the adjacent circus-prison-tribunal complex, he needed to discover martyrs; only martyrs could provide the conceptual link through the walls of the city from the extramural cemetery into the circus, the site of public assemblies, imperial pageants, and Roman-era imprisonments, agonies, and martyrdoms.

By gaining direct control over the corpses and their shrines, the bishop of Milan could improve his ability to control the way the historical image of the martyr was interpreted by onlookers. The Roman matrons who theretofore had presided over the martyrs' tombs could not necessarily be counted on to emphasize the persecutory excesses of the Roman imperial state. They were much more likely instead to explain the historical significance of the martyrs as testimonies to the importance of noncon-secrated, nonpriestly, nonoffice-holding Christians in the heroic age of Christian beginnings. But somewhat divergent interpretations of the historical significance of the martyr figure (for the matrons, antiepisco-pal/official and possibly anti-imperial, for Ambrose, simply anti-imperial) was not the only reason Ambrose wanted to appropriate the matrons' tomb shrines.[79] More was at stake in fourth-century Milan than a con-

---

78 Sannazaro, "Considerazioni sulla topografia," 102.

79 Various formulations besides "appropriation" have over the years been suggested to describe what precisely the bishops such as Ambrose did when they seized martyrial relics and shrines thereto-fore under the control of nonepiscopal (including female) commemorators, as well as to describe what the nonepiscopal commemorators themselves were doing. Describing the former process,

venient vision of the past; there also was a conflict over the organization
and constitution of the church in the present.

It cannot be emphasized enough how uncertain the constitution (as it
were) of "the" Christian church was in the fourth century, and indeed in
many centuries to come. That bishops already controlled the Latin churches
in the third and fourth centuries is too often asserted without being demonstrated.[80] To uncritically align oneself with bishops (such as Ambrose) who
claimed to control the churches, and who eventually perhaps did come to do
so, is to ignore the implications of the challenges constantly posed to episcopal authority by "heretics" (that is, persons hereticated by bishops), wander-
ing charismatic holy figures, and so forth. Those who opposed the (Catholic)
bishops were not necessarily mere schismatics or factional leaders but were
indeed questioning the general constitution of the church.[81] At least since
the publication of Brown's *The Cult of the Saints*, historians have been aware
of the fact that the constitution of an episcopally organized Latin church in
late antiquity was, in large part, precisely a function of the successful
exploitation of tomb power bases by bishops. This insight must be explored
more thoroughly, and with attention to gender.

Most historians now recognize that Ambrose did not innovate in adher-
ing to the cult of martyrs in the first place, but rather that he copied a
number of matrons. But why stop there? Let us return to Milan in June
of 386, where Ambrose had just built a new basilica. On June 19 he dedicated that basilica in what is usually described as a novel way, that is, by
moving into the structure the dead bodies of the martyrs Gervasius and
Protasius, which he had just "invented" in the cemetery. According to
ecclesiastical historians, until June 19, 386, all churches had been dedicated by a eucharistic sacrifice and a dedicatory prayer.[82] But what is a
church, and what is a church dedication?

McLynn wrote of "renationalization" (*Ambrose of Milan*, 234); describing the latter process, Dassmann ("Ambrosius und die Märtyrer," 55) and Brown (*Cult of the Saints*, passim) wrote of "pri-
vatization." I avoid such labels, for they are inapplicable (and indeed misleading when so applied)
to fourth-century Milan. For a sense of the thorny difficulties raised by scholarly utilization of
such terminology, see Peter Van Moos, "Die Begriffe 'Öffentlich' und 'Privat' in der Geschichte
und bei den Historikern," *Saeculum* 49 (1998): 161–2.

80 E.g., Martin, "Die Macht der Heiligen."
81 Richard Landes, *While God Tarried* (forthcoming), promises to provide an eye-opening panorama
    of the extent to which the official, episcopal leaders of the Christian churches constantly found
    their authority challenged and doubted.
82 Dassmann, "Ambrosius und die Märtyrer," 54. Heinzelmann claims that in the fourth century
    there were two kinds of churches: genuine *ecclesiae* or community churches and *martyria* or mere
    burial churches. The situation began to change when Ambrose's contemporary Damasus, bishop
    of Rome, began to attach (male) clergy to the *martyria*, turning them into real community
    churches (*Translationsberichte*, 26). We should perhaps not be so quick to assume that the martyria
    provided no focus for community worship.

Until now, the ecclesiastical historiography on martyr memorialization has departed from and operated on set theological definitions of Christian practice that are anachronistic to the fourth century, when constitutional details of Christian ecclesiology were still inchoate; those definitions tend to exclude female-led ceremonies, a priori, from consideration. For instance, Victor Saxer writes that what makes a cult a martyr cult (and therefore Christian) and not a dead cult (therefore pagan) is the presence of the bishop; by definition, if there is no bishop present, then a celebration is not communal and therefore is a mere familial celebration.[83] Bernhard Kötting has a similar a priori definition buttressed not by historical evidence but only by theological rationale. According to Kötting, a cult is a mere "cult of the dead" and is only about familial remembrance unless it is a "real" martyr cult; by definition, a "real" martyr cult is a celebration of someone who was a witness and imitator of Jesus Christ. A "real" martyr who imitated Christ therefore can only be properly remembered with a eucharistic celebration. Therefore, a martyr can only be properly remembered by a priest, and it is the presence of the priest that defines a community celebration.[84] Within the extant historiography of martyr cults, cultic sites associated with women have to be treated, by definition, as private, familial, and domestic simply by virtue of their association with women.

Assumptions about gender have prevented scholars from seeing the full range of cultic strategies that Ambrose appropriated from his female rivals. Although Kötting, for instance, recognized (before any other scholar did) that Ambrose possessed ulterior motives for associating martyr relics with his own episcopal person, namely, to increase the prestige of the sacer-

---

83 Victor Saxer, *Morts, martyrs, reliques en Afrique Chrétienne aux premiers siècles: Les temoignages de Tertullien, Cyprien, et Augustin à la lumière de l'archéologie africaine*, Théologie Historique 55 (Paris, 1980), 116.

84 Bernhard Kötting, "Die Tradition der Grabkirche," in Karl Schmid and Joachim Wollasch, eds., *Memoria: Der geschichtliche Zeugniswert des liturgischen Gedenkens im Mittelalter*, Münsterische Mittelalter–Schriften 48 (Munich, 1984), 71. Elsewhere, he argues that a martyr cult without a Eucharist falls by definition in the realm of "der verwandschaftlichen Pietät und der Familienreligiösität" (Bernhard Kötting, *Der frühchristliche Reliquienkult und die Bestattung im Kirchengebäude* [Cologne, 1965], 9), although at no point does he show that actual family members were being commemorated. Like Heinzelmann and Hermann-Mascard (see note 57 to this chapter), he attributed the first real development of martyr commemoration to the matron Asklepia, who constructed the first known full-scale martyr-based mausoleum, but relegated the development to the realm of "private Initiative" (*Der frühchristliche Reliquienkult*, 14). This earlier – and at the time groundbreaking – study remains a crucial contribution to the field, particularly insofar as both legal issues and the late ancient "pagan" background to Christian relic cults are concerned. However, Kötting's foundational studies of martyr commemoration were written from within a particularly sexist frame of mind; e.g., Kötting actually denied the historical existence of female martyrs beyond the famous Perpetua and Felicitas (62–4).

dotal office by solidifying a symbolic complex Christ-altar-martyr-priest, he never suspected that Ambrose's priestly power plays might have been directed *against* anyone, such as nonsacerdotal (including female) rivals![85] There is a telling story of the experience of female religious leaders even in the late twentieth century. A female minister, having conducted a funeral, later heard several (female) attendees lamenting that no minister had been present so that there could be a "proper" funeral; instead, the lamenting women complained, "some woman just got up there and did the talking – it was the darndest thing!"[86]

Perhaps, given that it was no innovation to venerate a martyr, it also was no innovation to consecrate a community church through the installation of martyrs' bones. Perhaps that liturgical ceremony in itself already was a current practice, a practice of the matrons who controlled the ceremonial martyr churches, when Ambrose appropriated it. Fourth-century matrons clearly performed the ritual of transferring martyrs' remains into structures that then hosted commemorations of the martyrs in question. What, precisely, prevents us from reading these rituals as church consecration ceremonies? Matrons have not been recognized as belonging in the category of persons who consecrate churches, so their ceremony for consecration has been, a priori, excluded from consideration as such. Their churches, likewise, have not been recognized as churches but rather have been given a series of other names, such as *memoriae*.

Women have long been recognized as active financiers and builders of public buildings (including churches) on the Italian peninsula;[87] yet the idea that women actually led the religious communities centered in the buildings they constructed has not been (to my knowledge) considered. Elizabeth A. Clark has amassed substantial evidence of female religious patronage in the fourth century; she concluded: "Excluded from the

---

85 Kötting, *Der frühchristliche Reliquienkult*, 29.

86 Elaine J. Lawless, "Writing the Body in the Pulpit: Female-Sexed Texts," *Journal of American Folklore* 107 (1994): 65–6. With that in mind, consider the complaint of Rufinus that Ambrose's rival Justina was going around Milan rousing sentiment against the Nicene bishop by "chattering in the churches" ("Garrire in ecclesiis"; Rufinus, *Historia Ecclesiastica* 2.15 [PL 21 coll. 523–4]).

87 Bryan Ward-Perkins, *From Classical Antiquity to the Middle Ages: Urban Public Building in Northern and Central Italy, A.D. 300–800* (Oxford, 1984), 8, 12, 54, 56–7, 71, 79–90, 236–45. Women apparently acted as major "builders" elsewhere in the Mediterranean world in the period as well; see Cándida Martínez Lopez, "Influencia social de las mujeres en las ciudades de Hispania meridional," in A. Lopez, C. Martínez, and A. Pociña, eds., *La Mujer en el mundo mediterráneo antiguo* (Granada, 1990), 229–36. A fascinating and suggestive work for those interested in female control of early Christian churches (from the era of house churches through the *domus ecclesiae* to the *aula ecclesiae* forms) even after the Constantinian imposition of the (official) basilical form on Christian assembly places, is White, *Building God's House*.

Christian priesthood as well as from secular office, elite women of late antiquity enjoyed fewer routes to prestige and power than did their male peers. . . . Thus, the dramatic increase in religious patronage in the fourth century gave women a new avenue for benefaction with its concomitant honor."[88] However, the fact that elite women were excluded from the imperially recognized episcopal ecclesiastical structure does not necessarily mean that all inhabitants of the newly Christianized Roman Empire accepted either the episcopal churches or women's exclusion from them. Scholars simply have too often aligned themselves with the eventually triumphant episcopal position; and so it has not been perceived that Ambrose sought to crush rival community leaders, not "overmighty patrons."[89]

The possibility that female (and nonclerical male) controllers of martyr shrines were in fact Christian community leaders must be considered in light of how much recent scholarship has argued for the existence of female religious leaders in early Christianity.[90] From the days of the apostle Paul, women such as Prisca (Priscilla) had been hosting churches in their houses at Corinth, at Ephesus, and (even before Paul himself arrived) at Rome (Acts 18:2–4; 1 Cor. 16:19; Rom. 16:5). Such traditions of assembly and worship could not have simply evaporated overnight in the fourth century, with the conversion of the imperial family to Christianity. Furthermore, there is no reason that they should have, given the fact that Roman women already played official roles (such as that of Vestal Virgin) in non-Christian religions of the empire.[91]

Paulinus, Ambrose's biographer, describes Ambrose's invention of Gervasius and Protasius in these terms: The problem in 386 was that so many people constantly flocked to the *memoria* where Felix and Nabor were commemorated and did not realize that underneath that structure lay the bones of Gervasius and Protasius, whom everyone had forgotten but who were in fact the most important historical martyrs of Milan. Accordingly, Ambrose exhumed Gervasius and Protasius, and with great ceremony took them to the new Ambrosian basilica and announced that

---

88 Elizabeth A. Clark, "Patrons not Priests: Gender and Power in Late Ancient Christianity," *Gender and History* 2 (1990): 253–73.

89 The latter formulation is that of Brown, *Cult of the Saints.*

90 Elizabeth Schüssler-Fiorenza, *In Memory of Her: A Feminist Theological Reconstruction of Christian Origins* (New York, 1983); Wayne A. Meeks, *The First Urban Christians: The Social World of the Apostle Paul* (New Haven, Conn., 1982); cf. Bernadette Brooten, *Women Leaders in the Synagogue* (Chico, Calif., 1982).

91 I owe this point to Jochen Martin, in private conversation.

the newly dedicated structure should thenceforth be the focal point for the veneration of Milanese martyrs.[92] Ambrose himself mentioned Felix and Nabor in sermons and composed a hymn to them;[93] therefore, he accepted the "fact" of their sanctity. So if the martyrs were genuine and their shrines accessible, what was wrong with their – highly popular – cult, wrong enough to motivate Ambrose to exhume the "forgotten" Gervasius and Protasius from beneath Felix and Nabor?

I suggest that the martyr churches of Milan posed a serious problem for Bishop Ambrose because they formed the power bases of rival religious leaders; those religious leaders were primarily Roman matrons (excluded from the hierarchy of the episcopal church), but I do not discount the possibility that a number of men also led commemorative services at nonepiscopal martyr shrines. The so-called *memoria* (I would say "church") of Felix and Nabor was a foundation by the matron Savina, who had deposed the martyrs' bodies in the cemetery and constructed a tomb.[94] Another nearby *memoria* to the martyr Victor still bore the name of its presumed founder, Fausta.[95] Both of these churches were soon to be overshadowed by Ambrose's massive Milanese basilicas. The shrines of Saints Felix, Nabor, and Victor have rightly been called "casualties" of Ambrose's construction campaigns.[96] Yet more than buildings were lost, and Ambrose triumphed over more than the Homoian-Arian party through his relic manipulations: The year 386 was a signal date in the process of creating an episcopal monopoly in Christian worship that excluded a number of actual and potential rival religious leaders. Ambrose's vigorous activities in that year, when he turned his back on a lifetime of rejecting martyr memorialization, can best be explained by recognizing the extent of the threat posed to his own position by Roman matrons and their tomb-centered communities. A number of late-ancient matrons were able to exploit the fact that no social or legal restrictions

92 Paulinus, Vita Ambrosii, 14. For a recent full account of this curious decision to dig under the memoria of Felix and Nabor, see McLynn, *Ambrose of Milan*, 209–19.

93 Alessandro Caretta, "Nabore e Felice," BSS IX coll. 689–93; Ambrose, *Explanatio Evangelii secundum Lucam* VII.178, CCSL XIV (Turnhout, 1957), 275–6; M. Simonetti, *Innologia Ambrosiana* (Alba, 1956), 7–9, 56–9.

94 Daniel Papebroch, "Gervasius et Protasius," *AASS* June III (Antwerp, 1701), 818.

95 Dassmann, "Ambrosius und die Märtyrer," 54; Antonio Rimaldi, "Vittore" BSS XII coll. 1274–5. While Ambrose rather dramatically dug under Felix and Nabor in order to neutralize that site and to identify Gervasius and Protasius as the "true" workers of miracles that had occurred there, he also "marked" the church of St. Victor by leaving the newly invented relics in that locale during a two-day vigil before moving them into Milan (Ambrose, Ep. 75 [22], CSEL 82/3). It is possible that the Fausta in question was the empress, wife of Constantine and daughter of Maximianus, whose residence had been in Milan (Sannozaro, "Considerazioni sulla topografia," 100).

96 McLynn, *Ambrose of Milan*, 226–7.

barred them from caring for and remembering the dead in order to become leaders of religious communities.

Neither Ambrose nor any other fourth-century bishop actually managed to definitively block female access to shrine-tombs as power bases. Indeed, the martyr relics of Vitalis and Agricola, which Ambrose brought to Florence in 394, ended up in a basilica built by the widow Juliana.[97] The relics of Vitalis and Agricola, which Ambrose himself brought to Milan from Bologna, left the city in 409 (along with the relics of Gervasius and Protasius) in the hands of Galla Placidia, who established a church for them in Ravenna.[98] The augusta Pulcheria used the relics of Stephen as a major power base for her politico-military policies in the late 410s and early 420s, when she established a chapel to Stephen in Constantinople.[99] Even the cult of Gervasius and Protasius was first exploited outside Milan and Ravenna by a woman, the matron Vestina, who built a church in Rome for the martyrs in the time of Innocent I (402–417).[100] It is unclear whether any of these shrines should be thought of as rival, nonepiscopal community churches.

After the fourth century, gender politics continued to be a factor in struggles over control of the dead bodies of significant martyrs. Indeed, the first known legal attempt to "reclaim" a body of a saint from its burial place was directed by the bishop of Clermont against the female community of Saint Pierre de Lyons.[101] But there are examples of a con-

---

97 Dassmann, "Ambrosius und die Märtyrer," 58.

98 Gian Domenico Gordini, "Vitale e Agricola," BSS XII coll. 1225–8. In Ravenna, Vitalis came to be identified as the father of Gervasius and Protasius, and the husband of Valeria; see subsequent discussion.

99 Kenneth G. Holum and Gary Vikan, "The Trier Ivory: Adventus Ceremonial and the Relics of St. Stephen," *Dumbarton Oaks Papers* 33 (1973): 128–32. Although Holum and Vikan's interpretation of the ivory itself is being vigorously challenged by Hans-Christoph Noeske's work in progress, the augusta's connection with Stephen in general would not be affected.

100 Ward-Perkins, *Urban Public Building*, 66; Dufourcq, *Etude*, 1:121; Gordini, "Vitale e Agricola"; Antonio Rimoldi, "Gervasio e Protasio," BSS VI coll. 298–302. The church in question is S. Vitale in via Nazionale. Furthermore, the church of St. Stephen in the via Latina in Rome, built by Leo I (440–61) was financed by Demetria Anicia (Ward-Perkins, *Urban Public Building*, 66). The dedication of another Roman church, founded in the fourth century by Fasciola, is not known (Dufourcq, *Etude*, 1:171).

101 Hermann-Mascard, *Les reliques des saints*, 336. Such battles for control of martyr relics continue today. Another early spur to this project was a 1994 visit to the Shrine of the Alamo in San Antonio, Texas, where the then-current controllers of the shrine, the Daughters of the Republic of Texas, were being challenged for control by the state government. The terms

sciousness of gender as an issue in connection with martyr corpses much closer to the ground I have already covered. The first example concerns the *revelatio Stephani*, presented by its author as an eyewitness account of the discovery of Stephen's relics in 415, and generally accepted by scholars as a late ancient text. In all versions of the accounts, only men (including male emperors) are shown as ever having had anything to do with the remains of the saint – a depiction that contrasts sharply with current scholarly understandings of the roles of empresses such as Eucheria and Pulcheria in Stephen's memorialization. Indeed, the men shown controlling the deacon's body in the *revelatio* make a particular point to emphasize in their accounts that the wife of the primary handler of the corpse had refused to convert to Christianity and had left her husband, therefore having had no contact with the body. That treatment of the gender issue, however, is subtle compared to the next example.

A late fifth- or early sixth-century pseudo-Ambrosian, synthetic account of all the martyrs invented by the bishop of Milan makes the gender-and-dead-bodies theme central to its depiction of events.[102] The pseudo-Ambrosian letter includes a *libellus*, quoted in full and ascribed to a certain Phillip. Phillip's putative *libellus* begins with the assertion that he and his son were the ones who originally took possession of and buried, in their own home, the bodies of Ambrose's most famous inventions, Gervasius and Protasius.[103] The author of the pseudonymous Ravennese tract considered it more important to assert that the bodies in question had been, from the moment of martyrdom, in male hands than to make any other preparatory point. Later in the work, when Saint Vitalis (supposedly the father of the twins Gervasius and Protasius and another of Ambrose's relic finds)[104] dies, his wife Valeria comes to claim his body, but the Christians of the area prevent her from taking the corpse of her martyred husband. She keeps trying and at the same time has visions telling her to

of the conflict were publicized at the shrine itself, and it is clear that a number of gender stereotypes (such as that women exploited the shrine only for their private benefit) were being pressed into service by representatives of the state of Texas. Some aspects of the controversy are discussed in Holly Beachly Brear, *Inherit the Alamo: Myth and Ritual at an American Shrine* (Austin, Tex., 1995). For the discussion that follows, see "Revelatio Sancti Stephani (BHL 7850–6)," ed. S. Vanderlinden, *Revue des etudes byzantines* 4 (1946): 192–200.

102 Pseudo-Ambrose, *Inventio et passio Gervasii et Protasii* (BHL 3514) in PL 17 coll. 742–7, written in the late fifth or early sixth century at Ravenna; see F. Savio, "Due lettere falsamente attribuite a s. Ambrogio," *Nuovo Bullettino di archeologia cristiana* 3 (1897): 153–77, and Michel Aubineau, "Jean Damascène et l'*Epistula de Inventione Gervasii et Protasii* attribuée à Ambroise," *Analecta Bollandiana* 90 (1972): 1–14.

103 "Ego servus Christi Philippus intra domum meam sanctorum corpora, quae cum filio meo rapui, sepelivi" (PL 17 col. 744).

104 Giovanni Lucchesi, "Vitale, Valeria ed Ursicino," BSS XII coll. 1229–31.

relent. Still she persists until finally Vitalis himself appears to her and says, "Do not molest me, woman, for you can never prepare for me a sepulchre as glorious as the one that the lord Jesus Christ has commanded to be made for me."[105] The fifth- or sixth-century Ravennese author of the pseudo-Ambrosian work was apparently disturbed by the fact that, despite Ambrose's efforts at the end of the fourth century, matrons still managed to use tombs for their own cultic purposes.

The most famous example of a female sponsor of a (male) martyr cult is Saint Genovefa of Paris, who in the fifth century established (against the opposition of the male clergy of Paris) a shrine to Dionysius as her power base; Dionysius's original tomb was even said to have been built by the matron Catulla.[106] Suzanne Wittern has recently argued that Genovefa exercised much less authority in the city of Paris than might seem to be the case when judging by a superficial reading of her *vita*.[107] However, Wittern completely ignores the possibility that the basilica of Dionysius in and of itself may have been a source of power for Genovefa; had she taken such a possibility into account, she might have been more willing to see the virgin of Paris as an authoritative figure. Precisely to what extent women could bolster their own noninstitutional/nonofficial power through control of powerful (male) dead bodies deserves further exploration.

PROBLEMATIC: WOMEN AND THE SEXIST CASTING OF THE *CHORUS SANCTORUM*[108]

Although specific percentages are impossible to determine, it is clear that "historically" or "factually" speaking, both female and male martyrs were available for memorialization after 313; it has even been argued – albeit by a nonspecialist – that 73 percent of those who suffered or sacrificed themselves to some degree for their Christian beliefs before the Con-

---

105 "Noli mihi molesta esse, mulier, quia numquam mihi tam gloriosum poteris parare sepulcrum, quale mihi Dominus Jesus Christus fieri jussit" (PL 17 col. 745). Male control of burials is a leitmotif in the work, which includes multiple deaths and entombments. The first is the burial of the martyr Ursicinus, killed at Ravenna by the judge Paulinus and then buried by Vitalis. It was Vitalis's decision to bury Ursicinus that began his family's fatal involvement with Roman state authorities.

106 For full references to all the relevant sources, see Martin Heinzelmann and Joseph-Claude Poulin, *Les vies anciennes de sainte Geneviève de Paris* (Paris, 1986).

107 Suzanne Wittern, *Frauen, Heiligkeit und Macht: Lateinische Frauenviten aus dem 4. bis 7. Jahrhundert* (Stuttgart, 1994), 67, 84–7.

108 Cf. Jane Tibbets Schulenberg, "Sexism and the Celestial Gynecaeum," *Journal of Medieval History* 4 (1978): 117–34.

stantinian "turn" were women.[109] Eusebius, the first large-scale memori-
alizer of historical martyrs, fully integrated women into his heroic depictions, sometimes lavishing particularly effusive praise on female martyrs.[110]
However, it will not have escaped most readers that the martyred figures
around whom elaborate memorial practices developed in late antiquity
were overwhelmingly male. All the female-sponsored martyr shrines discussed in this essay were centered on male heroes, beginning with the
most famous one, the shrine of the protomartyr Stephen. Stephen's female
sponsors also promoted the memory of other male martyrs: Eudocia composed an 800-line poem on the martyrdom of Saint Cyprian,[111] and both
Pulcheria and Melania commemorated Lawrence and the forty soldier-
martyrs of Sebaste.[112] It therefore seems that when late-ancient women
constructed martyrial power bases for themselves, they preferentially
selected male figures for that purpose.[113]

Thus, influential women in late antiquity seem to have actively labored
to represent the past as male or to highlight males as historical agents
while ignoring available and equivalent female heroines. Both parallels and
contrasts to the apparent late-antique pattern can be found. One might
compare how the almost exclusively female labor force of art museums
has consistently depicted the "artist" as male and relegated the works of
female artists to storage basements or worse.[114] By contrast, during the

---

109 Arthur Frederick Ide, *Martyrdom of Women: A Study of Death Psychology in the Early Christian
     church to 301 C.E.* (Garland, Tex., 1985), 7. For specialist treatments, see Frederick C. Klawiter,
     "The Role of Martyrdom and Persecution in Developing the Priestly Authority of Women in
     Early Christianity: A Case Study of Montanism," *Church History* 49 (1980): 251–61; Stuart G.
     Hall, "Women Among the Early Martyrs," and Chris Jones, "Women, Death, and the Law During
     the Christian Persecutions," both in Diane Wood, ed., *Martyrs and Martyrologies* (Oxford, 1993),
     1–21, 23–34.

110 Elizabeth Clark argues that female martyrs were so prominently featured in Eusebius's past
     because they could so well serve apologetic purposes, particularly by demonstrating the ability
     of Christianity to transform even lowly creatures into hero(ine)s. See Elizabeth Clark, "Eusebius
     on Women in Early Church History," in Attridge and Hata, eds., *Eusebius, Christianity, and Judaism,*
     256–69. I myself wonder whether it is necessary to attribute a fundamentally misogynistic atti-
     tude or rationale to male authors even when they do celebrate female heroism.

111 Josephine Balmer, ed., *Classical Women Poets* (Newcastle Upon Tyne, 1996), 115.

112 Clark, "Claims on the Bones," 143–6.

113 The case of the female martyr Agnes does not, when carefully examined, break the pattern.
     Bishop Honorius of Rome (625–38) built the first reliably documented shrine dedicated to
     Agnes (Hermann-Mascard, *Les reliques des saints,* 34) near certain ruins. Those ruins were at the
     time considered to stem from an earlier Agnes basilica that had been constructed by Con-
     stantia, Constantine's daughter; the traditions of associating Constantia with an earlier Agnes
     basilica or even simply of seeing Constantia as a particularly holy, pious woman do not go back
     beyond the sixth century. See Brandenburg, *Roms frühchristliche Basiliken,* 93–120; Dufourcq,
     Etude, 1:148–9, 214–17, 266.

114 Anne Higgonet, "A New Center: The National Museum of Women in the Arts," in Daniel J.
     Sherman and Irit Rogoff, eds., *Museum Culture: Histories, Discourses, Spectacles* (Minneapolis, 1994),
     250–64.

early Middle Ages female authors and female "patrons" tended to create or support the creation of historical narratives that treated women as an active part of the "past."[115] And, in a particularly convoluted example, ancient Greek heroines (themselves of course mythic figures) who were celebrated for having founded cults to deities (already a minority of heroines) normally were associated with the goddesses; oddly enough, however, the relations between heroines and goddesses whose cults they were believed to have promoted were frequently marked by antagonism and competition.[116]

The phenomenon of female construction of tomb-shrines to male martyrs eventually became a topos. Even (or perhaps particularly) those later authors who were (apparently) fabricating out of whole cloth depictions of Roman-era martyrdoms and their aftermaths repeatedly attributed the initial salvaging of male martyrial remains and the construction of *martyria* to matrons.[117] Nowhere is this more concentrated, or more striking, than in the dozens of "legendary" accounts of Roman city martyrs composed between the fifth and seventh centuries, in which the overwhelming majority of the original founders of martyrial tomb-shrines are "remembered" as having been women.[118] The development of the

---

115 Janet Nelson, "Perceptions du pouvoir chez les historiennes du Haut Moyen Age," in Michel Rouche, ed., *Les femmes au Moyen Age* (Paris, 1990), 77–85; Rosamond McKitterick, "Frauen und Schriftlichkeit im Frühmittelalter," in Hans-Werner Goetz, ed., *Weibliche Lebensgestaltung im frühen Mittelalter* (Cologne, 1991), 65–118; Elizabeth M. C. Van Houts, "Women and the Writing of History in the Early Middle Ages," *Early Medieval History* 1 (1992): 53–68.

116 Deborah Lyons, *Gender and Immortality: Heroines in Ancient Greek Myth and Cult* (Princeton, N.J., 1997), 134–70.

117 Some almost certainly "fictitious" matron-martyr pairs are Eusebia-Quintinus, Pientia-Nigasius, and Thecla-Eleutherius. Adele Simonetti also noticed this frequent connection in narrative sources between (cefalophoric) male saints' tombs and women, a connection that she took to be an expression of a deep-rooted Celtic substratum in European consciousness, which archetypically connects women and severed heads. She argued that the cultural association of women with the tombs of headless male martyrs functioned so as to exclude women from the Christian cult. See Adele Simonetti, "Santi cefalofori altomedioevali," *Studi Medievali* ser. 3, 28 (1987): 67–121. In contrast, I would read the topos of women as builders of male martyr shrines as itself evidence of a recognition of women's historical agency, as I have done with the topos of the female missionary. See Felice Lifshitz, "Des femmes missionnaires: L'exemple de la Gaule," *Revue d'Histoire Ecclésiastique* 83 (1988): 5–33; cf. Janet Nelson, "Women and the Word in the Earlier Middle Ages," in W. J. Sheils and Diana Wood, eds., *Women and the Church* (Oxford, 1990); Kate Cooper, "Insinuations of Womanly Influence: Aspects of the Christianization of the Roman Aristocracy," *Journal of Roman Studies* 82 (1992): 150–65; and Michelle Renee Salzman, "Aristocratic Women: Conductors of Christianity in the Fourth Century," *Helios* 16 (1989): 207–20.

118 See the detailed data compiled in Dufourcq, *Etude*, 1:124, 131, 137, 163–4, 166, 174, 177, 185, 187, 212, 214–17, 219–21, 224, 229–33, 235. In the cases where no woman is specified as having originally buried and/or memorialized a martyr's remains, the entombers/memorializers are simply referred to as "they" or "the Christians"; males are rarely specifically named. Dufourcq himself did not notice, or at least did not comment on, the gendered pattern in his material.

topos is particularly striking because it contrasts with all expectations that would be aroused by the legal "realities" of the late-Roman situation: Roman women had no obligation to memorialize the dead because widows were supposed to remarry, and *memoria* was one of the tasks associated with the *paterfamilias* and with male heirs.[119] The fact that such a topos did in fact develop in the course of the fifth century, precisely in the absence of any social expectation or legal obligation on the part of women to engage in commemorative practices, probably does point to the "reality" of matronal activities during the late third and fourth centuries.[120] The dialogue between topos and reality has recently been treated from a variety of perspectives: Some authors have utilized the concepts of topos and reality;[121] others have proposed alternative formulations such as "vertical" or "diachronic patterning" of events;[122] still others have tried to explicitly break out of the trap of reinforcing and reifying essentialist topoi completely.[123]

During late antiquity, both women and men were able to memorialize the dead, and some women exploited that possibility to its fullest potential.[124] In memorializing the martyrs of Roman imperial persecutions (or, often more accurately, in identifying unknown dead Christians as having been martyrs of Roman imperial persecutions), female and male cultic impresarios both constructed and represented the Roman past as a

---

119 Jocelyn M. C. Toynbee, *Death and Burial in the Roman World* (Ithaca, N.Y., 1971), 54; Jean Prieur, *La mort dans l'antiquité romaine* (Ouest-France, 1986); see Bernhard Jussen's essay in this book (Chapter 10). Meanwhile, fathers, mothers, husbands, wives, sons, and daughters all could and did erect and care for funerary monuments. See Toynbee, *Death and Burial*, 77–9, and passim for ownership of tombs; also Ian Morris, *Death-Ritual and Social Structure in Classical Antiquity* (Cambridge, 1992), 158–65.

120 Unfortunately, none of the scholarship on burial practices with which I am familiar has addressed the significance of the predominance of women (namely, Lucina, Domitilla, and Priscilla) among the proprietors of third- and fourth-century catacombs around Rome. See Toynbee, *Death and Burial*, 240.

121 E.g., Paul Strohm, *Hochon's Arrow: The Social Imagination of Fourteenth-Century Texts* (Princeton, N.J., 1992).

122 Giselle de Nie, *Views from a Many-Windowed Tower: Studies of Imagination in the Works of Gregory of Tours* (Amsterdam, 1987), 296.

123 Cordula Nolte, *Conversio und Christianitas: Frauen in der Christianisierung vom 5. bis 8. Jahrhundert* (Stuttgart, 1995). The particular topos of the matron who discovered the martyr corpse is now being investigated by Kate Cooper.

124 There is no serious evidence that women were considered or considered themselves ritually impure in any way that would have prevented them from presiding over sacred tombs. See Giselle de Nie, "Is een vrouw een mens? Voorschrift, vooroordell en praktijk in zesde-eeuws Gallië," *Jaarboek voor Vrouwengeschiedenis* 10 (1989): 51–74. Even Charlemagne, who sought to limit the ability of everyone except princes and upper clergy to orchestrate new cults, confided the imperial collection of martyr relics to the management of his sister at Chelles. See Jean Laporte, "Reliques du haut moyen age à Chelles," *Revue d'art et d'histoirre de la Brie et du pays de Meaux* 37 (1986): 45–58.

period marked by persecutions of Christians and constructed tomb-centered power bases for themselves. All the various memorializers and constructors instrumentalized the figure of the martyr in different ways, depending on their own circumstances and needs: Eusebius and Genovefa were both worlds and miles apart in this regard, just to name two examples. However, common to most commemorators was an apparent preference for the male heroes rather than the female heroines of early Christian times. The *chorus sanctorum*, as it exists today in the Roman calendar, for instance, has long been recognized as a chauvinistically con-stituted body; the active participation of late-ancient female impresarios in the discriminatory casting process that created that chorus has not, however, been sufficiently appreciated.

Index

Lightning Source UK Ltd.
Milton Keynes UK
UKOW042140170513

210871UK00002B/99/A